Pelican Books

The Origins and Growth
of Sociology

J. H. Abraham was educated at University College,
London. After serving as a lecturer at Mannheim
University, Germany, he joined the Egyptian
Educational Service in 1932. Along with other
British officials of the Egyptian Government he was
dismissed from his post as lecturer at Cairo
University in 1951. During his service in Egypt he
was literary adviser and a regular broadcaster on the
European Service of the Egyptian State
Broadcasting Services. From 1960 to 1965 he was
Extension Lecturer in Sociology at the University of
London, and from 1965 to 1968 he was Head of
Department of Social Science at the West Ham
College of Technology. In 1968 he was appointed to
the Chair of Sociology at the University of Ghana
and has since been Visiting Professor of Sociology at
Wayne State University, Detroit.

He is the author of *Sociology* (1966) and has
contributed to various journals including the
Listener and *British Journal of Sociology*; he has also
broadcast on several occasions for the B.B.C.

The Origins and Growth of Sociology

J. H. Abraham

Penguin Books

Penguin Books Ltd, Harmondsworth,
Middlesex, England
Penguin Books Inc., 7110 Ambassador Road,
Baltimore, Maryland 21207, U.S.A.
Penguin Books Australia Ltd, Ringwood,
Victoria, Australia

First published 1973
Copyright © J. H. Abraham, 1973

Made and printed in Great Britain by
Hazell Watson & Viney Ltd
Aylesbury, Bucks
Set in Monotype Times Roman

Contents

Acknowledgements

The author and publishers wish to thank all those who have given permission to reprint copyright material. Full details are given on the first page of each extract.

Preface

The Origins and Growth of Sociology has a very modest purpose, which is to give a broad idea of how certain writers and thinkers have conceived the problems of society from the time of ancient Greece to the present day. It is not, strictly speaking, a history of sociological thought – this would require several volumes; nor is it in any way a rounded picture of the sociological scene as it has unfolded in the course of time. It is in many respects an impressionistic, biased, but it is hoped not an untruthful, view of certain forces and movements that have gone to shape the subject as we know it today and of the people who articulated them. A deliberate policy has been to exclude any reference to the flourishing sociology that countries such as Japan, India, Mexico and others have managed to develop in the twentieth century. The reason is very simple. It was not so much due to lack of space, which was certainly an important factor, as because the seminal ideas that have given form and character to modern sociology were born largely in four countries, France, England, Germany and America; and wherever sociology is taught and practised, its starting point, its orientation and inspiration have been derived from these sources.

This short exposition of the development of sociological thought is supplemented by extensive extracts from major sociological works. In this way, the reader will better understand the kinds of problems the writers dealt with, the way they approached them, and their style of thought and expression; and, it is hoped, he will thus get the 'feel' of the writers' thoughts in addition to the direct acquaintance he will make with a few of the basic ideas underlying their works.

As well as providing such a clue as to how and why this widely

Preface

ramified discipline has come to be what it is, with the sort of ideas that have agitated the minds of writers over the centuries, and the trails, some false, others sound, which they followed, a parallel aim of this book is to make the reader participate in this exciting itinerary so that he can with greater confidence voice his own opinion concerning the status, claims and achievements of sociology. To help in this endeavour and with the object, not of convincing, but rather of stimulating thought, the author has felt it necessary to make his position on the matter perfectly clear: that a meaningful sociology as a scientific and humanistic discipline must be grounded on a sound philosophical and historical basis, that its practice in any area must be aimed at clarifying a situation in its social context, and that its study can only be justified by the greater understanding and knowledge it provides of how society is arranged and of the direction in which it is moving. This was essentially the framework in which the classical writers approached their work, and it is only within such a framework, continuously refined and improved, that any theoretical or empirical study can make headway. If this work can make even the tiniest contribution towards the creation of a critical and pervasive climate of sociological thought, so vitally essential for a progressive and enlightened sociology, I shall feel amply rewarded.

Finally I wish to thank Miss Sallie Westwood and Miss Carmel Dinan, both former Junior Research Fellows in the Department of Sociology at the University of Ghana, for their invaluable assistance in the preparation of this work.

J. H. ABRAHAM

Introduction

Any review of the historical growth of sociology would be incomplete without a preliminary consideration of three questions. The first is the subject matter of sociology, and why sociology is studied; the second is the reason for its late appearance in the corpus of academic disciplines; and the third is the meaning of science, and what kind of scientific discipline sociology is.

What is sociology?

The vagueness of the many definitions given to sociology must not mislead us into thinking that the subject matter of sociology is uncertain. Actually the various definitions of sociology as the science of society, of social behaviour, of social institutions, are all designed to emphasize a special way of looking at social behaviour which no other discipline can do as well. It is now accepted that history, politics and economics as well as sociology, because they all deal with man in society in one way or another, should be called social sciences. One can at once notice the respects in which history, politics and economics differ from one another. Each has its own well-defined subject matter and its own methods of investigation. Yet it seems obvious that although they all attempt to explain a great deal about man's social behaviour, each of them deals with only one part of it. In other words, it is possible to deal with social behaviour partially and in isolation. Thus, in history the course of events in the past is traced as it is determined by those who played a significant part in it as well as by those forces, human and material, without which no movement is possible. In economics one studies how the production and distribution of wealth in society is effected, given certain assumptions about human behaviour; and in political science one is concerned mainly with analysing how power or authority is distributed in society.

In what respects does sociology differ from these other sciences? In one sense it can be said to differ completely, and in another not at all. It is not too difficult to explain this paradox. If and when the historian or the economist or the political scientist operates in a way which makes him relate the subject matter under investigation to other parts or forces or institutions in society, he is also being a sociologist. Thus a historian who is not merely content to record the movements of events in the past, but is also concerned to show how and why such a movement took the direction it did in terms of other factors in the situation, is in effect explaining the events sociologically. To take two prominent examples, Gilbert Murray's analysis, in *Five Types of Greek Religion*, of the decline of Greek culture in terms of the political, social and intellectual factors has been described by S. K. Merton as one of the finest pieces of sociological analysis in literature; and Ibn Khaldun's explanation of the decline of Islamic political power in North Africa in the fourteenth century in terms of the breakdown of tribal solidarity is pure sociology.

Of all the social sciences economics is the one which has the greatest claim to be a closed science. Its numerous theoretical models and the advanced mathematical techniques it employs combine to make it resemble the physical sciences. Viewed in this light, economics becomes a very narrow science unrelated to the elements which comprise the structure of social life. It is evident, however, that no economic theory or practice can ever be treated in isolation and that the interplay of social factors and the economics of society is an essential prerequisite for understanding the economic development of society. Marx proved conclusively that the structure of society – in his terms it was the class structure of society – reflects the economic basis of society, and a change in the economic system will automatically entail a change in the social structure. The economic laws of society cannot therefore be understood in isolation from the social structure, nor do they have the same validity as laws in the natural sciences.

So sociology is not only closely allied to the other social

sciences; it borrows extensively from them because it is essentially dealing with identical problems, only from a broader perspective and from a special selective centre of interest.

The rise of modern sociology

The question then arises why sociology has taken a long time to emerge as a separate discipline with its own subject matter and methodology. Not only this, but even its inclusion in the university curriculum is a recent innovation, and has not come about without difficulties and struggles. The reasons are perfectly obvious. For one thing – and this is perhaps the most important reason of all – it is only in modern times that conditions have been propitious for an investigation into problems of society, and by implication for a critique of society. In the past, dissatisfaction with the existing state of affairs, where possible, led to some kind of violence perpetrated on the ruler or rulers. Society – and this was a universal phenomenon – moved in jolts, sometimes enjoying a sense of security and establishing a better and more just system of government, and sometimes retrogressing so that the elements of society fell apart. In this kind of situation neither the causes nor the effects of these changes were understood, much less assessed. This, of course, does not imply that if such understanding had been shown, or such an assessment made, society would have behaved differently; but it does imply that an awareness of why and how things happened might quite probably have made a difference. The fact is, however, that for historical reasons no such examination of society was possible.

This is certainly true of simple, homogeneous societies whose structure is unchanging and often unchangeable. Life revolves around a social system which, once established, is almost sacrosanct, and its permanence is guaranteed by the absence of any motive or desire for change. But even when a society is more highly organized and an interest in its history, either through oral tradition or written records, is shown, the idea of looking more closely into its institutions and system of life and discovering their rationale may not occur to it. What was common in history was the uncritical acceptance of a political system, and only when tyranny, incompetence or corruption could no longer be tolerated was there an attempt to question the legitimacy, not so much of the system but of the rulers. Only moral criteria were applied in judgements concerning the justice of any particular government. An important factor throughout history was the prohibition of any kind of criticism which questioned the accepted state of affairs, and it is obvious that one necessary condition for any critique of society must be unfettered freedom of expression.

Lastly, discursive thought, minute investigation and documentary evidence had not yet evolved to become the tools and techniques of pure disinterested knowledge. Only on two occasions in the past when society experienced a violent change were men found who were free to investigate the problems concerning it. The first of these occasions was in Athens at the time of Plato and Aristotle, and the second was North African society in the fourteenth century, at the time of Ibn Khaldun. Otherwise the world had to wait until the eighteenth century, when conditions were ripe for the emergence of a new discipline. The break-up of the feudal system in Europe, the vast changes being produced in social life and the promise of even vaster changes which the machine age or Industrial Revolution held, the complete and absolute freedom of expression that writers in Western Europe enjoyed, and the new techniques of investigation that were available, these were the factors which converged almost of necessity to bring about a desire to clarify and understand the complex problems of society. Hume and Ferguson in Britain, Rousseau, Montesquieu and Saint-Simon in France, and Vico in Italy were the fathers of modern sociology. It was left to Comte to gather all these strands of thought, to systematize them and give them a distinct form and shape, and in this way to demarcate the subject matter of sociology from all the other sciences.

Sociology and science

Perhaps one has to look for a reason for the existence of sociology in the fact that it is a science, as its practitioners are loud in claiming that it is. It shares with the other sciences a certain common origin. In much the same way as many sciences began as purely speculative or theoretical ideas which the urge for knowledge inspired, sociology can be regarded in the same light as having had a special interest for people to increase their knowledge and enhance their understanding. The parallel with the early sciences is in fact quite close. Like them, sociology can be said to have started as a body of speculative and theoretical ideas whose truths could only be validated when subjected to practical tests. As progress in the sciences became rapid when this occurred, so it can be said of sociology that the same progress can be expected when its ideas are put to the test to be verified or rejected. Can this claim be sustained?

No conclusive answer can be provided until we are clear in our minds as to what exactly we mean by science. This is not as easy as it sounds, for the precision we are after is not to be found in the common everyday connotation of the term. To most English-speaking people in particular, the term 'science' refers to what goes on in laboratories where all sorts of experiments are carried out to prove a theory or idea, and eventually to produce something new. Of course in some cases, like astronomy, only observations are made and inferences and deductions drawn in the light of these observations. In general, however, one requires from these sciences certain concrete results. This is why all these sciences are called 'natural sciences', because they are all concerned with natural phenomena, those hard, palpable, visible, concrete things that surround us. This is the narrow conception of science which is perpetuated in our educational system, which divides all school subjects into the sciences and the arts. In a more sophisticated form this division appears in the common assumption that our culture is of two kinds – scientific, and humanistic or literary. This division has no basis in either etymology, history or fact. Science simply means knowledge, in which case every subject in the world is entitled to be called a science if it is taught and studied as an intellectual exercise for the purpose of furthering our knowledge. This is how science is used in German, meaning knowledge (*Wissenschaft*). On the basis of this criterion, there is every reason for including, say, theology as well as logic, mathematics, politics, among the sciences. In this sense the idea of science is a body of specialized knowledge which can be regarded

15

as a system of thought consisting of facts and ideas. Sciences, of course, differ in the extent to which they have to rely on experiments, on observation, or merely on sifting of evidence; but in all of them the same process of reasoning and understanding has to be applied. Thus every scientific discipline must have its own subject matter, a body of knowledge which can be learnt and verified with the underlying assumption that existing knowledge is not final, and can be indefinitely extended and refined.

In short, science arises when people begin to look for answers to questions which have puzzled them. As long as they bring to bear upon these problems rational thought, and as long as they can devise answers which increase knowledge and understanding, they are behaving scientifically. Most people are content to regard the findings of their senses as final, and endeavour to make a practical job of their lives on that basis. Water is essential to life, and in so far as man knew the uses of water for all life-giving purposes he did not feel the need to go beyond this. Even today, a farmer is not concerned to know that water is composed of two gases, hydrogen and oxygen, in proportion of two to one. He knows from experience and trial and error what the effect of water is on plants and animals, and as long as the results of his husbandry are satisfactory he is quite content to let the matter rest there. One must not underestimate the extent of knowledge acquired by this means, or the practical results obtained; but curiosity, which is a basic human drive, will urge certain people to discover deeper reasons for the findings of everyday practical life. By probing deeper they are able to make good the deficiencies of common sense and give to the judgements of ordinary experience a more articulate formulation in order to discover, where possible, their underlying logic. In this respect science can be regarded, in Huxley's words, as refined common sense. The pursuit of science, however, is never successful in the absence of a certain attitude of mind, an attitude governed by the spirit of objectivity in the search for truth.

And so knowledge, in all disciplines of thought, if it is to serve a scientific purpose, must be pursued dispassionately, devoid of bias and subjective consideration. The true meaning of science, therefore, is that it is a method of learning and working, and as such it can be applied to all disciplines and not just to the natural or physical sciences, which hitherto have been erroneously regarded as the only true examples of what science really is.

A humanistic sociology

In making out a claim for sociology as a distinctive field of human inquiry, we are at the same time claiming for sociology a place not only in the sciences but also in the humanities. This latter aspect of sociology has not been given the prominence and importance by writers that it deserves. Rightly concerned as they were to bring a scientific approach to the problems of society, they overlooked the fact that sociology as a science is different from all the other sciences. The difference consists in the fact that the person who wishes to make sense of what is happening in society, to understand the 'web of relationships', as it has been put, that makes a society tick and gives it a distinct form, is himself a product of that society, so that in trying to understand it he is at the same time trying to understand himself and his position in society better. In this respect sociology becomes part of the culture of society, which means that no person who is at all interested in or concerned with his society can fail to benefit, intellectually and morally, from the observations and insights of people engaged in sociological pursuits. Sociology in this way is not merely an intellectual exercise or a profession having a certain practical end, it is an integral part of one's education, and is its own justification. Max Weber's insistence on distinguishing sociology from the other sciences, as it requires a special kind of understanding, was designed to underline the close relationship of sociology to the humanistic disciplines. We cannot, according to this view, deal fully with the actions and interactions of people in society without understanding the motives which make people act in the way they do, and we can only do so because we ourselves know that we would be moved in similar circumstances by the same motives.

To understand a sociological 'object' in this sense is more than just to know everything about it. It is also to feel something towards it, so that such understanding as is acquired is in the real sense sympathetic understanding. A sociologist cannot take an

17

entirely impersonal view of it. While he is trying to understand it he is concerned with its history, its fortunes, its future. Like a true scientist, he becomes wrapped up in it, but because it is a 'live' object he has a close and intimate relationship to it, while assuming an attitude towards it sufficiently distant to allow him to look at it in the round. This combination of a rounded perspective and a distant approach will enable him to overcome any partiality or bias, of which no one is entirely free in these matters. To look at everything with an open eye means that one should take nothing for granted; the most formally established principles of society may well be based on shaky foundations. This kind of scepticism in no way entails either wholesale condemnation or ribald mockery. On the contrary, such scepticism, in querying the present, is conscious of the awful uncertainty of change. In this sense sociology is a sceptical science attempting to derive new knowledge, new understanding and new explanation of existing facts and situations. Unlike the other sciences, which are all the time extending the sphere of knowledge by the discovery of new facts, sociology extends our knowledge only in the sense that, at its best, it provides us with a fresh insight into existing social facts. Social facts create themselves. They are known because they are 'lived'. The sociologist looks at them in a way which will bring out their significance in relation to other facts in the social world, and in this way we see them in a new light. To study social facts in isolation is the most profitless of undertakings. Every social fact must be seen from a broad perspective so that its place in the structure as a whole can be assessed more meaningfully. In saying this, we are implying that a social fact has a meaning. We abstract the meaning that it has for us, and relate it to the other meanings derived from the other related facts.

This abstraction of meaning concerning social facts is what separates sociology from the natural sciences, and this is one reason why it is futile to reduce it to the natural sciences. This was one of the aberrations of sociologists in the last hundred years or so, who felt that if any success was to be achieved in sociology it could only be done through the same methods as were applied so successfully in the natural sciences. What they regarded as the successful methods of the natural sciences were the discovery of laws of uniformities of nature, and with this the possibility of making exact predictions. Now these may well be the essence and objective of the natural sciences; but a moment's thought will show how impossible, not to say unsuitable, they are in sociology. The discovery of uniformities of behaviour is certainly an essential task of sociology, and it may well be possible to express these uniformities in terms of causal laws, but this is far from being the only task of sociology, for it is as certain as anything in social life that disformities are as frequent, and perhaps as important, as the uniformities, and it is the task of sociology to be able to account for these. This, therefore, implies that although up to a point we are enabled in sociology, as we are in the natural sciences, to make predictions, these predictions must not be thought of as exact, and they would only apply to the uniformities which we can observe. In other words, the unpredictability of man is one of the basic assumptions of any meaningful sociology. As we maintained before, this in no way detracts from the claim that sociology is a science, and an exact science at that; but this kind of science, and this kind of exactness, must not be confused with those that we expect from the natural sciences.

Change in society can, therefore, be seen as having arisen in two ways: the first as a historical movement from one state to another, determined by social causes, and the other as arising from certain unpredictable factors due to individual choice. An invention, a discovery, an artistic production, a prophetic message, all these have a social origin, no doubt; but they are unpredictable because they are the products of an individual's genius. Therefore social explanations must be in terms both of exceptional, or even ordinary, individuals and of social wholes. Short-range predictions can certainly be made of the latter, simply because in dealing with social wholes we are abstracting all the individual differences that separate the members who compose these wholes. In this way we are enabled to measure, and even measure accurately, trends and movements and opinions and so forth; but in the final resort any changes taking place in these trends, movements or opinions will be due to individual initiatives, and sociology must give due prominence to these. The effects of all these individual initiatives would be seen in the behaviour of the social group or whole, which is why we are enabled to make generalizations – and are justified in doing so – about both individuals and groups, always bearing in mind that these generalizations are tentative and could well be revised or modified in the light of changing circumstances.

In brief we can state the situation in this way: no social life is possible, and therefore no understanding of social life is possible, except on the assumption that most of the actions of people in society are predictable; but because society is never static, and is always undergoing changes, we are justified in attributing these changes to that residuum in some people's actions which is not predictable. With regard to group behaviour, predictions are more frequent and more exact for the reasons already adduced; but changes in society, and therefore in group behaviour, are due sometimes to external and sometimes to internal factors, and at other times to individual deviations within the group or whole, so that the individual plays a crucial part in the changes that occur in society.

In saying that social facts have meaning, we are implying that every social fact is value-laden. By 'value' here is meant an implicit or explicit judgement that the fact is good or bad, desirable or undesirable, worthwhile or not worthwhile. In this respect it can be said that the whole of social life consists of value systems which are inherited, learned and passed on to future generations, with the proviso of course that they are never static and undergo, frequently or infrequently, some modification. These value systems comprise the culture of society, using 'culture' in a very broad sense to mean the general attitudes, thoughts, aspirations, norms, all of which distinguish that society as a living unit of action. Thus a human society is a society which is culturally determined by virtue of the value systems which prevail, and the organization of society is a reflection and expression of these value systems.

1　Sociology in Ancient and Medieval Times

While sociology is a modern science, there is no doubt that a great deal of what was written in the past about social and political matters can well be described as sociological; such writings, however, were subsumed under other names – history, ethics, politics, or law. Once a problem concerning society is brought under scrutiny and made the subject of systematic analysis, it deserves to be called a sociological problem.

In this sense, Plato and Aristotle can be regarded as the first thinkers who dealt with problems of society systematically. Implicit in every form of society, however loosely organized and at whatever stage of development, is the recognition that the existence and survival of society depend on a system of norms binding on the members. Obedience or acquiescence to these norms is effected by a variety of mechanisms – custom, religion or law; and deviation will meet with various sanctions – disapproval and all kinds of punishment. At the same time a society must be organized to serve certain ends; so we have the equation: norms + organization = society. This organization is essentially political, and it was regarded as such by the Greek thinkers. Unfortunately 'political' in our more narrow sense is understood to refer to the purely governmental aspects of society – the person or persons who rule, and how they rule, and all the other matters concerning the business of government. There is here a clear distinction between what is political and what is non-political or social. To the Greeks this distinction was meaningless. Their *polis* referred to a fully organized city state in all its aspects, so that 'political' and 'social' were equivalent. The way in which the city state – or society – was organized described its political character; so when Aristotle described man as 'a political animal' it would be equally correct to substitute 'social' for 'political', and what he meant was that man is what he is by virtue of the fact that he is a member of society.

The Greeks went further. For them, social or political life was organized to serve a certain end or purpose. In other words, society must be viewed teleologically. What the end or purpose is, whether it is a good or a bad one, whether society is measuring up to this end or purpose, were questions which it was the task of a philosopher to determine. So politics or sociology in our terminology formed with the Greeks part of ethics, and should be concerned with the question as to what are the chief characteristics of a good society, and how far our existing society approximates to one; or in what respects it is deviating from it, and if so, what the remedy might be. If from our point of view there were two problems here which were inextricably confused, the factual or empirical on the one hand and the normative or prescriptive on the other, to the Greek mind these two problems were two aspects of one and the same problem. With them no problem as to how the state was organized could be separated from the problem as to whether the state was functioning well or not in accordance with certain ends or ideals.

There was no difference between Plato and Aristotle in their approach and attitude to this problem. The difference was rather a matter of emphasis, Plato concentrating more on the prescriptive aspects and Aristotle on the empirical. In consequence, Plato's political or sociological theories were related to a much more comprehensive and all-embracing philosophical theory. A reference to the latter is required in order to understand the grounds for the view he held concerning society.

A fundamental premise in Plato's philosophy is the distinction between appearance and reality. The first includes all the objects of our senses, and these are in a state of flux, continually changing, and cannot provide us with true knowledge. At most we can only have an opinion about them. But behind these objects of appearance there must be another realm of being, unchanging, fixed, eternal, an ideal of which the objects of sense are only a pale reflection. These 'ideal forms' are the true objects of knowledge, which only our faculty of reason is capable of apprehending. For Plato, these ideal forms can be and should be placed in a hierarchical order of importance, so that at the apex would be found the highest ideal form of all, namely goodness, or the good, to which all the others are subordinate in the sense that their existence depends on it and that they all contribute towards the achievement or attainment of goodness, or the good. The way in which we can assess the goodness of a thing is quite simple. We define the ideal of whatever it is we are judging – a sword, a man, or any other object – and this ideal becomes the unalterable, immutable standard of measurement, so that we will be in a position to say how far a sword, a man, or any other object falls short of this ideal standard or approximates to it. In the same way there is an ideal political state (*politeia*) of which the different forms of government are more or less imperfect copies. Plato's theory of society consisted not in considering the actual political institutions in order to make sense of them in terms of their legitimacy or function, but in demonstrating the imperfection of every form of human government and setting up instead an ideal government conforming to an *a priori* definition of social justice. His utopia, like all utopias modern or ancient, is in one sense anarchical because the institutions of society like law, morality and so forth, having been all perfectly realized, have really no further reason to exist. They just wither away. Now a critique of society is an expression of the dissatisfaction felt at the way in which society is organized, and its purpose is to demonstrate how it might be organized differently. The assumption is implicit that there is always room for indefinite change or improvement, not that a stage will have been reached when no further change or improvement is required. Plato's was the most far-reaching, profound and devastating critique of society of any writer in history, but it was vitiated because the object was not to analyse the existing institutions of society to show how they have arisen, and what their effects are, and what their future might hold, but rather to show that, short of a complete transformation, we have no ground for holding that one form of society is better than another except in the sense that one is more evil than another.

An added complication in Plato's theory was the peculiar view taken concerning Nature (*phusis*). There is, according to this view, a realm of Nature which is ruled by fixed and immutable laws. These are rational and good, because they were created by God. Being himself, in however infinitesimal a degree, possessed of godlike knowledge and reason, man can have an insight into these bodies of laws which govern Nature. This implies that although human society may have fallen short of what is rational and good, at one time man must have lived in a society which was ideal, rational and good. This was the backward-looking element of primitivism in Plato's thought. If, sociologically if not philosophically, Plato's advocacy of a kind of anarchism combining with a wistful nostalgia for a lost Paradise is logically and empirically unacceptable, his ineradicable belief in the rationality of Nature and of man at his best as part of Nature contributed more than anything else to the rise of the scientific spirit which has dominated Western thought. It implies, for one thing, that it is possible for man to organize his life and society rationally, and be in a position to criticize and condemn where this is justified.

Plato's criticism and condemnation of existing human institutions must be seen as springing from a passionate zeal for the welfare of man, and the conviction that it was possible to bring about a different state of affairs. His social thought must not be derived exclusively from the utopia which he outlined in *The Republic*: of much greater value sociologically were the views on society contained in *The Laws*. In this work Plato allowed for the possibility of setting up a state of society where the actual laws would approximate to ideal justice. It may be that his ideal justice on any interpretation involved a totalitarian view of law completely at variance with our modern concepts of freedom and equality; it may also be that Plato's view of society was one in which the system of law and the organization of economic and social life allowed for no variation or change; nevertheless, implicit in his theory was the view that society is not a mechanical thing without rhyme or reason and with no functions as such. It is, on the contrary, a conscious process of continual endeavour to achieve the good life, a process in which all the members participate for their mutual good, and from which no one is excluded. This is possible because man is endowed with the faculty of reason –

which, however, is continually at war with the other two faculties of his, spirit and appetite. His task is to try to overcome and control these two faculties. The way in which he organizes his life, or, in other words, the way in which society itself is organized, is a reflection of the success or failure of this task. Societies, therefore, can be changed in such a way that the predominant element, which is reason, prevails, so that all the three elements can co-exist harmoniously. This is sociologically an important discovery because it implies that man is responsible for creating those institutions in society which seem appropriate to him, and they can be changed with a more determined and sustained application of rationality.

No writer has had such a profound insight into the meaning and purpose of human society as Plato had. As has already been indicated, Aristotle's approach to the problems of society was identical with Plato's. Aristotle conceived of the state of society as a natural development of man's social impulses. In this view man exists only as a social animal, and without the society of people – in other words, without social organization – man is nothing. His whole progress in life is only possible within, and is determined by, his participation in a society of like-minded people. The modern ideas of socialization and internalization – those processes by which man learns his roles in society, how to live with others in co-operation, and how to conform to the norms of society – are implicit in Aristotle's theory. Like Plato, he regarded society teleologically as a process directed towards an end or purpose, and that end or purpose was moral in character. It was to achieve the good; and both defined the good in terms of the harmony or equilibrium of parts. They defined these terms *a priori* as having been unalterably fixed by Nature. To take one notorious example, they both justified the institution of slavery because for them some groups in society are by nature inferior to others, and should be in a subordinate position to carry out the orders of others. In this respect Aristotle, like Plato, must be ruled out as sociologically a significant thinker. On the other hand Aristotle, being more empirically minded, gave a brilliant and classic account of different types of society by analysing their political organization, their effects and ability to produce a stable and happy society. In this respect he was the first empiricist in politics and social science in general. By defining democracy in a less extreme form than Plato did, Aristotle concluded that, however numerous and serious were the defects of democracy, it was superior as a form of social and political organization to any others.

Like Plato, he rated reason or intellect as the highest quality for man to cultivate, quite convinced that true happiness resides in the exercise of intellect. As it was impossible for everyone in society to be equally endowed with this quality, for Aristotle therefore it was quite in keeping with the natural order of things, and in conformity with the demands of justice, that society should be graded hierarchically. There would be a few enlightened intellectual people at the top, who would be followed by others less well endowed but, within the limitations imposed by nature, knowing their place, vocation or role in society and being satisfied with it, until the most intellectually inferior group in society, like slaves, is reached. Here it is that Aristotle, in an endeavour to be more rigorous in his conceptual analysis, introduced valuable distinctions which were overlooked by Plato, but which were not refined enough to be immune from serious shortcomings. Unlike Plato, Aristotle realized that, however defective it is, some form of judicial system is required in every society, and therefore some kind of justice which is accepted and applied must prevail. This kind of justice, falling short of the ideal as it does, is nevertheless better than no justice. It is necessary, therefore, to distinguish between this kind of justice, which may be called conventional justice applying to a particular society, and the other kind of justice, which may be called natural justice applying to all men alike.

From this point onwards a process started in Western thought in which the concept of Nature has played a most significant role, so that henceforth it was possible to appeal to a higher norm, the norm of Nature, whenever the norms of society were no longer acceptable, or needed modification. It would be difficult to estimate the extent to which our legal and political systems have evolved and assumed new forms as a result of the use of such concepts as 'natural law', 'natural right' and 'natural justice'.

If for 2,000 years writers have been arguing interminably about these concepts, their possible meanings and the things to which they are to apply, it is no surprise that Aristotle gave a number of overlapping interpretations to this concept of Nature. With his biological bias he was impressed with the idea of development. He thought of the growth of anything – plant, animal, man – in terms of latent potentiality which can be actually realized. Such realization can be described as the fulfilment of one's nature. As far as man is concerned, by 'nature' we could mean just the way in which he behaves given his particular kind of make-up. It could also mean an ideal standard to which he is for ever aspiring if his full potentialities are to be realized. There is combined in the factual description of man's nature a normative element laying down a rule as to how man's nature might or should be fulfilled. The confusion between what is and what ought to be has persisted in Western thought ever since.

The Stoics took Nature to mean that realm of existence in which universal reason prevails, and whose laws are fixed and immutable, and which man, because he is endowed with reason, must obey. Natural law came thus to mean the opposite of man-made law, one which overrides the latter and is applicable to man as such irrespective of what he is or where he comes from by virtue of the sanction that derives from reason.

The disintegration of the political order in Europe following the fall of the Roman Empire not only caused a complete rupture with previous thought, but led to a fragmentation of local power inimical to a social organization sufficiently uniform and homogeneous to allow for a considered and historically determined view of the dynamics of society. Society in flux contains no point at which its past and future can be brought into a synthesis of understanding. Only a strong religious faith resting firmly on the belief in another existence can become the sheet anchor for the frightful hazards of the present. St Augustine's *City of God* becomes a model of what the real human society is like. The feudal system which took shape in Europe was a response to social and economic conditions which were narrowly circumscribed but which provided the possibility of a stable system of life and government. The division of society into separate rigid orders had

27

the sanction of both religion and the secular authority. Canon law, whose orientation and principles were derived to a great extent from Roman law, welded the feudal system together, while the Institutes of Justinian laid the foundations for the systems of law in Western Europe. Scholasticism, appropriating the doctrine of Aristotle in support of Christian dogma, set the tone for philosophical thought for many centuries. The Stoic doctrine of natural law had to be interpreted in the light of Christian theology. This was neatly done by Thomas Aquinas. Man-made law, which is conventional and clearly defective, must yield to the higher law of Nature, to which mankind as a whole owes allegiance. In addition there is Divine Law, which is supreme and must be obeyed by those to whom the faith of Christ has been revealed. In a Christian society the submission of man to the laws of God as defined by the Church is absolute, and social justice is what the Church decides is right. Henceforth, as de Tocqueville observed, the movement of society in Western Europe was one towards greater equality in the conditions of life.

It would be quite impossible to give a full explanation of the causes which led to this unique movement in modern history. All that can be asserted is that the various factors which might have been thought to be sufficiently powerful to resist this movement had to yield to its inexorable advance. It would not be wrong to say that the combination of the Stoic and Christian doctrines and the gradual supersession of Church authority by secular authority created a climate of opinion in which men's minds were turned to this ideal and their efforts were directed to ways of bringing it about. It was first necessary to limit the entrenched powers of monarchs, princes and nobles which perpetuated the rigid and unequal divisions of society. To the extent that their powers and privileges were limited, by so much, it was thought, would the social conditions be equalized. The political writings from Machiavelli right up to the present day may be said to have been concerned either to defend the existing and traditional form of society or to justify the reduction and limitation of power and privilege for the sake of greater equality. But change in this direction, once the process began and however uneven its course, could not be reversed. It is understandable that it had to be mainly political writings and controversies which exercised men's minds for so many centuries. It was only when the battle seemed to have been won, and change – political, social and economic – had assumed a new and unwonted aspect, that sociology addressed itself to its causes, ramifications and effects.

Long before this was attempted in Europe one man, Ibn Khaldun in the fourteenth century – who did not belong to and was ignorant of the European tradition of thought – formulated a theory of change, the most brilliant and original ever conceived by a writer. Ibn Khaldun called his monumental work *Prolegomena to Universal History*, intending to convey by this title that any historical account must be preceded by an analysis of the factors which contributed to shaping the events in question. In this way his *Prolegomena* covered a very broad compass, in spite of which, while it included a great deal of historical knowledge, it was a self-contained and self-sufficient sociological analysis of the contemporary society with which he was concerned.

North African society, or the Maghreb, presented a picture of a society which had known great power and influence, but which had declined to a position of weakness and decadence. Ibn Khaldun undertook to explain the reasons for this sudden decline, and in order to make his explanation as complete as possible he dealt with all aspects of society, economic, geographical, legal and religious, which has a bearing on this problem of change. As a result all societies, historical and contemporary, as far as they were known to him, came under scrutiny and were subjected to an analysis with the object of demonstrating why and how they came to be what they were. Concerning the Maghreb, Ibn Khaldun employed one basic concept, solidarity or community feeling (*asabieh*). According to his theory, solidarity formed through kinship and tribal ties reinforced by rigid and fanatical religious faith is the most irresistible force in society, capable of overcoming militarily numerically superior forces. This would account for the conquest by Arab tribal power of the settled populations of North Africa. Cultivating sedentary habits of life, with all that that implies in terms of trade, economic advance and refinement of luxury, the new dynasties experienced a progressive degeneration and decline of power within a few generations, until they became so weak that they would be a ready prey to external forces bound by stronger ties of solidarity like those which they themselves had possessed in their original and more primitive state.

Ibn Khaldun, like Vico in the eighteenth century in Europe, adopted a quasi-deterministic view of human society whereby events happened according to certain predetermined laws. In addition, judging from the cases he was examining, history moved in cyclical phases so that there was a continuous movement at regular periods from strong to weak solidarity and vice versa. In this view all social institutions are subject to laws of change and decay. Although change in the social situation of groups may be due to a number of factors, it never has anything to do with individual choice, but has a purely social cause. This view of human society was at bottom a pessimistic one, for it consisted in holding that any advance is only temporary, and is bound to be reversed. Mankind is faced, in fact, with two alternatives: either being closely knit in a simple but a durable form of society, or being loosely linked in a more complex but more vulnerable and unstable form of society. As a universal theory of human society, Ibn Khaldun's theory fails precisely because it is too universalistic. Human conditions being as variable as they are, a theory like this cannot possibly fit every case; but within the context of the society which he was investigating, the theory is as valid as any theory can be, and represents a most ambitious and original advance in sociological thought.

Plato 427–347 B.C.

Works of sociological importance

Major dialogues:
The Republic
The Laws
Minor dialogues:
The Apology
Crito

The following extract is reprinted from Plato, *The Republic*, translated by H. D. P. Lee (London: Penguin Books, 1955), Part II, §§ 1–2, pp. 102–8 (Book II, 369–73).

'Society originates, then,' said I, 'so far as I can see, because the individual is not self-sufficient, but has many needs which he can't supply himself. Or can you suggest any other origin for it?'

'No, I can't,' he said.

'And when we have got hold of enough people to satisfy our many varied needs, we have assembled quite a large number of partners and helpers together to live in one place; and we give the resultant settlement the name of a community or state?'

'Yes, I agree.'

'And in the community all mutual exchanges are made with the benefit of the partners in view?'

'Certainly.'

'Come then,' I said, 'let us proceed with our imaginary sketch of the origin of the state. It springs, as we have seen, from our needs.'

'Yes.'

'And our first and greatest need is clearly the provision of food to keep us alive.'

'Clearly.'

'Our second need is shelter, and our third clothing of various kinds.'

'Yes.'

'Well then, how will our state supply these needs? It will need a farmer, a builder, and a weaver, and also, I think, a shoemaker and one or two others to provide for our bodily needs. So that the minimum state would consist of four or five men.'

'Evidently.'

'Then should each of these men contribute the product of his labour to a common stock? For instance, should the farmer provide enough food for all four of them, and devote enough time and labour to food production to provide for all their common needs? Or, alternatively, should he disregard the others, and devote a quarter of his time to producing a quarter the amount of food, and the other three quarters one to building himself a house, one to making clothes, and another to making shoes? Should he, in other words, avoid the trouble of sharing with others and devote himself to providing for his own needs only?'

To which Adeimantus replied, 'The first alternative is perhaps the simpler.'

'Nor need that surprise us,' I rejoined. 'For as you were speaking, it occurred to me that, in the first place, no two of us are born exactly alike. We have different aptitudes, which fit us for different jobs.'

'We have indeed.'

'So do we do better to stick to one trade or to try to practise several?'

'To stick to one,' he said.

'And there is a further point. It is fatal in any job to miss the right moment for action. The workman must be at the call of his job; his job will not wait till he has leisure to spare for it. Quantity and quality are therefore more easily produced when a man specializes appropriately on a single job for which he is naturally fitted.'

'That's certainly true.'

'We shall need more than four citizens, then, Adeimantus, to supply the needs we mentioned. For the farmer, it seems, will not make his own plough or hoe, or any of his other agricultural implements, if they are to be well made. The same is true of the builder and the many tools he needs, and of the weaver and shoemaker. And so smiths and other craftsmen must share the work and swell the numbers of our small community.'

'They must.'

'And it will still not be unduly large, if we add cowherds and shepherds and stockmen of various kinds, to provide oxen for the plough and draught-animals for builder and farmer, as well as hides and wool for shoemaker and weaver.'

'No,' he answered; 'but it will no longer be so very small.'

'And yet it is almost impossible to found a state in a place where it will not need imports.'

'Quite impossible.'

'So we shall need another class in our community to fetch for it what it needs from abroad.'

'Yes.'

'And if our agent goes empty-handed, and takes with him nothing of which those from whom he is to get what we want are in need, he will return empty-handed. So we must produce at home not only enough for our own needs but also enough goods of the right kind for the foreigners who supply us. Which means an increase in the number of farmers and other workers in our state.'

'The increase will be necessary.'

'And it will of course include agents to handle the export and import of goods whom we call merchants. We shall need them too.'

'We shall.'

'And if our trade is to be overseas, we shall need a whole lot of experts on ships and seafaring.'

'Yes, a whole lot of them.'

'Then within our state, how are its citizens to exchange the products of their labour? For such mutual exchange was the reason for its foundation.'

'They will buy and sell.'

'And that will require a market, and a currency as the medium of exchange.'

'Certainly.'

'And if a farmer or any other producer brings his goods to market at a time when no one who wants to exchange with him is there, will he sit about in the market and neglect his own job?'

'Certainly not,' he replied. 'There is a class who see here a chance of doing a service. It consists, in a well-run community, of those who are least fit physically, and unsuitable for other work. For their job ties them to the market place, where they buy goods from those who want to sell and sell goods to those who want to buy.'

'And so this requirement produces a class of retailers in our state. For that is what we call those whose business is to trade with the public at home, as opposed to merchants who travel abroad.'

'Agreed.'

'There is another class whose services we need – those who have no great powers of mind to contribute, but whose physical strength makes them suitable for manual labour. They market their strength and call the return they get for it their wages, and in consequence are usually called wage-earners. And with them our population is complete.'

'Yes, I think it is.'

'Then can we say that our state is now full grown?'

'Perhaps we can.'

'If so, where are we to find justice and injustice in it? With which of the elements we have examined does it originate?'

'I don't know, Socrates,' he replied, 'unless it be in some relationship between them.'

'You may be right,' said I; 'we must press on with our enquiry. So let us first consider how our citizens, so equipped, will live. They will produce corn, wine, clothes, and shoes, and will build themselves houses. In the summer they will for the most part work unclothed and unshod, in the winter they will be clothed and shod suitably. For food they will prepare wheat-meal or barley-meal for baking or kneading. They will serve splendid cakes and loaves on rushes or fresh leaves, and will sit down to feast with their children on couches of myrtle and bryony;

and afterwards they will drink wine and pray to the gods with garlands on their heads and enjoy each other's company. And fear of poverty and war will make them keep the numbers of their families within their means.'

'I say,' interrupted Glaucon, 'that's pretty plain fare for a feast, isn't it?'

'You're quite right,' said I. 'I had forgotten; they will have a few luxuries. Salt, of course, and olive oil and cheese, and different kinds of vegetables from which to make various country dishes. And we must give them some dessert, figs and peas and beans, and myrtle-berries and acorns to roast at the fire as they sip their wine. So they will lead a peaceful and healthy life, and expect to die at a ripe old age, leaving their children to do the same in their turn.'

Civilized Society

'Really, Socrates,' Glaucon commented, 'you might be catering for a community of pigs!'

'And how would you do it, Glaucon?' I asked.

'Give them the ordinary comforts,' he replied. 'Let them sit on chairs and eat off tables, and have normal civilized food.'

'All right,' I said, 'I understand. We are to study not only the origins of society, but also society when it enjoys the luxuries of civilization. Not a bad idea, perhaps, for in the process we may discover how justice and injustice are bred in a community. For though the society we have described seems to me to be the true norm, just as a man in health is the norm, there's nothing to prevent us, if you wish, studying one whose temperature luxury has raised. Such a society will not be satisfied with the standard of living we have described. It will want chairs and tables and other furniture, and a variety of delicacies, scents, cosmetics, sweets, and mistresses. And we must no longer confine ourselves to the bare necessities of our earlier description, houses, clothing, and shoes, but must add the fine arts of painting and embroidery, and introduce materials like gold and ivory. Do you agree?'

'Yes,' he said.

'We shall have to enlarge our state again. Our healthy state is no longer big enough; its size must be enlarged to make room for a multitude of occupations none of which is concerned with necessaries. There will be hunters and fishermen, and there will be artists, sculptors, painters, and musicians; there will be poets and playwrights with their following of reciters, actors, chorus-trainers, and producers; there will be manufacturers of domestic furniture of all sorts, and fashion-experts for the women. And we shall need a lot more servants – tutors, nurses, ladies' maids, barbers, confectioners, and cooks. And we shall need swineherds too: there were none in our former state, as we had no need of them, but now we need pigs, and cattle in quantities too, if we are to eat meat. Agreed?'

'There's no denying it.'

'We shall need doctors too, far more than we did before.'

'With our new luxuries we certainly shall.'

'And the territory which was formerly enough to support us will now be too small. If we are to have enough for pasture and plough, we shall have to cut a slice off our neighbours' territory. And if they too are no longer confining themselves to necessities and have embarked on the pursuit of unlimited material possessions, they will want a slice of ours too.'

'The consequence is inevitable!'

'And that will lead to war, Glaucon, will it not?'

'It will.'

'For the moment,' I said, 'we are not concerned with the effects of war, good or bad; let us merely note that we have found its origin to be the same as that of most evil, individual or social.'

'Yes, I agree.'

Aristotle 384–322 B.C.

Works of sociological importance

The Politics
Nicomachean Ethics
Metaphysics

The following extract is reprinted from Aristotle, *The Politics*, translated by Ernest Barker (Oxford: Clarendon Press, 1946), with the permission of the publisher.

Theory of the Household

8. When we come to the final and perfect association, formed from a number of villages, we have already reached the polis – an association which may be said to have reached the height of full self-sufficiency; or rather (to speak more exactly) we may say that while it *grows* for the sake of mere life (and is so far, and at that stage, still short of full self-

sufficiency), it *exists* (when once it is fully grown) for the sake of a good life (and is therefore fully self-sufficient).

Because it is the completion of associations existing by nature, every polis exists by nature, having itself the same quality as the earlier associations from which it grew. It is the end or consummation to which those associations move, and the 'nature' of things consists in their end or consummation; for what each thing is when its growth is completed we call the nature of that thing, whether it be a man or a horse or a family. 9. Again (and this is a second reason for regarding the state as natural) the end, or final cause, is the best. Now self-sufficiency (which it is the object of the state to bring about) is the end, and so the best; (and on this it follows that the state brings about the best, and is therefore natural, since nature always aims at bringing about the best).

From these considerations it is evident that the polis belongs to the class of things that exist by nature, and that man is by nature an animal intended to live in a polis. He who is without a polis, by reason of his own nature and not of some accident, is either a poor sort of being, or a being higher than man: he is like the man of whom Homer wrote in denunciation: 'Clanless and lawless and heartless is he'.

10. The man who is such by nature (i.e. unable to join in the society of a polis) at once plunges into a passion of war; he is in the position of a solitary advanced piece in a game of draughts.

The reason why man is a being meant for political association, in a higher degree than bees or other gregarious animals can ever associate, is evident. Nature, according to our theory, makes nothing in vain; and man alone of the animals is furnished with the faculty of language. 11. The mere making of sounds serves to indicate pleasure and pain, and is thus a faculty that belongs to animals in general: their nature enables them to attain the point at which they have perceptions of pleasure and pain, and can signify those perceptions to one another. But language serves to declare what is advantageous and what is the reverse, and it therefore serves to declare what is just and what is unjust. 12. It is the peculiarity of man, in comparison with the rest of the animal world, that he alone possesses a perception of good and evil, of the just and the unjust, and of other similar qualities; and it is association in (a common perception of) these things which makes a family and a polis.

We may now proceed to add that (though the individual and the family are prior in the order of time) the polis is prior in the order of nature to the family and the individual. 13. The reason for this is that the whole is necessarily prior (in nature) to the part. If the whole body be destroyed, there will not be a foot or a hand, except in that ambiguous sense in which one uses the same word to indicate a different thing, as when one speaks of a 'hand' made of stone; for a hand, when destroyed (by the destruction of the whole body), will be no better than a stone 'hand'. All things derive their essential character from their function and their capacity: and it follows that if they are no longer fit to discharge their function, we ought not to say that they are still the same things, but only that, by an ambiguity, they still have the same names.

14. We thus see that the polis exists by nature and that it is prior to the individual. (The proof of both propositions is the fact that the polis is a whole, and that individuals are simply its parts.) Not being self-sufficient when they are isolated, all individuals are so many parts all equally depending on the whole (which alone can bring about self-sufficiency). The man who is isolated – who is unable to share in the benefits of political association, or has no need to share because he is already self-sufficient – is no part of the polis, and must therefore be either a beast or a god. 15. (Man is thus intended by nature to be a part of a political whole, and) there is therefore an immanent impulse in all men towards an association of this order. But the man who first *constructed* such an association was none the less the greatest of benefactors. Man, when perfected, is the best of animals; but if he be isolated from law and justice he is the worst of all.

16. Injustice is all the graver when it is armed injustice; and man is furnished from birth with arms (such as, for instance, language) which are intended to serve the purposes of moral prudence and virtue, but which may be used in preference for opposite ends. That is why, if he be without virtue, he is a most unholy and savage being, and worse than all others in the indulgence of lust and gluttony. Justice (which is his salvation) belongs to the polis; for justice, which is the determination of what is just, is an ordering of the political association.

(Book I, Chapter ii, §§ 8–16)

Actual Constitutions

4. In all states there may be distinguished three parts, or classes, of the citizen body – the very rich; the very poor; and the middle class which forms the mean. Now it is admitted, as a general principle, that moderation and the mean are always best. We may therefore conclude that in the ownership of all gifts of fortune a middle condition will be the best. 5. Men who are in this condition are the most ready to listen to reason. Those who belong to either extreme – the over-handsome, the over-strong, the over-noble, the over-wealthy; or at the opposite end the over-poor, the over-weak, the utterly ignoble – find it hard to follow the lead of reason. Men in the first class tend more to violence

and serious crime: men in the second tend too much to roguery and petty offences; and most wrongdoing arises either from violence or roguery. It is a further merit of the middle class that its members suffer least from ambition, which both in the military and civil sphere is dangerous to states. 6. It must also be added that those who enjoy too many advantages – strength, wealth, connexions, and so forth – are both unwilling to obey and ignorant how to obey. This is a defect which appears in them from the first, from childhood and in home-life: nurtured in luxury, they never acquire a habit of discipline, even in the matter of lessons. But there are also defects in those who suffer from the opposite extreme of a lack of advantages: they are far too mean and poor-spirited. 7. We have thus, on the one hand, people who are ignorant how to rule and only know how to obey, as if they were so many slaves, and, on the other hand, people who are ignorant how to obey any sort of authority and only know how to rule as if they were masters of slaves. The result is a state, not of freemen, but only of slaves and masters: a state of envy on the one side and on the other contempt. Nothing could be further removed from the spirit of friendship or the temper of a political community. Community depends on friendship; and when there is enmity instead of friendship, men will not even share the same path. 8. A state aims at being, as far as it can be, a society composed of equals and peers (who, as such, can be friends and associates); and the middle class, more than any other, has this sort of composition. It follows that a state which is based on the middle class is bound to be the best constituted in respect of the elements (i.e. equals and peers) of which, on our view, a state is naturally composed. The middle classes (besides contributing, in this way, to the security of the state) enjoy a greater security themselves than any other class. 9. They do not, like the poor, covet the goods of others; nor do others covet their possessions, as the poor covet those of the rich. Neither plotting against others, nor plotted against themselves, they live in freedom from danger; and we may well approve the prayer of Phocylides,

> Many things are best for the middling:
> Fain would I be of the state's middle class.

10. It is clear from our argument, first, that the best form of political society is one where power is vested in the middle class, and, secondly, that good government is attainable in those states where there is a large middle class – large enough, if possible, to be stronger than both of the other classes, but at any rate large enough to be stronger than either of them singly; for in that case its addition to either will suffice to turn the scale, and will prevent either of the opposing extremes from becoming

dominant. 11. It is therefore the greatest of blessings for a state that its members should possess a moderate and adequate property. Where some have greater possessions, and others have nothing at all. the result is either an extreme democracy or an unmixed oligarchy; or it may even be – indirectly, and as a reaction against both of these extremes – a tyranny. Tyranny is a form of government which may grow out of the headiest type of democracy, or out of oligarchy; but it is much less likely to grow out of constitutions of the middle order, or those which approximate to them (e.g. moderate oligarchies). 12. We shall explain the reason later, when we come to treat of revolutions and constitutional change.

Meanwhile, it is clear that the middle type of constitution is best (for the *majority* of states). It is the one type free from faction; where the middle class is large, there is least likelihood of faction and dissension among the citizens. 13. Large states are generally more free from faction just because they have a large middle class. In small states, on the other hand, it is easy for the whole population to be divided into only two classes; nothing is left in the middle, and all – or almost all – are either poor or rich. 14. The reason why democracies are generally more secure and more permanent than oligarchies is the character of their middle class, which is more numerous, and is allowed a larger share in the government, than it is in oligarchies. Where democracies have no middle class, and the poor are greatly superior in number, trouble ensues, and they are speedily ruined. 15. It must also be considered a proof of its value that the best legislators have come from the middle class. Solon was one, as his own poems prove; Lycurgus was another (and not, as is sometimes said, a member of the royal family); and the same is true of Charondas and most of the other legislators.

(Book IV, Chapter xi, §§ 4–15)

Ibn Khaldun 1332–1406

Major work

Al-Muqaddimah (The Prolegomena)

The following extracts are reprinted from Ibn Khaldun, *Prolego-mena*, translated by Charles Issawi as *An Arab Philosophy of History* (London: John Murray, 1950), pp. 50–52, 53–5, with the permission of the publisher.

Genealogists, noticing that each people has distinctive physical characteristics, have concluded that this is due to different racial origins ...

The cause of this error is the belief that distinctions between peoples can arise only from racial differences, which is not true. For although certain people have a common ancestry, e.g. the Arabs, the Jews, and the Persians, other people are distinguished by the regions they inhabit, or by their special characteristics as well as descent, e.g. the Arabs. And there are further possibilities as regards habits and distinctive qualities.

It is therefore false to generalize and to say that all who live in a given region, whether in the North or the South, and who share the same colour or traits or occupation are descended from a common ancestor. The error arises from a failure to observe the nature of things and of regions; for everything changes with successive generations and nothing remains constant.

Differences Between Groups are Cultural not Innate

In the East, however, learning did not cease, but it still flourishing and overflowing owing to the continued and unbroken prosperity of society. For although the great cities in which learning developed, such as Baghdad, Basra and Kufa, have been ruined, God Almighty has compensated this loss with other mightier cities. Thus learning shifted eastward to Khorasan, in Persia, and Transoxania, then westward to Cairo and the adjoining regions, which are still flourishing, and actively pursue learning.

The Easterners, then, are, generally speaking, deeply rooted in learning and teaching, as in all the other crafts. This is so true that many travellers who go from the Maghrib to the East in search of learning believe that the minds of the Easterners are more developed than those of the Westerners, [that they are innately quicker and more thoughtful], and that their reason is, by its very nature, more perfect. They even believe that there is a difference between us [i.e. the Westerners] and them in the very essence of humanity, [and get heated up over this theory owing] to what they see of the superiority of the Easterners in the sciences and the crafts. This is not so; there is no essential difference between the Easterners and the Westerners, except perhaps in the habitants of the extreme zones, such as the First and Seventh zones, whose temperaments, and hence their minds, are far removed from moderation, as we mentioned earlier. The differences between Easterners and Westerners are cultural, deriving from the intellectual capacities acquired [by those who practice the crafts].

We mentioned this point earlier and will now develop it further. Civilized townsmen follow certain codes in matters of living, dwelling, and building, in religious and worldly affairs, and, in general, in all their customs and transactions. These codes, which regulate all their behaviour and their actions, seem to constitute impassable limits. Yet, in fact, they are conventional things, made by man and learned by each generation from the preceding one. For there is no doubt that every organized craft affects the soul in such a way as to give it a new mind which will dispose it to acquire another craft and makes the mind readier and more capable of acquiring new knowledge.

The skills acquired in learning, in the crafts and in daily life sharpen men's intelligence and clear their vision by the imprints they leave on the mind. For, as was said before, the mind develops only through experience and the resulting skills which it acquires. Hence [those who live in a civilized environment] acquire a power of judgment derived from the effects of learning and this makes the common people think, wrongly, that they are different in their very nature.

The same holds true of the relation between townsmen and nomads. Townsmen are so much brighter and more intelligent that nomads sometimes think that they [i.e. townsmen] belong to a superior humanity. The truth is that the townsman has perfected certain skills, observed certain codes, and followed certain civilized customs which are unknown to the nomad. The townsman, having practised the crafts and acquired certain skills, thinks that anyone who is deficient in those skills, has not as good an intellect as he has and that the nomad is by birth mentally deficient and inferior to himself. This is not so, for among nomads we find persons endowed with the very highest forms of intellect and understanding. The difference between the two groups arises from the veneer left on the townsman by the crafts and sciences.

The Easterners being more deeply rooted in learning and, for the reasons given in the preceding chapter, the Westerners being nearer the nomadic stage, fools have thought that the differences between them are due to certain essential qualities possessed by the former and lacking in the latter . . .

Imitation of the Conquerors by the Vanquished

The vanquished always seek to imitate their victors in their dress, insignia, belief, and other customs and usages. This is because men are always inclined to attribute perfection to those who have defeated and subjugated them. Men do this either because the reverence they feel for their conquerors makes them see perfection in them or because they refuse to admit that their defeat could have been brought about by ordinary causes, and hence they suppose that it is due to the perfection of the conquerors. Should this belief persist long, it will change into a profound conviction and will lead to the adoption of all the tenets of the victors and the imitation of all their characteristics. This imitation may come about either unconsciously or because of a mistaken belief that the victory of the conquerers was due not to their superior solidarity and strength but to [inferiority of] the customs and beliefs of the conquered. Hence, arises the further belief that such an imitation will remove the causes of defeat.

Therefore we see the defeated always imitating the victors in their way of dressing, of carrying their arms, and in their equipment and in all their mode of living.

Notice, in the same way, how boys imitate their fathers, to whom they attribute all perfection. Notice, too, how, in all countries, the native population generally adopt the dress of the royal garrison stationed in their midst because the latter has imposed its rule upon them. In fact every country which has powerful, conquering neighbours tends, to a large extent, to imitate those neighbours, as we see among the Spanish Muslims today in respect to their Galician [Christian] neighbours. For the Muslims imitate the Galician in their dress and ornaments and indeed in many of their customs and institutions, even to the extent of having statues and pictures on the walls of their houses and shops. And in this the careful observer will mark a sign of inferiority . . .

The Arabs

Arabs, are, of all peoples, the least versed in the crafts. The reason for this is that they are deeply rooted in nomadism, far removed from sedentary society and its accompanying crafts and other activities. Non-Arabs, on the other hand, whether they are the inhabitants of the East or the Christians dwelling North of the Mediterranean, are, of all peoples, best fitted for practising the crafts, since they have a long tradition of sedentary life and are so far removed from nomadism that the camels which have helped the Arabs to remain in a state of nomadism and savagery and the pastures and sands in which camels thrive, are not to be found among them. This is why the lands of the Arabs, and those conquered by them under Islam, are so deficient in crafts that they [i.e. crafts or their products] are imported from abroad. Notice on the other hand how abundant are the crafts in non-Arab lands such as China, India, the land of the Turks, and the lands of the Christians, which export to other lands.

The Berbers of North Africa are in this respect like the Arabs, owing to their long traditions of nomadism, as may be seen from the scarcity of towns in their country. Hence crafts in North Africa are few and not deeply rooted [and consist] of the weaving of wool and the tanning and sewing of hides. Those two industries, in view of the great demand for their products and the abundance of wool and hides in any nomadic society, were developed when the Berbers settled down to sedentary life.

In the East, however, crafts have established themselves since the days of ancient Persian, Babylonian, Egyptian, Israelite, Greek and Roman rule. These lands have practised a sedentary mode of living for many generations, hence the civilized way of life – and therefore the crafts, as we said before – have been cultivated by the inhabitants and have not been wiped out. It is true that Yemen, Bahrain, Oman and the rest of the Arabian peninsula have always been under Arab rule. Yet this rule has persisted for thousands of years, under different peoples, such as 'Ad, Thamud, the Amalekites, the Himyarites and their successors, the Tubba'ites and the Adhwa, who built cities and reached the heights of civilization and luxury. In other words there was a long period of established rule and civilization, under which crafts multiplied and struck roots so that they did not disappear with the passing away of the ruling dynasties or the established state but remain flourishing until this day.

The Eighteenth Century

The seventeenth century can be said to have laid the foundations of the modern western world. The rationalistic attitude of mind, derived from medieval scholasticism, was no longer confined to theological controversies. Free to roam over the whole field of human endeavour, it became the starting point of a revolution in thought. In science there was a more determined effort to devise more simple explanations of phenomena, based on rational observation, experiment and calculation. The unproved assumptions of Aristotle and medieval thought were found wanting and discarded one after another. Nowhere was the revolution in thought more in evidence than in astronomy. The universe of Dante, with the earth as the fixed centre and heaven and hell occupying real and identifiable locations, had to yield to one in which the earth, a comparatively small planet, was divested of its pre-eminent place and accorded a role commensurate with its position and size, no more and no less. For the first time, astronomy allied itself with physics and mathematics to produce a more coherent picture of the universe. New conceptual tools were constantly being devised to facilitate the emergence of a fresh outlook and to account for a different theory of nature.

It might have been thought that, the earth having been displaced from the centre of the universe, man himself would shrink in size and no longer regard himself as possessing a unique status. Quite the reverse. For hundreds of years, man's function in the social system had been predetermined for him, allowing very little scope for individuality. Subject to the whims and ravages of fortune beyond his control, he had to accept his part, great or small, in a system which was greater than the sum of the parts which composed it. Side by side with the Copernican revolution in astronomy, there came about a no less far-reaching revolution in the concept of man. Many factors contributed to this revolution: the revival of humanistic studies, greater security of life, travel and the discovery of new lands, in particular the invention of printing and the wider dissemination of culture. All this was reinforced and given greater impetus by the mechanical philosophy according to which matter is composed of discrete units of atoms, all ultimately alike. Having regained his individuality, man was now alone and solitary, master of his own destiny. He was no longer a part of a system; he was the system himself, round which everything revolved. He had displaced the earth as the centre of the universe, and made himself the centre of his own universe. This mechanical concept of man, by analogy with the atom, as the unit of life and existence of supreme importance in his own right, became henceforth for good or ill an essential presupposition of thought.

This breakthrough in the science of matter and in the concept of man – the two were closely related – was not followed immediately by a total repudiation of the older, classical or medieval way of thought. If anything, the revolutionary element in seventeenth-century thought was consistently underestimated even by those who were its instigators, and its identity with the past over-emphasized. Newton's was the outstanding example. As Lord Keynes pointed out, for all the revolution in thought for which he was responsible, Newton always gave the impression that he was looking backwards, not forwards. It should come as no surprise that much of his life was devoted not to science, but to theology and chronology, whose tradition went back to the early chronicles of the Bible.

All the scientists of the day were people of extreme piety whose faith, they were convinced, would be strengthened by the discoveries of science. Indeed, each discovery or advance in science was regarded as a demonstrable proof of the existence of a beneficent Being and as tending to His greater glory. Even Descartes's philosophy with its principle of doubt and the primacy of the human consciousness was inspired by a rationalism that bore close affinities with medieval theology.

In political theory the revolution in thought, though less

spectacular, was no less significant. Its authors, Thomas Hobbes (1588–1679) and Spinoza (1632–77), were not, however, conscious of the revolutionary element in their thought. They were both men of conservative temperament, who had a horror of violent change. The doctrine which Hobbes so brilliantly expounded to give a philosophical justification for unquestioned obedience to state and authority was very simple. It consisted in assuming that in a state of nature men are virtually animals, but by virtue of a modicum of intelligence which they possess, they realize that it is better to live at peace than in constant warfare. By giving up their rights in a 'free-for-all' state of nature, and submitting to an authority who would maintain law and order in the state, they would be able to live peacefully and securely. A compact or a contract exists now between the ruler and the ruled, which carries with it a condition that the ruler is supreme and sovereign. Whatever issues from his lips is law, for he can't be wrong. His law is therefore a command demanding implicit obedience. None of these basic ideas about the state of nature, contract or law was original; one or other was found in Greek philosophy and could equally have been inspired by the Bible. But in combination and in Hobbes's hands, they were developed into a system of thought concerning society, politics and law unsurpassed for its audacity and depth. As a theory, however, it was frankly materialistic, based on the idea that men, like units of matter, come together and cohere mechanically. Their only purpose is self-preservation, and they are only moved by the prospect of pleasure or the fear of pain. In spite of his atheism, Hobbes was a theologian and a thinker of the old school who did not question, or even feel it necessary to investigate, the institutions of society.

Spinoza's theory differed in important respects from that of Hobbes. Where Hobbes's theory was negative and static, in the sense that it advocated restraint and condemned disobedience, Spinoza's theory was positive and constructive. It specified the conditions of a stable, secure and happy society, based not on fear but on mutual aid and sociability.

Unlike Hobbes, Spinoza put God at the centre of his philosophy, but a God unlike any conceived by man. His conception of God was even relevant to his social and political theory. He did not regard man, in the fashion of the mechanistic philosophy, as a self-contained, autonomous unit, but as one who finds fulfilment only in a community of people animated by a higher purpose. For Spinoza, this higher purpose is the best that our nature requires, and that best is the God in us. All thought, all philosophy, all wisdom had for Spinoza a very practical end, the happiness of the individual. Society was to be ordered in such a way that the conditions of such happiness must be assured, the most important of which are tolerance, freedom of thought and expression. Majority views and opinion must prevail. But whether society is poor or rich, organized one way or another, are insignificant issues compared to the overriding necessity of seeing to it that social life is lived in a climate conducive to the acquisition of wisdom and the attainment of happiness. His theory breathed the spirit of a scientific humanism for which Europe was not yet prepared. It required over a century for discerning minds to realize the dynamic, indeed explosive, character of Spinoza's thought. In the meantime, his political programme was being implemented by the sheer force of circumstance. So his revolution became finally an intellectual and emotional revolution, bringing relief to those who felt constrained by the fetters of custom and tradition. Spinoza did not ask or try to answer the question why things happened in a certain way. He was only concerned to show how things happened, without applauding or regretting the result. Only in this way could we bring a right attitude of mind to them, which must be one of understanding. Like Hobbes, Spinoza's mode of thought and his terminology had an old-fashioned, medieval ring about it.

Towards the end of the seventeenth century and at the beginning of the eighteenth, a subtle change occurred. The scientific revolution had really set in. Its lessons were being absorbed and applied. The accretions and excrescences that accompanied its inception were thrown overboard; only its bare principles were retained. This could be seen not only in speculative thought, but in art and literature. We need only compare Milton and Hobbes on the one hand with Locke and Dryden on the other to realize this. In modes of expression, style and terminology, they are worlds apart. The emphasis in the latter is on simplicity, directness of expression, a plain and unambiguous terminology, not unlike a mathematical equation.

We are not concerned for the moment with literature and art, but with social and political theory. Here Locke's approach was of crucial importance, destined to have a lasting influence. Less original than Hobbes or Spinoza, Locke (1632–1704) had a pragmatical turn of mind which appealed to the rising generation of writers who felt the need to approach the affairs of life in a practical business-like way in tune with the new mercantile spirit of the day. Locke's aim was very modest, to discover what limits should be set to the bounds of knowledge and to avoid speculation that could not be verified by experience. This was the start of empirical philosophy, whose pattern of thought has persisted to the present day. In France, even more than in England, Locke was hailed as the first philosopher who could be understood by the ordinary man and to whose views popular assent could readily be given. It didn't matter if his philosophy was a jumble of half-baked ideas, shot through with paradoxes, which showed how impossible it was to keep to the narrow path of empiricism. But at least Locke blazed the path which could only be ignored at one's peril. It was, however, in his political theory that he came to be widely known and revered, even if it was at bottom a rationalization of a situation that was precipitated by the Whig Revolution of 1688. Locke used the notions of natural rights and contract in a way which made them perfectly consistent with the liberal-bourgeoisie ascendancy in politics. There are natural rights, according to him, to property, equality and freedom. The contract between the ruler and ruled was conceived on the lines of a commercial contract which could be abrogated if one of the parties to it could not or would not adhere to its terms. Locke was the first to formulate the philosophy of representative government. Henceforth all the political movements in England, France, America and elsewhere were influenced, if not directly inspired, by his writings. Like Hobbes, Locke was not concerned to investigate the mechanism of society except in so far as the institutions were defective when judged by the criteria of Whiggism in politics and landlordism in economics.

Now that the political battle was won, at least theoretically, the world was ready for a new perspective in thought, a sociological investigation of history and human affairs. Innumerable factors contributed to bring this about. The conquest of the earth was now being achieved. Vast territories, it is true, were still to be discovered, colonized and exploited, Australasia, Central Africa, the Western States of America. But the consolidation of overseas territories was now firmly established to allow for the further expansion that was to come. The sea lanes round the coasts of Africa, America and Asia were operating regularly to foster trade, commerce and the insatiable curiosity of the European.

For the first time tales, based on first-hand observation, of far-off places and peoples were recounted to the delight, amazement and wonder of European readers. A curious phenomenon was witnessed. The world was being dominated by a few countries of Western Europe. This indisputable, unchallenged and unchallengeable superiority, far from engendering pride and self-esteem, produced the opposite effect. The lives and manners of other people were studied not to prove their inferiority but on the contrary to show how superior they were in many respects to the lives and manners of the Europeans. It was as though the consciousness of genuine superiority bred a no less genuine modesty. As was to be expected, the eighteenth century was also the age of satire, unequalled in the annals of literature. Conscious of the strength of their character and institutions, the Europeans could afford to laugh at themselves by exaggerating the weaknesses to which they, in common with the rest of mankind, were prone.

There was of course a more serious side to this. Nothing impressed the European more than the many-sidedness of human culture and the corollary that the institutions of society, religion, law, politics, manners, and trade were neither sacrosanct nor immutable, that they were human artefacts, and, in this sense, artificial. There was a vast untrodden field of comparative study, and European scholars in France, England, Germany and Italy were not slow to cultivate it. All kinds of ideas were appropriated and made to germinate in their minds. Nature, noble savage, civilization, law, religion, politics, customs, were all subjected to investigation, assigned a precise place in the scheme of things and made the basis of a superficial or profound theory.

Nature was the concept that proved most fruitful, becoming the focus of eighteenth-century thought. The writer who made it central to his thought was Rousseau. Neither a historian nor a philosopher, Rousseau gave impetus to movements of thought in literature, philosophy, education and politics which the intrinsic merits of his ideas hardly justified. Unlike Plato, who thought that you could change human nature by changing human institutions, Rousseau thought that, by abolishing human institutions, you could make human nature be what it was meant to be. For him everything that distorted and inhibited human nature must be wrong. The romantic element in Rousseau's thought must not be regarded as an aberration of mind incapable of facing reality. The idea of the 'noble savage' was not entirely a fiction; it did represent a true picture of a condition of life in which the simple, universal virtues could be expressed at their best. The natural man came, therefore, to mean the real man. So the return to nature meant the return to the essential humanity of man, which was to be free from all artificial restraints. Man is born free, that is, man is meant to be free, but lives in chains.

Living in a society, man can enjoy freedom only if he himself has willed the kind of government that will bring out the best in him. This voluntary submission on the part of all members of society will result in a General Will which cannot be or do wrong because it is the collective will of the community and because the participation of all wills in it is a precondition of its existence. Man's true nature consists in the fulfilment of this General Will. A government must be a personal government or it is not a government. It must be formed by all, known to all, and exist for all. The Geneva of Rousseau's day or the city-states of ancient Greece fulfilled all those conditions. He could conceive of no other form of government, because government and society in his view were virtually identical. For sociology, the idea that man lives best and most freely in a community of which he is an integral part, and which he has had a hand in shaping, anticipates the later important distinction made in sociology between society and community. Rousseau's General Will, however, was differently interpreted to mean that man must subordinate his will to the wider whole, namely, the state, of which he is a part – a doctrine which in the hands of the German thinkers became the most mischievous political doctrine of the nineteenth and twentieth centuries. In psychology, likewise, the idea of a 'collective consciousness', an equally mischievous doctrine, owed much to Rousseau's General Will.

However, the reversal of the idea of nature, which Rousseau did so much to bring about, was a characteristic feature of eighteenth-century thought. There was not the obvious distinction between the natural state of man and the artificial state. Far from being a state of ferocious competition and lawlessness, the natural state of man was conceived as one where freedom, harmony and real happiness prevailed. Not independently of this new view of Nature, the idea that there is a law of Nature discoverable by our Reason which should override all man-made law was revived to produce a revolution in historical jurisprudence. The thinkers of the modern era were not in a position, as the Stoics and Roman jurists had been 2,000 years before them, to dispense with Divine Law and make use of Natural Law alone to serve as the final arbiter of things. What people like Grotius (1583–1645) and Pufendorf (1632–94) did was more subtle and disingenuous. While not repudiating Divine Law, they merely suggested that the application of Natural Law in human affairs would mark a big step in the progress of man. The separation, however, was complete and irrevocable, not without violent opposition from the conservatives and theologians, who suspected that such a separation would undermine the basis of religious belief and practice. And they were right. For if we were to rely entirely on Reason not only to provide us with insight into how things behave, but to guide us towards the right ordering of life, to invoke any other principle for the task would be superfluous. The Age of Reason had begun.

Two types of causes could now be adduced to account for the course of events in history. The first could be called the Primary Cause, that is, Divine Providence, Divine intervention and mission in history. The second would comprise the Secondary Causes. Here it was enough to show, for example, that population is related to the fertility of the soil, that a tyranny would manifest such and such symptoms of behaviour and so forth, leaving the primary cause to those to whom it made an appeal. The most ingenious attempt to use both methods, but keeping them entirely separate, was made by Giambattista Vico (1668–1744), perhaps the greatest scholar of the eighteenth century. For Vico it was only possible to treat history through revealed religion if it could be proved that religion was actually revealed to a certain people. The history of the Jews, and presumably their successors, the Christians, was a different kind of history from that of the Gentile world. The history of the latter, it is true, is ruled by Divine Providence and shares in the common fate of fallen man. But it is a history that follows a course predetermined by its own inner logic. In this way Vico was able to trace the course of history through all the stages of its development, bringing to his interpretation the resources of a powerful mind, versed in law, psychology, philosophy, religion and literature. His was the first secular philosophy of history of modern times. His *Nuova Scienzia* (*New Science*) remains a masterpiece of brilliant insight and imaginative understanding. He was able – and in this he was the first of a long line of historians and social thinkers from Hegel through Comte and Marx to Spengler and Toynbee – to discern three stages in human development, which he called 'The Age of the Gods', 'The Heroic Age' and 'The Human Age'. For him, human history was a process of cyclical recurrence, of 'corsi e ricorsi'. The cycles may differ in detail and in scale, but they all exhibit the same pattern. To take one example: the Heroic Age of antiquity, in which heroic leaders emerged to form a ruling aristocracy, has a parallel in the Middle Ages with their chivalry, codes of honour and poetry. Vico was the pioneer of the concept of social evolution, basic to modern thought. In another respect he was more modern than many modern thinkers. Working within a rigid framework of a theory, he was naturally forced to fit the facts to his theory. But he never allowed the theory to run away with him and in the process distort the facts. He never deviated from the straight path of objective truth as he saw it. For him, as for Spinoza, the primary aim was 'to understand human actions, not to weep over them or hate them'.

Unfortunately, Vico's work, wide-ranging and profound as it was, received scant attention. It was in France that the transition was effected smoothly and successfully from interpreting history through revealed religion to interpreting it in terms of social origins. The difference between the two methods of approach is strikingly revealed in the contrast between Bossuet and Montesquieu. Bossuet (1627–1704), who has left his mark on French literature through his writings, in particular his funeral orations, was a central figure in the religious and political controversies of the time. As prelate, tutor to the Dauphin, and Bishop of Meaux, he had the power to change the course of European history. The aim of many far-sighted men of those times, lay and clerical, was to close ranks and heal the divisions of the Church. Bossuet refused to be a party to this attempt at reconciliation except on his own, that is Catholic, terms. The opportunity was never to arise again. In keeping with his intransigent, inflexible and uncompromising attitude, his *Discours sur l'histoire universelle* (*Discourse on Universal History*) was perhaps the last and greatest attempt to interpret history in terms of the operation of the Primary Cause on human affairs. Bossuet, however, was fighting a rear-guard action. In a matter of a few years the contest was over. The combination of the comparative study of institutions and the tracing of secondary causes, those immediately perceivable and empirically discovered, had produced a revolution in secular thought. Montesquieu was in the forefront of that revolution.

Montesquieu was not a profound or even a consistent thinker. Others in the eighteenth century towered high above him. He had not the literary graces of a Voltaire or a Rousseau, though he had the gift, which only French writers have succeeded in raising to an art, of turning a commonplace into a delightful, witty and clever saying only through the way in which it is expressed. As a historian he lacked the broad sweep and the massive stamina of a Gibbon, nor did he pioneer a new branch of learning as the Physiocrats and Adam Smith did. But he displayed a quality that nobody in the eighteenth century possessed in equal measure, a powerfully penetrating analytical mind. He took the whole world for his province. If he dealt with ancient history, it was not just with the well-known history of the Jews, Greeks and Romans, but also with the lesser-known history of the Egyptians and the Persians. If he dealt with modern history, it was not just with the history of Europe, but also with the little-known history of China, Japan and India. In this way he was able to put his finger invariably and unerringly at the right spot and, without deviating one inch from his prepared position, to show by an examination of human institutions, past and present, how they are affected by law, morals, religion, geography and climate. Patchy, disjointed and untidy as *The Spirit of Laws* is, it must take its place beside the great classics of sociological thought, the equally patchy, disjointed and untidy *Politics* of Aristotle and the *Prolegomena* of Ibn Khaldun. It is without question the first work in pure sociology of modern times and its influence and impact can hardly be exaggerated.

I have said that Montesquieu was not a consistent thinker. By this I mean that frequently he was not clear in his mind as to the direction to which his arguments were leading him, and that some of the generalizations he made either did not follow logically from the premises or were not formulated with that certainty that was required if they were to represent undoubted truths. Otherwise the charge that has been levelled against him by some of his critics, namely that he held contradictory views about human nature and societies, can be dismissed as without substance. To take one example: like Ibn Khaldun before him, or, for that matter, some of the earlier Greek thinkers, Montesquieu was impressed by the role that geography or environment played in human affairs. It was only right that he should devote a great deal of space to showing with copious illustrations, the extent of the influence that geography, taken in a very wide sense, has on the human mind and society at large. In this respect, it might be thought, as some of his critics averred, that he was a determinist or, in marxist jargon, a materialist. Yet no one was more insistent than Montesquieu that it was impossible to view man in mechanical terms as merely a creature of circumstance, that climate, locality and other material factors are not the only determining factors in shaping his life. Man's freedom to choose and determine his own fate was for Montesquieu a cardinal presupposition of thought. There is at bottom no contradiction whatsoever between these two views. Man remains free in the very unfreedom to which he is bound. If some of his customs, laws, conventions, modes of thought can be seen to arise from, and can only be explained by, the locality and the material circumstances in which he is placed, that does not in any way derogate from his essential freedom to make these serve his own ends.

Viewing man in society, Montesquieu could not accept Hobbes's account of him as a ferocious creature, nor Rousseau's idealization of him as a kind of angel. 'I assume', he says, 'that a savage, who has never lived anywhere but in the woods, meets for the first time in his life another man of the same species, and that neither the one nor the other is in a position to flee. Chance, based on the smallest gesture, or demeanour, will determine whether the two men will try to destroy each other or to give each other help. Likewise, the least circumstance will make a people anthropophagous or give it mores.' Although in principle man has a choice to live a social or a-social life, in reality he has always preferred to live in co-operation with other people, for this is the indispensable condition of enjoyment, life and development. It is not a matter of instinct. Man's sociableness is what distinguishes him as man and renders him unique. 'The beasts who have all separate interests always harm each other. Men alone, made to live in society, lose nothing of what they share.' But to live in society means to have a government.

We have now travelled a long way from Hobbes's theory based on contract, the surrender of rights and absolute obedience. Hobbes and Montesquieu are describing two different worlds, and it is easy to see which is mythical and which is real. Social life must then be conceived as resting on the mutual interests of its members and their adjustments must involve coercive sanctions. Central to Montesquieu's sociology is a theory of social control. For man to move about freely it is necessary for him to be constrained, 'for man is like a spring who works the better, the more it is repressed'.

Social control operates through broadly three fundamental institutions, mores, law and religion. Montesquieu was the first to work out the interrelations of these three forms of social control, showing for example that if laws are weakened, religion and mores come to the rescue of society, while on the other hand if religion is weak or less repressive, law is extremely strict. Montesquieu was inclined to give to law a rather more negative role as the repressor of evil, and to religion and mores a more positive role as the promoters of good.

Some of these views may be challenged on the grounds that they are not justified by the facts and they are based on certain *a priori* assumptions about the function of law, religion and mores. But these are insignificant blemishes compared to the outstanding service Montesquieu rendered in showing that society cannot be understood except in terms of the interrelations of parts. Again, Montesquieu's tripartite division of government into monarchical, republican and despotic is perhaps otiose. But the analysis of the institutions that function within the framework of each of these types retains its validity and transcends the compartmentalization into which he forces his thought.

From hundreds of examples, we will take one to illustrate Montesquieu's supreme talent for social analysis. This is how he accounts for the universal aversion in human society to incest. First he disposes of certain misconceptions. The incest-taboo cannot be said to be based on an instinctive revulsion from intercourse between near blood relatives, nor is such intercourse, as the glib phrase has it, 'against nature'. The universal prohibition of such sex contacts must be seen to arise from the human situation as such, which doesn't allow for contradictory sentiments to co-exist in the human mind. The relationship between father and daughter is based on authority, which in turn requires that a certain distance should come between the two parties in question. The relationship between husband and wife is based on a kind of equality, which is guaranteed as it were by the intimacy or nearness that the relationship entails. A human relationship cannot therefore be one of distance and nearness at one and the same time. 'How should a daughter have married herself to her father? As daughter, she would have owed him unlimited respect; as wife, there would have been equality between them. These two qualities would have been incompatible.' The taboo and its condemnation is easily transferred to the brother-sister relationship, though obviously it is somewhat weaker here. The universality of the incest-taboo does admit, however, of exceptions in which the sentiments existing among near blood relatives are such that intercourse between father and daughter, mother and son, and brother and sister can and does occur more frequently than is generally supposed. Nothing that has been written or said about the incest-taboo in the last two hundred years is more than an elaboration, if that, of Montesquieu's analysis. Montesquieu's most distinguished successor in this field, Claude Lévi-Strauss, simply takes the incest-taboo as a given, almost inexplicable, fact, and attributes to it the primary role in the institution of the human family, and hence of society and culture.

Charles de Secondat, Baron de Montesquieu 1689–1755

Major works

Persian Letters (*Les Lettres persanes*; 1721)
The Spirit of the Laws (*De l'Esprit des lois*; 1748)

The following extracts are reprinted from Montesquieu, *The Spirit of the Laws*, translated by Thomas Nugent (2 volumes, London: George Bell & Sons, 1878).

Of the Relation of Laws to Different Beings

Laws, in their most general signification, are the necessary relations arising from the nature of things. In this sense all beings have their laws: the Deity His laws, the material world its laws, the intelligences superior to man their laws, the beasts their laws, man his laws.

They who assert that a blind fatality produced the various effects we behold in this world talk very absurdly; for can anything be more unreasonable than to pretend that a blind fatality could be productive of intelligent beings?

There is, then, a prime reason; and laws are the relations subsisting between it and different beings, and the relations of these to one another.

God is related to the universe, as Creator and Preserver; the laws by which He created all things are those by which He preserves them. He acts according to these rules, because He knows them; He knows them, because He made them; He made them, because they are in relation to His wisdom and power.

Since we observe that the world, though formed by the motion of matter, and void of understanding, subsists through so long a succession

57

of ages, its motions must certainly be directed by invariable laws; and could we imagine another world, it must also have constant rules, or it would inevitably perish.

Thus the creation, which seems an arbitrary act, supposes laws as invariable as those of the fatality of the Atheists. It would be absurd to say that the Creator might govern the world without those rules, since without them it could not subsist.

These rules are a fixed and invariable relation. In bodies moved, the motion is received, increased, diminished, or lost according to the relations of the quantity of matter and velocity; each diversity is uniformity, each change is constancy.

Particular intelligent beings may have laws of their own making, but they have some likewise which they never made. Before there were intelligent beings, they were possible; they had therefore possible relations, and consequently possible laws. Before laws were made, there were relations of possible justice. To say that there is nothing just or unjust but what is commanded or forbidden by positive laws, is the same as saying that before the describing of a circle all the radii were not equal.

We must therefore acknowledge relations of justice antecedent to the positive law by which they are established: as, for instance, if human societies existed, it would be right to conform to their laws; if there were intelligent beings that had received a benefit of another being, they ought to show their gratitude; if one intelligent being had created another intelligent being, the latter ought to continue in its original state of dependence; if one intelligent being injures another, it deserves a retaliation; and so on.

But the intelligent world is far from being so well governed as the physical. For though the former has also its laws, which of their own nature are invariable, it does not conform to them so exactly as the physical world. This is because, on the one hand, particular intelligent beings are of a finite nature, and consequently liable to error; and on the other, their nature requires them to be free agents. Hence they do not steadily conform to their primitive laws; and even those of their own instituting they frequently infringe.

Whether brutes be governed by the general laws of motion, or by a particular movement, we cannot determine. Be that as it may, they have not a more intimate relation to God than the rest of the material world; and sensation is of no other use to them than in the relation they have either to other particular beings or to themselves.

By the allurement of pleasure they preserve the individual, and by the same allurement they preserve their species. They have natural laws, because they are united by sensation; positive laws they have none, because they are not connected by knowledge. And yet they do not invariably conform to their natural laws; these are better observed by vegetables, that have neither understanding nor sense.

Brutes are deprived of the high advantages which we have; but they have some which we have not. They have not our hopes, but they are without our fears; they are subject like us to death, but without knowing it; even most of them are more attentive than we to self-preservation, and do not make so bad a use of their passions.

Man, as a physical being, is like other bodies governed by invariable laws. As an intelligent being, he incessantly transgresses the law established by God, and changes those of his own instituting. He is left to his private direction, though a limited being, and subject, like all finite intelligences, to ignorance and error; even his imperfect knowledge he loses; and as a sensible creature, he is hurried away by a thousand impetuous passions. Such a being might every instant forget his Creator; God has therefore reminded him of his duty by the laws of religion. Such a being is liable every moment to forget himself; philosophy has provided against this by the laws of morality. Formed to live in society, he might forget his fellow-creatures; legislators have therefore by political and civil laws confined him to his duty.

Of the Laws of Nature

Antecedent to the above-mentioned laws are those of nature, so called, because they derive their force entirely from our frame and existence. In order to have a perfect knowledge of these laws, we must consider man before the establishment of society: the laws received in such a state would be those of nature.

The law which, impressing on our minds the idea of a Creator, inclines us towards Him, is the first in importance, though not in order, of natural laws. Man in a state of nature would have the faculty of knowing, before he had acquired any knowledge. Plain it is that his first ideas would not be of a speculative nature; he would think of the preservation of his being, before he would investigate its origin. Such a man would feel nothing in himself at first but impotency and weakness; his fears and apprehensions would be excessive; as appears from instances (were there any necessity of proving it) of savages found in forests, trembling at the motion of a leaf, and flying from every shadow.

In this state every man, instead of being sensible of his equality, would fancy himself inferior. There would therefore be no danger of their attacking one another; peace would be the first law of nature.

The natural impulse or desire which Hobbes attributes to mankind of subduing one another is far from being well founded. The idea of empire and dominion is so complex, and depends on so many other notions, that it could never be the first which occurred to the human understanding.

Hobbes inquires, for what reason go men armed, and have locks and keys to fasten their doors, if they be not naturally in a state of war? But is it not obvious that he attributes to mankind before the establishment of society what can happen but in consequence of this establishment, which furnishes them with motives for hostile attacks and self-defence?

Next to a sense of his weakness man would soon find that of his wants. Hence another law of nature would prompt him to seek for nourishment.

Fear, I have observed, would induce men to shun one another; but the marks of this fear being reciprocal, would soon engage them to associate. Besides, this association would quickly follow from the very pleasure one animal feels at the approach of another of the same species. Again, the attraction arising from the difference of sexes would enhance this pleasure, and the natural inclination they have for each other would form a third law.

Beside the sense or instinct which man possesses in common with brutes, he has the advantage of acquired knowledge; and thence arises a second tie, which brutes have not. Mankind have therefore a new motive of uniting; and a fourth law of nature results from the desire of living in society.

(Book I, Chapters 1–2, pp. 1–5)

Of the General Spirit of Mankind

Mankind are influenced by various causes: by the climate, by the religion, by the laws, by the maxims of government, by precedents, morals, and customs; whence is formed a general spirit of nations.

In proportion as, in every country, any one of these causes acts with more force, the others in the same degree are weakened. Nature and the climate rule almost alone over the savages; customs govern the Chinese; the laws tyrannise in Japan; morals had formerly all their influence at Sparta; maxims of government, and the ancient simplicity of manners, once prevailed at Rome.

How Far We Should be Attentive Lest the General Spirit of a Nation be Changed

Should there happen to be a country whose inhabitants were of a social temper, open-hearted, cheerful, endowed with taste and a facility in communicating their thoughts; who were sprightly and agreeable; sometimes imprudent, often indiscreet; and besides had courage, generosity, frankness, and a certain notion of honour, no one ought to endeavour to restrain their manners by law, unless he would lay a constraint on their virtues. If in general the character be good, the little foibles that may be found in it are of small importance.

They might lay a restraint upon women, enact laws to reform their manners and to reduce their luxury, but who knows but that by these means they might lose that peculiar taste which would be the source of the wealth of the nation, and that politeness which would render the country frequented by strangers?

It is the business of the legislature to follow the spirit of the nation, when it is not contrary to the principles of government; for we do nothing so well as when we act with freedom, and follow the bent of our natural genius.

If an air of pedantry be given to a nation that is naturally gay, the state will gain no advantage from it, either at home or abroad. Leave it to do frivolous things in the most serious manner, and with gaiety the things most serious.

That Everything Ought not to be Corrected

Let them but leave us as we are, said a gentleman of a nation which had a very great resemblance to that we have been describing, and nature will repair whatever is amiss. She has given us a vivacity capable of offending, and hurrying us beyond the bounds of respect: this same vivacity is corrected by the politeness it procures, inspiring us with a taste of the world, and, above all, for the conversation of the fair sex.

Let them leave us as we are; our indiscretions joined to our good nature would make the laws which should constrain our sociability not at all proper for us.

Of the Athenians and Lacedæmonians

The Athenians, this gentleman adds, were a nation that had some relation to ours. They mingled gaiety with business; a stroke of raillery was as agreeable in the senate as in the theatre. This vivacity, which discovered itself in their councils, went along with them in the execution of their resolves. The characteristic of the Spartans was gravity, seriousness, severity, and silence. It would have been as difficult to bring over an Athenian by teasing as it would a Spartan by diverting him.

The Eighteenth Century

Effects of a Sociable Temper

The more communicative a people are the more easily they change their habits, because each is in a greater degree a spectacle to the other; and the singularities of individuals are better observed. The climate which influences one nation to take pleasure in being communicative, makes it also delight in change, and that which makes it delight in change forms its taste.

The society of the fair sex spoils the manners and forms the taste; the desire of giving greater pleasure than others establishes the embellishments of dress; and the desire of pleasing others more than ourselves gives rise to fashions. This fashion is a subject of importance; by encouraging a trifling turn of mind, it continually increases the branches of its commerce.

Of the Vanity and Pride of Nations

Vanity is as advantageous to a government as pride is dangerous. To be convinced of this we need only represent, on the one hand, the numberless benefits which result from vanity, as industry, the arts, fashions, politeness, and taste; on the other, the infinite evils which spring from the pride of certain nations, as laziness, poverty, a total neglect of everything – in fine, the destruction of the nations which have happened to fall under their government, as well as of their own. Laziness is the effect of pride; labour, a consequence of vanity. The pride of a Spaniard leads him to decline labour; the vanity of a Frenchman to work better than others.

All lazy nations are grave; for those who do not labour regard themselves as the sovereigns of those who do.

If we search amongst all nations, we shall find that for the most part gravity, pride, and indolence go hand in hand.

The people of Achim are proud and lazy; those who have no slaves, hire one, if it be only to carry a quart of rice a hundred paces; they would be dishonoured if they carried it themselves.

In many places people let their nails grow, that all may see they do not work.

Women in the Indies believe it shameful for them to learn to read: this is, they say, the business of their slaves, who sing their spiritual songs in the temples of their pagods. In one tribe they do not spin; in another they make nothing but baskets and mats; they are not even to pound rice; and in others they must not go to fetch water. These rules are established by pride, and the same passion makes them followed.

There is no necessity for mentioning that the moral qualities, according as they are blended with others, are productive of different effects; thus pride, joined to a vast ambition and notions of grandeur, produced such effects among the Romans as are known to all the world.

Of the Character of the Spaniards and Chinese

The characters of the several nations are formed of virtues and vices, of good and bad qualities. From the happy mixture of these, great advantages result, and frequently where it would be least expected; there are others whence great evils arise – evils which one would not suspect.

The Spaniards have been in all ages famous for their honesty. Justin mentions their fidelity in keeping whatever was intrusted to their care; they have frequently suffered death rather than reveal a secret. They have still the same fidelity for which they were formerly distinguished. All the nations who trade at Cadiz trust their fortunes to the Spaniards, and have never yet repented it. But this admirable quality, joined to their indolence, forms a mixture whence such effects result as to them are most pernicious. The rest of the European nations carry on in their very sight all the commerce of their monarchy.

The character of the Chinese is formed of another mixture, directly opposite to that of the Spaniards; the precariousness of their subsistence inspires them with a prodigious activity, and such an excessive desire of gain, that no trading nation can confide in them. This acknowledged infidelity has secured them the possession of the trade to Japan. No European merchant has ever dared to undertake it in their name, how easy soever it might be for them to do it from their maritime provinces in the north.

A Reflection

I have said nothing here with a view to lessen that infinite distance which must ever be between virtue and vice. God forbid that I should be guilty of such an attempt! I would only make my readers comprehend that all political are not all moral vices; and that all moral are not political vices; and that those who make laws which shock the general spirit of a nation ought not to be ignorant of this.

Of Customs and Manners in a Despotic State

It is a capital maxim, that the manners and customs of a despotic empire ought never to be changed; for nothing would more speedily produce a revolution. The reason is, that in these states there are no laws, that is, none that can be properly called so; there are only manners and customs; and if you overturn these you overturn all.

Laws are established, manners are inspired; these proceed from a general spirit, those from a particular institution: now it is as dangerous, nay more so, to subvert the general spirit as to change a particular institution.

There is less communication in a country where each, either as superior or inferior, exercises or is oppressed by arbitrary power, than there is in those where liberty reigns in every station. They do not, therefore, so often change their manners and behaviour. Fixed and established customs have a near resemblance to laws. Thus it is here necessary that a prince or a legislator should oppose the manners and customs of the people than in any other country upon earth.

Their women are commonly confined, and have no influence in society. In other countries, where they have intercourse with men, their desire of pleasing, and the desire men also have of giving them pleasure, produce a continual change of customs. The two sexes spoil each other; they both lose their distinctive and essential quality; what was naturally fixed becomes quite unsettled, and their customs and behaviour alter every day.

Of the Behaviour of the Chinese

But China is the place where the customs of the country can never be changed. Besides their women being absolutely separated from the men, their customs, like their morals, are taught in the schools. A man of letters may be known by his easy address. These things being once taught by precept, and inculcated by grave doctors, become fixed, like the principles of morality, and are never changed.

What are the Natural Means of Changing the Manners and Customs of a Nation

We have said that the laws were the particular and precise institutions of a legislator, and manners and customs the institutions of a nation in general. Hence it follows that when these manners and customs are to be changed, it ought not to be done by laws; this would have too much the air of tyranny: it would be better to change them by introducing other manners and other customs.

Thus when a prince would make great alterations in his kingdom, he should reform by law what is established by law, and change by custom what is settled by custom; for it is very bad policy to change by law what ought to be changed by custom.

The law which obliged the Muscovites to cut off their beards and to shorten their clothes, and the rigour with which Peter I made them crop, even to their knees, the long cloaks of those who entered into the cities, were instances of tyranny. There are means that may be made use of to prevent crimes; these are punishments: there are those for changing our customs; these are examples.

The facility and ease with which that nation has been polished plainly shows that this prince had a worse opinion of his people than they deserved; and that they were not brutes, though he was pleased to call them so. The violent measures which he employed were needless; he would have attained his end as well by milder methods.

He himself experienced the faculty of bringing about these alterations. The women were shut up, and in some measure slaves; he called them to court; he sent them skills and fine stuffs, and made them dress like the German ladies. The sex immediately relished a manner of life which so greatly flattered their taste, their vanity, and their passions; and by their means it was relished by the men.

What rendered the change the more easy was that their manners at that time were foreign to the climate, and had been introduced amongst them by conquest and by a mixture of nations. Peter I, in giving the manners and customs of Europe to a European nation, found a faculty which he did not himself expect. The empire of the climate is the first, the most powerful, of all empires. He had then no occasion for laws to change the manners and customs of his country; it would have been sufficient to have introduced other manners and other customs.

Nations are in general very tenacious of their customs; to take them away by violence is to render them unhappy: we should not therefore change them, but engage the people to make the change themselves.

All punishment which is not derived from necessity is tyrannical. The law is not a mere act of power; things in their own nature indifferent are not within its province.

The Influence of Domestic Government on the Political

This alteration in the manners of women will doubtless have a great influence on the government of Muscovy. One naturally follows the other: the despotic power of the prince is connected with the servitude of women; the liberty of women with the spirit of monarchy.

How Some Legislators Have Confounded the Principles Which Govern Mankind

Manners and customs are those habits which are not established by legislators, either because they were not able or were not willing to establish them.

There is this difference between laws and manners, that the laws are most adapted to regulate the actions of the subject, and manners to regulate the actions of the man. There is this difference between manners and customs, that the former principally relate to the interior conduct, the latter to the exterior.

These things have been sometimes confounded. Lycurgus made the same code for the laws, manners, and customs; and the legislators of China have done the same.

We ought not to be surprised that the legislators of China and Sparta should confound the laws, manners, and customs; the reason is, their manners represent their laws, and their customs their manners.

The principal object which the legislators of China had in view was to make their subjects live in peace and tranquillity. They would have people filled with a veneration for one another, that each should be every moment sensible of his dependence on society, and of the obligations he owed to his fellow-citizens. They therefore gave rules of the most extensive civility.

Thus the inhabitants of the villages of China practise amongst themselves the same ceremonies as those observed by persons of an exalted station; a very proper method of inspiring mild and gentle dispositions, of maintaining peace and good order, and of banishing all the vices which spring from an asperity of temper. In effect, would not the freeing them from the rules of civility be to search out a method for them to indulge their own humours?

Civility is in this respect of more value than politeness. Politeness flatters the vices of others, and civility prevents ours from being brought to light. It is a barrier which men have placed within themselves to prevent the corruption of each other.

Lycurgus, whose institutions were severe, had no regard to civility in forming the external behaviour; he had a view to that warlike spirit with which he would fain inspire his people. A people who were in a continual state of discipline and instruction, and who were endued with equal simplicity and rigour, atoned by their virtues for their want of complaisance.

Of the Peculiar Quality of the Chinese Government

The legislators of China went further. They confounded their religion, laws, manners, and customs; all these were morality, all these were virtue. The precepts relating to these four points were what they called rites; and it was in the exact observance of these that the Chinese government triumphed. They spent their whole youth in learning them, their whole life in the practice. They were taught by their men of letters, they were inculcated by the magistrates; and as they included all the ordinary actions of life, when they found the means of making them strictly observed, China was well governed.

Two things have contributed to the ease with which these rites are engraved on the hearts and minds of the Chinese; one, the difficulty of writing, which during the greatest part of their lives wholly employs their attention, because it is necessary to prepare them to read and understand the books in which they are comprised; the other, that the ritual precepts having nothing in them that is spiritual, but being merely rules of common practice, are more adapted to convince and strike the mind than things merely intellectual.

Those princes who, instead of ruling these rites, governed by the force of punishments, wanted to accomplish that by punishments which it is not in their power to produce, that is, to give habits of morality. By punishments, a subject is very justly cut off from society, who, having lost the purity of his manners, violates the laws; but if all the world were to lose their moral habits, would these re-establish them? Punishments may be justly inflicted to put a stop to many of the consequences of the general evil, but they will not remove the evil itself. Thus when the principles of the Chinese government were discarded, and morality was banished, the state fell into anarchy, and revolutions succeeded.

A Consequence Drawn from the Preceding Chapter

Hence it follows that the laws of China are not destroyed by conquest. Their customs, manners, laws, and religion being the same thing, they cannot change all these at once; and as it will happen that either the conqueror or the conquered must change, in China it has always been the conqueror. For the manners of the conquering nation not being their customs, nor their customs their laws, nor their laws their religion, it has been more easy for them to conform by degrees to the vanquished people than the latter to them.

There still follows hence a very unhappy consequence, which is, that it is almost impossible for Christianity ever to be established in China. The vows of virginity, the assembling of women in churches, their necessary communication with the ministers of religion, their participation in the sacraments, auricular confession, extreme unction, the marriage of only one wife – all these overturn the manners and customs of the country, and with the same blow strike at their religion and laws.

The Christian religion, by the establishment of charity, by a public worship, by a participation of the same sacraments, seems to demand that all should be united; while the rites of China seem to ordain that all should be separated.

And as we have seen that this separation depends, in general, on the spirit of despotism, this will show us the reason why monarchies, and indeed all moderate governments, are more consistent with the Christian religion.

How this Union of Religion, Laws, Manners, and Customs Amongst the Chinese was Effected

The principal object of government which the Chinese legislators had in view was the peace and tranquillity of the empire; and subordination appeared to them as the most proper means to maintain it. Filled with this idea, they believed in their duty to inspire a respect for parents, and therefore exerted all their power to effect it. They established an infinite number of rites and ceremonies to do them honour when living, and after their death. It was impossible for them to pay such honours to deceased parents without being led to reverence the living. The ceremonies at the death of a father were more nearly related to religion; those for a living parent had a greater relation to the laws, manners, and customs: however, these were only parts of the same code; but this code was very extensive.

A veneration for their parents was necessarily connected with a suitable respect for all who represented them; such as old men, masters, magistrates, and the sovereign. This respect for parents supposed a return of love towards children, and consequently the same return from old men to the young, from magistrates to those who were under their jurisdiction, and from the emperor to his subjects. This formed the rites, and these rites the general spirit of the nation.

We shall now show the relation which things in appearance the most indifferent may bear to the fundamental constitution of China. This empire is formed on the plan of a government of a family. If you diminish the paternal authority, or even if you retrench the ceremonies which express your respect for it, you weaken the reverence due to magistrates, who are considered as fathers; nor would the magistrates have the same care of the people whom they ought to look upon as their children; and that tender relation which subsists between the prince and his subjects would insensibly be lost. Retrench but one of these habits and you overturn the state. It is a thing in itself very indifferent whether the daughter-in-law rises every morning to pay such and such duties to her mother-in-law; but if we consider that these exterior habits incessantly revive an idea necessary to be imprinted on all minds – an idea that forms the ruling spirit of the empire – we shall see that it is necessary that such or such a particular action be performed.

Explanation of a Paradox Relating to the Chinese

It is very remarkable that the Chinese, whose lives are guided by rites, are nevertheless the greatest cheats upon earth. This appears chiefly in their trade, which, in spite of its natural tendency, has never been able to make them honest. He who buys of them ought to carry with him his own weights; every merchant having three sorts, the one heavy for buying, another light for selling, and another of the true standard for those who are upon their guard. It is possible, I believe, to explain this contradiction.

The legislators of China had two objects in view: they were desirous that the people should be submissive and peaceful, and that they should also be laborious and industrious. By the nature of the soil and climate, their subsistence is very precarious; nor can it be in any other way secured than by industry and labour.

When every one obeys, and every one is employed, the state is in a happy situation. It is necessity, and perhaps the nature of the climate, that has given to the Chinese an inconceivable greediness for gain, and laws have never been made to restrain it. Everything has been forbidden when acquired by acts of violence; everything permitted when obtained by artifice or labour. Let us not then compare the morals of China with those of Europe. Every one in China is obliged to be attentive to what will be for his advantage; if the cheat has been watchful over his own interest, he who is the dupe ought to be attentive to his. At Sparta they were permitted to steal; in China they are suffered to deceive.

(Book XIX, Chapters 4–20, pp. 316–28)

Of Luxury

Luxury is ever in proportion to the inequality of fortunes. If the riches of a state are equally divided there will be no luxury; for it is founded merely on the conveniences acquired by the labour of others.

In order to have this equal distribution of riches, the law ought to give to each man only what is necessary for nature. If they exceed these bounds, some will spend, and others will acquire, by which means an inequality will be established.

Supposing what is necessary for the support of nature to be equal to a given sum, the luxury of those who have only what is barely necessary will be equal to a cipher: if a person happens to have double that sum, his luxury will be equal to one; he that has double the latter's substance will have a luxury equal to three; if this be still doubled, there will be a luxury equal to seven; so that the property of the subsequent individual being always supposed double to that of the preceding, the luxury will increase double, and a unit be always added, in this progression, 0, 1, 3, 7, 15, 31, 63, 127.

In Plato's republic, luxury might have been exactly calculated. There were four sorts of censuses or rates of estates. The first was exactly the term beyond poverty, the second was double, the third triple, the fourth quadruple to the first. In the first census, luxury was equal to a cipher; in the second to one, in the third to two, in the fourth to three: and thus it followed in an arithmetical proportion.

Considering the luxury of different nations with respect to one another, it is in each state a compound proportion to the inequality of wealth in different states. In Poland, for example, there is an extreme inequality of fortunes, but the poverty of the whole hinders them from having so much luxury as in a more opulent government.

Luxury is also in proportion to the populousness of the towns, and especially of the capital; so that it is in a compound proportion to the riches of the state, to the inequality of private fortunes, and to the number of people settled in particular places.

In proportion to the populousness of towns, the inhabitants are filled with notions of vanity, and actuated by an ambition of distinguishing themselves by trifles. If they are very numerous, and most of them strangers to one another, their vanity redoubles, because there are greater hopes of success. As luxury inspires these hopes, each man assumes the marks of a superior condition. But by endeavouring thus at distinction, every one becomes equal, and distinction ceases; as all are desirous of respect, nobody is regarded.

Hence arises a general inconvenience. Those who excel in a profession set what value they please on their labour; this example is followed by people of inferior abilities, and then there is an end of all proportion between our wants and the means of satisfying them. When I am forced to go to law, I must be able to fee counsel; when I am sick, I must have it in my power to fee a physician.

It is the opinion of several, that the assemblage of so great a multitude of people in capital cities is an obstruction to commerce, because the inhabitants are no longer at a proper distance from each other. But I cannot think so; for men have more desires, more wants, more fancies, when they live together.

(Book VII, Chapter 1, pp. 102–4)

Jean Jacques Rousseau 1712–78

Major works

Discourse on Inequality (Discours sur l'origine de l'inégalité; 1755)
La nouvelle Héloïse (1761)
Émile (1762)
The Social Contract (Le Contrat social; 1762)

The following extract is reprinted from Jean Jacques Rousseau, *Le Contrat social*, translated as *A Treatise on the Social Compact* in *The Miscellaneous Works of Mr J. J. Rousseau* (London: T. Becket and P. A. DeHondt, 1767), Book I, Chapters v–ix, and Book II, Chapters i–iii, pp. 16–37.

On the Necessity of Recurring Always to the Primitive Convention

On the supposition, that I should grant to be true what I have hitherto disproved, the advocate for despotism would, however, profit but little. There will be always a great difference between subjecting a multitude, and governing a society. Let individuals, in any number whatever, become severally and successively subject to one man, they are all, in that case, nothing more than master and slaves; they are not a people governed by their chief; they are an Aggregate if you will, but do not form an association; there subsists among them neither commonwealth nor body politic. Such a superior, though he should become the master of half the world, would be still a private person, and his interest, separate and distinct from that of his people, would be still no more than a private interest. When such a person dies, also the empire over which he presided is dissolved, and its component parts remain totally unconnected, just as an oak falls into a heap of ashes, when it is consumed by the fire.

A people, says Grotius, may voluntarily bestow themselves on a king: according to Grotius, therefore, a people are a people before they thus give themselves up to regal authority. Even this gift, however, is an act of society, and presupposes a public deliberation on the matter. Hence, before we examine into the act, by which a people make choice of a king, it is proper to examine into that by which a people became a people, for, on this, which is necessarily prior to the other, rests the true foundation of society.

For, if, in fact, there be no prior convention, whence arises (unless indeed the election was unanimous) the obligation of the smaller number to submit to the choice of the greater? and whence comes it, that an hundred persons, for instance, who might desire to have a master, had a right to vote for ten others who might desire to have none? The choice by a plurality of votes is itself an establishment of convention, and supposes, that unanimity must at least for once have subsisted among them.

On the Social Pact or Covenant

I suppose mankind arrived at that term, when the obstacles to their preservation, in a state of nature, prevail over the endeavours of individuals, to maintain themselves in such a state. At such a crisis this primitive state therefore could no longer subsist, and the human race must have perished, if they had not changed their manner of living.

Now as men cannot create new powers, but only compound and direct those which really exist, they have no other means of preservation, than that of forming, by their union, an accumulation of forces, sufficient to oppose the obstacles to their security, and of putting these in action by a first mover, capable of making them act in concert with each other.

This general accumulation of power cannot arise but from the concurrence of many particular forces; but the force and liberty of each individual being the principal instruments of his own preservation, how is he to engage them in the common interest, without hurting his own, and neglecting the obligations he lies under to himself? This difficulty, being applied to my present subject, may be expressed in the following terms:

'To find that form of association which shall protect and defend, with the whole force of the community, the person and property of each individual, and in which each person, by uniting himself to the rest, shall nevertheless be obedient only to himself, and remain as fully at liberty as before.' Such is the fundamental problem, of which the social compact gives the solution.

The clauses of this compact are so precisely determined by the nature of the act, that the least restriction or modification renders them void and of no effect; in so much, that, although they may perhaps never have been formally promulgated, they are yet universally the same, and are every where tacitly acknowledged and received. When the social pact, however, is violated, individuals recover their natural liberty, and are re-invested with their original rights, by losing that conventional liberty for the sake of which they had renounced them.

Again; these clauses, well understood are all reducible to one, *viz.* the total alienation of every individual, with all his rights and privileges, to the whole community. For, in the first place, as every one gives himself up entirely and without reserve, all are in the same circumstances, so that no one can be interested in making their common connection burthensome to others.

Besides, as the alienation is made without reserve, the union is as perfect as possible, nor hath any particular associate any thing to reclaim; whereas, if they should severally retain any peculiar privileges, there being no common umpire to determine between them and the public, each being his own judge in some cases, would, in time, pretend to be so in all, the state of nature would still subsist, and their association would necessarily become tyrannical or void.

In fine, the individual, by giving himself up to all, gives himself to none: and, as he acquires the same right over every other person in the community, as he gives them over himself, he gains an equivalent for what he bestows, and still a greater power to preserve what he retains.

If, therefore, we take from the social compact every thing that is not essential to it, we shall find it reduced to the following terms: 'We, the contracting parties, do jointly and severally submit our persons and abilities, to the supreme direction of the general will of all, and, in a collective body, receive each member into that body, as an indivisible part of the whole.'

This act of association accordingly converts the several individual contracting parties into one moral collective body, composed of as many members as there are votes in the assembly, which receives also from the same act its unity and existence. This public personage, which is thus formed by the union of all its members, used formerly to be denominated a CITY,[1] and, at present, takes the name of a *republic*,

1. The true sense of this word is almost entirely perverted among the moderns; most people take a town for a city, and an house-keeper for a citizen. Such are ignorant, however, that, though houses may form a town, it is the citizens only that constitute a city. This same errour formerly cost the Carthaginians very dear. I do not remember, in the course of my reading, to have ever found the title of *Cives* given to the subjects of a prince, not even formerly to the Macedonians, nor, in our times, to the English, though more nearly bordering on liberty than any other nation. The French are the only people who familiarly take on themselves the name of *citizens*, because they have no just idea of its meaning, as may be seen in their dictionaries; for, were it otherwise, indeed, they would be guilty of high treason in assuming it. This term is with them rather expressive of a virtue than a privilege. Hence, when Bodin spoke of the citizens and inhabitants of Geneva, he committed a wretched blunder, in mistaking one for the other. Mr d'Alembert indeed has avoided this mistake in the

or *body politic*. It is also called, by its several members, a *state*, when it is passive; the *sovereign*, when it is active; and simply a *power*, when it is compared with other bodies of the same nature. With regard to the associates themselves, they take collectively the name of the *people*, and are separately called *citizens*, as partaking of the sovereign authority, and *subjects*, as subjected to the laws of the state. These terms, indeed, are frequently confounded, and mistaken one for the other; it is sufficient, however, to be able to distinguish them, when they are used with precision.

Of the Sovereign

It is plain from the above formula, that the act of association includes a reciprocal engagement between particulars and the public; and that each individual, in contracting, if I may so say, with himself, is laid under a twofold engagement, *viz.* as a member of the sovereignty toward particular persons, and as a member of the state toward the sovereign. That maxim of the civil law, however, is inapplicable here, which says, that no one is bound by the engagements he enters into with himself; for, there is a wide difference between entering into a personal obligation with one's self, and with a whole, of which one may constitute a part.

It is farther to be observed, that the public determination, which is obligatory on the subject, with regard to the sovereign, on account of the twofold relation by which each stands contracted, is not, for the contrary reason, obligatory on the supreme power towards itself: and that it is consequently inconsistent with the nature of the body politic, that such supreme power should impose a law, which it cannot break. For, as the sovereign stands only in a single relation, it is in the same case as that of an individual contracting with himself; whence it is plain, that there neither is, nor can be, any fundamental law obligatory on the whole body of a people, even the social compact itself not being such. By this, however, it is not meant, that such a body cannot enter into engagements with others, in matters that do not derogate from this contract; for, with respect to foreign objects, it is a simple and individual person.

But, as the body politic, or the sovereign, derives its very existence from this inviolable contract, it can enter into no lawful engagement,

---

Encyclopædia, where he has properly distinguished the four orders of people (and even five reckoning mere strangers) that are found in our city, and of which two only compose the republic: No other French author than I know of hath ever comprehended the meaning of the word *citizen*.

even with any similar body, derogatory from the tenour of this primitive act; such as that of alienating any part of itself, or of submitting itself intirely to a foreign sovereign. To violate the act whereby it exists would be to annihilate itself, and from nothing can arise nothing.

No sooner are a multitude of individuals thus united in a body, than it becomes impossible to act offensively against any of the members, without attacking the whole, and still less to offend the whole body, without injuring the members. Hence both duty and interest equally oblige the two contracting parties to assist each other, and the same persons ought to endeavour to include, within this twofold relation, all the advantages which depend on it.

Now the sovereign, being formed only by the several individuals of which the state is composed, can have no interest contrary to theirs; of course the supreme power stands in no need of any guarantee toward the subjects, because it is impossible, that the body should be capable of hurting all its members; and we shall see hereafter, that it can as little tend to injure any of them in particular. Hence the sovereign is necessarily, and for the same reason that it exists, always such as it ought to be.

The case is different, however, as to the relation in which the subjects stand to the sovereign; as, notwithstanding their common interest, the latter can have no security that the former will discharge their engagements, unless means be found to engage their fidelity.

In fact, every individual may, as a man, entertain a particular will, either contradictory or dissimilar to his general will, as a citizen. His private interest may influence him, in a manner diametrically opposite to the common interest of the society. Reflecting on his own existence as positive and naturally independent, he may conceive what he owes to the common cause, to be a free and gratuitous contribution, the want of which will be less hurtful to others, than the discharge of it will be burthensome to himself; and, regarding the moral person of the state as an imaginery being, because it is not a man, he may be desirous of enjoying all the privileges of a citizen without fulfilling his engagement as a subject; an injustice, that, in its progresss, must necessarily be the ruin of the body politic.

To the end, therefore, that the social compact should not prove an empty form, it tacitly includes this engagement, which only can enforce the rest, *viz.* that whosoever refuses to pay obedience to the general will, shall be liable to be compelled to it by the force of the whole body. And this is in effect nothing more, than that they may be compelled to be free: for such is the condition which, in uniting every citizen to the state, secured him from all personal dependence; a condition, which forms the whole artifice and play of the political machine: it is this alone that renders all social engagements just and equitable which, without it, would be absurd, tyrannical, and subject to the most enormous abuses.

Of Civil Society in General

The transition of man from a state of nature to a state of society is productive of a very remarkable change in his being, by substituting justice instead of instinct, as the rule of his conduct, and attaching that morality to his actions, of which they were before destitute. It is in immediate consequence of this change, when the voice of duty succeeds to physical impulse and the law of appetite, that man, who hitherto regarded only his own gratification, finds himself obliged to act on other principles, and to consult his reason, before he follows the dictates of his passions. Although, by entering into a state of society, he is deprived also of many advantages which depend on that of nature, he gains by it others so very considerable, his faculties exert and expand themselves, his ideas are enlarged, his sentiments ennobled, and his whole soul is elevated to so great a degree, that, if the abuses of this new state do not degrade him below the former, he ought incessantly to bless that happy moment in which he was rescued from it, and converted from a stupid and ignorant animal into an intelligent and wise Being.

To state the balance of what is lost and gained by this change, we shall reduce it to comparative terms. By entering into the social compact, man gives up his natural liberty, or unlimited right to every thing which he is desirous of, and can attain. In return for this, he gains social liberty, and an exclusive property in all those things of which he is possessed. To avoid any mistake, however, in the nature of these compensations, it is necessary to make a just distinction between natural liberty, which is limited by nothing but the inabilities of the individual, and social liberty, which is limited by the general will of the community; and also, between that possession, which is only effected by force, or follows the right of prior occupancy, and that property, which is founded only on a positive title.

To the preceding also may be added, as the acquisition of a social state, moral liberty, which only renders a man truly master of himself: for to be under the direction of appetite alone is to be in a state of slavery, while to pay obedience only to those laws which we prescribe to ourselves, is liberty. But I have said too much already on this subject, the philosophical meaning of the word Liberty, being, in this place, out of the question.

Jean Jacques Rousseau

Of Real Demesnes

Each member of the community, in becoming such, devotes himself to the public from that moment, in such a state as he then is, with all his power and abilities, of which abilities his possessions make a part. Not that in consequence of this act the possession changes its nature, by changing hands, and becomes actual property in those of the sovereignty; but as the power of the community is incomparably greater than that of an individual, the public possession is in fact more fixed and irrevocable, without being more lawful, at least with regard to foreigners. For every state is, with respect to its members, master of all their possessions, by virtue of the social compact, which, in a state, serves as the basis of all other rights; but, with regard to other powers or states, it is master of them only, by the right of prior occupancy, which it derives from individuals.

The right of prior occupancy, although more real than that of the strongest, becomes not an equitable right, till after the establishment of property. Every man hath naturally a right to every thing which is necessary for his subsistence; but the positive act by which he is made the proprietor of a certain possession excludes him from the property of any other. His portion being assigned him, he ought to confine himself to that, and hath no longer any right to a community of possession. Hence it is that the right of prior occupancy, though but of little force in a state of nature, is so respectable in that of society. The point to which we are chiefly directed in the consideration of this right, is rather what belongs to another, than what does not belong to us.

To define the right of prior occupancy in general terms, it is founded on the following conditions. It is requisite, in the first place, that the lands in question should be unoccupied: secondly, that no greater quantity of it should be occupied than is necessary for the subsistence of the occupiers; and, in the third place, that possession should be taken of it, not by a vain ceremony, but by actual cultivation, the only mark of property, which, in defect of judicial titles, should be at all respected.

To allow the first occupier a right to as much territory as he may cultivate, and is necessary to his subsistence, is certainly carrying the matter as far as is reasonable. Otherwise we know not how to set bounds to this right. Is it sufficient for a man to set foot on an uninhabited territory, to pretend immediately an exclusive right to it? Is it sufficient for him to have power enough at one time to drive others from the spot, to deprive them for ever afterwards of the right of returning to it? How can a man, or even a whole people, possess themselves of an immense territory, and exclude from it the rest of mankind, without being guilty of an illegal usurpation, since, by so doing, they deprive the rest of mankind of an habitation, and those means of subsistence, which nature hath given in common to them all? When Nunez Balbao stood on the sea-shore, and, in the name of the crown of Castile, took possession of the Pacific Ocean, and of all South America, was this sufficient to dispossess all the inhabitants of that vast country, and exclude all the other sovereigns in the world? On such a supposition, the like idle ceremonies might have been ridiculously multiplied, and his Catholic Majesty would have had no more to do, than to have taken possession in his closet of all the countries in the world, and to have afterwards only deducted from his empire such as were before possessed by other princes.

It is easy to conceive, how the united and contiguous estates of individuals become the territory of the public, and in what manner the right of sovereignty, extending itself from the subjects to the lands they occupy, becomes at once both real and personal; a circumstance which lays the possessors under a state of the greatest dependence, and makes even their own abilities a security for their fidelity. This is an advantage which does not appear to have been duly attended to, by sovereigns among the ancients, who, by stiling themselves only kings of the Persians, the Scythians, the Macedonians, seemed to look on themselves only as chief of men, rather than as masters of a country. Modern princes more artfully stile themselves the kings of England, France, Spain &c. and thus, by claiming the territory itself, are secure of the inhabitants.

What is very singular in this alienation is, that the community, in accepting the possessions of individuals, is so far from despoiling them there-of, that, on the contrary, it only confirms them in such possessions, by converting an usurpation into an actual right, and a bare possession into a real property. The possessors also being considered as the depositaries of the public wealth, while their rights are respected by all the members of the state, and maintained by all its force against any foreign power, they acquire, if I may so say, by a cession advantageous to the public, and still more so to themselves, everything they ceded by it; a paradox which is easily explained by the distinction to be made between the rights which the sovereign and the proprietor have in the same fund, as will be seen hereafter.

It may also happen, that men may form themselves into a society, before they have any possessions; and that, acquiring a territory sufficient for all, they may possess it in common, or divide it among them, either equally or in such different proportions as may be determined by the sovereign. Now, in whatsoever manner such acquisition may be made, the right which each individual has to his own estate, must be always subordinate to the right which the community hath over the possessions of all; for, without this, there would be nothing binding in the social tie, nor any real force in the exercise of the supreme power.

I shall end this book, with a remark, that ought to serve as the basis of the whole social system: and this is, that, instead of annihilating the natural equality among mankind, the fundamental compact substitutes, on the contrary, a moral and legal equality, to make up for that natural and physical difference which prevails among individuals, who, though unequal in personal strength and mental abilities, become thus all equal by convention and right.[2]

That the Sovereignty is Unalienable

The first and most important consequence to be drawn from the principles already established, is, that the general *will* only can direct the forces of the state agreeable to the end of its original institution, which is the common good; for, though the opposition of private interests might make the establishment of societies necessary, it must have been through the coalition of those interests, that such establishment became possible. The bonds of society must have been formed out of something common to those several interests, for, if there had been no point to which they could have been reconciled, no society could possibly have subsisted. Now it is only on these points that the government of society should be founded.

I say, therefore, that the sovereignty, being only the exertion of the general will, cannot be alienated and that the sovereign, which is only a collective being, cannot be represented but by itself: the power of a people may be transmitted or delegated, but not their will.

It may not be absolutely impossible, that the will of an individual should agree, in some particular point, with the general will of a whole people; it is, however, impossible, that such agreement should be constant and durable, for the will of particulars always tends to make distinctions of preference, and the general will to a perfect equality. It is further still more impossible, such agreement might always subsist, to have any security that it would do so, as it could never be the effect of art, but of chance. The sovereign may say, My will is now agreeable to the will of

2. This equality, indeed, is under some governments merely apparent and delusive, serving only to keep the poor still in misery, and favour the oppression of the rich. And, in fact, the laws are always useful to persons of fortune, and hurtful to those who are destitute: whence it follows, that a state of society is advantageous to mankind in general, only when they all possess something, and none of them have anything too much.

such an individual, or at least to what he pretends to be his will; but it cannot pretend to say, I agree to whatever may be the will of such individual to morrow; as it is absurd for the will to lay itself under any restraint regarding the future, and as it is impossible for the will to consent to any thing contrary to the interest of the being whose will it is. Should a people therefore enter into the engagement of simply promising obedience, they would lose their quality, as a people, and be virtually dissolved by that very act. The moment there exists a master, there can be no longer a sovereign, the body politic being thereby destroyed.

I would not be understood to mean, that the orders of a chief may not pass for the dictates of the general will, when the sovereign, though at liberty to contradict, does not oppose it. In such a case, it is to be presumed, from the universal silence of the people, that they give their consent. This will be farther explained in the end.

That the Sovereignty is Indivisible

For the same reason that the sovereignty is unalienable, it is also indivisible; for the will is general,[3] or it is not; it is that of the body of the people, or only that of a part. In the first case, this will, when declared, is an act of sovereignty, and becomes a law: in the second, it is only a particular will, or an act of the magistracy, and is at most a decree.

But our politicians, incapable of dividing the sovereignty in its first principles, divide it in its object; they distinguish it into power and will; into a legislative and executive power; into the prerogatives of taxation, of executing justice, and of making war; into departments of domestic and foreign administration. Sometimes they blend all these confusedly together, and, at others, consider them as distinct and separate, making out the sovereign to be a fantastic compound, just as if they should compose a man out of several bodies, of which one should have only eyes, another arms, a third feet, and nothing more. It is said of the jugglers in Japan, that they will take a child, and cut it into pieces in the presence of the spectators, then, throwing up its dismembered limbs one after another into the air, they are united, and the child descends alive, and well as before. The legerdemain of our modern politicians greatly resembles this trick of the Japanese; for they, after having dismembered the body politic with equal dexterity, bring all its parts together by *hocus pocus* again, and represent it the same as before.

This error arises from their not having formed precise ideas of the

3. In order that this will should be general, it is not always necessary it should be unanimous; it is necessary, however, that every individual should be permitted to vote; every formal exclusion infringing the generality.

sovereign authority, and from their mistaking the simple emanations of this authority, for parts of its essence. Thus, for instance, the acts of declaring war and making peace are usually regarded as acts of sovereignty, which they are not; for neither of these acts are laws, but consist only of the application of the law. Each is a particular act, determinate only of the meaning of the law in such case, as will be seen more clearly when the idea attached to the word *law* shall be precisely settled.

By tracing, in like manner, their other divisions, we shall find that we are constantly mistaken, whenever we think the sovereignty divided; and that the prerogatives, which are supposed to be parts of the sovereignty, are all subordinate to it, and always suppose the predetermination of a superior will, which those prerogatives only serve to put in execution.

It is impossible to say, in how much obscurity this want of precision hath involved the reasonings of authors, on the subject of political law, when they came to examine into the respective rights of kings and people, on the principles they had established. By turning to the third and fourth chapters of the first book of Grotius, the reader may see, how that learned author and his translator, Barbeyrac, bewildered and entangled themselves in their own sophisms, thro' fear of saying too much or too little for their purpose, and of making those interests clash, which it was their business to reconcile. Grotius being dissatisfied with his own countrymen, a refugee in France, and willing to pay his court to Lewis XIII to whom his book is dedicated, spared no art nor pains to strip the people of their privileges, and to invest kings with prerogative. Barbeyrac also wrote with a similar view, dedicating his translation to George I of England. But, unluckily, the expulsion of James II which he calls an abdication, obliged him to be much on the reserve, to turn and wind about, as he saw occasion, in order not to make William III an usurper. Had these two writers adopted true principles, all these difficulties would have vanished, and they would have written consistently; in such a case, however, they could only, in sober sadness, have told the truth, and would have paid their court only to the people. Now, to tell the truth, is not the way to make a fortune; nor are ambassadors appointed, or places and pensions given away by the populace.

Whether the General Will Can Be in the Wrong

It follows, from what has been said, that the general Will is always in the right, and constantly tends to the public good; it does not follow, however, that the deliberations of the people will always be attended with the same rectitude. We are ever desirous of our own good, but we do not always distinguish in what it consists. A whole people never can be corrupted, but they may be often mistaken, and it is in such a case only that they appear to seek their own disadvantage.

There is often a considerable difference between the will of all the members and the general will of the whole body; the latter regards only the common interest, the other respects the private interest of individuals, and is the aggregated sum of their particular wills; but, if we take from this sum those contradictory wills that mutually destroy each other,[4] the sum of the remaining differences is the general will.

If a people, sufficiently informed of the nature of the subject under their consideration, should deliberate, without having any communication with each other, the general will would always result from the greater number of their little differences, and their deliberation would be such as it ought to be. But when they enter into cabals, and form partial associations, at the expence of the general one, the will of each of these associations becomes general, with regard to the particular members of each, and, in itself, particular, with regard to the state. In such a case, therefore, it may be said, there is no longer as many voters as individuals, but only as many voices as there are associations. The differences then become less numerous and give a less general result. Again, should one of these partial associations be so great, as to influence all the rest, the result would no longer be the sum of many little differences, but that of one great one; in which case, a general will would no longer subsist.

It is requisite, therefore, in order that each resolution may be dictated by the general will, that no such partial societies should be formed in a state, and that each citizen should think for himself. Such was the sublime institution of the great Lycurgus. But, if such partial societies must and will exist, it is then expedient to multiply their number, and prevent their inequality, as was done by Solon, Numa, and Servius. These are the only salutary precautions that can be taken, in order that the general will may be properly informed, and the people not be mistaken as to their true interest.

4. *Each interest*, says the Marquis d'A. *has different principles. A coalition between two particular interests may be formed, out of opposition to that of a third*. He might have added, that a coalition of all is formed out of opposition to the interest of each. Were there no different and clashing interests, that of the whole would be hardly distinguishable, as it would meet with no obstacle. All things would go regularly on of their own accord, and civil policy would cease to be an art.

3   Sociology in the Nineteenth Century – I

The nineteenth century began in the wake of three revolutions. The outcome of the American Revolution, which was a revolution in the sense that it was a rebellion of a colonial people against the mother country, resulted in the establishment of the first republican government of modern times, in which the ideals of human equality and happiness were made the cornerstone of its political and social system. Such a system of government – at once tradition-bound, for it was based on a common religious heritage and a common system of law, and forward-looking, for it was designed to herald a new kind of government functioning in a territory in which only natural and not human obstacles needed to be overcome – was destined to affect the social and political thought and practice of the rest of the world. Every future republican and democratic government was to be directly or indirectly inspired by the American example.

The French Revolution, more soul-searing and more violent, with immediate and profound repercussions negatively and positively on the political systems of Europe and America, became the model for all subsequent revolutions designed to substitute a new system of government for one which had become obsolete, antiquated and reactionary. The events which precipitated the revolution were unlike any which historically have been associated with revolutionary movements. In the context of conditions prevailing in the latter part of the eighteenth century France was not a country which suffered from administrative inefficiency, religious intolerance or dynastic feuds; but there was a consciousness among a growing class of people in town and country of the irksomeness of some of the vestiges that survived from medieval times, giving certain privileges and rights to an aristocracy which was no longer the powerful, affluent class it had once been. This consciousness was fed by a system of thought that suggested the possibility of inaugurating a new social system governed exclusively by the unfettered play of reason. Nowhere have the legacies of eighteenth-century thought been found in a more bankrupt form than in this attempt at making a complete sweep of the past. The idea that everything that the past represented was evil and should be discarded was so ingrained that the National Assembly wasted much of its energy in devising substitutes for previous institutions which were in fact no more than terminological ploys.

The third revolution, the Industrial Revolution, was a misnomer in the sense that it was not aimed at the overthrow of a political system, nor was it consciously planned or engineered by any group of people; but it was certainly a revolution, and a unique one, in the sense that it was destined to transform the basic structure, economic and social, first of Europe and then of the rest of the world. It grew slowly, stealthily even, from very small beginnings, owing everything to the skill and ingenuity of many people in all walks of life and of different levels of education. The progress of science and mathematics accelerated a process leading towards the invention of machinery to replace human labour and to increase production. The prospect of uninterrupted power and wealth was one to which all eyes were turned as the certain harbinger of the millennium. The time was therefore ripe for an appraisal of the implications that the new forces of production would have for the social system. Adam Smith had already laid the foundation of the science of economics, by which the complex factors of production, trade and commerce could be analysed on sound rational principles. The idea that the whole social system as such could be described and analysed in terms of broad generalizations was at the root of *An Essay on the History of Civil Society* by Adam Ferguson (1723–1816). Other strands of thought from many sources felt their way towards an understanding of the extent of change that the new industrial system was to bring about. They needed to be synthesized and systematized. To this end they seemed to converge on the thinking of one man, Saint-Simon (1760–1825), who was the first to have a profound insight into the social and political implications of industrialization.

Saint-Simon lived through a period which marked the change from a relatively stable and largely agricultural order to one which required a readjustment and reorientation of a radical kind. The political ferment in which France was involved provided him with the occasion for a comprehensive projection of the future of society, when the existing landmarks would be swept away and replaced by a new order. The society which could accommodate the new forces that were emerging was one which, for Saint-Simon, as for the men of the Enlightenment, would be able to sustain a growing and prosperous population under a political system capable of harmonizing all the antagonistic elements of society. A new science to deal with this problem would be required, and such a science of society, to be viable and constructive, must be underpinned by the same rigorous principles of thought as are used in the natural sciences. It could well be called social physiology.

Saint-Simon was not a systematic thinker. His work was conspicuous neither for its clarity of thought nor for its diction. He veered from one theme to another, unable to organize his ideas coherently. Nevertheless he had a conception of social development which in one form or another was appropriated by later thinkers and made the basis of a more comprehensive science of society. He can be said to have been responsible for launching what came to be known later as the Positivist Organisistic school of thought. His bent of mind was not revolutionary but evolutionary. He conceived of social development as a process that would be guided by a rational idea towards an end in which functional antagonism to the system would give way to a perfect equilibrium. His was a conservative ideal of evolutionary and organic growth towards an integrated society in which there would be a place both for a 'temporal' system of institutions and for a 'spiritual' ideology of conduct. Historically we can see this process at work, however imperfectly. Its beginnings were found in ancient Greece and Rome; the system collapsed and was supplanted by the one that prevailed in the Middle Ages, that of feudalism and Catholicism, which in turn gave way to a system founded on industry and science. The basic institutions of the past were not to be abolished but humanized and secularized. Saint-Simon's most famous work on Christianity outlined a kind of non-theistic or secular Christianity that could instil a heightened awareness in all classes of their common destiny. This may have been a brave, if pathetic and illusory, attempt to show how an integrative principle in social life might be applied, but at least it had the merit of proving that unless some such attempt was made, industrial man would be lost.

It was left to Auguste Comte, one-time secretary to Saint-Simon, to refine these ideas and carry them to their logical conclusion. In this way he constructed a comprehensive and all-embracing system of thought which not only outlined the historical process leading inevitably to the present upsurge in life, but also endeavoured to show how the same upsurge could be contained and utilized for the best possible purpose. Unlike Saint-Simon, Comte was an academician pure and simple, versed in the sciences and mathematics of his day, who neither felt the need nor had the inclination to subject his views to the test of verification. In the best tradition of Cartesian thought he approached the problems of society in a rationalistic spirit through a conceptual scheme of thought sustained by its own irrefragable logic. He put sociology on the map, not only because the term he invented for the science of society has come to stay, but, more importantly, because his was the first scientific study of society which in its alleged positivism claimed to be concerned with pure objective fact. Comte combined extreme naïveté of thought with a boldness of conception and large-scale manipulation of ideas which has few parallels in history. His naïveté of thought stemmed from a rationalization of sentiment that comes naturally to a timid and reserved character; his boldness of thought was derived from a deep awareness of the historical processes that have culminated in the positivism of science, and above all an awareness of the necessity of constructing a substantive system of thought whereby an understanding of these processes would contribute towards an amelioration of social life. Comte had a blueprint for this which he regarded as fool-proof. If sociology was to be, according to him, the most highly generalized science coming at the end of a series of ever more generalized sciences, beginning with mathematics and astronomy, followed by physics, chemistry and biology, it had to be shown in what respects it could confront and solve the problems of social life. For the first time – and this was a landmark in the history of sociological thought, and perhaps Comte's most original contribution to it – a distinction was made between two sets of separate but connected problems: those that concerned the structure of society as it is, its parts and their interrelations with each other and with the whole of which they form parts – in other words the morphology of society – to which Comte gave the name of Statics; and secondly, those problems dealing with the movements of society towards new ends as a result of change in ideas and institutions, to which he gave the name of Dynamics. To Comte, change must come through a change of ideas. This conviction of his was enshrined in his so-called three laws of human development, 'so-called' because they were not laws in any real sense of the word, but descriptions of mental processes that could conceivably have followed one another in the course of human development. The first stage was a theological one, when the human mind regarded all natural and human phenomena as divinely caused and dominated, that is, when nothing could be self-caused or due to chance but must have had a cause outside itself. In this stage the mind is a constant prey to purely subjective and irrational feeling, from one fanciful explanation to another, without logical coherence. No progress in knowledge and skill, no progress in social life, was possible. Somehow the human mind had managed to move forward, striking a new path in its conception of itself and its environment. This was the metaphysical stage, in which things were endowed with powers and entities which explained their behaviour. It was metaphysical because these powers or entities were no more than extrapolations from man's own ideas, and had no basis in reality. It was metaphysical in another sense, because such a system of thought cannot be put to the test and verified. It was, however, a definite advance on the previous stage in so far as it sought an explanation for things and events in those very things and events, however erroneous and misleading that explanation was.

The third and last stage had now been reached whereby the

mind, freed from supernatural and metaphysical speculations, could make a positive scientific approach to the problems of nature, including those of man himself and the society in which he lives. It is positive because it deals with bare facts brought to the light of day by pure reason; it is scientific because it is only through this positive approach that we can make verifiable generalizations and discover the laws underlying all the phenomena of nature and of society. Comte elaborated at length on these laws of human development for a special reason. To show the evolution of human thought in terms of these three stages was the only method he had of demonstrating that changes in human society are brought about exclusively by changes in human attitudes and mentality. Comte was not an academic recluse for nothing. He had a horror of violence and revolutionary change. He was much too near the events of the French Revolution and their aftermath to feel at ease with what they and similar events portended. Yet revolutionary changes of another kind were taking place before his very eyes which he could not ignore. He came to terms with these only by convincing himself that they were changes brought about by ideas alone, and these were changes for which science and science alone was responsible. Such changes did not require any change in the basic structure of society and its institutions. On the contrary, if well directed, they could have the effect of reinforcing these institutions and stabilizing society itself. This was why Comte laid great stress on the importance of conserving the family, which to him was the basic unit of society. Rather than being, as hitherto, a biological unit to which no rational explanation could be given, it would now be a social unit which could be strengthened through the rational scientific ideas which could be brought to bear on its maintenance and survival. No impending danger to the existence of society itself need be anticipated if the family assumed these new characteristics. Interaction of ideas and the material and other conditions of society was foreign to Comte's conservative bent of mind. It could never occur to him that there could come about a reverse trend whereby the material and other changes in society could well affect and modify our ideas.

Comte carried his rationalistic bias of mind to its logical

conclusion with disastrous results. To say that the basic institutions of society, not only that of the family, must be preserved is one thing; to say that they can and should be preserved by giving them a face-lift, as it were, by removing the dross of irrationalism from them and injecting them with the spirit of positive scientific rationalism is another, for here we are in the realm of pure arbitrariness, subjectivism and rationalization. At what point can we draw a line between the rational and the irrational? By what criteria are we to judge what is rational or irrational? Can we meaningfully speak of the rationality or otherwise of the family or religion? These institutions fulfil certain needs. These needs or ends are neither rational nor irrational: they are biological, psychological or social. Positivism and science simply do not enter in here, for their terms of reference are limited, and do not include the satisfaction or otherwise of needs or the fulfilment or otherwise of ends. We can study these latter positively and scientifically, but we cannot refer to their satisfaction or fulfilment as being positive and scientific.

The *reductio ad absurdum* of Comte's thought was reached in his advocacy of the religion of humanity, which was Catholicism without its God, mysteries and faith. The spectacle of a writer who brought so much erudition, scholarship and insight into the systematic study of society and who could descend to such a level of naïveté was pathetic in the extreme. Fortunately, his positive contributions to the study of society remain a permanent monument which neither his confusion of thought nor his distraught state of mind could shake or belittle. Through him sociology had come to stay, for the rapid changes that were overtaking society required a science to discover their causes and effects, and in this way to make sense of them. Nobody before Comte had seen so clearly the necessity for such a science. Equally important, he showed how this science could operate through a proper delimitation of subject matter. In his approach to these problems he anticipated the methods that later came to be known as the evolutionary, comparative, functional and organismic methods of analysis. In England his influence was great for a time through the sponsorship of J. S. Mill and the translation of some of his works by Harriet Martineau, and then it faded out completely. It revived in America, to become a potent influence on the new school of American sociologists which was steadily growing in importance and prominence.

The strain of conservatism in French social and political thought was given an original twist by Alexis de Tocqueville, the greatest political scientist of modern times. Possessed of great style of writing, as only a French writer can display, he had a rare kind of mind whose calm and judicious judgement, and in particular whose prophetic insight into the processes of historical development, past, present and future, were hardly ever equalled by any writer before or after him. Of aristocratic birth, he could be pardoned for expressing regret (but deserved only admiration for showing no bias) at the passing away of a social system which, however admirable in many ways, could not withstand the natural passion of man for equality. This was the clue to the understanding of modern history, and this in all its various guises was the central core and theme of de Tocqueville's writings. Whether he was writing about the origins of the French Revolution or the progress of American democracy, the burden of his thought was to prove how the modern world was being shaped by this stupendous movement, in which he saw the hand of Providence at work.

His classic work on American democracy was published in two volumes in 1835 and 1839, following a visit to America in 1830 lasting only eight months. Confined to a small number of states bordering the Atlantic coast, with a population of about 13 million, the America of his day had hardly begun that penetration and conquest of the West which turned it into the wealthiest and most powerful nation of the world. On this analysis of the processes at work de Tocqueville lavished immense resources of learning and interpretation which make his acute observations as valid today as they were in his own time. This was the measure of his genius. No work went deeper than his into the social effects of a political system which was inspired by a fundamental regard for human equality, this regard being enshrined in its legal, political and religious institutions. This equality neither de Tocqueville, nor anyone else in his day for that matter, ever regarded in any absolute sense. It was enough for them if equality signified essentially the absence of privilege due to rank, birth or other accidental condition. It was equivalent to what today we would call 'equality of opportunity'. Such equality was not incompatible with inequality of wealth, position or status in society acquired by merit or personal effort. Naturally, as in the American case, equality was inseparable from liberty. The two were intertwined so that without freedom of discussion or worship, freedom to organize and to vote as one wished – and all these freedoms were guaranteed in American democracy – equality would be meaningless. No thinker was more conscious than de Tocqueville of the possibility that equality could well be achieved, as he put it, in a state of servitude. There was a distinct possibility that this was precisely the direction in which future democracies were likely to move. Paradoxical as it may sound, the curtailment, or even the total suppression, of liberty can happen more easily in a democracy than in an aristocracy, provided some counter-vailing benefits derived from equality are manifestly being enjoyed. It has taken a hundred years or more to demonstrate the wisdom and truth of de Tocqueville's observations.

Up to a point de Tocqueville was a determinist – not, however, in the sense that he believed in the inexorability of events through the operation of certain iron laws of history, but only in the sense that once a process like that of equality began to animate the minds of men it would take a course that would culminate in the gradual achievement of equality among all people. On the other hand, he was an indeterminist in the sense that he never felt that this process, inevitable as it was, would follow the same invariable course everywhere. Innumerable factors arising from man's will could decelerate or accelerate it, deflect it for a time from its predetermined course, or give it a different shape.

De Tocqueville proved himself a supreme sociologist by trying to discover the answer to the most important question about American democracy: why was it so successful, and at what price was its success being achieved ? Starting from scratch in a new country, equality was the only basis on which a variable society could have a chance of achieving stability and progress. In addition, the Protestant ethic which the early Puritan settlers practised ensured that industry and thrift and co-operation would be the cardinal virtues animating their lives. One could not overlook, as de Tocqueville was at pains to show, the price that would have to be paid for achieving an egalitarian society. It had to lead to a kind of mediocrity and uniformity in all the institutions of life which contrasted very sharply with the kind of individualism that prevailed in aristocratic or élitist societies. But by conserving the liberty of the individual, by giving the individual the opportunity to form and join all kinds of associations, political, cultural and social, it might be possible, so de Tocqueville thought, to minimize the ugly effects that this decline to uniformity and mediocrity produces.

In his study of American democracy de Tocqueville had a particular object in view. By highlighting the extreme case of the American example he desired not only to make a comparison between America and in particular France, but also to show what effects on other countries the example of America would have in the long run. In this respect he showed himself immeasurably superior in depth of thought to Saint-Simon and Comte. The two latter – and in this respect they were identical in thought and sentiment – could not rid their minds of the nightmare which the French Revolution represented. Events assisted them to discover the means which they were convinced would make a repetition of this nightmare impossible. These they found in the scientific movements which produced the Industrial Revolution. Science, they thought, would rule out the possibility of any irrational and subversive upheavals. It was a form of escapism, which was why their sociology at bottom was indistinguishable from a kind of Utopianism which is the last refuge of a totally barren system of thought, obsessed as it was with an imaginary and illusory future. One of the fundamental tenets of de Tocqueville's social thought, on the other hand, was that the French Revolution was only the beginning of that process, which was a continuing one, and which would affect the fortunes and fate of the world as long as one could foresee. The freshness of his thought contrasts vividly with the arid lucubrations of these two writers. Nevertheless the fact of the Revolution, negatively for Saint-Simon and Comte and positively for de Tocqueville, was the cornerstone on which the new science of sociology was founded.

The conservative trend in French sociological thought was

given explicit formulation by Le Play (1806–82), who was that rare blend of a working scientist and engineer and an original social thinker. It was by accident and not design that he came up against certain social problems which no one before him had thought it worthwhile to examine, or had even regarded as problems at all. In the course of his extensive travels in Europe as a mining engineer and consultant, Le Play was impressed by the extraordinary effect that the social structure of society had on the organization of the family. This led him to conduct surveys – the first of their kind in sociology – into the types of family organization, and, by an examination of the kind of occupation in which it was engaged, its income and resources, into how far each type was affected by or causally related to the social and economic structure of society. For Le Play these problems were a sub-set of a wider problem concerning the political organization of the family, which was a reflection of the political organization of society as a whole.

Le Play's voluminous output reflected the enormous range of subjects he tackled, from the minutiae of family budgets to political theory. While he made a purely objective assessment and examination of the problems he studied, he did not conceal from his readers his own predilections, indeed even his prescriptions, concerning the right ordering of society. But these in no way involved him in any inconsistency or confusion with regard to the immediate problems which attracted his interest. As a man of deep religious feeling and sober habits, the recipe he prescribed for a good and enduring society was a very simple one – a return to the truths embodied in the Bible, and strict adherence to the Ten Commandments. For Le Play the solidarity of the family was the only guarantee of an ordered and harmonious society. The disintegration of the family is both the cause and the effect of a corrupt society. Society can endure and flourish only on the basis of law, order and moral ideals. He rejected completely the view that technical progress and affluence would solve the problems of society. On the contrary, prosperity is bound to lead to the corruption of the leaders, and this in turn will lead to the corruption of society. Industrialism creates pauperism and produces a rootless type of working class. The only means of restoring the integrity of society is by consolidating the working-class family, and by making it participate in a system of entrepreneurship whereby the owner of the business and his workmen share a common concern and a common end, all bound together by a mutual sentiment of love. In this way the working class will be encouraged to own their own property, and such ownership is not only desirable in itself, but would also be a means of supplementing their earnings.

In studying the family Le Play used the monographic method by which field data were collected for measurement purposes. What later came to be known simply as statistical techniques and index construction had their beginnings in Le Play's methodology. He was the first to classify the family into three types, the 'patriarchal', the 'stem' and the 'unstable'. The best type for him was the stem family, for its members are united by strong ties, spiritual and material; and as the family is the chief agency of socialization and social control, the stem family would be the best means of ensuring these ends and avoiding the latent conflict of classes in society. One hardly needs to mention the elements of a conservative mythology in these views and prescriptions. It is not surprising that it appealed to large sections of the public – to the Catholics, who were finding their position undermined by a powerful and growing anti-clerical movement among the intellectuals; to that section of the bourgeoisie who felt they were being threatened by the encroachment of a vast bureaucracy on the one hand and industrialization on the other; to provincial aristocratic notables who felt that they were being left behind in the changes overtaking society; and lastly even to certain kinds of socialists who hankered after the simplicity of the past when classes lived in harmony. Le Play was their spiritual leader. His pessimism found an echo among those affected by a pervasive feeling that things were not as fine as they looked, and that something was not quite right in society. Whether Le Play was fighting a losing battle or not, his insistence on the place of the family as the basic social unit, and the necessity of maintaining its solidarity, was timely and extraordinarily perceptive in view of the danger that threatened it from the blind, mad, haphazard and unplanned march of industrialization.

A school of thought inspired by his method and singleminded zeal, but not by his theories or propaganda, took up the story where he left off and produced remarkable surveys into the relationship of the family to other factors, environmental, educational, governmental and economic, of social life. Le Play's influence among social reformers elsewhere, in America and in England, was equally enduring, although among the intellectuals and in academic circles it had no impact whatsoever. The torch of sociology in France was henceforth to be carried aloft by a school of thought that claimed descent from Comte and the Enlightenment, rationalistic, free-thinking and anti-clerical. Its most outstanding representative and spokesman was Émile Durkheim.

The remarkable thing was that from different standpoints, seemingly utterly remote from each other, the views of Le Play and Durkheim converged by a kind of symbiotic process in a number of fundamental issues. It came about in this way. Three influences shaped Durkheim's thought: the Cartesian tradition of rationalism, with its emphasis on rigorous conceptual analysis, the Enlightenment, with its unqualified promise of a new age through the untrammelled use of reason; and the positivism of Comte, which blazed the trail towards a new science of society that by its methodology and approach took its place with the other sciences in its ability to discover laws, draw generalizations and make predictions. In addition to these formative influences the fashionable theory of evolution of his day could not fail to leave a mark on Durkheim's thought by enabling him to view society in terms of organic development and interrelations of parts. The stage was set, therefore, for the greatest contribution to sociology made by any one man; and without him the history of sociology would have turned out to be quite different. The paradox of Durkheim is that his influence steadily grew over the years – it is more potent now than it was even in his day – in inverse proportion to the credibility of his theories.

Durkheim was the first sociologist who conceived and constructed the framework within which sociology as a viable science can operate. It has its own subject matter as the natural sciences have theirs; the facts that it studies are as indubitably objective phenomena as those studied by the natural sciences, and their externality is as much a datum of experience as the externality of physical objects is. What distinguishes social facts from all other facts of experience, according to Durkheim, is the element of constraint. The language we speak, the laws we obey, the customs and conventions we follow, the rituals we perform and the contractual obligations we enter into – in short, all the inter- actional processes which enable us to live a social life – are characterized by this common element without which a social life would be inconceivable. Society itself is nothing else but a system of constraints. The individual as such does not count, for if as a social being his actions are determined by something outside him, then it is this something that is important for sociology, and not the individual himself. This rejection of psychological and individual explanation, extreme and one-sided as it was in the context of the intellectual atmosphere of his day, was absolutely essential if sociology was to survive as an independent science. This was Durkheim's greatest and most original contribution to sociology. Without it sociology was in imminent danger of being reduced to psychology, which was fast becoming an academic discipline in its own right. Moreover, the public mood was more receptive to a system of thought which explained the forces animating society in terms of psychological drives, instincts and satisfactions. The works of two of Durkheim's contemporaries, Gabriel Tarde (1843–1904) and Gustave Le Bon (1841–1931), attested to as well as satisfied this growing demand for psycho- logical explanation of social phenomena. Tarde attempted to explain all changes in society in terms of one basic human element, namely imitation, which follows a cyclical curve of routinization and innovation. Three great processes can be discerned in all areas of life, physical, biological and social, and they are repeti- tion, opposition and adaptation. All social phenomena can be explained in terms of the interaction of two persons one of whom exerts an influence on the other. Thus invention-imitation is a basic pattern of the social process. Invention obviously is a creative process and involves some element of change: imitation is a process through which an invention beomes socially adapted. Psychologically it is reducible to, or is indistinguishable from, suggestion. Tarde's theory of imitation was original, and a number of its elements have become part of accepted sociological theory. He was much less successful in his analysis of the other two processes, opposition and adaptation.

Le Bon acquired an international reputation through his popular work, *The Psychology of the Crowd*, which crystallized the view widely held in his day that people in certain situations would manifest a syndrome of mental disease. The behaviour of a crowd, according to Le Bon, is one example of that. Now this kind of emphasis on individual processes was in direct opposition to the view that Durkheim held. Durkheim's rejection of such a psychological approach was nowhere more in evidence than in his classic work on suicide. No act can be regarded more as an individual phenomenon having a cause in the individual psyche than suicide. It was precisely this subject which Durkheim chose to study in order to provide positive proof of his thesis that social phenomena can only be explained in terms of other social phenomena. In other words, we can discover the causes of suicide in the social environment. It was a most outstanding application of methodology employing positive empirical means to prove a theory which otherwise might have remained purely speculative. Durkheim's *Suicide* was a landmark in more ways than one. His statistical analysis of suicide rates was a *tour de force*, lacking as it did the refinement which later development in statistical techniques made possible. While Durkheim remained within the strict limits which his subject matter imposed he never lost sight of the wider implications his theory of suicide had for his general view of social cohesion and social solidarity – key elements in his theory of society. Yet with all the remarkable blend we find in *Suicide* of theory and empiricism, and with its superb artistry – for it was as much a work of art as a work of science – one is left with the impression that it tries to prove more than is justified by the facts, that it is a form of special pleading, and that Durkheim is trying to fit facts to a preconceived theory rather than testing the theory for its truth or falsity by a complete and not a selected set of facts. This is what led him to call one type of suicide, rather paradoxically, 'altruistic' suicide, as though a man who feels he has to avenge flouted honour is not affected by the same system of life as a man who no longer feels bound by family kinship or religious ties.

An identical flaw seems to run throughout his works. In his *Division of Labour*, his concern was to trace and elucidate the causal factors which made possible a transition from a simple to a complex society, characterized respectively by two contrasted types of solidarity which he called 'mechanical' and 'organic'. According to his theory the density and volume of a population reach a point when they have to be contained and controlled. This is affected by the division of labour, which has the one supreme advantage that it makes the members so interdependent that their cohesion becomes stronger. This idea was raised even to the status of a law, yet no law rested on such a shaky foundation. However, if we can ignore for a moment his theory and not take too seriously his rather arbitrary distinction between simple and complex societies, his work is of such a dazzling brilliance that it can be said of even the latest theories of society that they are no more than an extension and refinement of views and insights which were contained in it. His ideas that social life was a system of constraints because society is nothing but a moral community, that social life is governed by norms and values to which sanctions of one kind or another are attached, that civilization which is the hallmark of an advanced and complex society must not be confused with moral progress, and that what is built into every social system is a possibility, even a necessity, of deviance – these are some of Durkheim's contributions to sociology whose value became apparent only as more thought was given to the problems of society.

His *Elementary Forms of Religious Life* showed no diminution of analytic power or originality of thought. It is, however, his least successful work. It is true that he read everything that had been written on the Australian aborigines. He sifted the materials with a fine comb, and no detail escaped his sharp and inquiring mind. But to found a theory of religion on unquestioned reliance on second-hand and sometimes contradictory data was, if audacious, hardly scientific. Moreover, the basis of the theory itself was open to question, namely that by investigating the religious beliefs and practices of the simplest society in existence one could arrive at a complete understanding of the nature of the religion of the most highly civilized societies. And yet there was a subtle method in this quest for the meaning and significance of religion. Unlike the agnostics among his contemporaries, whose interest in primitive religion was a means of rationalizing their agnosticism by showing religion's fundamentally irrational origins, Durkheim, in spite of his agnosticism, had a profound respect for the religious sentiment. To him the solidarity of social life was a cardinal necessity, and one of the most effective means of ensuring, and even enhancing, that solidarity was religion. The Judaism which he renounced emerged in a new form. By substituting society for the God we worship, we are enabled to see the significance of religion in our lives. The rituals we observe, the beliefs we entertain, the distinctions we make between sacred and profane (the Judaic origin of this is unmistakable) all these fall into place and can be seen to have a sound reason in the scheme of things. Indeed, they can be seen to be even indispensable if cohesion, integration and solidarity in society are to be preserved. There is something pathetically touching in the spectacle of a man who cannot believe in a thing, yet clings to it passionately enough if he is allowed to call it by another name. In this way he killed two birds with one stone. He was able to justify his repudiation of traditional religion and claim at the same time that he had discovered the reality of religion behind the appearance.

If we draw his theory to its logical conclusion we arrive at views that are as absurd as they are naïve. Mankind has perpetrated the greatest deception on itself by believing it is doing something when in reality it is doing something else altogether. The forms in which it is doing it may appear to vary enormously, but at bottom they possess one thing in common – they are directed to serving the same ends, which are hidden from it but essential for its survival. In effect it does not much matter what religion a man worships – the cruder it is the clearer is the purpose behind it. The religious dissensions must be seen as merely different ways in which the protagonists wish to live in society, which is really their object of worship, and not as doctrinal differences. The differences between an agnostic and a believer are not, therefore, fundamental differences, for they both owe at bottom the same religious allegiance to one identical society. The question can be put thus: if two people are living in two societies but are worshipping the same religion, are they worshipping two societies or one? If two societies, then there are as many valid religions as there are societies; if one, then it is human society as such that is the object of religion – which is either saying so little as to be of no significance, for it boils down to the commonplace idea that religion is social and binds the members of society together, or it says too much, which is not borne out by the facts of experience, for society as such cannot be the object of anything, whereas *a* society can be. In many respects Durkheim's doctrine of bracketing society and religion comes perilously near Comte's ludicrous idea of a religion of humanity; but whereas Comte's idea was to be realized at some future time when science would reign supreme in society, Durkheim's view was that society is – always has been, in fact – the religion of man. This was an extreme example of realism and reification of an idea almost medieval in its implications.

As in *The Division of Labour*, if we can ignore for a while his theory of religion, Durkheim's *Elementary Forms of Religious Life* is a masterpiece of critical, incisive and at times highly original observations. He has nowhere displayed such superb acumen or skill as in the way he demolished the views of religion of the contemporary sociologists and anthropologists. Although he did not elaborate them at sufficient length, his views concerning the social origin of the categories of thought provided a new insight into the operations of the human mind whose genesis and growth can only be understood in terms of its social background. Social psychologists, philosophers and sociologists are still groping to assess the full implications of these powerful ideas.

By a curious irony, the views of Durkheim, the rationalist and progressive thinker proud of the intellectual traditions of which he was the standard-bearer, and those of Le Play, the traditional conservative and pessimistic thinker, converged in a number of points. Much as Durkheim wished to feel that the progress of society from simple to complex was a progress in civilization, the undertones of disillusionment and disenchantment could hardly be disguised. The division of labour, which had so many beneficent effects, not least by bringing about a more rational organization of society, if carried too far would destroy man's initiative and independence. Durkheim's distaste for traditional mechanical solidarity gave way gradually to a nostalgic sentiment towards the simple human virtues in a society whose firm binding ties, like those of mechanical solidarity, would ensure the smooth harmonious social relationship of its members. The individuality which modern advanced society extols is at bottom an anomic condition of life, lacking as it does the rich, satisfying community feeling of a kind that exists only in a simple society. Durkheim could not, as Le Play had no difficulty in doing, come out explicitly for a return to a religious way of life. Because of this – unlike Le Play whose hope was never extinguished that such a consummation was possible – Durkheim could draw no comfort from the prospect that stretched before him of a soul-destroying and never satisfied and rampant individualism. He had one or two prescriptions. He was one of the first to make clear the distinction between state and society, but in order to forestall the possibility of the state becoming, as it was fast threatening to become, an all-powerful, pervasive and unpredictable instrument of society, Durkheim advocated a kind of syndicalism whereby a partnership between the state and other institutions of society, namely industry and trade unions, would make for a more satisfactory equilibrium in which no section would be dominant. This was no more than a *cri de cœur*, a despairing attempt at salvaging a foundering wreck. So Durkheim was torn between the admiration he felt for the undoubted progress that Western civilization, not least in the industrial sphere, had made, and the deep concern and anxiety he felt for the future of society in its headlong rush towards what nobody could tell. His love for France as the greatest civilization on earth could not survive the fatal blow it received with the death of his son in the war. Durkheim died in 1919.

*

In sociology the nineteenth century was the French century. The French created sociology, and their contributions were unrivalled for their scope and depth. One could account for this as follows. To the philosophers and Encyclopedists of the eighteenth century the inequitable distribution of wealth, power and status in society was seen as inevitably giving rise to change. They turned their attention to answering two questions. The first was how did such inequality arise at all in the first place? Various answers were given, but sociologically the most important was Rousseau's, according to which property was the source of all evil in society. The second question was how should one cope with the inevitable processes of change? Theoretically we have views like those of the Physiocrats, with Quesnay at their head, who drew up a blueprint of the future of society that anticipated but was more rationally founded than the programme that Marx outlined a century later. The French Revolution must be seen to have been a practical, if violent, expression of the widespread desire for change towards a more equitable system of life. In the event the violence and destruction were not warranted by the kind of changes that were brought about. As a result, the most significant trend of thought in French sociology of the nineteenth century was the emphasis, variously expressed, on harmony and consensus. With industrialization becoming a dominant factor in society, Saint-Simon and Comte thought they could discern a basis for consensus in the industrial process itself. De Tocqueville saw the dangers of the growing power of mass democracy, but thought consensus was possible through the creation of voluntary organization which would give scope for individual initiative and independence, and thereby curb the tyrannical power of the mass. Le Play's remedy for the anarchy of modern industrial life consisted in the reinforcement of family unity, reciprocity of rights and obligations between all those engaged in economic activity, and the acceptance of the immutable teachings of religion. Durkheim's pessimism stemmed from doubt as to how far the division of labour, essential and desirable as it was in a complex society, was compatible with that cohesion, integration, solidarity and community feeling that were so essential for society.

Auguste Comte 1798–1857

Major works

The Positive Philosophy (6 volumes, 1830–42)
Discourse on the Positive Spirit (1844)
System of Positive Polity (4 volumes, 1851–4)
The Catechism of Positive Religion (1852)
Subjective Synthesis (1856)

The following extracts are reprinted from Auguste Comte, *The Positive Philosophy*, freely translated and condensed by Harriet Martineau (London: George Bell & Sons, 1896).

Having now ascertained the fundamental position of the problems of political philosophy, and thus obtained guidance as to the scientific aim to be attained, the next step is to exhibit the general spirit of Social Physics, whose conditions we have been deciding.

SPIRIT OF SOCIAL SCIENCE

The philosophical principle of the science being that social phenomena are subject to natural laws, admitting of rational prevision, we have to ascertain what is the precise subject, and what the peculiar character of those laws. The distinction between the Statical and Dynamical conditions of the subject must be extended to social science; and I shall treat of the conditions of social existence as, in biology, I treated of organization under the head of anatomy; and then on the laws of social movement, as in biology of those of life, under the head of physiology. This division, necessary for exploratory purposes, must not be stretched beyond that use: and, as we saw in Biology, that the distinction becomes weaker with the advance of science, so shall we see that when the science of social physics is fully constituted, this division will remain for analytical purposes, but not as a real separation of the science into two parts. The distinction is not between two classes of facts, but between two aspects of a theory. It corresponds with the double conception of order and progress: for order consists (in a positive sense) in a permanent harmony among the conditions of social existence; and progress consists in social development; and the conditions in the one case, and the laws of movement in the other, constitute the statics and dynamics of social physics. – And here we find again the constant relation between the

103

science and the art, – the theory and the practice. A science which proposes a positive study of the laws of order and of progress cannot be charged with speculative rashness by practical men of any intelligence, since it offers the only rational basis for the practical means of satisfying the needs of society, as to order and progress; and the correspondence in this case will be found to be analogous to that which we have seen to exist between biological science and the arts which relate to it, – the medical art especially. – One view of the deepest interest in this connection is that the ideas of order and progress which are in perpetual conflict in existing society, occasioning infinite disturbance, are thus reconciled, and made necessary to each other, becoming as truly inseparable as the ideas of organization and life in the individual being. The further we go in the study of the conditions of human society, the more clearly will the organizing and progressive spirit of the positive philosophy become manifest.

STATICAL STUDY

The statical study of sociology consists in the investigation of the laws of action and reaction of the different parts of the social system, – apart, for the occasion, from the fundamental movement which is always gradually modifying them. In this view, sociological prevision, founded upon the exact general knowledge of those relations, acts by judging by each other the various statical indications of each mode of social existence, in conformity with direct observation, – just as is done daily in the case of anatomy. This view condemns the existing philosophical practice of contemplating social elements separately, as if they had an independent existence; and it leads us to regard them as in mutual relation, and forming a whole which compels us to treat them in combination. By this method, not only are we furnished with the only possible basis for the study of social movement, but we are put in possession of an important aid to direct observation; since many social elements which cannot be investigated by immediate observation may be estimated by their scientific relation to others already known. When we have a scientific knowledge of the interior relation of the parts of any science or art; and again, of the relations of the sciences to each other: and again, of the relations of arts to their respective sciences, the observation of certain portions of the scheme enables us to pronounce on the state of other portions, with a true philosophical security. The case is the same when, instead of studying the collective social phenomena of a single nation, we include in the study those of contemporary nations, whose reciprocal influence cannot be disputed, though it is much reduced in modern times, and, as in the instance of western Europe and eastern Asia, apparently almost effaced.

SOCIAL ORGANIZATION

The only essential case in which this fundamental relation is misconceived or neglected is that which is the most important of all, – involving, as it does, social organization, properly so called. The theory of social organization is still conceived of as absolute and isolated, independent altogether of the general analysis of the corresponding civilization, of which it can, in fact, constitute only one of the principal elements. [This vice is chargeable in an almost equal degree upon the most opposite political schools, which agree in abstract discussions of political systems, without thinking of the coexisting state of civilization, and usually conclude with making their immutable political type coincide with an infantile state of human development.] If we ascend to the philosophical source of this error, we shall find it, I think, in the great theological dogma of the Fall of Man. This fundamental dogma, which reappears, in one form or another, in all religions, and which is supported in its intellectual influence by the natural propensity of men to admire the past, tends, directly and necessarily, to make the continuous deterioration of society coincide with the extension of civilization. We have noticed before how, when it passes from the theological into the metaphysical state, this dogma takes the form of the celebrated hypothesis of a chimerical state of nature, superior to the social state, and the more remote, the further we advance in civilization. We cannot fail to perceive the extreme seriousness, in a political as well as a philosophical sense, of an error so completely incorporated with existing doctrines, and so deeply influencing in an unconscious way, our collective social speculations, – the more disastrously perhaps for not being expressly maintained as a general principle. – If it were so presented, it must immediately give way before sound philosophical discussion; for it is in direct contradiction to many ideas in political philosophy which, without having attained any scientific consistency, are obtaining some intellectual ascendancy, through the natural course of events, or the expansion of the general mind. For instance, all enlightened political writers acknowledge more or less mutual relation between political institutions; and this is the first direct step towards the rational conception of the agreement of the special system of institutions with the total system of civilization. We now see the best thinkers admitting a constant mutual connection between the political and the civil power: which means, in scientific language, that preponderating social forces always end in assuming the direction of society. Such partial advances towards a right view, – such fortunate feeling after the right path, must not, however, induce us to relax in our requirements of a true philosophical conception of that general social agreement which can alone constitute organization. Desultory indications, more literary than scientific, can never supply the place of a strict philosophical doctrine, as we may see from the fact that, from Aristotle downwards, (and even from an earlier period,) the greater number of philosophers have constantly reproduced the famous aphorism of the necessary subordination of laws to manners, without this germ of sound philosophy having had any effect on the general habit of regarding institutions as independent of the coexisting state of civilization – however strange it may seem that such a contradiction should live through twenty centuries. This is, however, the natural course with intellectual principles and philosophical opinions, as well as with social manners and political institutions. When once they have obtained possession of men's minds, they live on, notwithstanding their admitted impotence and inconvenience, giving occasion to more and more serious inconsistencies, till the expansion of human reason originates new principles, of equivalent generality and superior rationality. We must not therefore take for more than their worth the desultory attempts that we see made in the right direction, but must insist on the principle which lies at the heart of every scheme of social organization, – the necessary participation of the collective political *régime* in the universal consensus of the social body.

The scientific principle of the relation between the political and the social condition is simply this; – that there must always be a spontaneous harmony between the whole and the parts of the social system, the elements of which must inevitably be, sooner or later, combined in a mode entirely conformable to their nature. It is evident that not only must political institutions and social manners on the one hand, and manners and ideas on the other, be always mutually connected; but, further, that this consolidated whole must be always connected, by its nature, with the corresponding state of the integral development of humanity, considered in all its aspects, of intellectual, moral, and physical activity: and the only object of any political system whatever, temporal or spiritual, is to regulate the spontaneous expansion so as best to direct it towards its determinate end. Even during revolutionary periods, when the harmony appears furthest from being duly realized, it still exists: for without it there would be a total dissolution of the social organism. During those exceptional seasons, the political *régime* is still, in the long run, in conformity with the corresponding state of civilization, as the disturbances which are manifest in the one proceed from equivalent derangements in the other. It is observable that when the popular theory attributes to the legislator the permanent power of infringing the harmony we are speaking of, it supposes him to be armed with a sufficient authority. But every social power, whether called authority or anything else, is constituted by a corresponding assent, spontaneous or deliberate, explicit or implicit, or various individual wills, resolved, from certain preparatory convictions, to concur in a common action, of which this power is first the organ, and then the regulator. Thus, authority is derived from concurrence, and not concurrence from authority, (setting aside the necessary reaction:) so that no great power can arise otherwise than from the strongly prevalent disposition of the society in which it exists: and when there is no strong preponderance, such powers as exist are weak accordingly: and the more extensive the society, the more irresistible is the correspondence. On the other hand, there is no denying the influence which, by a necessary reaction, the political system, as a whole, exercises over the general system of civilization, and which is so often exhibited in the action, fortunate or disastrous, of institutions, measures, or purely political events, even upon the course of the sciences and arts, in all ages of society, and especially the earliest. We need not dwell on this; for no one denies it. The common error, indeed, is to exaggerate it, so as to place the reaction before the primary action. It is evident, considering their scientific relation to each other, that both concur in creating that fundamental agreement of the social organism which I propose to set forth in a brief manner, as the philosophical principle of statical sociology. We shall have to advert repeatedly to the subject of the general correspondence between the political *régime* and the contemporary state of civilization, in connection with the question of the necessary limits of political action, and in the chapter which I must devote to social statics: but I did not think fit to wait for these explanations before pointing out that the political system ought always to be regarded as relative. The relative point of view, substituted for the absolute tendency of the ordinary theories, certainly constitutes the chief scientific character of the positive philosophy in its political application. If, on the one hand, the conception of this connection between government and civilization presents all ideas of political good or evil as necessarily relative and variable (which is quite another thing than being arbitrary), on the other hand, it provides a rational basis for a positive theory of the spontaneous order of human society, already vaguely perceived, in regard to some minor relations, by that part of the metaphysical polity which we call political economy; for, if the value of any political system can consist in nothing but its harmony with the corresponding social state, it follows that in the natural course of events, and in the absence of intervention, such a harmony must necessarily be established.

INTERCONNECTION OF THE SOCIAL ORGANISM

There are two principal considerations which induce me to insist on this elementary idea of the radical consensus proper to the social organism: first, the extreme philosophical importance of this master-thought of social statics, which must, from its nature, constitute the rational basis of any new political philosophy; and, secondly, in an accessory way, that dynamical considerations of sociology must prevail throughout the rest of this work, as being at present more interesting, and therefore better understood; and it is, on that account, the more necessary to characterize now the general spirit of social statics, which will henceforth be treated only in an indirect and implicit way. As all artificial and voluntary order is simply a prolongation of the natural and involuntary order to which all human society tends, every rational political institution must rest upon an exact preparatory analysis of corresponding spontaneous tendencies, which alone can furnish a sufficiently solid basis. In brief, it is our business to contemplate order, that we may perfect it; and not to create it; which would be impossible. In a scientific view, this master-thought of universal social interconnection becomes the consequence and complement of a fundamental idea established, in our view of biology, as eminently proper to the study of living bodies. Not that this idea of interconnection is peculiar to that study: it is necessarily common to all phenomena; but amidst immense differences in intensity and variety, and therefore in philosophical importance. It is, in fact, true that wherever there is any system whatever, a certain interconnection must exist. The purely mechanical phenomena of astronomy offer the first suggestion of it; for the perturbations of one planet may sensibly affect another, through a modified gravitation. But the relation becomes closer and more marked in proportion to the complexity and diminished generality of the phenomena, and thus, it is in organic systems that we must look for the fullest mutual connection. Hitherto, it had been merely an accessory idea; but then it becomes the basis of positive conceptions; and it becomes more marked, the more compound are the organisms, and the more complex the phenomena in question, – the animal interconnection being more complete than the vegetable, and the human more than the brute; the nervous system being the chief seat of the biological interconnection. The idea must therefore be scientifically preponderant in social physics even more than in biology, where it is so decisively recognized by the best order of students. But the existing political philosophy supposes the absence of any such interconnection among the aspects of society: and it is this which has rendered it necessary for me now to establish the point, – leaving the illustration of it to a future portion of the volume. Its consideration is, in fact, as indispensable in assigning its encyclopaedic rank to social science as we before saw it to be in instituting Social Physics a science at all.

It follows from this attribute that there can be no scientific study of society, either in its conditions or its movements, if it is separated into portions, and its divisions are studied apart. I have already remarked upon this, in regard to what is called political economy. Materials may be furnished by the observation of different departments; and such observation may be necessary for that object: but it cannot be called science. The methodical division of studies which takes place in the simple inorganic sciences is thoroughly irrational in the recent and complex science of society, and can produce no results. The day may come when some sort of subdivision may be practicable and desirable; but it is impossible for us now to anticipate what the principle of distribution may be; for the principle itself must arise from the development of the science; and that development can take place no otherwise than by our formation of the science as a whole. The complete body will indicate for itself, at the right season, the particular points which need investigation; and then will be the time for such special study as may be required. By any other method of proceeding, we shall only find ourselves encumbered with special discussions, badly instituted, worse pursued, and accomplishing no other purpose than that of impeding the formation of real science. It is no easy matter to study social phenomena in the only right way, – viewing each element in the light of the whole system. It is no easy matter to exercise such vigilance as that no one of the number of contemporary aspects shall be lost sight of. But it is the right and the only way; and we may perceive in it a clear suggestion that this lofty study should be reserved for the highest order of scientific minds, better prepared than others, by wise educational discipline, for sustained speculative efforts, aided by an habitual subordination of the passions to the reason. There is no need to draw out any lengthened comparison between this state of things as it should be and that which is. And no existing degree of social disturbance can surprise us when we consider how intellectual anarchy is at the bottom of such disturbance, and see how anarchical our intellectual condition appears in the presence of the principle I have laid down.

ORDER OF STATICAL STUDY

Before we go on to the subject of social dynamics, I will just remark that the prominent interconnection we have been considering prescribes a procedure in organic studies different from that which suits inorganic. The metaphysicians announce as an aphorism that we should always, in every kind of study, proceed from the simple to the compound: whereas, it appears most rational to suppose that we should follow that or the reverse method, as may best suit our subject. There can be no absolute merit in the method enjoined, apart from its suitableness. The rule should rather be (and there probably was a time when the two rules were one) that we must proceed from the more known to the less. Now, in the inorganic sciences, the elements are much better known to us than the whole which they constitute: so that in that case we must proceed from the simple to the compound. But the reverse method is necessary in the study of Man and of Society; Man and Society as a whole being better known to us, and more accessible subjects of study, than the parts which constitute them. In exploring the universe, it is as a whole that it is inaccessible to us; whereas, in investigating Man or Society, our difficulty is in penetrating the details. We have seen, in our survey of biology, that the general idea of animal nature is more distinct to our minds than the simpler notion of vegetable nature; and that man is the biological unity; the idea of Man being at once the most compound, and the starting-point of speculation in regard to vital existence. Thus, if we compare the two halves of natural philosophy, we shall find that in the one case it is the last degree of composition, and, in the other, the last degree of simplicity, that is beyond the scope of our research. As for the rest, it may obviate some danger of idle discussion to say that the positive philosophy, subordinating all fancies to reality, excludes logical controversies about the absolute value of this or that method, apart from its scientific application. The only ground of preference being the superior adaptation of any means to the proposed end, this philosophy may, without any inconsistency, change its order of proceeding when the one first tried is found to be inferior to its converse: – a discovery of which there is no fear in regard to the question we have now been examining.

DYNAMICAL STUDY

Passing on from statical to dynamical sociology, we will contemplate the philosophical conception which should govern our study of the movement of society. Part of this subject is already despatched, from the explanations made in connection with statics having simplified the chief difficulties of the case. And social dynamics will be so prominent throughout the rest of this work, that I may reduce within very small compass what I have to say now under that head.

Though the statical view of society is the basis of sociology, the dynamical view is not only the more interesting of the two, but the more marked in its philosophical character, from its being more distinguished from biology by the master-thought of continuous progress, or rather, of the gradual development of humanity. If I were writing a methodical treatise on political philosophy, it would be necessary to offer a preliminary analysis of the individual impulses which make up the progressive force of the human race, by referring them to that instinct which results from the concurrence of all our natural tendencies, and which urges man to develop the whole of his life, physical, moral, and intellectual, as far as his circumstances allow. But this view is admitted by all enlightened philosophers; so that I must proceed at once to consider the continuous succession of human development, regarded in the whole race, as if humanity were one. For clearness, we may take advantage of Condorcet's device of supposing a single nation to which we may refer all the consecutive social modifications actually witnessed among distinct peoples. This rational fiction is nearer the reality than we are accustomed to suppose; for, in a political view, the true successors of such or such a people are certainly those who, taking up and carrying out their primitive endeavours, have prolonged their social progress, whatever may be the soil which they inhabit, or even the race from which they spring. In brief, it is political continuity which regulates sociological succession, though the having a common country must usually affect this continuity in a high degree. As a scientific artifice merely, however, I shall employ this hypothesis, and on the ground of its manifest utility.

SOCIAL CONTINUITY

The true general spirit of social dynamics then consists in conceiving of each of these consecutive social states as the necessary result of the preceding, and the indispensable mover of the following, according to the axiom of Leibnitz, – *the present is big with the future*. In this view, the object of science is to discover the laws which govern this continuity, and the aggregate of which determines the course of human development. In short, social dynamics studies the laws of succession, while social statics inquires into those of coexistence; so that the use of the first is to furnish the true theory of progress to political practice, while the second performs the same service in regard to order; and this suitability to the needs of modern society is a strong confirmation of the philosophical character of such a combination.

PRODUCED BY NATURAL LAWS

If the existence of sociological laws has been established in the more difficult and uncertain case of the statical condition, we may assume that they will not be questioned in the dynamical province. In all times and places, the ordinary course of even our brief individual life has disclosed certain remarkable modifications which have occurred, in various ways, in the social state; and all the most ancient representations of human life bear unconscious and most interesting testimony to this, apart from all systematic estimate of the fact. Now it is the slow, continuous accumulation of these successive changes which gradually constitutes the social movement, whose steps are ordinarily marked by generations, as the most appreciable elementary variations are wrought by the constant renewal of adults. At a time when the average rapidity of this progression seems to all eyes to be remarkably accelerated, the reality of the movement cannot be disputed, even by those who most abhor it. The only question is about the constant subjection of these great dynamical phenomena to invariable natural laws, a proposition about which there is no question to any one who takes his stand on positive philosophy. It is easy however to establish, from any point of view, that the successive modifications of society have always taken place in a determinate order, the rational explanation of which is already possible in so many cases that we may confidently hope to recognize it ultimately in all the rest. So remarkable is the steadiness of this order, moreover, that it exhibits an exact parallelism of development among distinct and independent populations, as we shall see when we come to the historical portion of this volume. Since, then, the existence of the social movement is unquestionable, on the one hand, and, on the other, the succession of social states is never arbitrary, we cannot but regard this continuous phenomenon as subject to natural laws as positive as those which govern all other phenomena, though more complex. There is in fact no intellectual alternative; and thus it is evident that it is on the ground of social science that the great conflict must soon terminate which has gone on for three centuries between the positive and the theologico-metaphysical spirit. Banished for ever from all other classes of speculation, in principle at least, the old philosophies now prevail in social science alone; and it is from this domain that they have to be excluded, by the conception of the social movement being subject to invariable natural laws, instead of to any will whatever.

Though the fundamental laws of social interconnection are especially verified in this condition of movement, and though there is a necessary unity in this phenomenon, it may be usefully applied, for preparatory purposes, to the separate elementary aspects of human existence, physical, moral, intellectual and, finally, political, – their mutual relation being kept in view. Now, in whichever of these ways we regard, as a whole, the movement of humanity, from the earliest periods till now, we shall find that the various steps are connected in a determinate order; as we shall hereafter see, when we investigate the laws of this succession. I need refer here only to the intellectual evolution, which is the most distinct and unquestionable of all, as it has been the least impeded and most advanced of any, and has therefore been usually taken for guidance. The chief part of this evolution, and that which has most influenced the general progression, is no doubt the development of the scientific spirit, from the primitive labours of such philosophers as Thales and Pythagoras to those of men like Lagrange and Bichat. Now, no enlightened man can doubt that, in this long succession of efforts and discoveries, the human mind has pursued a determinate course, the exact preparatory knowledge of which might have allowed a cultivated reason to foresee the progress proper to each period. Though the historical considerations cited in my former volume were only incidental, any one may recognize in them numerous and indisputable examples of this necessary succession, more complex perhaps, but not more arbitrary than any natural law, whether in regard to the development of each separate science, or to the mutual influence of the different branches of natural philosophy. In accordance with the principles laid down at the beginning of this work, we have already seen in various signal instances, that the chief progress of each period, and even of each generation, was a necessary result of the immediately preceding state; so that the men of genius, to whom such progression has been too exclusively attributed, are essentially only the proper organs of a predetermined movement, which would, in their absence, have found other issues. We find a verification of this in history, which shows that various eminent men were ready to make the same great discovery at the same time, while the discovery required only one organ. All the parts of human evolution admit of analogous observations, as we shall presently see, though they are more complex and less obvious than that which I have just cited. The natural progression of the arts of life is abundantly evident; and in our direct study of social dynamics we shall find an explanation of the apparent exception of the fine arts, which will be found to oppose no contradiction to the general course of human progression. As to that part of the movement which appears at present to be least reducible to natural laws, the political movement (still supposed to be governed by wills of adequate power), it is clear as in any other case that political systems have exhibited an historical succession, according to a traceable filiation, in a determinate order, which I am prepared to show to be even more inevitable than that of the different states of human intelligence.

The interconnection which we have examined and established in a statical view may aid us in developing the conception of the existence of positive laws in social dynamics. Unless the movement was determined by those laws, it would occasion the entire destruction of the social system. Now, that interconnection simplifies and strengthens the preparatory indications of dynamic order; for, when it has once been shown in any relation, we are authorized to extend it to all others; and this unites all the partial proofs that we can successively obtain of the reality of this scientific conception. In the choice and the application of these verifications, we must remember that the laws of social dynamics are most recognizable when they relate to the largest societies in which secondary disturbances have the smallest effect. Again, these fundamental laws become the more irresistible, and therefore the more appreciable, in proportion to the advancement of the civilization upon which they operate, because the social movement becomes more distinct and certain with every conquest over accidental influences. As for the philosophical co-ordination of these preparatory evidences, the combination of which is important to science, it is clear that the social evolution must be more inevitably subject to natural laws, the more compound are the phenomena, and the less perceptible therefore the irregularities which arise from individual influences. This shows how inconsistent it is, for instance, to suppose the scientific movement to be subject to positive laws, while the political movement is regarded as arbitrary; for the latter, being more composite, must overrule individual disturbances, and be therefore more evidently predetermined than the former, in which individual genius must have more power. Any paradoxical appearance which this statement may exhibit will disappear in the course of further examination.

(Volume II, Book VI, Chapter iii, pp. 218–32)

THREE ASPECTS

Every sociological analysis supposes three classes of considerations, each more complex than the preceding: viz., the conditions of social existence of the individual, the family, and society; the last comprehending, in a scientific sense, the whole of the human species, and chiefly, the whole of the white race ...

THE FAMILY

As every system must be composed of elements of the same nature with itself, the scientific spirit forbids us to regard society as composed of individuals. The true social unit is certainly the family, – reduced, if necessary, to the elementary couple which forms its basis. This consideration implies more than the physiological truth that families become tribes, and tribes become nations: so that the whole human race might be conceived of as the grand development of a single family, if local diversities did not forbid such a supposition. There is a political point of view from which also we must consider this elementary idea, inasmuch as the family presents the true germ of the various characteristics of the social organism. Such a conception is intermediate between the idea of the individual and that of the species, or society. There would be as many scientific inconveniences in passing it over in a speculative sense as there are dangers in practice in pretending to treat of social life without the inevitable preparation of the domestic life. Whichever way we look at it, this necessary transition always presents itself, whether in regard to elementary notions of fundamental harmony, or for the spontaneous rise of social sentiment. It is by this avenue that Man comes forth from his mere personality, and learns to live in another, while obeying his most powerful instincts ...

SOCIETY

The third head of our statical analysis brings us to the consideration of society, as composed of families and not of individuals and from a point of view which commands all times and places.

The main cause of the superiority of the social to the individual organism is, according to an established law, the more marked speciality of the various functions fulfilled by organs more and more distinct, but interconnected; so that unity of aim is more and more combined with diversity of means. We cannot, of course, fully appreciate a phenomenon which is for ever proceeding before our eyes, and in which we bear a part; but if we withdraw ourselves in thought from the social system, and contemplate it as from afar, can we conceive of a more marvellous spectacle, in the whole range of natural phenomena, than the regular and constant convergence of an innumerable multitude of human beings, each possessing a distinct and, in a certain degree, independent existence, and yet incessantly disposed, amidst all their discordance of talent and character, to concur in many ways in the same general development, without concert, and even consciousness on the part of most of them, who believe that they are merely following their personal impulses? This is the scientific picture of the phenomenon: and no temporary disturbances can prevent its being, under all circumstances, essentially true. This reconciliation of the individuality of labour with co-operation of endeavours, which becomes more remarkable as society grows more complex and extended, constitutes the radical character of human operations when we rise from the domestic to the social point of view. The degree of association that we observe among the superior animals has something voluntary in it, but there is no organization which can make it resemble the human: and the first individual specializing of common functions is seen in our simple domestic life, which is thus a type of social organization. The division of labour can never, however, be very marked in the family, because the members are few; and yet more because such a division would soon show itself to be hostile to the spirit of the institution; for domestic training, being founded on imitation, must dispose the children to follow parental employments, instead of undertaking new ones; and again, any very marked separation in the employments of the members must impair the domestic unity which is the aim of the association. The more we look into the subject, the more we shall see that the appropriation of employments, which is the elementary principle of general society, cannot hold anything like so important a place in the family. In fact, the domestic relations do not constitute an association, but a *union*, in the full force of the term; and, on account of this close intimacy, the domestic connection is of a totally different nature from the social. Its character is essentially moral, and only incidentally intellectual; or, in anatomical language, it corresponds more to the middle than to the anterior part of the brain. Founded chiefly upon attachment and gratitude, the domestic union satisfies, by its mere existence, all our sympathetic instincts, quite apart from all idea of active and continuous co-operation towards any end, unless it be that of its own institution. Though more or less co-ordination of different employments must exist, it is so secondary an affair that when, unhappily, it remains the only principle of connection, the domestic union degenerates into mere association, and is even too likely to dissolve altogether. In society the elementary economy presents an inverse character, the sentiment of co-operation becoming preponderant, and the sympathetic instinct, without losing its steadiness, becoming secondary. No doubt there are a multitude of men well enough organized to love their fellow-labourers, however numerous or remote they may be, and however indirect may be their co-operation; but such a sentiment, arising from the reaction of the reason upon the social feelings, could never be strong enough to guide social life. Even under the best circumstances the intellectual mediocrity of the majority of men does not allow them to form any distinct idea of relations which are too extensive, too indirect, and too foreign to their own occupations to impart any sympathetic stimulus which could be of permanent use. It is only in domestic life that Man can habitually seek the full and free expansion of his social affections; and perhaps this is the chief reason why it is the last indispensable preparation for social life; for concentration is as necessary to the feelings as generalization to the thoughts. Even the most eminent men, who direct their sympathetic instincts upon their race at large or the society in which they live, are usually impelled to this by the moral disappointments of a domestic life which has failed in some of its conditions; and however genial the imperfect compensation may be to them, this abstract love of their species admits of nothing like that satisfaction of the affections which arises from a very limited, and especially an individual attachment. However this may be, such cases are besides too evidently exceptional to affect an inquiry into the social economy. Thus, though the sympathetic instinct exists wherever there is association, more or less, the principle of co-operation is that which must prevail, when we pass on from the consideration of the family to the general co-ordination of families. To attribute to it the formation of the social state, as it was the fashion of the last century to do, is a capital error; but, when the association has once begun, there is nothing like this principle of co-operation for giving consistency and character to the combination. In the lower stages of savage life we see families combining for a temporary purpose, and then returning, almost like the brutes, to their isolated independence, as soon as the expedition, which is usually one of war or the chase, is ended, though already some common opinions, expressed in a certain uniform language, are preparing them for permanent union in tribes, more or less numerous. It is upon the principle of co-operation, then, spontaneous or concerted, that we must found our analysis of the last division of social statics.

DISTRIBUTION OF EMPLOYMENTS

We must include in our view of the division of employments something much more extensive than the material arrangements which the expression is usually understood to convey. We must include under it all human operations whatever, regarding not only individuals and classes, but also, in many ways, different nations, as participating in a special mode and degree, in a vast common work, the gradual development of which connects the fellow-labourers with the whole series of their predecessors, and even with their successors. This is what is meant when we speak of the race being bound up together by the very distribution of their occupations; and it is this distribution which causes the extent and growing complexity of the social organism, which thus appears as comprising the whole of the human race. Man can hardly exist in a solitary state: the family can exist in isolation, because it can divide its employments and provide for its wants in a rough kind of way: a spontaneous approximation of families is incessantly exposed to temporary rupture, occasioned by the most trifling incidents. But when a regular division of employments has spread through any society, the social state begins to acquire a consistency and stability which place it out of danger from particular divergencies. The habit of partial co-operation convinces each family of its close dependence on the rest, and, at the same time, of its own importance, each one being then justified in regarding itself as fulfilling a real public function, more or less indispensable to the general economy, but inseparable from the system as a whole. In this view the social organization tends more and more to rest on an exact estimate of individual diversities, by so distributing employments as to appoint each one to the destination he is most fit for, from his own nature (which however is seldom very distinctly marked), from his education and his position, and, in short, from all his qualifications; so that all individual organizations, even the most vicious and imperfect (short of monstrosity), may be finally made use of for the general good. Such is, at least, the social type which we conceive of as the limit of the existing social order, and to which we may be for ever approximating, though without the hope of ever attaining it; and it is, in fact, a reproduction, with a large extension, of the domestic organism, with less power, in proportion to its extent, of appointing a due destination to every member; so that the social discipline must always be more artificial, and therefore more imperfect, than the domestic, which nature herself ordains and administers.

The necessities of this co-ordination and distribution of special offices, cause inconveniences which I am compelled to advert to; for it is in the investigation of these that we find the scientific germ of the relation between the idea of society and that of government.

INCONVENIENCES

Some economists have pointed out, but in a very inadequate way, the evils of an exaggerated division of material labour; and I have indicated, in regard to the more important field of scientific labour, the mischievous intellectual consequences of the spirit of speciality which at present prevails. It is necessary to estimate directly the principle of such an influence, in order to understand the object of the spontaneous system of requisites for the continuous preservation of society. In decomposing, we always disperse; and the distribution of human labours must occasion individual divergencies, both intellectual and moral, which require a permanent discipline to keep them within bounds. If the separation of social functions develops a useful spirit of detail, on the one hand, it tends, on the other, to extinguish or to restrict what we may call the aggregate or general spirit. In the same way, in moral relations, while each individual is in close dependence on the mass, he is drawn away from it by the expansion of his special activity, constantly recalling him to his private interest, which he but very dimly perceives to be related to the public. On both grounds the inconveniences of the division of functions increase with its characteristic advantages, without their being in the same relation, throughout the spontaneous course of the social evolution. The growing speciality of habitual ideas and familiar relations must tend to restrict the understanding more and more, while sharpening it in a certain direction, and to sever more and more the private interest from a public interest which is for ever becoming more vague and indirect; while, at the same time, the social affections, gradually concentrated among individuals of the same profession, become more and more alienated from all other classes, for want of a sufficient analogy of ways and ideas. Thus it is that the principle by which alone general society could be developed and extended, threatens, in another view, to decompose it into a multitude of unconnected corporations, which almost seem not to belong to the same species; and hence it is that the gradual expansion of human ability seems destined to produce such minds as are very common among civilized peoples, and prodigiously admired by them, – minds which are very able in some one respect and monstrously incapable in all others. If we have been accustomed to deplore the spectacle, among the artisan class, of a workman occupied during his whole life in nothing else but making knife-handles or pins' heads, we may find something quite as lamentable in the intellectual class, in the exclusive employment of a human brain in resolving some equations, or in classifying insects. The moral effect is, unhappily, analogous in the two cases. It occasions a miserable indifference about the general course of human affairs, as long as there are equations to resolve and pins to manufacture. This is an extreme case of human automatism; but the frequency, and the growing frequency, of the evil gives a real scientific importance to the case, as indicating the general tendency, and warning us to restrain it. Thus it appears to me that the social destination of government is to guard against and restrain the fundamental dispersion of ideas, sentiments, and interests, which is the inevitable result of the very principle of human development, and which, if left to itself, would put a stop to social progression in all important respects.

BASIS OF THE TRUE THEORY OF GOVERNMENT

Here we have, in my opinion, the basis of the elementary and abstract theory of government, regarded in its complete scientific extension; that is, as characterized by the universal necessary reaction, – first spontaneous and then regulated, – of the whole upon the parts. It is clear that the only way of preventing such a dispersion is by setting up this reaction as a new special function, which shall intervene in the performance of all the various functions of the social economy, to keep up the idea of the whole, and the feeling of the common interconnection: and the more energetically, the more individual activity tends to dissolve them. Not itself affecting any determinate social progress, it contributes to all that society can achieve, in any direction whatever, and which society could not achieve without its concentrating and protective care. The very nature of its action indicates that it cannot be merely material, but also, and much more, intellectual and moral; so as to show the double necessity of what has been called the temporal and spiritual government, the rational subordination of which was the best feature of the social organization that was happily effected in its day, under the influence of the prevalent Catholicism, Moreover, this ruling function must become more, instead of less necessary, as human development proceeds, because its essential principle is inseparable from that of the development itself. – Thus, it is the habitual predominance of the spirit of the whole which constitutes government, in whatever way it is regarded. The next consideration is, how such an action arises, independently of all systematic combination, in the natural course of the social economy.

ELEMENTARY SUBORDINATION

If the dispersive tendency arising from the distribution of functions naturally propagates itself, it is clear that any influence capable of neutralizing it must also be constantly expanding. In fact, an elementary subordination must always be growing out of the distribution of human operations, which gives birth to government, in the bosom of society itself, as we could easily discover by analysing any marked subdivision which has just taken place in any employment whatever. This subordination is not only material, but yet more intellectual and moral; that is, it requires, besides practical submission, a corresponding degree of real confidence in both the capacity and the probity of the special organs to whom a function, hitherto universal, is confided. Every one of us relies, even for life itself, on the aptitude and the morality of a multitude of almost unknown agents, whose folly or wickedness might affect the welfare of vast numbers of human beings. Such a condition belongs to all modes of social existence. If it is especially attributed to industrial societies, it is only because it must be most conspicuous where the division of labour goes furthest; and it is as certainly to be found in purely military societies; as the statical analysis of an army, a man-of-war, or any other active corporation shows in a moment.

This elementary subordination discloses its own law; which is, that the various operations in which individuals are engaged fall naturally under the direction of those which are next above them in generality. We may easily convince ourselves of this by analysing any special occupation at the moment when it assumes a separate character: because the task thus separated is necessarily more special than the function from which it proceeds, and to which its own fulfilment must be subordinated. This is not the occasion on which to expatiate on this law; but its political bearing concerns us here, – indicating as it does the germ of a true classification of social functions. We shall hereafter meet with a full verification of this law in regard to the industrial life of modern societies: the eminent regularity of military associations renders the law obvious at once; and when the law is once admitted, it discloses the spontaneous connection of this elementary social subordination with that political subordination, properly so called, which is the basis of government, and which presents itself as the last degree in the hierarchy formed by the subjection of the more special to the more general classes of phenomena. For, as the various particular functions of the social economy are naturally implicated in relations of greater generality, all must at length be subject to the direction of the most general function of all, which is characterized, as we have seen, by the constant action of the whole upon the parts. On the other hand, the organs of this direction must be much strengthened by the encouragement afforded to intellectual and moral inequality under a system of division of employments. It is clear that while men were obliged to do everything for themselves, they must have been confined to domestic life, devoting all their activity to supply the wants of the family; and there could be little expansion of individual ability and character. Though marked individuality must always have made itself felt, in every state of society, the division of labour, and the leisure which it brings, have been needful to the conspicuous development of that intellectual superiority on which all political ascendency must mainly rest. We must observe, moreover, that there can be no such division of intellectual as of material labour; so that the intellectual functions must be less affected than the industrial by the dispersive tendencies of such a division. We are familiar with the effect of civilization in developing moral, and yet more, intellectual inequalities; but we must bear in mind that moral and intellectual forces do not admit, like the physical, of being accumulated and compounded: so that, eminently as they can occur, and clearly as they are the creators of social concurrence, they are much less adapted for direct co-operation. A sufficient coalition of the most insignificant individuals can easily carry any point of physical conflict, or of acquisition of wealth, against the highest superiority in an individual or a family; so that, for example, the most enormous private fortune cannot sustain any competition with the financial power of a nation, whose treasury is filled by a multitude of the smallest contributions. But, on the contrary, if the enterprise depends on a high intellectual power, as in the case of a great scientific or poetical conception, there can be no association of ordinary minds, however extensive, which can compete with a Descartes or a Shakspere. It is the same in the moral case; as, for instance, if society is in need of any great resource of devotedness, the want cannot be supplied by accumulating any amount of moderate zeal furnished by individuals. The only use of a multitude in such a case is that it improves the chance of finding the *unique* organ of the proposed function; and when that singular agent is once found, there is no degree of multitude which can weigh down its preponderance. It is through this privilege that intellectual and moral forces tend to an ever-increasing social authority, from the time when a due division of employments admits of their proper development.

TENDENCY OF SOCIETY TO GOVERNMENT

Such is, then, the elementary tendency of all human society to a spontaneous government. This tendency accords with a corresponding system, inherent in us as individuals, of special dispositions towards command in some, and towards obedience in others. We must not, with regard to the first, confound the desire to rule with the fitness to do so; though the desire is one element of the fitness; and, on the other hand, there is a much stronger inclination to obedience in the generality of men than it is customary in our day to suppose. If men were as rebellious as they are at present represented, it would be difficult to understand how they could ever have been disciplined: and it is certain that we are all more or less disposed to respect any superiority, especially any intellectual or moral elevation, in our neighbours, independently of any view to our own advantage: and this instinct of submission is, in truth, only too often lavished on deceptive appearances. However excessive the desire of command may be in our revolutionary day, there can be no one who, in his secret mind, has not often felt, more or less vividly, how sweet it is to obey when he can have the rare privilege of consigning the burdensome responsibility of his general self-conduct to wise and trustworthy guidance: and probably the sense of this is strongest in those who are best fitted for command. In the midst of political convulsion, when the spirit of revolutionary destruction is abroad, the mass of the people manifest a scrupulous obedience towards the intellectual and moral guides from whom they accept direction, and upon whom they may even press a temporary dictatorship, in their primary and urgent need of a preponderant authority. Thus do individual dispositions show themselves to be in harmony with the course of social relations as a whole, in teaching us that political subordination is as inevitable, generally speaking, as it is indispensable. And this completes the elementary delineation of Social Statics.

My sketch has perhaps been so abstract and condensed that the conceptions of this chapter may appear obscure at present; but light will fall upon them as we proceed. We may already see, however, the practical advantage which arises from the scientific evolution of human relations. The individual life, ruled by personal instincts; the domestic, by sympathetic instincts; and the social, by the special development of intellectual influences, prepare for the states of human existence which are to follow: and that which ensues is, first, personal morality, which subjects the preservation of the individual to a wise discipline; next, domestic morality, which subordinates selfishness to sympathy; and lastly, social morality, which directs all dividual tendencies by enlightened reason, always having the general economy in view, so as to bring into concurrence all the faculties of human nature, according to their appropriate laws.

(Volume II, Book VI, Chapter v, pp. 275, 280–81, 289–98)

We have indicated the general direction of the human evolution, its rate of progress, and its necessary order. We may now proceed at once to investigate the natural laws by which the advance of the human mind proceeds. The scientific principle of the theory appears to me to consist in the great philosophical law of the succession of the three states – the primitive theological state, the transient metaphysical, and the final positive state – through which the human mind has to pass, in every kind of speculation. This seems to be the place in which we should attempt the direct estimate of this fundamental law, taking it as the basis of my historical analysis, which must itself have for its chief object to explain and expand the general notion of this law by a more and more extended and exact application of it in the review of the entire past of human history. I hope that the frequent statement and application of this law throughout the preceding part of my work will enable me to condense my demonstration of it here, without impairing its distinctiveness, or injuring its efficacy in such ulterior use as we shall have to make of it.

LAW OF THE THREE PERIODS

The reader is by this time abundantly familiar with the interpretation and destination of the law. All thoughtful persons can verify for themselves its operation in individual development, from infancy to manhood, as I pointed out at the beginning of this work. We can test it, as we have tested other laws, by observation, experiment, and comparison. I have done so through many years of meditation; and I do not hesitate to say that all these methods of investigation will be found to concur in the complete establishment of this historical proposition, which I maintain to be as fully demonstrated as any other law admitted into any other department of natural philosophy. Since the discovery of this law of the three periods, all positive philosophers have agreed on its special adaptation to the particular science in which each was interested, though all have not made the avowal with equal openness. The only objections that I have encountered have related merely to the universality of its application. I hold it to be now implicitly recognized with regard to all the sciences which are positive: that is, the triple evolution is admitted in regard to all cases in which it is accomplished. It is only in regard to social science that its application is supposed to be impossible: and I believe the objection to signify nothing more than that the evolution is in this case incomplete. Social science has, with all its complexity, passed through the theological state, and has almost everywhere fully attained the metaphysical; while it has nowhere yet risen to the positive, except in this book. I shall leave the assertion of the law in regard to sociology to the demonstration which my analysis will afford: for those who can not perceive in this volume, as a whole, the nascent realization of this last philosophical process could not be convinced by argument. Leaving the historical verification of the law, therefore, to the reader, I invite attention to its philosophical explanation. It is not enough that the succession of the three states is a general fact. Such generality would go for more in any other science than in sociology, because, as we have seen, our biological philosophy enables us to conceive of all the main relations of social phenomena *à priori*, independently of their direct investigation, and we need confirmation of our conceptions by a direct knowledge of human nature and experience. An *à-priori* conception of a law so important as this is of the deepest interest in the study of social dynamics; and, to confirm it, we must carefully mark the general grounds, derived from an exact knowledge, which have rendered indispensable on the one hand, and inevitable on the other, that succession of social phenomena which take their course under the operation of this law. The logical grounds have already been assigned, at the outset of the work, and repeatedly since: and it is with the moral and social that we now have to do, and we can review them without subjecting ourselves to the reproach of severing the parts of a philosophical demonstration which are in their nature bound up together.

THE THEOLOGICAL PERIOD

The necessity of the intellectual evolution I assert lies in the primary tendency of Man to transfer the sense of his own nature into the radical explanation of all phenomena whatever. Philosophers tell us of the fundamental difficulty of knowing ourselves; but this is a remark which could not have been made till human reason had achieved a considerable advance. The mind must have attained to a refined state of meditation before it could be astonished at its own acts – reflecting upon itself a speculative activity which must be at first incited by the external world. If, on the one hand, Man must begin by supposing himself the centre of all things, he must, on the other hand, next set himself up as a universal type. The only way that he can explain any phenomena is by likening them, as much as possible, to his own acts – the only ones whose mode of production he can suppose himself, by the accompanying sensations, to understand. We may therefore set up a converse statement, and say that Man knows nothing but himself; and thus, his philosophy, in his earliest stage, consists principally in transferring this spontaneous unity, more or less fortunately, into all subjects which may present themselves to his nascent attention. It is the highest proof of his philosophical maturity when he can, at length, apply the study of external nature to his own. When I laid this down as the basis of biological philosophy, I intimated the extreme rarity of such an attainment. At the outset, under the inverse process, the universe is always subordinated to Man, in speculative as well as in active respects. We shall not have attained a truly rational position till we can reconcile these two great philosophical views, at present antagonistic, but admitting of being made mutually complementary, and, in my opinion, prepared for being so, from this time forward. Such a harmony is even now barely conceivable in the brightest insight of philosophical genius, and there could have been no choice between the two courses in the earliest days of human development. The starting-point must have been that which

125

alone was naturally possible. This was the spontaneous origin of the theological philosophy, the elementary spirit of which consists in explaining the intimate nature of phenomena, and their mode of production, and in likening them, as much as possible, to the acts of human will, through our primary tendency to regard all beings as living a life analogous to our own, and often superior, from their greater habitual energy. This procedure is so eminently exclusive, that men are unable to emancipate themselves from it, even in the most advanced stages of evolution, except by abandoning altogether these inaccessible researches, and restricting themselves to the study of the laws of phenomena, apart from their causes. Whenever, at this day, the human mind attempts to pass these inevitable limits, it involuntarily falls again into the primary errors, even in regard to the simplest phenomena, because it recurs to an aim and point of view essentially analogous, in attributing the production of phenomena to special volitions, internal, or more or less external. One case presents itself as an example, of the simplest scientific character – that of the memorable philosophical error of the illustrious Malebranche in regard to the explanation of the mathematical laws of the elementary collision of solid bodies. If such a mind, in such an age, could explain such a theory in no other way than by an express recurrence to the continuous activity of a direct and special providence, we can not doubt the tendency of our reason towards a radically theological philosophy whenever we attempt to penetrate, on any ground whatever, the intimate nature of phenomena.

INTELLECTUAL INFLUENCE OF THE THEOLOGICAL PHILOSOPHY

This inevitableness of the theological philosophy is its most radical property, and the first cause of its long ascendency. We have seen before that it was necessary, as the only possible beginning of our intellectual evolution; for the facts which must form the basis of a positive theory could not be collected to any purpose without some preliminary theory which should guide their collection. Our understanding can not act without some doctrine, false or true, vague or precise, which may concentrate and stimulate its efforts, and afford ground for enough speculative continuity to sustain our mental activity. Our meteorological *observations*, as we call them, show us how useless may be vast compilations of facts, and how really unmeaning, while we are destitute of any theory whatever. Those who expect that the theory will be suggested by the facts, do not understand what is the course necessarily pursued by the human mind, which has achieved all real results by the only effectual method, – of anticipating scientific observations by some conception (hypothetical in the first instance) of the corresponding phenomena. Such a necessity has already been shown to be especially marked in the case of social speculations, not only from their complexity, but from the peculiarity that a long preparatory development of the human mind and of Society constitutes the phenomena of the case, independently of all preparation of observers, and all accumulation of observations. It may be worth observing, that all the partial verifica= tions of this fundamental proposition that we meet with in the different sciences confirm each other, on account of our tendency to unity of method and homogeneousness of doctrine, which would incline us to extend the theological philosophy from one class of speculations to another, even if we should not so treat each one of them separately.

The original and indispensable office of the theological philosophy is then to lead forth the human mind from the vicious circle in which it was confined by the two necessities of observing first, in order to form conceptions, and of forming theories first, in order to observe. The theological philosophy afforded an issue by likening all phenomena whatever to human acts; directly, in the first instance, by supposing all bodies to have a life more or less like our own, and indirectly afterwards, by means of the more durable and suggestive hypothesis which adds to the visible system of things an invisible world, peopled by super-human agents, who occasion all phenomena by their action on matter, otherwise inert. The second stage is especially suitable to the human mind which begins to feel its difficulties and its needs; for every new phenomenon is accounted for by the supposition of a fresh volition in the ideal agent concerned, or, at most, by easy creation of a new agent. However futile these speculations may now appear, we must remember that, in all times and everywhere, they have awakened human thought by offering to it the only material which it could at first accept. Besides that there was no choice, the infant reason can be interested by nothing but sublime solutions, obtained without any deep and sustained conflict of thought. We, at this day, find ourselves able, after suitable training, to devote ourselves to the study of the laws of phenomena, without heed to their first and final causes; but still we detect ourselves occasion-ally yielding to the infantine curiosity which pretends to a power of knowing the origin and the end of all things. But such severity of reason as we are capable of has become attainable only since the accumulation of our knowledge has yielded us a rational hope of finally discovering the natural laws that were altogether out of reach, in the early states of the human mind; and the only alternative from total inactivity was, in those days, in the pursuit of the inaccessible subjects which are represented by the theological philosophy. – The moral and social grounds of this philosophy were as necessary as the intellectual. Its moral influence was to inspire Man with confidence enough for action, by animating him with a sense of a position of supremacy. There is something astonishing in the contrast between the actual powers of Man in an infant state and the indefinite control which he aspires to exercise over external nature; just as there is in his expectation of understanding matters which are inaccessible to reason. The practical and the speculative expectation alike belong to the theological philosophy. Supposing all phenomena to be regulated by superhuman will, Man may hope to modify the universe by his desires; not by his personal resources, but by the access which he believes himself to have to the imaginary beings whose power is unlimited; whereas, if he was aware from the beginning that the universe is subject to invariable laws, the certainty that he could no more influence than understand them would so discourage him that he would remain for ever in his original apathy, intellectual and moral. We find ourselves able to dispense with supernatural aid in our difficulties and sufferings, in proportion as we obtain a gradual control over Nature by a knowledge of her laws: but the early races of men were in an opposite condition. They could obtain confidence, and therefore courage, only from above, and through the illusion of an illimitable power residing there, which could, on any occasion, afford them irresistible aid. I am not referring now to any hope of a future life. We shall see presently that it was not till a much later period that hope exercised any important social influence: and even in more recent times, we shall find that the effect of the religious spirit on the conduct of human life proceeds much more from belief in actual and special immediate aid than from the uniform perspective of a remote future existence. This seems to me the leading aspect of the remarkable state which is produced in the human brain by the important intellectual and moral phenomenon of prayer; the admirable properties of which, when it has attained its full physiological efficacy, are very manifest in the earliest stage of progress. After a long decline of the religious spirit, the notion of *miracle* was naturally formed, to characterize the events which had become exceptional, and were attributed to divine intervention: but the very conception shows that the general principle of natural laws had become familiar, and even preponderant, because the only sense of *miracle* was a transient suspension of natural laws.

While the theological philosophy was all in all, there were no miracles, because everything was equally marvellous, as we see by the artless descriptions of ancient poetry, in which the commonest incidents are mixed up with the most monstrous prodigies, and undergo analogous explanations. Minerva intervenes to pick up the whip of a warrior in military games, as well as to protect him against a whole army: and in our own time, the devotee is as importunate in praying for his smallest personal convenience as for the largest human interests. In all ages, the priest has been more occupied with the solicitations of his flock about immediate favours of Providence than with their care for their external state. However this may be, we see that it is a radical property of the theological philosophy to be the sole support and stimulus of Man's moral courage, as well as the awakener and director of his intellectual activity. – To this we must add, as another attraction of Man to this philosophy, that the affective influence comes in to fortify the speculative. Feeble as are the intellectual organs, relatively considered, the attractive moral perspective of an unbounded power of modifying the universe, by the aid of supernatural protectors, must have been most important in exciting mental action. In our advanced state of scientific progress, we can conceive of the perpetual pursuit of knowledge for the sake of the satisfaction of intellectual activity, joined to the tranquil pleasure which arises from the discovery of truth: yet it is doubtful whether such natural stimulus as this would always suffice without collateral instigations of glory, of ambition, or of lower and stronger passions, except in the case of a very few lofty minds; and with them, only after training in the requisite habits. And nothing of this kind can be supposed possible in the early days, when the intellect is torpid and feeble, and scarcely accessible to the strongest stimulus; nor yet afterwards, when science is so far advanced as to have attained some speculative success. In the working out of such speculation, the mental activity can be sustained by nothing short of the fictions of the theological philosophy about the supremacy of man and his unbounded empire over external nature; as we have seen in regard to astrology and alchemy. In our own time, when there are enlightened men who hold such delusions in regard to social speculations alone, we see how irrationally they expect to modify at will the whole course of political phenomena, in which they could not take any adequate scientific interest without such an expectation. What we see of the influence of this view in maintaining the old polities may give us some faint idea of its power when it pervaded every part of the intellectual system, and illusion beset the reason of Man, whichever way he turned. Such then was the moral operation of the theological philosophy, – stimulating Man's active energy by the offer, in the midst of the troubles of his infantine state, of absolute empire over the external world, as the prize of his speculative efforts.

SOCIAL INFLUENCES OF THE THEOLOGICAL PHILOSOPHY

The social evidences under this head will be fully treated in the following chapters, so that we may dismiss them now with a very short notice, important as they are; and the more easily, because this class of evidences is the most indisputable of the three. There are two views which must be considered, in relation to the high social office of the theological philosophy: first, its function in organizing society; and next, its provision for the permanent existence of a speculative class. – As to the first, we must perceive that the formation of any society, worthy to be so called, supposes a system of common opinions, such as may restrain individual eccentricity; and such an influence, if needful now, when men are connected together by such a concurrence of obligations as high civilization induces, must be absolutely indispensable in the infancy of society, when families adhere to each other so feebly, by means of relations as precarious as they are defective. No concurrence of interests, nor even sympathy in sentiment, can give durability to the smallest society, if there be not intellectual unanimity enough to obviate or correct such discordance as must inevitably arise. It has been shown that, indolent as our intellectual faculties are in comparison with the others, reason must rule, not domestic but social, and yet more political life: for through it alone can there be any organization of that reaction of society on the individual which appoints the function of government, and absolutely requires a system of common opinions about nature and Man. Such a system, then, is a political necessity; and especially in the infancy of society. But, on the other hand, we must admit that the human mind, having thus furnished a basis for social organization, must depend for its further development on society itself, whose expansion is really inseparable from that of human intelligence. Here we see that society is in a vicious circle in a political, as well as a logical view, through the opposition of two equal necessities, and here, again, the only possible issue is afforded by the theological philosophy. It directs the first social organization, as it first forms a system of common opinions, and by forming such a system. Because we see it now in such a state of decomposition that its advocates lose sight of the unity of opinions that it once secured and are themselves involved in intellectual discordance, we must not forget how, in those days of vigour by which it must be judged, it established an intellectual communion which constituted its most remarkable political function. The police consideration of a future life is wrongly attributed to this period of human society. It arose long after, and was of very inferior importance to the intellectual agreement which preceded it: and its operation would not be so erroneously exaggerated, but that religion has so far faded out of men's minds as to leave no other strong habitual remembrance than of its grossest impressions.

INSTITUTION OF A SPECULATIVE CLASS

Another way in which the theological philosophy was politically indispensable to human progress was by instituting, in the midst of society, a special class regularly devoted to speculative activity. In this view, the social supremacy of the theological philosophy has lasted to our own time. It is scarcely possible for us to form any but an indirect idea of the difficulty of establishing, in the earliest period of society, any permanent division between theory and practice, such as is effected by the existence of a class regularly occupied with speculation. Even now, amidst all the refinement of our mental habits, we find extreme difficulty in duly estimating any new operation which has no immediate practical bearing: and by this we may imperfectly understand how impossible it was, in the remotest ages, to institute among populations of warriors and slaves a corporation that should be disengaged from military and industrial employments, and whose activity should be mainly of an intellectual kind. Such a class could, in those times, have been neither established nor tolerated if it had not been introduced in the natural course of social movement, and invested with authority beforehand by the influence of the theological philosophy. The political function of that philosophy thus was to establish a speculative body whose social existence not only admitted of no preparatory discussion, but was itself an indispensable preparation for the regular organization of all other classes. Whatever might have been the confusion of intellectual labour, and the inanity of the leading investigations of the sacerdotal orders, it is not the less true that the human mind owes to them the first effectual separation between theory and practice, which could take place in no other manner. Mental progress, by which all other progress is directed, would certainly have been destroyed at its birth, if society had continued to be composed of families engaged in the cares of material existence, or, as the only alternative, in the excitement of a brutal military activity. Any spiritual expansion supposes the existence of a privileged class, enjoying the leisure indispensable to intellectual culture, and at the same time urged, by its social position, to develop to the utmost the kind of speculative activity compatible with the primitive state of humanity; and this description is answered by the sacerdotal institution established by the theological philosophy. Though, in the decrepitude of the old philosophy, we see the theological class sunk in mental lethargy, we must not forget that, but for their activity in the days of its prime, human society would have remained in a condition much like that of a company of superior monkeys. By forming this speculative class, then, the theological philosophy fulfilled the political conditions of a further progression of the human mind.

Such are the qualities, intellectual, moral and social, which secured the supremacy of the theological philosophy, at the outset of human progress. This is the only part of my sociological demonstration which is at all open to dispute; and this is one reason why I have dwelt so long upon it: but it is not the only reason. Another and a greater is that this view contains the radical principle of the whole demonstration, the remainder of which will not detain us long.

THE POSITIVE STAGE

If this starting-point of human development has been placed beyond dispute, the final or positive stage does not admit of it. We have seen enough of the establishment of the positive philosophy in other departments to be satisfied of its destined prevalence in sociology. For the same reasons which explain and justify the early supremacy of the theological philosophy, we see that it must be a provisional state, for its supremacy was owing to its aptitude to meet the needs of a primitive state of humanity; and those needs are not the same, not requiring the same philosophy to satisfy them, as those which arise in a more advanced stage of the human evolution. After having awakened human reason, and superintended its progress, in the absence of a more real philosophy, theology began to repress the human mind from the first moment of its coming into direct antagonism with the positive philosophy. And in the same way, in its moral relations, it imparted at first a consolatory confidence and active energy, which have become transmuted, by too long a duration, into oppressive terror and a faint apathy which have been too common a spectacle since it has been driven to struggle to retain its hold, instead of extending its dominion. There is no more question of the moral than of the intellectual superiority and final supremacy of the positive philosophy, capable as it is of developing in us an unshaken vigour and a deliberate steadfastness, directly derived from our own nature, without any external assistance, or any imaginary hindrance. And again, in regard to its social bearings, though the ascendency of the theological philosophy lasted longer on this ground than on the other two, it is evident enough at present that, instead of uniting men, which was its proper function at first, it now divides them, so that, after having created speculative activity, it has ended with radically hindering it. The function of reuniting, as of stimulating and directing, belongs more and more, as religious belief declines, to the conceptions of positive philosophy, which alone can establish that intellectual community all over the world on which the great future political organization is to be grounded. The intellectual destination of the two philosophies has been sufficiently established in our review of all the departments of natural philosophy. Their moral and social destination will be illustrated in succeeding chapters of this work. My historical analysis will explain to us the continuous decline of the one and the corresponding rise of the other, from the earliest period of human progression. It may appear paradoxical to regard the theological philosophy as in a steadily-declining state intellectually, at the very time that it was fulfilling its most exalted political mission; but we shall find satisfactory scientific evidence that Catholicism, its noblest social work, must necessarily be its last effort, on account of the germs of disorganization which must thenceforth grow more and more rapidly. We need here, therefore, only assign the general principle of the inevitable tendency of the human mind towards an exclusive positive philosophy, throughout the whole range of the intellectual system.

ATTEMPTED UNION OF THE TWO PHILOSOPHIES

The general, like the individual human mind, is governed by imagination first, and then, after a sufficient exercise of the faculties at large, more and more by reason. The same grounds on which the process takes place in the individual case determine that of the whole species; and with the more certainty and power on account of the greater complexity and perpetuity of the social organism. Supreme as the theological philosophy once was, it is certain that such a method of philosophizing was resorted to only because no other was possible. Wherever there has been a choice, in regard to any subject whatever, Man has always preferred the study of the laws of phenomena to that of their primary causes, though prior training, which there has been no rational education adapted to counteract, has often occasioned lapse into his old illusions. Theological philosophy has, however, never been absolutely universal. That is, the simplest and commonest facts in all classes of phenomena have always been supposed subject to natural laws, and not the arbitrary will of supernatural agents. (Adam Smith made the remark that there never was, in any age or country, a god of Weight). In more complex cases, if only the relations of phenomena are seen to be invariable, the most superficial observer recognizes the presence of law. Even among moral and social phenomena, where the entrance of positive philosophy has been interdicted, we are all obliged to act daily on the supposition of natural laws, in order to conduct the common affairs of life, for all forecast would be impossible if we supposed every incident to be ascribable to supernatural agency, and no other resource therefore possible than prayer, for influencing the course of human actions. It is even noticeable that the principle of the theological philosophy itself lies in the transference to the phenomena of external nature of the first beginnings of the laws of human action; and thus the germ of the positive philosophy is at least as primitive as that of the theological philosophy itself, though it could not expand till a much later time. This idea is very important to the perfect rationality of our social theory; because, as human life can never present any real creation, but only a gradual evolution, the final spread of the positive spirit would be scientifically incomprehensible, if we could not trace its rudiments from the very beginning. From that scarcely-appreciable presence at the beginning, the rise of the positive spirit has been recognizable, in proportion to the extension and generalization of our observations, and the theological philosophy has been slowly but steadily driven back within the narrowing limits of phenomena whose natural laws were still unknown. Thus was the function of the old philosophy clearly a provisional one – to maintain our mental activity by the only exercise open to it, till the positive philosophy should usher it into the wide field of universal knowledge, made accessible to the whole race. This destination has only recently exhibited itself in an unquestionable way since the disclosure of natural laws in phenomena, so numerous and so various as to suggest the necessary existence of analogous laws in all other departments, however remote their actual discovery may be.

It does not follow, from anything that I have said, that the two philosophies were always visibly opposed to each other. On the contrary, the physical study must have succumbed to the theological spirit if they had seemed at the outset to be incompatible. In fact the study of the laws of phenomena appeared, for a long course of time, to agree very well with the investigation into their causes. It was only when observations became more connected, and disclosed important relations, that the radical opposition of the two doctrines began to be felt. Before the antagonism was avowed, the positive spirit manifested its repugnance to the futile absolute explanations of the theological philosophy; and the theological spirit lavished its disdain on the circumspect march and modest investigations of the new school; while still there was no idea that the study of real laws was irreconcilable with that of essential causes. When natural laws of considerable scope were at length discovered, the incompatibility became clear between the preponderance of imagination and that of reason, between the absolute spirit and the relative; and, above all, between the ancient hypothesis of the sovereign direction of events by any arbitrary will, and the growing certainty that we can foresee and modify them by the rational access of human wisdom. It is only in our own time that the antagonism has been extended to all parts of the intellectual field; and even up to the last moment, the students of special subjects have believed that by confining themselves to the investigation of natural laws, and paying no attention to the nature of beings and mode of production of phenomena, they might find physical researches compatible with the explanations of theology; while theology made its own concessions in the form of a provisional notion of a universal providence, combined with special laws which it had imposed on itself. The conduct of Catholicism, in interdicting the habitual use of miracle and prophecy, which prevailed so largely in ancient times, seems to me to present, in religious affairs, a transient situation analogous to that which is exhibited by what is called the institution of constitutional monarchy in the political world; each being, in its own way, an indisputable symptom of decline. However this may be, the insufficiency of the theological philosophy manifests itself to popular observation in that form of popular evidence which can alone reach the majority of mankind, – in its comparison with its opponent in the application of means. The positive philosophy enables us to foresee and to modify natural events, and thus satisfies, more and more, as it advances, the most urgent intellectual needs of humanity, while the ancient philosophy remains barren; so that its fanciful explanations are more and more neglected, while the new philosophy obtains a perpetually firmer hold on the public reason. Those who have remained faithful in their attachment to the theological philosophy make no practical use of it in their daily life, and ground their predilection for it on its characteristic generality: so that when its antagonist shall have become systemized as fully as it is destined to be, the ancient philosophy will have lost the last attribute which has ever entitled it to social supremacy.

THE METAPHYSICAL PERIOD

We have now only to take a cursory survey of the intermediate state. I have pointed out more than once before, that any intermediate state can be judged of only after a precise analysis of the two extremes. The present case is a remarkable illustration of this necessity; for if it is once admitted that the human mind must set out from the theological state, and arrive certainly at the positive, we may easily understand how it must pass through the metaphysical, which has no other destination than to afford a transition from the one to the other. The bastard and mobile character of the metaphysical philosophy fits it for this office, as it reconciles, for a time, the radical opposition of the other two, adapting itself to the gradual decline of the one, and the preparatory rise of the other, so as to spare our dislike of abrupt change, and to afford us a transition almost imperceptible. The metaphysical philosophy takes possession of the speculative field after the theological has relinquished it, and before the positive is ready for it: so that in each particular case, the dispute about the supremacy of any of the three philosophies is reduced to the mere question of opportuneness, judged by a rational examination of the development of the human mind. The method of modification consists in substituting gradually the entity for a deity when religious conceptions become so generalized as to diminish perpetually the number of supernatural agents, as well as their active intervention, and at length arrive, professedly if not really, at rigorous unity. When supernatural action loses its original speciality, it consigns the immediate direction of the phenomenon to a mysterious entity, at first emanating from itself, but to which daily custom trains the human mind to refer more and more exclusively the production of each event. This strange process has favoured the withdrawal of supernatural causes, and the exclusive consideration of phenomena; that is, the decline of the theological and the rise of the positive spirit. Beyond this, the general character of this philosophy is that of the theological, of which it is only a modification, though the chief. It has an inferior intellectual consistency, and a much less intense social power; so that it is much better adapted for a critical function than for any real organization: and it is those very qualities which disable it for resistance to the growth of the positive spirit. On the one hand the increasing subtlety of metaphysical speculations is for ever reducing their characteristic entities to mere abstract denominations of the corresponding phenomena, so as to render their own impotence ridiculous when they attempt explanations: a thing which would not have been possible, in an equal degree, with purely theological forms. On the other hand, its deficiency of organizing power, in consequence of its radical inconsistency, must prevent its maintaining any such political struggle as theology maintained against the spread of positive social philosophy. However, it obtains a respite by its own equivocal and mobile nature, which enables it to escape from rational discussion even more than the theological philosophy itself, while the positive spirit is as yet too imperfectly generalized to be able to attack the only substantial ground of their common authority, – the universality which they can boast, but which it has not. However this may be, we must admit the aptitude of metaphysics to sustain, provisionally, our speculative activity on all subjects till it can receive more substantial aliment; at the same time carrying us over from the theological *régime* further and further in the direction of the positive. The same aptitude appears in its political action. Without overlooking the serious intellectual and moral dangers which distinguish the metaphysical philosophy, its transitional quality accounts to us for the universal ascendency which it has provisionally obtained among the most advanced societies, which can not but have an instinctive sense of some indispensable office to be fulfilled by such a philosophy in the evolution of humanity. The irresistible necessity of this temporary phase is thus, on all grounds, as unquestionable as it could be prior to the direct analysis to which it will be subjected in the course of our historical review.

COEXISTENCE OF THE THREE PERIODS

During the whole of our survey of the sciences, I have endeavoured to keep in view the great fact that all the three states, theological, metaphysical, and positive, may and do exist at the same time in the same mind in regard to different sciences. I must once more recall this consideration, and insist upon it; because in the forgetfulness of it lies the only real objection that can be brought against the grand law of the three states. It must be steadily kept in view that the same mind may be in the positive state with regard to the most simple and general sciences; in the metaphysical with regard to the more complex and special; and in the theological with regard to social science, which is so complex and special as to have hitherto taken no scientific form at all. Any apparent contradiction must certainly arise, even if it could be shown to exist, from the imperfection of our hierarchical arrangement, and not from the law of evolution itself. This once fully understood, the law itself becomes our guide in further investigation, as every proved theory does, by showing us by anticipation, what phenomena to look for, and how to use those which arise: and it supplies the place of direct exploration, when we have not the means of investigation. We shall find that by this law alone can the history of the human mind be rendered intelligible. Having convinced ourselves of its efficacy in regard to all other sciences, and in interpreting all that has yet come to pass in human history, we must adhere to it steadily, in analysing the present, and in forming such anticipation of the future as sociology, being a real science, enables us to rely upon.

To complete my long and difficult demonstration, I have only now to show that material development, as a whole, must follow a course, not only analogous, but perfectly correspondent with that of intellectual development, which, as we have seen, governs every other.

CORRESPONDING MATERIAL DEVELOPMENT

All political investigation of a rational kind proves the primitive tendency of mankind, in a general way, to a military life; and to its final issue in an industrial life. No enlightened mind disputes the continuous decline of the military spirit, and the gradual ascendency of the industrial. We see now, under various forms, and more and more indisputably, even in the very heart of armies, the repugnance of modern society to a military life. We see that compulsory recruiting becomes more and more necessary, and that there is less voluntary persistence in that mode of life. Notwithstanding the immense exceptional development of military activity which was occasioned by anomalous circumstances at the beginning of the present century, our industrial and pacific instincts have returned to their regular course of expansion, so as to render us secure of the radical tranquillity of the civilized world, though the peace of Europe must often appear to be endangered through the provisional deficiency of any systematic organization of international relations; a cause which, though insufficient to produce war, keeps us in a state of frequent uneasiness. We need not then go over again the proof of the first and last terms of the evolution: which will be abundantly illustrated by the historical analysis that I shall offer. We have only to refer the facts of human experience to the essential laws of human nature, and the necessary conditions of social development: – a scientific procedure which has never yet been attempted.

PRIMITIVE MILITARY LIFE

As long as primitive Man was averse from all regular toil, the military life alone furnished a field for his sustained activity. Apart from cannibalism, it offered the simplest means of subsistence. However deplorable the necessity, its universal prevalence and continuous development, even after subsistence might have been obtained by other means, proves that the military *régime* must have had some indispensable, though provisional office to fulfil in the progression of the race. It was indeed the only one under which human industry could make a beginning; in the same way that the scientific spirit could not have arisen without the protection of the religious. The industrial spirit supposed the existence of a considerable social development, such as could not have taken place till isolated families had been connected by the pursuits of war. The social, and yet more the political properties of military activity are, in their early stages, perfectly clear and decisive, and, in short, fully appropriate to the high civilizing function which they had to fulfil. It was thus that habits of regularity and discipline were instituted, and the families of men were brought into association for warlike expeditions, or for their common defence. The objects of association could not possibly be more obvious or urgent, nor the elementary conditions of concurrence more irresistible. In no other school could a primitive society learn order; as we may see at this day in the case of those types of ancient humanity, – the exceptional individuals who can not now be made amenable to industrial discipline. This ascendency of the military spirit was indispensable, not only to the original consolidation of political society, but yet more to its continuous extension, which could not otherwise have taken place but with excessive slowness; and such extension was, to a certain degree, indispensable to the final development of human industry. Thus, then, we find humanity involved in the same kind of vicious circle with regard to its temporal as we saw it to be with its spiritual progress; and in both cases an issue was afforded by the fortunate expansion of a preliminary tendency.

PRIMITIVE SLAVERY

In fact, the necessary basis of the military *régime* has everywhere been the individual slavery of the producing class, by which warriors were allowed the full and free development of their activity. We shall see hereafter that the great social operation which was to be accomplished, in due time, by the continuous progression of a military system, powerfully instituted and wisely carried out, must have failed in its earliest stages. We shall see how this ancient slavery was the necessary preparation for the final prevalence of the industrial life, by imposing on the majority of the race, irresistibly and exclusively, that toil to which Man is constitutionally averse, though an ultimate condition of laborious perseverance was in store for all. To view the case without prejudice, we must transport ourselves to those primitive times, and not regard the slavery of that age with the just horror with which we view that of modern times, – the colonial slavery of our day which is truly a social monstrosity, existing as it does in the heart of an industrial period, subjecting the labourer to the capitalist in a manner equally degrading to both. The ancient slavery was of the producer to the warrior; and it tended to develop their respective energies, so as to occasion their final concurrence in the same social progression.

THE MILITARY RÉGIME PROVISIONAL

Necessary as this military *régime* was, it was not the less merely provisional. While industrial activity has the fine quality of bearing the most energetic extension among all individuals and nations without making the rise of the one irreconcilable with that of the other, it is evident that the exaltation of the military life among any considerable portion of the race must occasion the restriction of all the rest; this being, in fact, the proper function of the *régime* in regard to the whole field of civilization. Thus, while the industrial period comprehends the whole term of human progress under natural laws – that is, the whole future that we can conceive of – the military period could last no longer than the formation of those preparatory conditions which it was its function to create. This end was attained when the chief part of the civilized world was at length united under the same rule; that is, in regard to Europe, when Rome had completed its conquests. From that time forward, military activity had neither object nor aliment; and from that time forward, therefore, it declined, so as no longer to disguise that gradual rise of the industrial spirit, which had been preparing during the interval. But, notwithstanding this connection, the industrial state was so radically different from the military as to require an intermediate term: and in the same way that, in the spiritual evolution, an intermediate term was required between the theological and the positive spirit. In both cases, the middle phase was fluctuating and equivocal. We shall see hereafter that, in the temporal case, it consisted first, in a substitution of a defensive for an offensive military organization, and afterwards in an involuntary general subordination, more and more marked, of the military spirit to the instinct of production. This transitory phase being the one in which we live, its proper nature, vague as it is, can be estimated by direct intuition.

Such is the temporal evolution, briefly surveyed in its three periods. No philosophical mind can help being struck by the analogy between this indisputable progression and our primary law of successsion of the three states of the human mind. But our sociological demonstration requires that we should establish the connection between them by exhibiting the natural affinity which has always existed, first between the theological and the military spirit, and afterwards between the scientific and the industrial; and, consequently, between the two transient functions of the metaphysicians and the legists. This elucidation will impart the last degree of precision and consistency to my demonstration and will thus establish it as the rational basis of the entire historical analysis which will follow.

Auguste Comte

AFFINITY BETWEEN THE THEOLOGICAL AND MILITARY RÉGIME

The occasional rivalry between the theological power and the military, which history presents, has sometimes disguised their radical affinity, even in the eyes of philosophers. But, if we consider, there can be no real rivalry but among the different elements of the same political system, in consequence of that spontaneous emulation which, in all cases of human concurrence, must become more earnest and extensive as the end is more important and indirect, and therefore the means more distinct and independent, without the participation, voluntary or instinctive, being thereby prevented. When two powers, equally energetic, rise, increase, and decline together, notwithstanding the difference of their natures, we may be assured that they belong to the same *régime*, whatever may be their habitual conflicts. Conflict indicates radical incompatibility only when it takes place between two elements employed in analogous functions, and when the gradual growth of the one coincides with the continuous decline of the other. As to the present case, it is evident that, in any political system, there must be an incessant rivalry between the speculative and the active powers, which, through the imperfection of our nature, must often be inclined to ignore their necessary co-ordination and to disdain the general limits of their reciprocal attributes. Notwithstanding the social affinity between science and industry, we must look for similar conflict between them hereafter, in proportion to the political ascendency which they will obtain together. We see signs of it already in the intellectual and moral antipathy of Science to the natural inferiority of these labours of Industry which yet are the means of wealth and in the instinctive repugnance of Industry to the abstraction which characterizes Science, and to the just pride by which it is animated.

Having despatched these objections, we may now contemplate the strong bond which united the theological and military powers, and which has in all ages been felt and honoured by all enlightened men who have borne a part in either, notwithstanding the passions of political rivalry. It is plain that no military system could arise and endure without the countenance of the theological spirit, which must secure for it the complete and permanent subordination essential to its existence. Each period imposes equal exigencies of this sort in its special manner. At the outset, when the narrowness and nearness of the aim required a less absolute submission of mind, social ties were so weak that nothing could have been done but for the religious authority with which military chiefs were naturally invested. In more advanced times the end became so vast and remote, and the participation so indirect that even long habits of discipline would not have secured the necessary co-operation without the aid of the theological convictions occasioning blind and involuntary confidence in military superiors. It was in very ancient times that the military spirit had its great social function to fulfil; and it was in those ancient times that the two powers were usually found concentrated in the same chiefs. We must observe also that it was not every spiritual authority whatever that would have sufficiently suited the foundation and consolidation of military government, which, from its nature, required the concurrence of the theological philosophy and no other: for instance, though natural philosophy has rendered eminent service in modern times to the art of war, the scientific spirit, which encourages habits of rational discussion, is radically incompatible with the military spirit; and we know that the subjection of their art to the principles of science has always been bitterly deplored by the most distinguished soldiers, on the introduction of every change, as a token of the decline of the military system. On this ground, then, the affinity of temporal military powers for spiritual theological powers is sufficiently accounted for. At the first glance we might suppose the converse relation to be less indispensable, since purely theocratic societies have existed, while an exclusively military one has never been known. But a closer examination will always show the necessity of the military system to consolidate, and yet more to extend, the theological authority, developed in this way by a continual political application, as the sacerdotal instinct has always been well aware. We shall see again that the theological spirit is as hostile to the expansion of industry as the military. Thus the two elements of the primitive political system have not only a radical affinity, but common antipathies and sympathies, as well as general interests; and it must be needless to enlarge further in this place on the sociological principle of the concurrence of these powers, which my historical analysis will present as constantly engaged in consolidating and correcting each other.

AFFINITY BETWEEN THE POSITIVE AND THE INDUSTRIAL SPIRIT

The latest case of political dualism is even more unquestionable than the earliest, and we are favourably circumstanced for observing it – the two elements not having yet attained their definite ascendency, though their social development is sufficiently marked. When the time arrives for their political rivalry, it may be more difficult than now to exhibit that resemblance in origin and destination, and that conformity of principles and interests, which could not be seriously disputed as long as their common struggle against the old political system acts as a restraint upon their divergencies. The most remarkable feature that we have to contemplate in their case is the aid which each renders to the political triumph of the other, by seconding its own efforts against its chief antagonist. I have already noticed, in another connection, the secret incompatibility between the scientific spirit and the military. There is the same hostility between the industrial spirit, when sufficiently developed, and the theological. The most zealous advocates of the old *régime* are very far removed from the old religious point of view; but we can transport ourselves to it for a moment, and see how the voluntary modification of phenomena by the rules of human wisdom must thence appear as impious as the rational prevision of them, as both suppose invariable laws, finally irreconcilable with all arbitrary will. According to the rigorous though barbarous logic of the least-civilized nations, all human intervention to improve the economy of nature is an injurious attack upon providential government. There is no doubt, in fact, that a strong preponderance of the religious spirit benumbs the industrial, by the exaggerated feelings of a stupid optimism, as has been abundantly clear on many decisive occasions. That this disastrous effect has not been more fatal is owing to priestly sagacity, which has so managed this dangerous power as to educe its civilizing influence, while neutralizing its injurious action by constant and vigilant effort, in a way which I shall presently exhibit. We can not, then, overlook the political influence by which the gradual expansion of human industry must aid the pro-gressive ascendency of the scientific spirit, in its antagonism to the religious; to say nothing of the daily stimulus which industry and science impart to each other, when once strong enough for mutual action. Thus far their office has chiefly been to substitute themselves for the ancient political powers which are yielding up their social influence; and our attention is necessarily drawn chiefly to the aid they have afforded to each other in this operation. But it is easy to perceive what force and what efficacy must reside in their connection, when it shall have assumed the organic character, in which it is at present deficient, and shall proceed to the final reorganization of modern society.

INTERMEDIATE RÉGIME

Now that we have examined the two extreme states, the intermediate dualism requires little notice. The interconnection of the convergent powers, spiritual and temporal, which constitutes the transitory *régime* is a necessary consequence of all that we have been observing. Indeed, we need but look at the labours of metaphysicians and legists to see what

143

their affinity is, amidst their rivalries; an affinity which stakes the philosophical ascendency of the one class on the political preponderance of the other. We may, then, regard as now complete the necessary explanation required by our fundamental law of human evolution, in order to its direct application to the study of this great phenomenon. That study will be guided by the consideration of the three dualisms which I have established as the only basis of sound historical philosophy. It is worth noticing the conformity of this law of succession, at once intellectual and material, social and political, with the historical order which popular reason has instinctively established by distinguishing the ancient and the modern world, separated and reunited by the Middle Ages. The sociological law which I have propounded may be found to have for its destination to take up a vague empirical notion, hitherto barren, and render it rational and prolific. I hail this spontaneous coincidence, as giving a sanction to my speculative labours; and I claim this confirmation, in virtue of that great aphorism of positive philosophy which I have quoted so often, which enjoins upon all sound scientific theories to start from a point sufficiently accordant with the spontaneous indications of popular reason, of which true science is simply a special prolongation.

The series of views of social dynamics sketched out in this chapter has established the fundamental law of human development, and therefore the bases of historical philosophy. We had before ascertained the spirit and method of that philosophy; and we may now therefore proceed to apply this great sociological conception to the analysis of the history of mankind.

(Volume II, Book VI, Chapter vi, pp. 522–40)

Alexis de Tocqueville 1805–59

Major works

Democracy in America (*La Démocratie en Amérique*; 2 volumes, 1835, 1840)

The Old Régime and the French Revolution (*L'Ancien Régime et la révolution*; 1856)

The following extracts are reprinted from Alexis de Tocqueville, *Democracy in America*, translated by George Lawrence, edited by G. P. Mayer and Max Lerner (2 volumes, New York: Harper & Row, 1966), with the permission of Harper & Row, Publishers,

Respect for Law in the United States

It is not always feasible to call on the whole people, either directly or indirectly, to take its part in lawmaking, but no one can deny that when that can be done the law derives great authority therefrom. This popular origin, though often damaging to the wisdom and quality of legislation, gives it peculiar strength.

There is prodigious force in the expression of the wills of a whole people. When it stands out in broad daylight, even the imagination of those who would like to contest it is somehow smothered.

Parties are well aware of this truth.

For that reason, whenever possible they cast doubts on the majority's validity. Having failed to gain a majority from those who voted, they claim it among those who abstained from voting, and if that fails them, they claim a majority among those who have no right to vote.

In the United States, except for slaves, servants, and paupers fed by the township, no one is without a vote and, hence, an indirect share in lawmaking. Therefore those who would like to attack the laws are forced to adopt ostensibly one of two courses: they must either change the nation's opinion or trample its wishes under foot.

There is a second reason, too, more direct and powerful in its effect, namely, that every American feels a sort of personal interest in obeying the laws, for a man who is not today one of the majority party may be so tomorrow, and so he may soon be demanding for laws of his choosing that respect which he now professes for the lawgiver's will. Therefore, however annoying a law may be, the American will submit to it, not only as the work of the majority but also as his own doing; he regards it as a contract to which he is one of the parties.

So in the United States there is no numerous and perpetually turbulent crowd regarding the law as a natural enemy to fear and to suspect. On the contrary, one is bound to notice that all classes show great confidence in their country's legislation, feeling a sort of paternal love for it.

I am wrong in saying all classes. As in America, the European ladder of power has been turned upside down; the wealthy find themselves in a position analogous to that of the poor in Europe: it is they who often mistrust the law. As I have said elsewhere, the real advantage of democratic government is not that it guarantees the interests of all, as is sometimes claimed, but just that it does protect those of the greatest number. In the United States, where the poor man rules, the rich have always some fear that he may abuse his power against them.

This state of mind among the wealthy may produce a silent discontent, but it creates no violent trouble for society, for the same reason which prevents the rich men from trusting the lawgiver also prevents him from defying his commands. Because he is rich he does not make the law, and because of his wealth he does not dare break it. Among civilized nations it is generally only those with nothing to lose who revolt. Hence, though democratic laws may not always deserve respect, they are almost always respected, for those who usually break the laws cannot fail to obey those they have made and from which they profit, and those citizens who might have an interest in infringing them are impelled both by character and by circumstance to submit to the lawgiver's will, whatever it may be. Moreover, in America the people obey the law not only because it is their work but also because they can change it if by any change it does injure them; they submit to it primarily as a self-imposed evil, and secondly as a passing one.

(Volume I, pp. 296–8)

Tyranny of the Majority

I regard it as an impious and detestable maxim that in matters of government the majority of a people has the right to do everything, and nevertheless I place the origin of all powers in the will of the majority. Am I in contradiction with myself?

There is one law which has been made, or at least adopted, not by the majority of this or that people, but by the majority of all men. That law is justice.

Justice therefore forms the boundary to each people's right.

A nation is like a jury entrusted to represent universal society and to apply the justice which is its law. Should the jury representing society have greater power than that very society whose laws it applies?

Consequently, when I refuse to obey an unjust law, I by no means deny the majority's right to give orders; I only appeal from the sovereignty of the people to the sovereignty of the human race.

There are those not afraid to say that in matters which only concern itself a nation cannot go completely beyond the bounds of justice and reason and that there is therefore no need to fear giving total power to the majority representing it. But that is the language of a slave.

What is a majority, in its collective capacity, if not an individual with opinions, and usually with interests, contrary to those of another individual, called the minority? Now, if you admit that a man vested with omnipotence can abuse it against his adversaries, why not admit the same concerning a majority? Have men, by joining together, changed their character? By becoming stronger, have they become more patient of obstacles? For my part, I cannot believe that, and I will never grant to several that power to do everything which I refuse to a single man.

It is not that I think that in order to preserve liberty one can mix several principles within the same government in such a way that they will be really opposed to one another.

I have always considered what is called a mixed government to be a chimera. There is in truth no such thing as a mixed government (in the sense usually given to the words), since in any society one finds in the end some principle of action that dominates all the others.

Eighteenth-century England, which has been especially cited as an example of this type of government, was an essentially aristocratic state, although it contained within itself great elements of democracy, for laws and mores were so designed that the aristocracy could always prevail in the long run and manage public affairs as it wished.

The mistake is due to those who, constantly seeing the interest of the great in conflict with those of the people, have thought only about the struggle and have not paid attention to the result thereof, which was more important. When a society really does have a mixed government, that is to say, one equally shared between contrary principles, either a revolution breaks out or that society breaks up.

I therefore think it always necessary to place somewhere one social power superior to all others, but I believe that freedom is in danger when that power finds no obstacle that can restrain its course and give it time to moderate itself.

Omnipotence in itself seems a bad and dangerous thing. I think that its exercise is beyond man's strength, whoever he be, and that only God can be omnipotent without danger because His wisdom and justice are always equal to His power. So there is no power on earth in itself so worthy of respect or vested with such a sacred right that I would wish to let it act without control and dominate without obstacles. So when I see the right and capacity to do all given to any authority whatsoever, whether it be called people or king, democracy or aristocracy, and whether the scene of actions is a monarchy or a republic, I say: the germ of tyranny is there, and I will go look for other laws under which to live.

My greatest complaint against democratic government as organized in the United States is not, as many Europeans make out, its weakness, but rather its irresistible strength. What I find most repulsive in America is not the extreme freedom reigning there but the shortage of guarantees against tyranny.

When a man or a party suffers an injustice in the United States, to whom can he turn? To public opinion? That is what forms the majority. To the legislative body? It represents the majority and obeys it blindly. To the executive power? It is appointed by the majority and serves as its passive instrument. To the police? They are nothing but the majority under arms. A jury? The jury is the majority vested with the right to pronounce judgment; even the judges in certain states are elected by the majority. So, however iniquitous or unreasonable the measure which hurts you, you must submit.

But suppose you were to have a legislative body so composed that it represented the majority without being necessarily the slave of its passions, an executive power having a strength of its own, and a judicial power independent of the other two authorities; then you would still have a democratic government, but there would be hardly any remaining risk of tyranny.

I am not asserting that at the present time in America there are frequent acts of tyranny. I do say that one can find no guarantee against it there and that the reasons for the government's gentleness must be sought in circumstances and in mores rather than in the laws.

(Volume I, pp. 309–13)

The Future

It must not be thought possible to halt the impetus of the English race in the New World. The dismemberment of the Union, bringing war into the continent, or the abolition of the republic, bringing tyranny, might slow expansion down, but cannot prevent the people ultimately fulfilling their inevitable destiny. No power on earth can shut out the immigrants from that fertile wilderness which on every side offers rewards to industry and a refuge from every affliction. Whatever the future may hold in store, it cannot deprive the Americans of their climate, their inland seas, their great rivers, or the fertility of their soil. Bad laws, revolutions, and anarchy cannot destroy their taste for well-being or that spirit of enterprise which seems the characteristic feature of their race; nor could such things utterly extinguish the lights of knowledge guiding them.

Thus, in all the uncertainty of the future, one event at least is sure. At a period which we may call near, for we are speaking of the life of nations, the Anglo-Americans alone will cover the whole of the immense areas between the polar ice and the tropics, extending from the Atlantic to the Pacific coast.

I think the land over which the Anglo-American race will spread will be three quarters of the size of Europe. The Union's climate is, on balance, better than that of Europe; its natural advantages are as great; it is clear that its population will one day be proportionate to our own.

Europe, divided into different nations, torn by constant renewal of warfare and held back by the barbarism of the Middle Ages, has come to have 410 inhabitants to the square league. What cause is powerful enough to prevent the United States one day having as many?

Many centuries will pass by before the various offshoots of the English race in America cease to present a common physiognomy. One cannot foresee a time when permanent inequality of conditions could be established in the New World.

Whatever differences – peace or war, freedom or tyranny, prosperity or affliction – may one day arise between the various branches of the great Anglo-American family, at least they will all preserve a similar social state and will share the usage and ideas which derive therefrom.

In the Middle Ages the link of religion alone was enough to unite all the various races of Europe in one civilization. The English of the New World have a thousand other links between them, and they live at a time when there is a general tendency toward equality in human affairs.

The Middle Ages were a time of divisions. Each people, each province, each city, and each family had a strong urge to assert its individuality. In our day an opposite tendency is noticeable, and nations seem to steer toward unity. There are intellectual links between the most distant parts of the earth, and men cannot remain strangers to each other for a single day or fail to know what happens in any corner of the world. That is why one now notices less difference between contemporary Europeans and their descendants in the New World, in spite of the ocean that divides them, than there was in the thirteenth century between towns separated only by a river.

If this tendency toward assimilation brings foreign nations closer to each other, it must *a fortiori* prevent branches of the same people becoming strangers to one another.

Therefore, the time must come when there will be in North America one hundred and fifty million people all equal one to the other, belonging to the same family, having the same point of departure, the same civilization, language, religion, habits, and mores, and among whom thought will circulate in similar forms and with like nuances. All else is doubtful, but that is sure. And this is something entirely new in the world, something, moreover, the significance of which the imagination cannot grasp.

There are now two great nations in the world which, starting from different points, seem to be advancing toward the same goal: the Russians and the Anglo-Americans.

Both have grown in obscurity and while the world's attention was occupied elsewhere, they have suddenly taken their place among the leading nations, making the world take note of their birth and of their greatness almost at the same instant.

All other peoples seem to have nearly reached their natural limits and to need nothing but to preserve them; but these two are growing. All the others have halted or advanced only through great exertions; they alone march easily and quickly forward along a path whose end no eye can yet see.

The American fights against natural obstacles; the Russian is at grips with men. The former combats the wilderness and barbarism; the latter civilization with all its arms. America's conquests are made with the ploughshare, Russia's with the sword.

To attain their aims, the former relies on personal interest and gives free scope to the unguided strength and common sense of individuals.

The latter in a sense concentrates the whole power of society in one man.

One has freedom as the principal means of action; the other has servitude.

Their point of departure is different and their paths diverse; nevertheless, each seems called by some secret design of Providence one day to hold in its hands the destinies of half the world.

(Volume I, pp. 509–12)

Why Democratic Nations Show a More Ardent and Enduring Love for Equality Than for Liberty

The first and liveliest of the passions inspired by equality is, I need not say, love of that equality itself. My readers will therefore not be surprised if I speak of that before all the others.

Everybody has noticed that in our age, and especially in France, this passion for equality is daily acquiring a greater hold over the human heart. It has been said a hundred times that our contemporaries love equality much more ardently and tenaciously than liberty. But I do not think that anyone has yet adequately explained the reason for this fact. I will try to do so.

It is possible to imagine an extreme point at which freedom and equality would meet and blend.

Let us suppose that all the citizens take a part in the government and that each of them has an equal right to do so.

Then, no man is different from his fellows, and nobody can wield tyrannical power; men will be perfectly free becuase they are entirely equal, and they will be perfectly equal because they are entirely free. Democratic peoples are tending toward that ideal.

That is the completest possible form for equality on this earth. But there are a thousand other forms which, though less perfect, are no less cherished by those nations.

There can be established equality in civil society, though there is none in the world of politics. One can have the right to enjoy the same pleasures, to engage in the same professions, and to meet in the same places – in a word, to live in the same manner and seek wealth by the same means – without all taking the same part in the government.

There can even be a sort of equality in the world of politics without any political freedom. A man may be the equal of all his fellows save one, who is the master of all without distinction and chooses the agents of his power equally from among all.

One can easily invent several other hypotheses in which a great deal of equality is easily combined with institutions more or less free, or even not free at all.

Although men cannot be absolutely equal without being entirely free, and consequently equality, in its more extreme forms, must merge with freedom, there is good reason to distinguish one from the other.

So men's taste for freedom and their taste for equality are in fact distinct, and, I have no hesitation in adding, among democracies they are two unequal elements.

On close inspection one finds in every age some peculiar and predominating element which controls all the rest. This element almost always engenders some seminal thought or ruling passion which in the end drags all other feelings and ideas along in its course. It is like a great river which seems to make all surrounding rivulets flow toward it.

Freedom is found in different times and in different forms; it is not exclusively dependent on one social state, and one finds it elsewhere than in democracies. It cannot therefore be taken as the distinctive characteristic of democratic ages.

The particular and predominating fact peculiar to those ages is equality of conditions, and the chief passion which stirs men at such times is the love of this same equality.

Do not ask what singular charm the men of democratic ages find in living as equals or what special reason they may have for clinging so tenaciously to equality rather than the other advantages society offers. Equality forms the distinctive characterstic of the age in which they live. That is enough to explain why they prefer it to all the rest.

But apart from that reason there are several others which at all times lead men to prefer equality to liberty.

If a people could ever succeed in destroying or even diminishing the equality prevailing in its body social, it could only do so by long and laborious efforts. They would have to modify their social condition, repeal their laws, supersede their opinions, change their habits, and alter their mores. But political liberty is easily lost; neglect to hold it fast, and it is gone.

Men therefore hold on to equality not only because it is precious to them; they are also attached to it because they think it will last for ever.

Nobody is so limited and superficial as not to realize that political liberty can, if carried to excess, endanger the peace, property and lives of individuals. But only perceptive and clearsighted men see the dangers with which equality threatens us, and they generally avoid pointing them out. They see that the troubles they fear are distant and console themselves that they will only fall on future generations, for which the present generation hardly cares. The ills which liberty brings may be immediate; all can see them and all, more or less, feel them. The ills produced by extreme equality only become apparent little by little; they gradually insinuate themselves into the body social; they are only occasionally noticed, and when they do become most excessive, habit has already made them pass unfelt.

The good things that freedom brings are seen only as time passes, and it is always easy to mistake the cause that brought them about.

The advantages of equality are felt immediately, and it is daily apparent where they come from.

Political liberty occasionally gives sublime pleasure to a few.

Equality daily gives each man in the crowd a host of small enjoyments. The charms of equality are felt the whole time and are within the reach of all; the noblest spirits appreciate them, and the commonest minds exult in them. The passion engendered by equality is therefore both strong and general.

Men cannot enjoy political liberty without some sacrifice, and they have never won it without great effort. But equality offers its pleasures free; each little incident in life occasions them, and to taste them one needs but to live.

Democratic peoples always like equality, but there are times when their passion for it turns to delirium. This happens when the old social hierarchy, long menaced, finally collapses after a severe internal struggle and the barriers of rank are at length thrown down. At such times men pounce on equality as their booty and cling to it as a precious treasure they fear to have snatched away. The passion for equality seeps into every corner of the human heart, expands, and fills the whole. It is no use telling them that by this blind surrender to an exclusive passion they are compromising their dearest interests; they are deaf. It is no use pointing out that freedom is slipping from their grasp while they look the other way; they are blind, or rather they can see but one thing to covet in the whole world.

The foregoing applies to all democratic nations, what follows only to the French.

Among most modern nations, especially those of Europe, the taste for freedom and the conception of it only began to take shape and grow at the time when social conditions were tending toward equality, and it was a consequence of that very equality. It was the absolute monarchs who worked hardest to level down ranks among their subjects. For the peoples equality had come before liberty, so equality was an established fact when freedom was still a novelty; the one had already shaped customs, opinions, and laws to its use when the other was first stepping lonely forward into broad daylight. Thus the latter was still only a matter of opinion and preference, whereas the former had already insinuated itself into popular habits, shaped mores, and given a particular twist to the slightest actions of life. Why, then, should we be surprised that our contemporaries prefer the one to the other?

I think democratic peoples have a natural taste for liberty; left to themselves, they will seek it, cherish it, and be sad if it is taken from them. But their passion for equality is ardent, insatiable, eternal, and invincible. They want equality in freedom, and if they cannot have that, they still want equality in slavery. They will put up with poverty, servitude, and barbarism, but they will not endure aristocracy.

This is true at all times, but especially in our own. All men and all powers who try to stand up against this irresistible passion will be overthrown and destroyed by it. In our day freedom cannot be established without it, and despotism itself cannot reign without its support.

(Volume II, pp. 647–51)

Émile Durkheim 1858–1917

Major works

The Division of Labour in Society (1893)
The Rules of Sociological Method (1895)
Suicide (1897)
The Elementary Forms of Religious Life (1912)
Sociology and Philosophy (1924)

The following extracts are reprinted from Émile Durkheim, *The Division of Labor in Society*, translated by George Simpson (New York: Macmillan, 1933), Preface, pp. 37–8; Book I, Chapter i, pp. 61–2, 64–5, 68–9; Chapter ii, pp. 109–10; Chapter iii, pp. 111–15, 127–31, with the permission of The Macmillan Company. Copyright © The Free Press, 1947.

This work had its origins in the question of the relations of the individual to social solidarity. Why does the individual, while becoming more autonomous, depend more upon society? How can he be at once more individual and more solidary? Certainly, these two movements, contradictory as they appear, develop in parallel fashion. This is the problem we are raising. It appeared to us that what resolves this apparent antimony is a transformation of social solidarity due to the steadily growing development of the division of labor. That is how we have been led to make this the object of our study . . .

The social relations to which the division of labor gives birth have often been considered only in terms of exchange, but this misinterprets what such exchange implies and what results from it. It suggests two beings mutually dependent because they are each incomplete, and translates this mutual dependence outwardly. It is, then, only the superficial expression of an internal and very deep state. Precisely because this state is constant, it calls up a whole mechanism of images which function with a continuity that exchange does not possess. The image of the one who completes us becomes inseparable from ours, not only because it is frequently associated with ours, but particularly because it is the natural complement of it. It thus becomes an integral and permanent part of our conscience, to such a point that we can no longer separate ourselves from it and seek to increase its force. That is why we enjoy the society of the one it represents, since the presence of the object that it expresses, by making us actually perceive it, sets it off more. On the other hand, we will suffer from all circumstances which, like absence or death, may have as effect the barring of its return or the diminishing of its vivacity.

As short as this analysis is, it suffices to show that this mechanism is not identical with that which serves as a basis for sentiments of sympathy whose source is resemblance. Surely there can be no solidarity between others and us unless the image of others unites itself with ours. But when the union results from the resemblance of two images, it consists in an agglutination. The two representations become solidary because, being indistinct, totally or in part, they confound each other, and become no more than one, and they are solidary only in the measure which they confound themselves. On the contrary, in the case of the division of labor, they are outside each other and are linked only because they are distinct. Neither the sentiments nor the social relations which derive from these sentiments are the same in the two cases.

We are thus led to ask if the division of labor would not play the same role in more extensive groups, if, in contemporary societies where it has developed as we know, it would not have as its function the integration of the social body to assure unity. It is quite legitimate to suppose that the facts which we have just observed reproduce themselves here, but with greater amplitude, that great political societies can maintain themselves in equilibrium only thanks to the specialization of tasks, that the division of labor is the source, if not unique, at least principal, of social solidarity . . .

But social solidarity is a completely moral phenomenon which, taken by itself, does not lend itself to exact observation nor indeed to measurement. To proceed to this classification and this comparison, we must substitute for this internal fact which escapes us an external index which symbolizes it and study the former in the light of the latter.

This visible symbol is law. In effect, despite its immaterial character, wherever social solidarity exists, it resides not in a state of pure potentiality, but manifests its presence by sensible indices. Where it is strong, it leads men strongly to one another, frequently puts them in contact, multiplies the occasions when they find themselves related. To speak correctly, considering the point our investigation has reached, it is not easy to say whether social solidarity produces these phenomena, or whether it is a result of them, whether men relate themselves because it is a driving force, or whether it is a driving force because they relate themselves. However, it is not, at the moment, necessary to decide this question; it suffices to state that the two orders of fact are linked and vary at the same time and in the same sense. The more solidary the members of a society are, the more they sustain diverse relations, one with another, or with the group taken collectively, for if their meetings were rare, they would depend upon one another only at rare intervals, and then tenuously. Moreover, the number of these relations is necessarily proportional to that of the juridical rules which determine them. Indeed, social life, especially where it exists durably, tends inevitably to assume a definite form and to organize itself, and law is nothing else than this very organization in so far as it has greater stability and precision. The general life of society cannot extend its sway without juridical life extending its sway at the same time and in direct relation. We can thus be certain of finding reflected in law all the essential varieties of social solidarity ...

To proceed scientifically, we must find some characteristic which, while being essential to juridical phenomena, varies as they vary. Every precept of law can be defined as a rule of sanctioned conduct. Moreover, it is evident that sanctions change with the gravity attributed to precepts, the place they hold in the public conscience, the role they play in society. It is right, then, to classify juridical rules according to the different sanctions which are attached to them.

They are of two kinds. Some consist essentially in suffering, or at least a loss, inflicted on the agent. They make demands on his fortune, or on his honor, or on his life, or on his liberty, and deprive him of something he enjoys. We call them repressive. They constitute penal law. It is true that those which are attached to rules which are purely moral have the same character, only they are distributed in a diffuse manner, by everybody indiscriminately, whereas those in penal law are applied through the intermediary of a definite organ; they are organized. As for the other type, it does not necessarily imply suffering for the agent, but consists only of *the return of things as they were*, in the reestablishment of troubled relations to their normal state, whether the incriminated act is restored by force to the type whence it deviated, or is annulled, that is, deprived of all social value. We must then separate juridical rules into two great classes, accordingly as they have organized repressive sanctions or only restitutive sanctions. The first comprise all penal law; the second, civil law, commercial law, procedural law, administrative and constitutional law, after abstraction of the penal rules which may be found there ...

There exists a social solidarity which comes from a certain number of states of conscience which are common to all the members of the same society. This is what repressive law materially represents, at least in so far as it is essential. The part that it plays in the general integration of society evidently depends upon the greater or lesser extent of the social life which the common conscience embraces and regulates. The greater the diversity of relations wherein the latter makes its action felt, the more also it creates links which attach the individual to the group; the more, consequently, social cohesion derives completely from this source and bears its mark. But the number of these relations is itself proportional to that of the repressive rules. In determining what fraction of the juridical system penal law represents, we, at the same time, measure the relative importance of this solidarity. It is true that in such a procedure we do not take into account certain elements of the collective conscience which, because of their smaller power or their indeterminateness, remain foreign to repressive law while contributing to the assurance of social harmony. These are the ones protected by punishments which are merely diffuse. But the same is the case with other parts of law. There is not one of them which is not complemented by custom, and as there is no reason for supposing that the relation of law and custom is not the same in these different spheres, this elimination is not made at the risk of having to alter the results of our comparison.

Organic Solidarity Due to the Division of Labor

The very nature of the restitutive sanction suffices to show that the social solidarity to which this type of law corresponds is of a totally different kind.

What distinguishes this sanction is that it is not expiatory, but consists of a simple *return in state*. Sufferance proportionate to the misdeed is not inflicted on the one who has violated the law or who disregards it; he is simply sentenced to comply with it. If certain things were done, the judge reinstates them as they would have been. He speaks of law; he says nothing of punishment. Damage-interests have no penal character; they are only a means of reviewing the past in order to reinstate it, as far as possible, to its normal form. Tarde, it is true, has tried to find a sort of civil penality in the payment of costs by the defeated party. But, taken in this sense, the word has only a metaphorical value. For punishment to obtain, there would at least have to be some relation between the punishment and the misdeed, and for that it would be necessary for the degree of gravity of the misdeed to be firmly established. In fact, however, he who loses the litigation pays the damages even when his intentions were pure, even when his ignorance alone was his culpability. The reasons for this rule are different from those offered by

Tarde: given the fact that justice is not rendered gratuitously, it appears equitable for the damages to be paid by the one who brought them into being. Moreover, it is possible that the prospect of such costs may stop the rash pleader, but that is not sufficient to constitute punishment. The fear of ruin which ordinarily follows indolence or negligence may keep the negotiant active and awake, though ruin is not, in the proper sense of the word, the penal sanction for his misdeeds.

Neglect of these rules is not even published diffusely. The pleader who has lost in litigation is not disgraced, his honor is not put in question. We can even imagine these rules being other than they are without feeling any repugnance. The idea of tolerating murder arouses us, but we quite easily accept modification of the right of succession, and can even conceive of its possible abolition. It is at least a question which we do not refuse to discuss. Indeed, we admit with impunity that the law of servitudes or that of usufructs may be otherwise organized, that the obligations of vendor and purchaser may be determined in some other manner, that administrative functions may be distributed according to different principles. As these prescriptions do not correspond to any sentiment in us, and as we generally do not scientifically know the reasons for their existence, since this science is not definite, they have no roots in the majority of us. Of course, there are exceptions. We do not tolerate the idea that an engagement contrary to custom or obtained either through violence or fraud can bind the contracting parties. Thus, when public opinion finds itself in the presence of such a case, it shows itself less indifferent than we have just now said, and it increases the legal sanction by its censure. The different domains of the moral life are not radically separated one from another, they are, rather, continuous, and, accordingly, there are among them marginal regions where different characters are found at the same time. However, the preceding proposition remains true in the great majority of cases. It is proof that the rules which a restitutive sanction either do not totally derive from the collective conscience, or are only feeble states of it. Repressive law corresponds to the heart, the centre of the common conscience; laws purely moral are a part less central; finally, restitutive law is born in very ex-centric regions whence it spreads further. The more it becomes truly itself, the more removed it is.

This characteristic is, indeed, made manifest by the manner of its functioning. While repressive law tends to remain diffuse within society, restitutive law creates organs which are more and more specialized: consular tribunals, councils of arbitration, administrative tribunals of every sort. Even in its most general part, that which pertains to civil law, it is exercised only through particular functionaries: magistrates, lawyers, etc., who have become apt in this role because of very special training.

But, although these rules are more or less outside the collective conscience, they are not interested solely in individuals. If this were so, restitutive law would have nothing in common with social solidarity, for the relations that it regulates would bind individuals to one another without binding them to society. They would simply be happenings in private life, as friendly relations are. But society is far from having no hand in this sphere of juridical life. It is true that, generally, it does not intervene of itself and through its own movements; it must be solicited by the interested parties. But, in being called forth, its intervention is none the less the essential cog in the machine, since it alone makes it function. It propounds the law through the organ of its representatives.

It has been contended, however, that this role has nothing properly social about it, but reduces itself to that of a conciliator of private interests; that, consequently, any individual can fill it, and that, if society is in charge of it, it is only for commodious reasons. But nothing is more incorrect than considering society as a sort of third-party arbitrator. When it is led to intervene, it is not to put to rights some individual interests. It does not seek to discover what may be the most advantageous solution for the adversaries and does not propose a compromise for them. Rather, it applies to the particular case which is submitted to it general and traditional rules of law. But law is, above all, a social thing and has a totally different object than the interest of the pleaders. The judge who examines a request for divorce is not concerned with knowing whether this separation is truly desirable for the married parties, but rather whether the causes which are adduced come under one of the categories foreseen by the law.

But better to appreciate the importance of social action, we must observe it, not only at the moment when the sanction is applied, when the troubled relation is adjudicated, but also when it is instituted.

It is, in effect, necessary either to establish or to modify a number of juridical relations which this law takes care of and which the consent of the interested parties suffices neither to create nor to change. Such are those, notably, which concern the state of the persons. Although marriage is a contract, the married persons can neither form it nor break it at their pleasure. It is the same with all the other domestic relations and, with stronger reason, with all those which administrative law regulates. It is true that obligations properly contractual can be entered into and abrogated solely through the efforts of those desiring them. But it must not be forgotten that, if the contract has the power to bind, it is society which gives this power to it. Suppose that society did not sanction the obligations contracted for. They become simply promises which have no more than moral authority.[1] Every contract thus supposes that behind the parties implicated in it there is society very ready to intervene in order to gain respect for the engagements which have been made. Moreover, it lends this obligatory force only to contracts which have in themselves a social value, which is to say, those which conform to the rules of law. We shall see that its intervention is sometimes even more positive. It is present in all relations which restitutive law determines, even in those which appear most completely private, and its presence, though not felt, at least in normal circumstances, is none the less essential.[2]

Since rules with restitutive sanctions are strangers to the common conscience, the relations that they determine are not those which attach themselves indistinctly everywhere. That is to say, they are established immediately, not between the individual and society, but between restricted, special parties in society whom they bind. But, since society is not absent, it must be more or less directly interested, it must feel the repercussions. Thus, according to the force with which society feels them, it intervenes more or less concomitantly and more or less actively, through the intermediary of special organs charged with representing it. These relations are, then, quite different from those which repressive law regulates, for the latter attach the particular conscience to the collective conscience directly and without mediation; that is, the individual to society.

To sum up: the relations governed by co-operative law with restitutive sanctions and the solidarity which they express, result from the division of social labor. We have explained, moreover, that, in general, co-operative relations do not convey other sanctions. In fact, it is in the nature of special tasks to escape the action of the collective conscience, for, in order for a thing to be the object of common sentiments, the first condition is that it be common, that is to say, that it be present in all consciences and that all can represent it in one and the same manner. To be sure, in so far as functions have a certain generality, everybody can have some idea of them. But the more specialized they are, the more circumscribed the number of those cognizant of each of them. Consequently, the more marginal they are to the common

1. And even this moral authority comes from custom, which is to say, from society.

2. We must restrict ourselves to general indications, common to all the norms of restitutive law.

conscience. The rules which determine them cannot have the superior force, the transcendent authority which, when offended, demands expiation. It is also from opinion that their authority comes, as is the case with penal rules, but from an opinion localized in restricted regions of society.

Moreover, even in the special circles where they apply and where, consequently, they are represented in people, they do not correspond to very active sentiments, nor even very often to any type of emotional state. For, as they fix the manner in which the different functions ought to concur in diverse combinations of circumstances which can arise, the objects to which they relate themselves are not always present to consciences. We do not always have to administer guardianship, trusteeship,[3] or exercise the rights of creditor or buyer, etc., or even exercise them in such and such a condition. But the states of conscience are strong only in so far as they are permanent. The violation of these rules reaches neither the common soul of society in its living parts, nor even, at least not generally, that of special groups, and, consequently, it can determine only a very moderate reaction. All that is necessary is that the functions concur in a regular manner. If this regularity is disrupted, it behooves us to re-establish it. Assuredly, that is not to say that the development of the division of labor cannot be affective of penal law. There are, as we already know, administrative and governmental functions in which certain relations are regulated by repressive law, because of the particular character which the organ of common conscience and everything that relates to it has. In still other cases, the links of solidarity which unite certain social functions can be such that from their break quite general repercussions result invoking a penal sanction. But, for the reason we have given, these counter-blows are exceptional.

This law definitely plays a role in society analogous to that played by the nervous system in the organism. The latter has as its task, in effect, the regulation of the different functions of the body in such a way as to make them harmonize. It thus very naturally expresses the state of concentration at which the organism has arrived, in accordance with the division of physiological labor. Thus, on different levels of the animal scale, we can measure the degree of this concentration according to the development of the nervous system. Which is to say that we can equally measure the degree of concentration at which a society has arrived in accordance with the division of social labor according to the

3. That is why the law which governs the relations of domestic function is not penal, although these functions are very general.

development of co-operative law with restitutive sanctions. We can foresee the great services that this criterion will render us.

Since negative solidarity does not produce any integration by itself, and since, moreover, there is nothing specific about it, we shall recognize only two kinds of positive solidarity which are distinguishable by the following qualities:

1. The first binds the individual directly to society without any intermediary. In the second, he depends upon society, because he depends upon the parts of which it is composed.

2. Society is not seen in the same aspect in the two cases. In the first, what we call society is a more or less organized totality of beliefs and sentiments common to all the members of the group: this is the collective type. On the other hand, the society in which we are solidary in the second instance is a system of different, special functions which definite relations unite. These two societies really make up only one. They are two aspects of one and the same reality, but none the less they must be distinguished.

3. From this second difference there arises another which helps us to characterize and name the two kinds of solidarity.

The first can be strong only if the ideas and tendencies common to all the members of the society are greater in number and intensity than those which pertain personally to each member. It is as much stronger as the excess is more considerable. But what makes our personality is how much of our own individual qualities we have, what distinguishes us from others. This solidarity can grow only in inverse ratio to personality. There are in each of us, as we have said, two consciences: one which is common to our group in its entirety, which, consequently, is not ourself, but society living and acting within us; the other, on the contrary, represents that in us which is personal and distinct, that which makes us an individual.[4] Solidarity which comes from likenesses is at its maximum when the collective conscience completely envelops our whole conscience and coincides in all points with it. But, at that moment, our individuality is nil. It can be born only if the community takes smaller toll of us. There are, here, two contrary forces, one centripetal, the other centrifugal, which cannot flourish at the same time. We cannot, at one and the same time, develop ourselves in two opposite senses. If we have a lively desire to think and act for ourselves, we cannot be strongly inclined to think and act as others do. If our ideal

4. However, these two consciences are not in regions geographically distinct from us, but penetrate from all sides.

is to present a singular and personal appearance, we do not want to resemble everybody else. Moreover, at the moment when this solidarity exercises its force, our personality vanishes, as our definition permits us to say, for we are no longer ourselves, but the collective life.

The social molecules which can be coherent in this way can act together only in the measure that they have no actions of their own, as the molecules of inorganic bodies. That is why we propose to call this type of solidarity mechanical. The term does not signify that it is produced by mechanical and artificial means. We call it that only by analogy to the cohesion which unites the elements of an inanimate body, as opposed to that which makes a unity out of the elements of a living body. What justifies this term is that the link which thus unites the individual to society is wholly analogous to that which attaches a thing to a person. The individual conscience, considered in this light, is a simple dependent upon the collective type and follows all of its movements, as the possessed object follows those of its owner. In societies where this type of solidarity is highly developed, the individual does not appear, as we shall see later. Individuality is something which the society possesses. Thus, in these social types, personal rights are not yet distinguished from real rights.

It is quite otherwise with the solidarity which the division of labor produces. Whereas the previous type implies that individuals resemble each other, this type presumes their difference. The first is possible only in so far as the individual personality is absorbed into the collective personality; the second is possible only if each one has a sphere of action which is peculiar to him; that is, a personality. It is necessary, then, that the collective conscience leave open a part of the individual conscience in order that special functions may be established there, functions which it cannot regulate. The more this region is extended, the stronger is the cohesion which results from this solidarity. In effect, on the one hand, each one depends as much more strictly on society as labor is more divided; and, on the other, the activity of each is as much more personal as it is more specialized. Doubtless, as circumscribed as it is, it is never completely original. Even in the exercise of our occupation, we conform to usages, to practices which are common to our whole professional brotherhood. But, even in this instance, the yoke that we submit to is much less heavy than when society completely controls us, and it leaves much more place open for the free play of our initiative. Here, then, the individuality of all grows at the same time as that of its parts. Society becomes more capable of collective movement, at the same time that each of its elements has more freedom of movement. This solidarity resembles that which we observe among the higher animals. Each organ, in effect, has its special physiognomy, its autonomy. And, moreover, the unity of the organism is as great as the individuation of the parts is more marked. Because of this analogy, we propose to call the solidarity which is due to the division of labor, organic.

The following extracts are reprinted from Émile Durkheim, *Suicide*, translated by John A. Spaulding and George Simpson (Glencoe, Ill.: The Free Press, 1951), Book II, Chapter iii, pp. 208–16; Chapter iv, pp. 217, 221–2, 227–8, 239–40, with the permission of Routledge & Kegan Paul Ltd and The Macmillan Company. Copyright © The Free Press, a Corporation, 1951; Routledge & Kegan Paul Ltd, 1952.

We have thus successively set up the three following propositions:

> *Suicide varies inversely with the degree of integration of religious society.*
> *Suicide varies inversely with the degree of integration of domestic society.*
> *Suicide varies inversely with the degree of integration of political society.*

This grouping shows that whereas these different societies have a moderating influence upon suicide, this is due not to special characteristics of each but to a characteristic common to all. Religion does not owe its efficacy to the special nature of religious sentiments, since domestic and political societies both produce the same effects when strongly integrated. This, moreover, we have already proved when studying directly the manner of action of different religions upon suicide. Inversely, it is not the specific nature of the domestic or political tie which can explain the immunity they confer, since religious society has the same advantage. The cause can only be found in a single quality possessed by all these social groups, though perhaps to varying degrees. the only quality satisfying this condition is that they are all strongly integrated social groups. So we reach the general conclusion: suicide varies inversely with the degree of integration of the social groups of which the individual form as a part.

But society cannot disintegrate without the individual simultaneously detaching himself from social life, without his own goals becoming preponderant over those of the community, in a word without his personality tending to surmount the collective personality. The more weakened the groups to which he belongs, the less he depends on them, the more he consequently depends only on himself and recognizes no other rules of conduct than what are founded on his private interests. If we agree to call this state egoism, in which the individual ego asserts itself to excess in the face of the social ego and at its expense, we may call egoistic the special type of suicide springing from excessive individualism.

But how can suicide have such an origin?

First of all, it can be said that, as collective force is one of the obstacles best calculated to restrain suicide, its weakening involves a development of suicide. When society is strongly integrated, it holds individuals under its control, considers them at its service and thus forbids them to dispose wilfully of themselves. Accordingly it opposes their evading their duties to it through death. But how could society impose its supremacy upon them when they refuse to accept this subordination as legitimate? It no longer then possesses the requisite authority to retain them in their duty if they wish to desert; and conscious of its own weakness, it even recognizes their right to do freely what it can no longer prevent. So far as they are the admitted masters of their destinies, it is their privilege to end their lives. They, on their part, have no reason to endure life's sufferings patiently. For they cling to life more resolutely when belonging to a group they love, so as not to betray interests they put before their own. The bond that unites them with the common cause attaches them to life and the lofty goal they envisage prevents their feeling personal troubles so deeply. There is, in short, in a cohesive and animated society a constant interchange of ideas and feelings from all to each and each to all, something like a mutual moral support, which instead of throwing the individual on his own resources, leads him to share in the collective energy and supports his own when exhausted.

But these reasons are purely secondary. Excessive individualism not only results in favoring the action of suicidogenic causes, but it is itself such a cause. It not only frees man's inclination to do away with himself from a protective obstacle, but creates this inclination out of whole cloth and thus gives birth to a special suicide which bears its mark. This must be clearly understood for this is what constitutes the special character of the type of suicide just distinguished and justifies the name we have given it. What is there then in individualism that explains this result?

It has been sometimes said that because of his psychological constitution, man cannot live without attachment to some object which transcends and survives him, and that the reason for this necessity is a need we must have not to perish entirely. Life is said to be intolerable unless some reason for existing is involved, some purpose justifying life's trials. The individual alone is not a sufficient end for his activity. He is too little. He is not only hemmed in spatially; he is also strictly limited temporally. When, therefore, we have no other object than ourselves we cannot avoid the thought that our efforts will finally end in nothingness, since we ourselves disappear. But annihilation terrifies us. Under these conditions one would lose courage to live, that is, to act and struggle, since nothing will remain of our exertions. The state of egoism, in other words, is supposed to be contradictory to human nature and, consequently, too uncertain to have chances of permanence.

In this absolute formulation the proposition is vulnerable. If the thought of the end of our personality were really so hateful, we could consent to live only by blinding ourselves voluntarily as to life's value. For if we may in a measure avoid the prospect of annihilation we cannot extirpate it; it is inevitable, whatever we do. We may push back the frontier for some generations, force our name to endure for some years or centuries longer than our body; a moment, too soon for most men, always comes when it will be nothing. For the groups we join in order to prolong our existence by their means are themselves mortal; they too must dissolve, carrying with them all our deposit of ourselves. Those are few whose memories are closely enough bound to the very history of humanity to be assured of living until its death. So, if we really thus thirsted after immortality, no such brief perspectives could ever appease us. Besides, what of us is it that lives? A word, a sound, an imperceptible trace, most often anonymous,[1] therefore nothing comparable to the violence of our efforts or able to justify them to us. In actuality, though a child is naturally an egoist who feels not the slightest craving to survive himself, and the old man is very often a child in this and so many other respects, neither ceases to cling to life as much or more than the adult; indeed we have seen that suicide is very rare for the first fifteen years and tends to decrease at the other extreme of life. Such too is the case with animals, whose psychological constitution differs from that of men only in degree. It is therefore untrue that life is only possible by its possessing its rationale outside of itself.

Indeed, a whole range of functions concern only the individual; these are the ones indispensable for physical life. Since they are made for this purpose only, they are perfected by its attainment. In everything con-

1. We say nothing of the ideal protraction of life involved in the belief in immortality of the soul, for (1) this cannot explain why the family or attachment to political society preserves us from suicide; and (2) it is not even this belief which forms religion's prophylactic influence, as we have shown above.

cerning them, therefore, man can act reasonably without thought of transcendental purposes. These functions serve by merely serving him. In so far as he has no other needs, he is therefore self-sufficient and can live happily with no other object than living. This is not the case, however, with the civilized adult. He has many ideas, feelings and practices unrelated to organic needs. The roles of art, morality, religion, political faith, science itself are not to repair organic exhaustion nor to provide sound functioning of the organs. All this supra-physical life is built and expanded not because of the demands of the cosmic environment but because of the demands of the social environment. The influence of society is what has aroused in us the sentiments of sympathy and solidarity drawing us toward others; it is society which, fashioning us in its image, fills us with religious, political and moral beliefs that control our actions. To play our social role we have striven to extend our intelligence and it is still society that has supplied us with tools for this development by transmitting to us its trust fund of knowledge.

Through the very fact that these superior forms of human activity have a collective origin, they have a collective purpose. As they derive from society they have reference to it; rather they are society itself incarnated and individualized in each one of us. But for them to have a raison d'être in our eyes, the purpose they envisage must be one not indifferent to us. We can cling to these forms of human activity only to the degree that we cling to society itself. Contrariwise, in the same measure as we feel detached from society we become detached from that life whose source and aim is society. For what purpose do these rules of morality, these precepts of law binding us to all sort of sacrifices, these restrictive dogmas exist, if there is no being outside us whom they serve and in whom we participate? What is the purpose of science itself? If its only use is to increase our chances for survival, it does not deserve the trouble it entails. Instinct acquits itself better of this role; animals prove this. Why substitute for a more hesitant and uncertain reflection? What is the end of suffering, above all? If the value of things can only be estimated by their relation to this positive evil for the individual, it is without reward and incomprehensible. This problem does not exist for the believer firm in his faith or the man strongly bound by ties of domestic or political society. Instinctively and unreflectively they ascribe all that they are and do, the one to his Church or his God, the living symbol of the Church, the other to his family, the third to his country or party. Even in their sufferings they see only a means of glorifying the group to which they belong and thus do homage to it. So, the Christian ultimately desires and seeks suffering to testify more fully to his contempt for the flesh and more fully resemble his divine model. But the more the believer doubts, that is, the less he feels himself a real participant in the religious faith to which he belongs, and from which he is freeing himself; the more the family and community become foreign to the individual, so much the more does he become a mystery to himself, unable to escape the exasperating and agonizing question: to what purpose?

If, in other words, as has often been said, man is double, that is because social man superimposes himself upon physical man. Social man necessarily presupposes a society which he expresses and serves. If this dissolves, if we no longer feel it in existence and action about and above us, whatever is social in us is deprived of all objective foundation. All that remains is an artificial combination of illusory images, a phantasmagoria vanishing at the least reflection; that is, nothing which can be a goal for our action. Yet this social man is the essence of civilized man; he is the masterpiece of existence. Thus we are bereft of reasons for existence; for the only life to which we could cling no longer corresponds to anything actual; the only existence still based upon reality no longer meets our needs. Because we have been initiated into a higher existence, the one which satisfies an animal or a child can satisfy us no more and the other itself fades and leaves us helpless. So there is nothing more for our efforts to lay hold of, and we feel them lose themselves in emptiness. In this sense it is true to say that our activity needs an object transcending it. We do not need it to maintain ourselves in the illusion of an impossible immortality; it is implicit in our moral constitution and cannot be even partially lost without this losing its raison d'être in the same degree. No proof is needed that in such a state of confusion the least cause of discouragement may easily give birth to desperate resolutions. If life is not worth the trouble of being lived, everything becomes a pretext to rid ourselves of it.

But this is not all. This detachment occurs not only in single individuals. One of the constitutive elements of every national temperament consists of a certain way of estimating the value of existence. There is a collective as well as an individual humor inclining peoples to sadness or cheerfulness, making them see things in bright or sombre lights. In fact, only society can pass a collective opinion on the value of human life; for this the individual is incompetent. The latter knows nothing but himself and his own little horizon; thus his experience is too limited to serve as a basis for a general appraisal. He may indeed consider his own life to be aimless; he can say nothing applicable to others. On the contrary, without sophistry, society may generalize its own feeling as to itself, its state of health or lack of health. For individuals share too deeply in the life of society for it to be diseased without their suffering infection. What it suffers they necessarily suffer. Because it is the whole, its ills are communicated to its paths. Hence it cannot disintegrate without awareness that the regular conditions of general existence are equally disturbed. Because society is the end on which our better selves depend, it cannot feel us escaping it without a simultaneous realization that our activity is purposeless. Since we are its handiwork, society cannot be conscious of its own decadence without the feeling that henceforth this work is of no value. Thence are formed currents of depression and disillusionment emanating from no particular individual but expressing society's state of disintegration. They reflect the relaxation of social bonds, a sort of collective asthenia, or social malaise, just as individual sadness, when chronic, in its way reflects the poor organic state of the individual. Then metaphysical and religious systems spring up which, by reducing these obscure sentiments to formulae, attempt to prove to men the senselessness of life and that it is self-deception to believe that it has purpose. Then new moralities originate which, by elevating facts to ethics, commend suicide or at least tend in that direction by suggesting a minimal existence. On their appearance they seem to have been created out of whole cloth by their makers who are sometimes blamed for the pessimism of their doctrines. In reality they are an effect rather than a cause; they merely symbolize in abstract language and systematic form the physiological distress of the body social.[2] As these currents are collective, they have, by virtue of their origin, an authority which they impose upon the individual and they drive him more vigorously on the way to which he is already inclined by the state of moral distress directly aroused in him by the disintegration of society. Thus, at the very moment that, with excessive zeal, he frees himself from the social environment, he still submits to its influence. However individualized a man may be, there is always something collective remaining – the very depression and melancholy resulting from this same exaggerated individualism. He effects communion through sadness where he no longer has anything else with which to achieve it.

Hence this type of suicide well deserves the name we have given it. Egoism is not merely a contributing factor in it; it is its generating cause. In this case the bond attracting man to life relaxes because that attaching him to society is itself slack. The incidents of private life which seem the direct inspiration of suicide and are considered its determining

2. This is why it is unjust to accuse these theorists of sadness of generalizing personal impressions. They are the echo of a general condition.

causes are in reality only incidental causes. The individual yields to the slightest shock of circumstance because the state of society has made him a ready prey to suicide.

Several facts confirm this explanation. Suicide is known to be rare among children and to diminish among the aged at the last confines of life; physical man, in both, tends to become the whole of man. Society is still lacking in the former, for it has not had the time to form him in its image; it begins to retreat from the latter or, what amounts to the same thing, he retreats from it. Thus both are more self-sufficient. Feeling a lesser need for self-completion through something not themselves, they are also less exposed to feel the lack of what is necessary for living. The immunity of an animal has the same causes. We shall likewise see in the next chapter that, though lower societies practice a form of suicide of their own, the one we have just discussed is almost unknown to them. Since their social life is very simple, the social inclinations of individuals are simple also and thus they need little for satisfaction. They readily find external objectives to which they become attached. If he can carry with him his gods and his family, primitive man, everywhere that he goes, has all that his social nature demands.

This is also why woman can endure life in isolation more easily than man. When a widow is seen to endure her condition much better than a widower and desires marriage less passionately, one is led to consider this ease in dispensing with the family a mark of superiority; it is said that woman's affective faculties, being very intense, are easily employed outside the domestic circle, while her devotion is indispensable to man to help him endure life. Actually, if this is her privilege it is because her sensibility is rudimentary rather than highly developed. As she lives outside of community existence more than man, she is less penetrated by it; society is less necessary to her because she is less impregnated with sociability. She has few needs in this direction and satisfies them easily. With a few devotional practices and some animals to care for, the old unmarried woman's life is full. If she remains faithfully attached to religious traditions and thus finds ready protection against suicide, it is because these very simple social forms satisfy all her needs. Man, on the contrary, is hard beset in this respect. As his thought and activity develop, they increasingly overflow these antiquated forms. But then he needs others. Because he is a more complex social being, he can maintain his equilibrium only by finding more points of support outside himself, and it is because his moral balance depends on a larger number of conditions that it is more easily disturbed.

Émile Durkheim

Altruistic Suicide

In the order of existence, no good is measureless. A biological quality can only fulfil the purposes it is meant to serve on condition that it does not transgress certain limits. So with social phenomena. If, as we have just seen, excessive individuation leads to suicide, insufficient individuation has the same effects. When man has become detached from society, he encounters less resistance to suicide in himself, and he does so likewise when social integration is too strong . . .

We thus confront a type of suicide differing by incisive qualities from the preceding one. Whereas the latter is due to excessive individuation, the former is caused by too rudimentary individuation. One occurs because society allows the individual to escape it, being insufficiently aggregated in some parts or even in the whole; the other, because society holds him in too strict tutelage. Having given the name of *egoism* to the state of the ego living its own life and obeying itself alone, that of *altruism* adequately expresses the opposite state, where the ego is not its own property, where it is blended with something not itself, where the goal of conduct is exterior to itself, that is, in one of the groups in which it participates. So we call the suicide caused by intense altruism *altruistic suicide*. But since it is characteristically performed as a duty, the terminology adopted should express this fact. So we will call such type *obligatory altruistic suicide*.

The combination of these two adjectives is required to define it; for not every altruistic suicide is necessarily obligatory. Some are not so expressly imposed by society, having a more optional character. In other words, altruistic suicide is a species with several varieties . . .

We have thus constituted a second type of suicide, itself consisting of three varieties: obligatory altruistic suicide, optional altruistic suicide, and acute altruistic suicide, the perfect pattern of which is mystical suicide. In these different forms, it contrasts most strikingly with egoistic suicide. One is related to the crude morality which disregards everything relating solely to the individual; the other is closely associated with the refined ethics which sets human personality on so high a pedestal that it can no longer be subordinated to anything. Between the two there is, therefore, all the difference between primitive people and the most civilized nations.

However, if lower societies are the theatre par excellence of altruistic suicide, it is also found in more recent civilizations. Under this head may notably be classified the death of some of the Christian martyrs.

All those neophytes who without killing themselves, voluntarily allowed their own slaughter, are really suicides. Though they did not kill themselves, they sought death with all their power and behaved so as to make it inevitable. To be suicide, the act from which death must necessarily result need only have been performed by the victim with full knowledge of the facts. Besides, the passionate enthusiasm with which the believers in the new religion faced final torture shows that at this moment they had completely discarded their personalities for the idea of which they had become the servants. Probably the epidemics of suicide which devastated the monasteries on several occasions during the Middle Ages, apparently caused by excesses of religious fervor, were of this nature.

In our contemporary societies, as individual personality becomes increasingly free from the collective personality, such suicides could not be widespread. Some may doubtless be said to have yielded to altruistic motives, such as soldiers who preferred death to the humiliation of defeat, like Commandant Beaurepaire and Admiral Villeneuve, or unhappy persons who kill themselves to prevent disgrace befalling their family. For when such persons renounce life, it is for something they love better than themselves. But they are isolated and exceptional cases. Yet even today there exists among us a special environment where altruistic suicide is chronic: namely, the army ...

It may now be better understood why we insisted on giving an objective definition of suicide and on sticking to it.

Because altruistic suicide, though showing the familiar suicidal traits, resembles especially in its most vivid manifestations some categories of actions which we are used to honoring with our respect and even admiration, people have often refused to consider it as self-destruction. It is to be remembered that the deaths of Cato and of the Girondins were not suicides for Esquirol and Falret. But if suicides with the spirit of renunciation and abnegation as their immediate and visible cause do not deserve the name, it can be no more appropriate for those springing from the same moral disposition, though less apparently; for the second differ by only a few shades from the first. If the inhabitant of the Canary Islands who throws himself into an abyss to do honor to his god is not a suicide, how give this name to a Jain sectary who kills himself to obtain entry to oblivion; to the primitive who, under the influence of the same mental state, renounces life for a slight insult done him or merely to express his contempt for existence; to the bankrupt who prefers not to survive his disgrace; and finally to the many soldiers who every year increase the numbers of voluntary deaths? All these cases have for their root the same state of altruism which is equally the cause of what might be called heroic suicide. Shall they alone be placed among the ranks of suicides and only those excluded whose motive is particularly pure? But first, according to what standard will the division be made? When does a motive cease to be sufficiently praiseworthy for the act it determines to be called suicide? Moreover, by separating these two classes of facts radically from each other, we inevitably misjudge their nature. For the essential characteristics of the type are clearest in obligatory altruistic suicide. Other varieties are only derivative forms. Either a considerable number of instructive phenomena will be eliminated or, if not all are eliminated, not only will a purely arbitrary choice be the only one possible among them, but it will be impossible to detect the common stock to which those that are retained belong. Such is the risk we incur in making the definition of suicide depend on the subjective feelings it inspires.

Besides, not even the reasons for the sentiment thought to justify this exclusion are well founded. The fact is stressed that the motives of certain altruistic suicides reappear in slightly different forms as the basis of actions regarded by everyone as moral. But is egoistic suicide any different? Has not the sentiment of individual autonomy its own morality as well as the opposite sentiment? If the latter serves as foundation to a kind of courage, strengthening and even hardening the heart, the other softens and moves it to pity. Where altruistic suicide is prevalent, man is always ready to give his life; however, at the same time, he sets no more value on that of another. On the contrary, when he rates individual personality above all other ends, he respects it in others. His cult for it makes him suffer from all that minimizes it even among his fellows. A broader sympathy for human suffering succeeds the fanatical devotions of primitive times. Every sort of suicide is then merely the exaggerated or deflected form of a virtue. In that case, however, the way they affect the moral conscience does not sufficiently differentiate them to justify their being separated into different types.

The following extract is reprinted from Émile Durkheim, *The Elementary Forms of Religious Life*, translated by Joseph W. Swain (London: George Allen & Unwin Ltd, 1915; Glencoe, Ill.: The Free Press, 1954, pp. 206–14), with the permission of George Allen & Unwin Ltd and The Macmillan Company. Copyright © George Allen & Unwin Ltd, 1915. First Free Press Paperback Edition 1963.

In a general way, it is unquestionable that a society has all that is necessary to arouse the sensation of the divine in minds, merely by the power that it has over them; for to its members it is what a god is to his worshippers. In fact, a god is, first of all, a being whom men think of as superior to themselves, and upon whom they feel that they depend. Whether it be a conscious personality, such as Zeus or Jahveh, or merely abstract forces such as those in play in totemism, the worshipper, in the one case as in the other, believes himself held to certain manners of acting which are imposed upon him by the nature of the sacred principle with which he feels that he is in communion. Now society also gives us the sensation of a perpetual dependence. Since it has a nature which is peculiar to itself and different from our individual nature, it pursues ends which are likewise special to it; but, as it cannot attain them except through our intermediacy, it imperiously demands our aid. It requires that, forgetful of our own interests, we make ourselves its servitors, and it submits us to every sort of inconvenience, privation and sacrifice, without which social life would be impossible. It is because of this that at every instant we are obliged to submit ourselves to rules of conduct and of thought which we have neither made nor desired, and which are sometimes even contrary to our most fundamental inclinations and instincts.

Even if society were unable to obtain these concessions and sacrifices from us except by a material constraint, it might awaken in us only the idea of a physical force to which we must give way of necessity, instead of that of a moral power such as religions adore. But as a matter of fact, the empire which it holds over consciences is due much less to the physical supremacy of which it has the privilege than to the moral authority with which it is invested. If we yield to its orders, it is not merely because it is strong enough to triumph over our resistance; it is primarily because it is the object of a venerable respect.

We say that an object, whether individual or collective, inspires respect when the representation expressing it in the mind is gifted with such a force that it automatically causes or inhibits actions, *without regard for any consideration relative to their useful or injurious effects*. When we obey somebody because of the moral authority which we recognize in him, we follow out his opinions, not because they seem wise, but because a certain sort of physical energy is imminent in the idea that we form of this person, which conquers our will and inclines it in the indicated direction. Respect is the emotion which we experience when we feel this interior and wholly spiritual pressure operating upon us. Then we are not determined by the advantages or inconveniences of the attitude which is prescribed or recommended to us; it is by the way in which we represent to ourselves the person recommending or prescribing it. This is why commands generally take a short, peremptory form leaving no place for hesitation; it is because, in so far as it is a command and goes by its own force, it excludes all idea of deliberation or calculation; it gets its efficacy from the intensity of the mental state in which it is placed. It is this intensity which creates what is called a moral ascendancy.

Now the ways of action to which society is strongly enough attached to impose them upon its members, are, by that very fact, marked with a distinctive sign provocative of respect. Since they are elaborated in common, the vigour with which they have been thought of by each particular mind is retained in all the other minds, and reciprocally. The representations which express them within each of us have an intensity which no purely private states of consciousness could ever attain; for they have the strength of the innumerable individual representations which have served to form each of them. It is society who speaks through the mouths of those who affirm them in our presence; it is society whom we hear in hearing them; and the voice of all has an accent which that of one alone could never have. The very violence with which society reacts, by way of blame or material suppression, against every attempted dissidence, contributes to strengthening its empire by manifesting the common conviction through this burst of ardour. In a word, when something is the object of such a state of opinion, the representation which each individual has of it gains a power of action from its origins and the conditions in which it was born, which even those feel who do not submit themselves to it. It tends to repel the representations which contradict it, and it keeps them at a distance; on the other hand, it commands those acts which will realize it, and it does so, not by a material coercion or by the perspective of something of this sort, but by the simple radiation of the mental energy which it contains. It has an efficacy coming solely from its psychical properties, and it is by just this sign that moral authority is recognized. So opinion, primarily a social thing, is a source of authority, and it might even be asked whether all authority is not the daughter of opinion.[1] It may be objected that science is often the antagonist of opinion, whose errors it combats and rectifies. But it cannot succeed in this task if it does not have sufficient authority, and it can obtain this authority only from opinion itself. If a people did not have faith in science, all the scientific demonstrations in the world would be without any influence whatsoever over their minds. Even to-day, if science happened to resist a

1. This is the case at least with all moral authority recognized as such by the group as a whole.

very strong current of public opinion, it would risk losing its credit there.[2]

Since it is in spiritual ways that social pressure exercises itself, it could not fail to give men the idea that outside themselves there exist one or several powers, both moral and, at the same time, efficacious, upon which they depend. They must think of these powers, at least in part, as outside themselves, for these address them in a tone of command and sometimes even order them to do violence to their most natural inclinations. It is undoubtedly true that if they were able to see that these influences which they feel emanate from society, then the mythological system of interpretations would never be born. But social action follows ways that are too circuitous and obscure, and employs psychical mechanisms that are too complex to allow the ordinary observer to see whence it comes. As long as scientific analysis does not come to teach it to them, men know well that they are acted upon, but they do not know by whom. So they must invent by themselves the idea of these powers with which they feel themselves in connection, and from that, we are able to catch a glimpse of the way by which they were led to represent them under forms that are really foreign to their nature and to transfigure them by thought.

But a god is not merely an authority upon whom we depend; it is a force upon which our strength relies. The man who has obeyed his god and who, for this reason, believes the god is with him, approaches the

2. We hope that this analysis and those which follow will put an end to an inexact interpretation of our thought, from which more than one misunderstanding has resulted. Since we have made constraint the *outward sign* by which social facts can be the most easily recognized and distinguished from the facts of individual psychology, it has been assumed that according to our opinion, physical constraint is the essential thing for social life. As a matter of fact, we have never considered it more than the material and apparent expression of an interior and profound fact which is wholly ideal: this is *moral authority*. The problem of sociology – if we can speak of *a* sociological problem – consists in seeking, among the different forms of external constraint, the different sorts of moral authority corresponding to them and in discovering the causes which have determined these latter. The particular question which we are treating in this present work has as its principal object, the discovery of the form under which that particular variety of moral authority which is inherent in all that is religious has been born, and out of what elements it is made. It will be seen presently that even if we do make social pressure one of the distinctive characteristics of sociological phenomena, we do not mean to say that it is the only one. We shall show another aspect of the collective life, nearly opposite to the preceding one, but none the less real.

world with confidence and with the feeling of an increased energy. Likewise, social action does not confine itself to demanding sacrifices, privations and efforts from us. For the collective force is not entirely outside of us; it does not act upon us wholly from without; but rather since society cannot exist except in and through individual consciousness,[3] this force must also penetrate us and organize itself within us; it thus becomes an integral part of our being and by that very fact this is elevated and magnified.

There are occasions when this strengthening and vivifying action of society is especially apparent. In the midst of an assembly animated by a common passion, we become susceptible of acts and sentiments of which we are incapable when reduced to our own forces; and when the assembly is dissolved and when, finding ourselves alone again, we fall back to our ordinary level, we are then able to measure the height to which we have been raised above ourselves. History abounds in examples of this sort. It is enough to think of the night of the Fourth of August, 1789, when an assembly was suddenly led to an act of sacrifice and abnegation which each of its members had refused the day before, and at which they were all surprised the day after. This is why all parties, political economic or confessional, are careful to have periodical reunions where their members may revivify their common faith by manifesting it in common. To strengthen those sentiments which, if left to themselves, would soon weaken, it is sufficient to bring those who hold them together and to put them into closer and more active relations with one another. This is the explanation of the particular attitude of a man speaking to a crowd, at least if he has succeeded in entering into communion with it. His language has a grandiloquence that would be ridiculous in ordinary circumstances; his gestures show a certain domination; his very thought is impatient of all rules, and easily falls into all sorts of excesses. It is because he feels within him an abnormal oversupply of force which overflows and tries to burst out from him; sometimes he even has the feeling that he is dominated by a moral force which is greater than he and of which he is only the interpreter. It is by this trait that we are able to recognize what has often been called the demon of oratorical inspiration. Now this exceptional increase of force is something very real; it comes to him from the very group which he addresses. The sentiments provoked by his words come back to him, but enlarged and amplified, and to this degree they strengthen his own sentiment. The passionate energies he arouses

3. Of course this does not mean to say that the collective consciousness does not have distinctive characteristics of its own.

re-echo within him and quicken his vital tone. It is no longer a simple individual who speaks; it is a group incarnate and personified.

Besides these passing and intermittent states, there are other more durable ones, where this strengthening influence of society makes itself felt with greater consequences and frequently even with greater brilliancy. There are periods in history when, under the influence of some great collective shock, social interactions have become much more frequent and active. Men look for each other and assemble together more than ever. That general effervescence results which is characteristic of revolutionary or creative epochs. Now this greater activity results in a general stimulation of individual forces. Men see more and differently now than in normal times. Changes are not merely of shades and degrees; men become different. The passions moving them are of such an intensity that they cannot be satisfied except by violent and unrestrained actions, actions of superhuman heroism or of bloody barbarism. This is what explains the Crusades, for example, or many of the scenes, either sublime or savage, of the French Revolution. Under the influence of the general exaltation, we see the most mediocre and inoffensive bourgeois become either a hero or a butcher. And so clearly are all these mental processes the ones that are also at the root of religion that the individuals themselves have often pictured the pressure before which they thus gave way in a distinctly religious form. The Crusaders believed that they felt God present in the midst of them, enjoining them to go to the conquest of the Holy Land; Joan of Arc believed that she obeyed celestial voices.

But it is not only in exceptional circumstances that this stimulating action of society makes itself felt; there is not, so to speak, a moment in our lives when some current of energy does not come to us from without. The man who has done his duty finds in the manifestations of every sort expressing the sympathy, esteem or affection which his fellows have for him, a feeling of comfort, of which he does not ordinarily take account, but which sustains him, none the less. The sentiments which society has for him raise the sentiments which he has for himself. Because he is in moral harmony with his comrades, he has more confidence, courage and boldness in action, just like the believer who thinks that he feels the regard of his god turned graciously towards him. It thus produces, as it were, a perpetual sustenance for our moral nature. Since this varies with a multitude of external circumstances, as our relation with the groups about us are more or less active and as these groups themselves vary, we cannot fail to feel that this moral support depends upon an external cause; but we do not perceive where this cause is nor what it is. So we ordinarily think of it under the form of a moral power which, though immanent in us, represents within us something not ourselves: this is the moral conscience, of which, by the way, men have never made even a slightly distinct representation except by the aid of religious symbols.

In addition to these free forces which are constantly coming to renew our own, there are others which are fixed in the methods and traditions which we employ. We speak a language that we did not make; we use instruments that we did not invent; we invoke rights that we did not found; a treasury of knowledge is transmitted to each generation that it did not gather itself, etc. It is to society that we owe these varied benefits of civilization, and if we do not ordinarily see the source from which we get them, we at least know that they are not our own work. Now it is these things that give man his own place among things; a man is a man only because he is civilized. So he could not escape the feeling that outside of him there are active causes from which he gets the characteristic attributes of his nature and which, as benevolent powers, assist him, protect him and assure him of a privileged fate. And of course he must attribute to these powers a dignity corresponding to the great value of the good things he attributes to them.

Thus the environment in which we live seems to us to be peopled with forces that are at once imperious and helpful, august and gracious, and with which we have relations. Since they exercise over us a pressure of which we are conscious, we are forced to localize them outside ourselves, just as we do for the objective causes of our sensations. But the sentiments which they inspire in us differ in nature from those which we have for simple visible objects. As long as these latter are reduced to their empirical characteristics as shown in ordinary experience, and as long as the religious imagination has not metamorphosed them, we entertain for them no feeling which resembles respect, and they contain within them nothing that is able to raise us outside ourselves. Therefore, the representations which express them appear to us to be very different from those aroused in us by collective influences. The two form two distinct and separate mental states in our consciousness, just as do the two forms of life to which they correspond. Consequently, we get the impression that we are in relations with two distinct sorts of reality and that a sharply drawn line of demarcation separates them from each other: on the one hand is the world of profane things, on the other, that of sacred things.

Also, in the present day just as much as in the past, we see society constantly creating sacred things out of ordinary ones. If it happens to fall in love with a man and if it thinks it has found in him the principal aspirations that move it, as well as the means of satisfying them, this man will be raised above the others, and, as it were, deified. Opinion will invest him with a majesty exactly analogous to that protecting the gods. This is what has happened to so many sovereigns in whom their age had faith: if they were not made gods, they were at least regarded as direct representatives of the deity. And the fact that it is society alone which is the author of these varieties of apotheosis, is evident since it frequently chances to consecrate men thus who have no right to it from their own merit. The simple deference inspired by men invested with high social functions is not different in nature from religious respect. It is expressed by the same movements: a man keeps at a distance from a high personage; he approaches him only with precautions; in conversing with him, he uses other gestures and language than those used with ordinary mortals. The sentiment felt on these occasions is so closely related to the religious sentiment that many peoples have confounded the two. In order to explain the consideration accorded to princes, nobles and political chiefs, a sacred character has been attributed to them. In Melanesia and Polynesia, for example, it is said that an influential man has *mana*, and that his influence is due to this *mana*. However, it is evident that his situation is due solely to the importance attributed to him by public opinion. Thus the moral power conferred by opinion and that with which sacred beings are invested are at bottom of a single origin and made up of the same elements. That is why a single word is able to designate the two.

In addition to men, society also consecrates things, especially ideas. If a belief is unanimously shared by a people, then, for the reason which we pointed out above, it is forbidden to touch it, that is to say, to deny it or to contest it. Now the prohibition of criticism is an interdiction like the others and proves the presence of something sacred. Even to-day, howsoever great may be the liberty which we accord to others, a man who should totally deny progress or ridicule the human ideal to which modern societies are attached, would produce the effect of a sacrilege. There is at least one principle which those the most devoted to the free examination of everything tend to place above discussion and to regard as untouchable, that is to say, as sacred: this is the very principle of free examination.

This aptitude of society for setting itself up as a god or for creating gods was never more apparent than during the first years of the French Revolution. At this time, in fact, under the influence of the general enthusiasm, things purely laïcal by nature were transformed by public opinion into sacred things: these were the Fatherland, Liberty, Reason. A religion tended to become established which had its dogmas, symbols, altars and feasts. It was to these spontaneous aspirations that the cult of

Reason and the Supreme Being attempted to give a sort of official satisfaction. It is true that this religious renovation had only an ephemeral duration. But that was because the patriotic enthusiasm which at first transported the masses soon relaxed. The cause being gone, the effect could not remain. But this experiment, though short-lived, keeps all its sociological interest. It remains true that in one determined case we have seen society and its essential ideas become, directly and with no transfiguration of any sort, the object of a veritable cult.

All these facts allow us to catch glimpses of how the clan was able to awaken within its members the idea that outside of them there exist forces which dominate them and at the same time sustain them, that is to say in fine, religious forces: it is because there is no society with which the primitive is more directly and closely connected. The bonds uniting him to the tribe are much more lax and more feebly felt. Although this is not at all strange or foreign to him, it is with the people of his own clan that he has the greatest number of things in common; it is the action of this group that he feels the most directly; so it is this also which, in preference to all others, should express itself in religious symbols.

But this first explanation has been too general, for it is applicable to every sort of society indifferently, and consequently to every sort of religion. Let us attempt to determine exactly what form this collective action takes in the clan and how it arouses the sensation of sacredness there. For there is no place where it is more easily observable or more apparent in its results.

The following extract is reprinted from Émile Durkheim, *The Elementary Forms of Religious Life*, translated by Joseph W. Swain (London: George Allen & Unwin Ltd, 1915; Glencoe, Ill.: The Free Press, 1954, Conclusion, section 1, pp. 416–27), with the permission of George Allen & Unwin Ltd and The Macmillan Company. Copyright © George Allen & Unwin Ltd, 1915. First Free Press Paperback Edition 1963.

The theorists who have undertaken to explain religion in rational terms have generally seen in it before all else a system of ideas, corresponding to some determined object. This object has been conceived in a multitude of ways: nature, the infinite, the unknowable, the idea, etc.; but these differences matter but little. In any case, it was the conception and beliefs which were considered as the essential elements of religion. As for the rites, from this point of view they appear to be only an external translation, contingent and material, of these internal states which alone pass as having any intrinsic value. This conception is so commonly held that generally the disputes of which religion is the theme turn about the question whether it can conciliate itself with science or not, that is to say, whether or not there is a place beside our scientific knowledge for another form of thought which would be specifically religious.

But the believers, the men who lead the religious life and have a direct sensation of what it really is, object to this way of regarding it, saying that it does not correspond to their daily experience. In fact, they feel that the real function of religion is not to make us think, to enrich our knowledge, nor to add to the conceptions which we owe to science others of another origin and another character, but rather, it is to make us act, to aid us to live. The believer who has communicated with his god is not merely a man who sees new truths of which the unbeliever is ignorant; he is a man who is *stronger*. He feels within him more force, either to endure the trials of existence, or to conquer them. It is as though he were raised above the miseries of the world, because he is raised above his condition as a mere man; he believes that he is saved from evil, under whatever form he may conceive this evil. The first article in every creed is the belief in salvation by faith. But it is hard to see how a mere idea could have this efficacy. An idea is in reality only a part of ourselves; then how could it confer upon us powers superior to those which we have of our own nature? Howsoever rich it might be in affective virtues, it could add nothing to our natural vitality; for it could only release the motive powers which are within us, neither creating them nor increasing them. From the mere fact that we consider an object worthy of being loved and sought after, it does not follow that we feel ourselves stronger afterwards; it is also necessary that this object set free energies superior to these which we ordinarily have at our command and also that we have some means of making these enter into us and unite themselves to our interior lives. Now for that, it is not enough that we think of them; it is also indispensable that we place ourselves within their sphere of action, and that we set ourselves where we may best feel their influence; in a word, it is necessary that we act, and that we repeat the acts thus necessary every time we feel the need of renewing their effects. From this point of view, it is readily seen how that group of regularly repeated acts which form the cult get their importance. In fact, whoever has really practised a religion knows very well that it is the cult which gives rise to these impressions of joy, of interior peace, of serenity, of enthusiasm which are, for the believer, an experimental proof of his beliefs. The cult is not simply a system of signs by which the faith is outwardly translated; it is a collection of the means by which this is created and recreated periodically. Whether it consists in material acts or mental operations, it is always this which is efficacious.

Our entire study rests upon this postulate that the unanimous sentiment of the believers of all times cannot be purely illusory. Together with a recent apologist of the faith[1] we admit that these religious beliefs rest upon a specific experience whose demonstative value is, in one sense, not one bit inferior to that of scientific experiments, though different from them. We, too, think that 'a tree is known by its fruits,'[2] and that fertility is the best proof of what the roots are worth. But from the fact that a 'religious experience,' if we choose to call it this, does exist and that it has a certain foundation – and, by the way, is there any experience which has none? – it does not follow that the reality which is its foundation conforms objectively to the idea which believers have of it. The very fact that the fashion in which it has been conceived has varied infinitely in different times is enough to prove that none of these conceptions express it adequately. If a scientist states it as an axiom that the sensations of heat and light which we feel correspond to some objective cause, he does not conclude that this is what it appears to the senses to be. Likewise, even if the impressions which the faithful feel are not imaginary, still they are in no way privileged intuitions; there is no reason for believing that they inform us better upon the nature of their object than do ordinary sensations upon the nature of bodies and their properties. In order to discover what this object consists of, we must submit them to an examination and elaboration analogous to that which has substituted for the sensuous idea of the world another which is scientific and conceptual.

This is precisely what we have tried to do, and we have seen that this reality, which mythologies have represented under so many different forms, but which is the universal and eternal objective cause of these sensations *sui generis* out of which religious experience is made, is society. We have shown what moral forces it develops and how it awakens this sentiment of a refuge, of a shield and of a guardian support which attaches the believer to his cult. It is that which raises him outside himself; it is even that which made him. For that which makes a man is the totality of the intellectual property which constitutes civilization, and civilization is the work of society. Thus is explained the preponderating rôle of the cult in all religions, which ever they may be. This is

1. William James, *The Varieties of Religious Experience.*
2. Quoted by James, op. cit., p. 20.

because society cannot make its influence felt unless it is in action, and it is not in action unless the individuals who compose it are assembled together and act in common. It is by common action that it takes consciousness of itself and realizes its position; it is before all else an active co-operation. The collective ideas and sentiments are even possible only owing to these exterior movements which symbolize them, as we have established. Then it is action which dominates the religious life, because of the mere fact that it is society which is its source.

In addition to all the reasons which have been given to justify this conception, a final one may be added here, which is the result of our whole work. As we have progressed, we have established the fact that the fundamental categories of thought, and consequently of science, are of religious origin. We have seen that the same is true for magic and consequently for the different processes which have issued from it. On the other hand, it has long been known that up until a relatively advanced moment of evolution, moral and legal rules have been indistinguishable from ritual prescriptions. In summing up, then, it may be said that nearly all the great social institutions have been born in religion.[3] Now in order that these principal aspects of the collective life may have commenced by being only varied aspects of the religious life, it is obviously necessary that the religious life be the eminent form and, as it were, the concentrated expression of the whole collective life. If religion has given birth to all that is essential in society, it is because the idea of society is the soul of religion.

Religious forces are therefore human forces, moral forces. It is true that since collective sentiments can become conscious of themselves only by fixing themselves upon external objects, they have not been able to take form without adopting some of their characteristics from other things: they have thus acquired a sort of physical nature: in this way they have come to mix themselves with the life of the material world, and then have considered themselves capable of explaining what passes there. But when they are considered only from this point of view and in this rôle, only their most superficial aspect is seen. In reality, the essential elements of which these collective sentiments are made have

3. Only one form of social activity has not yet been expressly attached to religion: that is economic activity. Sometimes processes that are derived from magic have, by that fact alone, an origin that is indirectly religious. Also, economic value is a sort of power or efficacy, and we know the religious origins of the idea of power. Also richness can confer *mana*; therefore it has it. Hence it is seen that the ideas of economic value and of religious value are not without connection. But the question of the nature of these connections has not yet been studied.

been borrowed by the understanding. It ordinarily seems that they should have a human character only when they are conceived under human forms;[4] but even the most impersonal and the most anonymous are nothing else than objectified sentiments.

It is only by regarding religion from this angle that it is possible to see its real significance. If we stick closely to appearances, rites often give the effect of purely manual operations: they are anointings, washings, meals. To consecrate something, it is put in contact with a source of religious energy, just as to-day a body is put in contact with a source of heat or electricity to warm or electrize it; the two processes employed are not essentially different. Thus understood, religious technique seems to be a sort of mystic mechanics. But these material manoeuvres are only the external envelope under which the mental operations are hidden. Finally, there is no question of exercising a physical constraint upon blind and, incidentally, imaginary forces, but rather of reaching individual consciousnesses, of giving them a direction and of disciplining them. It is sometimes said that inferior religions are materialistic. Such an expression is inexact. All religions, even the crudest, are in a sense spiritualistic: for the powers they put in play are before all spiritual, and also their principal object is to act upon the moral life. Thus it is seen that whatever has been done in the name of religion cannot have been done in vain: for it is necessarily the society that did it, and it is humanity that has reaped the fruits.

But, it is said, what society is it that has thus made the basis of religion? Is it the real society, such as it is and acts before our very eyes, with the legal and moral organization which it has laboriously fashioned during the course of history? This is full of defects and imperfections. In it, evil goes beside the good, injustice often reigns supreme, and the truth is often obscured by error. How could anything so crudely organized inspire the sentiments of love, the ardent enthusiasm and the spirit of abnegation which all religions claim of their followers? These perfect beings which are gods could not have taken their traits from so mediocre, and sometimes even so base a reality.

But, on the other hand, does someone think of a perfect society, where justice and truth would be sovereign, and from which evil in all its forms would be banished for ever? No one would deny that this is in close relations with the religious sentiment; for, they would say, it is towards the realization of this that all religions strive. But that society is not an empirical fact, definite and observable; it is a fancy, a dream

4. It is for this reason that Frazer and even Preuss set impersonal religious forces outside of, or at least on the threshold of religion, to attach them to magic.

with which men have lightened their sufferings, but in which they have never really lived. It is merely an idea which comes to express our more or less obscure aspirations towards the good, the beautiful and the ideal. Now these aspirations have their roots in us; they come from the very depths of our being; then there is nothing outside of us which can account for them. Moreover, they are already religious in themselves; thus it would seem that the ideal society presupposes religion, far from being able to explain it.[5]

But, in the first place, things are arbitrarily simplified when religion is seen only on its idealistic side: in its way, it is realistic. There is no physical or moral ugliness, there are no vices or evils which do not have a special divinity. There are gods of theft and trickery, of lust and war, of sickness and of death. Christianity itself, howsoever high the idea which it has made of the divinity may be, has been obliged to give the spirit of evil a place in its mythology. Satan is an essential piece of the Christian system; even if he is an impure being, he is not a profane one. The anti-god is a god, inferior and subordinated, it is true, but nevertheless endowed with extended powers; he is even the object of rites, at least of negative ones. Thus religion, far from ignoring the real society and making abstraction of it; is in its image; it recalls all its aspects, even the most vulgar and the most repulsive. All is to be found there, and if in the majority of cases we see the good victorious over evil, life over death, the powers of light over the powers of darkness, it is because reality is not otherwise. If the relation between these two contrary forces were reversed, life would be impossible; but, as a matter of fact, it maintains itself and even tends to develop.

But if, in the midst of these mythologies and theologies we see reality clearly appearing, it is none the less true that it is found there only in an enlarged, transformed and idealized form. In this respect, the most primitive religions do not differ from the most recent and the most refined. For example, we have seen how the Arunta place at the beginning of time a mythical society whose organization exactly reproduces that which still exists to-day; it includes the same clans and phratries, it is under the same matrimonial rules and it practices the same rites. But the personages who compose it are ideal beings, gifted with powers and virtues to which common mortals cannot pretend. Their nature is not only higher, but it is different, since it is at once animal and human. The evil powers there undergo a similar metamorphosis: evil itself is, as it were, made sublime and idealized. The question now raises itself of whence this idealization comes.

Some reply that men have a natural faculty for idealizing, that is to

5. Boutroux, *Science et Religion*, pp. 206–7.

say, of substituting for the real world another different one, to which they transport themselves by thought. But that is merely changing the terms of the problem; it is not resolving it or even advancing it. This systematic idealization is an essential characteristic of religions. Explaining them by an innate power of idealization is simply replacing one word by another which is the equivalent of the first; it is as if they said that men have made religions because they have a religious nature. Animals know only one world, the one which they perceive by experience, internal as well as external. Men alone have the faculty of conceiving the ideal, of adding something to the real. Now where does this singular privilege come from? Before making it an initial fact or a mysterious virtue which escapes science, we must be sure that it does not depend upon empirically determinable conditions.

The explanation of religion which we have proposed has precisely this advantage, that it gives an answer to this question. For our definition of the sacred is that it is something added to and above the real: now the ideal answers to this same definition; we cannot explain one without explaining the other. In fact, we have seen that if collective life awakens religious thought on reaching a certain degree of intensity, it is because it brings about a state of effervescence which changes the conditions of psychic activity. Vital energies are over-excited, passions more active, sensations stronger; there are even some which are produced only at this moment. A man does not recognize himself; he feels himself transformed and consequently he transforms the environment which surrounds him. In order to account for the very particular impressions which he receives, he attributes to the things with which he is in most direct contact properties which they have not, exceptional powers and virtues which the objects of every-day experience do not possess. In a word, above the real world where his profane life passes he has placed another which, in one sense, does not exist except in thought, but to which he attributes a higher sort of dignity than to the first. Thus, from a double point of view it is an ideal world.

The formation of the ideal world is therefore not an irreducible fact which escapes science; it depends upon conditions which observation can touch; it is a natural product of social life. For a society to become conscious of itself and maintain at the necessary degree of intensity the sentiments which it thus attains, it must assemble and concentrate itself. Now this concentration brings about an exaltation of the mental life which takes form in a group of ideal conceptions where is portrayed the new life thus awakened; they correspond to this new set of physical forces which is added to those which we have at our disposition for the daily tasks of existence. A society can neither create itself nor recreate itself without at the same time creating an ideal. This creation is not a sort of work of supererogation for it, by which it would complete itself, being already formed; it is the act by which it is periodically made and remade. Therefore when some oppose the ideal society to the real society, like two antagonists which would lead us in opposite directions, they materialize and oppose abstractions. The ideal society is not outside of the real society; it is a part of it. Far from being divided between them as between two poles which mutually repel each other, we cannot hold to one without holding to the other. For a society is made up merely of the mass of individuals who compose it, the ground which they occupy, the things which they use and the movements which they perform, but above all is the idea which it forms of itself. It is undoubtedly true that it hesitates over the manner in which it ought to conceive itself; it feels itself drawn in divergent directions. But these conflicts which break forth are not between the ideal and reality, but between two different ideals, that of yesterday and that of to-day, that which has the authority of tradition and that which has the hope of the future. There is surely a place for investigating whence these ideals evolve; but whatever solution may be given to this problem, it still remains that all passes in the world of the ideal.

Thus the collective ideal which religion expresses is far from being due to a vague innate power of the individual, but it is rather at the school of collective life that the individual has learned to idealize. It is in assimilating the ideals elaborated by society that he has become capable of conceiving the ideal. It is society which, by leading him within its sphere of action, has made him acquire the need of raising himself above the world of experience and has at the same time furnished him with the means of conceiving another. For society has constructed this new world in constructing itself, since it is society which this expresses. Thus both with the individual and in the group, the faculty of idealizing has nothing mysterious about it. It is not a sort of luxury which a man could get along without, but a condition of his very existence. He could not be a social being, that is to say, he could not be a man, if he had not acquired it. It is true that incarnating themselves in individuals, collective ideals tend to individualize themselves. Each understands them after his own fashion and marks them with his own stamp; he suppresses certain elements and adds others. Thus the personal ideal disengages itself from the social ideal in proportion as the individual personality develops itself and becomes an autonomous source of action. But if we wish to understand this aptitude, so singular in appearance, of living outside of reality, it is enough to connect it with the social conditions upon which it depends.

Therefore it is necessary to avoid seeing in this theory of religion a simple restatement of historical materialism: that would be misunderstanding our thought to an extreme degree. In showing that religion is something essentially social, we do not mean to say that it confines itself to translating into another language the material forms of society and its immediate vital necessities. It is true that we take it as evident that social life depends upon its material foundation and bears its mark, just as the mental life of an individual depends upon his nervous system and in fact his whole organism. But collective consciousness is something more than a mere epiphenomenon of its morphological basis, just as individual consciousness is something more than a simple efflorescence of the nervous system. In order that the former may appear, a synthesis *sui generis* of particular consciousnesses is required. Now this synthesis has the effect of disengaging a whole world of sentiments, ideas and images which, once born, obey laws all their own. They attract each other, repel each other, unite, divide themselves, and multiply, though these combinations are not commanded and necessitated by the condition of the underlying reality. The life thus brought into being even enjoys so great an independence that it sometimes indulges in manifestations with no purpose or utility of any sort, for the mere pleasure of affirming itself. We have shown that this is often precisely the case with ritual activity and mythological thought.

But if religion is the product of social causes, how can we explain the individual cult and the universalistic character of certain religions? If it is born *in foro externo*, how has it been able to pass into the inner conscience of the individual and penetrate there ever more and more profoundly? If it is the work of definite and individualized societies, how has it been able to detach itself from them, even to the point of being conceived as something common to all humanity?

In the course of our studies, we have met with the germs of individual religion and of religious cosmopolitanism, and we have seen how they were formed; thus we possess the more general elements of the reply which is to be given to this double question.

We have shown how the religious force which animates the clan particularizes itself, by incarnating itself in particular consciousnesses. Thus secondary sacred beings are formed; each individual has his own, made in his own image, associated to his own intimate life, bound up with his own destiny; it is the soul, the individual totem, the protecting ancestor, etc. These beings are the object of rites which the individual can celebrate by himself, outside of any group; this is the first form of the individual cult. To be sure, it is only a very rudimentary cult; but since the personality of the individual is still only slightly marked, and but little value is attributed to it, the cult which expresses it could hardly be expected to be very highly developed as yet. But as individuals have differentiated themselves more and more and the value of an individual has increased, the corresponding cult has taken a relatively greater place in the totality of the religious life and at the same time it is more fully closed to outside influences.

Thus the existence of individual cults implies nothing which contradicts or embarrasses the sociological interpretation of religion; for the religious forces to which it addresses itself are only the individualized forms of collective forces. Therefore, even when religion seems to be entirely within the individual conscience, it is still in society that it finds the living source from which it is nourished. We are now able to appreciate the value of the radical individualism which would make religion something purely individual: it misunderstands the fundamental conditions of the religious life. If up to the present it has remained in the stage of theoretical aspirations which have never been realized, it is because it is unrealizable. A philosophy may well be elaborated in the silence of the interior imagination, but not so a faith. For before all else, a faith is warmth, life, enthusiasm, the exaltation of the whole mental life, the raising of the individual above himself. Now how could he add to the energies which he possesses without going outside himself? How could *he surpass himself merely by his own forces*? The only source of life at which we can morally re-animate ourselves is that formed by the society of our fellow beings; the only moral forces with which we can sustain and increase our own are those which we get from others. Let us even admit that there really are beings more or less analogous to those which the mythologies represent. In order that they may exercise over souls the useful direction which is their reason for existence, it is necessary that men believe in them. Now these beliefs are active only when they are partaken by many. A man cannot retain them any length of time by a purely personal effort; it is not thus that they are born or that they are acquired; it is even doubtful if they can be kept under these conditions. In fact, a man who has a veritable faith feels an invincible need of spreading it: therefore he leaves his isolation, approaches others and seeks to convince them, and it is the ardour of the convictions which he arouses that strengthens his own. It would quickly weaken if it remained alone.

It is the same with religious universalism as with this individualism. Far from being an exclusive attribute of certain very great religions, we have found it, not at the base, it is true, but at the summit of the Australian system. Bunjil, Daramulun or Baiame are not simple tribal gods; each of them is recognized by a number of different tribes. In a

Émile Durkheim

sense, their cult is international. This conception is therefore very near to that found in the most recent theologies. So certain writers have felt it their duty to deny its authenticity, howsoever incontestable this may be.

And we have been able to show how this has been formed.

Neighbouring tribes of a similar civilization cannot fail to be in constant relations with each other. All sorts of circumstances give an occasion for it; besides commerce, which is still rudimentary, there are marriages; these international marriages are very common in Australia. In the course of these meetings, men naturally become conscious of the moral relationship which united them. They have the same social organization, the same division into phratries, clans and matrimonial classes; they practice the same rites of initiation, or wholly similar ones. Mutual loans and treaties result in reinforcing these spontaneous resemblances. The gods to which these manifestly identical institutions were attached could hardly have remained distinct in their minds. Everything tended to bring them together and consequently, even supposing that each tribe elaborated the notion independently, they must necessarily have tended to confound themselves with each other. Also, it is probable that it was in inter-tribal assemblies that they were first conceived. For they are chiefly the gods of initiation, and in the initiation ceremonies, the different tribes are usually represented. So if sacred beings are formed which are connected with no geographically determined society, that is not because they have an extra-social origin. It is because there are other groups above these geographically determined ones, whose contours are less clearly marked: they have no fixed frontiers, but include all sorts of more or less neighbouring and related tribes. The particular social life thus created tends to spread itself over an area with no definite limits. Naturally the mythological personages who correspond to it have the same character; their sphere of influence is not limited; they go beyond the particular tribes and their territory. They are the great international gods.

Now there is nothing in this situation which is peculiar to Australian societies. There is no people and no state which is not a part of another society, more or less unlimited, which embraces all the people and all the States with which the first comes in contact, either directly or indirectly; there is no national life which is not dominated by a collective life of an international nature. In proportion as we advance in history, these international groups acquire a greater importance and extent. Thus we see how, in certain cases, this universalistic tendency has been able to develop itself to the point of affecting not only the higher ideas of the religious system, but even the principles upon which it rests.

4

Sociology in the Nineteenth Century – II

The development of French sociology followed a course that had no parallel elsewhere. One can discern in French sociology, in spite of the many forms it took, an unbroken strand of thought from the time of the Encyclopedists to the end of the nineteenth century, grounded on philosophical reflection.

The same can hardly be said of British sociology. It followed an erratic course, more in keeping with the insular, independent and eccentric British temperament. The early promise of a real and momentous breakthrough towards a new science of society was not fulfilled. In response to the final dissolution of the feudal system in Europe and the imminence of industrial transformation, a remarkable group of Scots thinkers, from a standpoint not too remote but sufficiently distant to view objectively the course of events, turned their attention to the analysis of the conditions and prospects of an industrial society. David Hume (1711–76) may be said to have been the founder of this movement of thought, which is associated equally with the names of John Miller (1735–1801), the author of *The Origin of the Distinction of Ranks*, Adam Ferguson (1723–1816), and Adam Smith (1723–90). Miller and Ferguson may be entitled to claim, with Montesquieu, to be the founders of modern sociology. The movement petered out, with Hume's social and political writings taking a subordinate place to the purely empirical philosophy which survived in the first half of the nineteenth century in the Associationist psychology, and with Miller's and Ferguson's works virtually forgotten.

It was perhaps Adam Smith, unknowingly, who gave the *coup de grâce* to the movement. It was no coincidence that the country which felt the greatest impact of the Industrial Revolution should be the one that gave the world a classic work on political economy.

Adam Smith's *Wealth of Nations* did not merely lay the foundation of the new science of economics; it had the effect of diverting British thought away from a concern with social problems and towards the elaboration and refinement of economic theory and principles. This was the preserve and prerogative of British writers and thinkers throughout the nineteenth century and right into the twentieth. Here it is that we can trace a continuous line of development from Adam Smith to J. M. Keynes. It was as though British society was completely taken by surprise at the enormous productive power that the steam machines were able to generate, and it was far too engrossed in the business of accumulating wealth to pay much attention to the social problems that the industrial process brought in its wake. The utilitarian doctrine could have been used to effect a change in attitude. It certainly was instrumental in bringing about legal reform, but it could also be interpreted – as indeed it was – to suit the convenience of the new industrial class. Even the genius of Buckle, under the influence of Comte, could not penetrate into the heart of the social problems, obsessed as it was by two extreme ideas. The first was the role geography plays in the formation, development and character of society; and the second was the static position of our moral thought in comparison with the dynamic forward movement of man's scientific and intellectual thought. It was a barren sociology, all the more regrettable in view of the vast erudition and learning that Buckle deployed in his unfinished work on the civilization of England.

Herbert Spencer was the greatest sociologist England produced. He dominated social thinking for half a century. He had to contend with two forces which, when combined, made his unequal struggle for recognition and acceptance hopeless from the start, and led to his undoing. The first was internal – a kind of demon which seized Spencer and prevented him from ever relaxing, driving him into a frenzy of writing with the object of embracing every known subject on earth, not forgetting even the Unknown. Carlyle's jibe that Spencer was 'the most unending ass in Christendom' was no doubt inspired by malice, but it contained a suspicion of truth. If Spencer had written less and reflected more his work might have withstood the assaults of criticism and given proof of sound and judicious judgement. The other force was external, and made him the victim of intellectual snobbery – a form of social snobbery which is perhaps the most offensive quality in the British character. Under the influence of the German academic tradition, British universities became the preserve of a select group of people to whom an interloper like Spencer, who had no academic standing, was by definition inferior, to be excluded from the charmed membership of a mutual-admiration club. In addition, the empiricism which is the greatest glory of British philosophy, to whose general viewpoint Spencer adhered, came under fire from the new idealistic movement in thought, again inspired by German philosophy. Poor Spencer did not have a chance. Rebuffed and mauled, he stood his ground unflinchingly, and his influence during his lifetime remained undiminished; but it died with him. His works since then have remained unread, and he himself has become a historic nonentity to whom not even the passing homage of respect is paid. In America, however, his works continued to make a considerable impact, while in France Durkheim's theory of society was directly influenced by Spencer's sociological theory, and Bergson's philosophy was partly a reaction to Spencer's biological theories.

Spencer's *Principles of Sociology*, in three volumes, took thirty years to complete. It was a masterpiece of vast erudition and boring irrelevancies. The central theme was the analogy between the biological organism and society, and here for the first time the theory of evolution, which was designed to explain the development of organic life, was applied to account for the development of human society. As a biological organism has to be studied in all its parts if it is to be understood, so society in all its various institutions, the development of the latter in their present form and their contribution to the continued life of society, has to be studied if society is to be understood as a functioning whole. For this purpose Spencer devised a conceptual scheme for analysis which is his greatest contribution to sociological theory. By the method of evolution Spencer traced the steps that led from a homogeneous simple (agricultural) undifferentiated society to one that is heterogeneous, complex (industrial) and differentiated. By what process such a change was effected Spencer failed to say.

Durkheim after him made a valiant effort to show how this occurred, but he too failed, because the premise from which they started was invalid. The simplicity which they attributed to an early stage of society was one of their own devising, defined and interpreted in their own terms, and could hardly refer to the cultural and institutional complexity which even a so-called primitive society can be seen to display. The whole thing was arbitrary and artificial, useful only for heuristic purposes.

Spencer's utilitarianism and his evolutionary bias of thought led him to take a view of progress that was paradoxically voluntaristic and deterministic. Man's conscious effort through a proper social organization and a political system strictly limited in function would enable him to enjoy the fruits of industrialization. Such material advancement is, however, the culmination of a long historical process of natural selection in which the survival of the fittest in human society operates in the same way as it does in nature. There is no limit to this movement towards a greater control of the environment for man's enjoyment. The optimism that such a view engendered was not tempered by any doubt or qualified by any reservations. Spencer's teeming brain was full of shrewd observations, ingenious hypotheses and confident explanations, but no system of thought was less systematic, because it failed to be conceptually coherent and logically consistent. Spencer welcomed industrialization for the benefits it could have, but failed to see that there is no logical connection between industrialization as such and its benefits, nor between industrialization as such and progress or happiness. Unlike de Tocqueville, who could project his mind towards a future fraught with serious problems, Spencer was totally unaware that there were any problems at all that would require a solution.

A movement of thought stemming from Darwin's theory of evolution and inspired by writers like Spencer grew up to play a considerable role in the second half of the nineteenth century. The use of biological analogies and the fascination with the idea of evolution as a process from a lower to a higher form of life was developed into a new and what the writers regarded as an entirely rational, scientific and water-tight theory of society. Social Darwinism, as the theory came to be called, was essentially an attempt to justify in Darwinian terms the existing individualistic laissez-faire, competitive and stratified system of society. To understand how social Darwinism arose, two strands of thought must be disentangled in Darwin's theory. The first was the perfectly straightforward, uncontroversial description of the process of evolution itself in terms of the appearance of new species. Such a description would make it possible to work out, as it were, the composition of species and to distinguish the relationship they hold to one another. Side by side with this morphologically important and useful exercise was an attempt to give an explanation of how and why each species appeared and survived. Here Darwin indulged in question-begging, misleading metaphors and unverifiable assumptions. This is how he put it: 'As many more individuals of each species are born than can possibly survive; and as, consequently, there is a frequently recurring struggle for existence, it follows that any being, if it vary however slightly in any manner profitable to itself, under the complex and sometimes varying conditions of life, will have a better chance of surviving, and thus be naturally selected' (*The Origin of Species*, 1859, p. 5). The redundant phrase 'naturally selected' was to become henceforth the cliché for a whole host of distorted ideas. Though the theory does not spell it out very clearly, two apparently simultaneous processes are at work in evolution. The first is this. Only those individuals survive who have a better chance of surviving owing to some superior quality they have acquired by chance. In other words, a species appears which is an advance on the older species through the acquisition of new variations which enable it to survive. In this case, the quality acquired is passed on by some mysterious inheritable mechanism to the next generation bringing about an improvement in the species or even changing it into an entirely new species for purposes of survival.

The second is this. Because the limited resources of nature cannot provide enough sustenance for all the individuals within the same species there must always be a few superior individuals who survive while the weaker and inferior ones do not, and this survival depends on the acquisition by a few of a favoured quality which makes them the fittest and the strongest of that species. This is what the Social Darwinists took 'natural selection' to mean. They were not concerned with the variations, environmentally determined as Darwin supposed, which improved and changed the stock. They were concerned to emphasize what they took to be an ineluctable fact of nature that the less fit varieties are eliminated in the struggle for existence while the fitter ones are maintained. Applied to society, this would imply that inequalities among individuals are natural, which in turn implies that the stratified divisions of society are natural too. Morality must be seen to be no more than a branch of biology. In society, it is right that certain individuals endowed with 'superior' gifts should possess and control property at the expense of those, the vast majority, who, lacking these gifts, must remain propertyless and subordinate. It is taken for granted that only those in possession and control of property are entitled to exercise power and domination. That is their 'natural' prerogative.

The doctrine, surprisingly enough, assumed an intellectually respectable form in the writings of Walter Bagehot (1826–77). For him the development of human society occurred through the possession and exercise of certain superior qualities which enabled one society, not only to survive, but to advance and dominate other societies. But in showing why certain societies remained backward and stagnant in comparison with others, an easy prey to conquest, assimilation or total annihilation, Bagehot never for a moment suggested that, even if this was historically an inevitable process of 'natural selection', it could not be reversed through the cultivation by all societies of the appropriate social qualities.

In its most extreme and usually degrading form, the doctrine, whose adherents were found mainly, for obvious reasons, among political writers, reached its apotheosis in America in the writings of Sumner. But even in America where, often for obvious reasons, it survived longest, it finally petered out without a whimper from sheer lack of scientific and moral credibility. For it was quite evident, as T. H. Huxley, himself a Darwinian, insisted, that the biological sphere of social life must not be confused with the ethical sphere, but kept totally distinct from it. Furthermore, far from being, as its early adherents supposed, in the liberal tradition of thought, the doctrine was soon revealed in its true colours as a conservative 'ideology', wedded to conformity, opposed to change and immune to modification.

However, there was one redeeming feature in the British scene. The conscience of the British people happens to be a little more sensitive to the iniquities and abuses of society than that of any other people. At the very moment when Spencer was extolling the virtues of industrialization and, true to the laissez-faire philosophy, warning against the interference of the state in the affairs of society, many thoughtful people were revolted by the degradation to which the working class – the vast majority of the population – was reduced by the inbuilt and free-for-all economic system. As wealth grew, the problems created by wealth also grew, in size and scope, and the price of industrial wealth was paid in malnutrition, ignorance, crime and disease. Bring to light these problems, and you would create that climate of opinion which would put pressure on existing agencies – governmental, public and private – to alleviate the burden of life. At no period in the history of the world did freedom of speech and expression prove such a boon in enabling people to discuss openly, without fear or hindrance, the serious problems that had assailed society, materially and spiritually. The aristocrats like Shaftesbury, writers like Carlyle, Ruskin and Arnold, philosophers like J. S. Mill and T. H. Green – all these, each in his own way, made their voices heard to arouse the public to a sense of guilt. The beneficial results of these cumulative efforts on the part of so many Victorians are a sufficient answer to the cheap jibe that comes so easily to the lips of ignorant people when the term 'Victorian' is used.

Of far-reaching significance was the impact made on a growing number of educated people by the meticulous detail and lifelike descriptions of East End life by Henry Mayhew, and works by others who followed in his footsteps, which disclosed the horrors of living from which the teeming community that formed the greater part of the population of London were suffering. Mayhew's work in particular was a survey of the London poor, the first of its kind, and the real ancestor of the more scientific and carefully compiled surveys of the social conditions of life in the larger towns with the aim of formulating proposals for remedial action. Here was something which was typically British, very much in tune with the national temperament, pragmatic, empirical, factual, and concerned with a specific practical issue. This movement was led by members of learned societies or by officially-constituted bodies of men as well as by interested individuals, who through speech and writing constituted a pressure group and were responsible in the long run for bringing about needed social reforms. There was hardly a political issue or a social problem – unemployment, slums, wages, working hours, trade unionism, education – on which some research was not done or survey made. This was the pattern of social writing in Britain right up to the present day. Such people as Booth, Rowntree, the Webbs, and members of the Fabian Society produced literature and created a climate of thought which was destined to have a profound influence on social policy, culminating as it did in the Welfare State of modern times. These writers were not interested in theory as such, and the distrust of the intellectual was more evident here than in any other branch of learning. While sociology was an established discipline in other countries, it was non-existent in England.

The paradox of sociology as an intellectual discipline is that it arose in modern times precisely in response to practical situations – the break-up of feudalism, the French Revolution, the Industrial Revolution, and the newly awakened desire for freedom and equality. The British movement towards social reform was not, therefore, so remote from sociological theory. It is true that a social problem that requires solution is not the same as a sociological problem that requires sorting out on the basis of sound logic and theory. Nevertheless the actual approach to a social problem is as a rule made from a sociological standpoint and through sociological means. The empirical studies into social problems, though producing no theory, have proved an indispensable source material for any sociological theory at all.

One branch of sociology, however, appears to have had a peculiar appeal to British writers. The penetration of the European into every nook and cranny of the habitable world brought to light an immense amount of material on primitive society. This gave rise to two related theories, the first concerning the origin of human institutions, and the second concerning the development and progress of society. The problem that these early anthropologists posed was this: if we take any institution as we know it – family, law, religion and so forth – and if we assume that it arises from somewhere, what was its earliest form? If we could find that out, we could then trace its development in the course of history, and discover how and why it was modified. Darwin's theory of evolution served as a model for this kind of investigation. The answer was very simple. The existing primitive societies must be survivals of the earliest type of human society, so that by studying them we would understand how our own institutions originated. Unlike American anthropologists, who studied Indian societies at first hand by actually living among the Indians, British anthropologists studied at home and formed their views on the basis of accounts they read of travellers, missionaries and others. It was taken for granted that all these societies were archaic, doomed to extinction because they were hidebound by false ideas and horrible practices. According to Frazer, our advanced science must have originated in the kind of magic practised by these people. In fact, magic was just a very inferior kind of science.

There was perhaps a more subtle reason for tracing the development of human institutions from the early beginnings as they have been preserved in primitive society to the present day. Wherever these writers turned, whatever account of a primitive society they studied, it was clear to them that religion, whether they called it animism, fetishism or totemism, played a predominant part in the life of primitive people. As it was impossible – or they made no effort – to give a rational explanation of these barbarous beliefs and practices, the conclusion seemed to follow that religion as such was irrational. Not daring to make a frontal attack on religion, they used this indirect but very convenient way of dealing what they deemed were fatal blows at religion, and of rationalizing their own agnosticism or repudiation of religion.

Nevertheless, in spite of their own far-fetched and often contradictory explanations of primitive beliefs and practices, the mere fact that primitive society was regarded as worthy of study was in itself a stimulus to anthropological research. In this respect the work of these nineteenth-century anthropologists, wildly unscientific and misguided as it was, laid the foundation of what later became in England the foremost school of anthropology in modern times.

In general, whether one considers the works of English writers in pure sociology like those of Buckle, Bagehot or Spencer, or the works of the social anthropologists like Tylor and Frazer, one can discover a common strand of thought underlying all of them. It could be defined simply as a confident and unbounded optimism in the prospects of society. Triumphant science and abundant wealth were an infallible index of a progress that was guaranteed to endure indefinitely. If the benighted savages of Africa and other parts of the world could be converted by force, casuistry or persuasion to our way of thinking, there could be some hope for them. If not, the sooner they disappeared the better. At no time did the suspicion enter the minds of these writers that the progress which they extolled was being bought at a heavy price. The harangues of Ruskin, Arnold, Morris and Mill could be ignored as the habitual diatribes of poets and writers; but scholars, reflecting the mood of the times, knew better. The gnawing doubt that assailed French thinkers hardly touched them.

In Germany sociology made a late start and took a more circuitous route to reach a stage of development where it could take its place beside the one that had already been established in France. The reason was not far to seek. The philosophical tradition in Germany was more firmly entrenched than anywhere else. It was Kant who gave philosophy that stamp of authority which made it the most intensively studied discipline in that country. Henceforth it was to philosophy that people turned for an answer to the great issues of the day.

Kant's own philosophical works contained views on law, society, moral life and equality which, if elaborated, might well have served as a theoretical basis for a new science of society. After his death philosophy in Germany developed in new directions, and Hegel's reputation soon eclipsed that of Kant. For a generation or so Hegel's system of thought was the starting point for every speculative doctrine concerning man and society. In particular, Hegel's view of the state provided no place for a theory of society as an ongoing process which follows its own laws. For Hegel the state was the political system par excellence;

it was the spirit of man incarnate, embodying its highest expression and making possible its highest fulfilment. A distinction, therefore, between state and society did not exist for him. It was only the state that counted, and society, like everything else, simply marched with the state. Thus all the institutions which are necessary for man's social welfare were institutions that were ultimately derived from the state, and had no status, meaning or justification without it. No sociology can be founded on such a doctrine. Certain attempts were made to escape from the stranglehold of Hegel's doctrine, the most successful of which was the work of Lorenz von Stein, who drew up the first draft of a systematic science of society. Influenced as he was by French socialism, von Stein advocated a programme of social reform to ward off the inevitable social revolution of the proletariat. He thought this could be undertaken by the upper classes with the assistance of the state, the state thus becoming a part, if a very integral part, of society.

However, it was Karl Marx who, having been brought up on and under the influence of Hegel's philosophy, turned Hegel upside down while employing an identical approach to the study of history; only for Marx it was not 'spirit' that gave rise to the developing institutions of society, but rather the material institutions of society, in particular its system of economic production, that were responsible for the way in which society lived and functioned, thought and felt. So Marx constructed a system of thought which embraced economics, politics, sociology and history in a way which made these disciplines all aspects of one total and comprehensive view of society, to which was given the name of historical materialism. According to this doctrine – and this is what constituted its distinguishing feature – every human society wherever it existed could be defined by its ruling class, which controls the means of production and dominates the other classes. The concept of class is, therefore, central to Marx's thought. Class for Marx has no meaning except in terms of its place in the process of production. The form which it assumes in society varies according to the technology that prevails. The present stage of society is one where the means of production, through land and factory ownership, are held by a few people, and the rest of the population have to sell their labour to the owners for the bare means of subsistence. This kind of economic or productive system is called capitalism. Society is therefore polarized between these two opposing classes, the bourgeoisie and the proletariat. The history of man is one of conflict between the rulers and the ruled, and we can expect the same conflict in an even more acute form to develop between these two classes. This will only be resolved when the proletariat, conscious of its strength and united in its purpose, overcomes the bourgeoisie.

What is interesting about this over-simplification of the problems of society is that Marx, like many another sociologist, was trying to show how consensus could be achieved in society. For him it could and will be achieved with the abolition of class; but unlike de Tocqueville, Marx never attempted to show what society would be like once consensus has been achieved.

Marx's theory was thus an evolutionary one of society, and also a theory of social structure and change. Again not unlike other sociologists, his theory emphasized a single determining factor in social change. This was both its strength and its weakness. Having polarized society in this way into two classes in conflict with each other, Marx was able to draw attention to an aspect of society that tended to be overlooked – those who sold their labour constituted the exploited and depressed class, and those who profited from that labour constituted another and different class. This was Marx's permanent contribution to sociological thought, and henceforth our whole attitude to society was influenced by Marx's view of class. At the same time, while Marx's analysis of the structure of capitalist society may have been applicable in certain respects to the conditions of his day, the different conditions of capitalist society of our day would render such an analysis altogether inapplicable.

One fundamental departure from Hegel's philosophy followed from this polarization. Since society is divided between rulers and ruled, exploiters and exploited, therefore government or the state is always included in the exploiting or ruling class. The distinction between society and the state is brought out very clearly in this theory. It follows, therefore, that with the abolition of all classes in society, government or the state will also be abolished.

The most interesting thing about Marxism is that it is deterministic in the sense that society develops and moves from one inevitable conflict to another. Once conflict is abolished it follows logically that there is no more movement, no more development, and no more history. This is another form of Utopianism which is not only impractical but inhuman.

Marx's works became a blueprint for revolutionary political action. As a result, neither economics nor political science nor sociology as an academic discipline were much influenced by them. It is only recently that sociology in particular has found Marx's methodology and approach, as well as his theory of classes, very powerful tools of thought. The dogmatists among the Marxists today are determined in their attempt to retain the pattern that Marx outlined to describe the capitalist society of his day in their explanation of present-day conditions. In spite, therefore, of the enormous changes that have occurred in the capitalist structure of society, they believe that these changes do not affect the pattern as such, and that society is still divided between the two classes, the owners of capital and the working class. Indeed, some reinforcement has been derived from the recent revival of Marx's view of alienation, which is seen as a necessary consequence of the division of society, and which is the condition of the majority of workers. One thing, however, which both Marxist dogmatists and their critics have in common is their agreement that the productive forces of society are of fundamental importance in their effect on people's lives and thoughts.

To return to the German scene. By the middle of the nineteenth century industrialization was beginning to make inroads into the age-old institutions of the Prussian state. Just when Hegel's influence was on the wane the state, through the growth of its power, was approaching more and more to the image that Hegel conceived for it. The natural sciences were beginning to attract the talent and effort of an increasing number of students and scholars. A revival of Kantianism in its more empirical, as opposed to its idealistic, aspects was now under way, to be given the name of Neo-Kantianism. A fresh look at the newly emerging pattern of society was called for.

Ferdinand Tönnies was the one who provided this, in a classical statement that has retained its force and validity to the present day. The very title of his book *Gemeinschaft und Gesellschaft* indicated its theme as well as the orientation of his thought. The two terms cannot be adequately translated without sacrifice of vital meaning: 'community' and 'association' would be the closest that one could get in English to describe them. They bore an uncanny resemblance to Durkheim's distinction between simple and complex societies, between mechanical and organic solidarity; but while Durkheim's intention, not very successfully carried out, was to demonstrate the essentially 'civilized' advance from simple to complex, Tönnies's view was that although *Gesellschaft* was an inevitable development of society, it was bought at a price that society could ill afford – the loss of vital societal elements that could only be found in a *Gemeinschaft*, that closely integrated and emotionally satisfying community of a small-scale society. This bold distinction between the community of a small-scale society and the association of a large-scale society cannot do justice to the analytical power that went to its formulation and elaboration, nor to the rich illustrative details which made it so real. What is important to remember is that Tönnies was the first sociologist to have taken an uncompromising stand against the new industrial order, pointing out that unless it retained some of the elements of the old it was irretrievably lost. Again unlike speculative thinkers before and after him, Tönnies founded his analysis on solid empirical data. The only disputable point was whether the distinction he drew was really as rigid as he made it out to be. He did not rule out a reconciliation between the two, although the signs were – and he produced perfectly valid arguments in support of his judgement – altogether to the contrary.

Again, Tönnies was one of the earliest pioneers of the empirical school of sociology. He carried out, among others, a number of surveys into dock labour at Hamburg. Thus he combined in himself a deep philosophical insight with a practical bent that was put to very good use. This was not altogether typical of German sociology. To a large extent the philosophical tradition of German thought gave sociology in Germany that historical and theoretical bias which was its most distinctive characteristic. Two of the greatest sociologists of all time, Weber and Simmel, were profound scholars imbued with a deep historical sense as well as philosophical thinkers of the highest calibre. In time Weber came to have a greater impact on sociology than Simmel. Less philosophical than Simmel's sociology, Weber's was more wide-ranging, touched on more aspects of society and pioneered a theoretically more fruitful approach to sociological problems. As a legal historian, which is how he began his academic career, he published as a young man a work on the legal aspects of trade in the Middle Ages that gave a foretaste of that comprehensive historical perspective which was such a marked feature of his later, more purely sociological works. He then turned to more contemporary problems, still legal-economic in character, concerning the archaic, anomalous position of the Junker class in the modern world of industry. A nervous breakdown interrupted his work for some ten years. When he resumed writing after his recovery, he applied himself with such unremitting vigour and vitality that in the course of a few years he produced outstanding original work that left an indelible mark on sociological thinking. At the same time his liberal sympathies were freely put to the service of progressive measures in German politics. He died in 1919, just when the new republican regime in Germany could ill afford to lose the support of a dedicated thinker of his stature.

Throughout his work Weber was preoccupied with the economic status of society. For him that was fundamental, and no theory of society would be complete and meaningful if it did not include a consideration of the economics of social organization. But in this matter he parted company from Marx, to whose views he brought all the powers he could muster of implacable hostility. Weber was the greater scholar of the two, and never made a statement without supporting it by irrefragable evidence. Hence arose those remarkable series of works on the sociology of religion beginning with his famous *Protestant Ethic and the Spirit of Capitalism*, in which he endeavoured to show that economic factors do not represent a constant and independent variable to which all others stand in dependence. They are one variable, and a very important one, in close relationship with others, affected by them as in fact it in turn can affect them. He found this to be the case in every great instance he studied – the rise of capitalism in Western Europe, the religions of Confucianism, Buddhism or ancient Judaism. As history willed it, Weber's theories were of interest only to scholars. Marx's theories were destined to shake the world to its foundations; but unlike Weber's theories, they will not stand the test of rigorous logic. Their success was due to their practical and simplicistic appeal, not to their truth.

One of Weber's most distinctive contributions was his view of sociology as a science. It is no exaggeration to say that sociology would have taken a different course if Weber's view had prevailed. Durkheim, as we have seen, in his concern to give sociology a scientific status so that it could take its place as a science alongside the other natural sciences, went so far as to maintain that a social fact studied by sociology must be regarded as – indeed, is in essence – a thing, as objective, external and concrete as any 'thing' studied by physics, chemistry or geology. He showed, too, how a social fact could be recognized as a thing through the element of constraint which governs every case of social interaction. He therefore had to eliminate all psychological factors in dealing with social facts, individual motives, intentions and dispositions. This is open to a very simple objection, namely that, try as we can, we can never define a social fact as we can define a thing in the natural sciences. It has neither shape nor form; it cannot be manipulated or become an object for experiment. Assuming that we know what a social fact is, and that we can observe it, we must never lose sight of the fact that it is also experienced by the individual. To put it on a par with the 'things' of the natural sciences is really misrepresenting it, and to think that it can be studied in the same way as things can be in the natural sciences is a presumptuous absurdity. Weber was the first sociologist to appreciate and make explicit the distinction between the natural sciences and sociology. The sociologist cannot study his subject without bringing to it a special form of 'understanding' (*Verstehen*). It in no way detracts from the importance of sociology to say that it is a special kind of science, and it would be doing it a disservice if we thought it could be studied by the same methods and techniques as are employed by the natural sciences, even on the erroneous assumption that there are identical methods and techniques for all the sciences. Moreover, because individuals in a social situation undergo certain experiences, the sociologist cannot avoid including in his purview the psychological causes and effects of these experiences. To do this he must not be thought of as attempting to reduce the subject to a form of psychologism whereby all the statements he makes can be converted to psychological statements. On the contrary, the psychological antecedents and components of social interaction would reinforce and clarify the essentially social causes of the act, not replace them. There is a further consequence. The sociologist is involved in the situation that he is studying in a way that a natural scientist is not when he is studying his objects. He does not merely observe, he has also to understand. It must have a 'meaning' to him. He has, in other words, to bring to bear on anything he studies a special mental endowment not given to everyone to possess, and only acquired after prolonged effort and training.

In these two respects Weber was diametrically opposed in his approach and methodology to Durkheim. Never afraid, as Durkheim was, that sociology might be overtaken by psychology, which made Durkheim define sociology in the way he did, Weber was quite certain that sociology would be a useless science unless it was grounded on history, psychology, philosophy, economics and law. These are all sources which feed the one broad stream which we call sociology.

The third characteristic of Weber's sociology was its methodology. Weber was acutely conscious, as others had been, of the vagueness and imprecision of terms used in ordinary discourse. To use them for analytical purposes it is necessary to redefine them to suit the sense that we desire to give them. Weber's use of key terms in his sociology must be seen in the light of the special meaning he gave them, quite different from the one they ordinarily bear. More importantly, in order to explain the causal relationships of social phenomena Weber used a method which was as original as it was confusing. The rich kaleidoscopic character of social phenomena makes it virtually impossible to study them as such without a grave risk of distortion or omission. What is needed, therefore, is to isolate certain essential features of a phenomenon so that (a) no one case of that phenomenon ever completely comprehends or corresponds to those features; and (b) every case of that phenomenon can be said to be one falling within this predetermined definition. This is the origin of Weber's famous 'typology', according to which a social phenomenon under study answers to, or is, a 'type' only of that phenomenon. There is no other way of understanding it nor of showing its relationship to other 'typical' phenomena, each of which is an 'ideal type' because it conforms to certain ideas formed about it, but is no less real for being 'ideal'.

When Weber wished to relate the Protestant ethic to the spirit of modern capitalism he was at pains to make clear that the Protestant ethic was not the complete ethic that prevailed in any one society at a particular period of history. If that were so, then in each particular case an account of the ethic would have to be so clarified as to take into account the variations through time and space. As such it would fail to provide a base for a historical judgement. What is needed for this purpose is a view of it, in other words an 'ideal type' which could be applied in a sufficiently general manner so that each particular case of it can be unmistakably identified as approximating to it. On this basis a valid judgement can be made and an explanatory model of it devised to trace a causal relationship between it and the other variables. The same holds with all the other concepts he used for sociological explanations. It is, however, questionable whether Weber's 'ideal type' is such a radical departure from the usually accepted and well-tried doctrines of scientific explanation. It would seem that Weber, to obtain his 'ideal type', selected only those features which he thought were essential for explanatory purposes. This is no more than what every scientist does when he defines an object. The definition never includes more than what serves the particular purpose in hand, and the object in this way can be regarded as an 'ideal type'.

Be this as it may, Weber employed the formidable techniques he devised to range over the most fundamental problems of society in a spirit of pure objectivity. It is here that we must refer to the controversy in which Weber was involved, and which rent

German social scientists into two hostile and warring factions. From the outset Weber, in speech and writing, took a firm stand in maintaining that sociology, like the other social sciences, must be value-free (*wertfrei*). This was misunderstood to mean that no personal judgement must intrude in social writing, that a writer must have no personal views of his own concerning the issues at hand, and that any expression of his attitudes and feelings must be rigorously suppressed. This was far from what Weber had in mind. What he was violently opposed to was the growing tendency among academic people to use their platform for propaganda and partisan purposes. He thought that this was not only prostituting one's integrity but was fatal to any kind of genuine scholarship. Nobody was more morally and passionately committed as a scholar to what he thought was the truth than Weber, and nobody was a greater apostle of the liberal ideal in society. He would not have been the scholar that he was without these moral qualities. Yet he was right in thinking that his works stood the test of scientific objectivity without reference to his own bias or partiality. The weakness of many of the professors in German universities, against whom he inveighed with all the power he could command, was precisely their failure to be objective in this sense. This is what caused the schism in the social sciences in Germany, a symptom of a deep-rooted division in the social and political life of Germany which came to a head in the events of the twenties and thirties.

To summarize Weber's contributions and achievements it is no exaggeration to say that the central issues in sociology – value, freedom, the development of western society – were first made explicit by Weber and dominated his thinking. In addition, the concrete problems he dealt with – the three-fold division of authority into *charismatic*, *traditional* and *rational-legal*, legitimation of power in the state and society, and bureaucracy, class and status, to take the most notable ones – feature prominently in modern sociology as being of fundamental importance, and Weber's inspiration, method and example are evident.

Georg Simmel's name is associated with what has come to be known as the Formal or Formalistic school of sociology. What is this formalism which is alleged to characterize Simmel's sociology?

A great deal has been written, some complimentary and some derogatory, concerning formalism in sociology. As it affects Simmel the misconception and misunderstanding would not have arisen if a closer study had been made of his methodology. To understand it we must take account of Simmel's general epistemological standpoint. He accepted Kant's view of what human knowledge consists of, namely, of content and form. According to Kant, what is given in knowledge is unorganized and diffuse. It is inchoate content which has to be given shape and form to be meaningful and take its place among other items of knowledge. When known, it must not be thought of as a discrete bit of knowledge just added to the other bits that we already have; it must enter into a meaningful relationship with them, to be transformed and to make in turn its own impact on them. An analogy would make this clearer. A wife who enters the household of her husband's family is not just one extra member added to the household, for new relationships are established, not only between the new member and the rest of the family, but also between the members of the family among themselves. The same applies to every new knowledge that we acquire. It affects and is affected by all the existing knowledge that we possess. Now this process of giving form and shape to the contents supplied to us in experience is made by the mind. Its constitution is such that it applies certain ways or forms of thought to the content of experience in order to appropriate it and make it part of its intellectual equipment. Simmel applied this epistemological scheme to society. According to him we can discern in every process of society a content and a form, and we can separate the two. The only thing to remember is that the form, unlike the form of knowledge, is part and parcel of the societal process. Thus we find in some personal or group interactions one person who dominates and others who are dominated. Having extracted what is of the essence of this in action, namely domination, we can study what this domination is, how it affects the person dominating and the persons dominated, and a host of other problems arising from this factor. Simmel's originality was to have discovered and classified the forms of the relationships in which groups enter. To make his object clearer he himself used a famous analogy with grammar. The kinds of words we use to make a sentence, the relationships that exist between the words of a sentence and between one sentence and another, all these make the subject matter of grammar, which is the only way of ascertaining whether what we are saying conforms to the appropriate rules, and so forth. Now we cannot isolate the grammatical forms from the contents, that is, the actual words we use, for this is the only way in which we can illustrate the rules of grammar. It is, therefore, misleading to think that Simmel was engaged in compiling what can be called a grammar of society; he did this but much more besides. To go behind the contents and discover the forms in which they enter is not to abandon the contents; it is to understand them better. He would not have been the versatile and profound scholar he was if he had confined himself only to a scholastic jugglery with conceptual schemes. His mind ranged far and wide – literature, poetry, sculpture, architecture, history, philosophy, ethics. He examined all of them; and not only this, he wrote on subjects which nobody before him had thought could be treated philosophically. Some of his brilliant essays were on such themes as *The Handle*, *The Key*, *The Stranger*; and nobody before him had brought out more the significance of money and the transformation experienced by man in the city, or 'metropolitan man'. Only recently the principles of conflict which he adumbrated have been made the basis of an extended modern theory of social conflict by L. Coser. In all these works Simmel displayed an extraordinary talent for bringing together instances that are seemingly so dissimilar, abstracting common features from them in order to serve as the basis for theoretical exposition.

Like his contemporaries Durkheim and Weber, Simmel was concerned to define the subject matter of sociology and to trace clear boundaries between sociology and the other social sciences, in particular between sociology on the one hand and psychology, social philosophy and history on the other. We are more or less familiar with the distinction today, but in Simmel's day it was vague, and he spelt it out brilliantly.

Herbert Spencer 1820–1903

Major works

Social Statics (1851)
First Principles of a New System of Philosophy (1862)
The Principles of Sociology (3 volumes, 1876–96)

The following extract is reprinted from Herbert Spencer, *The Study of Sociology* (New York: D. Appleton & Co., 1873), Chapter x, pp. 241–6.

Many years ago a solicitor, sitting by me at dinner, complained bitterly of the injury which the then lately-established County Courts were doing his profession. He enlarged on the topic in a way implying that he expected me to agree with him in therefore condemning them. So incapable was he of going beyond the professional point of view that what he regarded as a grievance he thought I also ought to regard as a grievance – oblivious of the fact that the more economical administration of justice of which his lamentation gave me proof, was to me, not being a lawyer, matter of rejoicing.

The bias thus exemplified is a bias by which nearly all have their opinions warped. Naval officers disclose their unhesitating belief that we are in imminent danger because the cry for more fighting ships and more sailors has not been met to their satisfaction. The debates on the purchase-system proved how strong was the conviction of military men that our national safety depended on the maintenance of an army-organization like that in which they were brought up and had attained their respective ranks. Clerical opposition to the Corn-Laws showed how completely that view which Christian ministers might have been expected to take was shut out by a view more congruous with their interests and alliances. In all class and sub-classes it is the same. Hear the murmurs uttered when, because of the Queen's absence, there is less expenditure in entertainments and the so-called gaieties of the season, and you perceive that London traders think the nation suffers if the consumption of superfluities is checked. Study the pending controversy about co-operative stores *versus* retail shops, and you find the shop-keeping mind possessed by the idea that Society commits a wrong if it deserts shops and goes to stores – is quite unconscious that the present distributing system rightly exists only as a means of economically and conveniently supplying consumers, and must yield to another system if that should prove more economical and convenient. Similarly with other trading bodies, general and special . . .

The class-bias, like the bias of patriotism, is a reflex egoism, and like it has its uses and abuses. As the strong attachments citizens feel for their nation cause that enthusiastic co-operation by which its integrity is maintained in presence of other nations, severally tending to spread and subjugate their neighbours, so the *esprit de corps* more or less manifest in each specialized part of the body politic prompts measures to preserve the integrity of that part in opposition to other parts, all somewhat antagonistic. The egoism of individuals leads to an egoism of the class they form; and besides the separate efforts, generates a joint effort to get an undue share of the aggregate proceeds of social activity. The aggressive tendency of each class thus produced, has to be balanced by like aggressive tendencies of other classes. The implied feelings do, in short, develop one another; and the respective organizations in which they embody themselves develop one another. Large classes of the community marked-off by rank, and sub-classes marked-off by special occupations, severally combine, and severally set up organs advocating their interests: the reason assigned being in all cases the same – the need for self-defence.

Along with the good which a society derives from this self-asserting and self-preserving action, by which each division and sub-division keeps itself strong enough for its functions, there goes, among other evils, this which we are considering – the aptness to contemplate all social arrangements in their bearings on class-interests, and the resulting inability to estimate rightly their effects on Society as a whole. The habit of thought produced perverts not merely the judgments on questions which directly touch class-welfare, but it perverts the judgments on questions which touch class-welfare very indirectly, if at all. It fosters an adapted theory of social relations of every kind, with sentiments to fit the theory; and a characteristic stamp is given to the beliefs on public matters in general. . . .

More recently, this same class-bias has been shown by the protest made when Mr Cowan was dismissed for executing the Kooka rioters who had surrendered. The Indian Government, having inquired into the particulars, found that this killing of many men without form of law and contrary to orders, could not be defended on the plea of pressing danger; and finding this, it ceased to employ the officer who had committed so astounding a deed, and removed to another province the superior officer who had approved of the deed. Not excessive punishment, one would say. Some might contend that extreme mildness was shown in thus inflicting no greater evil than is inflicted on a labourer when he does not execute his work properly. But now mark what is thought by one who displays in words the bias of the governing classes, intensified by life in India. In a letter published in the *Times* of May 15, 1872, the late Sir Donald M'Leod writes concerning this dismissal and removal: –

> All the information that reaches me tends to prove that a severe blow has been given to all chance of vigorous or independent action in future, when emergencies may arise. The whole service appears to have been astonished and appalled by the mode in which the officers have been dealt with.

That we may see clearly what amazing perversions of sentiment and idea are caused by contemplating actions from class points of view, let us turn from this feeling of sympathy with Mr Cowan, to the feeling of detestation shown by members of the same class in England towards a man who kills a fox that destroys his poultry. Here is a paragraph from a recent paper: –

> Five poisoned foxes have been found in the neighbourhood of Penzance, and there is consequently great indignation among the western sportsmen. A reward of 20*l*. has been offered for information that shall lead to the conviction of the poisoner.

So that wholesale homicide, condemned alike by religion, by equity, by law, is approved, and the mildest punishment of it blamed; while vulpicide, committed in defence of property, and condemned neither by religion, nor by equity, nor by any law save that of sportsmen, excites an anger that cries aloud for positive penalties!

I need not further illustrate the more special distortions of sociological belief which result from the class-bias. They may be detected in the conversations over every table, and in the articles appearing in every party-journal or professional publication. The effects here most worthy of our attention are the general effects – the effects produced on the minds of the upper and lower classes.

The following extracts are reprinted from Herbert Spencer, *The Principles of Sociology*, Volume II (New York: D. Appleton & Co., 1898), pp. 447–53, 456, 593–7.

212. This question has to be asked and answered at the outset. Until we have decided whether or not to regard a society as an entity; and until we have decided whether, if regarded as an entity, a society is to be classed as absolutely unlike all other entities or as like some others; our conception of the subject-matter before us remains vague.

It may be said that a society is but a collective name for a number of individuals. Carrying the controversy between nominalism and realism into another sphere, a nominalist might affirm that just as there exist only the members of a species, while the species considered apart from them has no existence; so the units of a society alone exist, while the existence of the society is but verbal. Instancing a lecturer's audience as an aggregate which by disappearing at the close of the lecture, proves itself to be not a thing but only a certain arrangement of persons, he might argue that the like holds of the citizens forming a nation.

But without disputing the other steps of his argument, the last step may be denied. The arrangement, temporary in the one case, is permanent in the other; and it is the permanence of the relations among component parts which constitutes the individuality of a whole as distinguished from the individualities of its parts. A mass broken into fragments ceases to be a thing; while, conversely, the stones, bricks, and wood previously separate, become the thing called a house if connected in fixed ways.

Thus we consistently regard a society as an entity, because, though formed of discrete units, a certain concreteness in the aggregate of them is implied by the general persistence of the arrangments among them throughout the area occupied. And it is this trait which yields our idea of a society. For, withholding the name from an ever-changing cluster such as primitive men form, we apply it only where some constancy in the distribution of parts has resulted from settled life.

213. But now, regarding a society as a thing, what kind of thing must we call it? It seems totally unlike every object with which our senses acquaint us. Any likeness it may possibly have to other objects, cannot be manifest to perception, but can be discerned only by reason. If the constant relations among its parts make it an entity; the question arises whether these constant relations among its parts are akin to the constant relations among the parts of other entities. Between a society and anything else, the only conceivable resemblance must be one due to *parallelism of principle in the arrangement of components*.

There are two great classes of aggregates with which the social aggregate may be compared – the inorganic and the organic. Are the attributes of a society in any way like those of a not-living body? or are they in any way like those of a living body? or are they entirely unlike those of both?

The first of these questions needs only to be asked to be answered in the negative. A whole of which the parts are alive, cannot, in its general characters, be like lifeless wholes. The second question, not to be thus promptly answered, is to be answered in the affirmative. The reasons for asserting that the permanent relations among the parts of a society, are analogous to the permanent relations among the parts of a living body, we have now to consider.

A Society Is an Organism

214. When we say that growth is common to social aggregates and organic aggregates, we do not thus entirely exclude community with inorganic aggregates. Some of these, as crystals, grow in a visible manner; and all of them, on the hypothesis of evolution, have arisen by integration at some time or other. Nevertheless, compared with things we call inanimate, living bodies and societies so conspicuously exhibit augmentation of mass, that we may fairly regard this as characterizing them both. Many organisms grow throughout their lives: and the rest grow throughout considerable parts of their lives. Social growth usually continues either up to times when the societies divide, or up to times when they are overwhelmed.

Here, then, is the first trait by which societies ally themselves with the organic world and substantially distinguish themselves from the inorganic world.

215. It is also a character of social bodies, as of living bodies, that while they increase in size they increase in structure. Like a low animal, the embryo of a high one has few distinguishable parts; but while it is acquiring greater mass, its parts multiply and differentiate. It is thus with a society. At first the unlikenesses among its groups of units are inconspicuous in number and degree; but as population augments, divisions and sub-divisions become more numerous and more decided. Further, in the social organism as in the individual organism, differentiations cease only with that completion of the type which marks maturity and precedes decay.

Though in inorganic aggregates also, as in the entire Solar System and in each of its members, structural differentiations accompany the integrations; yet these are so relatively slow, and so relatively simple, that they may be disregarded. The multiplication of contrasted parts in bodies politic and in living bodies, is so great that it substantially constitutes another common character which marks them off from inorganic bodies.

216. This community will be more fully appreciated on observing that progressive differentiation of structures is accompanied by progressive differentiation of functions.

The divisions, primary, secondary, and tertiary, which arise in a developing animal, do not assume their major and minor unlikenesses to no purpose. Along with diversities in their shapes and compositions go diversities in the actions they perform: they grow into unlike organs having unlike duties. Assuming the entire function of absorbing nutriment at the same time that it takes on its structural characters, the alimentary system becomes gradually marked off into contrasted portions; each of which has a special function forming part of the general function. A limb, instrumental to locomotion or prehension. acquires divisions and sub-divisions which perform their leading and their subsidiary shares in this office. So is it with the parts into which a society divides. A dominant class arising does not simply become unlike the rest, but assumes control over the rest; and when this class separates into the more and the less dominant these, again, begin to discharge distinct parts of the entire control. With the classes whose actions are controlled it is the same. The various groups into which they fall have various occupations: each of such groups also, within itself, acquiring minor contrasts of parts along with minor contrasts of duties.

And here we see more clearly how the two classes of things we are comparing, distinguish themselves from things of other classes; for such differences of structure as slowly arise in inorganic aggregates, are not accompanied by what we can fairly call differences of function.

217. Why in a body politic and in a living body, these unlike actions of unlike parts are properly regarded by us as functions, while we cannot so regard the unlike actions of unlike parts in an inorganic body, we shall perceive on turning to the next and most distinctive common trait.

Evolution establishes in them both, not differences simply, but definitely-connected differences – differences such that each makes the others possible. The parts of an inorganic aggregate are so related that one may change greatly without appreciably affecting the rest. It is otherwise with the parts of an organic aggregate or of a social aggregate. In either of these, the changes in the parts are mutually determined, and the changed actions of the parts are mutually dependent. In both, too, this mutuality increases as the evolution advances. The lowest type of animal is all stomach, all respiratory surface, all limb. Development of a type having appendages by which to move about or lay hold of food, can take place only if these appendages, losing power to absorb nutriment directly from surrounding bodies, are supplied with nutriment by parts which retain the power of absorption. A respiratory surface to which the circulating fluids are brought to be ærated, can be formed only on condition that the concomitant loss of ability to supply itself with materials for repair and growth, is made good by the development of a structure bringing these materials. Similarly in a society. What we call with perfect propriety its organization, necessarily implies traits of the same kind. While rudimentary, a society is all warrior, all hunter, all hut-builder, all tool-maker: every part fulfils for itself all needs. Progress to a stage characterized by a permanent army, can go on only as there arise arrangements for supplying that army with food, clothes, and munitions of war by the rest. If here the population occupies itself solely with agriculture and there with mining – if these manufacture goods while those distribute them, it must be on condition that in exchange for a special kind of service rendered by each part to other parts, these other parts severally give due proportions of their services.

This division of labour, first dwelt on by political economists as a social phenomenon, and thereupon recognized by biologists as a phenomenon of living bodies, which they called the 'physiological division of labour,' is that which in the society, as in the animal, makes it a living whole. Scarcely can I emphasize enough the truth that in respect of this fundamental trait, a social organism and an individual organism are entirely alike. When we see that in a mammal, arresting the lungs quickly brings the heart to a stand: that if the stomach fails absolutely in its office all other parts by-and-by cease to act; that paralysis of its limbs entails on the body at large death from want of food, or inability to escape; that loss of even such small organs as the eyes, deprives the rest of a service essential to their preservation; we cannot but admit that mutual dependence of parts is an essential characteristic. And when, in a society, we see that the workers in iron stop if the miners do not supply materials, that makers of clothes cannot carry on their business in the absence of those who spin and weave textile fabrics; that the manufacturing community will cease to act unless the food-producing and food-distributing agencies are acting, that the controlling powers, governments, bureaux, judicial officers, police, must fail to keep order when the necessaries of life are not supplied to them by the parts kept in order; we are obliged to say that this mutual dependence of parts is similarly rigorous. Unlike as the two kinds of aggregates otherwise are, they are unlike in respect of this fundamental character, and the characters implied by it . . .

223. From this last consideration, which is a digression rather than

a part of the argument, let us now return and sum up the reasons for regarding a society as an organism.

It undergoes continuous growth. As it grows, its parts become unlike: it exhibits increase of structure. The unlike parts simultaneously assume activities of unlike kinds. These activities are not simply different, but their differences are so related as to make one another possible. The reciprocal aid thus given causes mutual dependence of the parts. And the mutually-dependent parts, living by and for one another, form an aggregate constituted on the same general principle as is an individual organism. The analogy of a society to an organism becomes still clearer on learning that every organism of appreciable size is a society; and on further learning that in both, the lives of the units continue for some time if the life of the aggregate is suddenly arrested, while if the aggregate is not destroyed by violence, its life greatly exceeds in duration the lives of its units. Though the two are contrasted as respectively discrete and concrete, and though there results a difference in the ends subserved by the organization, there does not result a difference in the laws of the organization: the required mutual influences of the parts, not transmissible in a direct way, being, in a society, trasmitted in an indirect way.

Having thus considered in their most general forms the reasons for regarding a society as an organism, we are prepared for following out the comparison in detail . . .

270. But now let us drop this alleged parallelism between individual orgainizations and social organizations. I have used the analogies elaborated, but as a scaffolding to help in building up a coherent body of sociological inductions. Let us take away the scaffolding: the inductions will stand by themselves.

We saw that societies are aggregates which grow; that in the various types of them there are great varieties in the growths reached; that types of successively larger sizes result from the aggregation and re-aggregation of those of smaller sizes; and that this increase by coalescence, joined with interstitial increase, is the process through which have been formed the vast civilized nations.

Along with increase of size in societies goes increase of structure. Primitive hordes are without established distinction of parts. With growth of them into tribes habitually come some unlikenesses; both in the powers and occupations of their members. Unions of tribes are followed by more unlikenesses, governmental and industrial – social grades running through the whole mass, and contrasts between the differently-occupied parts in different localities. Such differentiations multiply as the compounding progresses. They proceed from the general to the special. First the broad division between ruling and ruled; then within the ruling part divisions into political, religious, military, and within the ruled part divisions into food producing classes and handicraftsmen; then within each of these divisions minor ones, and so on.

Passing from the structural aspect to the functional aspect, we note that so long as all parts of a society have like natures and activities, there is hardly any mutual dependence, and the aggregate scarcely forms a vital whole. As its parts assume different functions they become dependent on one another, so that injury to one hurts others; until, in highly-evolved societies, general perturbation is caused by derangement of any portions. This contrast between undeveloped and developed societies, arises from the fact that with increasing specialization of functions comes increasing inability in each part to perform the functions of other parts.

The organization of every society begins with a contrast between the division which carries on relations, habitually hostile, with environing societies, and the division which is devoted to procuring necessaries of life; and during the earlier stages of development these two divisions constitute the whole. Eventually there arises an intermediate division serving to transfer products and influences from part to part. And in all subsequent stages, evolution of the two earlier systems of structures depends on evolution of this additional system.

While the society as a whole has the character of its sustaining system determined by the character of its environment; inorganic and organic, the respective parts of this system differentiate in adaptation to local circumstances; and, after primary industries have been thus localized and specialized, secondary industries dependent on them arise in conformity with the same principle. Further, as fast as societies become compounded and re-compounded, and the distributing system develops, the parts devoted to each kind of industry, originally scattered, aggregate in the most favourable localities; and the localized industrial structures, unlike the governmental structures, grow regardless of the original lines of division.

Increase of size, resulting from the massing of groups, necessitates means of communication; both for achieving combined offensive and defensive actions, and for exchange of products. Faint tracks, then paths, rude roads, finished roads, successively arise; and as fast as intercourse is thus facilitated, there is a transition from direct barter to trading carried on by a separate class; out of which evolves a complex mercantile agency of wholesale and retail distributors. The movement of commodities effected by this agency, beginning as a slow flux to and re-flux from certain places at long intervals, passes into rhythmical, regular, rapid currents; and materials for sustentation distributed hither and thither, from being few and crude become numerous and elaborated. Growing efficiency of transfer with greater variety of transferred products, increases the mutual dependence of parts at the same time that it enables each part to fulfil its function better.

Unlike the sustaining system, evolved by converse with the organic and inorganic environments, the regulating system is evolved by converse, offensive and defensive, with environing societies. In primitive headless groups temporary chieftainship results from temporary war; chronic hostilities generate permanent chieftainship and gradually from the military control results the civil control. Habitual war, requiring prompt combination in the actions of parts, necessitates subordination. Societies in which there is little subordination disappear, and leave outstanding those in which subordination is great; and so there are produced, societies in which the habit fostered by war and surviving in peace, brings about permanent submission to a government. The centralized regulating thus evolved, is in early stages the sole regulating system. But in large societies which have become predominantly industrial, there is added a decentralized regulating system for the industrial structures; and this, at first subject in every way to the original system, acquires at length substantial independence. Finally there arises for the distributing structures also, an independent controlling agency.

Societies fall firstly into the classes of simple compound, doubly-compound, trebly-compound; and from the lowest the transition to the highest is through these stages. Otherwise, though less definitely, societies may be grouped as militant and industrial; of which the one type in its developed form is organized on the principle of compulsory co-operation, while the other in its developed form is organized on the principle of voluntary co-operation. The one is characterized not only by a despotic central power, but also by unlimited political control of personal conduct; while the other is characterized not only by a democratic or representative central power, but also by limitation of political control over personal conduct.

Lastly we noted the corollary that change in the predominant social activities brings metamorphosis. If, where the militant type has not elaborated into so rigid a form as to prevent change, a considerable industrial system arises, there come mitigations of the coercive restraints characterizing the militant type, and weakening of its structures. Conversely, where an industrial system largely developed has established freer social forms, resumption of offensive and defensive activites causes reversion towards the militant type.

271. And now, summing up the results of this general survey, let us observe the extent to which we are prepared by it for further inquiries.

The many facts contemplated unite in proving that social evolution forms a part of evolution at large. Like evolving aggregates in general, societies show *integration*, both by simple increase of mass and by coalescence and re-coalescence of masses. The change from *homogeneity* to *heterogeneity* is multitudinously exemplified: up from the simple tribe, alike in all its parts, to the civilized nation, full of structural and functional unlikenesses. With progressing integration and heterogeneity goes increasing *coherence*. We see the wandering group dispersing, dividing, held together by no bonds; the tribe with parts made more coherent by subordination to a dominant man; the cluster of tribes united in a political plexus under a chief with sub-chiefs; and so on up to the civilized nation, consolidated enough to hold together for a thousand years or more. Simultaneously comes increasing *definiteness*. Social organization is at first vague; advance brings settled arrangements which grow slowly more precise: customs pass into laws which, while gaining fixity, also become more specific in their applications to varieties of actions; and all institutions, at first confusedly intermingled, slowly separate, at the same time that each within itself marks off more distinctly its component structures. Thus in all respects is fulfilled the formula of evolution. There is progress towards greater size, coherence, multiformity, and definiteness.

Besides these general truths, a number of special truths have been disclosed by our survey. Comparisons of societies in their ascending grades, have made manifest certain cardinal facts respecting their growths, structures, and functions – facts respecting the systems of structures, sustaining, distributing, regulating, of which they are composed; respecting the relations of these structures to the surrounding conditions and the dominant forms of social activities entailed; and respecting the metamorphoses of types caused by changes in the activities. The inductions arrived at, thus constituting in rude outline an Empirical Sociology, show that in social phenomena there is a general order of co-existence and sequence; and that therefore social phenomena form the subject-matter of a science reducible, in some measure at least, to the deductive form.

Guided, then, by the law of evolution in general, and, in subordination to it, guided by the foregoing inductions, we are now prepared for following out the synthesis of social phenomena. We must begin with those simplest ones presented by the evolution of the family.

Sociology in the Nineteenth Century – II

The following extract is reprinted from Herbert Spencer, *The Principles of Sociology*, Volume I (New York: D. Appleton & Co., 1897), pages 8–15.

1. The behaviour of a single inanimate object depends on the co-operation between its own forces and the forces to which it is exposed: instance a piece of metal, the molecules of which keep the solid state or assume the liquid state, according partly to their natures and partly to the heat-waves falling on them. Similarly with any groups of inanimate objects. Be it a cart-load of bricks shot down, a barrowful of gravel turned over, or a boy's bag of marbles emptied, the behaviour of the assembled masses – here standing in a heap with steep sides, here forming one with sides much less inclined, and here spreading out and rolling in all directions – is in each case determined partly by the properties of the individual members of the group, and partly by the forces of gravitation, impact, and friction, they are subjected to.

It is equally so when the discrete aggregate consists of organic bodies, such as the members of a species. For a species increases or decreases in numbers, widens or contracts its habitat, migrates or remains stationary, continues an old mode of life or falls into a new one, under the combined influences of its intrinsic nature and the environing actions, inorganic and organic.

It is thus, too, with aggregates of men. Be it rudimentary or be it advanced, every society displays phenomena that are ascribable to the character of its units and to the conditions under which they exist. Here, then, are the factors as primarily divided.

2. These factors are re-divisible. Within each there are groups of factors that stand in marked contrasts.

Beginning with the extrinsic factors, we see that from the outset several kinds of them are variously operative. We have climate; hot, cold, or temperate, moist or dry, constant or variable. We have surface much or little of which is available, and the available part of which is fertile in greater or less degree; and we have configuration of surface, as uniform or multiform. Next we have the vegetal productions; here abundant in quantities and kinds, and there deficient in one or both. And besides the Flora of the region we have its Fauna, which is influential in many ways; not only by the numbers of its species and individuals, but by the proportion between those that are useful and those that are injurious. On these sets of conditions, inorganic and organic, characterizing the environment, primarily depends the possibility of social evolution.

When we turn to the intrinsic factors we have to note first, that, considered as a social unit, the individual man has physical traits, such as degrees of strength, activity, endurance, which affect the growth and structure of the society. He is in every case distinguished by emotional traits which aid, or hinder, or modify, the activities of the society, and its developments. Always, too, his degree of intelligence and the tendencies of thought peculiar to him, become co-operating causes of social quiescence or social change.

Such being the original sets of factors, we have now to note the secondary or derived sets of factors, which social evolution itself brings into play.

3. First may be set down the progressive modifications of the environment, inorganic and organic, which societies effect.

Among these are the alterations of climate caused by clearing and by drainage. Such alterations may be favourable to social growth, as where a rainy region is made less rainy by cutting down forests, or a swampy surface rendered more salubrious and fertile by carrying off water;[1] or they may be unfavourable, as where, by destroying the forests, a region already dry is made arid: witness the seat of the old Semitic civilizations, and, in a less degree, Spain.

Next come the changes wrought in the kinds and quantities of plant-life over the surface occupied. These changes are three-fold. There is the increasing culture of plants conducive to social growth, replacing plants not conducive to it; there is the gradual production of better varieties of these useful plants, causing, in time, great divergences from their originals; and there is, eventually, the introduction of new useful plants.

Simultaneously go on the kindred changes which social progress works in the Fauna of the region. We have the diminution or destruction of some or many injurious species. We have the fostering of useful species, which has the double effect of increasing their numbers and making their qualities more advantageous to society. Further, we have the naturalization of desirable species brought from abroad.

1. It is worth noting that drainage increases what we may figuratively call terrestrial respiration; and that on terrestrial respiration the lives of land-plants, and therefore of land-animals, and therefore of men, depend. Every change of atmospheric pressure produces exits or entrances of the air into all the interstices of the soil. The depth to which these irregular inspirations and expirations reach, is increased by freedom from water; since interstices occupied by water cannot be filled by air. Thus those chemical decompositions effected by the air that is renewed with every fall and rise of the barometer, are extended to a greater depth by drainage; and the plant-life depending on such decompositions is facilitated.

It needs but to think of the immense contrast between a wolf-haunted forest or a boggy moor peopled with wild birds, and the fields covered with crops and flocks which eventually occupy the same area, to be reminded that the environment, inorganic and organic, of a society undergoes a continuous transformation during the progress of the society; and that this transformation becomes an all-important secondary factor in social evolution.

4. Another secondary factor is the increasing size of the social aggregate, accompanied, generally, by increasing density.

Apart from social changes otherwise produced, there are social changes produced by simple growth. Mass is both a condition to, and a result of, organization. It is clear that heterogeneity of structure is made possible only by multiplicity of units. Division of labour cannot be carried far where there are but few to divide the labour among them. Complex co-operations, governmental and industrial, are impossible without a population large enough to supply many kinds and gradations of agents. And sundry developed forms of activity, both predatory and peaceful, are made practicable only by the power which large masses of men furnish.

Hence, then, a derivative factor which, like the rest, is at once a consequence and a cause of social progress, is social growth. Other factors co-operate to produce this; and this joins other factors in working further changes.

5. Among derived factors we may next note the reciprocal influence of the society and its units – the influence of the whole on the parts, and of the parts on the whole.

As soon as a combination of men acquires permanence, there begin actions and reactions between the community and each member of it, such that either affects the other in nature. The control exercised by the aggregate over its units, tends ever to mould their activities and sentiments and ideas into congruity with social requirements; and these activities, sentiments, and ideas, in so far as they are changed by changing circumstances, tend to remould the society into congruity with themselves.

In addition, therefore, to the original nature of the individuals and the original nature of the society they form, we have to take into account the induced natures of the two. Eventually, mutual modification becomes a potent cause of transformation in both.

6. Yet a further derivative factor of extreme importance remains. I mean the influence of the super-organic environment – the action and reaction between a society and neighbouring societies.

While there exist only small, wandering, unorganized hordes, the conflicts of these with one another work no permanent changes of arrangement in them. But when there have arisen the definite chieftainships which frequent conflicts tend to initiate, and especially when the conflicts have ended in subjugations, there arise the rudiments of political organization; and, as at first, so afterwards, the wars of societies with one another have all-important effects in developing social structures, or rather, certain of them. For I may here, in passing, indicate the truth to be hereafter exhibited in full, that while the industrial organization of a society is mainly determined by its inorganic and organic environments, its governmental organization is mainly determined by its superorganic environment – by the actions of those adjacent societies with which it carries on the struggle for existence.

7. There remains in the group of derived factors one more, the potency of which can scarcely be over-estimated. I mean that accumulation of super-organic products which we commonly distinguish as artificial, but which, philosophically considered, are no less natural than all other products of evolution. There are several orders of these.

First come the material appliances, which beginning with roughly-chipped flints, end in the complex automatic tools of an engine-factory driven by steam; which from boomerangs rise to eighty-ton guns; which from huts of branches and grass grow to cities with their palaces and cathedrals. Then we have language, able at first only to eke out gestures in communicating simple ideas, but eventually becoming capable of expressing involved conceptions with precision. While from that stage in which it conveys thoughts only by sounds to one or a few persons, we pass through picture-writing up to steam-printing: multiplying indefinitely the numbers communicated with, and making accessible in voluminous literatures the ideas and feelings of countless men in various places and times. Concomitantly there goes on the development of knowledge, ending in science. Numeration on the fingers grows into far-reaching mathematics; observation of the moon's changes leads in time to a theory of the solar system; and there successively arise sciences of which not even the germs could at first be detected. Meanwhile the once few and simple customs, becoming more numerous, definite, and fixed, end in systems of laws. Rude superstitions initiate elaborate mythologies, theologies, cosmogonies. Opinion getting embodied in creeds, gets embodied, too, in accepted codes of ceremony and conduct, and established social sentiments. And then there slowly evolve also the products we call aesthetic; which of themselves form a highly-complex group. From necklaces of fishbones we advance to dresses elaborate, gorgeous, and infinitely varied; out of discordant war-chants come symphonies and operas; cairns develop into magnificent temples; in place of caves with rude markings there arise at length galleries of paintings; and the recital of a chief's deeds with mimetic accompaniment gives origin to epics, dramas, lyrics, and the vast mass of poetry, fiction, biography, and history.

These various orders of super-organic products, each developing within itself new genera and species while growing into a larger whole, and each acting on the other orders while reacted on by them, constitute an immensely-voluminous, immensely-complicated, and immensely-powerful set of influences. During social evolution they are ever modifying individuals and modifying society, while being modified by both. They gradually form what we may consider either as a non-vital part of the society itself, or else as a secondary environment, which eventually becomes more important than the primary environments – so much more important that there arises the possibility of carrying on a high kind of social life under inorganic and organic conditions which originally would have prevented it.

8. Such are the factors in outline. Even when presented under this most general form, the combination of them is seen to be of an involved kind.

Recognizing the primary truth that social phenomena depend in part on the natures of the individuals and in part on the forces the individuals are subject to, we see that these two fundamentally-distinct sets of factors, with which social changes commence, give origin to other sets as social changes advance. The pre-established environing influences, inorganic and organic, which are at first almost unalterable, become more and more altered by the actions of the evolving society. Simple growth of population brings into play fresh causes of transformation that are increasingly important. The influences which the society exerts on the natures of its units, and those which the units exert on the nature of society, incessantly co-operate in creating new elements. As societies progress in size and structure, they work on one another, now by their war-struggles and now by their industrial intercourse, profound metamorphoses. And the ever-accumulating, ever-complicating super-organic products, material and mental, constitute a further set of factors which become more and more influential causes of change. So that, involved as the factors are at the beginning, each step in advance increases the involution, by adding factors which themselves grow more complex while they grow more powerful.

Karl Marx 1818–83

Major works

The Poverty of Philosophy (1847)
The Communist Manifesto (1848)
Capital: A Critique of Political Economy (3 volumes, 1867–79)

The following extracts are reprinted from Karl Marx, *A Contribution to the Critique of Political Economy*, translated by N. I. Stone, from the second German edition (New York: International Library Publishing Co., 1904), Appendix, sections 1, 2, pp. 265–9, 291–2, Author's Preface, 11–13.

The subject of our discussion is first of all *material* production by individuals as determined by society, which naturally constitutes the starting point. The individual and isolated hunter or fisher who forms the starting point with Smith and Ricardo, belongs to the insipid illusions of the eighteenth century. They are Robinsonades which do not by any means represent, as students of the history of civilization imagine, a reaction against over-refinement and a return to a misunderstood natural life. They are no more based on such a naturalism than is Rousseau's 'contrat social,' which makes naturally independent individuals come in contact and have mutual intercourse by contract. They are the fiction and only the aesthetic fiction of the small and great Robinsonades. They are, moreover, the anticipation of 'bourgeois society,' which had been in course of development since the sixteenth century and made gigantic strides towards maturity in the eighteenth. In this society of free competition the individual appears free from the bonds of nature, etc., which in former epochs of history made him a part of a definite, limited human conglomeration. To the prophets of the eighteenth century, on whose shoulders Smith and Ricardo are still standing, this eighteenth century individual, constituting the joint product of the dissolution of the feudal form of society and of the new forces of production which has developed since the sixteenth century, appears as an ideal whose existence belongs to the past; not as a result of history, but as its starting point.

Since that individual appeared to be in conformity with nature and [corresponded] to their conception of human nature, [he was regarded] not as a product of history, but of nature. This illusion has been characteristic of every new epoch in the past. Steuart, who, as an aristocrat, stood more firmly on historical ground, contrary to the spirit of the eighteenth century, escaped this simplicity of view. The further back we go into history, the more the individual and, therefore, the producing individual seems to depend on and constitute a part of a larger whole: at first it is, quite naturally, the family and the clan, which is but an enlarged family; later on, it is the community growing up in its different forms out of the clash and the amalgamation of clans. It is but in the eighteenth century, in 'bourgeois society,' that the different forms of social union confront the individual as a mere means to his private ends, as an outward necessity. But the period in which this view of the isolated individual becomes prevalent, is the very one in which the inter-relations of society (general from this point of view) have reached the highest state of development. Man is in the most literal sense of the word a *zoon politikon* not only a social animal, but an animal which can develop into an individual only in society. Production by isolated individuals outside of society – something which might happen as an exception to a civilized man who by accident got into the wilderness and already dynamically possessed within himself the forces of society – is as great an absurdity as the idea of the development of language without individuals living together and talking to one another. We need not dwell on this any longer. It would not be necessary to touch upon this point at all, were not the vagary which had its justification and sense with the people of the eighteenth century transplanted in all earnest into the field of political economy by Bastiat, Carey, Proudhon and others. Proudhon and others naturally find it very pleasant, when they do not know the historical origin of a certain economic phenomenon, to give it a quasi historical-philosophical explanation by going into mythology. Adam or Prometheus hit upon the scheme cut and dried, whereupon it was adopted, etc. Nothing is more tediously dry than the dreaming *locus communis*.

Whenever we speak, therefore, of production, we always have in mind production at a certain stage of social development, or production by social individuals. Hence, it might seem that in order to speak of production at all, we must either trace the historical process of development through its various phases, or declare at the outset that we are dealing with a certain historical period, as, e.g., with modern capitalistic production which, as a matter of fact, constitutes the subject proper of this work. But all stages of production have certain land-marks in common, common purposes. *Production in general* is an abstraction, but it is a rational abstraction, in so far as it singles out and fixes the common features, thereby saving us repetition. Yet these general or common features discovered by comparison constitute something very complex, whose constituent elements have different destinations. Some of these elements belong to all epochs, others are common to a few. Some of them are common to the most modern as well as to the most ancient epochs. No production is conceivable without them; but while even the most completely developed languages have laws and conditions in common with the least developed ones, what is characteristic of their development are the points of departure from the general and common. The conditions which generally govern production must be differentiated in order that the essential points of difference be not lost sight of in view of the general uniformity which is due to the fact that the subject, mankind, and the object, nature, remain the same. The failure to remember this one fact is the source of all the wisdom of modern economists who are trying to prove the eternal nature and harmony of existing social conditions ...

The result we arrive at is not that production, distribution, exchange and consumption are identical, but that they are all members of one entity, different sides of one unit. Production predominates not only over production itself in the opposite sense of that term, but over the other elements as well. With it the process constantly starts over again. That exchange and consumption can not be the predominating elements is self evident. The same is true of distribution in the narrow sense of distribution of products; as for distribution in the sense of distribution of the agents of production, it is itself but a factor of production. A definite [form of] production thus determines the [forms of] consumption, distribution, exchange, and *also the mutual relations between these various elements*. Of course, production *in its one-sided form* is in its turn influenced by other elements; e.g. with the expansion of the market, i.e. of the sphere of exchange, production grows in volume and is subdivided to a greater extent.

With a change in distribution, production undergoes a change; as e.g. in the case of concentration of capital, of a change in the distribution of population in city and country, etc. Finally, the demands of consumption also influence production. A mutual interaction takes place between the various elements. Such is the case with every organic body ...

In the social production which men carry on they enter into definite relations that are indispensable and independent of their will; these relations of production correspond to a definite state of development of their material powers of production. The sum total of these relations of production constitutes the economic structure of society – the real foundation, on which rise legal and political super-structures and to which correspond definite forms of social consciousness. The mode of production in material life determines the general character of the social, political and spiritual processes of life. It is not the consciousness of men that determines their existence, but, on the contrary, their social existence determines their consciousness. At a certain stage of their development, the material forces of production in society come in conflict with the existing relations of production or – what is but a legal expression for the same thing – with the property relations within which they had been at work before. From forms of development of the forces of production these relations turn into their fetters. Then comes the period of social revolution. With the change of the economic foundation the entire immense superstructure is more or less rapidly transformed. In considering such transformations the distinction should always be made between the material transformation of the economic conditions of production which can be determined with the precision of natural science, and the legal, political, religious, aesthetic or philosophic – in short ideological forms in which men become conscious of this conflict and fight it out. Just as our opinion of an individual is not based on what he thinks of himself, so can we not judge of such a period of transformation by its own consciousness: on the contrary, this consciousness must rather be explained from the contradictions of material life, from the existing conflict between the social forces of production and the relations of production. No social order ever disappears before all the productive forces, for which there is room in it, have been developed; and new higher relations of production never appear before the material conditions of their existence have matured in the womb of the old society. Therefore, mankind always takes up only such problems as it can solve; since, looking at the matter more closely, we will always find that the problem itself arises only when the material conditions necessary for its solution already exist or are at least in the process of formation. In broad outlines we can designate the Asiatic, the ancient, the feudal and the modern bourgeois methods of production as so many epochs in the progress of the economic formation of society. The bourgeois relations of production are the last antagonistic form of social process of production – antagonistic not in the sense of individual antagonism, but of one arising from conditions surrounding the life of individuals in society; at the same time the productive forces developing in the womb of bourgeois society create the material conditions for the solution of that antagonism. This social formation constitutes, therefore, the closing chapter of the pre-historic stage of human society.

Karl Marx

The following extract is reprinted from Karl Marx, *Manifesto of the Communist Party* (Chicago: Charles H. Kerr, 1888), section 1, pp. 12–32.

The history of all hitherto existing society[1] is the history of class struggles.

Freemen and slave, patrician and plebeian, lord and serf, guild-master[2] and journeyman, in a word, oppressor and oppressed, stood in constant opposition to one another, carried on an uninterrupted, now hidden, now open fight, a fight that each time ended, either in a revolutionary re-constitution of society at large, or in the common ruin of the contending classes.

In the earlier epochs of history, we find almost everywhere a complicated arrangement of society into various orders, a manifold gradation of social rank. In ancient Rome we have patricians, knights, plebeians, slaves; in the middle ages, feudal lords, vassals, guild-masters, journeymen, apprentices, serfs; in almost all of these classes, again, subordinate gradations.

The modern bourgeois[3] society that has sprouted from the ruins of feudal society, has not done away with class antagonisms. It has but established new classes, new conditions of oppression, new forms of struggle in place of the old ones.

1. That is, all written history. In 1847, the pre-history of society, the social organization existing previous to recorded history, was all but unknown. Since then Haxthausen discovered common ownership of land in Russia, Maurer proved it to be the social foundation from which all Teutonic races started in history, and by and bye village communities were found to be, or to have been, the primitive form of society everywhere from India to Ireland. The inner organization of this primitive Communistic society was laid bare, in its typical form, by Morgan's crowning discovery of the true nature of the gens and its relation to tribe. With the dissolution of these primaeval communities society begins to be differentiated into separate and finally antagonistic classes. I have attempted to retrace this process of dissolution in: 'Der Ursprung der Familie, des Privateigenthums und des Staats,' 2nd edit. Stuttgart 1886.

2. Guild-master, that is a full member of a guild, a master within, not a head of, a guild.

3. By bourgeoisie is meant the class of modern Capitalists, owners of the means of social production and employers of wage-labour. By proletariat, the class of modern wage-labourers who, having no means of production of their own, are reduced to selling their labour-power in order to live.

Our epoch, the epoch of the bourgeoisie, possesses, however, this distinctive feature; it has simplified the class antagonisms. Society as a whole is more and more splitting up into two great hostile camps, into two great classes directly facing each other: Bourgeoisie and Proletariat.

From the serfs of the middle ages sprang the chartered burghers of the earliest towns. From these burgesses the first elements of the bourgeoisie were developed.

The discovery of America, the rounding of the Cape, opened up fresh ground for the rising bourgeoisie. The East-Indian and Chinese markets, the colonization of America, trade with the colonies, the increase in the means of exchange and in commodities generally, gave to commerce, to navigation, to industry, an impulse never before known, and thereby, to the revolutionary element in the tottering feudal society, a rapid development.

The feudal system of industry, under which industrial production was monopolized by close guilds, now no longer sufficed for the growing wants of the new markets. The manufacturing system took its place. The guild-masters were pushed on one side by the manufacturing middle-class; division of labour between the different corporate guilds vanished in the face of division of labour in each single workshop.

Meantime the markets kept ever growing, the demand, ever rising, Even manufacture no longer sufficed. Thereupon, steam and machinery revolutionized industrial production. The place of manufacture was taken by the giant, Modern Industry, the place of the industrial middle-class, by industrial millionaires, the leaders of whole industrial armies, the modern bourgeois.

Modern industry has established the world-market, for which the discovery of America paved the way. This market has given an immense development to commerce, to navigation, to communication by land. This development has, in its turn, reacted on the extension of industry; and in proportion as industry, commerce, navigation, railways extended, in the same proportion the bourgeoisie developed, increased its capital and pushed into the background every class handed down from the Middle Ages.

We see, therefore, how the modern bourgeoisie is itself the product of a long course of development, of a series of revolutions in the modes of production and of exchange.

Each step in the development of the bourgeoisie was accompanied by a corresponding political advance of that class. An oppressed class under the sway of the feudal nobility, an armed and self-governing association in the mediaeval commune,[4] here independent urban republic (as in Italy and Germany), there taxable 'third estate' of the monarchy (as in France), afterwards, in the period of manufacture proper, serving either the semi-feudal or the absolute monarchy as a counterpoise against the nobility, and, in fact, corner stone of the great monarchies in general, the bourgeoisie has at last, since the establishment of Modern Industry and of the world-market, conquered for itself, in the modern representative State, exclusive political sway. The executive of the modern State is but a committee for managing the common affairs of the whole bourgeoisie.

The bourgeoisie, historically, has played a most revolutionary part.

The bourgeoisie, wherever it has got the upper hand, has put an end to all feudal patriarchal, idyllic relations. It has pitilessly torn asunder the motley feudal ties that bound man to his 'natural superiors' and has left remaining no other nexus between man and man than naked self-interest, than callous 'cash payment.' It has drowned the most heavenly ecstacies of religious fervour, of chivalrous enthusiasm, of philistine sentimentalism, in the icy water of egotistical calculation. It has resolved personal worth into exchange value, and in place of the numberless indefeasible chartered freedoms, has set us that single, unconscionable freedom – Free Trade. In one word, for political exploitation, veiled by religious and political illusions, it has substituted naked, shameless, direct, brutal exploitation.

The bourgoisie has stripped of its halo every occupation hitherto honoured and looked up to with reverent awe. It has converted the physician, the lawyer, the priest, the poet, the man of science, into its paid wage-labourers.

The bourgeoisie has torn away from the family its sentimental veil, and has reduced the family relation to a mere money relation.

The bourgeoisie has disclosed how it came to pass that the brutal display of vigour in the Middle Ages, which Reactionists so much admire, found its fitting complement in the most slothful indolence. It has been the first to shew what man's activity can bring about. It has accomplished wonders far surpassing Egyptian pyramids, Roman aqueducts, and Gothic cathedrals; it has conducted expeditions that put in the shade all former Exoduses of nations and crusades.

The bourgeoisie cannot exist without constantly revolutionizing the

4. 'Commune' was the name, taken in France, by the nascent towns even before they had conquered from their feudal lords and masters, local self-government and political rights as 'the Third Estate.' Generally speaking, for the economical development of the bourgeoisie, England is here taken as the typical country, for its political development, France.

instruments of production, and thereby the relations of production, and with them the whole relations of society. Conservation of the old modes of production in unaltered form, was, on the contrary, the first condition of existence for all earlier industrial classes. Constant revolutionizing of production, uninterrupted disturbance of all social conditions, everlasting uncertainty and agitation distinguish the bourgeois epoch from all earlier ones. All fixed, fast-frozen relations, with their train of ancient and venerable prejudices and opinions, are swept away, all new-formed ones become antiquated before they can ossify. All that is solid melts into air, all that is holy is profaned, and man is at last compelled to face with sober senses, his real conditions of life, and his relations with his kind,

The need of a constantly expanding market for its products chases the bourgeoisie over the whole surface of the globe. It must nestle everywhere, settle everywhere, establish connexions everywhere.

The bourgeoisie has through its exploitation of the world-market given a cosmopolitan character to production and consumption in every country. To the great chagrin of Re-actionists, it has drawn from under the feet of industry the national ground on which it stood. All old-established national industries have been destroyed or are daily being destroyed. They are dislodged by new industries, whose introduction becomes a life and death question for all civilized nations, by industries that no longer work up indigenous raw material, but raw material drawn from the remotest zones; industries whose products are consumed, not only at home, but in every quarter of the globe. In place of the old wants, satisfied by the productions of the country, we find new wants, requiring for their satisfaction the products of distant lands and climes. In place of the old local and national seclusion and self-sufficiency, we have intercourse in every direction, universal interdependence of nations. And as in material, so also in intellectual production. The intellectual creations of individual nations become common property. National one-sidedness and narrow-mindedness become more and more impossible, and from the numerous national and local literatures there arises a world-literature.

The bourgeoisie, by the rapid improvement of all instruments of production, by the immensely facilitated means of communication, draws all, even the most barbarian, nations into civilization. The cheap prices of its commodities are the heavy artillery with which it batters down all Chinese walls, with which it forces the barbarians' intensely obstinate hatred of foreigners to capitulate. It compels all nations, on pain of extinction, to adopt the bourgeois mode of production; it compels them to introduce what it calls civilization into their midst, i.e., to become bourgeois themselves. In a word, it creates a world after its own image.

The bourgeoisie has subjected the country to the rule of the towns. It has created enormous cities, has greatly increased the urban population as compared with the rural, and has thus rescued a considerable part of the population from the idiocy of rural life. Just as it has made the country dependent on the towns, so it has made barbarian and semi-barbarian countries dependent on the civilized ones, nations of peasants on nations of bourgeois, the East on the West.

The bourgeoisie keeps more and more doing away with the scattered state of the population, of the means of productions, and of property. It has agglomerated population, centralized means of production, and has concentrated property in a few hands. The necessary consequence of this was political centralization. Independent, or but loosely connected provinces, with separate interests, laws, governments and systems of taxation, became lumped together in one nation, with one government, one code of laws, one national class-interest, one frontier and one customs-tariff.

The bourgeoisie, during its rule of scarce one hundred years, has created more massive and more colossal productive forces than have all preceding generations together. Subjection of Nature's forces to man, machinery, application of chemistry to industry and agriculture, steam-navigation, railways, electric telegraphs, clearing of whole continents for cultivation, canalization of rivers, whole populations conjured out of the ground – what earlier century had even a presentiment that such productive forces slumbered in the lap of social labour?

We see then: the means of production and of exchange on whose foundation the bourgeoisie built itself up, were generated in feudal society. At a certain stage in the development of these means of production and of exchange, the conditions under which feudal society produced and exchanged, the feudal organization of agriculture and manufacturing industry, in one word, the feudal relations of property became no longer compatible with the already developed productive forces; they became so many fetters. They had to burst asunder; they were burst asunder.

Into their places stepped free competition, accompanied by a social and political constitution adapted to it, and by the economical and political sway of the bourgeois class.

A similar movement is going on before our own eyes. Modern bourgeois society with its relations of production, of exchange and of property, a society that has conjured up such gigantic means of production and of exchange, is like the sorcerer, who is no longer able to control the powers of the nether world whom he has called up by his spells. For many a decade past the history of industry and commerce is but the history of the revolt of modern productive forces against modern conditions of production, against the property relations that are the conditions for the existence of the bourgeoisie and of its rule. It is enough to mention the commercial crises that by their periodical return put on its trial, each time more threateningly, the existence of the entire bourgeois society. In these crises a great part not only of the existing products, but also of the previously created productive forces, are periodically destroyed. In these crises there breaks out an epidemic that, in all earlier epochs, would have seemed an absurdity – the epidemic of over-production. Society suddenly finds itself put back into a state of momentary barbarism; it appears as if a famine, a universal war of devastation had cut off the supply of every means of subsistence; industry and commerce seem to be destroyed; and why? Because there is too much civilization, too much means of subsistence, too much industry, too much commerce. The productive forces at the disposal of society no longer tend to further the development of the conditions of bourgeois property; on the contrary, they have become too powerful for these conditions, by which they are fettered, and so soon as they overcome these fetters, they bring disorder into the whole of bourgeois society, endanger the existence of bourgeois property. The conditions of bourgeois society are too narrow to comprise the wealth created by them. And how does the bourgoisie get over these crises? On the one hand by enforced destruction of a mass of productive forces; on the other, by the conquest of new markets, and by the more thorough exploitation of the old ones. That is to say, by paving the way for more extensive and more destructive crises, and by diminishing the means whereby crises are prevented.

The weapons with which the bourgeoisie felled feudalism to the ground are now turned against the bourgeoisie itself.

But not only has the bourgeoisie forged the weapons that bring death to itself; it has also called into existence the men who are to wield those weapons – the modern working-class – the proletarians.

In proportion as the bourgeoisie, i.e., capital, is developed, in the same proportion is the proletariat, the modern working-class, developed, a class of labourers, who live only so long as they find work, and who find work only so long as their labour increases capital. These labourers who must sell themselves piecemeal, are a commodity, like every other article of commerce, and are consequently exposed to all the vicissitudes of competition, to all the fluctuations of the market.

Owing to the extensive use of machinery and to division of labour, the work of the proletarians has lost all individual character, and, consequently, all charm for the workman. He becomes an appendage of the machine, and it is only the most simple, most monotonous, and most easily acquired knack that is required of him. Hence, the cost of production of a workman is restricted, almost entirely, to the means of subsistence that he requires for his maintenance, and for the propagation of his race. But the price of a commodity, and also of labour, is equal to its cost of production. In proportion, therefore, as the repulsiveness of the work increases, the wage decreases. Nay more, in proportion as the use of machinery and division of labour increases, in the same proportion the burden of toil also increases, whether by prolongation of the working hours, by increase of the work enacted in a given time, or by increased speed of the machinery, etc.

Modern industry has converted the little workshop of the patriarchal master into the great factory of the industrial capitalist. Masses of labourers, crowded into the factory, are organized like soldiers. As privates of the industrial army they are placed under the command of a perfect hierarchy of officers and sergeants. Not only are they the slaves of the bourgeois class, and of the bourgeois State, they are daily and hourly enslaved by the machine, by the over-looker, and, above all, by the individual bourgeois manufacturer himself. The more openly this despotism proclaims gain to be its end and aim, the more petty, the more hateful and the more embittering it is.

The less the skill and exertion or strength implied in manual labour, in other words, the more modern industry becomes developed, the more is the labour of men superseded by that of women. Differences of age and sex have no longer any distinctive social validity for the working class. All are instruments of labour, more or less expensive to use, according to their age and sex.

No sooner is the exploitation of the labourer by the manufacturer, so far, at an end, that he receives his wages in cash, than he is set upon by the other portions of the bourgeoisie, the landlord, the shop-keeper the pawnbroker, etc.

The lower strata of the Middle class – the small tradespeople, shopkeepers, and retired tradesmen generally, the handicraftsmen and peasants – all these sink gradually into the proletariat, partly because their diminutive capital does not suffice for the scale on which Modern Industry is carried on, and is swamped in the competition with the large capitalists, partly because their specialized skill is rendered worthless by new methods of production. Thus the proletariat is recruited from all classes of the population.

The proletariat goes through various stages of development. With its birth begins its struggle with the bourgeoisie. At first the contest is carried on by individual labourers, then by the workpeople of a factory, then by the operatives of one trade, in one locality, against the individual bourgeois who directly exploits them. They direct their attacks not against the bourgeois conditions of production, but against the instruments of production themselves; they destroy imported wares that compete with their labour, they smash to pieces machinery, they set factories ablaze, they seek to restore by force the vanished status of the workman of the Middle Ages.

At this stage the labourers still form an incoherent mass scattered over the whole country, and broken up by their mutual competition. If anywhere they unite to form more compact bodies, this is not yet the consequence of their own active union, but of the union of the bourgeoisie, which class, in order to attain its own political ends, is compelled to set the whole proletariat in motion, and is moreover yet, for a time, able to do so. At this stage, therefore, the proletarians do not fight their enemies, but the enemies of their enemies, the remnants of absolute monarchy, the land-owners, the non-industrial bourgeois, the petty bourgeoisie. Thus the whole historical movement is concentrated in the hands of the bourgeoisie; every victory so obtained is a victory for the bourgeoisie.

But with the development of industry the proletariat not only increases in number; it becomes concentrated in greater masses, its strength grows, and it feels that strength more. The various interests and conditions of life within the ranks of the proletariat are more and more equalized, in proportion as machinery obliterates all distinctions of labour, and nearly everywhere reduces wages to the same low level. The growing competition among the bourgeois, and the resulting commercial crises, make the wages of the workers ever more fluctuating. The unceasing improvement of machinery, ever more rapidly developing, makes their livelihood more and more precarious; the collisions between individual workmen and individual bourgeois take more and more the character of collisions between two classes. Thereupon the workers begin to form combinations (Trades' Unions) against the bourgeois; they club together in order to keep up the rate of wages; they found permanent associations in order to make provision beforehand for these occasional revolts. Here and there the contest breaks out into riots.

Now and then the workers are victorious, but only for a time. The real fruit of their battles lies, not in the immediate result, but in the ever expanding union of the workers. This union is helped on by the improved means of communication that are created by modern industry, and that place the workers of different localities in contact with one another. It was just this contact that was needed to centralize the numerous local struggles, all of the same character, into one national struggle between classes. But every class struggle is a political struggle. And that union, to attain which the burghers of the Middle Ages, with their miserable highways, required centuries, the modern proletarians, thanks to railways, achieve in a few years.

This organization of the proletarians into a class, and consequently into a political party, is continually being upset again by the competition between the workers themselves. But it ever rises up again, stronger, firmer, mightier. It compels legislative recognition of particular interests of the workers, by taking advantage of the divisions among the bourgeoisie itself. Thus the ten-hours'-bill in England was carried.

Altogether collisions between the classes of the old society further, in many ways, the course of development of the proletariat. The bourgeoisie finds itself involved in a constant battle. At first with the aristocracy; later on, with those portions of the bourgeoisie itself, whose interests have become antagonistic to the progress of industry; at all times, with the bourgeoisie of foreign countries. In all these battles it sees itself compelled to appeal to the proletariat, to ask for its help, and thus, to drag it into the political arena. The bourgeoisie itself, therefore, supplies the proletariat with its own elements of political and general education, in other words, it furnishes the proletariat with weapons for fighting the bourgeoisie.

Further, as we have already seen, entire sections of the ruling classes are, by the advance of industry, precipitated into the proletariat, or are at least threatened in their conditions of existence. These also supply the proletariat with fresh elements of enlightenment and progress.

Finally, in times when the class-struggle nears the decisive hour, the process of dissolution going on within the ruling class, in fact within the whole range of old society, assumes such a violent, glaring character, that a small section of the ruling class cuts itself adrift, and joins the revolutionary class, the class that holds the future in its hands. Just as, therefore, at an earlier period, a section of the nobility went over to the bourgeoisie, so now a portion of the bourgeoisie goes over to the proletariat, and in particular, a portion of the bourgeois ideologists, who have raised themselves to the level of comprehending theoretically the historical movements as a whole.

Of all the classes that stand face to face with the bourgeoisie today, the proletariat alone is a really revolutionary class. The other classes decay and finally disappear in the face of modern industry; the proletariat is its special and essential product.

The lower middle-class, the small manufacturer, the shopkeeper, the artisan, the peasant, all these fight against the bourgeoisie, to save from extinction their existence as fractions of the middle class. They are therefore not revolutionary, but conservative. Nay more, they are reactionary, for they try to roll back the wheel of history. If by chance they are revolutionary, they are so, only in view of their impending transfer into the proletariat, they thus defend not their present, but their future interests, they desert their own standpoint to place themselves at that of the proletariat.

The 'dangerous class', the social scum, that passively rotting mass thrown off by the lowest layers of old society, may, here and there, be swept into the movement by a proletarian revolution; its conditions of life, however, prepare it far more for the part of a bribed tool of reactionary intrigue.

In the conditions of the proletariat, those of old society at large are already virtually swamped. The proletarian is without property; his relation to his wife and children has no longer anything in common with the bourgeois family-relations; modern industrial labour, modern subjection to capital, the same in England as in France, in America as in Germany, has stripped him of every trace of national character. Law, morality, religion, are to him so many bourgeois prejudices, behind which lurk in ambush just as many bourgeois interests.

All the preceding classes that got the upper hand, sought to fortify their already acquired status by subjecting society at large to their conditions of appropriation. The proletarians cannot become masters of the productive forces of society, except by abolishing their own previous mode of appropriation, and thereby also every other previous mode of appropriation. They have nothing of their own to secure and to fortify; their mission is to destroy all previous securities for, and insurances of, individual property.

All previous historical movements were movements of minorities, or in the interest of minorities. The proletarian movement is the self-conscious, independent movement of the immense majority, in the interest of the immense majority. The proletariat, the lowest stratum of our present society, cannot stir, cannot raise itself up, without the whole superincumbent strata of official society being sprung into the air.

Though not in substance, yet in form, the struggle of the proletariat with the bourgeoisie is at first a national struggle. The proletariat of each country must, of course, first of all settle matters with its own bourgeoisie.

In depicting the most general phases of the development of the proletariat, we traced the more or less veiled civil war, raging within existing society, up to the point where that war breaks out into open revolution, and where the violent over-throw of the bourgeoisie, lays the foundation for the sway of the proletariat.

Hitherto, every form of society has been based, as we have already seen, on the antagonism of oppressing and oppressed classes. But in order to oppress a class, certain conditions must be assured to it under which it can, at least, continue its slavish existence. The serf, in the period of serfdom, raised himself to membership in the commune, just as the petty bourgeois, under the yoke of feudal absolutism, managed to develop into a bourgeois. The modern labourer, on the contrary, instead of rising with the progress of industry, sinks deeper and deeper below the conditions of existence of his own class. He becomes a pauper, and pauperism develops more rapidly than population and wealth. And here it becomes evident, that the bourgeoisie is unfit any longer to be the ruling class in society, and to impose its conditions of existence upon society as an over-riding law. It is unfit to rule, because it is incompetent to assure an existence to its slave within his slavery, because it cannot help letting him sink into such a state, that it has to feed him, instead of being fed by him. Society can no longer live under this bourgeoisie, in other words, its existence is no longer compatible with society.

The essential condition for the existence, and for the sway of the bourgeois class, is the formation and augmentation of capital; the condition for capital is wage-labour. Wage-labour rests exclusively on competition between the labourers. The advance of industry, whose involuntary promoter is the bourgeoisie, replaces the isolation of the labourers, due to competition, by their involuntary combination, due to association. The development of Modern Industry, therefore, cuts from under its feet the very foundation on which the bourgeoisie produces and appropriates products. What the bourgeoisie therefore produces, above all, are its own gravediggers. Its fall and the victory of the proletariat are equally inevitable.

Ferdinand Tönnies 1855–1936

Major works

Community and Society (Gemeinschaft und Gesellschaft; 1887)
Thomas Hobbes's Life and Teachings (1896)
Marx: Life and Teaching (1921)

The following extracts are reprinted from Ferdinand Tönnies, *Community and Society*, translated and introduced by Charles P. Loomis (East Lansing, Michigan: Michigan State University Press, 1957), Book I, sections 1, 2, pp. 33–40, 42–4, 46–8, 64–9, 75–8, with the permission of Michigan State University Press.

Subject

RELATIONS BETWEEN HUMAN WILLS – GEMEINSCHAFT (COMMUNITY) AND GESELLSCHAFT (SOCIETY) FROM A LINGUISTIC POINT OF VIEW[1]

Human wills stand in manifold relations to one another. Every such relationship is a mutual action, inasmuch as one party is active or gives while the other party is passive or receives. These actions are of such a nature that they tend either towards preservation or towards destruction of the other will or life; that is, they are either positive or negative. This study will consider as its subject of investigation only the relationships of mutual affirmation. Every such relationship represents unity in plurality or plurality in unity. It consists of assistance, relief, services, which are transmitted back and forth from one party to another and are to be considered as expressions of wills and their forces. The group which is formed through this positive type of relationship is called an association (*Verbindung*) when conceived of as a thing or being which acts as a unit inwardly and outwardly. The relationship itself, and also the resulting association, is conceived of either as real and organic life – this is the essential characteristic of the *Gemeinschaft* (community), – or as imaginary and mechanical structure – this is the concept of *Gesellschaft* (society).

  1. The parenthetical English renditions of the words *Gemeinschaft* and *Gesellschaft* found in this section indicate the difficulty which would be encountered if one attempted their translation by any one pair of terms. Elsewhere in the text these two substantives and their adjective forms are not translated when they are used in the ideal typological sense.

Through the application of these two terms we shall see that the chosen expressions are rooted in their synonymic use in the German language. But to date in scientific terminology they have been customarily confused and used at random without any distinction. For this reason, a few introductory remarks may explain the inherent contrast between these two concepts. All intimate, private, and exclusive living together, so we discover, is understood as life in Gemeinschaft (community). Gesellschaft (society) is public life – it is the world itself. In Gemeinschaft (community) with one's family, one lives from birth on bound to it in weal and woe. One goes into Gesellschaft (society) as one goes into a strange country. A young man is warned against bad Gesellschaft (society), but the expression bad Gemeinschaft (community) violates the meaning of the word. Lawyers may speak of domestic (*häusliche*) Gesellschaft (society) thinking only of the legalistic concept of a social association, but the domestic Gemeinschaft (community) or home life with its immeasurable influence upon the human soul has been felt by everyone who ever shared it. Likewise, each member of a bridal couple knows that he or she goes into marriage as a complete Gemeinschaft (community) of life (*communio totius vitae*). A Gesellschaft (society) of life would be a contradiction in and of itself. One keeps or enjoys another's Gesellschaft (society or company) but not his Gemeinschaft (community) in this sense. One becomes a part of a religious Gemeinschaft (community); religious Gesellschaften (associations, or societies) like any other groups formed for given purposes, exist only in so far as they, viewed from without, take their places among the institutions of a political body or as they represent conceptual elements of a theory; they do not touch upon the religious Gemeinschaft as such. There exists a Gemeinschaft (community) of language, of folkways, or mores, or of beliefs; but, by way of contrast, Gesellschaft (society or company) exists in the realm of business, travel, or sciences. So of special importance are the commercial Gesellschaften (societies or companies), whereas, even though a certain familiarity and Gemeinschaft (community) may exist among business partners, one could indeed hardly speak of commercial Gemeinschaft (community). To make the word combination, 'joint-stock Gemeinschaft,' would be abominable. On the other hand, there exists a Gemeinschaft (community) of ownership in fields, forest, and pasture. The Gemeinschaft (community) of property between man and wife cannot be called Gesellschaft (society) of property. Thus many differences become apparent.

In the most general way, one could speak of a Gemeinschaft (community) comprising the whole of mankind, such as the church wishes to be regarded. But human Gesellschaft (society) is conceived as mere coexistence of people independent of each other. Recently, the concept of Gesellschaft as opposed to and distinct from the state has been developed. This term will also be used in this treatise, but can only derive its adequate explanation from the underlying contrast to the Gemeinschaft of the people.

Gemeinschaft (community) is old; Gesellschaft (society) is new as a name as well as a phenomenon. This has been recognized by an author who otherwise taught political science in all its aspects without penetrating to its fundamentals. 'The entire concept of Gesellschaft (society) in a social and political sense,' says Bluntschli (*Staatswörterbuch* IV), 'finds its natural foundation in the folkways, mores, and ideas of the third estate. It is not really the concept of a people (*Volks-Begriff*) but the concept of the third estate . . . Its Gesellschaft has become the origin and expression of common opinions and tendencies . . . Wherever urban culture blossoms and bears fruits, Gesellschaft appears as its indispensable organ. The rural people know little of it.' On the other hand, all praise of rural life has pointed out that the Gemeinschaft (community) among people is stronger there and more alive; it is the lasting and genuine form of living together. In contrast to Gemeinschaft, Gesellschaft (society) is transitory and superficial. Accordingly, Gemeinschaft (community) should be understood as a living organism, Gesellschaft (society) as a mechanical aggregate and artifact.

ORGANIC AND MECHANICAL FORMATIONS

Everything real is organic in so far as it can be conceived only as something related to the totality of reality and defined in its nature and movements by this totality. Thus attraction in its manifold forms makes the universe, in so far as it is accessible to our knowledge, into a totality, the action of which expresses itself in the movements by which any two bodies change their mutually held positions. But for observation and scientific theory based thereupon, a totality must be limited to be effective, and each such totality will consist of smaller totalities which have a certain direction and speed in relation to each other. Attraction itself remains either unexplained (as force in space) or is understood as mechanical force (by exterior contact) making itself effective, perhaps in some unknown manner.

Thus the masses of matter may be divided into homogeneous molecules which attract each other with more or less energy and which in their aggregate state appear as bodies. The molecules are divided into dissimilar (chemical) atoms, the dissimilarity of which remains to be explained by further analysis of the different arrangement which similar atom constituents take within the atom. Pure theoretical mechanics, however, presupposes the existence of centers of force without dimension as sources of real actions and reactions. The concept of these centers is very close to the concept of metaphysical atoms and it excludes from the calculation all influence of the movements, or tendencies thereto, of the parts. For all practical applications the physical molecules, when thought of in relation to the same body as their systems, can be considered equally well as carriers of energy, as substance itself, since these molecules are equal in size and no attention is given to their possible subdivision. All real masses may be compared by weight and expressed as quantities of a similar definite substance when their parts are conceived as being in a perfectly solid state of aggregation.

In every case the unit, which is assumed as the subject of a movement or as an integral part of a totality (a higher unit), is the product of a fiction necessary for scientific analysis. Strictly speaking, only the ultimate units, metaphysical atoms, could be accepted as their adequate representatives: somethings which are nothings or nothings which are somethings (*Etwasse, welche Nichtse, oder Nichtse, welche Etwasse sind*). But in so reasoning, the relative meaning of all concepts of size must be kept in mind.

In reality, however, even if they may be anomalies in the mechanical concept, there exist bodies other than these combinable and combining particles of matter conceived as dead. Such bodies appear to be natural totalities which, as totalities, have movement and action in relation to their parts. These are the organic bodies. To these we human beings, who strive for knowledge and understanding, ourselves belong. Each of us has, in addition to imparted knowledge of all possible bodies, an immediate knowledge of his own. We are driven to the conclusion that psychic life is connected with every living body, existing as an entity in the same way as we know ourselves to exist. But objective observation teaches not less clearly that in the case of a living body we deal each time with a totality which is not a mere aggregation of its parts but one which is made up of these parts in such a manner that they are dependent upon and conditioned by the totality, and that such a body as a totality and hence as a form possesses reality and substance.

As human beings we are able to produce only inorganic things from organic materials, dividing and recombining them. In the same way things are also made into a unity through scientific manipulation and are a unity in our concepts. Naïve interpretation or attitudes and artistic imagination, folk belief, and inspired poetry lend life to the phenomena. This creative element is also apparent in the fictions of science. But science also reduces the living to the dead in order to grasp its relations and conditions. It transforms all conditions and forces into movements and interprets all movements as quantities of labor performed, i.e., expended energy, in order to comprehend processes as similar and commensurable. This last is true to the same extent that the assumed units are realities, and the possibility for thought is unlimited. Thus understanding, as an end, is attained, and therewith other objectives.

However, the tendencies and inevitableness of organic growth and decay cannot be understood through mechanical means. In the organic world the concept itself is a living reality, changing and developing as does the idea of the individual being. When science enters this realm it changes its own nature and develops from a logical and rational to an intuitive and dialectic interpretation; it becomes philosophy. However, the present study does not deal with genus and species, i.e., in regard to human beings it is not concerned with race, people, or tribe as biological units. Instead, we have in mind their sociological interpretation, which sees human relationships and associations as living organisms or, in contrast, mechanical constructions. This has its counterpart and analogy in the theory of individual will, and in this sense to present the psychological problem will be the text of the second book of this treatise.

Theory of Gemeinschaft

EMBRYO OR EMERGENT FORMS

In accordance with the preliminary explanations, the theory of Gemeinschaft starts from the assumption of perfect unity of human wills as an original or natural condition which is preserved in spite of actual separation. This natural condition is found in manifold forms because of dependence on the nature of the relationship between individuals who are differently conditioned. The common root of this natural condition is the coherence of vegetative life through birth and the fact that the human wills, in so far as each one of these wills is related to a definite physical body, are and remain linked to each other by parental descent and by sex, or by necessity become so linked. This close interrelation as a direct and mutual affirmation is represented in its most intense form by three types of relationships, namely: (1) the relation between a mother and her child; (2) the relation between husband and wife in its natural or general biological meaning; (3) the relation among brothers and sisters, that is, at least among those who know each other as being the offspring of the same mother. If in the relations of kindred individuals one may assume the embryo of Gemeinschaft or the tendency and force thereto, rooted in the individual wills, specific significance must be attributed to the three above-mentioned relationships, which are the strongest and most capable of development. Each, however, is important in a special way:

(A) The relation between mother and child is most deeply rooted in liking or in pure instinct. Also, in this case the transition from an existing physical to a purely psychic bond is evident. But the physical element is the more apparent the closer the relation remains to its origin (birth). The relationship implies long duration as the mother has to feed, protect, and educate the child until it becomes capable of doing this alone. With this development the relation loses in essentiality, and separation of mother and child becomes more probable. This tendency toward separation, however, can be counterbalanced, or at least restrained, by other tendencies, namely, through the mother and child becoming accustomed to one another and through remembrance of the pleasures which they have given each other, especially the gratitude of the child for the care and painstaking attention of the mother. To these direct mutual relations other common and indirectly binding relations involving other things are added: pleasure, habit, remembrance of objects in the environments which were, or have become, pleasant. The same holds also of shared remembrances of intimate, helpful, beloved persons such as the father, if he lives with the mother, or the brothers and sisters of the mother or child, etc.

(B) The sexual instinct does not in any way necessitate a permanent living together. Moreover, in the beginning it does not lead so much to a fixed mutual relationship as to one-sided subjugation of the woman, who, weaker by nature, can be reduced to an object of mere possession or to servitude. For this reason the relationship between man and wife, if considered independent from kinship and from all social forces based thereupon, has to be supported mainly by habituation to one another in order that the relationship may shape itself into one of mutual affirmation. Besides this, there are, as will be readily understood, the other previously mentioned factors which assist in strengthening the bond. Especially in this connection may be mentioned the relationship to the children as common possession, and further, the common possessions and household.

(C) Among brothers and sisters there is no such innate and instinctive affection and natural liking or preference as between mother and children or between husband and wife. This is true even though the husband-wife relationship may resemble that among brothers and sisters, and there are many reasons to believe that this has frequently been the case with some tribes in an earlier period in the history of man. It must be remembered, however, that among such tribes, as long as descent was reckoned only from the mother, the relationship between brothers and sisters was extended in name, as well as in its emotional aspects, to the corresponding generations of cousins. This practice was so general that the more limited meaning of the concept was, as in many other cases, developed only in a later period. It was through a similar development in the most important ethnic groups that marriage between brothers and sisters came to be regarded as illicit, and where exogamy prevailed, marriage and clan membership (but not kinship) also became mutually exclusive. Therefore, one is justified in considering love between brother and sister, although essentially based upon blood kinship, as the most 'human' relationship between human beings. The intellectual quality of this relationship as compared to the two others discussed above is also apparent from the fact that while instinct plays only a small part, the intellectual force of memory is the foremost in creating, conserving, and consolidating this bond of hearts. For where children of the same mother, in living with her, are also living together with each other, the reminiscences of each of them about pleasant impressions and experiences will necessarily include the person and the activities of the other one. This all the more so, the more closely the group is tied together, especially where, endangered from the outside, it is compelled to strive and act in unison. Thus habit makes such life easier and dearer. At the same time the greatest possible *similarity* of nature and equality of strength may be expected among brothers even though the differences in intelligence and experience, as a purely human or mental element, may easily be perceived.

THEIR UNITY

Many other less intimate relationships are linked to those most fundamental and familiar types. They find their unity and perfection in the relationships between father and children. The existence of an organic basis which keeps the intelligent being connected with the offspring of his body makes this relationship in the most important aspect similar to the first one mentioned (A), from which it differs in that the instinctive part of it is so much weaker. Thus it resembles more closely the husband-wife relationship and is, therefore, more readily conceived as merely coercive. But while the affection of the husband, as to duration more than as to intensity, is inferior to that of the mother, the love of a father differs from the love of a mother in the opposite direction. If present to any considerable degree, therefore, it is similar through its spiritual nature to the affection among brothers and sisters, but, in contrast to the latter, it is defined by an inequality of nature, especially that of age and intellectual power.

Thus the idea of authority is, within the Gemeinschaft, most adequately represented by fatherhood or paternity. However, authority, in this sense, does not imply possession and use in the interest of the master; it means education and instruction as the fulfilment of procreation, i.e., sharing the fullness of one's own life and experiences with the children who will grow gradually to reciprocate these gifts and thus to establish a truly mutual relationship. In this regard the first-born son has a natural preference – he is the closest to the father and will occupy the place which the aging father leavès. The full authority of the father is, therefore, at least implicitly, passed on to the first-born son at his very birth. Thus the idea of an ever-renewed vital force finds its expression in the continuous succession of fathers and sons. We know that this rule of inheritance is not the original one. Apparently the patriarchate has been preceded by the matriarchate and the rule of the brother on the mother's side, and even if collateral succession (the system of tanistry) has precedence over primogeniture, this precedence is based only on the relation to a former generation: the succeeding brother does not derive his right from the brother but from the common father . . .

GEMEINSCHAFT BY BLOOD – OF PLACE – OF MIND.
KINSHIP – NEIGHBORHOOD – FRIENDSHIP

The Gemeinschaft by blood, denoting unity of being, is developed and differentiated into Gemeinschaft of locality, which is based on a common habitat. A futher differentiation leads to the Gemeinschaft of mind which implies only co-operation and co-ordinated action for a common goal. Gemeinschaft of locality may be conceived as a community of physical life, just as Gemeinschaft of mind expresses the community of mental life. In conjunction with the others, this last type of Gemeinschaft represents the truly human and supreme form of community. The first or kinship Gemeinschaft signifies a common relation to, and share in, human beings themselves, while in the second one such a common relation is established through collective ownership of land, and in the third the common bond is represented by sacred places and worshiped deities. All three types of Gemeinschaft are closely inter-related in space as well as in time. They are, therefore, also related in all such single phenomena and in their development as well as in general human culture and its history. Wherever human beings are related through their wills in an organic manner and affirm each other, we find Gemeinschaft of one or another of the three types. Either the earlier type involves the later one, or the later type has developed to relative independence from some earlier one. It is, therefore, possible to deal with (1) kinship, (2) neighborhood, and (3) friendship as definite and meaningful derivations of these original categories.

The house constitutes the realm and, as it were, the body of kinship. Here people live together under one protecting roof, here they share their possessions and their pleasures, they feed from the same supply, they sit at the same table. As invisible spirits the dead are venerated here, as if they were still powerful and held a protecting hand over their family. Thus common fear and common honor ensure with greater certainty peaceful living and co-operation. The will and spirit of kinship is not confined within the walls of the house nor bound up with physical proximity; but where it is strong and alive in the closest and most intimate relationship, it can live on itself, thrive on memory alone, and overcome any distance by its feeling and its imagination of nearness and common activity. But, nevertheless, it seeks all the more for physical proximity and is loath to give it up, because such nearness alone will fulfill the desire for love. The ordinary human being, therefore – in the long run and for the average of cases – feels best and most cheerful if he is surrounded by his family and relatives. He is among his own (*chez soi*).

Neighborhood describes the general character of living together in the rural village. The proximity of dwellings, the communal fields, and even the mere contiguity of holdings necessitate many contacts of human beings and cause inurement to and intimate knowledge of one another. They also necessitate co-operation in labor, order, and management, and lead to common supplication for grace and mercy to the gods and spirits of land and water who bring blessing or menace with disaster. Although essentially based upon proximity of habitation, this neighborhood type of Gemeinschaft can nevertheless persist during separation from the locality, but it then needs to be supported still more than before by well-defined habits of reunion and sacred customs.

Friendship is independent of kinship and neighborhood, being conditioned by and resulting from similarity of work and intellectual attitude. It comes most easily into existence when callings or crafts are the same or of similar character. Such a tie, however, must be made and maintained through easy and frequent meetings, which are most likely to take place in a town. A worshiped deity, created out of a common mentality, has an immediate significance for the preservation of such a bond, since only, or at least mainly, this deity is able to give it living and lasting form. Such good spirit, therefore, is not bound to any place but lives in the conscience of its worshipers and accompanies them on their travels into foreign countries. Thus, those who are brethren of such a common faith feel, like members of the same craft or rank, everywhere united by a spiritual bond and the co-operation in a common task. Urban community of life may be classified as neighborhood, as is also the case with a community of domestic life in which nonrelated members or servants participate. In contradistinction, spiritual friendship forms a kind of invisible scene or meeting which has to be kept alive by artistic intuition and creative will. The relations between human beings themselves as friends and comrades have the least organic and intrinsically necessary character. They are the least instinctive and they are based less upon habit of neighborhood. They are of a mental nature and seem to be founded, therefore, as compared with the earlier relationships, upon chance or free choice . . .

AUTHORITY AND SERVICE – INEQUALITY AND ITS LIMITS

All authority is characterized by particular and enhanced freedom and honor, and thus represents a specific sphere of will. As such it must be derived from the general and equal share of will of the Gemeinschaft. It finds its corollary in service as a particular and diminished freedom and honor. Each authority can be regarded as service and each service as authority, provided the particularity involved is taken into consideration. The realm of will and therefore the will of the Gemeinschaft is a mass of determined force, power, or right. And right is, in essence, will as being able or being allowed and will as obligation or duty. This is the nature of all derived realms of will in which rights and duties are the two corresponding aspects of the same thing, or nothing but the subjective modalities of the same objective substance of right or force. In this way, through increased and diminished duties and rights, real inequalities exist and develop within the Gemeinschaft through its will. These inequalities can be increased only to a certain limit, however, because beyond this limit the essence of the Gemeinschaft as the unity of unequal beings would be disolved: In case the superiors' legal power would become too great, their relation to the common sphere of right would become indifferent and without value and the inferiors' legal power would become too small and their relationship thereto unreal and insignificant.

The less human beings who remain or come into contact with each other are bound together in relation to the same Gemeinschaft, the more they stand opposite each other as free agents of their wills and abilities. The less this freedom is dependent upon a preconditioned will of the individual himself, which is to say the less this will is dependent upon or influenced by a common will, the greater is the freedom. For, besides the inherited forces and instincts, the influence of a community as an educating and guiding will is the most important factor determining the condition and formation of every individual habit and disposition. Especially is the family spirit (*Familiengeist*) important, but so also is every spirit (*Geist*) which is similar to it and has the same effects.

COMMON WILL – UNDERSTANDING – NATURAL LAW – LANGUAGE – MOTHER TONGUE – CONCORD

Reciprocal, binding sentiment as a peculiar will of a Gemeinshaft we shall call understanding (*consensus*).[2] It represents the special social force and sympathy which keeps human beings together as members of a totality. As everything instinctive in the man is related to reasons and requires the capacity of speech, this mentality can be regarded also as the reason and significance of such a relationship. This mentality exists, for instance, between the parent and the child only to the degree in which the child is conceived as possessing speech, intellect, and reason. In the same way it can be said that everything that conforms to the conception of a Gemeinschaft relationship and what in and for this situation has meaning, forms its laws. Everything that conforms to the conception of this Gemeinschaft relationship is to be considered as the proper and real will of those bound together. In so far as enjoyment and labor are differentiated according to the very nature and capability of individuals, especially in such a manner that one part is entitled to guidance, the other bound to obedience, this constitutes a natural law as an order of group life, which assigns a sphere and function, incorporating duties and privileges, to every will. Understanding is based upon intimate knowledge of each other in so far as this is conditioned and advanced by direct interest of one being in the life of the other, and readiness to take part in his joy and sorrow. For that reason understanding is the more probable, the more alike the constitution and experience or the more the natural disposition, character, and intellectual attitude are similar or harmonize.

The real organ of understanding, through which it develops and improves, is language. Language given by means of gestures and sounds enables expressions of pain and pleasure, fear and desire, and all other feelings and emotions to be imparted and understood. Language has – as we all know – not been invented and, as it were, agreed upon as a means and tool by which one makes oneself understood. It is itself the living understanding both in its content and in its form. Similar to all

2. *Verständnis* is translated 'understanding'. The concept as here used should also carry the meaning of mutual understanding and possession of similar sentiments, hopes, aspirations, desires, attitudes, emotions, and beliefs.

other conscious activities of expression, the manifestation of language is the involuntary outcome of deep feelings and prevailing thoughts. It is not merely an artificial means of overcoming a natural lack of understanding, nor does it serve merely the purpose of enabling one to make oneself understood. Language can be used, however, among those who do understand each other, as a mere system of symbols, the same as other symbols which have been agreed upon. All these manifestations can be expressions of hostile as well as friendly passions. This justifies the general statement that friendly and hostile moods and passions underlie the same or very similar conditions. We must, however, distinguish between the hostility which springs from the rupture or loosening of natural and existing ties and the other type of hostility which is based upon strangeness, misunderstanding, and distrust. Both are instinctive, but the first one is anger, hatred, displeasure; the second one is fear, abhorrence, dislike. The first one is acute, the second one chronic. Of course language, like any other means of communication between minds, did not spring from either of these two kinds of hostility – which is only an unnatural and diseased state – but from intimacy, fondness, and affection. Especially from the deep understanding between mother and child, mother tongue should develop most easily and vigorously. Underlying the open hostility associated with an intimate understanding, on the contrary, we can always think of a certain friendship and unity.

The real foundation of unity, and consequently the possibility of Gemeinschaft, is in the first place closeness of blood relationship and mixture of blood, secondly physical proximity, and finally – for human beings – intellectual proximity. In this gradation are, therefore, to be found the sources of all kinds of understanding.

We may now establish the great main laws of Gemeinschaft. (1) Relatives and married couples love each other or easily adjust themselves to each other. They speak together and think along similar lines. Likewise do neighbors and other friends. (2) Between people who love each other there is understanding. (3) Those who love and understand each other remain and dwell together and organize their common life. A mixed or complex form of common determinative will, which has become as natural as language itself and which consists of a multitude of feelings of understanding which are measured by its norm, we call concord (*Eintracht*) or family spirit (*concordia* as a cordial allegiance and unity). Understanding and concord are one and the same thing; namely, will of the Gemeinschaft in its most elementary forms, including understanding in their separate relations and actions and concord in their total force and nature . . .

Sociology in the Nineteenth Century – II

Theory of Gesellschaft
THE FUNDAMENTAL CHARACTERISTIC OF THE
GESELLSCHAFT, A NEGATION – EQUALITY OF VALUE –
THE OBJECTIVE JUDGMENT

The theory of the Gesellschaft deals with the artificial construction of an aggregate of human beings which superficially resembles the Gemeinshaft in so far as the individuals peacefully live and dwell together. However, in the Gemeinshaft they remain essentially united in spite of all separating factors, whereas in the Gesellshaft they are essentially separated in spite of all uniting factors. In the Gesellschaft, as contrasted with the Gemeinschaft, we find no actions that can be derived from an a priori and necessarily existing unity; no actions, therefore, which manifest the will and the spirit of the unity even if performed by the individual; no actions which, in so far as they are performed by the individual, take place on behalf of those united with him. In the Gesellschaft such actions do not exist. On the contrary, here everybody is by himself and isolated, and there exists a condition of tension against all others. Their spheres of activity and power are sharply separated, so that everybody refuses to everyone else contacts with and admittance to his sphere; i.e., intrusions are regarded as hostile acts. Such a negative attitude towards one another becomes the normal and always underlying relation of these power-endowed individuals, and it characterizes the Gesellschaft in the condition of rest; nobody wants to grant and produce anything for another individual, nor will he be inclined to give ungrudgingly to another individual, if it be not in exchange for a gift or labor equivalent that he considers at least equal to what he has given. It is even necessary that it be more desirable to him than what he could have kept himself; because only for the sake of receiving something that seems better to him will he be moved to give away a good. Inasmuch as each and every one is possessed of such will it is self-evident that for the individual 'B' the object 'a' may possibly be better than the object 'b,' and correspondingly, for the individual 'A' the object 'b' better than the object 'a'; it is, however, only with reference to these relations that 'a' is better than 'b' and at the same time 'b' is better than 'a.' This leads us to the question, With what meaning may one speak of the worth or of the value of things, independently of such relationships?

The answer runs as follows: In the concept presented here, all goods are conceived to be separate, as are also their owners. What somebody has and enjoys, he has and enjoys to the exclusion of all others. So, in reality, something that has a common value does not exist. Its existence may, however, be brought about through fiction on the part of the individuals, which means that they have to invent a common personality and his will, to whom this common value has to bear reference. Now, a manipulation of this kind must be warranted by a sufficient occasion. Such an occasion is given when we consider the simple action of the delivery of an object by one individual and its acceptance by another one. For there a contact takes place and there is brought into existence a common sphere which is desired by both individuals and lasts through the same length of time as does the 'transaction'. This period of time may be so small as to be negligible, but, on the other hand, it may also be extended indefinitely. At any rate, during this period the piece which is getting separated from the sphere of, for example, the individual 'A' has ceased to be under the exclusive dominion of 'A' and has not yet begun to be entirely under the dominion of 'B'; it is still under the partial dominion of 'A' and already under the partial dominion of 'B'. It is still dependent upon both individuals, provided that their wills with reference to it are in accord. This is, however, the case as long as the act of giving and receiving continues. During this time it is a common good and represents a social value. Now the will that is directed to this common good is combined and mutual and *can* also be regarded as homogeneous in that it keeps demanding from either individual the execution of the two-fold act until it is entirely completed. This will *must* however, be regarded as a unity inasmuch as it is conceived as a personality or inasmuch as a personality is assigned to it; for to conceive something as existing or as a thing is the same as conceiving it as a unity. There, however, we must be careful to discern whether and to what extent such an *ens fictivum* (artificial being) exists only in the theory, i.e., in scientific thinking, or whether and under which conditions it is also implanted in the thinking of the individuals who are its thinking agents. This last-mentioned possiblity presupposes, of course, that the individuals are already capable of common willing and acting. For, again, it is quite a different proposition if they are imagined to be only participants in the authorship of something that is conceived as objective in the scientific sense because it is that which under given conditions 'each and every one' is compelled to think.

Now, it is to be admitted that each act of giving and receiving implicitly includes a social will, in the way just indicated. These acts are, furthermore, not conceivable except in connection with their purpose or end, i.e., the receipt of the compensating gift. As, however, this latter act is conditioned in like manner, neither act can precede the other; they must concur. Or, expressing the same thought in other words, the acceptance equals the delivery of an accepted compensation. Thus, the exchange itself, considered as a united and single act, represents the content of the assumed social will. With regard to this will the exchanged goods are of equal value. This equality is the judgment of the will and is valid for both individuals, since they have passed it when their wills were in concord; hence it is binding only for the moment in which the act of exchange takes place or for the space of time during which it continues. In order that the judgment may even with this qualification become objective and universally valid, it must appear as a judgment passed by 'each and every one'. Hence, each and every one must have this single will; in other words, the will of the exchange becomes universal; i.e., each and every one becomes a participant in the single act and he confirms it; thus it becomes an absolute and public act. On the contrary, the Gesellschaft may deny this act and declare 'a' is not equal to 'b,' but smaller than 'b' or greater than 'b,' i.e., the objects are not being exchanged according to their values. The true value is explained as that value which each and every one attributes to a thing that we thus regard as a general Gesellschaft-conditioned good. Hence, the true value is ascertained if there is nobody who estimates either object as higher or lower in terms of the other. Now, a general consensus of each and every one that is not accidental, but necessary, will be effected only with reference to what is sensible, right and true. Since all individuals are thus of one mind we may imagine them as concentrated in the person of a measuring, weighing, and knowing judge who passes the objective judgment. The judgment must be recognizable by each and every one, and each and every one must conform to it inasmuch as they themselves are endowed with judgment and objective thinking, or, figuratively speaking, as they use the same yardstick or weigh with the same scales.

VALUE AS AN OBJECTIVE QUALITY – QUANTITIES OF NECESSARY LABOR

We are now confronted with the following question: What shall we consider to be the yardstick or balances in this procedure of deliberative comparing? We know the 'quality' which is to be determined quantitatively by means of this constant tester, and we call it 'value.' Value must not, however, be identified with 'worth,' since worth is a quality which is perceived by the real individual. Moreover, the very difference of worth as it is sensed by real individuals, in relation to the same object is the basis of a reasonable exchange. We, however, are concerned to find equality of value in objective judgment of different objects. In natural and naïve evaluation one takes things of the same category in order to compare them. The evaluation take the form of a question, the answer to which consists of an affirmation or negation, in a stronger or lesser degree, according as the objects submit to the idea of such a comparison. In this sense we may establish a general category of service-able (or useful) things. Some may be considered as necessary, some as superfluous, some may be given prominence as very useful, and others rejected as very harmful. In this connection humanity would have to be pictured as a whole, or at least as a Gemeinschaft of human beings which – like the real individual – lives and therefore has needs; it has to be regarded as uniform in its will, so that it shares profit and loss (since the judgment is at the same time considered as a subjective one).

Now, if one asserts the equality of value of two exchanged objects, this does not at all mean that they are equally useful and necessary for an aggregate being. Otherwise the possiblity of someone buying absolutely harmful things would have to be set up. But that would be monstrous and utopian. One may assert on good grounds that a judgment is wrong when conditioned by desire, so that many a one acquires through exchange an object that is harmful to himself. But it is self-evident that the same liquor which is harmful to the workman is positively useful to the owner of the distillery, since he does not drink it but sells it. In order that a thing may be at all of value in the Gesell-schaft, it is only necessary that it be possessed by one party to the exclusion of another and be desired by one or another individual of this latter party. Apart from this requirement all its other characteristics are insignificant. Saying that a thing has a certain value does not mean that it is endowed with an equal amount of usefulness. Value is an objective quality; as length is an objective quality for the senses of vision and of touch, and as weight for the muscular sense and the sense of touch, so value is an objective quality for the understanding that examines and comprehends social facts. This understanding takes note of and examines the objects as to whether they can be manufactured quickly, or whether they require much time; as to whether they can be easily provided, or whether they require toil and drudgery. In other words, the understanding analyzes the actuality of the objects by examining the possibility of their existence, and it then determines their probability. For determining value the probability of existence is the only test, being subjective in regard to the sensible exchanging individual, and objective in regard to the Gesellschaft. This dictum in the first place carries only the following purport: if a sensible individual is confronted with objects being offered for sale, the thought comes (must come) to him that those objects naturally have a cost in order to be there at all, and particularly to be at that special place at that special time, be this cost represented by other objects against which they have been exchanged, or by labor, or by both items. However, the Gesellschaft, as it is an *ens fictivum* (artificial being) does not exchange anything, unless it be conceived of as an individual person, which here is quite out of the question. Therefore, since the exchange takes place only between human individuals, there is no being that could confront the Gesellschaft. From the viewpoint of the Gesellschaft the cost of the objects is, therefore, represented only by toil and labor. Robbery, as well as exchange, when considered as a means of acquiring objects, is based upon the assumption that goods already exist. Only producing, nurturing, creating, and fashioning labor is to be considered in this connection as the cause of the existence of things at a particular time. To this inherent labor can be added the extraneous labor of movement in space, as the cause of the existence of a given good at a particular place.

Things are considered as equal in so far as each object or each quantity of objects stands merely for a certain quantity of necessary labor. Thus the Gesellschaft disregards the fact that some producers work faster or with better yield (more productively) than others, so that with greater skill or better tools the same objects can be produced with less labor. All such individual differences can be reduced to a common denominator. This process becomes all the more complete in the degree that the exchange of commodities becomes general or Gesellschaft-like. That is to say: each individual offers his commodity to everyone else, and all are capable of producing the same commodities, but everyone, through his own insight and free choice, confines himself to that commodity with presents the least difficulties to him. Thus we exclude here the case of a work which is essentially Gemeinschaft-like but which is divided or divides itself up so that special arts are developed, inherited, and taught. But here we rather have in mind that each individual takes that piece of work which most closely approaches the price that the Gesellschaft attributes to it; that is to say, a piece of work which requires as little extra labor as possible. Thus the Gesellschaft can be imagined to be in reality composed of such separate individuals all of whom are busy for the general Gesellschaft inasmuch as they seem to be active in their own interests and who are working for their own interests while they seem to be working for the Gesellschaft. As a consquence of repeated dividing (of labors) and of indefinite exercise of free choice, there finally falls to each individual an actually equal and simple or elementary labor, representing an atom that he contributes and which forms and integrating part of the total labor of the Gesellschaft. By means of exchange each individual disposes of value not useful to him in order to acquire an equal value that he can use. The present investigation will show what relationship the real structure of the Gesellschaft bears to the concept presented here ...

ACTIVITY AS OBJECT OF A PROMISE – POWER TO ENFORCE IT – RELATION – NATURAL LAW – CONVENTION

In every exchange the place of a perceivable object can be taken by an activity. The activity itself is given and received. It must be useful or agreeable to the receiver as a commodity. This activity is thought of as a commodity the production and consumption of which coincide in time. Although the performance which is not given but only promised may be contrasted with the thing which is not given and only promised, the result in both cases is similar. It belongs to the receiver legally; after the term expires he can force the promising party legally to perform the activity promised, just as he could legally force the debtor to give that which is owed or have it taken with force. A performance which is owed can be acquired only by force. The promise of a performance can as well be mutual as one-sided; therefore, resulting rights to coercion can also be mutual or one-sided as the case may be. In this respect several people can bind themselves for a certain equal activity in such a manner that everyone uses the performance of the other as an aid to himself. Finally, several people can agree to regard their association as an existing and independent being of the same individual nature as they are themselves, and to grant this fictitious person a special will and the capacity to act and therefore to make contracts and to incur obligations. Like all other things related to contracts, this so-called person is to be conceived as objective and real only in so far as the Gesellschaft seems to co-operate with it and to confirm its existence. Only in this way is this so-called person a thinking agent of the legal order of the Gesellschaft, and it is called a society, an association or special-interest group, a corporation, or any such name. The natural content of such an order can be comprised in the one formula: '*Pacta esse observanda*' – contracts must be executed. This includes the presupposition of a condition of separate realms or spheres of will so that an accepted and consequently legal change of each sphere can take place by contract in favor or in disfavor of spheres which are outside the system, or within the system. This means that the agreement of all is involved. Such concurrence of wills is according to its nature momentarily punctual so that the change, as creation of a new situation, does not have to have a duration in time. This necessitates no modification of the most important rule, that everyone can do legally within his realm that which he wishes, but nothing outside. If, however, a common realm originates, as might be the case in a lasting obligation and in an organization, freedom itself, as the total of rights to act freely, must be divided and altered or a new artificial or fictitious form of freedom created. The simple form of the general will of the Gesellschaft, in so far as it postulates this law of nature, I call *convention*. Positive definitions and regulations of all kinds, which according to their origin are of very different style, can be recognized as conventional, so that convention is often understood as a synonym for tradition and custom. But what springs from tradition and custom or the folkways and mores is conventional only in so far as it is wanted and maintained for its general use, and in so far as the general use is maintained by the individual for his use. Convention is not, as in the case of tradition, kept as sacred inheritence of the ancestors. Consequently, the words tradition, customs, or folkways and mores, are not adequate to convey the meaning of convention.

BOURGEOIS SOCIETY (*bürgerliche Gesellschaft*) – EVERYONE A MERCHANT – UNIVERSAL COMPETITION – GESELLSCHAFT IN A MORAL SENSE

Gesellschaft, an aggregate by convention and law of nature, is to be understood as a multitude of natural and artificial individuals, the wills and spheres of whom are in many relations with and to one another, and remain nevertheless independent of one another and devoid of mutual familiar relationships. This gives us the general description of 'bourgeois society' or 'exchange Gesellschaft,' the nature and movements of which legislative economy attempts to understand; a condition in which, according to the expression of Adam Smith, 'Every man . . . becomes in some measure a merchant, . . .' Where merchants, companies, or firms or associations deal with one another in international or national markets and exchanges, the nature of the Gesellschaft is erected as in a concave mirror or as in an extract.

The generality of this situation is by no means, as the famous Scotchman imagined, the immediate or even probable result of the innovation that labor is divided and products exchanged. It is more a remote goal with respect to which the development of the Gesellschaft must be understood. To the extent that this goal is realized, the existence of a Gesellschaft in the sense that it is used here is real at a given time. It is something in the process of becoming, something which should be conceived here as personality of the general will or the general reason, and at the same time (as we know) it is fictitious and nominal. It is like an emanation, as if it had emerged from the heads of the persons in whom it rests, who join hands eagerly to exchange across all distances, limits, and scruples, and establish this speculative Utopia as the only country, the only city, in which all fortune seekers and all merchant adventurers have a really common interest. As the fiction of money is represented by metal or paper, it is represented by the entire globe, or by a circumscribed territory.

In the conception of Gesellschaft the original or natural relations of human beings to each other must be excluded. The possibility of a relation in the Gesellschaft assumes no more than a multitude of mere persons who are capable of delivering something and consequently of promising something. Gesellschaft as a totality to which a system of conventional rules applies is limitless; it breaks through its chance and real boundaries constantly. In Gesellschaft every person strives for that which is to his own advantage and affirms the actions of others only in so far as and as long as they can further his interest. Before and outside of convention and also before and outside of each special contract, the relation of all to all may therefore be conceived as potential hostility or latent war. Against this condition all agreements of the will stand as so many treaties and peace pacts. This conception is the only one which does justice to all facts of business and trade where all rights and duties can be reduced to mere value and definitions of ability to deliver. Every theory of pure private law or law of nature understood as pertaining to the Gesellschaft has to be considered as being based upon this conception. Buyer and seller in their manifold types stand in relation one to the other in such a manner that each one, for as little of his own wealth as possible, desires and attempts to obtain as much of the wealth of others as possible. The real commercial and business people race with each other on many sprinting tracks, as it were, trying each to get the better of the other and to be the first to reach the goal: the sale of their goods and of as large a quantity as possible. Thus they are forced to crowd each other out or to trip each other up. The loss of one is the profit of the other, and this is the case in every individual exchange, unless owners exchange goods of actually equal value. This constitutes general competition which takes place in so many other spheres, but is nowhere so evident and so much in the consciousness of people as in trade, to which, consequently, the conception is limited in its common use. Competition has been described by many pessimists as an illustration of the war of all against all, which a famous thinker has conceived as the natural state of mankind.

However, even competition carries within it, as do all forms of such

263

war, the possibility of being ended. Even enemies like these – although among these it may be the least likely – recognize that under certain conditions it is to their advantage to agree and to spare each other. They may even unite themselves together for a common purpose (or also – and this is the most likely – against a common enemy). Thus competition is limited and abolished by coalition.

In analogy to this situation, based upon the exchange of material goods, all conventional society life, in the narrower sense of the word, can be understood. Its supreme rule is politeness. It consists of an exchange of words and courtesies in which everyone seems to be present for the good of everyone else and everyone seems to consider everyone else as his equal, whereas in reality everyone is thinking of himself and trying to bring to the fore his importance and advantages in competition with the others. For everything pleasant which someone does for someone else, he expects, even demands, at least an equivalent. He weighs exactly his services, flatteries, presents, and so on, to determine whether they will bring about the desired result. Formless contracts are made continuously, as it were, and constantly many are pushed aside in the race by the few fortunate and powerful ones.

Since all relations in the Gesellschaft are based upon comparison of possible and offered services, it is evident that the relations with visible, material matters have preference, and that mere activities and words form the foundation for such relationships only in an unreal way. In contrast to this, Gemeinschaft as a bond of 'blood' is in the first place a physical relation, therefore expressing itself in deeds and words. Here the common relation to the material objects is of a secondary nature and such objects are not exchanged as often as they are used and possessed in common.

Max Weber 1864–1920

Major works

The Protestant Ethic and the Spirit of Capitalism (1904–5)
The City (1921)
Wirtschaft und Gesellschaft: Grundriss der Verstehenden Soziologie
    (1927; Part I translated as *The Theory of Social and Economic
    Organization*)
The Sociology of Religion (1922)

The following extracts are reprinted from Max Weber, *The Theory of Social and Economic Organization*, translated by A. M. Henderson and Talcott Parsons, edited by Talcott Parsons (Glencoe, Ill.: The Free Press, 1947), with the permission of The Macmillan Company. Copyright © Talcott Parsons, 1947.

The Definition of Sociology and of Social Action

1. Sociology (in the sense in which this highly ambiguous word is used here) is a science which attempts the interpretive understanding of social action in order thereby to arrive at a causal explanation of its course and effects. In 'action' is included all human behaviour when and in so far as the acting individual attaches a subjective meaning to it. Action in this sense may be either overt or purely inward or subjective; it may consist of positive intervention in a situation, or of deliberately refraining from such intervention or passively acquiescing in the situation. Action is social in so far as, by virtue of the subjective meaning attached to it by the acting individual (or individuals), it takes account of the behaviour of others and is thereby oriented in its course ...[1]

1. In this series of definitions Weber employs several important terms which need discussion. In addition to *Verstehen*, which has already been commented upon, there are four important ones: *Deuten, Sinn, Handeln*, and *Verhalten. Deuten* has generally been translated as 'interpret'. As used by Weber in this context it refers to the interpretation of subjective states of mind and the meanings which can be imputed as intended by an actor. Any other meaning of the word 'interpretation' is irrelevant to Weber's discussion. The term *Sinn* has generally been translated as 'meaning'; and its variations, particularly the corresponding adjectives, *sinnhaft, sinnvoll, sinnfremd*, have been dealt with by appropriately modifying the term

Sociology in the Nineteenth Century – II

THE CONCEPT OF SOCIAL ACTION

1. Social action, which includes both failure to act and passive acquiescence, may be oriented to the past, present, or expected future behaviour of others. Thus it may be motivated by revenge for a past attack, defence against present, or measures of defence against future aggression. The 'others' may be individual persons, and may be known to the actor as such, or may constitute an indefinite plurality and may be entirely unknown as individuals. Thus 'money' is a means of exchange which the actor accepts in payment because he orients his action to the expectation that a large but unknown number of individuals he is personally unacquainted with will be ready to accept it in exchange on some future occasion.

2. Not every kind of action, even of overt action, is 'social' in the sense of the present discussion. Overt action is non-social if it is oriented solely to the behaviour of inanimate objects. Subjective attitudes constitute social action only so far as they are oriented to the behaviour of others. For example, religious behaviour is not social if it is simply a matter of contemplation or of solitary prayer. The economic activity of an individual is only social if, and then only in so far as, it takes account of the behaviour of someone else. Thus very generally in formal terms it becomes social in so far as the actor's actual control over economic goods is respected by others. Concretely it is social, for instance, if in relation to the actor's own consumption the future wants of others are taken into account and this becomes one consideration affecting the actor's own saving. Or, in another connexion, production may be oriented to the future wants of other people.

---

meaning. The reference here again is always to features of the content of subjective states of mind or of symbolic systems which are ultimately referable to such states of mind.

The terms *Handeln* and *Verhalten* are directly related. *Verhalten* is the broader term referring to any mode of behaviour of human individuals, regardless of the frame of reference in terms of which it is analysed. 'Behaviour' has seemed to be the most appropriate English equivalent. *Handeln*, on the other hand, refers to the concrete phenomenon of human behaviour only in so far as it is capable of 'understanding', in Weber's technical sense, in terms of subjective categories. The most appropriate English equivalent has seemed to be 'action'. This corresponds to the editor's usage in *The Structure of Social Action* and would seem to be fairly well established. 'Conduct' is also closely similar and has sometimes been used. *Deuten*, *Verstehen*, and *Sinn* are thus applicable to human behaviour only in so far as it constitutes action or conduct in this specific sense. – ED.

3. Not every type of contact of human beings has a social character, this is rather confined to cases where the actor's behaviour is meaningfully oriented to that of others. For example, a mere collision of two cyclists may be compared to a natural event. On the other hand, their attempt to avoid hitting each other, or whatever insults, blows, or friendly discussion might follow the collision, would constitute 'social action.'

4. Social action is not identical either with the similar actions of many persons or with action influenced by other persons. Thus, if at the beginning of a shower a number of people on the street put up their umbrellas at the same time, this would not ordinarily be a case of action mutually oriented to that of each other, but rather of all reacting in the same way to the like need of protection from the rain. It is well known that the actions of the individual are strongly influenced by the mere fact that he is a member of a crowd confined within a limited space. Thus, the subject matter of studies of 'crowd psychology,' such as those of Le Bon, will be called 'action conditioned by crowds.' It is also possible for large numbers, though dispersed, to be influenced simultaneously or successively by a source of influence operating similarly on all the individuals, as by means of the press. Here also the behaviour of an individual is influenced by his membership in the crowd and by the fact that he is aware of being a member. Some types of reaction are only made possible by the mere fact that the individual acts as part of a crowd. Others become more difficult under these conditions. Hence it is possible that a particular event or mode of human behaviour can give rise to the most diverse kinds of feeling – gaiety, anger, enthusiasm, despair, and passions of all sorts – in a crowd situation which would not occur at all or not nearly so readily if the individual were alone. But for this to happen there need not, at least in many cases, by any meaningful relation between the behaviour of the individual and the fact that he is a member of a crowd. It is not proposed in the present sense to call action 'social' when it is merely a result of the effect on the individual of the existence of a crowd as such and the action is not oriented to that fact on the level of meaning. At the same time the borderline is naturally highly indefinite. In such cases as that of the influence of the demagogue, there may be a wide variation in the extent to which his mass clientele is affected by a meaningful reaction to the fact of its large numbers; and whatever this relation may be, it is open to varying interpretations.

But furthermore, mere 'imitation' of the action of others, such as that on which Tarde has rightly laid emphasis, will not be considered a case of specifically social action if it is purely reactive so that there is no meaningful orientation to the actor imitated. The borderline is, however, so indefinite that it is often hardly possible to discriminate. The mere fact that a person is found to employ some apparently useful procedure which he learned from someone else does not, however, constitute, in the present sense, social action. Action such as this is not oriented to the action of the other person, but the actor has, through observing the other, become acquainted with certain objective facts; and it is these to which his action is oriented. His action is then *causally* determined by the action of others, but not meaningfully. On the other hand, if the action of others is imitated because it is 'fashionable' or traditional or exemplary, or lends social distinction, or on similar grounds, it is meaningfully oriented either to the behaviour of the source of imitation or of third persons or of both. There are of course all manner of transitional cases between the two types of imitation. Both the phenomena discussed above, the behaviour of crowds and imitation, stand on the indefinite borderline of social action. The same is true, as will often appear, of traditionalism and charisma. The reason for the indefiniteness of the line in these and other cases lies in the fact that both the orientation to the behaviour of others and the meaning which can be imputed to the actor himself, are by no means always capable of clear determination and are often altogether unconscious and seldom fully self-conscious. Mere 'influence' and meaningful orientation cannot therefore always be clearly differentiated on the empirical level. But conceptually it is essential to distinguish them, even though merely 'reactive' imitation may well have a degree of sociological importance at least equal to that of the type which can be called social action in the strict sense. Sociology, it goes without saying, is by no means confined to the study of 'social action'; this is only, at least for the kind of sociology being developed here, its central subject matter, that which may be said to be decisive for its status as a science. But this does not imply any judgment on the comparative importance of this and other factors.

The Types of Social Action

Social action, like other forms of action, may be classified in the following four types according to its mode of orientation: (1) in terms of rational orientation to a system of discrete individual ends (*zweckrational*), that is, through expectations as to the behaviour of objects in the external situation and of other human individuals, making use of these expectations as 'conditions' or 'means' for the successful attainment of the actor's own rationally chosen ends; (2) in terms of rational orientation to an absolute value (*wertrational*); involving a conscious belief in the absolute value of some ethical, aesthetic, religious, or other form of behaviour, entirely for its own sake and independently of any prospects of external success; (3) in terms of affectual orientation, especially emotional, determined by the specific affects and states of feeling of the actor; (4) traditionally oriented, through the habituation of long practice.[2]

1. Strictly traditional behaviour, like the reactive type of imitation discussed above, lies very close to the borderline of what can justifiably be called meaningfully oriented action, and indeed often on the other side. For it is very often a matter of almost automatic reaction to habitual stimuli which guide behaviour in a course which has been repeatedly followed. The great bulk of all everyday action to which people have become habitually accustomed approaches this type.

2. The two terms *zweckrational* and *wertrational* are of central significance to Weber's theory, but at the same time present one of the most difficult problems to the translator. Perhaps the keynote of the distinction lies in the absoluteness with which the values involved in *Wertrationalität* are held. The sole important consideration to the actor becomes the realization of the value. In so far as it involves ends, rational considerations, such as those of efficiency, are involved in the choice of means. But there is no question either of rational weighing of this end against others, nor is there a question of 'counting the cost' in the sense of taking account of possible results other than the attainment of the absolute end. In the case of *Zweckrationalität*, on the other hand, Weber conceives action as motivated by a plurality of relatively independent ends, none of which is absolute. Hence, rationality involves on the one hand the weighing of the relative importance of their realization, on the other hand, consideration of whether undesirable consequences would outweigh the benefits to be derived from the projected course of action. It has not seemed possible to find English terms which would express this distinction succinctly. Hence the attempt has been made to express the ideas as clearly as possible without specific terms.

It should also be pointed out that, as Weber's analysis proceeds, there is a tendency of the meaning of these terms to shift, so that *Wertrationalität* comes to refer to a system of ultimate ends, regardless of the degree of their absoluteness, while *Zweckrationalität* refers primarily to considerations respecting the choice of means and ends which are in turn means to further ends, such as money. What seems to have happened is that Weber shifted from a classification of ideal types of action to one of elements in the structure of action. In the latter context 'expediency' is often an adequate rendering of *Zweckrationalität*. This process has been analysed in the editor's *Structure of Social Action*, chap. XVI.

The other two terms *affektuell* and *traditional* do not present any difficulty of translation. The term affectual has come into English psychological usage from the German largely through the influence of psychoanalysis.

Hence, its place in a systematic classification is not merely that of a limiting case because, as will be shown later, attachment to habitual forms can be upheld with varying degrees of self-consciousness and in a variety of senses. In this case the type may shade over into number two (*Wertrationalität*).

2. Purely affectual behaviour also stands on the borderline of what can be considered 'meaningfully' oriented, and often it, too, goes over the line. It may, for instance, consist in an uncontrolled reaction to some exceptional stimulus. It is a case of sublimation when affectually determined action occurs in the form of conscious release of emotional tension. When this happens it is usually, though not always, well on the road to rationalization in one or the other or both of the above senses.

3. The orientation of action in terms of absolute value is distinguished from the affectual type by its clearly self-conscious formulation of the ultimate values governing the action and the consistently planned orientation of its detailed course to these values. At the same time the two types have a common element, namely that the meaning of the action does not lie in the achievement of a result ulterior to it, but in carrying out the specific type of action for its own sake. Examples of affectual action are the satisfaction of a direct impulse to revenge, to sensual gratification, to devote oneself to a person or idea, to contemplative bliss, or, finally, toward the working off of emotional tensions. Such impulses belong in this category regardless of how sordid or sublime they may be.

Examples of pure rational orientation to absolute values would be the action of persons who, regardless of possible cost to themselves, act to put into practice their convictions of what seems to them to be required by duty, honour, the pursuit of beauty, a religious call, personal loyalty, or the importance of some 'cause' no matter in what it consists. For the purposes of this discussion, when action is oriented to absolute values, it always involves 'commands' or 'demands' to the fulfilment of which the actor feels obligated. It is only in cases where human action is motivated by the fulfilment of such unconditional demands that it will be described as oriented to absolute values. This is empirically the case in widely varying degrees, but for the most part only to a relatively slight extent. Nevertheless, it will be shown that the occurrence of this mode of action is important enough to justify its formulation as a distinct type; though it may be remarked that there is no intention here of attempting to formulate in any sense an exhaustive classification of types of action.

4. Action is rationally oriented to a system of discrete individual ends (*zweckrational*) when the end, the means, and the secondary results are

all rationally taken into account and weighed. This involves rational consideration of alternative means to the end, of the relations of the end to other prospective results of employment of any given means, and finally of the relative importance of different possible ends. Determination of action, either in affectual or in traditional terms, is thus incompatible with this type. Choice between alternative and conflicting ends and results may well be determined by considerations of absolute value. In that case, action is rationally oriented to a system of discrete individual ends only in respect to the choice of means. On the other hand, the actor may, instead of deciding between alternative and conflicting ends in terms of a rational orientation to a system of values, simply take them as given subjective wants and arrange them in a scale of consciously assessed relative urgency. He may then orient his action to this scale in such a way that they are satisfied as far as possible in order of urgency, as formulated in the principle of 'marginal utility.' The orientation of action to absolute values may thus have various different modes of relation to the other type of rational action, in terms of a system of discrete individual ends. From the latter point of view, however, absolute values are always irrational. Indeed, the more the value to which action is oriented is elevated to the status of an absolute value, the more 'irrational' in this sense the corresponding action is. For, the more unconditionally the actor devotes himself to this value for its own sake, to pure sentiment or beauty, to absolute goodness or devotion to duty, the less is he influenced by considerations of the consequences of his action. The orientation of action wholly to the rational achievement of ends without relation to fundamental values is, to be sure, essentially only a limiting case.

5. It would be very unusual to find concrete cases of action, especially of social action, which were oriented *only* in one or another of these ways. Furthermore, this classification of the modes of orientation of action is in no sense meant to exhaust the possibilities of the field, but only to formulate in conceptually pure form certain sociologically important types, to which actual action is more or less closely approximated or, in much the more common case, which constitute the elements combining to make it up. The usefulness of the classification for the purposes of this investigation can only be judged in terms of its results.

The Concept of Social Relationship

The term 'social relationship' will be used to denote the behaviour of a plurality of actors in so far as, in its meaningful content, the action of each takes account of that of the others and is oriented in these terms.

The social relationship thus *consists* entirely and exclusively in the existence of a *probability* that there will be, in some meaningfully understandable sense, a course of social action. For purposes of definition there is no attempt to specify the basis of this probability.

1. Thus, as a defining criterion, it is essential that there should be at least a minimum of mutual orientation of the action of each to that of the others. Its content may be of the most varied nature; conflict, hostility, sexual attraction, friendship, loyalty, or economic exchange. It may involve the fulfilment, the evasion, or the denunciation of the terms of an agreement; economic, erotic, or some other form of 'competition'; common membership in national or class groups or those sharing a common tradition of status. In the latter cases mere group membership may or may not extend to include social action; this will be discussed later. The definition, furthermore, does not specify whether the relation of the actors is 'solidary' or the opposite.

2. The 'meaning' relevant in this context is always a case of the meaning imputed to the parties in a given concrete case, on the average or in a theoretically formulated pure type – it is never a normatively 'correct' or a metaphysically 'true' meaning. Even in cases of such forms of social organization as a state, church, association, or marriage, the social relationship consists exclusively in the fact that there has existed, exists, or will exist a probability of action in some definite way appropriate to this meaning. It is vital to be continually clear about this in order to avoid the 'reification' of these concepts. A 'state,' for example, ceases to exist in a sociologically relevant sense whenever there is no longer a probability that certain kinds of meaningfully oriented social action will take place. This probability may be very high or it may be negligibly low. But in any case it is only in the sense and degree in which it does exist or can be estimated that the corresponding social relationship exists. It is impossible to find any other clear meaning for the statement that, for instance, a given 'state' exists or has ceased to exist.

3. The subjective meaning need not necessarily be the same for all the parties who are mutually oriented in a given social relationship; there need not in this sense be 'reciprocity.' 'Friendship,' 'love,' 'loyalty,' 'fidelity to contracts,' 'patriotism,' on one side, may well be faced with an entirely different attitude on the other. In such cases the parties associate different meanings with their actions and the social relationship is in so far objectively 'asymmetrical' from the points of view of the two parties. It may nevertheless be a case of mutual orientation in so far as, even though partly or wholly erroneously, one party presumes a particular attitude toward him on the part of the other and orients

his action to this expectation. This can, and usually will, have consequences for the course of action and the form of the relationship. A relationship is objectively symmetrical only as, according to the typical expectations of the parties, the meaning for one party is the same as that for the other. Thus the actual attitude of a child to its father may be at least approximately that which the father, in the individual case, on the average or typically, has come to expect. A social relationship in which the attitudes are completely and fully corresponding is in reality a limiting case. But the absence of reciprocity will, for terminological purposes, be held to exclude the existence of a social relationship only if it actually results in the absence of a mutual orientation of the action of the parties. Here as elsewhere all sorts of transitional cases are the rule rather than the exception.

4. A social relationship can be of a temporary character or of varying degrees of permanence. That is, it can be of such a kind that there is a probability of the repeated recurrence of the behaviour which corresponds to its subjective meaning, behaviour which is an understandable consequence of the meaning and hence is expected. In order to avoid fallacious impressions, let it be repeated and continually kept in mind, that it is *only* the existence of the probability that, corresponding to a given subjective meaning complex, a certain type of action will take place, which constitutes the 'existence' of the social relationship. Thus that a 'friendship' or a 'state' exists or has existed means this and only this: that we, the observers, judge that there is or has been a probability that on the basis of certain kinds of known subjective attitude of certain individuals there will result in the average sense a certain specific type of action. For the purposes of legal reasoning it is essential to be able to decide whether a rule of law does or does not carry legal authority, hence whether a legal relationship does or does not 'exist.' This type of question is not, however, relevant to sociological problems.

5. The subjective meaning of a social relationship may change, thus a political relationship, once based on solidarity, may develop into a conflict of interests. In that case it is only a matter of terminological convenience and of the degree of continuity of the change whether we say that a new relationship has come into existence or that the old one continues but has acquired a new meaning. It is also possible for the meaning to be partly constant, partly changing.

6. The meaningful content which remains relatively constant in a social relationship is capable of formulation in terms of maxims which the parties concerned expect to be adhered to by their partners, on the average and approximately. The more rational in relation to values or to given ends the action is, the more is this likely to be the case. There

is far less possibility of a rational formulation of subjective meaning in the case of a relation of erotic attraction or of personal loyalty or any other affectual type than, for example, in the case of a business contract.

7. The meaning of a social relationship may be agreed upon by mutual consent. This implies that the parties make promises covering their future behaviour, whether toward each other or toward third persons. In such cases each party then normally counts, so far as he acts rationally, in some degree on the fact that the other will orient his action to the meaning of the agreement as he (the first actor) understands it. In part, they orient their action rationally to these expectations as given facts with, to be sure, varying degrees of subjectively 'loyal' intention of doing their part. But in part also they are motivated each by the value to him of his 'duty' to adhere to the agreement in the sense in which he understands it. This much may be anticipated.

Modes of Orientation of Social Action

It is possible in the field of social action to observe certain empirical uniformities. Certain types, that is, of action which correspond to a typically appropriate subjective meaning attributable to the same actors, are found to be wide-spread, being frequently repeated by the same individual or simultaneously performed by many different ones. Sociological investigation is concerned with these typical modes of action. Thereby it differs from history, the subject of which is rather the causal explanation of important individual events; important, that is, in having an influence on human destiny.

An actually existent probability of a uniformity in the orientation of social action will be called 'usage' (*Brauch*), if and in so far as the probability of its maintenance among a group of persons is determined entirely by its actual practice. Usage will be called 'custom' (*Sitte*) if the actual performance rests on long familiarity. On the other hand, a uniformity of action may be said to be 'determined by the exploitation of the opportunities of his situation in the self-interest of the actor.' This type of uniformity exists in so far as the probability of its empirical performance is determined by the purely rational (*zweckrational*) orientation of the actors to similar ulterior expectations.[3]

3. In the above classification as well as in some of those which follow, the terminology is not standardized either in German or in English. Hence, just as there is a certain arbitrariness in Weber's definitions, the same is true of any corresponding set of definitions in English. It should be kept in mind that all of them are modes of orientation of action to patterns which contain a normative element. 'Usage' has seemed to be the most appropriate

1. Usage also includes 'fashion' (*Mode*). As distinguished from custom and in direct contrast to it, usage will be called fashion so far as the mere fact of the novelty of the corresponding behaviour is the basis of the orientation of action, Its place is closely related to that of 'convention,'[4] since both of them usually spring from a desire for social prestige. It will not, however, be further discussed here.

2. As distinguished from both 'convention' and 'law,' 'custom' refers to rules devoid of any external sanction. The actor conforms with them of his own free will, whether his motivation lies in the fact that he merely fails to think about it, that it is more comfortable to conform, or whatever else the reason may be. But always it is justified expectation on the part of the members of the group that a customary rule will be adhered to. Thus custom is not 'valid'[5] in anything like the legal sense; conformity with it is not 'demanded' by anybody. Naturally, the transition from this to validly enforced convention and to law is gradual. Everywhere what has been traditionally handed down has been an important source of what has come to be enforced. To-day it is customary every morning to eat a breakfast which, within limits, conforms to a certain pattern. But there is no obligation to do so, except possibly for hotel guests ('American plan'), and it has not always been customary. On the other hand, the current mode of dress, even though it has partly

---

translation of *Brauch* since, according to Weber's own definition, the principal criterion is that 'it is done to conform with the pattern.' There would also seem to be good precedent for the translation of *Sitte* by 'custom.' The contrast with fashion, which Weber takes up in his first comment, is essentially the same in both languages. The term *Interessenlage* presents greater difficulty. It involves two components; the motivation in terms of self-interest and orientation to the opportunities presented by the situation. It has not seemed possible to use any single term to convey this meaning in English and hence, a more roundabout expression has had to be resorted to. – ED.

4. The term 'convention' in Weber's usage is narrower than *Brauch*. The difference consists in the fact that a normative pattern to which action is oriented is conventional only in so far as it is regarded as part of a legitimate order, whereas the question of moral obligation to conformity which legitimacy implies is not involved in 'usage.' The distinction is closely related to that of W. G. Sumner between 'mores' and 'folkways.' It has seemed best to retain the English term closest to Weber's own. – ED.

5. The German term which has been translated as 'validity' is *Geltung*. The primary use of this term is in a legal context and hence the validity in question is not empirical or logical validity, but legal. A legal rule is 'valid' in so far as it is judged binding upon those who recognize the legitimacy of the legal order. – ED.

originated in custom, is to-day very largely no longer customary alone, but conventional.

3. Many of the especially notable uniformities in the course of social action are not determined by orientation to any sort of norm which is held to be valid, nor do they rest on custom, but entirely on the fact that the corresponding type of social action is in the nature of the case best adapted to the normal interest of the actors as they themselves are aware of them. This is above all true of economic action, for example, the uniformities of price determination in a 'free' market, but is by no means confined to such cases. The dealers in a market thus treat their own actions as means for obtaining the satisfaction of the ends defined by what they realize to be their own typical economic interests, and similarly treat as conditions the corresponding typical expectations as to the prospective behaviour of others. The more strictly rational their action is, the more will they tend to react similarly to the same situation. In this way there arise similarities, uniformities, and continuities in their attitudes and actions which are often far more stable than they would be if action were oriented to a system of norms and duties which were considered binding on the members of a group. This phenomenon – the fact that orientation to the situation in terms of the pure self-interest of the individual and of the others to whom he is related can bring about results which are very similar to those which an authoritarian agency, very often in vain, has attempted to obtain by coercion – has aroused a lively interest, especially in economic affairs. Observation of this has, in fact, been one of the important sources of economics as a science. But it is true in all other spheres of action as well. This type, with its clarity of self-consciousness and freedom from subjective scruples, is the polar antithesis of every sort of unthinking acquiescence in customary ways, as well as, on the other hand, of devotion to norms consciously accepted as absolute values. One of the most important aspects of the process of 'rationalization' of action is the substitution for the unthinking acceptance of ancient custom, of deliberate adaptation to situations in terms of self-interest. To be sure this process by no means exhausts the concept of rationalization of action. For in addition this can proceed in a variety of other directions; positively in that of a conscious rationalization of ultimate values; or negatively, at the expense not only of custom, but of emotional values; and, finally, in favour of a morally sceptical type of rationality, at the expense of any belief in absolute values. The many possible meanings of the concept of rationalization will often enter into the discussion.[6]

6. It is, in a sense, the empirical reference of this statement which constitutes the central theme of Weber's series of studies in the Sociology of

Further remarks on the analytical problem will be found below.[7]

4. The stability of merely customary action rests essentially on the fact that the person who does not adapt himself to it is subjected to both petty and major inconveniences and annoyances as long as the majority of the people he comes in contact with continue to uphold the custom and conform with it.

Similarly, the stability of action in terms of self-interest rests on the fact that the person who does not orient his action to the interests of others, does not 'take account' of them, arouses their antagonism or may end up in a situation different from that which he had foreseen or wished to bring about. He thus runs the risk of damaging his own interests.

(pp. 88, 112–23)

I. The Basis of Legitimacy
THE DEFINITION, CONDITIONS, AND TYPES OF IMPERATIVE CONTROL

'Imperative co-ordination' was defined as the probability that certain specific commands (or all commands) from a given source will be obeyed by a given group of persons. It thus does not include every mode of exercising 'power' or 'influence' over other persons. The motives of obedience to commands in this sense can rest on considerations varying over a wide range from case to case; all the way from simple habituation to the most purely rational calculation of advantage. A criterion of every true relation of imperative control, however, is a certain minimum of voluntary submission; thus an interest (based on ulterior motives or genuine acceptance) in obedience.

Not every case of imperative co-ordination makes use of economic means; *still less* does it always have economic objectives. But normally (not always) the imperative co-ordination of the action of a considerable number of men requires control of a staff of persons. It is necessary,

Religion. In so far as he finds it possible to attribute importance to 'ideas' in the determination of action, the most important differences between systems of ideas are not so much those in the degree of rationalization as in the direction which the process of rationalization in each case has taken. This series of studies was left uncompleted at his death, but all the material which was in a condition fit for publication has been assembled in the three volumes of the *Gesammelte Aufsätze zur Religionssoziologie*. – ED.

7. It has not been possible to identify this reference of Weber's. It refers most probably to a projected conclusion of the whole work which was never written. – ED.

that is, that there should be a relatively high probability that the action of a definite, supposedly reliable group of persons will be primarily oriented to the execution of the supreme authority's general policy and specific commands.

The members of the administrative staff may be bound to obedience to their superior (or superiors) by custom, by affectual ties by a purely material complex of interests or by ideal (*wertrational*) motives. *Purely* material interests and calculations of advantage as the basis of solidarity between the chief and his administrative staff result, in this as in other connexions, in a relatively unstable situation. Normally other elements, affectual and ideal, supplement such interests. In certain exceptional, temporary cases the former may be alone decisive. In everyday routine life these relationships, like others, are governed by custom and in addition, material calculation of advantage. But these factors, custom and personal advantage, purely affectual or ideal motives of solidarity, do not, even taken together, form a sufficiently reliable basis for a system of imperative co-ordination. In addition there is normally a further element, the belief in legitimacy.

It is an induction from experience that no system of authority voluntarily limits itself to the appeal to material or affectual or ideal motives as a basis for guaranteeing its continuance. In addition every such system attempts to establish and to cultivate the belief in its 'legitimacy.' But according to the kind of legitimacy which is claimed, the type of obedience, the kind of administrative staff developed to guarantee it, and the mode of exercising authority, will all differ fundamentally. Equally fundamental is the variation in effect. Hence, it is useful to classify the types of authority according to the kind of claim to legitimacy typically made by each. In doing this it is best to start from modern and therefore more familiar examples.

1. The choice of this rather than some other basis of classification can only be justified by its results. The fact that certain other typical criteria of variation are thereby neglected for the time being and can only be introduced at a later stage is not a decisive difficulty. The 'legitimacy' of a system of authority has far more than a merely 'ideal' significance, if only because it has very definite relations to the legitimacy of property.

2. Not every 'claim' which is protected by custom or by law should be spoken of as involving a relation of authority. Otherwise the worker, in his claim for fulfilment of the wage contract, would be exercising 'authority' over his employer because his claim can, on occasion, be enforced by order of a court. Actually his formal status is that of party to a contractual relationship with his employer, in which he has certain

'rights' to receive payments. At the same time, the concept of a relation of authority naturally does not exclude the possibility that it has originated in a formally free contract. This is true of the authority of employers over the worker as manifested in the former's rules and instructions regarding the work process; and also of the authority of a feudal lord over a vassal who has freely entered into the relation of fealty. That subjection to military discipline is formally 'involuntary' while that to the discipline of the factory is voluntary does not alter the fact that the latter is also a case of subjection to authority. The position of a bureaucratic official is also entered into by contract and can be freely resigned, and even the status of 'subject' can often be freely entered into and (in certain circumstances) freely repudiated. Only in the limiting case of the slave is formal subjection to authority absolutely involuntary.

Another case, in some respects related, is that of economic 'power' based on monopolistic position; that is, in this case, the possibility of 'dictating' the terms of exchange to contractual partners. This will not, taken by itself, be considered to constitute 'authority' any more than any other kind of 'influence' which is derived from some kind of superiority, as by virtue of erotic attractiveness, skill in sport or in discussion. Even if a big bank is in a position to force other banks into a cartel arrangement, this will not alone be sufficient to justify calling it a relation of imperative co-ordination. But if there is an immediate relation of command and obedience such that the management of the first bank can give orders to the others with the claim that they shall, and the probability that they will, be obeyed purely as such regardless of particular content, and if their carrying out is supervised, it is another matter. Naturally, here as everywhere the transitions are gradual; there are all sorts of intermediate steps between mere indebtedness and debt slavery. Even the position of a 'salon' can come very close to the borderline of authoritarian domination and yet not necessarily constitute a system of authority. Sharp differentiation in concrete fact is often impossible, but this makes clarity in the analytical distinctions all the more important.

3. Naturally, the legitimacy of a system of authority may be treated sociologically only as the probability that to a relevant degree the appropriate attitudes will exist, and the corresponding practical conduct ensue. It is by no means true that every case of submissiveness to persons in positions of power is primarily (or even at all) oriented to this belief. Loyalty may be hypocritically simulated by individuals or by whole groups on purely opportunistic grounds, or carried out in practice for reasons of material self-interest. Or people may submit

from individual weakness and helplessness because there is no acceptable alternative. But these considerations are not decisive for the classification of types of imperative co-ordination. What is important is the fact that in a given case the particular claim to legitimacy is to a significant degree and according to its type treated as 'valid'; that this fact confirms the position of the persons claiming authority and that it helps to determine the choice of means of its exercise.

Furthermore a system of imperative co-ordination may – as often occurs in practice – be so completely assured of dominance, on the one hand by the obvious community of interests between the chief and his administrative staff as opposed to the subjects (bodyguards, Pretorians, 'red' or 'white' guards), on the other hand by the helplessness of the latter, that it can afford to drop even the pretence of a claim to legitimacy. But even then the mode of legitimation of the relation between chief and his staff may vary widely according to the type of basis of the relation of authority between them, and, as will be shown, this variation, is highly significant for the structure of imperative co-ordination.

4. 'Obedience' will be taken to mean that the action of the person obeying follows in essentials such a course that the content of the command may be taken to have become the basis of action for its own sake. Furthermore, the fact that it is so taken is referable only to the formal obligation, without regard to the actor's own attitude to the value or lack of value of the content of the command as such.

5. Subjectively, the causal sequence may vary, especially as between 'submission' and 'sympathetic agreement.' This distinction is not, however, significant for the present classification of types of authority.

6. The scope of determination of social relationships and cultural phenomena by authority and imperative co-ordination is considerably broader than appears at first sight. For instance, the authority exercised in the school has much to do with the determination of the forms of speech and of written language which are regarded as orthodox. The official languages of autonomous political units, hence of their ruling groups, have often become in this sense orthodox forms of speech and writing and have even led to the formation of separate 'nations' (for instance, the separation of Holland from Germany). The authority of parents and of school, however, extends far beyond the determination of such cultural patterns which are perhaps only apparently formal, to the formation of the character of the young, and hence of human beings generally.

7. The fact that the chief and his administrative staff often appear formally as servants or agents of those they rule, naturally does nothing whatever to disprove the authoritarian character of the relationship.

There will be occasion later to speak of the substantive features of so-called 'democracy.' But a certain minimum of assured power to issue commands, thus of 'authority,' must be provided for in nearly every conceivable case.

THE THREE PURE TYPES OF LEGITIMATE AUTHORITY

There are three pure types of legitimate authority. The validity of their claims to legitimacy may be based on:

1. Rational grounds – resting on a belief in the 'legality' of patterns of normative rules and the right of those elevated to authority under such rules to issue commands (legal authority).

2. Traditional grounds – resting on an established belief in the sanctity of immemorial traditions and the legitimacy of the status of those exercising authority under them (traditional authority); or finally,

3. Charismatic grounds – resting on devotion to the specific and exceptional sanctity, heroism or exemplary character of an individual person, and of the normative patterns or order revealed or ordained by him (charismatic authority).

In the case of legal authority, obedience is owed to the legally established impersonal order. It extends to the persons exercising the authority of office under it only by virtue of the formal legality of their commands and only within the scope of authority of the office. In the case of traditional authority, obedience is owed to the *person* of the chief who occupies the traditionally sanctioned position of authority and who is (within its sphere) bound by tradition. But here the obligation of obedience is not based on the impersonal order, but is a matter of personal loyalty within the area of accustomed obligations. In the case of charismatic authority, it is the charismatically qualified leader as such who is obeyed by virtue of personal trust in him and his revelation, his heroism or his exemplary qualities so far as they fall within the scope of the individual's belief in his charisma.

1. The usefulness of the above classification can only be judged by its results in promoting systematic analysis. The concept of 'charisma' (the gift of grace) is taken from the vocabulary of early Christianity. For the Christian religious organization, Rudolf Sohm, in his *Kirchenrecht*, was the first to clarify the substance of the concept, even though he did not use the same terminology. Others (for instance, Hollin, *Enthusiasmus und Bussgewalt*) have clarified certain important consequences of it. It is thus nothing new.

2. The fact that none of these three ideal types, the elucidation of which will occupy the following pages, is usually to be found in historical

cases in 'pure' form, is naturally not a valid objection to attempting their conceptual formulation in the sharpest possible form. In this respect the present case is no different from many others. Later on the transformation of pure charisma by the process of routinization will be discussed and thereby the relevance of the concept to the understanding of empirical systems of authority considerably increased. But even so it may be said of every empirically historical phenomenon of authority that it is not likely to be 'as an open book.' Analysis in terms of sociological types has, after all, as compared with purely empirical historical investigation, certain advantages which should not be minimized. That is, it can in the particular case of a concrete form of authority determine what conforms to or approximates such types as 'charisma,' 'hereditary charisma,' 'the charisma of office,' 'patriarchy,' 'bureaucracy' the authority of status groups [*Ständische*], and in doing so it can work with relatively unambiguous concepts. But the idea that the whole of concrete historical reality can be exhausted in the conceptual scheme about to be developed is as far from the author's thoughts as anything could be.

II. Legal Authority with a Bureaucratic Administrative Staff
LEGAL AUTHORITY: THE PURE TYPE WITH EMPLOYMENT OF A BUREAUCRATIC ADMINISTRATIVE STAFF

The effectiveness of legal authority rests on the acceptance of the validity of the following mutually inter-dependent ideas.

1. That any given legal norm may be established by agreement or by imposition, on grounds of expediency or rational values or both, with a claim to obedience at least on the part of the members of the corporate group. This is, however, usually extended to include all persons within the sphere of authority or of power in question – which in the case of territorial bodies is the territorial area – who stand in certain social relationships or carry out forms of social action which in the order governing the corporate group have been declared to be relevant.

2. That every body of law consists essentially in a consistent system of abstract rules which have normally been intentionally established. Furthermore, administration of law is held to consist in the application of these rules to particular cases; the administrative process in the rational pursuit of the interests which are specified in the order governing the corporate group within the limits laid down by legal precepts and following principles which are capable of generalized formulation and are approved in the order governing the group, or at least not disapproved in it.

3. That thus the typical person in authority occupies an 'office.' In the action associated with his status, including the commands he issues to others, he is subject to an impersonal order to which his actions are oriented. This is true not only for persons exercising legal authority who are in the usual sense 'officials,' but, for instance, for the elected president of a state.

4. That the person who obeys authority does so, as it is usually stated, only in his capacity as a 'member' of the corporate group and what he obeys is only 'the law.' He may in this connexion be the member of an association, of a territorial commune, of a church, or a citizen of a state.

5. In conformity with point 3, it is held that the members of the corporate group, in so far as they obey a person in authority, do not owe this obedience to him as an individual, but to the impersonal order. Hence, it follows that there is an obligation to obedience only within the sphere of the rationally delimited authority which, in terms of the order, has been conferred upon him.

The following may thus be said to be the fundamental categories of rational legal authority: –

(1) A continuous organization of official functions bound by rules.

(2) A specified sphere of competence. This involves (a) a sphere of obligations to perform functions which has been marked off as part of a systematic division of labour. (b) The provision of the incumbent with the necessary authority to carry out these functions. (c) That the means of compulsion are clearly defined and their use is subject to definite conditions. A unit exercising authority which is organized in this way will be called an 'administrative organ' [*Behörde*].

There are administrative organs in this sense in large-scale private organizations, in parties and armies, as well as in the state and the church. An elected president, a cabinet of ministers, or a body of elected representatives also in this sense constitute administrative organs. This is not, however, the place to discuss these concepts. Not every administrative organ is provided with compulsory powers. But this distinction is not important for present purposes.

(3) The organization of offices follows the principle of hierarchy; that is, each lower office is under the control and supervision of a higher one. There is a right of appeal and of statement of grievances from the lower to the higher. Hierarchies differ in respect to whether and in what case complaints can lead to a ruling from an authority at various points higher in the scale, and as to whether changes are imposed from higher up or the responsibility for such changes is left to the lower office, the conduct of which was the subject of complaint.

The rules which regulate the conduct of an office may be technical rules or norms. In both cases, if their application is to be fully rational, specialized training is necessary. It is thus normally true that only a person who has demonstrated an adequate technical training is qualified to be a member of the administrative staff of such an organized group, and hence only such persons are eligible for appointment to official positions. The administrative staff of a rational corporate group thus typically consists of 'officials,' whether the organization be devoted to political, religious, economic – in particular, capitalistic – or other ends.

(5) In the rational type it is a matter of principle that the members of the administrative staff should be completely separated from ownership of the means of production or administration. Officials, employees, and workers attached to the administrative staff do not themselves own the non-human means of production and administration. These are rather provided for their use in kind or in money, and the official is obligated to render an accounting of their use. There exists, furthermore, in principle complete separation of the property belonging to the organization, which is controlled within the sphere of office, and the personal property of the official, which is available for his own private uses. There is a corresponding separation of the place in which official functions are carried out, the 'office' in the sense of premises, from living quarters.

(6) In the rational type case, there is also a complete absence of appropriation of his official position by the incumbent. Where 'rights' to an office exist, as in the case of judges, and recently of an increasing proportion of officials and even of workers, they do not normally serve the purpose of appropriation by the official, but of securing the purely objective and independent character of the conduct of the office so that it is oriented only to the relevant norms.

(7) Administrative acts, decisions, and rules are formulated and recorded in writing, even in cases where oral discussion is the rule or is even mandatory. This applies at least to preliminary discussions and proposals, to final decisions, and to all sorts of order and rules. The combination of written documents and a continuous organization of official functions constitutes the 'office' which is the central focus of all types of modern corporate action.

(8) Legal authority can be exercised in a wide variety of different forms which will be distinguished and discussed later. The following analysis will be deliberately confined for the most part to the aspect of imperative co-ordination in the structure of the administrative staff. It will consist in an analysis in terms of ideal types of officialdom or 'bureaucracy.'

In the above outline no mention has been made of the kind of supreme head appropriate to a system of legal authority. This is a consequence of certain considerations which can only be made entirely understandable at a later stage in the analysis. There are very important types of rational imperative co-ordination which, with respect to the ultimate source of authority, belong to other categories. This is true of the hereditary charismatic type, as illustrated by hereditary monarchy and of the pure charismatic type of president chosen by plebiscite. Other cases involve rational elements at important points, but are made up of a combination of bureaucratic and charismatic components, as is true of the cabinet form of government. Still others are subject to the authority of the chief of other corporate groups, whether their character be charismatic or bureaucratic; thus the formal head of a government department under a parliamentary regime may be a minister who occupies his position because of his authority in a party. The type of rational, legal administrative staff is capable of application in all kinds of situations and contexts. It is the most important mechanism for the administration of everyday profane affairs. For in that sphere, the exercise of authority and, more broadly, imperative co-ordination, consists precisely in administration.

LEGAL AUTHORITY: THE PURE TYPE WITH EMPLOYMENT OF A BUREAUCRATIC ADMINISTRATIVE STAFF – (*Continued*)

The purest type of exercise of legal authority is that which employs a bureaucratic administrative staff. Only the supreme chief of the organization occupies his position of authority by virtue of appropriation, of election, or of having been designated for the succession. But even *his* authority consists in a sphere of legal 'competence.' The whole administrative staff under the supreme authority then consists, in the purest type, of individual officials who are appointed and function according to the following criteria:

(1) They are personally free and subject to authority only with respect to their impersonal official obligations.

(2) They are organized in a clearly defined hierarchy of offices.

(3) Each office has a clearly defined sphere of competence in the legal sense.

(4) The office is filled by a free contractual relationship. Thus, in principle, there is free selection.

(5) Candidates are selected on the basis of technical qualifications.

In the most rational case, this is tested by examination or guaranteed by diplomas certifying technical training, or both. They are *appointed*, not elected.

(6) They are remunerated by fixed salaries in money, for the most part with a right to pensions. Only under certain circumstances does the employing authority, especially in private organizations, have a right to terminate the appointment, but the official is always free to resign. The salary scale is primarily graded according to rank in the hierarchy; but in addition to this criterion, the responsibility of the position and the requirements of the incumbent's social status may be taken into account.

(7) The office is treated as the sole, or at least the primary, occupation of the incumbent.

(8) It constitutes a career. There is a system of 'promotion' according to seniority or to achievement, or both. Promotion is dependent on the judgment of superiors.

(9) The official works entirely separated from ownership of the means of administration and without appropriation of his position.

(10) He is subject to strict and systematic discipline and control in the conduct of the office.

This type of organization is in principle applicable with equal facility to a wide variety of different fields. It may be applied in profit-making business or in charitable organizations, or in any number of other types of private enterprises serving ideal or material ends. It is equally applicable to political and to religious organizations. With varying degrees of approximation to a pure type, its historical existence can be demonstrated in all fields.

1. For example, this type of bureaucracy is found in private clinics, as well as in endowed hospitals or the hospitals maintained by religious orders. Bureaucratic organization has played a major role in the Catholic Church. It is well illustrated by the administrative role of the priesthood [*Kablanokratie*] in the modern church, which has expropriated almost all of the old church benefices, which were in former days to a large extent subject to private appropriation. It is also illustrated by the conception of the universal Episcopate, which is thought of as formally constituting a universal legal competence in religious matters. Similarly, the doctrine of Papal infallibility is thought of as in fact involving a universal competence, but only one which functions 'ex cathedra' in the sphere of the office, thus implying the typical distinction between the sphere of office and that of the private affairs of the incumbent. The same phenomena are found in the large-scale capitalistic enterprise; and the larger it is, the greater their role. And this is not less true of political parties, which will be discussed separately. Finally, the

modern army is essentially a bureaucratic organization administered by that peculiar type of military functionary, the 'officer.'

2. Bureaucratic authority is carried out in its purest form where it is most clearly dominated by the principle of appointment. There is no such thing as a hierarchy of elected officials in the same sense as there is a hierarchical organization of appointed officials. In the first place, election makes it impossible to attain a stringency of discipline even approaching that in the appointed type. For it is open to a subordinate official to compete for elective honours on the same terms as his superior, and his prospects are not dependent on the superior's judgment.

3. Appointment by free contract, which makes free selection possible, is essential to modern bureaucracy. Where there is a hierarchical organization with impersonal spheres of competence, but occupied by unfree officials – like slaves or dependents, who, however, function in a formally bureaucratic manner – the term 'patrimonial bureaucracy' will be used.

4. The role of technical qualifications in bureaucratic organizations is continually increasing. Even an official in a party or a trade-union organization is in need of specialized knowledge, though it is usually of an empirical character, developed by experience, rather than by formal training. In the modern state, the only 'offices' for which no technical qualifications are required are those of ministers and presidents. This only goes to prove that they are 'officials' only in a formal sense, and not substantively, as is true of the managing director or president of a large business corporation. There is no question but that the 'position' of the capitalistic entrepreneur is as definitely appropriated as is that of a monarch. Thus, as the top of a bureaucratic organization, there is necessarily an element which is at least not purely bureaucratic. The category of bureaucracy is one applying only to the exercise of control by means of a particular kind of administrative staff.

5. The bureaucratic official normally receives a fixed salary. By contrast, sources of income which are privately appropriated will be called 'benefices' [*Pfründen*]. Bureaucratic salaries are also normally paid in money. Though this is not essential to the concept of bureaucracy, it is the arrangement which best fits the pure type. Payments in kind are apt to have the character of benefices, and the receipt of a benefice normally implies the appropriation of opportunities for earnings and of positions. There are, however gradual transitions in this field with many intermediate types. Appropriation by virtue of leasing or sale of offices or the pledge of income from office are phenomena foreign to the pure type of bureaucracy.

6. 'Offices' which do not constitute the incumbent's principal occupation, in particular 'honorary' offices, belong in other categories.

The typical 'bureaucratic' official occupies the office as his principal occupation.

7. With respect to the separation of the official from ownership of the means of administration, the situation is essentially the same in the field of public administration and in private bureaucratic organizations, such as the large-scale capitalistic enterprise.

8. Collegial bodies at the present time are rapidly decreasing in importance in favour of types of organization which are in fact, and for the most part formally as well, subject to the authority of a single head. For instance, the collegial 'governments' in Prussia have long since given way to the monocratic 'district president' [*Regierungs präsident*]. The decisive factor in this development has been the need for rapid, clear decisions, free of the necessity of compromise between different opinions and also free of shifting majorities.

9. The modern army officer is a type of appointed official who is clearly marked off by certain class distinctions. In this respect such officers differ radically from elected military leaders, from charismatic condottieri, from the type of officers who recruit and lead mercenary armies as a capitalistic enterprise, and, finally, from the incumbents of commissions which have been purchased. There may be gradual transitions between these types. The patrimonial 'retainer,' who is separated from the means of carrying out his function and the proprietor of a mercenary army for capitalistic purposes have, along with the private capitalistic entrepreneur, been pioneers in the organization of the modern type of bureaucracy.   (pp. 324–36)

Georg Simmel 1858–1918

Major works

Soziologie (1908)
The Sociology of Georg Simmel (edited and translated by Kurt H. Wolff, 1950)

The following extract is reprinted from Georg Simmel, 'The Sociology of Sociability' ('Soziologie der Geselligkeit'; 1910), translated by Everett C. Hughes, *American Journal of Sociology*, LV, No. 3 (November 1949), 254–61, with the permission of the University of Chicago Press. Copyright © University of Chicago, 1949. All rights reserved.

There is an old conflict over the nature of society. One side mystically exaggerates its significance, contending that only through society is human life endowed with reality. The other regards it as a mere abstract concept by means of which the observer draws the realities, which are individual human beings, into a whole, as one calls trees and brooks, houses and meadows, a 'landscape.' However one decides this conflict, he must allow society to be a reality in a double sense. On the one hand are the individuals in their directly perceptible existence, the bearers of the processes of association, who are united by these processes into the higher unity which one calls 'society'; on the other hand, the interests which, living in the individuals, motivate such union: economic and ideal interests, warlike and erotic, religious and charitable. To satisfy such urges and to attain such purposes, arise the innumerable forms of social life, all the with-one-another, for-one-another, in-one-another, against-one-another, and through-one-another, in state and commune, in church and economic associations, in family and clubs. The energy effects of atoms upon each other bring matter into the innumerable forms which we see as 'things.' Just so the impulses and interests, which a man experiences in himself and which push him out toward other men, bring about all the forms of association by which a mere sum of separate individuals are made into a 'society.'

Within this constellation, called society, or out of it, there develops a special sociological structure corresponding to those of art and play, which draw their form from these realities but nevertheless leave their reality behind them. It may be an open question whether the concept of a play impulse or an artistic impulse possesses explanatory value; at least it directs attention to the fact that in every play or artistic activity there is contained a common element not affected by their differences of content. Some residue of satisfaction lies in gymnastics, as in card-playing, in music, and in plastic, something which has nothing to do with the peculiarities of music or plastic as such but only with the fact that both of the latter are art and both of the former are play. A common element, a likeness of psychological reaction and need, is found in all these various things – something easily distinguishable from the special interest which gives each its distinction. In the same sense one may speak of an impulse to sociability in man. To be sure, it is for the sake of special needs and interests that men unite in economic associations or blood fraternities, in cult societies or robber bands. But, above and beyond their special content, all these associations are accompanied by a feeling for, by a satisfaction in, the very fact that one is associated with others and that the solitariness of the individual is resolved into togetherness, a union with others. Of course, this feeling can, in individual cases, be nullified by contrary psychological factors; association can be felt as a mere burden endured for the sake of our objective aims. But typically there is involved in all effective motives for association a feeling of the worth of association as such, a drive which presses toward this form of existence and often only later calls forth that objective content which carries the particular association along. And as that which I have called artistic impulse draws its form from the complexes of perceivable things and builds this form into a special structure corresponding to the artistic impulse, so also the impulse to sociability distils, as it were, out of the realities of social life the pure essence of association, of the associative process as a value and a satisfaction. It thereby constitutes what we call sociability in the narrower sense. It is no mere accident of language that all sociability, even the purely spontaneous, if it is to have meaning and stability, lays such great value on form, on good form. For 'good form' is mutual self-definition, interaction of the elements, through which a unity is made; and since in sociability the concrete motives bound up with life-goals fall away, so must the pure form, the free-playing, interacting interdependence of individuals stand out so much the more strongly and operate with so much the greater effect.

And what joins art with play now appears in the likeness of both to sociability. From the realities of life play draws its great, essential themes: the chase and cunning; the proving of physical and mental powers, the contest and reliance on chance and the favor of forces which one cannot influence. Freed of substance, through which these activites make up the seriousness of life, play gets its cheerfulness but also that symbolic significance which distinguishes it from pure pastime. And just this will show itself more and more as the essence of sociability; that it makes up its substance from numerous fundamental forms of serious relationships among men, a substance, however, spared the frictional relations of real life; but out of its formal relations to real life, sociability (and the more so as it approaches pure sociability) takes on a symbolically playing fulness of life and a significance which a superficial rationalism always seeks only in the content. Rationalism, finding no content there, seeks to do away with sociability as empty idleness, as did the savant who asked concerning a work of art, 'What does that prove?' It is nevertheless not without significance that in many, perhaps in all, European languages, the word 'society' (Gesellschaft) indicates literally 'togetherness.' The political, economic, the society held together by some purpose is, nevertheless, always 'society.' But only the sociable is a 'society' without qualifying adjective, because it alone presents the pure, abstract play of form, all the specific contents of the one-sided and qualified societies being dissolved away.

Sociability is, then, the play-form of association and is related to the content-determined concreteness of association as art is related to reality. Now the great problem of association comes to a solution possible only in sociability. The problem is that of the measure of significance and accent which belongs to the individual as such in and as against the social milieu. Since sociability in its pure form has no ulterior end, no content, and no result outside itself, it is oriented completely about personalities. Since nothing but the satisfaction of the impulse to sociability – although with a resonance left over – is to be gained, the process remains, in its conditions as in its results, strictly limited to its personal bearers; the personal traits of amiability, breeding, cordiality, and attractiveness of all kinds determine the character of purely sociable association. But precisely because all is oriented about them, the personalities must not emphasize themselves too individually. Where real interests, co-operating or clashing, determine the social form, they provide of themselves that the individual shall not present his peculiarities and individuality with too much abandon and aggressiveness. But where this restraint is wanting, if association is to be possible at all, there must prevail another restriction of personal pushing, a restriction springing solely out of the form of the association. It is for this reason that the sense of tact is of such special significance in society, for it guides the self-regulation of the individual in his personal relations to others where no outer or directly egoistic interests provide regulation. And perhaps it is the specific function of tact to mark out for individual impulsiveness, for the ego and for outward demands, those limits which the rights of others require. A very remarkable sociological structure appears at this point. In sociability, whatever the personality has of objective importance, of features which have their orientation toward something outside the circle, must not interfere. Riches and social position, learning and fame, exceptional capacities and merits of the individual have no role in sociability or, at most, as a slight nuance of that immateriality with which alone reality dares penetrate into the artificial structure of sociability. As these objective qualities which gather about the personality, so also must the most purely and deeply personal qualities be excluded from sociability. The most personal things – character, mood, and fate – have thus no place in it. It is tactless to bring in personal humor, good or ill, excitement and depression, the light and shadow of one's inner life. Where a connection, begun on the sociable level – and not necessarily a superficial or conventional one – finally comes to center about personal values, it loses the essential quality of sociability and becomes an association determined by a content – not unlike a business or religious relation, for which contact exchange, and speech are but instruments for ulterior ends, while for sociability they are the whole meaning and content of the social processes. This exclusion of the personal reaches into even the most external matters; a lady would not want to appear in such extreme *décolletage* in a really personal, intimately friendly situation with one or two men as she would in a large company without any embarrassment. In the latter she would not feel herself personally involved in the same measure and could therefore abandon herself to the impersonal freedom of the mask. For she is, in the larger company, herself, to be sure, but not quite completely herself, since she is only an element in a formally constituted gathering.

A man, taken as a whole, is, so to speak, a somewhat unformed complex of contents, powers, potentialities; only according to the motivations and relationships of a changing existence is he articulated into a differentiated, defined structure. As an economic and political agent, as a member of a family or of a profession, he is, so to speak, an *ad hoc* construction; his life-material is ever determined by a special idea, poured into a special mold, whose relatively independent life is, to be sure, nourished from the common but somewhat undefinable source of energy, the ego. In this sense, the man, as a social creature, is also a unique structure, occurring in no other connection. On the one hand, he has removed all the objective qualities of the personality and entered into the structure of sociability with nothing but the capacities, attractions and interests of his pure humanity. On the other hand, this structure stops short of the purely subjective and inward parts of his personality. That discretion which is one's first demand upon others in sociability is also required of one's own ego, because a breach of it in either direction causes the sociological artifact of sociability to break down into a sociological naturalism. One can therefore speak of an upper and a lower sociability threshold for the individual. At the moment when people direct their association toward objective content and purpose, as well as at the moment when the absolutely personal and subjective matters of the individual enter freely into the phenomenon, sociability is no longer the central and controlling principle but at most a formalisitc and outwardly instrumental principle.

From this negative definition of the nature of sociability through boundaries and thresholds, however, one can perhaps find the positive motif. Kant set it up as the principle of law that everyone should have that measure of freedom which could exist along with the freedom of every other person. If one stands by the sociability impulse as the source or also as the substance of sociability, the following is the principle according to which it is constituted: everyone should have as much satisfaction of this impulse as is consonant with the satisfaction of the impulse for all others. If one expresses this not in terms of the impulse but rather in terms of success, the principle of sociability may be formulated thus: everyone should guarantee to the other that maximum of sociable values (joy, relief, vivacity) which is consonant with the maximum of values he himself receives. As justice upon the Kantian basis is thoroughly democratic, so likewise this principle shows the democratic structure of all sociability, which to be sure every social stratum can realize only within itself, and which so often makes sociability between members of different social classes burdensome and painful. But even among social equals the democracy of their sociability is a play. Sociability creates, if one will, an ideal sociological world, for in it – so say the enunciated principles – the pleasure of the individual is always contingent upon the joy of others; here, by definition, no one can have his satisfaction at the cost of contrary experiences on the part of others. In other forms of association such lack of reciprocity is excluded only by the ethical imperative which governs them but not by their own immanent nature. This world of sociability, the only one in which a democracy of equals is possible without friction, is an *artificial* world, made up of beings who have renounced both the objective and the purely personal features of the intensity and extensiveness of life in order to bring about among themselves a pure interaction, free of any disturbing material accent. If we now have the conception that we enter into sociability purely as 'human beings,' as that which we really are, lacking all the burdens, the agitations, the inequalities with which real life disturbs the purity of our picture, it is because modern life is overburdened with objective content and material demands. Ridding ourselves of this burden in sociable circles, we believe we return to our natural-personal being and overlook the fact that this personal aspect also does not consist in its full uniqueness and natural completeness, but only a certain reserve and stylizing of the sociable man. In earlier epochs, when a man did not depend so much upon the purposive, objective content of his associations, his 'formal personality' stood out more clearly against his personal existence: hence personal bearing in the society of earlier times was much more ceremonially rigidly and impersonally regulated than now. This reduction of the personal periphery of the measure of significance which homogeneous interaction with others allowed the individual has been followed by a swing to the opposite extreme; a specific attitude in society is that courtesy by which the strong, outstanding person not only places himself on a level with the weaker but goes so far as to assume the attitude that the weaker is the more worthy and superior. If association is interaction at all, it appears in its purest and most stylized form when it goes on among equals, just as symmetry and balance are the most outstanding forms of artistic stylizing of visible elements. Inasmuch as sociability is the abstration of association – an abstraction of the character of art or of play – it demands the purest, most transparent, most engaging kind of interaction – that among *equals*. It must, because of its very nature, posit beings who give up so much of their objective content, who are so modified in both their outward and their inner significance, that they are sociably equal, and every one of them can win sociability values for himself only under the condition that the others, interacting with him, can also win them. It is a game in which one 'acts' as though all were equal, as though he especially esteemed everyone. This is just as far from being a lie as is play or art in all their departures from reality. But the instant the intentions and events of practical reality enter into the speech and behavior of sociability, it does become a lie – just as a painting does when it attempts, panorama fashion, to be taken for reality. That which is right and proper within the self-contained life of sociability, concerned only with the immediate play of its forms, becomes a lie when this is mere pretense, which in reality is guided by purposes of quite another sort than the sociable or is used to conceal such purposes – and indeed sociability may easily get entangled with real life.

It is an obvious corollary that everything may be subsumed under sociability which one can call sociological play-form; above all, play itself, which assumes a large place in the sociability of all epochs. The expression 'social game' is significant in the deeper sense which I have indicated. The entire interactional or associational complex among men: the desire to gain advantage, trade, formation of parties and the desire to win from another, the movement between opposition and co-operation, outwitting and revenge – all this, fraught with purposive content in the serious affairs of reality, in play leads a life carried along only and completely by the stimulus of these functions. For even when play turns about a money prize, it is not the prize, which indeed could be won in many other ways, which is the specific point of the play; but the attraction for the true sportsman lies in the dynamics and in the chances of that sociologically significant form of activity itself. The social game has a deeper double meaning – that it is played not only *in* a society as its outward bearer but that *with* the society actually 'society' is played. Further, in the sociology of the sexes, eroticism has elaborated a form of play: coquetry, which finds in sociability its lightest, most playful, and yet its widest realization. If the erotic question between the sexes turns about consent or denial (whose objects are naturally of endless variety and degree and by no means only of strictly physiological nature), so is it the essence of feminine coquetry to play hinted consent and hinted denial against each other to draw the man on without letting matters come to a decision, to rebuff him without making him lose all hope. The coquette brings her attractiveness to its climax by letting the man hang on the verge of getting what he wants without letting it become too serious for herself; her conduct swings between yes and no, without stopping at one or the other. She thus playfully shows the simple and pure form of erotic decision and can bring its polar opposites together in a quite integrated behavior, since the decisive and fateful content, which would bring it to one of the two decisions, by definition, does not enter into coquetry. And this freedom from all the weight of firm content and residual reality gives coquetry that character of vacillation, of distance, of the ideal, which allows one to speak with some right of the 'art' – not of the 'arts' – of coquetry. In order, however, for coquetry to spread as so natural a growth on the soil of sociability, as experience shows it to be, it must be countered by a special attitude on the part of men. So long as the man denies himself the stimulation of coquetry, or so long as he is – on the contrary – merely a victim who is involuntarily carried along by her vacillations from a half-yes to a half-no – so long does coquetry lack the adequate structure of sociability. It lacks that free interaction and equivalence of the elements which is the fundamental condition of sociability. The latter appears only when the man desires nothing more than this free moving play, in which something definitively erotic lurks only as a remote symbol, and when he does not get his pleasure in these gestures and preliminaries from erotic desire or fear of it. Coquetry, as it unfolds its grace on the heights of sociable cultivation, has left behind the reality of erotic desire, of consent or denial, and becomes a play of shadow pictures of these serious matters. Where the latter enter or lurk, the whole process becomes a private affair of the two persons, played out on the level of reality; under the sociological sign of sociability, however, in which the essential orientation of the person to the fulness of life does not enter, coquetry is the teasing or even ironic play with which eroticism has distilled the pure essence of its interaction out from its substantive or individual content. As sociability plays at the forms of society, so coquetry plays out the forms of eroticism.

In what measure sociability realizes to the full the abstraction of the forms of sociological interaction otherwise significant because of their content and gives them – now turning about themselves, so to speak – a shadow body is revealed finally in that most extensive instrument of all human common life, conversation. The decisive point is expressed in the quite banal experience that in the serious affairs of life men talk for the sake of the content which they wish to impart or about which they want to come to an understanding – in sociability talking is an end in itself; in purely sociable conversation the content is merely the indispensable carrier of the stimulation, which the lively exchange of talk as such unfolds. All the forms with which this exchange develops: argument and the appeals to the norms recognized by both parties; the conclusion of peace through compromise and the discovery of common convictions; the thankful acceptance of the new and the parrying-off of that on which no understanding is to be hoped for – all these forms of conversational interaction, otherwise in the service of innumerable contents and purposes of human intercourse, here have their meaning in themselves; that is to say, in the excitement of the play of relations which they establish between individuals, binding and loosening, conquering and being vanquished, giving and taking. In order that this play may retain its self-sufficiency at the level of pure form, the content must receive no weight on its own account; as soon as the discussion gets business-like, it is no longer sociable; it turns its compass point around as soon as the verification of a truth becomes its purpose. Its character as sociable converse is disturbed just as when i t turns into a serious argument. The form of the common search of the truth, the form of the argument, may occur; but it must not permit the seriousness of the momentary content to become its substance any more than one may put a piece of three-dimensional reality into the perspective of a painting. Not that the content of sociable conversation is a matter of indifference; it must be interesting, gripping, even significant – only it is not the purpose of the conversation that these qualities should square with objective results, which stand by definition outside the conversation. Outwardly, there-fore, two conversations may run a similar course, but only that one of them is sociable in which the subject matter, with all its value and stimulation, finds its justification, its place, and its purpose only in the functional play of conversation as such, in the form of repartee with its special unique significance. It therefore inheres in the nature of sociable conversation that its object matter can change lightly and quickly; for, since the matter is only the means, it has an entirely interchangeable and accidental character which inheres in means as against fixed purposes. Thus sociability offers, as was said, perhaps the only case in which talk is a legitimate end in itself. For by the fact that it is two-sided – indeed with the possible exception of looking-each-other-over the purest and most sublimated form of mutuality among all sociological phenomena – it becomes the most adequate fulfilment of a relation, which is, so to speak, nothing but relationship, in which even that which is otherwise pure form of interaction is its own self-sufficient content. It results from this whole complex that also the telling of tales, witticisms, anecdotes, although often a stopgap and evidence of conversational poverty, still can show a fine tact in which all the motives of sociability are apparent. For, in the first place, the conversation is by this means kept above all individual intimacy, beyond everything purely personal which would not fit into the categories of sociability. This objective element is brought in not for the sake of its content but in the interest of sociability; that something is said and accepted is not an end in itself but a mere means to maintain the liveliness, the mutual understanding, the common consciousness of the group. Not only thereby is it given a content which all can share but it is a gift of the individual to the whole, behind which the giver can remain invisible; the finest sociably told story is that in which the narrator allows his own person to remain completely in the background; the most effective story holds itself in the happy balance of the sociable ethic, in which the subjectively individual as well as the objectively substantive have dissolved themselves completely in the service of pure sociability.

It is hereby indicated that sociability is the play-form also for the ethical forces of concrete society. The great problems placed before these forces are that the individual has to fit himself into a whole system and live for it; that, however, out of this system values and enhancement must flow back to him, that the life of the individual is but a means for the ends of the whole, the life of the whole but an instrument for the purposes of the individual. Sociability carries the seriousness, indeed the frequent tragedy of these requirements, over into its shadow world, in which there is no friction, because shadows cannot impinge upon one another. If it is, further, the ethical task of association to make the coming-together and the separation of its elements an exact and just expression of their inner relations, determined by the wholeness of their lives, so within sociability this freedom and adequacy are freed of their concrete and substantively deeper limitations; the manner in which in a 'society' groups form and break up, conversation spins itself out, deepens, loosens, cuts itself off purely according to impulse and opportunity, that is a miniature picture of the social ideal that man might call the freedom of bondage.

If all association and separation shall be the strictly appropriate representation of inner realities, so are the latter here fallen by the way, and only the former phenomenon is left, whose play, obedient to its own laws, whose closed charm, represents *aesthetically* that moderation which the seriousness of realities otherwise demands of its ethical decisions.

This total interpretation of sociability is evidently realized by certain historical developments. In the earlier German Middle Ages we find knightly fraternities which were founded by friendly patrician families. The religious and practical ends of these unions seem to have been lost rather early, and in the fourteenth century the chivalrous interests and conduct remain their only specific content. Soon after, this also disappears, and there remain only purely sociable unions of aristocratic strata. Here the sociability apparently develops as the residuum of a society determined by a content – as the residuum which, because the content has been lost, can exist only in form and in the forms of with-one-another and for-one-another. That the essential existence of these forms can have only the inner nature of play or, reaching deeper, of art appears even more clearly in the court society of the *ancien régime*. Here by the falling-off of the concrete life-content, which was sucked away from the French aristocracy in some measure by the monarchy, there developed free-moving forms, toward which the consciousness of this class was crystallized – forms whose force, definitions, and relations were purely sociable and in no way symbols or functions of the real meanings and intensities of persons and institutions. The etiquette of court society became an end in itself; it 'etiquetted' no content any longer but had elaborated immanent laws, comparable to those of art, which have validity only from the viewpoint of art and do not at all have the purpose of imitating faithfully and strikingly the reality of the model, that is, of things outside art.

With this phenomenon, sociability attains its most sovereign expression but at this same time verges on caricature. To be sure, it is its nature to shut out realities from the interactive relations of men and to build its castle in air according to the formal laws of these relations which move within themselves and recognize no purpose outside themselves. But the deep-running source, from which this empire takes its energies, is nonetheless to be sought not in these self-regulating forms but only in the vitality of real individuals, in their sensitivities and attractions, in the fulness of their impulses and convictions. All sociability is but a symbol of life, as it shows itself in the flow of a lightly amusing play; but, even so, a symbol of *life*, whose likeness it only so far alters as is required by the distance from it gained in the play, exactly as also the freest and most fantastic art, the furthest from all reality, nourishes itself from a deep and true relation to reality, if it is not to be empty and lying. If sociability cuts off completely the threads which bind it to real life and out of which it spins its admittedly stylized web, it turns from play to empty farce, to a lifeless schematization proud of its woodenness.

From this context it becomes apparent that men can complain both justly and unjustly of the superficiality of social intercourse. It is one of the most pregnant facts of mental life that, if we weld certain elements taken from the whole of being into a realm of their own, which is governed by its own laws and not by those of the whole, this realm, if completely cut off from the life of the whole, can display in its inner realization an empty nature suspended in the air; but then, often altered only by imponderables, precisely in this state of removal from all immediate reality, its deeper nature can appear more completely, more integrated and meaningful, than any attempt to comprehend it realistically and without taking distance. Accordingly as the former or the latter experience predominates, will one's own life, running its own course according to its own norms, be a formal, meaningless dead thing – or a symbolic play, in whose aesthetic charm all the finest and most highly sublimated dynamics of social existence and its riches are gathered. In all art, in all the symbolism of the religious life, in great measure even in the complex formulations of science, we are thrown back upon this belief, upon this feeling, that autonomies of mere parts of observed reality, that the combinations of certain superficial elements possess a relation to the depth and wholeness of life, which, although often not easy to formulate, makes such a part the bearer and the representative of the fundamental reality. From this we may understand the saving grace and blessing effect of these realms built out of the pure forms of existence, for in them we are released from life but have it still. The sight of the sea frees us inwardly, not in spite of but because of the fact that in its rushing up only to recede, its receding only to rise again, in the play and counterplay of its waves, the whole of life is stylized to the simplest expression of its dynamic, quite free from all reality which one may experience and from all the baggage of individual fate, whose final meaning seems nevertheless to flow into this stark picture. Just so art perhaps reveals the secret of life; that we save ourselves not by simply looking away from it but precisely in that in the apparently self-governing play of its forms we construct and experience the meaning and the forces of its deepest reality but without the reality itself. Sociability would not hold for so many thoughtful men who feel in every moment the pressure of life, this emancipating and saving exhilaration if it were only a flight from life, the mere momentary lifting of its seriousness. It can often enough be only this negative thing, a conventionalism and inwardly lifeless exchange of formulas; so perhaps in the *ancien régime*, where gloomy anxiety over a threatening reality drove men into pure escape, into severance from the powers of actual life. The freeing and lightening, however, that precisely the more thoughtful man finds in sociability is this; that association and exchange of stimulus, in which all the tasks and the whole weight of life are realized, here is consumed in an artistic play, in that simultaneous sublimation and dilution, in which the heavily freighted forces of reality are felt only as from a distance, their weight fleeting in a charm.

The following extracts are reprinted from *The Sociology of Georg Simmel*, edited and translated by Kurt H. Wolff (Glencoe, Ill.: The Free Press, 1950), Part III, Chapter i, pp. 181–9, and Chapter iv, pp. 250–67, with the permission of The Macmillan Company. Copyright © The Free Press, 1950.

Introduction

1. DOMINATION, A FORM OF INTERACTION

Nobody, in general, wishes that his influence completely determine the other individual. He rather wants this influence, this determination of the other, to act back upon *him*. Even the abstract will-to-dominate, therefore, is a case of interaction. This will draws its satisfaction from the fact that the acting or suffering of the other, his positive or negative condition, offers itself to the dominator as the product of *his* will. The significance of this solipsistic exercise of domination (so to speak) consists, for the superordinate himself, exclusively in the consciousness of his efficacy. Sociologically speaking, it is only a rudimentary form. By virtue of it alone, sociation occurs as little as it does between a sculptor and his statue, although the statue, too, acts back on the artist through his consciousness of his own creative power. The practical function of this desire for domination, even in this sublimated form, is not so much the exploitation of the other as the mere consciousness of this possibility. For the rest, it does not represent the extreme case of egoistic inconsiderateness. Certainly, the desire for domination is designed to break the *internal* resistance of the subjugated (whereas egoism usually aims only at the victory over his *external* resistance). But still, even the desire for domination has some interest in the other person, who constitutes a value for it. Only when egoism does not even amount to a desire for domination; only when the other is absolutely indifferent and a mere means for purposes which lie beyond him, is the last shadow of any sociating process removed.

The definition of later Roman jurists shows, in a relative way, that the elimination of *all* independent significance of one of the two interacting parties annuls the very notion of society. This definition was to the effect that the *societas leonina* must not be conceived of as a social contract. ['sociation with a lion', that is, a partnership in which all the advantage is on one side – Tr.] A comparable statement has been made regarding the lowest-paid workers in modern giant enterprises which preclude all effective competition among rivaling entrepreneurs for the services of these laborers. It has been said that the difference in the strategic positions of workers and employers is so overwhelming that the work contract ceases to be a 'contract' in the ordinary sense of the word, because the former are unconditionally at the mercy of the latter. It thus appears that the moral maxim never to use a man as a mere means is actually the formula of every sociation. Where the significance of the one party sinks so low that its effect no longer enters the relationship with the other, there is as little ground for speaking of sociation as there is in the case of the carpenter and his bench.

Within a relationship of subordination, the exclusion of all spontaneity whatever is actually rarer than is suggested by such widely used popular expressions as 'coercion,' 'having no choice,' 'absolute necessity,' etc. Even in the most oppressive and cruel cases of subordination, there is still a considerable measure of personal freedom. We merely do not become aware of it, because its manifestation would entail sacrifices which we usually never think of taking upon ourselves. Actually, the 'absolute' coercion which even the most cruel tyrant imposes upon us is always distinctively relative. Its condition is our desire to escape from the threatened punishment or from other consequences of our disobedience. More precise analysis shows that the super-subordination relationship destroys the subordinate's freedom only in the case of direct physical violation. In every other case, this relationship only demands a price for the realization of freedom – a price, to be sure, which we are not willing to pay. It can narrow down more and more the sphere of external conditions under which freedom is clearly realized, but, except for physical force, never to the point of the complete disappearance of freedom. The moral side of this analysis does not concern us here, but only its sociological aspect. This aspect consists in the fact that interaction, that is, action which is mutually determined, action which stems exclusively from personal origins, prevails even where it often is not noted. It exists even in those cases of superordination and subordination – and therefore makes even those cases *societal* forms – where according to popular notions the 'coercion' by one party deprives the other of every spontaneity, and thus of every real 'effect,' or contribution to the process of interaction.

2. AUTHORITY AND PRESTIGE

Relationships of superordination and subordination play an immense role in social life. It is therefore of the utmost importance for its analysis to clarify the spontaneity and co-efficiency of the subordinate subject and thus to correct their widespread minimization by superficial notions about them. For instance, what is called 'authority' presupposes, in a much higher degree than is usually recognized, a freedom on the part of the person subjected to authority. Even where authority seems to 'crush' him, it is based not *only* on coercion or compulsion to yield to it.

The peculiar structure of 'authority' is significant for social life in the most varied ways; it shows itself in beginnings as well as in exaggerations, in acute as well as in lasting forms. It seems to come about in two different ways. A person of superior significance or strength may acquire, in his more immediate or remote milieu, an overwhelming weight of his opinions, a faith, or a confidence which have the character of objectivity. He thus enjoys a prerogative and an axiomatic trustworthiness in his decisions which excel, at least by a fraction, the value of mere subjective personality, which is always variable, relative, and subject to criticism. By acting 'authoritatively,' the quantity of his significance is transformed into a new quality; it assumes for his environment the physical state – metaphorically speaking – of objectivity.

But the same result, authority, may be attained in the opposite direction. A super-individual power – state, church, school, family or military organizations – clothes a person with a reputation, a dignity, a power of ultimate decision, which would never flow from his individuality. It is the nature of an authoritative person to make decisions with a certainty and automatic recognition which logically pertain only to impersonal, objective axioms and deductions. In the case under discussion, authority descends upon a person from above, as it were, whereas in the case treated before, it arises from the qualities of the person himself, through a *generatio aequivoca*. ['Equivocal birth' or 'spontaneous generation.' – Tr.] But evidently, at this point of transition and change-over [from the personal to the authoritative situation], the more or less voluntary faith of the party subjected to authority comes into play. This transformation of the value of personality into a super-personal value gives the personality something which is beyond its demonstrable and rational share, however slight this addition may be. The believer in authority himself achieves the transformation. He (the subordinate element) participates in a sociological event which requires his spontaneous cooperation. As a matter of fact, the very feeling of the 'oppressiveness' of authority suggests that the autonomy of the subordinate party is actually presupposed and never wholly eliminated.

Another nuance of superiority, which is designated as 'prestige,' must be distinguished from 'authority.' Prestige lacks the element of super-subjective significance; it lacks the identity of the personality with an objective power or norm. Leadership by means of prestige is determined entirely by the strength of the individual. This individual force always remains conscious of itself. Moreover, whereas the average type of leadership always shows a certain mixture of personal and superadded-objective factors, prestige leadership stems from pure personality, even as authority stems from the objectivity of norms and forces. Superiority through prestige consists in the ability to 'push' individuals and masses and to make unconditional followers of them. Authority does not have this ability to the same extent. The higher, cooler, and normative character of authority is more apt to leave room for criticism, even on the part of its followers. In spite of this, however, prestige strikes us as the more voluntary homage to the superior person. Actually, perhaps, the recognition of authority implies a more profound freedom of the subject than does the enchantment that emanates from the prestige of a prince, a priest, a military or spiritual leader. But the matter is different in regard to the *feeling* on the part of those led. In the face of authority, we are often defenseless, whereas the *élan* with which we follow a given prestige always contains a consciousness of spontaneity. Here, precisely because devotion is only to the wholly personal, this devotion seems to flow only from the ground of personality with its inalienable freedom. Certainly, man is mistaken innumerable times regarding the measure of freedom which he must invest in a certain action. One reason for this is the vagueness and uncertainty of the explicit conceptions by means of which we account for this inner process. But in whatever way we interpret freedom, we can say that some measure of it, even though it may not be the measure we suppose, is present wherever there is the feeling and the conviction of freedom.

3. LEADER AND LED

The seemingly wholly passive element is in reality even more active in relationships such as obtain between a speaker and his audience or between a teacher and his class. Speaker and teacher appear to be nothing but leaders; nothing but, momentarily, superordinate. Yet whoever finds himself in such or a similar situation feels the determining and controlling re-action on the part of what seems to be a purely receptive and guided mass. This applies not only to situations where the two parties confront one another physically. All leaders are also led; in innumerable cases, the master is the slave of his slaves. Said one of the greatest German party leaders referring to his followers: 'I am their leader, therefore I must follow them.'

In the grossest fashion, this is shown by the journalist. The journalist gives content and direction to the opinions of a mute multitude. But he is nevertheless forced to listen, combine, and guess what the tendencies of his multitude are, what it desires to hear and have confirmed, and whither it wants to be led. While apparently it is only the public which is exposed to *his* suggestions, actually he is as much under the sway of the *public's* suggestion. Thus, a highly complex interaction (whose two mutually spontaneous forces, to be sure, appear under very different forms) is hidden here beneath the semblance of the pure superiority of the one element and a purely passive being-led of the other.

The content and significance of certain personal relations consist in the fact that the exclusive function of one of the two elements is service for the other. But the perfect measure of this devotion of the first element often depends on the condition that the other element surrenders to the first, even though on a different level of the relationship. Thus, Bismarck remarked concerning his relation to William I: 'A certain measure of devotion is determined by law; a greater measure, by political conviction; beyond this, a personal feeling of *reciprocity* is required. – My devotion had its principal ground in my loyalty to royalist convictions. But in the special form in which this royalism existed, it is after all possible only under the impact of a certain reciprocity – the reciprocity between master and servant.' The most characteristic case of this type is shown, perhaps, by hypnotic suggestion. An outstanding hypnotist pointed out that in every hypnosis the hypnotized has an effect upon the hypnotist; and that, although this effect cannot be easily determined, the result of the hypnosis could not be reached without it. Thus here, too, appearance shows an absolute influence, on the one side, and an absolute being-influenced, on the other; but it conceals an interaction, an exchange of influences, which transforms the pure one-sidedness of superordination and subordination into a *sociological* form.

4. INTERACTION IN THE IDEA OF 'LAW'

I shall cite some cases of superordination and subordination in the field of law. It is easy to reveal the interaction which actually exists in what seems a purely unilateral situation. If the absolute despot accompanies his order by the threat of punishment or the promise of reward, this implies that he himself wishes to be bound by the decrees he issues. The subordinate is expected to have the right to request something of him; and by establishing the punishment, no matter how horrible, the despot commits himself not to impose a more severe one. Whether or not afterward he actually abides by the punishment established or the reward promised is a different question: the *significance* of the relation is that, although the superordinate wholly determines the subordinate, the subordinate nevertheless is assured of a claim on which he can insist or which he can waive. Thus even this extreme form of the relationship still contains some sort of spontaneity on his part.

The motive of interaction within an apparently one-sided and passive subordination appears in a peculiar modification in a medieval theory of the state. According to this theory, the state came into existence because men mutually obligated one another to submit to a common chief. Thus, the ruler – including, apparently, the unconditional ruler – is appointed on the basis of a mutual contract among his subjects. Whereas contemporaneous theories of domination saw its reciprocal character in the contract between ruler and ruled, the theory under discussion located this mutual nature of domination in its very basis, the people: the obligation to the prince is conceived to be the mere articulation, expression, or technique of a reciprocal relation among the individuals of whom his people is composed. In Hobbes, in fact, the ruler has no means of breaking the contract with his subjects because he has not made one; and the corollary to this is that the subject, even if he rebels against his ruler, does not thereby break a contract concluded with *him*, but only the contract he has entered with all other members of the society, to the effect of letting themselves be governed by this ruler.

It is the *absence* of this reciprocity which accounts for the observation that the tyranny of a group over its own members is worse than that of a prince over his subjects. The group – and by no means the political group alone – conceives of its members, not as confronting it, but as being included by it as its own links. This often results in a peculiar inconsiderateness toward the members, which is very different from a ruler's personal cruelty. Wherever there is, formally, confrontation (even if, contentually, it comes *close* to submission), there is interaction; and, in principle, interaction always contains some limitation of *each* party to the process (although there may be individual exceptions to this rule). Where superordination shows an extreme inconsiderateness, as in the case of the group that simply *disposes* of its members, there no longer is any confrontation with its form of interaction, which involves spontaneity, and hence limitation, of both superordinate and subordinate elements.

This is very clearly expressed in the original conception of Roman law. In its purity, the term 'law' implies a submission which does not involve any spontaneity or counter-effect on the part of the person subordinate to the law. And the fact that the subordinate has actually cooperated in making it – and more, that *he* has given himself the law which binds him – is irrelevant. For in doing so, he has merely decomposed himself into the subject and object of lawmaking; and the law which the subject applies to the object does not change its significance only by the fact that both subject and object are accidentally lodged in the same physical person. Nevertheless, in their conception of law, the Romans directly allude to the idea of interaction. For originally, *'lex'* means 'contract,' even though in the sense that the conditions of the contract are fixed by its proponent, and the other party can merely accept or reject it in its totality. In the beginning, the *lex publica populi romani* implied that the King proposed this legislation, and the people were its acceptors. Hence the very concept which most of all seems to exclude interaction is, nevertheless, designed to refer to it by its linguistic expression. In a certain sense this is revealed in the prerogative of the Roman king that he alone was allowed to speak to the people. Such a prerogative, to be sure, expressed the jealously guarded exclusiveness of his rulership, even as in ancient Greece the right of everybody to speak to the people indicated complete democracy. Nevertheless, this prerogative implies that the significance of speaking to the people and, hence, of the people themselves, was recognized. Although the people merely *received* this one-sided action, they were nonetheless a *contractor* (whose party to the contract, of course, was only a single person, the king).

The purpose of these preliminary remarks was to show the properly sociological, social-formative character of superordination and subordination even where it appears as if a social relationship were replaced by a purely mechanical one – where, that is, the position of the subordinate seems to be that of a means or an object for the superordinate, without any spontaneity. It has been possible, at least in many cases, to show the sociologically decisive *reciprocal effectiveness*, which was concealed under the one-sided character of influence and being influenced . . .

Subordination under a Principle

1. SUBORDINATION UNDER A PRINCIPLE VS. A PERSON

I now come, finally, to the third typical form of subordination, subordination neither to an individual nor to a plurality, but to an impersonal, objective principle. The fact that here a real interaction, at least an immediate interaction, is precluded, seems to deprive this form of the element of freedom. The individual who is subordinate to an objective law feels himself determined by it; while he, in turn, in no way determines the law, and has no possibility of reacting to it in a manner which could influence it – quite in contrast to even the most miserable slave, who, in some fashion at least, can still in this sense react to his master. For if one simply does not obey the law, one is, to this extent, not *really* subjected to it; and if one changes the law, one is not subordinate to the old law at all, but is again, in the same entirely unfree manner, subject to the new law. In spite of this, however, for modern, objective man, who is aware of the difference between the spheres of spontaneity and of obedience, subordination to a law which functions as the emanation of impersonal, uninfluenceable powers, is the more dignified situation. This was quite different at a time when the personality could preserve its self-esteem only in situations characterized by full spontaneity, which even in case of complete subordination were still associated with inter-personal effect and counter-effect. For this reason, as late as in the sixteenth century, princes in France, Germany, Scotland, and the Netherlands often met with considerable resistance, if they let their countries be ruled by administrative bodies or erudite substitutes – that is, more nearly by laws. The ruler's order was felt to be something personal; the individual wanted to lend him obedience only from personal devotion; and personal devotion, in spite of its unconditional character, is always in the form of free reciprocity.

This passionate personalism of the subordination relationship almost becomes its own caricature in the following circumstance, reported from Spain at the beginning of the modern period. An impoverished nobleman who became a cook or lackey, did not thereby definitely lose his nobility: it only became latent and could be awakened again by a favorable turn of fate. But once he became a craftsman, his nobility was destroyed. This is entirely contrary to the modern conception, which separates the person from his achievement and, therefore, finds personal dignity to be preserved best if the content of subordination is as objective as possible. Thus, an American girl, who would work in a factory without the slightest feeling of humiliation, would feel wholly degraded as a family cook. Already in thirteenth-century Florence, the *lower* guilds comprised occupations in the immediate service of persons, such as cobblers, hosts, and school teachers; whereas the *higher* guilds were composed of occupations which, though still serving the public, were yet more objective and less dependent on particular individuals – for instance, clothiers and grocers. On the other hand, in Spain, where knightly traditions, with their engagement of the whole person in all activity, were still alive, every relationship which (in any sense) took place between person and person, was bound to be considered at least bearable; while every subordination to more objective claims, every integration into a system of impersonal duties (impersonal, because serving many and anonymous persons), was bound to be regarded as wholly disgraceful. An aversion to the objectivity of law can still be felt in the legal theories of Althusius: the *summus magistratus* legislates, but he does so, not because he represents the state, but because he is appointed by the people. The notion that the ruler could be designated as the representative of the state by appointment through law, not by personal appointment (actual or presumed) by the people – is still alien to Althusius.

In antiquity, on the contrary, subordination to law appeared thoroughly adequate, precisely because of the idea that law is free from any personal characteristics. Aristotle praised law as '*tó méson*,' that is, as that which is moderate, impartial, free from passions. Plato, in the same sense, had already recognized government by impersonal law as the best means for counteracting selfishness. His, however, was only a psychological motivation. It did not touch the core of the question, namely, the fundamental transition of the relationship of obedience from personalism to objectivism, a transition which cannot be derived from the anticipation of utilitarian consequence. Yet, in Plato, we also find this other theory: that, in the ideal state, the insight of the ruler stands above the law; and as soon as the welfare of the whole seems to require it of the ruler, he must be able to act even against the laws laid down by him. There must be laws which may not be broken under any circumstances, only if there are no true statesmen. The law, therefore, appears here as the lesser evil – but not, as in the Germanic feeling, mentioned before, because subordination under a person has an element of freedom and dignity in comparison with which all obedience to laws has something mechanical and passive. Rather, it is the rigidity of the law which is felt to be its weakness: in its rigidity, it confronts the changing and unforeseeable claims of life in a clumsy and inadequate way; and this is an evil from which only the entirely unprejudiced insight of a personal ruler can escape: and only where there is no such insight, does law become relatively advantageous. Here, therefore, it is always the *content* of the law, its physical state, as it were, which determines its value or disvalue as compared with subordination under persons. The fact that the relationship of obedience is totally different in its inner principle and in terms of the whole feeling of life, on the part of the obeyer, according to whether it originates in a person or in a law – this fact does not enter these considerations. The most general, or formal relation between government by law and government by person can (of course) be expressed in a preliminary, practical manner by saying that where the law is not forceful or broad enough, a person is necessary, and where the person is inadequate, the law is required. But, far beyond this, whether rule by man is considered as something provisional in lieu of rule by perfect law, or, inversely, rule by law is considered a gap-filler or an inferior substitute for government by a personality which is absolutely qualified to rule – this choice depends upon decisions of ultimate, indiscussable feelings concerning sociological values.

2. SUBORDINATION UNDER OBJECTS

There is still another form in which an objective principle may become the turning point in the relationship between superordinates and subordinates, namely, when neither a law nor an ideal norm, but rather a concrete object governs the domination, as, for instance, in the principle of patrimony. Here – most radically under the system of Russian bondage – bonded subjects are only appurtenances of the land – 'the air bonds the people.' The terrible hardship of bondage at least excluded personal slavery which would have permitted the sale of the slave. Instead, it tied subordination to the land in such a way that the bondsman could be sold only along with the land. In spite of all contentual and quantitative differences, nevertheless, sometimes this same form occurs in the case of the modern factory worker, whose own interest, through certain arrangements, binds him to a given factory. For instance, the acquisition of his house was made possible for him, or he participated out of his own purse in certain welfare expenditures, and all these benefits are lost once he leaves the factory, etc. He is thus bound, merely by objects, in a way which in a very specific manner makes him powerless in respect to the entrepreneur. Finally, it was this same form of domination which, under the most primitive patriarchal conditions, was governed not by a merely spatial, but by a living object: children did not belong to the father because he was their progenitor, but because the mother belonged to him (as the fruits of the tree belong to the tree's owner); therefore, children begotten by other fathers were no less his property.

This type of domination usually involves a humiliatingly harsh and unconditional kind of subordination. For, inasmuch as a man is subordinate by virtue of belonging to a thing, he himself psychologically sinks to the category of mere thing. With the necessary reservations, one could say that where law regulates domination, the superordinate belongs in the sphere of objectivity; while, where a *thing* regulates it, the *subordinate* does. The condition of the subordinate, therefore, is usually more favorable in the first case, and more unfavorable in the second, than in many cases of purely personal subordination.

3. CONSCIENCE

Immediate sociological interest in subordination under an objective principle attaches to two chief cases of it. One case is when this ideal, superordinate principle can be interpreted as a psychological crystallization of an actual social power. The other is when, among those who are commonly subject to it, it produces particular and characteristic relationships. The first case must be taken into consideration, above all, when dealing with moral imperatives. In our moral consciousness, we feel subordinate to a command which does not seem to derive from any human, personal power. The voice of conscience we hear only in ourselves, although in comparison with all subjective egoism, we hear it with a force and decisiveness which apparently can stem only from a tribunal *outside* the individual. An attempt has been made, as is well-known, to solve this contradiction by deriving the contents of morality from social norms. What is useful to the species and the group, the argument runs, and what the group, therefore, requests of its members for the sake of its own maintenance, is gradually bred into the individual as an instinct. He thus comes to contain it in himself, as his own, autonomous feeling, in addition to his personal feelings properly speaking, and thus often in contrast to them. This, it is alleged, explains the dual character of the moral command: that on the one hand, it confronts us as an impersonal order to which we simply have to submit, but that, on the other, no external power, but only our most private and internal impulses, imposes it upon us. At any rate, here is one of the cases where the individual, within his own consciousness, repeats the relationships which exist between him, as a total personality, and the group. It is an old observation that the conceptions of the single individual, with all their relations of association and dissociation, differentiation, and unification, behave in the same way in which individuals behave in regard to one another. It is merely a peculiar case of this correspondence that those intra-psychological relations are repeated, not only between individuals in general, but also between the individual and his group. All that society asks of its members – adaptation and loyalty, altruism and work, self-discipline and truthfulness – the individual also asks of himself.

In all this, several very important motives cut across one another.

Society confronts the individual with precepts. He becomes habituated to their compulsory character until the cruder and subtler means of compulsion are no longer necessary. His nature may thereby be so formed or deformed that he acts by these precepts as if on impulse, with a consistent and direct will which is not conscious of any law. Thus, the pre-Islamic Arabs were without any notion of an objectively legal compulsion; in all instances, purely personal decision was their highest authority, although this decision was thoroughly imbued with tribal consciousness and the requirements of tribal life, which gave it its norms. Or else, the law, in the form of a command which is carried by the authority of the society, does live in the individual consciousness, but irrespective of the question whether society actually backs it with its compulsory power or even itself supports it solely with its explicit will. Here then, the individual represents society to himself. The external confrontation, with its suppressions, liberations, changing accents, has become an interplay between his social impulses and the ego impulses in the stricter sense of the word; and both are included by the ego in the larger sense.

But this is not yet the really objective lawfulness, indicated above, in whose consciousness of which no trace of any historical-social origin is left. At a certain higher stage of morality, the motivation of action lies no longer in a real-human, even though super-individual power; at this stage, the spring of moral necessities flows beyond the contrast between individual and totality. For, as little as these necessities derive from society, as little do they derive from the singular reality of individual life. In the free conscience of the actor, in individual reason, they only have their bearer, the locus of their efficacy. Their power of obligation stems from these necessities themselves, from their inner, super-personal validity, from an objective ideality which we must recognize, whether or not we want to, in a manner similar to that in which the validity of a truth is entirely independent of whether or not the truth becomes real in any consciousness. The *content*, however, which fills these forms is (not necessarily but often) the societal requirement. But this requirement no longer operates by means of its social impetus, as it were, but rather as if it had undergone a metapsychosis into a norm which must be satisfied for its own sake, not for my sake nor for yours.

We are dealing here with differences which not only are psychologically of the greatest delicacy, but whose boundaries are also constantly blurred in practice. Yet this mixture of motivations in which psychic reality moves, makes it all the more urgent that it be isolated analytically. Whether society and individual confront one another like two powers and the individual's subordination is effected by society through

311

energy which seems to flow from an uninterrupted source and constantly seems to renew itself; or whether this energy changes into a psychological impulse in the very individual who considers himself a social being and, therefore, fights and suppresses those of his impulses that lean toward his 'egoistic' part; or whether the Ought, which man finds above himself as an actuality as objective as Being, is merely filled with the content of societal life conditions – these are constellations which only begin to exhaust the kinds of individual subordination to the group. In them, the three powers which fill historical life – society, individual, and objectivity – become norm-giving, in this order. But they do so in such a way that each of them absorbs the social content, the quantity of superordination of society over the individual; in a specific manner, each of them forms and presents the power, the will, and the necessities of society.

4. SOCIETY AND 'OBJECTIVITY'

Among these three potencies, objectivity can be defined as the un-questionably valid law which is enthroned in an ideal realm above society and the individual. But it can also be defined in still another dimension, as it were. Society often is the third element, which solves conflicts between the individual and objectivity or builds bridges where they are disconnected. As regards the genesis of cognition, the concept of society has liberated us from an alternative characteristic of earlier times, namely, that a cultural value either must spring from an individual or must be bestowed upon mankind by an objective power. Practically speaking, it is societal labor by means of which the individual can satisfy his claims upon the objective order. The cooperation of the many, the efforts of society as a unit, both simultaneously and successively, wrest from nature not only a greater quantity of need-satisfactions than can be achieved by the individual, but also new qualities and types of need-satisfactions which the labor of the individual alone cannot possibly attain. This fact is merely a symbol of the deeper and funda-mental phenomenon of society standing between individual man and the sphere of general natural laws. As something psychologically concrete, society blends with the individual; as something general, it blends with nature. It is the general, but it is not abstract. To be sure, every historical group is an individual, as is every historical human being; but it is this only in relation to other groups; for its members, it is a super-individual. But it is super-individual, not as a concept is in regard to its single, concrete realizations, where the concept synthesizes what is common to all of them. The group is super-individual, rather in a specific manner of generality – similar to the organic body, which is 'general' above its organs, or to 'room furniture,' which is 'general' above table, chair, chest, and mirror. And this specific generality coincides with the specific objectivity which society possesses for its members as subjects.

But the individual does not confront society as he confronts nature. The objectivity of nature denotes the irrelevance of the question of whether or not the subject spiritually participates in nature; whether he has a correct, a false, or no conception of it. Its being exists, and its laws are valid, independently of the significance which either of them may have for any subject. Certainly, society, likewise, transcends the individual and lives its own life which follows its own laws; it, too, confronts the individual with a historical, imperative firmness. Yet, society's 'in front of' the individual is, at the same time, a 'within.' The harsh indifference toward the individual also is an interest: social objectivity needs general individual subjectivity, although it does not need any particular individual subjectivity. It is these characteristics which make society a structure intermediate between the subject and an absolutely impersonal generality and objectivity.

The following observation, for instance, points in this direction. As long as the development of an economy does not yet produce objective prices, properly speaking, as long as knowledge and regulation of demand, offer, production costs, amounts at risk, gain, etc., do not yet lead to the idea that a given piece of merchandise is worth so much and must have such and such a fixed price – so long is the immediate interference of society and its organs and laws with the affairs of commerce (particularly in regard to the price and stability of commerce) much more strong and rigorous than under other conditions. Price taxes, the surveillance of quantity and quality of production, and, in a larger sense, even sumptuary laws and consumers' obligations, often emerged at that stage of economic development at which the subjective freedom of commerce strove after stable objectivity, without, however, yet being able to attain any pure, abstract objectivity in determining prices. It is at this stage that the concrete generality, the living objectivity of society enters, often clumsily, obstructively, schematically, but yet always as a super-subjective power which supplies the individual with a norm before he derives this norm directly from the structure of the matter at issue and its understood regularity.

On a much larger scale, this same formal development, from sub-ordination under society to subordination under objectivity, occurs in the intellectual sphere. All of intellectual history shows to what extent the individual intellect fills the content of its truth-concepts only with traditional, authoritative conceptions which are 'accepted by all,' long before he confronts the object directly and derives the content of the truth-concepts from its objectivity. Initially, the support and the norm of the inquiring mind are not the object, whose immediate observation and interpretation the mind is entirely unable to manipulate, but the general opinion of the object. It is this general opinion which mediates theoretical conceptions, from the silliest superstition to the subtlest prejudices, which almost entirely conceal the lacking independence of their recipient and the un-objective nature of their contents. It seems as if man could not easily bear looking the object in the eye; as if he were equal neither to the rigidity of its lawfulness nor to the freedom which the object, in contrast to all coercion coming from men, gives him. By comparison, to bow to the authority of the many or their representatives, to traditional opinion, to socially accepted notions, is something intermediate. Traditional opinion, after all, is more modifiable than is the law of the object; in it, man can feel some psychological mediation; it transmits, as it were, something which is already digested psychologically. At the same time, it gives us a hold, a relief from responsibility – the compensation for the lack of that autonomy which we derive from the purely intrinsic relationship between ego and object.

The concept of objective justice, no less than the concept of truth, finds its intermediate stage, which leads toward the objective sense of 'justice,' in social behavior. In the field of criminal law, as well as in all other regulations of life, the correlation between guilt and expiation, merit and reward, service and counter-service, is first, evidently, a matter of social expediency or of social impulses. Perhaps the equivalence of action and reaction, in which justice consists, is never an analytical equivalence directly resulting from these elements, but always requires a third element, an ideal, a purpose, a norm-setting situation, in which the first two elements create or demonstrate their mutual correspondence synthetically. Originally, this third element consists in the interests and forms of the general life which surrounds the individuals, that is, the subjects of the realization of justice. This general life creates, and acts on, the criteria of justice or injustice in the relation between action and reaction – of justice or injustice which cannot be ascertained in the action-and-reaction in isolation. Above this process, and mediated by it, there rises, at an objectively and historically later stage, the necessity of the 'just' correspondence between action and reaction, a correspondence which emerges in the comparison of these two elements themselves. The higher norm, which perhaps even in this later phase continues to determine weight and counter-weight according to its own scale, is completely absorbed by the elements themselves; it has become a value which seems to originate with them and operates out of them. Justice now appears as an objective relationship which follows necessarily from the intrinsic significance of sin and pain, good deed and happiness, offer and response. It must be realized for its own sake: *fiat justitia, pereat mundus*. It was, by contrast, the very preservation of the world which, from the earlier standpoint, constituted the ground of justice. Whatever the ideal sense of justice may be (which is not the topic of discussion here), the *objective* law, in which justice, purely for its own sake, embodies itself, and which claims compliance in its own right, is historically and psychologically a later stage of development. It is preceded, prepared, and mediated by the claim to justice stemming from merely *social* objectivity.

This same development, finally, prevails within the moral sphere, in the stricter sense of this term. The original content of morality is of an altruistic-social nature. The idea is not that morality has its own life independent of this content and merely absorbs it. Rather, the devotion of the 'I' to the 'thou' (in the singular or plural) is the very idea, the definition, of the moral. Philosophical doctrines of ethics represent, by comparison, a much later phase. In them, an absolutely objective Ought is separated from the question of 'I' and 'thou.' If it is important to Plato that the Idea of the Good be realized; to Kant, that the principle of individual action be suitable as a general law; to Nietzsche, that the human species transcend its momentary stage of development; then, occasionally, these norms may also refer to reciprocal relations among individuals. But, essentially this is no longer important. What is important is the realization of an objective law, which not only leaves behind the subjectivity of the actor but also the subjectivity of the individuals whom the action may concern. For, now, even the reference to the societal complex of the subjects is merely an accidental satisfaction of a much more general norm and obligation, which may legitimate socially and altruistically oriented action, but may also refuse to do so. In the development of the individual as of the species, ethical obedience to the claims of the 'thou' and of society characterizes the first emergence from the pre-ethical stage of naïve egoism. Innumerable individuals never go beyond obedience to the 'thou.' But, in principle, this stage is preparatory and transitory to subordination under an objectively ethical law, which transcends the 'I' as much as the 'thou,' and only on its own initiative admits the interests of the one or the other as ethical contents.

5. THE EFFECT OF SUBORDINATION UNDER A PRINCIPLE UPON THE RELATIONS BETWEEN SUPERORDINATES AND SUBORDINATES

The second sociological question in regard to subordination under an impersonal-ideal principle concerns the effect of this common subordination upon the reciprocal relations among the subordinates. Here, also, it must above all be remembered that ideal subordination is often preceded by real subordination. We frequently find that a person or class exerts superordination in the name of an ideal principle to which the person or class themselves are allegedly subordinated. This principle, therefore, seems to be logically prior to the social arrangement; the actual organization of domination among people seems to develop in consequence of that ideal dependency. Historically, however, the road has usually run in the opposite direction. Superordinations and subordinations develop out of very real, personal power relations. Through the spiritualization of the superordinate power or through the enlargement and de-personalization of the whole relationship, there gradually grows an ideal, objective power over and above these superordinations and subordinations. The superordinate then exerts his power merely in the capacity of the closest representative of this ideal, objective force.

These successive processes are shown very distinctly in the development of the position of *pater familias* among the Aryans. Originally – this is how the type is presented to us – his power was unlimited and wholly subjective. That is, the *pater familias* decided all arrangements by momentary whim and in terms of personal advantage. Yet this arbitrary power was gradually replaced by a feeling of responsbility. The unity of the family group, embodied (for instance) in the *spiritus familiaris*, became an ideal force, in reference to which even the master of the whole felt himself to be merely an executor and obeyer. It is in this sense that custom and habit, rather than subjective preference, determined his actions, his decisions, and judicial decrees; that he no longer behaved as the unconditional master of the family property, but rather as its administrator in the interest of the whole; that his position had more the character of an office than that of an unlimited right. The relation between superordinates and subordinates was thus placed upon an entirely new basis. Whereas, at the first stage, the subordinates constituted, so to speak, only at a personal appurtenance of the superordinates, later there prevailed the objective idea of the family which stands above all individuals and to which the leading patriarch is as much subordinated as is every other member. The patriarch can give orders to the other members of the family only in the name of that ideal unit.

Here we encounter an extremely important form-type, namely, that the very commander subordinates himself to the law which he has made. The moment his will becomes law, it attains objective character, and thus separates itself from its subjective-personal origin. As soon as the ruler gives the law as law, he documents himself, to this extent, as the organ of an ideal necessity. He merely reveals a norm which is plainly valid on the ground of its inner sense and that of the situation, whether or not the ruler actually enunciates it. What is more, even if instead of this more or less distinctly conceived legitimation, the will of the ruler itself becomes law, even then the ruler cannot avoid transcending the sphere of subjectivity: for in this case, he carries the super-personal legitimation *a priori* in himself, so to speak. In this way, the inner form of law brings it about that the law-giver, in giving the law, subordinates himself to it as a person, in the same way as all others. Thus, the Privileges of the medieval Flemish cities stated expressly that the jurors must give everybody a fair trial, including even the Count who had bestowed this privilege upon the city. And such a sovereign ruler as the Great Elector introduced a head-tax without asking the estates for their consent – but then he not only made his court pay it, but he also paid it himself.

The most recent history gives an example of the growth of an objective power, to which the person, who is originally and subsequently in command, must subordinate himself in common with his subordinates. The example is formally related to the case cited from the history of the family. In modern economic production, objective and technical elements dominate over personal elements. In earlier times, many superordinations and subordinations had a personal character, so that in a given relationship, one person simply was superordinate, and the other subordinate. Many of these super-subordinations have changed in the sense that both superordinates and subordinates alike stand under an objective purpose; and it is only within this common relationship to the higher principle that the subordination of the one to the other continues to exist as a technical necessity. As long as the relationship of wage labor is conceived of as a rental contract (in which the worker is rented), it contains as an essential element the worker's subordination to the entrepreneur. But, once the work contract is considered, not as the renting of a person, but as the purchase of a piece of merchandise, that is, labor, then this element of personal subordination is eliminated. In this case, the subordination which the employer requests of the worker is only – so it has been expressed – subordination 'under the cooperative process, a subordination as compulsive for the entrepreneur, once he engages in any activity at all, as for the worker.' The worker is no longer subject as a person but only as the servant of an objective, economic procedure. In this process, the element which in the form of entrepreneur or manager is superordinated to the worker, operates no longer as a personal element but only as one necessitated by objective requirements.

The increased self-feeling of the modern worker must, at least partly, be connected with this process, which shows its purely sociological character also in the circumstance that it often has no influence upon the material welfare of the laborer. He merely sells a quantitatively defined service, which may be smaller or larger than what was required of him under the earlier, personal arrangement. As a man, he thus frees himself from the relationship of subordination, to which he belongs only as an element in the process of production; and to this extent, he is coordinate with those who direct the production. This technical objectivity has its symbol in the legal objectivity of the contract relation: once the contract is concluded, it stands as an objective norm above *both* parties. In the Middle Ages, this phenomenon marked the turning point in the condition of the journeyman, which originally implied full personal subordination under the master: the journeyman was generally called 'servant' [*Knecht*]. The gathering of journeymen in their own estate was centered upon the attempt at transforming the personal-service relationship into a contractual relationship: as soon as the organization of the 'servants' was achieved, their name, most characteristically, was replaced by that of 'journeymen.' In general, it is relative coordination, instead of absolute subordination, which is correlated with the contractual form, no matter what the material content of the contract may be.

This form further strengthens its objective character if the contract is not concluded between individuals, but consists in collective regulations between a group of workers on the one side, and a group of employers on the other. It has been developed especially by the English Trade Unions, which in certain, highly advanced industries conclude contracts regarding wage rates, working time, overtime, holidays, etc., with associations of entrepreneurs. These contracts may not be ignored by any sub-contract that might be made between individual members of these larger categories. In this manner, the impersonality of the labor relationship is evidently increased to an extraordinary degree. The objectivity of this relationship finds an appropriate instrument and expression in the super-individual collectivity. This objective character, finally, is assured in an even more specific manner if the contracts are concluded for very brief periods. English Trade Unions have always urged this brevity, in spite of the increased insecurity which results from it. The explanation of the recommendation has been that the worker distinguishes himself from the slave by the right to leave his place of work; but, if he surrenders this right for a long time, he is, for the whole duration of this period, subject to all conditions which the entrepreneur imposes upon him, with the exception of those expressly stipulated; and he has lost the protection offered him by his right to suspend the relationship. Instead of the breadth, or comprehensiveness, of the bond which in earlier times committed the total personality, there emerges, if the contract lasts very long, the length, or duration, of the bond. In the case of short contracts, objectivity is guaranteed, not by something positive, but only by the necessity of preventing the objectively regulated contractual relationship from changing into a relationship determined by subjective arbitrariness – whereas in the case of long contracts there is no corresponding, sufficient protection.

In the condition of domestic servants – at least, on the whole, in contemporary central Europe – it is still the total individual, so to speak, who enters the subordination. Subordination has not yet attained the objectivity of an objectively, clearly circumscribed service. From this circumstance derive the chief inadequacies inherent in the institution of domestic service. This institution does approach that more perfect form when it is replaced by services of persons who perform only certain, objective functions in the house, and who are, to this extent, coordinated with the housewife. The earlier, but still existing, relationship involved them as total personalities and obliged them – as is most strikingly shown by the concept of the 'all-round girl' ['*Madchen fur alles*'] – to 'unlimited services'; they became subordinate to the housewife as a person, precisely because there were no objective delimitations. Under thoroughly patriarchal (as contrasted with contemporary) conditions, the 'house' is considered an objective, intrinsic purpose and value, in behalf of which housewife and servants cooperate. This results, even if there is a completely personal subordination, in a certain coordination sustained by the interest which the servant, who is solidly and permanently connected with the house, usually feels for it. The 'thou,' used in addressing him, on the one hand, gives expression to his personal subordination, but on the other, makes him comparable to the children of the house and thus ties him more closely to its organization. Strangely enough, it thus appears that in some measure, obedience to an objective idea occurs at the extreme stages in the development of obedience: under the condition of full patriarchal subordination, where the house still has, so to speak, an absolute value, which is served by the work of the housewife (though in a higher position) as well as by that of the servant; and then, under the condition of complete differentiation, where service and reward are objectively pre-determined, and the personal attachment, which characterizes the stage of an undefined quantity of subordination, has become extraneous to the relationship. The contemporary position of the servant who shares his master's house, particularly in the large cities, has lost the first of these two kinds of objectivity, without having yet attained the second. The total personality of the servant is no longer claimed by the objective idea of the 'house'; and yet, in view of the general way in which his services are requested, it cannot really separate itself from it.

Finally, this form-type may be illustrated by the relationship between officers and common soldiers. Here, the cleavage between subordination within the organization of the group, and coordination which results from common service in defense of one's country, is as wide as can be imagined. Understandably enough, the cleavage is most noticeable at the front. On the one hand, discipline is most merciless there, but on the other hand, fellowship between officers and privates is furthered, partly by specific situations, partly by the general mood. During peace-time, the army remains arrested in the position of a means which does not attain its purposes; it is, therefore, inevitable for its technical structure to grow into a psychologically ultimate aim, so that super-subordination, on which the technique of the organization is based, stands in the foreground of consciousness. The peculiar sociological mixture with coordination, which results from the common subordination under an objective idea, becomes important only when the changed situation calls attention to this idea, as the real purpose of the army.

Within the group organization of his specific content of life, the individual thus occupies a superordinate or subordinate position. But the group as a whole stands under a dominating idea which gives each of its members an equal, or nearly equal, position in comparison with all outsiders. Hence, the individual has a double role which makes his purely formal, sociological situation the vehicle for peculiarly mixed life-feelings. The employee of a large business may have a leading position in his firm, which he lets his subalterns feel in a superior and imperious way. But, as soon as he confronts the public, and acts under the idea of his business as a whole, he will exhibit serviceable and devout behavior. In the opposite direction, these elements are interwoven in the frequent haughtiness of subalterns, servants in noble houses, members of decimated intellectual or social circles, who actually stand at the periphery of these groups, but to the outsider represent all the more energetically the dignity of the whole circle and of its idea. For, the kind of positive relation to the circle which they have, gives them only a semi-solid position in it, internally and externally; and they seek to improve it in a negative way, by differentiating themselves from others. The richest formal variety of this type is offered, perhaps, by the Catholic hierarchy. Although every member of it is bound by a blind obedience which admits of no contradiction, nevertheless, in comparison with the layman, even the lowest member stands at an absolute elevation, where the idea of the eternal God rises above all temporal matters. At the same time, the highest member of this hierarchy confesses himself to be the 'servant of servants.' The monk, who within his order may have absolute power, dresses himself in deepest humility and servility in the face of a beggar; but the lowest brother of an order is superior to the secular prince by all the absolute sovereignty of church authority.

5

Twentieth-century Sociology: The Pioneers of the American School

The story of twentieth-century sociology, certainly of the first half of the century, is largely the story of American sociology. This is not to say that sociology elsewhere declined, remained stagnant or was without influence. On the contrary, as will be shown presently, the sociological tradition that was firmly established in Germany and France at the end of the nineteenth century grew and was strengthened, in Germany right up to the early thirties, and in France it never really ceased to exercise a potent influence in various areas of research, while in England certain movements, especially in social anthropology, represented a new depature in sociological understanding of immense and lasting significance. Curiously enough, however, sociology in Europe to the end of the Second World War became increasingly insulated, with the three main centres pursuing their own course with very little interchange of ideas between them. This being the case, it is not surprising that American sociology, while drawing much inspiration from the historical and contemporary movements of thought in Europe, provided in turn at most only a peripheral interest to European sociologists. So it grew and flourished independently in its own way, ultimately stamping sociology everywhere with its own imprint of positive as well as negative elements.

American sociology in the twentieth century can be neatly divided into two periods, the first of which may be called the Pioneering Period. It was a period which started with the work of the ethnographers or cultural anthropologists of the second half of the nineteenth century and continued with the work of the sociologists of the latter part of the nineteenth and early part of the twentieth centuries. Of the former the most outstanding figures were undoubtedly Franz Boas (1858–1942) and L. H. Morgan (1818–81). Boas was the first scholar to have actually lived among Indians, learnt their language and written about their way of life. No anthropological research henceforth, if it were to claim any scientific validity, could fail to employ Boas's pioneering methodology or follow his example. Morgan's work, for obvious reasons, influenced a much wider circle of readers. Formulating a theory of social evolution, Morgan stressed the paramount significance of technological factors in the evolution of society. The history of man, according to him, can best be understood by taking these factors into account, in terms of definite stages of evolution through which men have passed everywhere. Like Comte and Spencer, he distinguished three main stages of cultural advance: savagery, barbarism and civilization, and each of the first two was divided into three sub-stages, all of them initiated by major technological inventions. In this way all developments in social institutions were correlated with certain advances in technology. Morgan's *Ancient Society*, because of the crucial importance he attached to material or technological factors, impressed many writers, including Marx and Engels, as being an authoritative or source work on the origin and development of social institutions. His real originality for which he is remembered today, consisted in his classification of family terms and his insight into the social significance of the language used to denote categories of kin. The lesson has only been slowly learnt that names of kin are of social origin and have a different connotation according to the social arrangement of the society in question. This is equally true of all categories of thought.

This preoccupation with primitive thought and culture was going to play a much larger part in research later on. In the meantime the vast expansion of American society in the last quarter of the nineteenth century led to an intensified interest in the contemporary American society as such. The rise of American sociology dates from this period. It drew its initial inspiration from the movements of thought in Europe. Comte, Spencer, Le Play, the German School of Psychology, all provided material for what developed into a distinct school of sociology in America. Largely eclectic at first, it soon acquired an individual and unmistakable trend, holding sway where sociology elsewhere was, if not languishing, still seeking admittance into respectable academic circles.

Three influences converged to give an individual stamp to American sociology. The first was the old tradition of rural life which was being slowly supplanted by the rise of urbanism and large-scale industrial organization. This movement was accepted, even welcomed, because of its quite obvious result in the extra-ordinarily rapid increase of national wealth. Technical and educational resources required to meet this new phase of industrial capitalism produced that pragmatic approach to problems which was a peculiarly American characteristic and inhibited the kind of scholarly and broad theorizing by which the founders of sociology in Europe formulated their ideas.

The combination of these two factors, while producing an ambivalence in the minds of sociologists, posed a problem concerning the value system which they were determined to uphold. Since most of them came from small-town or rural areas, they could not but hold the view that the only kind of stability, order and harmony would be found in the life of a small or rural community. Hence came the emphasis in American sociology on the small group as being in itself a self-contained and self-sufficient unit of society. No other society was really conceivable, so that the same features and compositions of one will be seen to be reproduced in any number of other societies. An inevitable corollary to this view was that every case of disorder, disorganiza-tion and disharmony was to be found only in a large-scale urban centre. The virtues of the one and the vices of the other were wildly exaggerated. From another angle, there were not wanting sociologists who welcomed the advent of industrial capitalism, with all its attendant and acknowledged evils, as a confirmation of a species of natural selection operating in human society whereby might, in this case wealth, is not only right but is the only good.

A third influence, absent in the older European societies, made an indelible mark on American society. The ubiquitous immigrant was the new and disturbing phenomenon. He was the outsider, the stranger, the queer character with his strange ways and language. The problem now was how he was to be assimilated, accommodated and adjusted to the norms and values of the other and dominant society. Here we observe why and how the idea of adjustment came to play such a disproportionate, even an obsessive, role in American sociology.

The Pioneers

We will now proceed to review the works and theories of those representatives of early American sociology whom we have described as the pioneers. We shall refer first to those who, like their contemporaries in Europe, were influenced by the fashionable theory of natural selection and the idea of progress. The most distinguished was undoubtedly W. G. Sumner (1840–1910). His chief work, *Folkways*, was a landmark in American sociology. He embraced in an extreme form the laissez-faire doctrine, quite in keeping with the anarchical free-for-all competitive struggle of early industrial capitalism. For Sumner, social development, like biological development, was blind, mechanical and irrevocable. Any attempt to tamper with this movement, as for example by government action, was useless and against the natural order of things. Somehow society always arrived at a certain measure of social behaviour by which it was always adapted to the struggle for survival. Social behaviour was of two kinds. First there was customary behaviour, largely unconscious, which was determined by the convention, usage and religion whose authority makes it very difficult, if not impossible, for the individual to resist. These customs Sumner called folkways. They become, as the second kind of social behaviour, mores, or morals, when people begin to think about them consciously. In this respect, morals are really rationalizations of customs, and it is this kind of morality which holds a group together and which determines what is good or bad, right or wrong. There are as many moralities as there are groups and the group which triumphs over another can claim that its morality is superior.

No other sociologist had such an extreme and inhuman approach to society. Others expressed the view that there was, after all, a place for governmental action to deal with the possible effects of unrestrained competition. Nevertheless behind all these views was the implicit or explicit assumption that some societies were superior to others by reason of their wealth and power. Such unquestioned superiority entitles them to lay down the rules for others and serve as an example for emulation and imitation. F. L. Ward (1841–1913) was a typical representative of this mode of thought. Ward introduced a large number of neologisms in his works, with the result that these have remained largely unread. He was greatly influenced by both Comte and Spencer, but what was most interesting in his sociology was the place it accorded to the social processes of conflict and opposition. If these are endemic it is also necessary to resolve them. Society cannot function or survive without a measure of compromise and cooperation. In a developed society there is a dual process of work, that of differentiation and homogeneity, to use Spencer's terminology, coexisting together in perfect adjustment. The U.S. is the greatest example of this and can be regarded as the model of world history.

A. W. Small (1854–1926) was less original than these two writers, and lacked their flamboyance; yet no man contributed more than he towards establishing sociology as an on-going academic discipline in America. Small founded the first department of sociology at the University of Chicago. In 1895 he founded the *American Journal of Sociology*, and he helped to found in 1905 the American Sociological Society. What is more, Small was one of the foremost exponents of the view that sociology, concerned as it is with the problems of society, must also point the means by which these problems are to be solved. In one form or another, this advocacy of social meliorism was a marked feature of the writings of most of the early American sociologists. This was only to be expected in view of the many serious problems attending the vast expansion which was overtaking American society.

At first, Small held the view, following Comte's idea of static sociology, that sociology was the study and analysis of social structures and functions. He soon abandoned this view in favour of a more dynamic concept directed to a broad-based and historical study whose aim was the understanding of the process of social development and change. In such a study, the interrelations of various social groups and the class struggle would figure prominently. This would eventually – an almost marxian prophecy, but without the revolutionary element – lead to a change in social policy towards the achievement of a more equitable social order. Like his contemporaries and successors, Small regarded the group as the unit on which sociological interest is focused.

One question, however, was left unanswered. What was the factor which brought individuals together in social groups? In Europe, the Hegelians, the Marxists, the French sociologists came out with different answers. The first American sociologist to provide an original answer based on a psychological theory was F. H. Giddings (1855–1931). Drawing largely on Adam Smith's famous theory of sentiments, Giddings developed his own theory of 'the consciousness of kind'. It is thanks to this factor, by which people recognize that they are of the same kind and therefore belong together, that they merge into an organized social unit. Rather than take some of the determinants of society which could presumably be responsible for the organization and cohesion of social units, property or lack of it, religion, language and so forth, Giddings, faithful to the evolutionary and biological analogies of his day, attempted to trace the stages of this development from the early instinctive periods of the childhood of the race to finally the norms of society which demand obedience and conformity. In doing this, Giddings virtually ceased to employ his valuable concept of the consciousness of kind in any meaningful way, for it was impossible by its means to account for the existence of norms, much less for the process whereby these norms undergo a change. So Giddings's sociology resolved itself finally into a hotch-potch of crude speculations and equally crude rationalizations. For him, as for Ward, society must go through the phases of competition and struggle for survival to arrive at tolerance and cooperation. Discipline is required to maintain social life, and therefore a body of people must arise in society to see that this discipline is upheld. This immediately leads to the view that there is constantly forming in society an élite which Giddings called a 'protocracy', composed of individuals who by virtue of their superior endowments are acknowledged and function as leaders of society. Here once again the more efficient and therefore the morally superior individual needs no justification, as he is a resounding confirmation of the universally established law of the survival of the fittest.

Other aspects of Giddings's sociology had a more lasting effect. He was one of the first advocates of the view that sociology is a science whose methods must be statistical; also that sociology must be psychologized without its being reduced to psychology. Henceforth American sociology could not be completely divorced from what has come to be known as 'social psychology', and the development of this branch of sociology owes much to the later work of American sociologists.

Giddings's work may be said to represent an intersection of two trends of thought, one that was slowly receding into the background, consisting of half-baked ideas, speculations and biological analogies, the other more forward-looking, determined to see sociology firmly based on sound theoretical and empirical foundations. Matters in which individuals and groups were involved were thought to be eminently qualified to be brought under observation and tested. Their interactions and the resultant pattern of behaviour would be seen to spring from some fundamental human or psychological process which it is the business of sociology to bring to light. If American sociology can be characterized by one unmistakable feature, it is its effort to bring together, and weld into one, the psychological and sociological. If, as will be shown in the course of the exposition, it had to pay a heavy penalty for this, its success in this matter, nevertheless, was remarkable.

Three people were mainly responsible for this new orientation. The first was E. A. Ross (1866–1951), who first used the term 'social psychology', in the title of one of his books. Ross was an unusual character. He was a sociologist, social reformer and a roving journalist. Among the social problems he dealt with were family, labour, big business, the press and over-population. He found problems everywhere, in Mexico, India and China, on all of which he wrote with perspicacity, sympathy and indignation. As a result of a visit he paid to Russia when the revolution broke out in 1917, he published extensively on the new régime. In his primarily sociological writings, he introduced a concept which is basic in sociology, viz. 'social control'. But unlike most sociologists, who have used this concept to denote the sanctions which society, whatever its forms, imposes on the individual, Ross believed that the individual himself, moved by certain inborn feelings, imposes control upon himself, from which are derived the public sanctions of the group. On this interpretation, public sanctions are a kind of guiding principle in society. Social psychology is the study of this control, and concerns itself with the static and dynamic factors which result from the psychological relationships of individuals. Ross naturally started with the view that it was instinct which brought people together in cooperation or drove them apart into conflict, but he later came to realize that this human drive, if it could ever be located, described and categorized, was only one of the many social forces which are determined by culture and civilization. In sociology, according to Ross, the main object of study was 'the social process', which was not the development of society but was itself the causal factor in all personal relationships. Ross distinguished five main types of social processes, those which might be due to external factors and those which were inherent in the very structure of society. It is from the interplay of these latter, like opposition and adaptation, conflict and co-operation, that different groups in society are continually being formed and re-formed. However crude this classification of human relationships was, in terms of pairs of polarized attitudes, it was the first of its kind, and has proved of inestimable value in having led the way to a much better understanding of social pressures.

The psychological character of sociology was even more evident in the works of C. H. Cooley (1864–1929). In one of his early works, *Human Nature and the Social Order*, Cooley expounded the theme that a man developed his individuality, his 'nature' only within society. The ego, in his famous metaphor, was 'a looking-glass ego', since it saw itself only as it appeared to others and in the minds of others. It was in this way that self-consciousness grew out of self-feeling. In another work, *Social Organization*, Cooley introduced and developed another concept, 'the primary group', the group that was characterized by close and intimate relationships like the family, neighbours, etc. The experiences generated by primary groups were the most vital and fundamental experiences of man, and all the great ideals of life were only possible and were reinforced by the existence of these groups. As Cooley was firmly convinced that sociology was primarily concerned with group phenomena, to understand which an artist's insight and a scientist's observation are required, he viewed with scepticism the increasing encroachments of statistics into sociological investigations.

A similar approach to sociology was found in the works of C. A. Ellwood (1873–1946). Like Cooley, Ellwood thought that psychology and sociology should enter into a marriage, not only of convenience, but of necessity. However, Ellwood's interests were more broadly based than Cooley's and he was more internationally minded. He, too, held the view that the methods of natural science and of statstics were insufficient to allow a proper understanding of social life. The individual in society had a role to play in the production of social consciousness. This role can only be understood in terms of the historical background and the culture of the society of which the individual happens to be a member. Again, like Cooley, Ellwood believed in the force of tradition, of which the primary group was the vehicle. Whatever changes happen in society result from the interactions of the members of the group with each other; these interactions or relationships he called 'communications', which are the most important elements in social development. Everything in society can therefore be said to be the product of collective consciousness, which is always kept alive as a result of 'discussion' taking place between individuals and groups.

Perhaps the most outstanding influence on American sociology, growing with the years, was that of G. H. Mead (1863–1931). Nobody was ever able, before or after Mead, to make a real synthesis between the individual, in all his biological and psychological aspects, and society. While Mead's method was that of behaviourism in the sense that human behaviour can be regarded in terms of reactions to the environment, nevertheless, unlike the behaviourists, Mead took account of the social factors which determine the consciousness of the individual. All man's biological urges and strivings (Mead never spoke of instincts) were moulded and given shape by social pressure. Here was the first attempt made to show how ways of life are internalized and individuals become socialized. The interactions of individuals have meaning in so far as each individual plays the 'role' that others expect of him. Thus, an individual's actual behaviour, including his ideas, is dominated by the social role that he assumes. He conforms to it because that is expected of him and it becomes agreeable to him because it is more or less common to the group and receives its sanctions from it.

*

These were the master-builders of American sociology. In respect of the number of people engaged in this discipline, and in respect of their published works as well as the new perspectives that were opened up, American sociology was firmly established with its own distinctive features and peculiar orientations. If it can be described by one word, it can be said to have been fragmentary, which was both its weakness and strength. It eschewed the kind of theorizing and wide-ranging speculations that characterized sociology in Europe, in spite of one or two attempts at formulating generalizations applicable to human society as such. It was not rooted in history, because the American system, being enlarged continuously through immigration and territorial expansion and its increasing preoccupation with new tasks, was essentially forward-looking. The practical task of ensuring the continued security and prosperity of an expanding population drawn from many parts of the world taxed the ingenuity of the leaders of society without the benefit of the advantage, which every settled community enjoys, of seeing itself as a historical entity. In these circumstances, it was impossible to expect American sociologists to look at the structure of society as a whole, to observe the interplay of forces inherent in it and the interrelations of its parts with one another.

The beginnings of American sociology, not surprisingly, coincided with that movement in American philosophy known as pragmatism. The principal idea behind pragmatism, as expounded by Peirce, James and Dewey, is the futility of any attempt to arrive at absolute truth. Since a high degree of probability is all that can be expected in scientific matters, it is sufficient if in theory

331

and practice we think of truth as something which works and produces the desired consequences. In other words, there can be degrees of truth, so that experimentation and innovation are the criteria of any advance in knowledge. This was in keeping with a system of social life that never questioned its basic principles, but was confident that it was moving towards a greater measure of power, control, and affluence.

Finally, early American sociology was imbued with a warm, benevolent, if hazy, kind of idealism. It felt itself involved in the welfare of society, confident in its unbounded optimism that sooner or later the problems of society would be solved. It was part of the business of sociology, it was thought, to prescribe remedies. But the sociologists were extremely vague and uncertain about these remedies. Society and its official policy proceeded in its own sweet way, conscious of its growing power, whose complacency could not be shaken even by such fulminatious and righteous indignation as the inexhaustible energy of Ross displayed.

William Graham Sumner 1840–1910

Major works

What Social Classes Owe to Each Other (1883)
Folkways (1906)
The Science of Society (4 volumes, 1927; completed by A. G. Keller, published in their joint names)

The following extracts are reprinted from William Graham Sumner, *Folkways* (Boston: Ginn & Co., 1906), §§ 64, 67, 68, 80, 82–4, 88, 91–3, 97–100, 102–3, 105, 112, 114, 117–21, with the permission of the publisher. Copyright © Ginn & Company, a Xerox company, 1940; Graham Sumner, 1934; William Graham Sumner, 1906. All rights reserved.

Difference between Mores and Some Cognate Things. – Products of intentional investigation or of rational and conscious reflection, projects formally adopted by voluntary associations, rational methods consciously selected, injunctions and prohibitions by authority, and all specific conventional arrangements are not in the mores. They are differentiated by the rational and conscious element in them. We may also make a distinction between usages and mores. Usages are folkways which contain no principle of welfare, but serve convenience so long as all know what they are expected to do. For instance, Orientals, to show respect, cover the head and uncover the feet; Occidentals do the opposite. There is no inherent and necessary connection between respect and either usage, but it is an advantage that there should be a usage and that all should know and observe it. One way is as good as another, if it is understood and established. The folkways as to public decency belong to the mores, because they have real connection with welfare which determines the only tenor which they can have. The folkways about propriety and modesty are sometimes purely conventional and sometimes inherently real. Fashions, fads, affectations, poses, ideals, manias, popular delusions, follies, and vices must be included in the mores. They have characteral qualities and characteral effect. However frivolous or foolish they may appear to people of another age, they have the form of attempts to live well, to satisfy some interest, or to win some good. The ways of advertisers who exaggerate, use tricks to win attention, and appeal to popular weakness and folly; the ways of journalism; electioneering devices; oratorical and dithyrambic extravagances in politics; current methods of humbug and sensationalism – are not properly part of the mores but symptoms of them. They are not products of the concurrent and coöperative effort of all members of the society to live well. They are devices made with conscious ingenuity to exert suggestion on the minds of others. The mores are rather the underlying facts in regard to the faiths, notions, tastes, desires, etc., of that society at that time, to which all these modes of action appeal and of whose existence they are evidence ...

Ritual. – The process by which mores are developed and established is ritual. Ritual is so foreign to our mores that we do not recognize its power. In primitive society it is the prevailing method of activity, and primitive religion is entirely a matter of ritual. Ritual is the perfect form of drill and of the regulated habit which comes from drill. Acts which are ordained by authority and are repeated mechanically without intelligence run into ritual. If infants and children are subjected to ritual they never escape from its effects through life. Galton says that he was, in early youth, in contact with the Mohammedan ritual idea that the left hand is less worthy than the right, and that he never overcame it ...

The Pioneers of the American School

The Ritual of the Mores. – The mores are social ritual in which we all participate unconsciously. The current habits as to hours of labor, meal hours, family life, the social intercourse of the sexes, propriety, amusements, travel, holidays, education, the use of periodicals and libraries, and innumerable other details of life fall under this ritual. Each does as everybody does. For the great mass of mankind as to all things, and for all of us for a great many things, the rule to do as all do suffices. We are led by suggestion and association to believe that there must be wisdom and utility in what all do. The great mass of the folkways give us discipline and the support of routine and habit. If we had to form judgments as to all these cases before we could act in them, and were forced always to act rationally, the burden would be unendurable. Beneficent use and wont save us this trouble . . .

The Mores Have the Authority of Facts. – The mores come down to us from the past. Each individual is born into them as he is born into the atmosphere, and he does not reflect on them, or criticize them any more than a baby analyses the atmosphere before he begins to breathe it. Each one is subjected to the influence of the mores, and formed by them, before he is capable of reasoning about them. It may be objected that nowadays, at least, we criticize all traditions, and accept none just because they are handed down to us. If we take up cases of things which are still entirely or almost entirely in the mores, we shall see that this is not so. There are sects of free-lovers amongst us who want to discuss pair marriage. They are not simply people of evil life. They invite us to discuss rationally our inherited customs and ideas as to marriage, which, they say, are by no means so excellent and elevated as we believe. They have never won any serious attention. Some others want to argue in favor of polygamy on grounds of expediency. They fail to obtain a hearing. Others want to discuss property. In spite of some literary activity on their part, no discussion of property, bequest, and inheritance has ever been opened. Property and marriage are in the mores. Nothing can ever change them but the unconscious and imperceptible movement of the mores. Religion was originally a matter of the mores. It became a societal institution and a function of the state. It has now to a great extent been put back into the mores. Since laws with penalties to enforce religious creeds or practices have gone out of use any one may think and act as he pleases about religion. Therefore it is not now 'good form' to attack religion. Infidel publications are now tabooed by the mores, and are more effectually repressed than ever before. They produce no controversy. Democracy is in our American mores. It is a product of our physical and economic conditions. It is impossible to discuss or criticize it. It is glorified for popularity, and is a subject of dithyrambic rhetoric. No one treats it with complete candor and sincerity. No one dares to analyse it as he would aristocracy or autocracy. He would get no hearing and would only incur abuse. The thing to be noticed in all these cases is that the masses oppose a deaf ear to every argument against the mores. It is only in so far as things have been transferred from the mores into laws and positive institutions that there is discussion about them or rationalizing upon them. The mores contain the norm by which, if we should discuss the mores, we should have to judge the mores. We learn the mores as unconsciously as we learn to walk and eat and breathe. The masses never learn how we walk, and eat, and breathe, and they never know any reason why the mores are what they are. The justification of them is that when we wake to consciousness of life we find them facts which already hold us in the bonds of tradition, custom, and habit. The mores contain embodied in them notions, doctrines, and maxims, but they are facts. They are in the present tense. They have nothing to do with what ought to be, will be, may be, or once was, if it is not now . . .

The Mores Are Unrecorded. – A society is never conscious of its mores until it comes in contact with some other society which has different mores, or until, in higher civilization, it gets information by literature. The latter operation, however, affects only the literary classes, not the masses, and society never consciously sets about the task of making mores. In the early stages mores are elastic and plastic; later they become rigid and fixed. They seem to grow up, gain strength, become corrupt, decline, and die, as if they were organisms. The phases seem to follow each other by an inherent necessity, and as if independent of the reason and will of the men affected, but the changes are always produced by a strain towards better adjustment of the mores to conditions and interests of the society, or of the controlling elements in it. A society does not record its mores in its annals, because they are to it unnoticed and unconscious. When we try to learn the mores of any age or people we have to seek our information in incidental references, allusions, observations of travelers, etc. Generally works of fiction, drama, etc., give us more information about the mores than historical records. It is very difficult to construct from the Old Testament a description of the mores of the Jews before the captivity. It is also very difficult to make a complete and accurate picture of the mores of the English colonies in North America in the seventeenth century. The mores are not recorded for the same reason that meals, going to bed, sunrise, etc., are not recorded, unless the regular course of things is broken.

Inertia and Rigidity of the Mores. – We see that we must conceive of the mores as a vast system of usages, covering the whole of life, and serving all its interests; also containing in themselves their own justification by tradition and use and wont, and approved by mystic sanctions until, by rational reflection, they develop their own philosophical and ethical generalizations, which are elevated into 'principles' of truth and right. They coerce and restrict the newborn generation. They do not stimulate to thought, but the contrary. The thinking is already done and is embodied in the mores. They never contain any provision for their own amendment. They are not questions, but answers, to the problem of life. They present themselves as final and unchangeable, because they present answers which are offered as 'the truth.' No world philosophy, until the modern scientific world philosophy, and that only within a generation or two, has ever presented itself as perhaps transitory, certainly incomplete, and liable to be set aside to-morrow by more knowledge. No popular world philosophy or life policy ever can present itself in that light. It would cost too great a mental strain. All the groups whose mores we consider far inferior to our own are quite as well satisfied with theirs as we are with ours. The goodness or badness of mores consists entirely in their adjustment to the life conditions and the interests of the time and place. Therefore it is a sign of ease and welfare when no thought is given to the mores, but all coöperate in them instinctively. The nations of southeastern Asia show us the persistency of the mores, when the element of stability and rigidity in them becomes predominant. Ghost fear and ancestor worship tend to establish the persistency of the mores by dogmatic authority, strict taboo, and weighty sanctions. The mores then lose their naturalness and vitality. They are stereotyped. They lose all relation to expediency. They become an end in themselves. They are imposed by imperative authority without regard to interests or conditions (caste, child marriage, widows). When any society falls under the dominion of this disease in the mores it must disintegrate before it can live again. In that diseased state of the mores all learning consists in committing to memory the words of the sages of the past who established the formulæ of the mores. Such words are 'sacred writings,' a sentence of which is a rule of conduct to be obeyed quite independently of present interests, or of any rational considerations.

Persistency. – Asiatic fixity of the mores is extreme, but the element of persistency in the mores is always characteristic of them. They are elastic and tough, but when once established in familiar and continued use they resist change. They give stability to the social order when they are well understood, regular, and undisputed. In a new colony, with a sparse population, the mores are never fixed and stringent. There is great 'liberty.' As the colony always has traditions of the mores of the mother country, which are cherished with respect but are never applicable to the conditions of a colony, the mores of a colony are heterogeneous and are always in flux. That is because the colonists are all the time learning to live in a new country and have no traditions to guide them, the traditions of the old country being a hindrance. Any one bred in a new country, if he goes to an old country, feels the 'conservatism' in its mores. He thinks the people stiff, set in their ways, stupid, and unwilling to learn. They think him raw, brusque, and uncultivated. He does not know the ritual, which can be written in no books, but knowledge of which, acquired by long experience, is the mark of fit membership in the society ...

Variability. – No less remarkable than the persistency of the mores is their changeableness and variation. There is here an interesting parallel to heredity and variation in the organic world, even though the parallel has no significance. Variation in the mores is due to the fact that children do not perpetuate the mores just as they received them. The father dies, and the son whom he has educated, even if he continues the ritual and repeats the formulæ, does not think and feel the same ideas and sentiments as his father. The observance of Sunday; the mode of treating parents, children, servants, and wives or husbands; holidays; amusements; arts of luxury; marriage and divorce; wine drinking, – are matters in regard to which it is easy to note changes in the mores from generation to generation, in our own times. Even in Asia, when a long period of time is taken into account, changes in the mores are perceptible. The mores change because conditions and interests change. It is found that dogmas and maxims which have been current do not verify; that established taboos are useless or mischievous restraints; that usages which are suitable for a village or a colony are not suitable for a great city or state; that many things are fitting when the community is rich which were not so when it was poor; that new inventions have made new ways of living economical and healthful. It is necessary to prosperity that the mores should have a due degree of firmness, but also that they should be sufficiently elastic and flexible to conform to changes in interests and life conditions. A herding or an agricultural people, if it moves into a new country, rich in game, may revert to a hunting life. The Tunguses and Yakuts did so as they moved northwards. In the early days of the settlement of North America many whites 'Indianized'; they took to the mode of life of Indians. The Iranians separated from the Indians of Hindostan and became agriculturists. They adopted a

337

new religion and new mores. Men who were afraid of powerful enemies have taken to living in trees, lake dwellings, caves, and joint houses. Mediæval serfdom was due to the need of force to keep the peasant on his holding, when the holding was really a burden to him in view of the dues which he must pay. He would have run away if he had not been kept by force. In the later Middle Ages the villain had a valuable right and property in his holding. Then he wanted security of tenure so that he could not be driven away from it. In the early period it was the duty of the lord to kill the game and protect the peasant's crops. In the later period it became the monopoly right of the lord to kill game. Thus the life conditions vary. The economic conjuncture varies. The competition of life varies. The interests vary with them. The mores all conform, unless they have been fixed by dogma with mystic sanctions so that they are ritual obligations, as is, in general, the case now in southeastern Asia. The rights of the parties, and the right and wrong of conduct, after the mores have conformed to new life conditions, are new deductions. The philosophers follow with their systems by which they try to construe the whole new order of acts and thoughts with reference to some thought fabric which they put before the mores, although it was found out after the mores had established the relations. In the case in which the fixed mores do not conform to new interests and needs crises arise. Moses, Zoroaster, Manu, Solon, Lycurgus, and Numa are either mythical or historical culture heroes, who are said to have solved such crises by new 'laws,' and set the society in motion again. The fiction of the intervention of a god or a hero is necessary to account for a reconstruction of the mores of the ancestors without crime . . .

Possibility of Modifying Mores. – The combination in the mores of persistency and variability determines the extent to which it is possible to modify them by arbitrary action. It is not possible to change them, by any artifice or device, to a great extent, or suddenly, or in any essential element; it is possible to modify them by slow and long-continued effort if the ritual is changed by minute variations. The German emperor Frederick II was the most enlightened ruler of the Middle Ages. He was a modern man in temper and ideas. He was a statesman and he wanted to make the empire into a real state of the absolutist type. All the mores of his time were ecclesiastical and hierocratic. He dashed himself to pieces against them. Those whom he wanted to serve took the side of the papacy against him. He became the author of the laws by which the civil institutions of the time were made to serve ecclesiastical domination. He carried the purpose of the crusades to a higher degree of fulfillment than they ever reached otherwise, but this brought him no credit or peace. The same drift in the mores of the time bore down the Albigenses when they denounced the church corporation, the hierarchy, and the papacy. The pope easily stirred up all Europe against them. The current opinion was that every state must be a Christian state according to the mores of the time. The people could not conceive of a state which could answer its purpose if it was not such. But a 'Christian state' meant one which was in harmony with the pope and the ecclesiastical organization. This demand was not affected by the faults of the organization, or the corruption and venality of the hierarchy. The popes of the thirteenth century rode upon this tide, overwhelming opposition and consolidating their power. In our time the state is charged with the service of a great number of interests which were then intrusted to the church. It is against our mores that ecclesiastics should interfere with those interests. There is no war on religion. Religion is recognized as an interest by itself, and is treated with more universal respect than ever before, but it is regarded as occupying a field of its own, and if there should be an attempt in its name to encroach on any other domain, it would fail, because it would be against the mores of our time.

Russia. – When Napoleon said: 'If you scratch a Russian you find a Tartar,' what he had perceived was that, although the Russian court and the capital city have been westernized by the will of the tsars, nevertheless the people still cling to the strongly marked national mores of their ancestors. The tsars, since Peter the Great, have, by their policing and dragooning, spoilt one thing without making another, and socially Russia is in the agonies of the resulting confusion. Russia ought to be a democracy by virtue of its sparse population and wide area of unoccupied land in Siberia. In fact all the indigenous and most ancient usages of the villages are democratic. The autocracy is exotic and military. It is, however, the only institution which holds Russia together as a unit. On account of this political interest the small intelligent class acquiesce in the autocracy. The autocracy imposes force on the people to crush out their inherited mores, and to force on them western institutions. The policy is, moreover, vacillating. At one time the party which favored westernizing has prevailed at court; at another time the old Russian or pan-Slavic party. There is internal discord and repression. The ultimate result of such an attempt to control mores by force is an interesting question of the future. It also is a question which affects most seriously the interests of western civilization. The motive for the westernizing policy is to get influence in European politics. All the interference of Russia in European politics is harmful, menacing, and unjustifiable. She is not, in character, a European power, and she brings no contribution to European civilization, but the contrary. She has neither the capital not the character to enable her to execute the share in the world's affairs which she is assuming. Her territorial extensions for two hundred years have been made at the cost of her internal strength. The latter has never been at all proportioned to the former. Consequently the debt and taxes due to her policy of expansion and territorial greatness have crushed her peasant class, and by their effect on agriculture have choked the sources of national strength. The people are peaceful and industrious, and their traditional mores are such that they would develop great productive power and in time rise to a strong civilization of a truly indigenous type, if they were free to use their powers in their own way to satisfy their interests as they experience them from the life conditions which they have to meet.

Emancipation in Russia and the United States. – In the time of Peter the Great the ancient national mores of Russia were very strong and firmly established. They remain to this day, in the mass of the population, unchanged in their essential integrity. There is, amongst the upper classes, an imitation of French ways, but it is unimportant for the nation. The autocracy is what makes 'Russia,' as a political unit. The autocracy is the apex of a military system, by which a great territory has been gathered under one control. That operation has not affected the old mores of the people. The tsar Alexander II was convinced by reading the writings of the great literary coterie of the middle of the nineteenth century that serfdom ought to be abolished, and he determined that it should be done. It is not in the system of autocracy that the autocrat shall have original opinions and adopt an independent initiative. The men whom he ordered to abolish serfdom had to devise a method, and they devised one which was to appear satisfactory to the tsar, but was to protect the interests which they cared for. One is reminded of the devices of American politicians to satisfy the clamor of the moment, but to change nothing. The reform had but slight root in public opinion, and no sanction in the interests of the influential classes; quite the contrary. The consequence is that the abolition of serfdom has thrown Russian society into chaos, and as yet reconstruction upon the new system has made little growth. In the United States the abolition of slavery was accomplished by the North, which had no slaves and enforced emancipation by war on the South, which had them. The mores of the South were those of slavery in full and satisfactory operation, including social, religious, and philosophical notions adapted to slavery. The abolition of slavery in the northern states had been brought about by changes in conditions and interests. Emancipation in the South was produced by outside force against the mores of the whites there. The consequence has been forty years of economic, social, and political discord. In this case free institutions and mores in which free individual initiative is a leading element allow efforts towards social readjustment out of which a solution of the difficulties will come. New mores will be developed which will cover the situation with customs, habits, mutual concessions, and coöperation of interests, and these will produce a social philosophy consistent with the facts. The process is long, painful, and discouraging, but it contains its own guarantees . . .

Reforms of Joseph II. – The most remarkable case of a reform attempted by authority, and arbitarary in its method, is that of the reforms attempted by Joseph II, emperor of Germany. His kingdoms were suffering from the persistence of old institutions and mores. They needed modernizing. This he knew and, as an absolute monarch, he ordained changes, nearly all of which were either the abolition of abuses or the introduction of real improvements. He put an end to survivals of mediæval clericalism, established freedom of worship, made marriage a civil contract, abolished class privilege, made taxation uniform, and replaced serfdom in Bohemia by the form of villanage which existed in Austria. In Hungary he ordered the use of the German language instead of Latin, as the civil language. Interferences with language act as counter suggestion. Common sense and expediency were in favor of the use of the German language, but the order to use it provoked a great outburst of national enthusiasm which sought demonstration in dress, ceremonies, and old usages. Many of the other changes made by the emperor antagonized vested interests of nobles and ecclesiastics, and he was forced to revoke them. He promulgated orders which affected the mores, and the mental or moral discipline of his subjects. If a man came to enroll himself as a deist a second time, he was to receive twenty-four blows with the rod, not because he was a deist, but because he called himself something about which he could not know what it is. No coffins were to be used, corpses were to be put in sacks and buried in quicklime. Probably this law was wise from a purely rational point of view, but it touched upon a matter in regard to which popular sentiment is very tender even when the usage is most irrational. 'Many a usage and superstition was so closely interwoven with the life of the people that it could not be torn away by regulation, but only by education.' Non-Catholics were given full civil rights. None were to be excluded from the cemeteries. The unilluminated Jews would have preferred that there should be no change in the laws. Frederick of Prussia said that Joseph always took the second step without having taken the first. In the end the emperor revoked all his changes and innovations except the abolition of serfdom and religious toleration. Some of his measures were gradually realized through the nineteenth century. Others are now an object of political effort.

Adoption of Mores of Another Age. – The Renaissance was a period in which an attempt was made by one age to adopt the mores of another, as the latter were known through literature and art. The knowledge was very imperfect and mistaken, as indeed it necessarily must be, and the conceptions which were formed of the model were almost as fantastic as if they had been pure creations of the imagination . . .

. . . The New England Puritans, in the seventeenth century, tried to build a society on the Bible, especially the books of Moses. The attempt was in every way a failure. It may well be doubted if any society ever existed of which the books referred to were a description, and the prescriptions were found ill adapted to seventeenth-century facts. The mores made by any age for itself are good and right for that age, but it follows that they can suit another age only to a very limited extent.

What Changes are Possible. – All these cases go to show that changes which run with the mores are easily brought about, but that changes which are opposed to the mores require long and patient effort, if they are possible at all. The ruling clique can use force to warp the mores towards some result which they have selected, especially if they bring their effort to bear on the ritual, not on the dogmas, and if they are contented to go slowly. The church has won great results in this way, and by so doing has created a belief that religion, or ideas, or institutions, make mores. The leading classes, no matter by what standard they are selected, can lead by example, which always affects ritual. An aristocracy acts in this way. It suggests standards of elegance, refinement, and nobility, and the usages of good manners, from generation to generation, are such as have spread from the aristocracy to other classes. Such influences are unspoken, unconscious, unintentional. If we admit that it is possible and right for some to undertake to mold the mores of others, of set purpose, we see that the limits within which any such effort can succeed are very narrow, and the methods by which it can operate are strictly defined. The favorite methods fail because they do not affect ritual, and because they always aim at great results in a short time. Above all, we can judge of the amount of serious attention which is due to plans for 'reorganizing society,' to get rid of alleged errors and inconveniences in it. We might as well plan to reorganize our globe by redistributing the elements in it.

Dissent from the Mores: Group Orthodoxy. – Since it appears that the old mores are mischievous if they last beyond the duration of the conditions and needs to which they were adapted, and that constant, gradual, smooth, and easy readjustment is the course of things which is conducive to healthful life, it follows that free and rational criticism of traditional mores is essential to societal welfare. We have seen that the inherited mores exert a coercion on every one born in the group. It follows that only the greatest and best can react against the mores so as to modify them. It is by no means to be inferred that every one who sets himself at war with the traditional mores is a hero of social correction and amelioration. The trained reason and conscience never have heavier tasks laid upon them than where questions of conformity to, or dissent from, the mores are raised. It is by the dissent and free judgment of the best reason and conscience that the mores win flexibility and automatic readjustment. Dissent is always unpopular in the group. Groups form standards of orthodoxy as to the 'principles' which each member must profess and the ritual which each must practice. Dissent seems to imply a claim of superiority. It evokes hatred and persecution. Dissenters are rebels, traitors, and heretics. We see this in all kinds of subgroups. Noble and patrician classes, merchants, artisans, religious and philosophical sects, political parties, academies and learned societies, punish by social penalties dissent from, or disobedience to, their code of group conduct. The modern trades union, in its treatment of a 'scab,' only presents another example. The group also, by a majority, adopts a programme of policy and then demands of each member that he shall work and make sacrifices for what has been resolved upon for the group interest. He who refuses is a renegade or apostate with respect to the group doctrines and interests. He who adopts the mores of another group is a still more heinous criminal. The mediæval definition of a heretic was one who varied in life and conversation, dress, speech, or manner (that is, the social ritual) from the ordinary members of the Christian community. The first meaning of 'Catholic' in the fourth century was a summary of the features which were common to all Christians in social and ecclesiastical behavior; those were Catholic who conformed to the mores and were characteristic of Christians. If a heretic was better than the Catholics, they hated him more. That never excused him before the church authorities. They wanted loyalty to the ecclesiastical corporation. Persecution of a dissenter is always popular in the group which he has abandoned. Toleration of dissent is no sentiment of the masses . . .

Social Policy. – In Germany an attempt has been made to develop social policy into an art (*Socialpolitik*). Systematic attempts are made to study demographical facts in order to deduce from them conclusions as to the things which need to be done to make society better. The scheme is captivating. It is one of the greatest needs of modern states, which have gone so far in the way of experimental devices for social amelioration and rectification, at the expense of tax payers, that those devices should be tested and that the notions on which they are based should be verified. So far as demographical information furnishes these tests it is of the highest value. When, however, the statesmen and social philosophers stand ready to undertake any manipulation of institutions and mores, and proceed on the assumption that they can obtain data upon which to proceed with confidence in that undertaking, as an architect or engineer would obtain data and apply his devices to a task in his art, a fallacy is included which is radical and mischievous beyond measure. We have, as yet, no calculus for the variable elements which enter into social problems and no analysis which can unravel their complications. The discussions always reveal the dominion of the prepossessions in the minds of the disputants which are in the mores. We know that an observer of nature always has to know his own personal equation. The mores are a societal equation. When the mores are the thing studied in one's own society, there is an operation like begging the question. Moreover, the convictions which are in the mores are 'faiths.' They are not affected by scientific facts or demonstration. We 'believe in' democracy, as we have been brought up in it, or we do not. If we do, we accept its mythology. The reason is because we have grown up in it, are familiar with it, and like it. Argument would not touch this faith. In like manner the people of one state believe in 'the state,' or in militarism, or in commercialism, or in individualism. Those of another state are sentimental, nervous, fond of rhetorical phrases, full of group vanity. It is vain to imagine that any man can lift himself out of these characteristic features in the mores of the group to which he belongs, especially when he is dealing with the nearest and most familiar phenomena of everyday life. It is vain to imagine that a 'scientific man' can divest himself of prejudice or previous opinion, and put himself in an attitude of neutral independence towards the mores. He might as well try to get out of gravity or the pressure of the atmosphere. The most learned scholar reveals all the philistinism and prejudice of the man-on-the-curbstone when mores are in discussion. The most elaborate discussion only consists in resolving on one's own axis. One only finds again the prepossessions which he brought to the consideration of the subject, returned to him with a little more intense faith. The philosophical drift in the mores of our time is towards state regulation, militarism, imperialism, towards petting and flattering the poor and laboring classes, and in favor of whatever is altruistic and humanitarian. What man of us ever gets out of his adopted attitude, for or against these now ruling tendencies, so that he forms judgments, not by his ruling interest or conviction, but by the supposed impact of demographic data on an empty brain. We have no grounds for confidence in these ruling tendencies of our time. They are only the present phases in the endless shifting of our philosophical generalizations, and it is only proposed, by the application of social policy, to subject society to another set of arbitrary interferences, dictated by a new set of dogmatic prepossessions that would only be a continuation of old methods and errors.

Degenerate and Evil Mores. Mores of Advance and Decline. – The case is somewhat different when attempts are made by positive efforts to prevent the operation of bad mores, or to abolish them. The historians have familiarized us with the notion of corrupt or degenerate mores. Such periods as the later Roman empire, the Byzantine empire, the Merovingian kingdom, and the Renaissance offer us examples of evil mores. We need to give more exactitude to this idea. Bad mores are those which are not well fitted to the conditions and needs of the society at the time. But, as we have seen, the mores produce a philosophy of welfare, more or less complete, and they produce taboos which are concentrated inhibitions directed against conduct which the philosophy regards as harmful, or positive injunctions to do what is judged expedient and beneficial. The taboos constitute morality or a moral system which, in higher civilization, restrains passion and appetite, and curbs the will. Various conjunctures arise in which the taboos are weakened or the sanctions on them are withdrawn. Faith in the current religion may be lost. Then its mystic sanctions cease to operate. The political institutions may be weak or unfit, and the civil sanctions may fail. There may not be the necessary harmony between economic conditions and political institutions, or the classes which hold the social forces in their hands may misuse them for their selfish interest at the expense of others. The philosophical and ethical generalizations which are produced by the mores rise into a realm of intellect and reason which is proud, noble, and grand. The power of the intelligence is a human prerogative. If the power is correctly used the scope of achievement in the satisfaction of needs is enormously extended. The penalty of error in that domain is correspondingly great. When the mores go wrong it is, above all, on account of error in the attempt to employ the philosophical and ethical generalizations in order to impose upon mores and institutions a movement towards selected and 'ideal' results which the ruling powers of the society have determined to aim at. Then the energy of the society may be diverted from its interests. Such a drift of the mores is exactly

345

analogous to a vice of an individual, i.e. energy is expended on acts which are contrary to welfare. The result is a confusion of all the functions of the society, and a falseness in all its mores. Any of the aberrations which have been mentioned will produce evil mores, that is, mores which are not adapted to welfare, so that a group may fall into vicious mores just as an individual falls into vicious habits . . .

The Correction of Aberrations. – It is impossible to arrest or avert such an aberration in the mores at its beginning or in its early stages. It is, however, very difficult to do so, and it would be very difficult to find a case in which it has been done. Necessarily the effort to do it consists in a prophecy of consequences. Such prophecy does not appeal to any one who does not himself foresee error and harm. Prophets have always fared ill, because their predictions were unwelcome and they were unpopular. The pension system which has grown up in the United States since the civil war has often been criticized. It is an abuse of extreme peril in a democracy. Demagogues easily use it to corrupt voters with their own money. It is believed that it will soon die out by its own limitations. There is, however, great doubt of this. It is more likely to cause other evil measures, in order that it may not die out. If we notice the way in which, in this case, people let a thing go in order to avoid trouble, we may see how aberrant mores come in and grow strong . . .

Antagonism between an Individual and the Mores. – The case of dissent from the mores, which was considered above (§100), is the case in which the individual voluntarily sets himself in antagonism to the mores of the society. There are cases in which the individual finds himself in involuntary antagonism to the mores of the society, or of some subgroup to which he belongs. If a man passes from one class to another, his acts show the contrast between the mores in which he was bred and those in which he finds himself. The satirists have made fun of the *parvenu* for centuries. His mistakes and misfortunes reveal the nature of the mores, their power over the individual, their pertinacity against later influences, the confusion in character produced by changing them, and the grip of habit which appears both in the persistence of old mores and the weakness of new ones. Every emigrant is forced to change his mores. He loses the sustaining help of use and wont. He has to acquire a new outfit of it. The traveler also experiences the change from life in one set of mores to life in another. The experience gives him the best power to criticize his native mores from a standpoint outside of them. In the north American colonies white children were often stolen by Indians and brought up by them in their ways. Whether they would later, if opportunity offered, return to white society and white mores, or would prefer to remain with Indians, seems to have depended on the age at which they were captured. Missionaries have often taken men of low civilization out of the society in which they were born, have educated them, and taught them white men's mores. If a single clear and indisputable case could be adduced in which such a person was restored to his own people and did not revert to their mode of life, it would be a very important contribution to ethnology. We are forced to believe that, if a baby born in New England was taken to China and given to a Chinese family to rear and educate, he would become a Chinaman in all which belongs to the mores, that is to say, in his character, conduct and code of life . . .

Antagonism between Groups in Respect to Mores. – When different groups come in contact with each other their mores are brought into contrast and antagonism. Some Australian girls consider that their honor requires that they shall be knocked senseless and carried off by the men who thereby become their husbands. If they are the victims of violence, they need not be ashamed. Eskimo girls would be ashamed to go away with husbands without crying and lamenting, glad as they are to go. They are shocked to hear that European women publicly consent in church to be wives, and then go with their husbands without pretending to regret it. In Homer girls are proud to be bought and to bring to their fathers a bride price of many cows. In India *gandharva* marriage is one of the non-honorable forms. It is love marriage. It rests on passion and is considered sensual; moreover, it is due to a transitory emotion. If property is involved in marriage the institution rests on a permanent interest and is guaranteed. Kaffirs also ridicule Christian love marriage. They say that it puts a woman on a level with a cat, the only animal which, amongst them, has no value. Where polygamy prevails women are ashamed to be wives of men who can afford only one each; under monogamy they think it is a disgrace to be wives of men who have other wives. The Japanese think the tie to one's father the most sacred. A man who should leave father and mother and cleave to his wife would become an outcast. Therefore the Japanese think the Bible immoral and irreligious. Such a view in the mores of the masses will long outlast the 'adoption of western civilization.' The Egyptians thought the Greeks unclean. Herodotus says that the reason was because they ate cow's flesh. The Greeks, as wine drinkers, thought themselves superior to the Egyptians, who drank beer. A Greek people was considered inferior if it had no city life, no agora, no athletics, no share in the games, no group character, and if it kept on a robber life.

The Pioneers of the American School

The real reason for the hatred of Jews by Christians has always been the strange and foreign mores of the former. When Jews conform to the mores of the people amongst whom they live prejudice and hatred are greatly diminished, and in time will probably disappear. The dislike of the colored people in the sold slave states of the United States and the hostility to whites who 'associate with negroes' is to be attributed to the difference in the mores of whites and blacks. Under slavery the blacks were forced to conform to white ways, as indeed they are now if they are servants. In the North, also, where they are in a small minority, they conform to white ways. It is when they are free and form a large community that they live by their own mores. The civil war in the United States was due to a great divergence in the mores of the North and the South, produced by the presence or absence of slavery. The passionate dislike and contempt of the people of one section for those of the other was due to the conception each had formed of the other's character and ways. Since the abolition of slavery the mores of the two sections have become similar and the sectional dislike has disappeared. The contrast between the mores of English America and Spanish America is very great. It would long outlast any political combination of parts of the two, if such should be brought about . . .

Modification of the Mores by Agitation. – To this point all projects of missions and reform must come. It must be recognized that what is proposed is an arbitrary action on the mores. Therefore nothing sudden or big is possible. The enterprise is possible only if the mores are ready for it. The conditions of success lie in the mores. The methods must conform to the mores. That is why the agitator, reformer, prophet, reorganizer of society, who has found out 'the truth' and wants to 'get a law passed' to realize it right away, is only a mischief-maker. He has won considerable prestige in the last hundred years, but if the cases are examined it will be found that when he had success it was because he took up something for which the mores were ready. Wilberforce did not overthrow slavery. Natural forces reduced to the service of man and the discovery of new land set men 'free' from great labor, and new ways suggested new sentiments of humanity and ethics. The mores changed and all the wider deductions in them were repugnant to slavery. The free-trade agitators did not abolish the corn laws. The interests of the English population had undergone a new distribution. It was the redistribution of population and political power in the United States which made the civil war. Witchcraft and trial by torture were not abolished by argument. Critical knowledge and thirst for reality made them absurd. In Queen Anne's reign prisons in England were frightful sinks of vice, misery, disease, and cruel extortion. 'So the prisons continued until the time of Howard,' seventy-five years later. The mores had then become humanitarian. Howard was able to get a response.

Capricious Interest of the Masses. – Whether the masses will think certain things wrong, cruel, base, unjust, and disgusting; whether they will think certain pleas and demands reasonable; whether they will regard certain projects as sensible, ridiculous, or fantastic, and will give attention to certain topics, depends on the convictions and feelings which at the time are dominant in the mores. No one can predict with confidence what the response will be to any stimulus which may be applied . . .

How the Group becomes Homogeneous. – The only way in which, in the course of time, remnants of foreign groups are apparently absorbed and the group becomes homogeneous, is that the foreign element dies out. In like manner people who live by aberrant mores die. The aberrant forms then cease to be, and the mores become uniform. In the meantime, there is a selection which determines which mores shall survive and which perish. This is accomplished by syncretism.

Syncretism. – Although folkways for the same purpose have a great similarity in all groups, yet they present variations and characteristic differences from group to group. These variations are sometimes due to differences in the life conditions, but generally causes for them are unascertainable, or the variations appear capricious. Therefore each in-group forms its own ways, and looks with contempt and abhorrence upon the ways of any out-group. Dialectical differences in language or pronunciation are a sufficient instance. They cannot be accounted for, but they call out contempt and ridicule, and are taken to be signs of barbarism and inferiority. When groups are compounded by inter-marriage, intercourse, conquest, immigration, or slavery, syncretism of the folkways takes place. One of the component groups takes precedence and sets the standards. The inferior groups or classes imitate the ways of the dominant group, and eradicate from their children the traditions of their own ancestors . . .

The Art of Societal Administration. – It is not to be inferred that reform and correction are hopeless. Inasmuch as the mores are a phenomenon of the society and not of the state, and inasmuch as the machinery of administration belongs to the state and not to the society, the administration of the mores presents peculiar difficulties. Strictly speaking, there is no administration of the mores, or it is left to voluntary organs acting by moral suasion. The state administration fails if it tries to deal with the mores, because it goes out of its province. The voluntary organs which try to administer the mores (literature, moral teachers, schools, churches, etc.) have no set method and no persistent effort. They very often make great errors in their methods. In regard to divorce, for instance, it is idle to set up stringent rules in an ecclesiastical body, and to try to establish them by extravagent and false interpretation of the Bible, hoping in that way to lead opinion; but the observation and consideration of cases which occur affect opinion and form convictions. The statesman and social philosopher can act with such influences, sum up the forces which make them, and greatly help the result. The inference is that intelligent art can be introduced here as elsewhere, but that it is necessary to understand the mores and to be able to discern the elements in them, just as it is always necessary for good art to understand the facts of nature with which it will have to deal. It belongs to the work of publicists and statesmen to gauge the forces in the mores and to perceive their tendencies. The great men of a great epoch are those who have understood new currents in the mores. The great reformers of the sixteenth century, the great leaders of modern revolutions, were, as we can easily see, produced out of a protest or revulsion which had long been forming under and within the existing system. The leaders are such because they voice the convictions which have become established and because they propose measures which will realize interests of which the society has become conscious. A hero is not needed. Often a mediocre, common-place man suffices to give the critical turn to thought or interest. 'A Gian Angelo Medici, agreeable, diplomatic, benevolent, and pleasure-loving, sufficed to initiate a series of events which kept the occidental races in perturbation through two centuries.' (Symonds, *Catholic Reaction*, I, 1944.) Great crises come when great new forces are at work changing fundamental conditions, while powerful institutions and traditions still hold old systems intact. The fifteenth century was such a period. It is in such crises that great men find their opportunity. The man and the age react on each other. The measures of policy which are adopted and upon which energy is expended become components in the evolution. The evolution, although it has the character of a nature process, always must issue by and through men whose passions, follies, and wills are a part of it but are also always dominated by it. The inter-action defies our analysis, but it does not discourage our reason and conscience from their play on the situation, if we are content to know that their function must be humble. Stoll boldly declares that if one of us had been a judge in the times of the witch trials he would have reasoned as the witch judges did, and would have tortured like them. (Stoll, *Suggestion und Hypnotismus*, 248.) If that is so, then it behooves us by education and will, with intelligent purpose, to criticize and judge even the most established ways of our time, and to put courage and labor into resistance to the current mores where we judge them wrong. It would be a mighty achievement of the science of society if it could lead up to an art of societal administration which should be intelligent, effective, and scientific.

Charles Horton Cooley 1864–1929

Major works

Genius, Fame and the Comparison of Races (1897)
Human Nature and the Social Order (1902)
Social Organization (1909)
Social Process (1918)

The following extract is reprinted from Charles Horton Cooley, *Social Organization* (New York: Charles Scribner's Sons, 1909), Chapter iii, with the permission of Charles Scribner's Sons. Copyright © Charles Scribner's Sons, 1909; renewal copyright Elsie Jones Cooley, 1937.

Primary Groups

MEANING OF PRIMARY GROUPS – FAMILY, PLAYGROUND, AND NEIGHBORHOOD – HOW FAR INFLUENCED BY LARGER SOCIETY – MEANING AND PERMANENCE OF 'HUMAN NATURE' – PRIMARY GROUPS, THE NURSERY OF HUMAN NATURE

By *primary groups* I mean *those characterized by intimate face-to-face associations and cooperation*. They are primary in several senses, but chiefly in that they are fundamental in forming the social nature and ideals of the individual. The result of intimate association, psychologically, is a certain fusion of individualities in a common whole, so that one's very self, for many purposes at least, is the common life and purpose of the group. Perhaps the simplest way of describing this wholeness is by saying that it is a 'we'; it *involves the sort of sympathy and mutual identification for which 'we' is the natural expression*. One lives in the feeling of the whole and finds the chief aims of his will in that feeling.

It is not to be supposed that the unity of the primary group is one of mere harmony and love. It is always a differentiated and usually

351

a competitive unity, admitting of self-assertion and various appropriative passions; but these passions are socialized by sympathy, and come, or tend to come, under the discipline of a common spirit. *The individual will be ambitious, but the chief object of his ambition will be some desired place in the thought of the others, and he will feel allegiance to common standards of service and fair play.* So the boy will dispute with his fellows a place on the *team*, but above such disputes will place the common glory of his class and school.

The most important spheres of this intimate association and cooperation – though by no means the only ones – are the *family, the play-group of children, and the neighborhood or community group of elders.* These are practically universal, belonging to all times and all stages of development; and are accordingly a chief basis of what is universal in human nature and human ideals. The best comparative studies of the family, such as those of Westermarck[1] or Howard,[2] show it to us as not only a universal institution, but as more alike the world over than the exaggeration of exceptional customs by an earlier school had led us to suppose. Nor can any one doubt the general prevalence of play-groups among children or of informal assemblies of various kinds among their elders. Such association is clearly the nursery of human nature in the world about us, and there is no apparent reason to suppose that the case has anywhere or at any time been essentially different.

As regards play, I might, were it not a matter of common observation, multiply illustrations of the universality and spontaneity of the group discussion and cooperation to which it gives rise. The general fact is that children, especially boys after about their twelfth year, live in fellowships in which their sympathy, ambition, and honor are engaged even more, often, than they are in the family. Most of us can recall examples of the endurance by boys of injustice and even cruelty, rather than appeal from their fellows to parents or teachers – as, for instance, in the hazing so prevalent at schools, and so difficult, for this very reason, to repress. And how elaborate the discussion, how cogent the public opinion, how hot the ambitions in these fellowships.

Nor is this facility of juvenile association, as is sometimes supposed, a trait peculiar to English and American boys; since experience among our immigrant population seems to show that the offspring of the more restrictive civilizations of the continent of Europe form self-governing play-groups with almost equal readiness. Thus, Miss Jane Addams, after pointing out that the 'gang' is almost universal, speaks of the interminable discussion which every detail of the gang's activity

1. *The History of Human Marriage.*
2. *A History of Matrimonial Institutions.*

receives, remarking that 'in these social folk-motes, so to speak, the young citizen learns to act upon his own determination.'[3]

Of the neighborhood group it may be said, in general, that from the time men formed permanent settlements upon the land, down, at least, to the rise of modern industrial cities, it has played a main part in the primary, heart-to-heart life of the people. Among our Teutonic forefathers the village community was apparently the chief sphere of sympathy and mutual aid for the commons all through the 'dark' and Middle Ages, and for many purposes it remains so in rural districts at the present day. In some countries we still find it with its ancient vitality, notably in Russia, where the *mir*, or self-governing village group, is the main theatre of life, along with the family, for perhaps fifty millions of peasants.

In our own life the intimacy of the neighborhood has been broken up by the growth of an intricate mesh of wider contacts which leaves us strangers to people who live in the same house. And even in the country the same principle is at work, though less obviously, diminishing our economic and spiritual community with our neighbors. How far this change is a healthy development, and how far a disease, is perhaps still uncertain.

Besides these almost universal kinds of primary association, there are many others whose form depends upon the particular state of civilization; the only essential thing, as I have said, *being a certain intimacy and fusion of personalities. In our own society, being little bound by place, people easily form clubs, fraternal societies, and the like, based on congeniality, which may give rise to real intimacy.* Many such relations are formed at school and college, and among men and women brought together in the first instance by their occupations – as workmen in the same trade, or the like. Where there is a little common interest and activity, kindness grows like weeds by the roadside.

But the fact that the family and neighborhood groups are ascendant in the open and plastic time of childhood makes them even now incomparably more influential than all the rest.

Primary groups are primary in the sense that they give the individual his earliest and most complete experience of social unity, and also in the sense that they do not change in the same degree as more elaborate relations, but form a comparatively permanent source out of which the latter are ever springing. Of course they are not independent of the larger society, but to some extent reflect its spirit; as the German family and the German school bear somewhat distinctly the print of German militarism. But this, after all, is like the tide setting back into creeks, and

3. *Newer Ideals of Peace*, p. 177.

does not commonly go very far. Among the German, and still more among the Russian, peasantry are found habits of free cooperation and discussion almost uninfluenced by the character of the state; and it is a familiar and well-supported view that the village commune, self-governing as regards local affairs and habituated to discussion, is a very widespread institution in settled communities, and the continuator of a similar autonomy previously existing in the clan. 'It is man who makes monarchies and establishes republics, but the commune seems to come directly from the hand of God.'[4]

In our own cities the crowded tenements and the general economic and social confusion have sorely wounded the family and the neighborhood, but it is remarkable, in view of these conditions, what vitality they show; and there is nothing upon which the conscience of the time is more determined than upon restoring them to health.

These groups, then, are springs of life, not only for the individual but for social institutions. They are only in part moulded by special traditions, and, in larger degree, express a universal nature. The religion or government of other civilizations may seem alien to us, but the children or the family group wear the common life, and with them we can always make ourselves at home.

By human nature, I suppose, we may understand those sentiments and impulses that are human in being superior to those of lower animals, and also in the sense that they belong to mankind at large, and not to any particular race or time. It means, particularly, sympathy and the innumerable sentiments into which sympathy enters, such as love, resentment, ambition, vanity, hero-worship, and the feeling of social right and wrong.[5]

Human nature in this sense is justly regarded as a comparatively permanent element in society. Always and everywhere men seek honor and dread ridicule, defer to public opinion, cherish their goods and their children, and admire courage, generosity, and success. It is always safe to assume that people are and have been human.

It is true, no doubt, that there are differences of race capacity, so great that a large part of mankind are possibly incapable of any high kind of social organization. But these differences, like those among individuals of the same race, are subtle, depending upon some obscure intellectual deficiency, some want of vigor, or slackness of moral fibre, and do not involve unlikeness in the generic impulses of human nature. In these, all races are very much alike. The more insight one gets into

4. De Tocqueville, *Democracy in America*, Vol. I, chap. v.

5. These matters are expounded at some length in the writer's *Human Nature and the Social Order*.

the life of savages, even those that are reckoned the lowest, the more human, the more like ourselves, they appear. Take for instance the natives of central Australia, as described by Spencer and Gillen,[6] tribes having no definite government or worship and scarcely able to count to five. They are generous to one another, emulous of virtue as they understand it, kind to their children and to the aged, and by no means harsh to women. Their faces as shown in the photographs are wholly human and many of them attractive.

And when we come to a comparison between different stages in the development of the same race, between ourselves, for instance, and the Teutonic tribes of the time of Caesar, the difference is neither in human nature nor in capacity, but in organization, in the range and complexity of relations, in the diverse expression of powers and passions essentially much the same.

There is no better proof of this generic likeness of human nature than in the ease and joy with which the modern man makes himself at home in literature depicting the most remote and varied phases of life – in Homer, in the Nibelung tales, in the Hebrew Scriptures, in the legends of the American Indians, in stories of frontier life, of soldiers and sailors, of criminals and tramps, and so on. The more penetratingly any phase of human life is studied, the more an essential likeness to ourselves is revealed.

To return to primary groups: the view here maintained is that human nature is not something existing separately in the individual, but a *group-nature or primary phase of society*, a relatively simple and general condition of the social mind. It is something more, on the one hand, than the mere instinct that is born in us – though that enters into it – and something less, on the other, than the more elaborate development of ideas and sentiments that makes up institutions. It is the nature which is developed and expressed in those simple, face-to-face groups that are somewhat alike in all societies; groups of the family, the playground, and the neighborhood. In the essential similarity of these is to be found the basis, in experience, for similar ideas and sentiments in the human mind. In these, everywhere, human nature comes into existence. Man does not have it at birth; he cannot acquire it except through fellowship, and it decays in isolation.

If this view does not recommend itself to common sense I do not know that elaboration will be of much avail. It simply means the application at this point of the idea that society and individuals are inseparable phases of a common whole, so that wherever we find an individual fact

6. *The Native Tribes of Central Australia*. Compare also Darwin's views and examples given in chap. vii of his *Descent of Man*.

we may look for a social fact to go with it. If there is a universal nature in persons there must be something universal in association to correspond to it.

What else can human nature be than a trait of primary groups? Surely not an attribute of the separate individual – supposing there were any such thing – since its typical characteristics, such as affection, ambition, vanity, and resentment, are inconceivable apart from society. If it belongs, then, to man in association, what kind or degree of association is required to develop it? Evidently nothing elaborate, because elaborate phases of society are transient and diverse, while human nature is comparatively stable and universal. In short, the family and neighborhood life is essential to its genesis and nothing more is.

Here, as everywhere in the study of society, we must learn to see mankind in psychical wholes, rather than in artificial separation. We must see and feel the communal life of family and local groups as immediate facts, not as combinations of something else. And perhaps we shall do this best by recalling our own experience and extending it through sympathetic observation. What, in our life, is the family and the fellowship; what do we know of the we-feeling? Thought of this kind may help us to get a concrete perception of that primary group-nature of which everything social is the outgrowth.

The following extracts are reprinted from Charles Horton Cooley, *Human Nature and the Social Order* (New York: Charles Scribner's Sons, 1902; Glencoe, Ill.: The Free Press, 1956, pp. 168–70, 171, 179–85, 187–8, 189–92, 193–4, 196–200, 202–7), with the permission of Charles Scribner's Sons.

It is well to say at the outset that by the word 'self' in this discussion is meant simply that which is designated in common speech by the pronouns for the first person singular, 'I,' 'me,' 'my,' 'mine,' and 'myself.' 'Self' and 'ego' are used by metaphysicians and moralists in many other senses, more or less remote from the 'I' of daily speech and thought, and with these I wish to have as little to do as possible. What is here discussed is what psychologists call the empirical self, the self that can be apprehended or verified by ordinary observation. I qualify it by the word social not as implying the existence of a self that is not social – for I think that the 'I' of common language always has more or less distinct reference to other people as well as the speaker – but because I wish to emphasize and dwell upon the social aspect of it . . .

Charles Horton Cooley

The distinctive thing in the idea for which the pronouns of the first person are names is apparently a characteristic kind of feeling which may be called the my-feeling of some sense of appropriation. Almost any sort of ideas may be associated with this feeling, and so come to be named 'I' or 'mine,' but the feeling, and that alone it would seem, is the determining factor in the matter. As Professor James says in his admirable discussion of the self, the words 'me' and 'self' designate 'all the things which have the power to produce in a stream of consciousness excitement of a certain peculiar sort.' This view is very fully set forth by Professor Hiram M. Stanley, whose work, 'The Evolutionary Psychology of Feeling,' has an extremely suggestive chapter on self-feeling.

I do not mean that the feeling aspect of the self is necessarily more important than any other, but that it is the immediate and decisive sign and proof of what 'I' is; there is no appeal from it; if we go behind it it must be to study its history and conditions, not to question its authority. But, of course, this study of history and conditions may be quite as profitable as the direct contemplation of self-feeling. What I would wish to do is to present each aspect in its proper light.

The emotion or feeling of self may be regarded as instinctive, and was doubtless evolved in connection with its important function in stimulating and unifying the special activities of individuals.[1] It is thus very profoundly rooted in the history of the human race and apparently indispensable to any plan of life at all similar to ours. It seems to exist in a vague though vigorous form at the birth of each individual, and, like other instinctive ideas or germs of ideas, to be defined and developed by experience, becoming associated, or rather incorporated, with muscular, visual, and other sensations; with perceptions, apperceptions, and conceptions of every degree of complexity and of infinite variety of content; and, especially, with personal ideas. Meantime the feeling itself does not remain unaltered, but undergoes differentiation and refinement just as does any other sort of crude innate feeling. Thus, while retaining under every phase its characteristic tone or flavor, it breaks up into innumerable self-sentiments. And concrete self-feeling, as it exists in mature persons, is a whole made up of these various sentiments, along with a good deal of primitive emotion not thus broken up. It partakes fully of the general development of the mind, but never loses that peculiar gusto of appropriation that causes us to name a thought with a first-personal pronoun . . .

1. It is, perhaps, to be thought of as a more general instinct, of which anger, etc., are differentiated forms, rather than as standing by itself.

The social self is simply any idea, or system of ideas, drawn from the communicative life, that the mind cherishes as its own. Self-feeling has its chief scope *within* the general life, not outside of it; the special endeavor or tendency of which it is the emotional aspect finds its principal field of exercise in a world of personal forces, reflected in the mind by a world of personal impressions.

As connected with the thought of other persons the self idea is always a consciousness of the peculiar or differentiated aspect of one's life, because that is the aspect that has to be sustained by purpose and endeavor, and its more aggressive forms tend to attach themselves to whatever one finds to be at once congenial to one's own tendencies and at variance with those of others with whom one is in mental contact. It is here that they are most needed to serve their function of stimulating characteristic activity, of fostering those personal variations which the general plan of life seems to require. Heaven, says Shakespeare, doth divide

> The state of man in divers functions,
> Setting endeavor in continual motion,

and self-feeling is one of the means by which this diversity is achieved.

Agreeably to this view we find that the aggressive self manifests itself most conspicuously in an appropriativeness of objects of common desire, corresponding to the individual's need of power over such objects to secure his own peculiar development, and to the danger of opposition from others who also need them. And this extends from material objects to lay hold, in the same spirit, of the attentions and affections of other people, of all sorts of plans and ambitions, including the noblest special purposes the mind can entertain, and indeed of any conceivable idea which may come to seem a part of one's life and in need of assertion against some one else. The attempt to limit the word self and its derivatives to the lower aims of personality is quite arbitrary; at variance with common sense as expressed by the emphatic use of 'I' in connection with the sense of duty and other high motives, and unphilosophical as ignoring the function of the self as the organ of specialized endeavor of higher as well as lower kinds.

That the 'I' of common speech has a meaning which includes some sort of reference to other persons is involved in the very fact that the word and the ideas it stands for are phenomena of language and the communicative life. It is doubtful whether it is possible to use language at all without thinking more or less distinctly of some one else, and certainly the things to which we give names and which have a large place in reflective thought are almost always those which are impressed upon us by our contact with other people. Where there is no communication there can be no nomenclature and no developed thought. What we call 'me,' 'mine,' or 'myself' is, then, not something separate from the general life, but the most interesting part of it, a part whose interest arises from the very fact that it is both general and individual. That is, we care for it just because it is that phase of the mind that is living and striving in the common life, trying to impress itself upon the minds of others. 'I' is a militant social tendency, working to hold and enlarge its place in the general current of tendencies. So far as it can it waxes, as all life does. To think of it as apart from society is a palpable absurdity of which no one could be guilty who really *saw* it as a fact of life.

> Der Mensch erkennt sich nur im Menschen, nur
> Das Leben lehret jedem was er sei.[2]

If a thing has no relation to others of which one is conscious he is unlikely to think of it at all, and if he does think of it he cannot, it seems to me, regard it as emphatically *his*. The appropriative sense is always the shadow, as it were, of the common life, and when we have it we have a sense of the latter in connection with it. Thus, if we think of a secluded part of the woods as 'ours,' it is because we think, also, that others do not go there. As regards the body I doubt if we have a vivid my-feeling about any part of it which is not thought of, however vaguely, as having some actual or possible reference to some one else. Intense self-consciousness regarding it arises along with instincts or experiences which connect it with the thought of others. Internal organs, like the liver, are not thought of as peculiarly ours unless we are trying to communicate something regarding them, as, for instance, when they are giving us trouble and we are trying to get sympathy.

'I,' then, is not all of the mind, but a peculiarly central, vigorous, and well-knit portion of it, not separate from the rest but gradually merging into it, and yet having a certain practical distinctness, so that a man generally shows clearly enough by his language and behavior what his 'I' is as distinguished from thoughts he does not appropriate. It may be thought of, as already suggested, under the analogy of a central colored area on a lighted wall. It might also, and perhaps more justly, be compared to the nucleus of a living cell, not altogether separate from the surrounding matter, or of which indeed it is formed, but more active and definitely organized.

The reference to other persons involved in the sense of self may be

2. 'Only in man does man know himself; life alone teaches each one what he is.' – Goethe, *Tasso*, act 2, sc. 3.

distinct and particular, as when a boy is ashamed to have his mother catch him at something she has forbidden, or it may be vague and general, as when one is ashamed to do something which only his conscience, expressing his sense of social responsibility, detects and disapproves; but it is always there. There is no sense of 'I,' as in pride or shame, without its correlative sense of you, or he, or they. Even the miser gloating over his hidden gold can feel the 'mine' only as he is aware of the world of men over whom he has secret power; and the case is very similar with all kinds of hid treasure. Many painters, sculptors, and writers have loved to withhold their work from the world, fondling it in seclusion until they were quite done with it; but the delight in this, as in all secrets, depends upon a sense of the value of what is concealed . . .

In a very large and interesting class of cases the social reference takes the form of a somewhat definite imagination of how one's self – that is any idea he appropriates – appears in a particular mind, and the kind of self-feeling one has is determined by the attitude toward this attributed to that other mind. A social self of this sort might be called the reflected or looking-glass self:

> Each to each a looking-glass
> Reflects the other that doth pass.

As we see our face, figure, and dress in the glass, and are interested in them because they are ours, and pleased or otherwise with them according as they do or do not answer to what we should like them to be; so in imagination we perceive in another's mind some thought of our appearance, manners, aims, deeds, character, friends, and so on, and are variously affected by it.

A self-idea of this sort seems to have three principal elements: the imagination of our appearance to the other person; the imagination of his judgment of that appearance and some sort of self-feeling, such as pride or mortification. The comparison with a looking-glass hardly suggests the second element, the imagined judgment, which is quite essential. The thing that moves us to pride or shame is not the mere mechanical reflection of ourselves, but an imputed sentiment, the imagined effect of this reflection upon another's mind. This is evident from the fact that the character and weight of that other, in whose mind we see ourselves, makes all the difference with our feeling. We are ashamed to seem evasive in the presence of a straightforward man, cowardly in the presence of a brave one, gross in the eyes of a refined one, and so on. We always imagine, and in imagining share, the judgments of the other mind. A man will boast to one person of an action – say some sharp transaction in trade – which he would be ashamed to own to another ...

As suggested in the previous chapter, self-feeling may be regarded as in a sense the antithesis, or better perhaps, the complement, of that disinterested and contemplative love that tends to obliterate the sense of a divergent individuality. Love of this sort has no sense of bounds, but is what we feel when we are expanding and assimilating new and indeterminate experience, while self-feeling accompanies the appropriating, delimiting, and defending of a certain part of experience; the one impels us to receive life, the other to individuate it. The self, from this point of view, might be regarded as a sort of citadel of the mind, fortified without and containing selected treasures within, while love is an undivided share in the rest of the universe. In a healthy mind each contributes to the growth of the other: what we love intensely or for a long time we are likely to bring within the citadel, and to assert as part of ourself. On the other hand, it is only on the basis of a substantial self that a person is capable of progressive sympathy or love ...

The view that 'self' and the pronouns of the first person are names which the race has learned to apply to an instinctive attitude of mind, and which each child in turn learns to apply in a similar way, was impressed upon me by observing my child M. at the time when she was learning to use these pronouns. When she was two years and two weeks old I was surprised to discover that she had a clear notion of the first and second persons when used possessively. When asked, 'Where is your nose?' she would put her hand upon it and say 'my.' She also understood that when some one else said 'my' and touched an object, it meant something opposite to what was meant when she touched the same object and used the same word. Now, any one who will exercise his imagination upon the question how this matter must appear to a mind having no means of knowing anything about 'I' and 'my' except what it learns by hearing them used, will see that it should be very puzzling. Unlike other words, the personal pronouns have, apparently, no uniform meaning, but convey different and even opposite ideas when employed by different persons. It seems remarkable that children should master the problem before they arrive at considerable power of abstract reasoning. How should a little girl of two, not particularly reflective, have discovered that 'my' was not the sign of a definite object like other words, but meant something different with each person who used it? And, still more surprising, how should she have

361

achieved the correct use of it with reference to herself which, it would seem, *could not be copied from any one else*, simply because no one else used it to describe what belonged to her? The meaning of words is learned by associating them with other phenomena. But how is it possible to learn the meaning of one which, as used by others, is never associated with the same phenomenon as when properly used by one's self? Watching her use of the first person, I was at once struck with the fact that she employed it almost wholly in a possessive sense, and that, too, when in an aggressive, self-assertive mood. It was extremely common to see R. tugging at one end of a plaything and M. at the other, screaming, 'My, my.' 'Me' was sometimes nearly equivalent to 'my,' and was also employed to call attention to herself when she wanted something done for her. Another common use of 'my' was to demand something she did not have at all. Thus if R. had something the like of which she wanted, say a cart, she would exclaim, 'Where's *my* cart?'

It seemed to me that she might have learned the use of these pronouns about as follows. The self-feeling had always been there. From the first week she had wanted things and cried and fought for them. She had also become familiar by observation and opposition with similar appropriative activities on the part of R. Thus she not only had the feeling herself, but by associating it with its visible expression had probably divined it, sympathized with it, resented it, in others. Grasping, tugging, and screaming would be associated with the feeling in her own case and would recall the feeling when observed in others. They would constitute a language, precedent to the use of first-personal pronouns, to express the self-idea. All was ready, then, for the word to name this experience. She now observed that R., when contentiously appropriating something, frequently exclaimed, '*my*,' '*mine*,' 'give it to *me*,' '*I* want it,' and the like. Nothing more natural, then, than that she should adopt these words as names for a frequent and vivid experience with which she was already familiar in her own case and had learned to attribute to others. Accordingly it appeared to me, as I recorded in my notes at the time, that '"my" and "mine" are simply names for concrete images of appropriativeness,' embracing both the appropriative feeling and its manifestation. If this is true the child does not at first work out the I-and-you idea in an abstract form. The first-personal pronoun is a sign of a concrete thing after all, but that thing is not primarily the child's body, or his muscular sensations as such, but the phenomenon of aggressive appropriation, practised by himself, witnessed in others, and incited and interpreted by a hereditary instinct. This seems to get over the difficulty above mentioned, namely, the seeming lack of a common content between the meaning of 'my' when used by another and when used by one's self. This common content is found in the appropriative feeling and the visible and audible signs of that feeling. An element of difference and strife comes in, of course, in the opposite actions or purposes which the 'my' of another and one's own 'my' are likely to stand for. When another person says 'mine' regarding something which I claim, I sympathize with him enough to understand what he means, but it is a hostile sympathy, overpowered by another and more vivid 'mine' connected with the idea of drawing the object my way.

In other words, the meaning of 'I' and 'mine' is learned in the same way that the meanings of hope, regret, chagrin, disgust, and thousands of other words of emotion and sentiment are learned: that is, by having the feeling, imputing it to others in connection with some kind of expression, and hearing the word along with it. As to its communication and growth the self-idea is in no way peculiar that I see, but essentially like other ideas. In its more complex forms, such as are expressed by 'I' in conversation and literature, it is a social sentiment, or type of sentiments, defined and developed by intercourse, in the manner suggested in a previous chapter . . .

I imagine, then, that as a rule the child associates 'I' and 'me' at first only with those ideas regarding which his appropriative feeling is aroused and defined by opposition. He appropriates his nose, eye, or foot in very much the same way as a plaything – by antithesis to other noses, eyes, and feet, which he cannot control. It is not uncommon to tease little children by proposing to take away one of these organs, and they behave precisely as if the 'mine' threatened were a separable object – which it might be for all they know. And, as I have suggested, even in adult life, 'I,' 'me,' and 'mine' are applied with a strong sense of their meaning only to things distinguished as peculiar to us by some sort of opposition or contrast. They always imply social life and relation to other persons. That which is most distinctively mine is very private, it is true, but it is that part of the private which I am cherishing in antithesis to the rest of the world, not the separate but the special. The aggressive self is essentially a militant phase of the mind, having for its apparent function the energizing of peculiar activities, and, although the militancy may not go on in an obvious, external manner, it always exists as a mental attitude . . .

The process by which self-feeling of the looking-glass sort develops in children may be followed without much difficulty. Studying the movements of others as closely as they do they soon see a connection between their own acts and changes in these movements, that is, they perceive their own influence or power over persons. The child appropriates the visible actions of his parent or nurse, over which he finds he has some control, in quite the same way as he appropriates one of his own members or a plaything, and he will try to do things with this new possession. just as he will with his hand or his rattle. A girl six months old will attempt in the most evident and deliberate manner to attract attention to herself, to set going by her actions some of those movements of other persons that she has appropriated. She has tasted the joy of being a cause, of exerting social power, and wishes more of it. She will tug at her mother's skirts, wriggle, gurgle, stretch out her arms, etc., all the time watching for the hoped-for effect. These performances often give the child, even at this age, an appearance of what is called affectation, that is, she seems to be unduly preoccupied with what other people think of her. Affectation, at any age, exists when the passion to influence others seems to over-balance the established character and give it an obvious twist or pose. It is instructive to find that even Darwin was, in his childhood, capable of departing from truth for the sake of making an impression. 'For instance,' he says in his autobiography, 'I once gathered much valuable fruit from my father's trees and hid it in the shrubbery, and then ran in breathless haste to spread the news that I had discovered a hoard of stolen fruit.'[3]

The young performer soon learns to be different things to different people, showing that he begins to apprehend personality and to foresee its operation. If the mother or nurse is more tender than just she will almost certainly be 'worked' by systematic weeping. It is a matter of common observation that children often behave worse with their mother than with other and less sympathetic people. Of the new persons that a child sees it is evident that some make a strong impression and awaken a desire to interest and please them, while others are indifferent or repugnant. Sometimes the reason can be perceived or guessed, sometimes not; but the fact of selective interest, admiration, prestige, is obvious before the end of the second year. By that time a child already cares much for the reflection of himself upon one personality and little for that upon another. Moreover, he soon claims intimate and tractable persons as *mine*, classes them among his other possessions, and maintains his ownership against all comers. M., at three years of age, vigorously resented R.'s claim upon their mother. The latter was '*my* mamma,' whenever the point was raised.

Strong joy and grief depend upon the treatment this rudimentary social self receives. In the case of M. I noticed as early as the fourth

3. Life and Letters of Charles Darwin, by F. Darwin, p. 27.

month a 'hurt' way of crying which seemed to indicate a sense of personal slight. It was quite different from the cry of pain or that of anger, but seemed about the same as the cry of fright. The slightest tone of reproof would produce it. On the other hand, if people took notice and laughed and encouraged, she was hilarious. At about fifteen months old she had become 'a perfect little actress,' seeming to live largely in imaginations of her effect upon other people. She constantly and obviously laid traps for attention, and looked abashed or wept at any signs of disapproval or indifference. At times it would seem as if she could not get over these repulses, but would cry long in a grieved way, refusing to be comforted. If she hit upon any little trick that made people laugh she would be sure to repeat it, laughing loudly and affectedly in imitation. She had quite a repertory of these small performances, which she would display to a sympathetic audience, or even try upon strangers. I have seen her at sixteen months, when R. refused to give her the scissors, sit down and make-believe cry, putting up her under lip and snuffling, meanwhile looking up now and then to see what effect she was producing.

In such phenomena we have plainly enough, it seems to me, the germ of personal ambition of every sort. Imagination co-operating with instinctive self-feeling has already created a social 'I,' and this has become a principal object of interest and endeavor.

Progress from this point is chiefly in the way of a greater definiteness, fulness, and inwardness in the imagination of the other's state of mind. A little child thinks of and tries to elicit certain visible or audible phenomena, and does not go back on them; but what a grown-up person desires to produce in others is an internal, invisible condition which his own richer experience enables him to imagine, and of which expression is only the sign. Even adults, however, make no separation between what other people think and the visible expression of that thought. They imagine the whole thing at once, and their idea differs from that of a child chiefly in the comparative richness and complexity of the elements that accompany and interpret the visible or audible sign. There is also a progress from the naïve to the subtle in socially self-assertive action. A child obviously and simply, at first, does things for effect. Later there is an endeavor to suppress the appearance of doing so; affection, indifference, contempt, etc., are simulated to hide the real wish to affect the self-image. It is perceived that an obvious seeking after good opinion is weak and disagreeable.

I doubt whether there are any regular stages in the development of social self-feeling and expression common to the majority of children. The sentiments of self develop by imperceptible gradations out of the crude appropriative instinct of new-born babes, and their manifestations vary indefinitely in different cases. Many children show 'self-consciousness' conspicuously from the first half-year; others have little appearance of it at any age. Still others pass through periods of affectation whose length and time of occurrence would probably be found to be exceedingly various. In childhood, as at all times of life, absorption in some idea other than that of the social self tends to drive 'self-consciousness' out . . .

Sex-difference in the development of the social self is apparent from the first. Girls have, as a rule, a more impressible social sensibility; they care more obviously for the social image, study it, reflect upon it more, and so have even during the first year an appearance of subtlety, *finesse*, often of affectation, in which boys are comparatively lacking. Boys are more taken up with muscular activity for its own sake and with construction, their imaginations are occupied somewhat less with persons and more with things. In a girl *das ewig Weibliche*, not easy to describe but quite unmistakable, appears as soon as she begins to take notice of people, and one phase of it is certainly an ego less simple and stable, a stronger impulse to go over to the other person's point of view and to stake joy and grief on the image in his mind. There can be no doubt that women are as a rule more dependent upon immediate personal support and corroboration than are men. The thought of the woman needs to fix itself upon some person in whose mind she can find a stable and compelling image of herself by which to live. If such an image is found, either in a visible or an ideal person, the power of devotion to it becomes a source of strength. But it is a sort of strength dependent upon this personal complement, without which the womanly character is somewhat apt to become a derelict and drifting vessel. Men, being built more for aggression, have, relatively, a greater power for standing alone. But no one can really stand alone, and the appearance of it is due simply to a greater momentum and continuity of character which stores up the past and resists immediate influences. Directly or indirectly the imagination of how we appear to others is a controlling force in all normal minds.

The vague but potent phases of the self associated with the instinct of sex may be regarded, like other phases, as expressive of a need to exert power and as having reference to personal function. The youth, I take it, is bashful precisely because he is conscious of the vague stirring of an aggressive instinct which he does not know how either to effectuate or to ignore. And it is perhaps much the same with the other sex: the bashful are always aggressive at heart; they are conscious of an interest in the other person, of a need to be something to him. And the more developed sexual passion, in both sexes, is very largely an emotion of power, domination, or appropriation. There is no state of feeling that says 'mine, mine,' more fiercely. The need to be appropriated or dominated which, in women at least, is equally powerful, is of the same nature at bottom, having for its object the attracting to itself of a masterful passion. 'The desire of the man is for the woman, but the desire of the woman is for the desire of the man.'[4]

Although boys have generally a less impressionable social self than girls, there is great difference among them in this regard. Some of them have a marked tendency to *finesse* and posing, while others have almost none. The latter have a less vivid personal imagination: they are un-affected chiefly, perhaps, because they have no vivid idea of how they seem to others, and so are not moved to seem rather than to be; they are unresentful of slights because they do not feel them, not ashamed or jealous or vain or proud or remorseful, because all these imply imagination of another's mind. I have known children who showed no tendency whatever to lie; in fact, could not understand the nature or object of lying or of any sort of concealment, as in such games as hide-and-coop. This excessively simple way of looking at things may come from unusual absorption in the observation and analysis of the impersonal, as appeared to be the case with R., whose interest in other facts and their relations so much preponderated over his interest in personal attitudes that there was no temptation to sacrifice the former to the latter. A child of this sort gives the impression of being non-moral; he neither sins nor repents, and has not the knowledge of good and evil. We eat of the tree of this knowledge when we begin to imagine the minds of others, and so become aware of that conflict of personal impulses which conscience aims to allay.

Simplicity is a pleasant thing in children, or at any age, but it is not necessarily admirable, nor is affectation altogether a thing of evil. To be normal, to be at home in the world, with a prospect of power, useful-ness, or success, the person must have that imaginative insight into other minds that underlies tact and *savoir-faire*, morality and beneficence. This insight involves sophistication, some understanding and sharing of the clandestine impulses of human nature. A simplicity that is merely the lack of this insight indicates a sort of defeat. There is, however, another kind of simplicity, belonging to a character that is subtle and sensitive, but has sufficient force and mental clearness to keep in strict

4. Attributed to Mme. de Staël.

order the many impulses to which it is open, and so preserve its directness and unity. One may be simple like Simple Simon, or in the sense that Emerson meant when he said, 'To be simple is to be great.' Affectation, vanity, and the like, indicate the lack of proper assimilation of the influences arising from our sense of what others think of us. Instead of these influences working upon the individual gradually and without disturbing his equilibrium, they overbear him so that he appears to be not himself, posing, out of function, and hence silly, weak, contemptible. The affected smile, the 'foolish face of praise' is a type of all affectation, an external, put-on thing, a weak and fatuous petition for approval. Whenever one is growing rapidly, learning eagerly, preoccupied with strange ideas, he is in danger of this loss of equilibrium; and so we notice it in sensitive children, especially girls, in young people between fourteen and twenty, and at all ages in persons of unstable individuality.

This disturbance of our equilibrium by the outgoing of the imagination toward another person's point of view means that we are undergoing his influence. In the presences of one whom we feel to be of importance there is a tendency to enter into and adopt, by sympathy, his judgment of ourself, to put a new value on ideas and purposes, to recast life in his image. With a very sensitive person this tendency is often evident to others in ordinary conversation and in trivial matters. By force of an impulse springing directly from the delicacy of his perceptions he is continually imagining how he appears to his interlocutor, and accepting the image, for the moment, as himself. If the other appears to think him well-informed on some recondite matter, he is likely to assume a learned expression; if thought judicious he looks as if he were, if accused of dishonesty he appears guilty, and so on. In short, a sensitive man, in the presence of an impressive personality, tends to become, for the time, his interpretation of what the other thinks he is. It is only the heavy-minded who will not feel this to be true, in some degree, of themselves. Of course it is usually a temporary and somewhat superficial phenomenon; but it is typical of all ascendancy, and helps us to understand how persons have power over us through some hold upon our imaginations, and how our personality grows and takes form by divining the appearance of our present self to other minds.

So long as a character is open and capable of growth it retains a corresponding impressibility, which is not weakness unless it swamps the assimilating and organizing faculty. I know men whose careers are a proof of stable and aggressive character and who have an almost feminine sensitiveness regarding their seeming to others. Indeed, if one sees a man whose attitude toward others is always assertive, never receptive, he may be confident that man will never go far, because he will never learn much. In character, as in every phase of life, health requires a just union of stability with plasticity.

George H. Mead 1863–1931

Major works

Mind. Self and Society From the Standpoint of a Social Behaviorist (1934)
Movements of Thought in the Nineteenth Century (1936)
The Philosophy of the Act (1938)

The Background of the Genesis of the Self

The problem now presents itself as to how, in detail, a self arises. We have to note something of the background of its genesis. First of all there is the conversation of gestures between animals involving some sort of co-operative activity. There the beginning of the act of one is a stimulus to the other to respond in a certain way, while the beginning of this response becomes again a stimulus to the first to adjust his action to the oncoming response. Such is the preparation for the completed act, and ultimately it leads up to the conduct which is the outcome of this preparation. The conversation of gestures, however, does not carry with it the reference of the individual, the animal, the organism, to itself. It is not acting in a fashion which calls for a response from the form itself, although it is conduct with reference to the conduct of others. We have seen, however, that there are certain gestures that do affect the organism as they affect other organisms and may, therefore, arouse in the organism responses of the same character as aroused in the other. Here, then, we have a situation in which the individual may at least arouse responses in himself and reply to these responses, the condition being that the social stimuli have an effect on the individual which is like that which they have on the other. That, for example, is what is implied in language; otherwise language as significant symbol would disappear, since the individual would not get the meaning of that which he says . . .

Another set of background factors in the genesis of the self is reprinted in the activities of play and the game.

Among primitive people, as I have said, the necessity of distinguishing the self and the organism was recognized in what we term the 'double'; the individual has a thing-like self that is affected by the individual as it affects other people and which is distinguished from the immediate organism in that it can leave the body and come back to it. This is the basis for the concept of the soul as a separate entity.

We find in children something that answers to this double, namely, the invisible, imaginary companions which a good many children produce in their own experience. They organize in this way the responses which they call out in other persons and call out also in themselves. Of course, this playing with an imaginary companion is only a peculiarly interesting phase of ordinary play. Play in this sense, especially the stage which precedes the organized games, is a play at something. A child plays at being a mother, at being a teacher, at being a policeman; that is, it is taking different rôles, as we say. We have something that suggests this in what we call the play of animals: a cat will play with her kittens, and dogs play with each other. Two dogs playing with each other will attack and defend, in a process which if carried through would amount to an actual fight. There is a combination of responses which checks the depth of the bite. But we do not have in such a situation the dogs taking a definite rôle in the sense that a child deliberately takes the rôle of another. This tendency on the part of the children is what we are working with in the kindergarten where the rôles which the children assume are made the basis for training. When a child does assume a rôle he has in himself the stimuli which call out that particular response or group of responses. He may, of course, run away when he is chased, as the dog does, or he may turn around and strike back just as the dog does in his play. But that is not the same as playing at something. Children get together to 'play Indian.' This means that the child has a certain set of stimuli which call out in itself the responses that they would call out in others, and which answer to an Indian. In the play period the child utilizes his own responses to these stimuli which he makes use of in building a self. The response which he has a tendency to make to these stimuli organizes them. He plays that he is, for instance, offering himself something, and he buys it; he gives a letter to himself and takes it away; he addresses himself as a parent, as a teacher; he arrests himself as a policeman. He has a set of stimuli which call out in himself the sort of responses they call out in others. He takes this group of responses and organizes them into a certain whole. Such is the simplest form of being another to one's self. It involves a temporal situation. The child says something in one character and responds in another character, and then his responding in another character is a stimulus to himself in the first character, and so the conversation goes on. A certain organized structure arises in him and in his other which replies to it, and these carry on the conversation of gestures between themselves.

If we contrast play with the situation in an organized game, we note the essential difference that the child who plays in a game must be ready to take the attitude of everyone else involved in that game, and that these different rôles must have a definite relationship to each other. Taking a very simple game such as hide-and-seek, everyone with the exception of the one who is hiding is a person who is hunting. A child does not require more than the person who is hunted and the one who is hunting. If a child is playing in the first sense he just goes on playing, but there is no basic organization gained. In that early stage he passes from one rôle to another just as a whim takes him. But in a game where a number of individuals are involved, then the child taking one rôle must be ready to take the rôle of everyone else. If he gets in a ball nine he must have the responses of each position involved in his own position. He must know what everyone else is going to do in order to carry out his own play. He has to take all of these rôles. They do not all have to be present in consciousness at the same time, but at some moments he has to have three or four individuals present in his own attitude, such as the one who is going to throw the ball, the one who is going to catch it, and so on. These responses must be, in some degree, present in his own make-up. In the game, then, there is a set of responses of such others so organized that the attitude of one calls out the appropriate attitudes of the other.

This organization is put in the form of the rules of the game. Children take a great interest in rules. They make rules on the spot in order to help themselves out of difficulties. Part of the enjoyment of the game is to get these rules. Now, the rules are the set of responses which a particular attitude calls out. You can demand a certain response in others if you take a certain attitude. These responses are all in yourself as well. There you get an organized set of such responses as that to which I have referred, which is something more elaborate than the rôles found in play. Here there is just a set of responses that follow on each other indefinitely. At such a stage we speak of a child as not yet having a fully developed self. The child responds in a fairly intelligent fashion to the immediate stimuli that come to him, but they are not organized. He does not organize his life as we would like to have him do, namely, as a whole. There is just a set of responses of the type of play. The child reacts to a certain stimulus, and the reaction is in himself that is called out in others, but he is not a whole self. In his game he has to have an organization of these rôles; otherwise he cannot play the game. The game represents the passage in the life of the child from taking the rôle of others in play to the organized part that is essential to self-consciousness in the full sense of the term.

The following extract is reprinted from George H. Mead, 'The Psychology of Punitive Justice', *American Journal of Sociology*, XXIII (1918), 577–602, with the permission of the University of Chicago Press. Copyright © University of Chicago Press, 1918.

The study of instincts on the one side and of the motor character of human conduct upon the other has given us a different picture of human nature from that which a dogmatic doctrine of the soul and an intellectualistic psychology presented to an earlier generation.

The instincts even in the lower animal forms have lost their rigidity. They are found to be subject to modification by experience, and the nature of the animal is found to be not a bundle of instincts but an organization within which these congenital habits function to bring about complex acts – acts which are in many cases the result of instincts which have modified each other. Thus new activities arise which are not the simple expression of bare instincts. A striking illustration of this is found in play, especially among young animal forms, in which the hostile instinct is modified and held in check by the others that dominate the social life of the animals. Again the care which the parent form gives to the infant animal admits of hostile features which, however, do not attain the full expression of attack and destruction usually involved in the instinct from which they arise. Nor is this merging and interaction of such divergent instinctive acts a process of alternate dominance of now one and now another instinct. Play and parental care may be and generally are of a piece, in which the inhibition of one tendency by the others has entered into the structure of the animal's nature and seemingly even of its congenital nervous organization. Another illustration of such a merging of divergent instincts is found in the elaborate wooing of the female among the birds.

Back of all this type of organization of instinctive conduct lies the social life within which there must be co-operation of the different individuals, and therefore a continual adjustment of the responses to the changing attitudes of the animals that participate in the corporate acts. It is this body of organized instinctive reactions to one another which makes up the social nature of these forms, and it is from a social nature of this kind exhibited in the conduct of lower forms that our human nature is evolved. An elaborate analysis of this is still in the making, but certain great features in it stand out with sufficient clearness to warrant comment. We find two opposing groups of instincts, those which we have named hostile and those which may be termed friendly, the latter being largely combinations of the parental and sexual instincts. The import of a herding instinct lying back of them all is still very uncertain if not dubious. What we do find is that individuals adjust themselves to each other in common social processes, but come into conflict with each other frequently in the process, that the expression of this individual hostility within the whole social act is primarily that of the destructive hostile type, modified and molded by the organized social reaction, that where this modification and control breaks down, as, e.g., in the rivalry of males in the herd or pack, the hostile instinct may assert itself in its native ruthlessness.

If we turn to the human nature that has developed out of the social nature of lower animals, we find in addition to the organization of social conduct that I have indicated a vast elaboration of the process of adjustment of individuals to each other. This elaboration of gesture, to use Wundt's generalized term, reaches its most developed expression in language. Now language was first the attitude, glance of the eye, movement of the body and its parts indicating the oncoming social act to which the other individuals must adjust their conduct. It becomes language in the narrower sense when it is a common speech of whatever form; that is when through his gesture the individual addresses *him*self as well as the others who are involved in the act. His speech is their speech. He can address himself in their gestures and thus present to himself the whole social situation within which he is involved, so that not only is conduct social but consciousness becomes social as well.

It is out of this conduct and this consciousness that human society grows. What gives it its human character is that the individual through language addresses himself in the rôle of the others in the group and thus becomes aware of them in his own conduct. But while this phase of evolution is perhaps the most critical in the development of man, it is after all only an elaboration of the social conduct of lower forms. Self-conscious conduct is only an exponent which raises the possible complications of group activity to a higher degree. It does not change the character of the social nature that is elaborated and complicated, nor does it change the principles of its organization. Human nature still remains an organization of instincts which have mutually affected each other. Out of such fundamental instincts as those of sex, parenthood, and hostility has arisen an organized type of social conduct, the conduct of the individual within the group. The attack upon the other individuals of the group has been modified and softened so that the individual asserts himself as over against the others in play, in courting, in care of the young, in certain common attitudes of attack and defense, without the attempted destruction of the individuals attacked. If we use the common terminology we shall account for these modifications by the process of trial and error within the evolution out of which has arisen the social form. Out of the hostile instinct has arisen conduct modified by the social instincts that has served to delimit the conduct springing from sex, parenthood, and mutual defense and attack. It has been the function of the hostile instinct to provide the reaction by which the individual asserts himself within a social process, thus modifying that process while the hostile conduct is itself modified *pro tanto*. The result is the appearance of new individuals, certain types of sex mates, playmates, parent and child forms, mates in fight and mates in defense. While this assertion of the individual within the social process delimits and checks the social act at various points, it leads to a modified social response with a new field of operation which did not exist for the unmodified instincts. The source of these higher complexes of social conduct appears suddenly when through a breakdown of the organization of the social act there is enacted a crime of passion, the direct outcome of self-assertion within sex, family, or other group responses. Unmodified self-assertion under these conditions means the destruction of the individual attacked.

When now, through the exponent of self-consciousness, the complexities of social conduct are raised to the nth power, when the individual addresses himself as well as the others, by his gestures, when in the rôle of another he can respond to his own stimulus, all the range of possible activities is brought within the field of social conduct. He finds himself within groups of varied sorts. The size of the group to which he can belong is limited only by his ability to co-operate with its members. Now the common control over the food process lifts these instincts out of the level of the mechanical response to biologically determined stimuli and brings them within the sweep of self-conscious direction inside of the larger group activity. And these varied groupings multiply the occasions of individual oppositions. Here again the instinct of hostility becomes the method of self-assertion, but while the oppositions are self-conscious the process of readjustment and the molding of the hostile attitudes by the larger social process remains in principle the same, though the long road of trial and error may be at times abandoned for the short cuts which the symbolism of language provides.

On the other hand the consciousness of self through consciousness of others is responsible for a more profound sense of hostility – that of the members of the groups to those opposed to it, or even to those merely outside it. And this hostility has the backing of the whole inner organization of the group. It provides the most favorable condition for the sense of group solidarity because in the common attack upon the common enemy the individual differences are obliterated. But in the development of these group hostilities we find the same self-assertion with the attempted elimination of the enemy giving way before the larger social whole within which the conflicting groups find themselves. The hostile self-assertion passes over into functional activities in the new type of conduct as it has taken place in play even among lower animal forms. The individual becomes aware of himself, not through the conquest of the other but through the distinction of function. It is not so much that the actual hostile reactions are themselves transformed as that the individual who is conscious of himself as over against the enemy finds other opportunities for conduct which remove the immediate stimuli for destroying the enemy. Thus the conqueror who realized himself in his power of life or death over the captive found in the industrial value of the slave a new attitude which removed the sense of hostility and opened the door to that economic development which finally placed the two upon the same ground of common citizenship.

It is in so far as the opposition reveals a larger underlying relationship within which the hostile individuals arouse non-hostile reactions that the hostile reactions themselves become modified into a type of self-assertion which is balanced against the self-assertion of those who had been enemies, until finally these oppositions became the compensating activities of different individuals in a new social conduct. In other words the hostile instinct has the function of the *assertion* of the social self when self comes into existence in the evolution of human behavior. The man who has achieved an economic, a legal, or any type of social triumph does not feel the impulse to physically annihilate his opponent, and ultimately the mere sense of the security of his social position may rob the stimulus to attack of all of its power.

The moral of this is, and one is certainly justified in emphasizing it at this time of a profound democratic movement in the midst of a world-war, that advance takes place in bringing to consciousness the larger social whole within which hostile attitudes pass over into self-assertions that are functional instead of destructive.

The following pages discuss the hostile attitude as it appears especially in punitive justice.

In the criminal court it is the purpose of the proceeding to prove that the defendant did or did not commit a certain act, that in case the defendant did commit the act this act falls under such and such a category of crime or misdemeanor as defined by the statute, and that, as a consequence, he is subject to such and such punishment. It is the assumption of this procedure that conviction and punishment are the accomplishment of justice and also that it is for the good of society, that is, that it is both just and expedient, though it is not assumed that in any particular case the meting out to a criminal of the legal recompense of his crime will accomplish an immediate social good which will outweigh the immediate social evil that may result to him, his family, and society itself from his conviction and imprisonment. Galsworthy's play *Justice* turns upon the wide discrepancy between legal justice and social good in a particular case. On the other side lies the belief that without this legal justice with all its miscarriages and disintegrating results society itself would be impossible. In the back of the public mind lie both these standards of criminal justice, that of retribution and that of prevention. It is just that a criminal should suffer in proportion to the evil that he has done. On the other hand it is just that the criminal should suffer so much and in such a manner that his penalty will serve to deter him and others from committing the like offense in the future. There has been a manifest shift in the emphasis upon these two standards. During the Middle Ages, when courts of justice were the antechambers to chambers of torture, the emphasis lay upon the nice proportioning of the suffering to the offense. In the grand epic manner Dante projected this torture chamber, as the accomplishment of justice, against the sphere of the heavens, and produced those magnificent distortions and magnifications of human primitive vengeance that the mediaeval heart and imagination accepted as divine.

There existed, however, even then no commensurability between retributory sufferings and the evil for which the criminal was held responsible. In the last analysis he suffered until satisfaction had been given to the outraged sentiments of the injured person, or of his kith and kin, or of the community, or of an angry God. To satisfy the latter an eternity might be too short, while a merciful death ultimately carried away from the most exacting community the victim who was paying for his sin in the coin of his own agony. Commensurability does not exist between sin and suffering but does exist roughly between the sin and the amount and kind of suffering that will satisfy those who feel themselves aggrieved and yet it has become the judgment of our common moral consciousness that satisfaction in the suffering of the criminal has no legitimate place in assessing his punishment. Even in its sublimated form, as a part of righteous indignation, we recognize its legitimacy only in resenting and condemning injury, not in rendering justice for the evil done. It was therefore natural that in measuring the punishment the emphasis should shift from retribution to prevention, for there is a rough quantitative relation between the severity of the penalty and the fear which it inspires. This shift to the standard of expediency in determining the severity of the penalty does not mean that retribution is no longer the justification for punishment either in the popular mind or in legal theory, for however expedient it may be to visit crimes with condign punishments in the interest of the welfare of society, the justification for inflicting the suffering at all is found in the assumption that the criminal owes retributive suffering to the community; a debt which the community may collect in the form and amount which is most expedient to itself.

The curious combination of the concepts of retributive suffering which is the justification for punishment but may not be the standard for the amount and degree of the punishment, and of a social expediency which may not be the justification for the punishment itself but is the standard of the amount and kind of punishment inflicted, is evidently not the whole story. If retribution were the only justification for punishment it is hard to believe that punishment would not itself have disappeared when society came to recognize that a possible theory of punishment could not be worked out or maintained on the basis of retribution; especially when we recognize that a system of punishments assessed with reference to their deterrent powers not only works very inadequately in repressing crime but also preserves a criminal class. This other part of the story, which neither retribution nor social expediency tells, reveals itself in the assumed solemnity of criminal court procedure, in the majesty of the law, in the supposedly impartial and impersonal character of justice. These characters are not involved in the concept of retribution nor in that of deterrence. Lynch law is the very essence of retribution and is inspired with the grim assurance that such summary justice must strike terror into the heart of the prospective criminal, and lynch law lacks solemnity, and majesty, and is anything but impersonal or impartial. These characters inhere, not in the primitive impulses out of which punitive justice has arisen nor in the cautious prudence with which society devises protection for its goods, but in the judicial institution which theoretically acts on rule and not upon impulse and whose justice is to be done though the heavens fall. What, then, are these values evidenced in and maintained by the laws of punitive justice? The most patent value is the theoretically impartial enforcement of the common will. It is a procedure which untertakes to recognize and protect the individual in the interest of the common good and by the common will. In his acceptance of the law and dependence upon it the individual is at one with the community, while this very attitude carries with it the recognition of his responsibility to obey and support the law in its enforcement. So conceived the common law is an affirmation of citizenship. It is, however, a grave mistake to assume that the law itself and men's attitudes toward it can exist *in abstracto*. It is a grave mistake, for too often the respect for law as law is what we demand of members of the community, while we are able to regard with comparative indifference defects both in the concrete laws and in their administration. It is not only a mistake, it is also a fundamental error, for all emotional attitudes – and even respect for law and a sense of responsibility are emotional attitudes – arise in response to concrete impulses. We do not respect law in the abstract but the values which the laws of the community conserve. We have no sense of responsibility as such but an emotional recognition of duties which our position in the community entails. Nor are these impulses and emotional reactions less concrete because they are so organized into complex habits that some slight but appropriate stimulus sets a whole complex of impulses into operation. A man who defends an apparently unimportant right on principle is defending the whole body of analogous rights which a vast complex of social habits tends to preserve. His emotional attitude, which is seemingly out of proportion to the immediate issue, answers to all of those social goods toward which the different impulses in the organized body of habits are directed. Nor may we assume that because our emotions answer to concrete impulses they are therefore necessarily egoistic or self-regarding. No small portion of the impulses which make up the human individual are immediately concerned with the good of others. The escape from selfishness is not by the Kantian road of an emotional response to the abstract universal, but by the recognition of the genuinely social character of human nature. An important instance of this illusory respect for abstract law appears in our attitude of dependence upon the law and its enforcement for the defense of our goods and those of others with whom we identify our interests.

A threatened attack upon these values places us in an attitude of defense, and as this defense is largely intrusted to the operation of the laws of the land we gain a respect for the laws which is in proportion to the goods which they defend. There is, however, another attitude more easily aroused under these conditions which is, I think, largely responsible for our respect for law as law. I refer to the attitude of hostility of the lawbreaker as an enemy to the society to which we belong. In this attitude we are defending the social structure against an enemy with all the animus which the threat to our own interests calls out. It is not the detailed operation of the law in defining the invasion of rights and their proper preservation that is the centre of our interest but the capture and punishment of the personal enemy, who is also the public enemy. The law is the bulwark of our interests, and the hostile procedure against the enemy arouses a feeling of attachment due to the means put at our disposal for satisfying the hostile impulse. The law has become the weapon for overwhelming the thief of our purses, our good names, or even of our lives. We feel toward it as we feel toward the police officer who rescues us from a murderous assault. The respect for the law is the obverse side of our hatred for the criminal aggressor. Furthermore the court procedure, after the man accused of the crime is put under arrest and has been brought to trial, emphasizes this emotional attitude. The state's attorney seeks a conviction. The accused must defend himself against this attack. The aggrieved person and the community find in this officer of the government their champion. A legal battle takes the place of the former physical struggle which led up to the arrest. The emotions called out are the emotions of battle. The impartiality of the court who sits as the adjudicator is the impartiality of the umpire between the contending parties. The assumption that contending parties will each do his utmost to win, places upon each, even upon the state's attorney, the obligation to get a verdict for his own side rather than to bring about a result which will be for the best interests of all concerned. The doctrine that the strict enforcement of the law in this fashion is for the best interest of all concerned has no bearing upon the point which I am trying to emphasize. This point is that the emotional attitude of the injured individual and of the other party to the proceedings – the community – toward the law is that engendered by a hostile enterprise in which the law has become the ponderous weapon of defense and attack.[1]

1. I am referring here to criminal law and its enforcement, not only because respect for the law and the majesty of the law have reference almost entirely to criminal justice, but also because a very large part, perhaps the largest part, of civil law proceedings are undertaken and carried out with the intent of defining and readjusting social situations without the hostile attitudes which characterize the criminal procedure. The parties to the civil proceedings belong to the same group and continue to belong to this group, whatever decision is rendered. No stigma attaches to the one who loses. Our emotional attitude toward this body of law is that of interest, of condemnation and approval as it fails or succeeds in its social function.

There is another emotional content involved in this attitude of respect for law as law, which is perhaps of like importance with the other. I refer to that accompanying stigma placed upon the criminal. The revulsions against criminality reveal themselves in a sense of solidarity with the group, a sense of being a citizen which on the one hand excludes those who have transgressed the laws of the group and on the other inhibits tendencies to criminal acts in the citizen himself. It is this emotional reaction against conduct which excludes from society that gives to the moral taboos of the group such impressiveness. The majesty of the law is that of the angel with the fiery sword at the gate who can cut one off from the world to which he belongs. The majesty of the law is the dominance of the group over the individual, and the paraphernalia of criminal law serves not only to exile the rebellious individual from the group, but also to awaken in law-abiding members of society the inhibitions which make rebellion impossible to them. The formulation of these inhibitions is the basis of criminal law. The emotional content that accompanies them is a large part of the respect for law as law. In both these elements of our respect for law as law, in the respect for the common instrument of defense from and attack upon the enemy of ourselves and of society, and in the respect for that body of formulated custom which at once identifies us with the whole community and excludes those who break its commandments, we recognize concrete impulses – those of attack upon the enemy of ourselves and at the same time of the community, and those of inhibition and restraint through which we feel the common will, in the identity of prohibition and of exclusion. They are concrete impulses which at once identify us with the predominant whole and at the same time place us on the level of every other member of the group, and thus set up that theoretical impartiality and even-handedness of punitive justice which calls out in no small degree our sense of loyalty and respect. And it is out of the universality that belongs to the sense of common action springing out of these impulses that the institutions of law and of regulative and repressive justice arise. While these impulses are concrete in respect of their immediate object, i.e., the criminal, the values which this hostile attitude toward the criminal protects either in society or in ourselves are negatively and abstractly conceived. Instinctively we estimate the worth of the goods protected by

It is not an institution that must be respected even in its disastrous failures. On the contrary it must be changed. It is hedged about in our feelings by no majesty. It is efficient or inefficient and as such awakens satisfaction or dissatisfaction and an interest in its reform which is in proportion to the social values concerned.

the procedure against the criminal and in terms of this hostile procedure. These goods are not simply the physical articles but include the more precious values of self-respect, in not allowing one's self to be over-ridden, in downing the enemy of the group, in affirming the maxims of the group and its institutions against invasions. Now in all of this we have our backs toward that which we protect and our faces toward the actual or potential enemy. These goods are regarded as valuable because we are willing to fight and even die for them in certain exigencies, but their intrinsic value is neither affirmed nor considered in the legal proceeding. The values thus obtained are not their values in use but sacrifice values. To many a man his country has become infinitely valu-able because he finds himself willing to fight and die for it when the common impulse of attack upon the common enemy has been aroused, and yet he may have been, in his daily life, a traitor to the social values he is dying to protect because there was no emotional situation within which these values appeared in his consciousness. It is difficult to bring into commensurable relationship to each other a man's willingness to cheat his country out of its legitimate taxes and his willingness to fight and die for the same country. The reactions spring from different sets of impulses and lead to evaluations which seem to have nothing in common with each other. The type of valuation of social goods that arises out of the hostile attitude toward the criminal is negative, because it does not present the positive social function of the goods that the hostile procedure protects. From the standpoint of protection one thing behind the wall has the same import as anything else that lies behind the same defense. The respect for law as law thus is found to be a respect for a social organization of defense against the enemy of the group and a legal and judicial procedure that are oriented with reference to the criminal. The attempt to utilize these social attitudes and procedures to remove the causes of crime, to assess the kind and amount of punishment which the criminal should suffer in the interest of society, or to reinstate the criminal as a law-abiding citizen has failed utterly. For while the institutions which inspire our respect are concrete institutions with a definite function, they are responsible for a quite abstract and inadequate evaluation of society and its goods. These legal and political institutions organized with reference to the enemy or at least the outsider give a statement of social goods which is based upon defense and not upon function. The aim of the criminal proceeding is to determine whether the accused is innocent, i.e., still belongs to the group or whether he is guilty, i.e., is put under the ban which criminal punishment carries with it. The tech-nical statement of this is found in the loss of the privileges of a citizen, in sentences of any severity, but the more serious ban is found in the fixed attitude of hostility on the part of the community toward a jailbird. One effect of this is to define the goods and privileges of the members of the community as theirs in virtue of their being law-abiding, and their responsibilities as exhausted by the statutes which determine the nature of criminal conduct. This effect is not due alone to the logical tendency to maintain the same definition of the institution of property over against the conduct of the thief and that of the law-abiding citizen. It is due in far greater degree to the feeling that we all stand together in the protection of property. In the positive definition of property, that is in terms of its social uses and functions, we are met by wide diversity of opinion, especially where the theoretically wide freedom of control over private property, asserted over against the thief, is restrained in the interest of problematic public goods. Out of this attitude toward the goods which the criminal law protects arises that fundamental difficulty in social reform which is due, not to mere difference in opinion nor to conscious selfishness, but to the fact that what we term opinions are profound social attitudes which, once assumed, fuse all conflicting tendencies over against the enemy of the people. The respect for law as law in its positive use in defense of social goods becomes unwittingly a respect for the conceptions of these goods which the attitude of defense has fashioned. Property becomes sacred not because of its social uses but because all the community is as one in its defense, and this conception of property, taken over into the social struggle to make property serve its functions in the community, becomes the bulwark of these in possession, *beati possidentes*.

Beside property other institutions have arisen, that of the person with its rights, that of the family with its rights, and that of the government with its rights. Wherever rights exist, invasion of these rights may be punished, and a definition of these institutions is formulated in protecting the right against trespass. The definition is again the voice of the community as a whole proclaiming and penalizing the one whose conduct has placed him under the ban. There is the same unfortunate circumstance that the law speaking against the criminal gives the sanction of the sovereign authority of the community to the negative definition of the right. It is defined in terms of its contemplated invasion. The individual who is defending his own rights against the trespasser is led to state even his family and more general social interests in abstract individualistic terms. Abstract individualism and a negative conception of liberty in terms of the freedom from restraints become the working ideas in the community. They have the prestige of battle cries in the fight for freedom against privilege. They are still the countersigns of the descendants of those who cast off the bonds of political and social restraint in their defense and assertion of the rights their forefathers won. Wherever criminal justice, the modern elaborate development of the taboo, the ban, and their consequences in a primitive society, organizes and formulates public sentiment in defense of social goods and institutions against actual or prospective enemies, there we find that the definition of the enemies, in other words the criminals, carries with it the definition of the goods and institutions. It is the revenge of the criminal upon the society which crushes him. The concentration of public sentiment upon the criminal which mobilizes the institution of justice, paralyses the undertaking to conceive our common goods in terms of their uses. The majesty of the law is that of the sword drawn against a common enemy. The even-handedness of justice is that of universal conscription against a common enemy, and that of the abstract definition of rights which places the ban upon anyone who falls outside of its rigid terms.

Thus we see society almost helpless in the grip of the hostile attitude it has taken toward those who break its laws and contravene its institutions. Hostility toward the lawbreaker inevitably brings with it the attitudes of retribution, repression, and exclusion. These provide no principles for the eradication of crime, for returning the delinquent to normal social relations, nor for stating the transgressed rights and institutions in terms of their positive social functions.

On the other side of the ledger stands the fact that the attitude of hostility toward the lawbreaker has the unique advantage of uniting all members of the community in the emotional solidarity of aggression. While the most admirable of humanitarian efforts are sure to run counter to the individual interests of very many in the community, or fail to touch the interest and imagination of the multitude and to leave the community divided or indifferent, the cry of thief or murder is attuned to profound complexes, lying below the surface of competing individual effort, and citizens who have separated by divergent interests stand together against the common enemy. Furthermore, the attitude reveals common, universal values which underlie like a bedrock the divergent structures of individual ends that are mutually closed and hostile to each other. Seemingly without the criminal the cohesiveness of society would disappear and the universal goods of the community would crumble into mutually repellent individual particles. The criminal does not seriously endanger the structure of society by his destructive activities, and on the other hand he is responsible for a sense of solidarity, aroused among those whose attention would be otherwise centered upon interests quite divergent from those of each other. Thus courts of criminal justice may be essential to the preservation of society even when we take account of the impotence of the criminal over against society, and the clumsy failure of criminal law in the repression and suppression of crime. I am willing to admit that this statement is distorted, not however in its analysis of the efficacy of the procedure against the criminal, but in its failure to recognize the growing consciousness of the many common interests which is slowly changing our institutional conception of society, and its consequent exaggerated estimate upon the import of the criminal. But it is important that we should realize what the implications of this attitude of hostility are within our society. We should especially recognize the inevitable limitations which the attitude carries with it. Social organization which arises out of hostility at once emphasizes the character which is the basis of the opposition and tends to suppress all other characters in the members of the group. The cry of 'stop thief' unites us all as property owners against the robber. We all stand shoulder to shoulder as Americans against a possible invader. Just in proportion as we organize by hostility do we suppress individuality. In a political campaign that is fought on party lines the members of the party surrender themselves to the party. They become simply members of the party whose conscious aim is to defeat the rival organization. For this purpose the party member becomes merely a republican or a democrat. The party symbol expresses everything. Where simple social aggression or defense with the purpose of eliminating or encysting an enemy is the purpose of the community, organization through the common attitude of hostility is normal and effective. But as long as the social organization is dominated by the attitude of hostility the individuals or groups who are the objectives of this organization will remain enemies. It is quite impossible psychologically to hate the sin and love the sinner. We are very much given to cheating ourselves in this regard. We assume that we can detect, pursue, indict, prosecute, and punish the criminal and still retain toward him the attitude of reinstating him in the community as soon as he indicates a change in social attitude himself, that we can at the same time watch for the definite transgression of the statute to catch and overwhelm the offender, and comprehend the situation out of which the offense grows. But the two attitudes, that of control of crime by the hostile procedure of the law and that of control through comprehension of social and psychological conditions, cannot be combined. To understand is to forgive and the social procedure seems to deny the very responsibility which the law affirms, and on the other hand the pursuit by criminal justice inevitably awakens the hostile attitude in the offender and renders the attitude of mutual comprehension practically impossible. The social worker in the court is the sentimentalist, and the legalist in the social settlement in spite of his learned doctrine is the ignoramus.

While then the attitude of hostility, either against the transgressor of the laws or against the external enemy, gives to the group a sense of solidarity which most readily arouses like a burning flame and which consumes the differences of individual interests, the price paid for this solidarity of feeling is great and at times disastrous. Though human attitudes are far older than any human institutions and seem to retain identities of structure that make us at home in the heart of every man whose story has come down to us from the written and unwritten past, yet these attitudes take on new forms as they gather new social contents. The hostilities which flamed up between man and man, between family and family, and fixed the forms of old societies have changed as men came to realize the common whole within which these deadly struggles were fought out. Through rivalries, competitions, and co-operations men achieved the conception of a social state in which they asserted themselves while they at the same time affirmed the status of the others, on the basis not only of common rights and privileges but also on the basis of differences of interest and function, in an organization of more varied individuals. In the modern economic world a man is able to assert himself much more effectively against others through his acknowledgement of common property rights underlying their whole economic activity; while he demands acknowledgement for his individual competitive effort by recognizing and utilizing the varied activities and economic functions of others in the whole business complex.

This evolution reaches still richer content when the self-assertion appears in the consciousness of social contribution that obtains the esteem of the others whose activities it complements and renders possible. In the world of scientific research rivalries do not preclude the warm recognition of the service which the work of one scientist renders to the whole co-operative undertaking of the *monde savant*. It is evident that such a social organization is not obtainable at will, but is dependent upon the slow growth of very varied and intricate social mechanisms. While no clearly definable set of conditions can be presented as responsible for this growth, it will I think be admitted that a very necessary condition, perhaps the most important one, is that of overcoming the temporal and spatial separations of men so that they are brought into closer interrelation with each other. Means of intercommunications have been the great civilizing agents. The multiple social stimulation of an indefinite number of varied contacts of a vast number of individuals with each other is the fertile field out of which spring social organizations, for these make possible the larger social life that can absorb the hostilities of different groups. When this condition has been supplied there seems to be an inherent tendency in social groups to advance from the hostile attitudes of individuals and groups toward each other through rivalries, competitions, and co-operations toward a functional self-assertion which recognizes and utilizes other selves and groups of selves in the activities in which social human nature expresses itself. And yet the attitude of hostility of a community toward those who have transgressed its law or customs, i.e., its criminals, and toward the outer enemies has remained as a great solidifying power. The passionate appreciation of our religious, political, property, and family institutions has arisen in the attack upon those who individually or collectively have assailed or violated them, and hostility toward the actual or prospective enemies of our country has been the never-failing source of patriotism.

If then we undertake to deal with the causes of crime in a fundamental way, and as dispassionately as we are dealing with the causes of disease, and if we wish to substitute negotiation and international adjudication for war in settling disputes between nations, it is of some importance to consider what sort of emotional solidarity we can secure to replace that which the traditional procedures have supplied. It is in the juvenile court that we meet the undertaking to reach and understand the causes of social and individual breakdown, to mend if possible the defective situation and reinstate the individual at fault. This is not attended with any weakening of the sense of the values that are at stake, but a great part of the paraphernalia of hostile procedure is absent. The judge sits down with the child who has been committed to the court, with members of the family, parole officers, and others who may help to make the situation comprehensible and indicates what steps can be taken to bring matters to a normal condition. We find the beginnings of scientific technique in this study in the presence of the psychologist and medical officer who can report upon the mental and physical condition of the child, of the social workers who can report upon the situation of the families and neighborhood involved. Then there are other institutions beside the jails to which the children can be sent for prolonged observation and change of immediate environment. In centering interest upon reinstatement the sense of forward-looking moral responsibility is not only not weakened but is strengthened, for the court undertakes to determine what the child must do and be to take up normal social relations again. Where the responsibility rests upon others this can be brought out in much greater detail and with greater effect since it is not defined under abstract legal categories and the aim in determining responsibility is not to place punishment but to obtain future results. Out of this arises a much fuller presentation of the facts that are essential for dealing with the problem than can possibly appear in a criminal court procedure that aims to establish simply responsibility for a legally defined offense with the purpose of inflicting punishment. Of far greater importance is the appearance of the values of family relations, of schools, of training of all sorts, of opportunities to work, and of all the other factors that go to make up that which is worth while in the life of a child or an adult. Before the juvenile court it is possible to present all of these and all of them can enter the consideration of what action is to be taken. These are the things that are worth while. They are the ends that should determine conduct. It is impossible to discover their real import unless they can all be brought into relationship with each other.

It is impossible to deal with the problem of what the attitude and conduct of the community should be toward the individual who has broken its laws, or what his responsibility is in terms of future action, unless all the facts and all the values with reference to which the facts must be interpreted are there and can be impartially considered, just as it is impossible to deal scientifically with any problem without recognizing all the facts and all the values involved. The attitude of hostility which places the criminal under the ban, and thus takes him out of society, and prescribes a hostile procedure by which he is secured, tried, and punished can take into account only those features of his conduct which constitute infraction of the law, and can state the relation of the criminal and society only in the terms of trial for fixing guilt and of punishment. All else is irrelevant. The adult criminal court is not undertaking to readjust a broken-down social situation, but to determine by the application of fixed rules whether the man is a member of society in good and regular standing or is an outcast. In accordance with these fixed rules what does not come under the legal definition not only does not naturally appear but it is actually excluded. Thus there exists a field of facts bearing upon the social problems that come into our courts and governmental administrative bureaus, facts which cannot be brought into direct use in solving these problems. It is with this material that the social scientist and the voluntary social worker and his organizations are occupied. In the juvenile court we have a striking instance of this material forcing its way into the institution of the court itself and compelling such a change in method that the material can be actually used. Recent changes of attitude toward the family permit facts bearing upon the care of children which earlier lay outside the purview of the court to enter into its consideration.

Other illustrations could be cited of this change in the structure and function of institutions by the pressure of data which the earlier form of the institution had excluded. One may cite the earlier theory of charity that it was a virtue of those in fortunate circumstances which is exercised toward the poor whom we have always with us, in its contrast with the conception of organized charity whose aim is not the exercise of an individual virtue but such a change in the condition of the individual case and of the community within which the cases arise that a poverty which requires charity may disappear. The author of a mediaeval treatise on charity considering the lepers as a field for good works contemplated the possibility of their disappearance with the ejaculation 'which may God forbid!' The juvenile court is but one instance of an institution in which the consideration of facts which had been regarded as irrelevant or exceptional has carried with it a radical change in the institution. But it is of particular interest because the court is the objective form of the attitude of hostility on the part of the community toward the one who transgresses its laws and customs, and it is of further interest because it throws into relief the two types of emotional attitudes which answer to two types of social organization. Over against the emotional solidarity of the group opposing the enemy we find the interests which spring up around the effort to meet and solve a social problem. These interests are at first in opposition to each other. The interest in the individual delinquent opposes the interest in property and the social order dependent upon it. The interest in the change of the conditions which foster the delinquent is opposed to that identified with our positions in society as now ordered, and the resentment at added responsibilities which had not been formerly recognized or accepted.

But the genuine effort to deal with the actual problem brings with it tentative reconstructions which awaken new interests and emotional values. Such are the interests in better housing conditions, in different and more adequate schooling, in play-grounds and small parks, in controlling child labor and in vocational guidance, in improved sanitation and hygiene, and in community and social centers. In the place of the emotional solidarity which makes us all one against the criminal there appears the cumulation of varied interests unconnected in the past which not only bring new meaning to the delinquent but which also bring the sense of growth, development, and achievement. This reconstructive attitude offers the cumulative interest which comes with interlocking diversified values. The discovery that tuberculosis, alcoholism, unemployment, school retardation, adolescent delinquency, among other social evils, reach their highest percentages in the same areas not only awakens the interest we have in combatting each of these evils, but creates a definite object, that of human misery, which focuses endeavor and builds up a concrete object of human welfare which is a complex of values. Such an organization of effort gives rise to an individual or self with a new content of character, a self that is effective since the impulses which lead to conduct are organized with reference to a clearly defined object.

It is of interest to compare this self with that which responds to the community call for defense of itself or its institutions. The dominant emotional coloring of the latter is found in the standing together of all the group against the common enemy. The consciousness which one has of others is stripped of the instinctive oppositions which in varying forms are aroused in us by the mere presence of others. These may be merely the slight rivalries and differences of opinion and of social attitude and position, or just the reserves which we all preserve over against those about us. In the common cause these can disappear. Their disappearance means a removal of resistance and friction and adds exhilaration and enthusiasm to the expression of one of the most powerful of human impulses. The result is a certain enlargement of the self in which one seems to be at one with everyone else in the group. It is not a self-consciousness in the way of contrasting one's self with others. One loses himself in the whole group in some sense, and may attain the attitude in which he undergoes suffering and death for the common cause. In fact just as war removes the inhibitions from the attitude of hostility so it quickens and commends the attitude of self-assertion of a self which is fused with all the others in the community. The ban upon self-assertion which the consciousness of others in the group to which one belongs carries with it disappears when the assertion is directed against an object of common hostility or dislike. Even in times of peace we feel as a rule little if any disapproval of arrogance toward those of another nationality, and national self-conceit and the denigration of the achievements of other peoples may become virtues. The same tendency exists in varying degree among those who unite against the criminal or against the party foe. Attitudes of difference and opposition between members of the community or group are in abeyance and there is given the greater freedom for self-assertion against the enemy. Through these experiences come the powerful emotions which serve to evaluate for the time being what the whole community stands for in comparison with the interests of the individual who is opposed to the group. These experiences, however, serve only to set off against each other what the group stands for and the meager birthright of the individual who cuts himself off from the group.

What we all fight for, what we all protect, what we all affirm against the detractor, confers upon each in some measure the heritage of all, while to be outside the community is to be an Esau without heritage and with every man's hand against him. Self-assertion against the common enemy, suppressing as it does the oppositions of individuals within the group and thus identifying them all in a common effort, is after all the self-assertion of the fight in which the opposing selves strive each to eliminate the other, and in so doing are setting up their own survival and the destruction of the others as the end. I know that many ideals have been the ends of war, at least in the minds of many of the fighters; that in so far the fighting was not to destroy the fighters but some pernicious institution, such as slavery, that many have fought bloody wars for liberty and freedom. No champions however, of such causes have ever failed to identify the causes in the struggle with themselves. The battle is for the survival of the right party and the death of the wrong. Over against the enemy we reach the ultimate form of self-assertion, whether it is the patriotic national self, or the party, or the schismatic self, or the institutional self, or simply the self of the hand to hand mêlée. It is the self whose existence calls for the destruction, or defeat, or subjection, or reduction of the enemy. It is a self that finds expression in vivid, concentrated activity and under appropriate conditions of the most violent type. The instinct of hostility which provides the structure for this self when fully aroused and put in competition with the other powerful human complexes of conduct, those of sex, of hunger, and of parenthood and of possession has proved itself as more dominant than they. It also carries with it the stimulus for readier and, for the time being, more complete socialization than any other instinctive organization. There is no ground upon which men get together so readily as that of a common enemy, while a common object of the instinct of sex, of possession, or of hunger leads to instant opposition, and even the common object of the parental instinct may be the spring of jealousy. The socializing agency of common hostility is marked, as I have above indicated, by its own defects. In so far as it is the dominant instinct it does not organize the other instincts for its object. It suppresses or holds the others in abeyance. While hostility itself may be a constituent part of the execution of any instinct, for they all involve oppositions, there is no other instinctive act of the human self which is a constituent part of the immediate instinctive process of fighting, while struggle with a possible opponent plays its part in the carrying out of every other instinctive activity. As a result those who fight together against common enemies instinctively tend to ignore the other social activities within which oppositions between the individuals engaged normally arise.

It is this temporary relief from the social frictions which attend upon all other co-operative activities which is largely responsible for the emotional upheavals of patriotism, of mob consciousness, and the extremes of party warfare, as well as for the gusto of malicious gossiping and scandalmongering. Furthermore, in the exercise of this instinct success implies the triumph of the self over the enemy. The achievement of the process is the defeat of certain persons and the victory of others.

The end takes the form of that sense of self-enlargement and assurance which comes with superiority of the self over others. The attention is directed toward the relative position of the self toward others. The values involved are those that only can be expressed in terms of interests and relations of the self in its differences from others. From the standpoint of one set of antagonists their victory is that of efficient civilization while the other regards their victory as that of liberal ideas. All the way from the Tamerlanes who create a desert and call it peace to the idealistic warriors who fight and die for ideas, victory means the survival of one set of personalities and the elimination of others, and the ideas and ideals that become issues in the contest must perforce be personified if they are to appear in the struggles that arise out of the hostile instinct. War, whether it is physical, economic, or political, contemplates the elimination of the physical, economic, or political opponent. It is possible to confine the operation of this instinct within certain specific limitations and fields. In the prize fights as in the olden tourneys the annihilation of the enemy is ceremonially halted at a fixed stage in the struggle. In a football game the defeated team leaves the field to the champion. Successful competition in its sharpest form eliminates its competitor. The victor at the polls drives the opponent from the field of political administration. If the struggle can be *à outrance* within any field and contemplates the removal of the enemy from that field, the instinct of hostility has this power of uniting and fusing the contesting groups, but since victory is the aim of the fight and it is the victory of one party over the other, the issues of battle must be conceived in terms of the victor and the vanquished.

Other types of social organization growing out of the other instincts, such as possession, hunger, or parenthood, imply ends which are not as such identified with selves in their oppositions to other selves, though the objects toward which these instinctive activities are directed may be occasion for the exercise of the hostile instinct. The social organizations which arise about these objects are in good part due to the inhibitions placed upon the hostile impulse, inhibitions which are exercised by the other groups of impulses which the same situations call out. The possession by one individual in a family or clan group of a desirable object is an occasion for an attack on the part of other members of the group, but his characters as a member of the group are stimuli to family and clan responses which check the attack. It may be mere repression with smoldering antagonisms, or there may be such a social reorganization that the hostility can be given a function under social control, as in the party, political, and economic contests, in which certain party, political, and economic selves are driven from the field leaving others that carry out the social activity. Here the contest being restricted the most serious evils of the warfare are removed, while the contest has at least the value of the rough selection. The contest is regarded in some degree from the standpoint of the social function, not simply from that of the elimination of an enemy. As the field of constructive social activity widens the operation of the hostile impulse in its instinctive form decreases. This does not, however, mean that the reactions that go to make up the impulse or instinct have ceased to function. It does mean that the impulse ceases to be an undertaking to get rid of the offending object by injury and destruction, that is, an undertaking directed against another social being with capacities for suffering and death – physical, economical or political – like his own. It becomes in its organization with other impulses an undertaking to deal with a situation by removing obstacles. We will speak of him as fighting against his difficulties. The force of the original impulse is not lost but its objective is no longer the elimination of a person, but such a reconstruction that the profounder social activities may find their continued and fuller expression. The energy that expressed itself in burning witches as the causes of plagues expends itself at present in medical research and sanitary regulations and may still be called a fight with disease.

In all these changes the interest shifts from the enemy to the reconstruction of social conditions. The self-assertion of the soldier and conqueror becomes that of the competitor in industry or business or politics, of the reformer, the administrator, of the physician or other social functionary. The test of success of this self lies in the change and construction of the social conditions which make the self possible, not in the conquest and elimination of other selves. His emotions are not those of mass consciousness dependent upon suppressed individualities, but arise out of the cumulative interest of varied undertakings converging upon a common problem of social reconstruction. This individual and his social organization are more difficult of accomplishment and subject to vastly greater friction than those which spring out of war. Their emotional content may not be so vivid, but they are the only remedy for war, and they meet the challenge which the continued existence of war in human society has thrown down to human intelligence.

6   Twentieth-century Sociology: Modern American Sociology

By the early 1920s the work of the stalwart pioneers of American sociology was virtually over. Their reputation lingered on and many of them survived into a ripe old age right up to the 1940s. But if sociology came of age in America while elsewhere it was still struggling to gain acceptance, its adult progress in America was most uneven. The basic orientation of the earlier writers of examining society structurally, if from a narrow and often mistaken perspective, was abandoned. The trend towards parochialism and eclecticism was intensified. Much of the work was concerned with small-scale and isolated problems. While this led the way towards a new methodology in social science and new techniques of investigation, it saw for the first time the inclusion of a multitude of unrelated problems in the corpus of sociological research. The rapid growth of urbanism and the rapid shift from a largely agricultural economy to large-scale industrialization, which threw up a large number of new problems, helped in this process. No other society felt the impact of this change more forcibly than American society. The aftermath of the First World War, which heralded a new type of economic structure, witnessed a new realignment in social life. This was reflected in the decline of the dominant value system of rural America and in the divisive elements which were becoming more prominent in urban centres. But the spate of work published in America during the twenties and thirties failed lamentably to provide a basic understanding of what the problems under investigation were really about, much less of what sociology was really about. Lacking historical knowledge, philosophical understanding and conceptual clarity, American sociologists floundered in a morass of meaningless jargon, superfluous technicalities and crudities of thought. As though to escape from an unbearable reality, when society was shaking to its foundations, American sociologists, in the sheltered cloisters of academic centres, retreated into the self-comforting illusion that they were fulfilling their vocation if they made a public show of saying something about their totally misconceived social problems. The misconception consisted in the assumption that if there was a problem at all, it must be one which reflected a certain disorganization and deviation from the norm, the norm being, of course, the accepted value system of middle-class society. Wright Mills had this to say about these works:

> The level of abstraction which characterizes them is so low that often they seem to be empirically confused for lack of abstraction to knit them together. They display bodies of meagerly connected facts, ranging from rape in rural districts to public housing, and intellectually sanction this low level of abstraction . . . Collecting and dealing in a fragmentary way with scattered problems and facts of *milieux*, these books are not focussed on larger stratifications or upon structured wholes.
>
> 'The Professional Ideology of Social Pathologists',
> *Power, Politics and People*, p. 527

Fortunately, amidst this welter of disconnected facts, confusion of thought and arbitrary assumptions, other trends could be discerned in American sociology which gave it lustre, rescued it from trivialization and redeemed it from complete collapse and ineffectiveness. A breakthrough into real sociological under-standing was made by three different types of works, those by W. I. Thomas and F. Znaniecki, Pitirim A. Sorokin and Robert and Helen Lynd.

The most compelling influence on American sociology of the time was that of W. I. Thomas (1863–1947). Thomas may not have been a very deep or systematic thinker but he was one of the few who felt that sociology, if it was to be scientific, must have a solid base in theory. As all science basically is the discovery of causal relations between phenomena, so must social theory consist of laws demonstrating necessary relations between units of social reality. For Thomas, fundamental units of social reality are attitudes and values. This is the central theme of the famous work which he wrote in collaboration with F. Znaniecki, *The*

Polish Peasant in Europe and America (1918–21). Thomas's social theory was constructed on the idea that it was the action of the individual in a social situation that was being studied. This approach has come to be known as the situational approach. The concept of value had, of course, already been used by the classical sociologists. Thomas and Znaniecki introduced the concept of attitude. While value represents the actor's goal, attitude is the tendency to act, moved by a drive or wish. In their work the authors, in showing what the causal relations between attitudes and values are, expounded the thesis that the cause of an attitude or a value is never an attitude or a value alone, but always a combination of attitudes and values. The different reactions of people to the same influence would illustrate this. However, values are only one part, although a crucial part, of the total situation. The other two parts are the objective conditions, which include norms of behaviour and also the definition of the situation by the actor himself, as he has learnt to see it. The established systems of these social norms or rules form social institutions and these in turn make up a social organization.

Thomas was responsible for a number of other concepts, of which he made use in his major work, but which were not essential to his main theory. They have therefore only historical interest now. He held that 'every individual has a vast variety of wishes which can be satisfied only by his incorporation in society'. He thought he could detect four fundamental wishes: the desires for new experience, for security, for recognition, and for mastery. Another set of concepts refers to three types of personality, the Philistine, the Bohemian and the Creative Personality. The significance, however, of *The Polish Peasant* lies in the introduction of a novel research technique which consisted in the use of personal documents, such as letters, diaries and life histories of individuals.

One can criticize the vagueness of some of the basic concepts Thomas used and in particular the lack of proportion between actual results obtained and the ambitious scheme of his work. Nevertheless, Thomas made a significant contribution to sociological theory. He insisted on the absolute necessity of using scientific procedure in sociology but at the same time he did not minimize the difficulties of empirical social research. He rejected completely the evolutionary doctrine, holding that it is impossible to interpret social facts on the basis of some one factor. In America, at least, Thomas was one of the first to stress the primacy of norms in society and although his definition between attitude and value was imprecise, it was of great importance in bringing to light both the subjective and objective elements in the analysis of action. Lastly, Thomas made it quite clear that no problem can be dealt with in social theory unless it takes into account the interdependence of the individual and the social organization and culture. More important still, in this new field of research, Thomas set an example of a dedicated worker and thinker who, in his search for truth, never claimed that he discovered ultimate truth. He was never afraid to change his views in the light of new knowledge. He was the experimental thinker *par excellence*.

A new star in the firmament of American sociology appeared in the person of Pitirim A. Sorokin (1889–1968). Born in Russia and having been engaged in teaching, writing and in political activity, Sorokin was exiled as an opponent of the new régime in 1918. After a short spell as Professor of Sociology at the University of Minnesota, where he wrote two outstanding works, *Social Mobility* (1927) and *Contemporary Sociological Theories* (1928), he became a Professor of Sociology at Harvard University in 1930 and established there the first Harvard Department of Sociology. In the next twenty years, Sorokin was a prolific writer, publishing a large number of works whose impact on American and indeed world sociology was of enormous significance. His *magnum opus*, *Social and Cultural Dynamics*, was published in four volumes between 1937 and 1941, and that was followed by a unique work in American sociology, a systematic treatise on sociology, *Society, Culture and Personality*. Like many of his predecessors, Sorokin accepted the view that *interaction* was the unit into which social phenomena should be analysed and the subjects of interaction are either human individuals or organized groups of human individuals. For Sorokin, interaction is a sociocultural phenomenon consisting of three interrelated elements: ' 1. *Personality* as a subject of interaction; 2. *Society* as a totality of interacting personalities . . .; 3. *Culture* as the totality of the meanings, values, and norms possessed by the interacting personalities and the totality of the vehicles which objectify, socialize, and convey these meanings' (*Society, Culture and Personality*, p. 63). From his definition of interaction Sorokin derives the proposition that any group of interacting individuals is first and foremost a *causal-functional unity* which makes the group a *social system*. A social system cannot exist without a culture system, which can be defined as a system of meanings or ideas. The two together become a *sociocultural system*, which is a key concept in Sorokin's theory. The social system can thus be regarded as the bare bones of the structure of society, which is given a form, shape and vitality by the cultural system, the two combined making an integrated functional unity.

Sorokin's concern with culture was directed to discovering the hierarchy of sociocultural systems and the degree of their integration. He conceived of the total sociocultural system as a 'supersystem' which may be more or less integrated. This qualification was necessary because, for Sorokin, a society's total culture includes a certain number of *congeries*. Congeries are elements which happen to exist in a system but are not inherently indispensable to it. They are just a kind of epiphenomena which come and go in a cultural system without affecting it positively.

With regard to each supersystem, Sorokin held that it can be characterized by a dominant theme or idea which is a view or, better still, criterion of truth in a specific culture. If people ascribe validity to the evidence of their senses, Sorokin calls such a supersystem *sensate*. If, however, people believe that behind sense impressions there lies another deeper reality which is revealed to the truth of faith, such a supersystem is *ideational*. When these two approaches are combined, a third system of truth, that of reason or rationality, is invoked. This supersystem is *idealistic,* if the combination is harmonious, and mixed, if the two systems of truth are merely juxtaposed. Thus culture has a style according to the system of truth prevailing in a society. Sorokin's treatment of personality, which was not a fully developed aspect of his work, was intended to show that each of the broad sociocultural systems produced characteristic personality types.

Sorokin's views on the different systems of truth and in particular the distinction he draws between 'logico-rational' and intuitive systems can be challenged on philosophical grounds.[1] But Sorokin in these works did not only formulate an original and logically consistent theory of society but, through wide-ranging historical research, opened up new perspectives into many unknown and unexplored regions of our cultural past.

In this respect Sorokin was *the* scholar in American sociology at a time when scholarship in this discipline, let alone a broad philosophical training, was not rated high or not rated at all. It is not surprising therefore that Sorokin, for almost one generation, was totally ignored. But with the optimism that characterized his outlook, he made no concession to current fashion, refused to be beguiled by spurious and sham research and never ceased to proclaim the sound and proper goals of sociology as an intellectual discipline. In this respect he can be said to have been the gadfly of American sociology, always on the look-out to see where it erred and strayed, and leading it back to the right path. Only in the last few years of Sorokin's life did American sociologists awake to his extraordinary achievement and accord him the tribute and praise that he so richly earned.

Another breakthrough in American sociology was represented by Robert S. and Helen M. Lynd, who published their famous Middletown volumes between 1929 and 1937. The first volume, *Middletown*, was an attempt to understand a representative American community, Muncie in Indiana, and in what respects it could be regarded as a more or less self-contained social and cultural system satisfying the basic needs of its members, like getting a living, making a home, using leisure, etc. All kinds of data were used, statistical and historical, but the investigation was carried out largely by direct or participant observation. The conclusion reached was that the population could be basically divided into two classes, the business and working classes, each of which carries out the essential social functions in its own way and somewhat differently. The idea that a modern community is a fully integrated unit had to be rejected, for the life of the community was characterized by a large number of over-lapping

1. For a more detailed criticism of these views, see the author's review article on Sorokin in the *British Journal of Sociology*, January 1969.

activities which were often in conflict with each other. At the same time, the authors discovered certain uniformities in social change as, for example, the ready acceptance by all classes of technological innovations.

This work was followed in 1937 by *Middletown in Transition*, which was a follow-up study of Muncie in the depression years, and in this work the class structure and economic and political power relations were brought into sharper focus. None of the subsequent works in the same style, certainly not the over-praised and sociologically valueless work of William L. Warner and his team on *The Social Life of a Modern Community*, surpassed those of the Lynds in meticulous observation, respect for facts and in conceptual clarity.

Reinforcing these major influences, and side by side with the large mass of mediocre works to which reference has already been made, was the slow, almost imperceptible impact on American sociological thought made by some continental thinkers, notably Max Weber and Vilfredo Pareto (1848–1923).From 1930 onwards, Talcott Parsons was mainly responsible for the English translations of Max Weber's principal works and for introducing, through articles and prefaces, Weber's sociological theories to English readers. English readers owe an immeasurable debt to Parsons for placing Max Weber at the centre of modern sociological thought.

The appeal of Pareto to American sociologists was of a different kind and its explanation must be found in other than the mere desire to learn something from the muddled and obscure thoughts of a continental writer. Like the appeal of Freud at the same period, it can be attributed in part to that predilection of American writers for psychological theories and explanations.

Pareto began his career as a consulting engineer and then turned to economics, of which he became a professor at the University of Lausanne in 1892. His outstanding contribution to mathematical economics and his profound study of socialism in *The Socialist Systems* do not concern us here. His work in sociology was embodied in a number of volumes under the title *The General Treatise on Sociology*, published in 1916.

Pareto's central idea is his conception of society as a system in equilibrium; it is a whole consisting of interdependent parts. A change in one would affect the others and the whole. Pareto used physical and biological terms to describe the social forces which affect individuals in society. Among a number of conditions which determine the state of the social system, he regarded one set of conditions to be of central importance; these were interests, knowledge, and 'residues' and 'derivations'. What Pareto meant by 'residues' is what we mean by sentiments, those constant, innate and invariant mechanisms of human behaviour. But these, according to Pareto, do not reveal themselves in their pure form, but as 'derivations'. These, which are manifestations of sentiments, stand for the rationalizations by which a man justifies his actions. This very important distinction, couched as it unfortunately is in difficult language, bears some resemblance to Freud's distinction between the 'unconscious' and the 'conscious'.

All other cultural phenomena, such as law, politics, religion, play their part in maintaining a social system, but only in so far as they manifest basic sentiments. When such a system is subject to pressure for some form of change, it will encounter other forces which will tend to restore it to its former state of equilibrium. This sentiment of resistance or revulsion serves as a brake to any kind of change that threatens to disturb the equilibrium.

This view of the forces at work in society is based on the distinction between logical and non-logical action. Logical action can be defined, in short, as one which is objectively defined, and the means to attain it are based on the best and most scientific knowledge available. All other action is non-logical, which must not be confused with 'illogical', and, for Pareto, non-logical action is predominant in social life. It is related to residues and derivations. The sentiments of which these are manifestations are instincts or innate impulses. The tendency of people in society is to justify their actions by formulating non-logical theories which they consider to be logical. It is by a knowledge of the residues that we can arrive at a deeper penetration into the causation of human action. In Pareto's view, men do not first think or formulate theories and then act. Quite the reverse. They act first and then they rationalize. Thus, in analysing behaviour, we must not look at the theoretical justification of it but rather at the basic sentiments revealed by it. In other words, the residues are the underlying forces in social life and the derivations are merely their surface manifestations or explanations or justifications. There is no need to refer to the six classes of residues and the number of sub-classes in each class, nor to the four principal classes of derivations. They are merely *jeux d'esprit*, without psychological or logical consistency.

However, it is necessary to refer to Pareto's first two classes of residues, viz. the instinct of combinations and the persistence of aggregates, because these are related to social change. A result of this study leads to another basic theorem in Pareto's sociology, the theory of the circulation of *élites*. There are two principal classes of élites: a governing élite and a non-governing élite. The former comprises individuals who directly or indirectly are involved in the manipulation of political power; the latter consists of capable men not holding power. If the residue of class one is dominant, the type of men prevailing in society is designated by the term *speculator*. If on the other hand the residue of class two is dominant, the type of men prevailing in society is designated by the term *rentier*. In the first case, society is subject to fairly rapid change; in the second place change occurs more slowly. There is a central tendency for the élites of the two types to rotate in positions of political power. It is when an élite of one of these types has been in power too long or commits mistakes that the other type of men come to the fore and take over, and they in their turn sooner or later get supplanted in the same way as they have supplanted their predecessors.

Here we have a cyclic theory of social change characterized by the dominance of one or other attitudes or fashions in politics, conservative or progressive. 'History', Pareto asserts, 'is a graveyard of aristocracies.'

It is not difficult to see why Pareto exercised such a profound appeal for American sociologists. They were gratified to feel that the underlying assumptions about their own society were given explicit confirmation by an outsider. They were attracted to the idea of society being always in equilibrium, as they assumed it to be in their own society, and that it could be dynamic, because the forces maintaining the structure of society allowed for continuous change. Secondly the idea that our actions are not intellectual found an echo in a philosophy of life which emphasized the practical or pragmatic aspect as against the theoretical. Thirdly the idea of a governing élite, because, and not in spite of, the egalitarian tradition of American life, was attractive to those who were divided, in wealth, position, or power, from the rest of the people. And lastly, Pareto's insistence that sociology must be based on the logico-experimental method confirmed American sociologists in their view that the refined methodologies they were employing in sociology made their research really scientific, immune to all captious criticism.

Two other trends came to play a significant role in American sociology, cultural anthropology and psychoanalysis. It seemed obvious that what distinguished one group of people from another was culture, which came to mean the whole intellectual, material and social life of a community. It is culture then which is responsible for integrating the individual with his environment, carried out through education in its formal or informal aspects. In the United States, there were not only the American Indians but also a number of different immigrant groups whose cultural characteristics distinguished them from the older settled population. Not surprisingly, therefore, cultural anthropology became a firmly established discipline. The works of A. A. Goldenweiser (1880–1940), author of *Anthropology* (1937), A. L. Kroeber (1878–1960) and C. Kluckhohn (1905–60), joint authors of *Culture* (1952), among many others, testify to the growing importance of this branch of sociology in American thought. In addition, the works of the British anthropologists, in particular those of Malinowski and A. R. Radcliffe-Brown, made their own distinctive contribution to American sociology.[2] Already American sociologists had abandoned evolutionism as a causal explanation of social phenomena, except in the obvious sense that there is a historical continuity which must be assumed as a factor in society. Malinowski and Radcliffe-Brown brought a massive reinforcement to this way of thought by their emphasis on the importance of functionalism. It did not matter that 'function', like 'culture', was a very ambiguous concept. It served a function to bring out

2. See also Chapter 7, pp. 555–6.

what these writers thought about society and how it should be studied. According to them, if we know what the function of the institution is, we are on the way to explaining it and understanding it. Thus, function is used to refer to the basic needs or requirements which must be satisfied if the group is to survive. Through function we see how institutions are established as behaviour patterns which conform to certain norms and values. Institutions in this sense include not only the technical equipment used in society for its daily life but also all the spiritual ideas underlying its morality, religion, law, etc., by which it regulates its thought and conduct. Functionalism in this sense, dealing with 'institutions' as socio-psychological concepts, dispenses with all problems about historical origins and the processes of change. In this respect functionalism represents a distinct conservative trend in thought. Everything which can be shown to be 'functional' is *ipso facto* essential and therefore good.

In this way cultural anthropology and sociology became virtually indistinguishable. Ruth Benedict (1887–1948) used the ethnological material in her book *Patterns of Culture* to illustrate and confirm hypotheses concerning the general structure of society. Likewise, all the early ethnological works of Margaret Mead were of considerable value and relevance to sociological thought. If sociology can no longer dispense with 'culture' as a concept, however varied its use may be, it is largely due to the central place which the concept occupied in the works of anthropologists and ethnographers.

The interest shown by American writers in the problems of character and personality merely continued a tradition which had a long history in American sociology. Works were published, with a great deal of statistical and experimental data, on 'social character' and 'personality type'. The concept of 'social character', however, seemed to provide greater scope for sociological analysis than personality type. Nevertheless, Ralph Linton (1893–1953), who introduced 'basic personality type' into American sociology, was also responsible for introducing a new concept, which has since become basic in sociological thought: the concept of 'role'.

All these psychological studies, carried out in America in the twenties and thirties, incorporated a great number of ideas derived from psychoanalysis. Unlike Great Britain or France, which either despised or merely ignored the theories of psychoanalysis, America displayed no such inhibitions and made use, even if indiscriminately, of these theories. This was also helped by a number of prominent continental writers, familiar with these theories, who settled and taught in America.

The idea that human action is largely non-rational, if not irrational, which figured so prominently in the sociological theory of Pareto, now received confirmation from psychoanalysis. But psychoanalysis went even further than anything that had been thought of previously, because it set out to show that we can trace the origins of adult action, personal and social, in the early life of childhood. Malinowski, Ruth Benedict and Margaret Mead used a psychoanalytical approach in their anthropological work, though none of them subscribed completely to psychoanalytical theory. In this way psychoanalysis influenced sociological thought through cultural anthropology. In America, psychoanalysis was combined with behaviourism, whereby a theory of human behaviour was provided which seemed to fit together and could explain human motivation. Thus the learning process was dealt with in terms of the child's adaptation to the group. Although this adaptation is accompanied by constant failure, it also yields compensations in the form of new satisfactions. Side by side with frustration and aggression, we have acquiescence and obedience. Already in the thirties, a number of writers were inspired by psychoanalytic theory to account for and illuminate the deep-seated irrational drives which lie at the root of race prejudice. In a very remarkable work, *Psycho-Pathology and Politics*, published in 1930, Harold D. Lasswell established a direct connection between psychoanalysis and practical social research.

The most outstanding neo-Freudian of the time was Erich Fromm. Among his early important works in German may be mentioned *Studies on Authority and Family*, published from 1930 onwards in Paris. The ideas which he developed on 'analytical and socio-psychology' were used in his influential work *Fear of Freedom* (1941). In this work Fromm deals with social character, a general term which referred to the common character structure of the members of the social group or class. Fromm was specially concerned to free psychoanalysis from its extremes of 'libidinism' or 'pan-sexualism'. This laudable attempt to use psychoanalysis for sociological purposes could not conceal the rift caused between the socially critical elements in Freudism and the new emphasis on the need for a therapy which will contribute to the adaptation of society. The idea of a sacrosanct society, adaptation to which is a criterion of normality, is an underlying theme in American sociology.

The pattern of sociology that emerged in the United States up to the Second World War was not very clear or consistent. It was many-sided, uncoordinated and perhaps too ambitious. It still lacked basis in theory and philosophical understanding. The latent signs of opposition in American sociology were beginning to come to the surface, the opposition between empiricism and theory, between micro-sociology and macro-sociology. This opposition, not yet resolved, has taken many forms. It has divided those who believed that sociology is a science only if it is quantifiable from those who believed that qualitative interpretation is essential in sociology. It divided those who saw sociology as a purely parochial undertaking concerned with piecemeal matters of limited interest or significance from those, albeit very few, who regarded sociology from a wide perspective whose object is the understanding of interrelations of parts to the whole. It divided those who thought of sociology as a practical science to which scientific and mathematical models are indispensable tools from those who felt that sociology is a humanistic discipline. The Second World War accentuated this division. While certain foundations like the Russell Sage Foundation had long been established in America to provide funds for research and were responsible for the large number of social surveys carried out in America, it was only during the war that sociologists were engaged in government departments as consultants and researchers. This had the double effect of enhancing the professional status of sociologists and opening lucrative jobs for them outside the academic establishments. The post-war period accelerated this trend. Not only did the government departments, in particular the Defence Department, extend the range of research, but the proliferation of the new foundations and trusts, with almost unlimited resources, created new avenues of research, which were warranted neither by the intrinsic importance of the subject matter to be studied nor by the calibre of those who were engaged in it. Industry too was prepared to invest from its colossal profits on sociological research, with the full and prior knowledge that no harm would result from it, but that on the contrary the conclusions, couched in involved and newly minted language, would confirm it in its own good judgement. Much to the credit of American sociology, voices were heard and views were expressed that what was being done in the name of sociology was not sociology at all, that the marriage between empiricism and theory was possible, and that a return to sound academic teaching and research was the only condition for the growth and development of sociology.

That these voices and these views have not prevailed must be seen against the background of American ideology. It is not so much that easy access to funds has caused social research to be fragmented and directed to trivial goals and in this way its immunity to criticism would be assured. It is mainly because American ideology favours the manipulative techniques. What has proved successful, and even indispensable, in the physical sciences is quite fatal in the social sciences concerned with human relationships, and yet these manipulative techniques have been regarded as the sole means of restoring a situation that appeared to have got out of hand. It would seem that all the new mathematical and other quantitative methods devised, however different they are, have one object in view: to highlight a problem by isolating it, formalizing it and treating all the other factors involved in the situation as constants. This is, of course, quite indefensible and devoid of any scientific validity. Which is why this type of research, in addition to its sociological vacuity, is not empirical enough because it is not scientific. A short review of this trend in American sociology would make this clearer. The ostensible aim of these new techniques – to comply with the demands for scientific procedure and to observe the canons of inductive logic – is not in question.

To conduct social research under effective control conditions, and if possible to repeat experiments and compare results with the object of understanding, on the basis of processed data, the relationship between groups and individuals is eminently desirable and often necessary. Therefore questions of research techniques must be constantly kept in mind. The powerful progress that social research has made in America since the thirties was only possible in an economy which henceforth was geared towards increasing consumption. In this way, opinion and market research were in commercial demand to assist sales planning. The refinement and improvement of these and other techniques serving ever wider applications are a testimony to the ingenuity and inventiveness of the practitioners. The popularity of the Gallup and other polls for the analysis and forecasting of political and other opinions, by the method of the sampling process, was an indication of the extent to which the public came to rely on professional bodies for making choices and forming judgements. The method of approach is either the questionnaire, with questions structured in such a way as to elicit straight answers, or the intensive interview without previously formulated questions. There are other types of interview, like 'free' or 'depth' interviews, in which the questions asked may be either 'determined', allowing only very few answers, or 'open', in which the person interviewed can answer in any way he pleases.

The depression years in America in the thirties provoked a whole series of works on the effect of the depression on the family and the unemployed man. A revival of interest in the specific nature of modern industrial society, which had already been examined by Thorstein Veblen years before, produced such works as *The Modern Corporation and Private Property* (1935) by A. A. Berle and G. C. Means, and *The Managerial Revolution* (1941) by James Burnham. It was only natural that the increasing rationalization of industry should draw the attention of research workers to problems affecting the adaptation of work people to the work situation. Two disciplines seemed to vie with each other in dealing with these problems, industrial sociology and industrial psychology. The results of the investigations conducted by Elton Mayo and his colleagues in Hawthorne proved conclusively what was a perfectly obvious fact: that workmen in the factory are human beings and that human factors are important in labour morale. However, to overlook the fact that morale is not entirely determined by what occurs in the factory was a reflection of a philosophy that refused to question the assumptions of the economic system, and it led to the comforting illusion that the study of 'human relations' amongst work people would lead to the solution of industrial problems.

Once again, however, sociology turned to the study of groups, whence arose the distinction between 'formal' and 'informal' groups. Here experimental psychology was merged with sociology to investigate social life by using, on a purely *a priori* and quite unscientific basis, the statements of individuals as valid facts towards the formulation of sociological hypotheses.

Among the many schools adopting group investigation, two in particular must be mentioned. First is the school of sociometry, the work of Jacob L. Moreno, which was described in his book *Who Shall Survive* (1934). Moreno emphasized the remedial character of sociometry, which offered a solution to all the problems of society. The exaggerated claim made for sociometry was based on the fact that some people feel drawn to each other, others feel repelled by each other, and a few remain isolated. By means of questioning and observation, the exact relationships in a group can be discovered and recorded graphically in a 'sociogram'. In this way the real structure of groups among schoolchildren would become apparent. These so-called 'psychic distances' are worked out mathematically on a matrix.

Mathematical models were also adopted by Curt Luwin and his followers. They used the mathematical concept of 'field' to describe the totality of a situation to be investigated, and 'vectors' to describe various tensions, stresses and so forth in this field. Questionnaires, tests, and observation tables were used as material for the analysis. They called this kind of research 'action research', because it was believed that, in the course of an investigation of the dynamics of a group, the participants themselves undergo a certain change, which persists after the experiment is over.

The most successful of these attempts to translate qualitative differences in opinions, attitudes and behaviour into quantitative terms was *The Authoritarian Personality* (1950), edited by T. W. Adorno. By and large, however, all these sublte analyses of group behaviour and group dynamics failed because a group cannot be isolated as such and measured, since the individuals forming the group are, in other respects, as different from each other as the group is from other groups. The group as such can only be studied meaningfully in terms of its strucutal relationship within a persistent and recognizable complex in society like the family, the factory and any other institution. Furthermore, reductions of qualitative differences into quantitative results are retranslated into qualitative terms to confirm or disprove a hypothesis or theory.

To turn now to theoretical sociology. After Sorokin, the most influential writer in the development of systematic sociology was Talcott Parsons (1902–   ). Beginning as a biologist and then turning to economics, Parsons was convinced that social laws can be discovered and expressed that are identical with those in the natural sciences. He came in turn under the influence of Veblen, of Malinowski with his championing of 'functionalism' and of Max Weber with his theory of social action and the elements that go with it, and lastly of Durkheim, who confirmed Parsons in his belief that sociology can and must be developed as a system of thought whose reality is found in the processes of social life. Pareto and Freud were other influences which moulded Parsons's thinking. His first major work, *The Structure of Social Action* (1937), is a brilliant critique of the theories of Marshall, Pareto, Durkheim, and Weber. The most interesting feature of this work is a somewhat forced attempt by Parsons to see in all these authors, widely different as there were, a certain identical standpoint from which they developed their ideas, the standpoint of what he called 'voluntaristic' social action. This book, at the same time, revealed an almost fatal flaw in Parsons's work as a whole. His analytical thinking, brilliant as it is, is couched in language that is ponderous, often involved, and sometimes obscure. One has the impression that anything of value that Parsons has to say could have been said in simpler language and at less length. His own theory, which was already foreshadowed in *The Structure of Social Action*, was expanded in works that appeared in rapid succession in the next twenty years. The most important of these were *Essays in Sociological Theory, Pure and Applied* (1949), *Toward a General Theory of Action* (1951), *The Social System* (1951), and *Working Papers in the Theory of Action* (1953), written with Bales.

Parsons's theory is based on the idea that social action must be seen as a system of behaviour. It is a complex system, which can be broken down into its different parts so that these can be studied in their interrelationship and interdependence. In every system of behaviour we have the 'actor' and the symbols and values which guide him. A study of this system of behaviour will enable us, according to Parsons, to understand how an individual, or the social system as a whole, or even a whole culture, acts, functions and operates.

The three factors involved in 'social action' are thus the actor, a situation and the orientation of the actor to the situation. In the latter, we can distinguish *motivational* and *value* orientations. It can be represented schematically in this way:

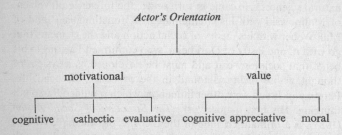

On the basis of this scheme, Parsons constructs three analytical systems: the *social system*, the *personality system*, and the *cultural system*.

The social system is given various meanings by Parsons. It is sometimes defined as a plurality of individual actors interacting with one another. At other times it is said to be a network of relations between actors. It is also referred to in terms of the motivations that guide a plurality of individuals. In other words, to understand a social system we must understand the *motivational orientation* of individuals, for they are 'motivated by tendency to optimum gratification' of needs. Values and norms are central to Parsons's theory, so what he is trying to do in the third description of the social system is to imply that no orientation to the situation is possible without the *value orientation*.

Parsons's views on *culture* are fairly straightforward in comparison. It is 'on the one hand the product, on the other hand a determinant of, systems of human social interaction'. A cultural system is composed of (1) systems of ideas; (2) systems of expressive symbols; and (3) systems of value orientations.

The personality system refers to the statuses and roles of actors in a social situation. *Status* refers to the place of the actor in a system of social relationships regarded as a structure; *role* refers to the behaviour of the actor in his relations with others, such behaviour being regarded as functionally significant for the social system. The various social roles persons play can be defined in terms of culturally determined patterns of expectations. A plurality of interrelated role patters forms an *institution*.

On this view, institutions are the focal point of sociology, for the efficient functioning of institutions is a condition of social stability. Social Theory must therefore be concerned with *institutionalization*. The link between society and culture on the one hand and personality and motivation on the other is formed by institutionalization. It involves the patterning of value orientations in society and the internalization of value systems in the human personality. To describe these processes adequately, Parsons has recourse to psychoanalytic theory and concepts.

One of the most original and most controversial contributions to sociological theory is Parsons's so-called discovery of 'the pattern variables'. These denote the *alternatives* which appear in norms of individual choices. Though not exhaustive, five of these are singled out by Parsons: (1) affectivity *versus* affective neutrality; (2) self-interest *versus* collective interest; (3) universalism *versus* particularism; (4) performance *versus* quality; and lastly (5) specificity *versus* diffuseness. One can easily think of other alternatives, or fewer alternatives which will comprehend the rest, so it is not surprising that Parsons himself made a number of revisions to this scheme of pattern variables.

What Parsons's theory emphasizes is the *normative* aspect of social life. He is saying in other words what his predecessors,

Durkheim, Thomas and Sumner, had said, viz. that society is rooted in morally sanctioned norms, and social action must be seen as conduct involving value orientation and patterned by cultural norms.

Viewing Parsons's theory as a whole one is struck by a feature which he shares with the empirical school of sociology, the extreme formalism of his treatment. To take one example: since the analysis of a social system becomes in his hands a study of 'roles', Parsons nowhere shows what determines these roles and how they are related to the history of society. His 'social system' is reduced to a static system of interrelated behaviour patterns. What he expects a study of the social system to reveal is a relatively stable uniformity, which is why he can speak of the structure of the system, so that its function is one which maintains the existence of behaviour patterns and values. The charge that Parsons's sociology is a 'conservative sociology' is one that cannot easily be refuted.

Parsons's approach to methodology was altogether different from that of another American sociologist, who appeared like a meteor trailing a dazzling flash of light momentarily and then as quickly disappearing. Wright Mills was steeped in history and the pragmatic philosophy of Peirce, James and Dewey on which he was nurtured. He never took up a theme without relating it to the wider context from which it sprang. His opposition to parochialism in sociology was absolute. His voluminous writings in the course of a very short working life were marked by a quality of style and thought that hardly ever varied. Though he held a chair of sociology at Columbia University, he was no doubt the odd man out in American sociology, an inevitable fate of one who towered far above his contemporaries, whose pretensions he ridiculed and whom he denounced (and offended) for their academic obscurantism. Wright Mills's influence today is greater than it was during his lifetime and is steadily growing. This is because his analysis of the social situation in general and of the social situation of America in particular is now seen to have been the right one, as the issues to which he devoted his attention twenty years ago appear in a more acute form today. The titles of his works indicate what in Mills's view are some of the basic

Modern American Sociology

issues of contemporary society: *White Collar*, *The Power Elite*, *The Causes of World War Three*, *The Sociological Imagination* and lastly *The Marxists*. The range of topics which he treated bears witness to his versatile interests and, even more, to his awareness of the importance they hold in society; and he brought to bear on them a power of analysis of a very rare kind. Some of Mills's most original contributions to sociological thought and theory are found in his scattered writings, which can now be read in a collected edition, *Power, Politics and People*, edited by I. L. Horowitz.

Mills's theory of society is expounded in a book which he wrote in collaboration with Hans Gerth, *Character and Social Structure* (1953). In this book *social role* is used as a central concept of society, and is viewed as a structure which is composed of numerous institutional roles. The total social structure can be analysed into a number of institutional orders, as, for example, the political, religious, economic, and so forth. Each institutional order is a combination of a number of institutions. This method of describing the structure of society leads unfortunately to confusion in so far as the same vaguely defined term, 'institution', is used to demarcate both one aspect of society and the parts composing that aspect. However, all institutional orders are characterized by a number of aspects of social conduct, namely technology, symbols, status and education. The question that Gerth and Mills endeavoured to answer was: how is society integrated? They presented four alternative principles: (1) *correspondence*, which refers to the integration of society through a common structural principle which can be seen to operate in all the institutional orders; (2) *coincidence*, referring to a partial, though viable, unity resulting from the development of different structural principles; (3) *co-ordination*, which refers to a kind of an imposed unity through one or more of the institutional orders becoming dominant, as a totalitarian society; and lastly (4) *convergence*, which occurs when two or more institutional orders coincide and are fused together. *Character and Social Structure* is one of the few books in America which sets out to formulate theoretical propositions of general applicability by drawing extensively on historical materials.

A sociologist who has tried to combine in a working synthesis a theoretical and empirical approach to sociological problems is Robert K. Merton. What has given a special flavour to Merton's writings is their stylistic charm and clarity. Perhaps no other work in sociological literature of recent times has been more widely read and studied or had such a profound impact in and outside America than his *Social Theory and Social Structure*, first published in 1949 and since considerably enlarged and reprinted.

Conscious of the failure of what Mills called abstract empiricism and metaphysical theorizing, Merton has adopted a middle course by showing that a special type of theory, which he calls 'the middle-range theory', would avoid the vacuity of untested theory and would be at the same time empirical. He means to demonstrate that no sociology is worth doing unless it starts with some idea or hypothesis, but in the course of empirical investigation the idea or hypothesis may well require to be modified. It must not be regarded, to start with, as more than tentative, liable to modification in the light of the subsequent investigation. Moreover, it is not an uncommon thing in sociology to meet with an unexpected and happy discovery, for which Merton uses the term 'serendipity'. All the more reason, according to Merton, for not committing ourselves completely to the same idea or hypothesis.

Merton is a functionalist, in spite of being by far the severest critic of the other kind of functionalism. Function is defined by Merton as 'those observed consequences which make for the adaptation and adjustment of a given system'. It is not a satisfactory definition. The observed consequences of any institution or custom in society do not enlighten us very much about its *raison d'être:* much less do they tell us anything about its origin, nor is 'the adaptation and adjustment of a given system' logically or causally related to these consequences.

Merton nevertheless makes an important contribution to functional theory with his distinction, implicit in the works of many writers before him, between *manifest* and *latent* functions. The first refer to those objective consequences of any specific social institution or practice which are intended by the participants, while the second refer to the unintended consequences.

There is no doubt that the distinction is fundamental and is invaluable because it draws attention to functions that could well be and have often been overlooked. Merton gives a large number of illustrations. A manifest function of economic consumption is use, but one of its latent functions is maintaining prestige or snobbery. Merton devotes a whole essay to a brilliant description of the urban political machine in America, which meets numerous needs of neglected groups that official institutions have ignored. Merton insists that it is wrong to assume that these needs cannot be met differently under a different political system. It is always necessary, therefore, to keep in mind the possibility of functional alternatives. As Merton puts it, we must be constantly on the lookout for 'the range of possible variation in the items which can, in the given instance, subserve a functional requirement. It unfreezes the identity of the existent and the inevitable'. Not only this, but, in order to guard against the easy way out by taking things for granted, Merton employs the concept of *dysfunction* to define those observed consequences which lessen the adaptation and adjustment of the system and increase tension and conflict in society. Merton believes that this concept provides an analytic approach to the study of dynamics and change. It may well be useful to add to these powerful functional concepts another one, *afunctional*, to refer to those numerous cases of the persistence of those customs and practices which have no necessary or obvious function but are not dysfunctional either.

Pitirim A. Sorokin 1889–1968

Major works

Social Mobility (1927, 1941)
Contemporary Sociological Theories (1928)
Social and Cultural Dynamics (4 volumes, 1937–41)
Fads and Foibles in Modern Sociology and Related Sciences (1956)

The following extract is reprinted from Pitirim A. Sorokin, *Social Mobility*, in *Social and Cultural Mobility* (Glencoe, Ill.: The Free Press, 1959), Chapter ii, pp. 11–17, with the permission

Modern American Sociology

of The Macmillan Company. Copyright © The Free Press, a Corporation, 1959.

CONCEPTIONS AND DEFINITIONS

Social stratification means the differentiation of a given population into hierarchically superposed classes. It is manifested in the existence of upper and lower layers. Its basis and very essence consist in an unequal distribution of rights and privileges, duties and responsibilities, social values and privations, social power and influences among the members of a society. Concrete forms of social stratification are different and numerous. If the economic status of the members of a society is unequal, if among them there are both wealthy and poor, the society is *economically stratified*, regardless of whether its organization is communistic or capitalistic, whether in its constitution it is styled 'the society of equal individuals' or not. Labels, signboards and 'speech reactions' cannot change nor obliterate the real fact of the economic inequality manifested in the differences of incomes, economic standards, and in the existence of the rich and the poor strata. If the social ranks within a group are hierarchically superposed with respect to their authority and prestige, their honors and titles; if there are the rulers and the ruled, then whatever are their names (monarchs, executives, masters, bosses), these things mean that the group is *politically stratified*, regardless of what is written in its constitution or proclaimed in its declarations. If the members of a society are differentiated into various occupational groups, and some of the occupations are regarded as more honorable than others, if the members of an occupational group are divided into bosses of different authority and into members who are subordinated to the bosses, the group is *occupationally stratified*, independently of the fact whether the bosses are elected or appointed, whether their position is acquired by social inheritance or personal achievement.

PRINCIPAL FORMS OF SOCIAL STRATIFICATION AND THEIR INTERRELATIONS

Concrete forms of social stratification are numerous. The majority of them may, however, be reduced to three principal classes: the economic, the political, and the occupational stratification. As a general rule, these forms are closely intercorrelated with each other. Usually, those who occupy the upper strata in one respect happen to be in the upper strata also in other respects, and *vice versa*. The men who dwell in the upper economic layers happen also to be in the upper political and occupational strata. The poor, as a rule, are politically disfranchised and dwell in the

416

lowest strata of the occupational hierarchy. Such is the general rule, though there are, however, many exceptions to it. Not always are the wealthiest men at the apex of the political or occupational pyramid; and not always are the poor men the lowest in the political or the occupational gradations. This means that the intercorrelation among the three forms of stratification is far from being perfect; the strata of each form do not coincide completely with one another. There is always a certain degree of overlapping among them. This fact does not permit us to analyse in a summary way all three fundamental forms of social stratification. For the sake of a greater accuracy each form has to be studied separately. A real picture of social stratification in any society is very complex. In order to make its analysis easier, only the most fundamental traits must be taken. Many details must be omitted, and the situation simplified, without, however, disfiguring it. This is done in any science and has to be done especially here where the problem is so complex and so little studied. In such cases the Roman *minima non curat prœtor* is completely justified.

SOCIAL STRATIFICATION IS A PERMANENT
CHARACTERISTIC OF ANY ORGANIZED SOCIAL GROUP

Any organized social group is always a stratified social body. There has not been and does not exist any permanent social group which is 'flat,' and in which all members are equal. Unstratified society, with a real equality of its members, is a myth which has never been realized in the history of mankind. This statement may sound somewhat paradoxical and yet it is accurate. The forms and proportions of stratification vary, but its essence is permanent, as far as any more or less permanent and organized social group is concerned. This is true not only in human society, but even in plant and animal communities. Let us consider the principal corroborations.

Plant and Animal Communities. – As far as it is possible to apply the conceptions of human sociology to plant and animal communities, social stratification may be said to exist here also. In the plant communities there are different 'social' classes, the phenomena of parasitism and exploitation, suppression and domination, different 'economic' standards of living (the amount of air, sunlight, moisture, and soil ingredients consumed) and so on. Of course, these phenomena are but roughly analogous to those of social stratification in human society; and yet they signify clearly that the plant community is in no way a community of 'equal units,' whose positions are equal and whose interrelations are identical within the community.

With still greater reason the same may be said of animal societies. Within them social stratification is manifested in: (a) the existence of different and sharply divided classes in the communities of bees, ants, and other insects; (b) the existence of leaders among gregarious mammals; (c) the general facts of parasitism, exploitation, domination, subordination, and so on. In brief, one cannot find here any society which may be styled an unstratified group.

Pre-literate Human Tribes. – Except, perhaps, the few cases where the members of a population are leading an isolated life, where no permanent social life and interaction exist, where, therefore, we do not have a social organization in the proper sense of the word, as soon as organization begins primitive social groups exhibit the trait of stratification. It is manifested in various forms. First, in the existence of the sex and age groups with quite different privileges and duties. Second, in the existence of a privileged and influential group of the tribe's leaders. Third, in the existence of the most influential chieftain or headman. Fourth, in the existence of outcasts and outlawed men. Fifth, in the existence of inter- and intratribal division of labor. Sixth, in the existence of different economic standards, and in that of economic inequality generally. Traditional opinion about primitive groups as communistic societies which do not have any commerce or private property or economic inequality, or inheritance of fortune, are far from being correct. 'The primitive economy (*Urwirtschaft*) is neither an economy of isolated individuals searching for food (as K. Bucher thinks), nor the economy of communism or collective production. What we really have is the economic group composed of mutually dependent and economically active individuals and of the smaller parts of the group which have a system of commerce and barter with each other.'[1] If in many tribes economic differentiation is very slight, and customs of mutual aid approach communism, this is due only to the general poverty of the group. These facts support the contention that primitive groups also are stratified bodies.

More Advanced Societies and Groups. – If we cannot find a non-

1. SOMLÓ, F., *Der Guterverkehr in der Urgesellschaft, Inst. of Solvay*, pp. 65–67, 155, 177 ff., 1909. See also PANSKOW, H., 'Betrachtungen über das Wirtschaftsleben der Natürvölker,' *Zeitschrift der Gesellschaft für Erdkunde zu Berlin*, Vol. XXXI, 1896; MAUNIER, R., 'Vie Religieuse et vie économique,' *Revue International de Sociologie*, December, 1907, January and February, 1908; LOWIE, R. H., *Primitive Society*, Chap. IX, New York, 1920; THURNWALD, R., *Die Gestaltung d. Wirtschaftsentwicklung aus ihren Anfangen heraus*, 1923; MALINOWSKI, B., 'The Argonauts in the West Pacific,' *Economics Journal*, March, 1921.

stratified society among the most primitive groups, it is useless to try to find it among more advanced, larger and compound societies. Here, without any single exception the fact of stratification is universal. Its forms and proportions vary; its essence has existed everywhere and at all times. Among all agricultural and, especially, industrial societies social stratification has been conspicuous and clear. The modern democracies also do not present any exception to the rule. Though in their constitutions it is said that 'all men are equal,' only a quite naïve person may infer from this a non-existence of social stratification within these societies. It is enough to mention the gradations: from Henry Ford to a beggar; from the President of the United States to a policeman; from a foreman to the most subordinate worker; from the president of a university to a janitor; from an 'LL.D.' or 'Ph.D.' to a 'B.A.'; from a 'leading authority' to an average man; from a commander-in-chief of an army to a soldier; from a president of a board of directors of a corporation to its common laborer; from an editor-in-chief of a newspaper to a simple reporter; it is enough to mention these various ranks and social gradations to see that the best democracies have social stratification scarcely less than the non-democratic societies.

It is needless to insist on these obvious facts. What should be stressed here is, that not only large social bodies, but any organized social group whatever, once it is organized, is inevitably stratified to some degree.

Gradations, hierarchies, shining leaders, cumulative aspirations – all these appear spontaneously whenever men get together, whether for play, for mutual help, for voluntary association, of for the great compulsory association of the State. Every Englishman is said to love a lord; every American is said to love a title.[2]

Family, church, sect, political party, faction, business organization, gang of brigands, labor union, scientific society – in brief, any organized social group is stratified at the price of its permanency and organization. The organization even of groups of ardent levelers, and the permanent failure of all attempts to build a non-stratified group, testify to the imminency and unavoidability of stratification in an organized social group. This remark may appear somewhat strange to many people who, under the influence of high-sounding phraseology, may believe that, at least, the societies of the levelers themselves are non-stratified. This belief, as many another one, is utterly wrong. Different attempts to exterminate social feudalism have been successful, in the best cases, only in ameliorating some of the inequalities, and in changing the concrete forms of

2. TAUSSIG, F. W., Inventors and Money Makers, p. 126, New York, 1915.

stratification. They have never succeeded in annihilating stratification itself. And the regularity with which all these efforts have failed once more witnesses the 'natural' character of stratification. Christianity started its history with an attempt to create an equal society; very soon, especially after 313 A.D., it already had a complicated hierarchy, and soon finished by the creation of a tremendous pyramid, with numerous ranks and titles, beginning with the omnipotent pope and ending with that of a lawless heretic. The institution of Fratres Minorum was organized by St Francis of Assisi on the principle of perfect equality. Seven years later equality disappeared. Without any exceptions, all attempts of the most ardent levelers in the history of all countries have had the same fate. They could not avoid it even when the faction of the levelers has been victorious. The failure of the Russian Communism is only an additional example in a long series of similar experiments performed on small and large scale, sometimes peacefully, as in many religious sects, sometimes violently, as in social revolutions of the past and present. If many forms of stratification were destroyed for a moment they regularly reappeared again in the old or in a modified form, often being built by the hands of the levelers themselves.

Present democracies and Socialist, Communist, Syndicalist, and other organizations, with their slogan of 'equality' do not present any exception to the rule. In regard to democracies this has been shown above. The inner organization of different socialist and similar groups pleading 'equality' shows that perhaps in no other organization does such and enormous hierarchy and 'bossism' exist as in these groups of levelers. 'The Socialist leaders regard the masses only as the passive tools in the hands, as a series of zeros destined only to increase the significance of the figure on the left' (the importance of the leaders themselves), says E. Fournière, himself one of these socialists.[3] If in the statement there is an exaggeration, it is hardly considerable. At least, the best and most competent investigators of the situation are unanimous in their conclusions of an enormous development of oligarchy and stratification within all these groups. The enormous potential taste for inequality of numerous 'levelers' becomes at once conspicuous, as soon, indeed, as they happen to be victorious. In such cases they often exhibit a greater cruelty and contempt toward the masses than former kings and rulers. This has been repeated regularly in victorious revolutions where the levelers become dictators. Classical descriptions of the situation given by Plato and Aristotle, on the basis of the ancient Greek social revolutions, may be literally applied to all such cases, including the Bolshevist experiment.

3. FOURNIÉRE, E., *La Sociocratie*, p. 117, 1910.

To sum up: social stratification is a permanent characteristic of any organized society. 'Varying in form, social stratification has existed in all societies which proclaimed the equality of men.'[4] Feudalism and oligarchy continue to exist in science and arts, in politics and administration, in a gang of bandits, in democracies, among the levelers, everywhere.

This, however, does not mean that the stratification quantitatively or qualitatively is identical in all societies and at all times. In its concrete forms, defects or virtues, it certainly varies. The problem to be discussed now is these quantitative and qualitative variations. Begin with the quantitative aspect of social stratification in its three forms; economic, political and occupational. This is what is meant by the height and the profile of social stratification, and, correspondingly, the height and the profile of a 'social building.' How high is it? How long is the distance from the bottom to the top of a social cone? Of how many stories is it composed? Is its profile steep, or does it slope gradually? These are the problems of the quantitative analysis of social stratification. It deals, so to speak, exclusively with the exterior architecture of a social building. Its inner structure, in its entirety, is the object of the qualitative analysis. The study should begin with the height and the profile of the social pyramid. After that the pyramid should be entered and an investigation of its inner organization made from the standpoint of stratification.

The following extract is reprinted from Pitirim A. Sorokin, *Social and Cultural Dynamics* (1937–41; one-volume edition Boston, Mass.: Porter Sargent Publisher, Extending Horizon Books, 1957, pp. 639–46), with the permission of Mrs Pitirim A. Sorokin and Porter Sargent Publisher.

Some Implications of the Principle of Immanent Change

(A) PRINCIPLE OF IMMANENT GENERATION OF CONSEQUENCES

The first implication of the principle of immanent change may be formulated as follows: *As long as it exists and functions, any sociocultural system incessantly generates consequences which are not the results of the external factors to the system, but the consequences of the existence of the system and of its activities. As such, they must be imputed to it, regard-*

4. PARETO, V., *Traité de sociologie générale*, Vol. I, p. 613, Paris, 1917–1919.

less of whether they are good or bad, desirable or not, intended or not by the system. One of the specific forms of this immanent generation of consequences is an incessant change of the system itself, due to its existence and activity. Let us have a sociocultural system X (individual, family, State, any social organization, any cultural system). Since it exists, it incessantly works or acts. Let it, at a given moment, in a milieu B, perform act A (the performance of some act, as explained, is inevitable to any going concern or system as long as it exists). The very performance of the act – inevitable in some form – generates a series of infinitesimal or great changes in the milieu, as well as in the system itself. After its performance, and due to it, the system ceases to be what it was before: it greatly or infinitesimally changes. Thus, among other consequences of the discharge of the act, there is the consequence of a modification of the system itself.

Since the system is changed, it will react in the same milieu B (identical with the first) in a somewhat different way compared with the first reaction. Thus, the milieu (theoretically) remains the same; meanwhile the system changes and its reactions change. For the same reason, its third reaction in the same milieu B will again be different from the first and second reactions. And so on. Thus the milieu or the stimuli remaining constant, the system and its reactions to the milieu incessantly change. As some actions have to be performed incessantly by any sociocultural system so long as it exists, the incessant generation of the change of the system itself becomes immanent in it.

In the preceding case I took the milieu B as constant (which, in many experiments with the biological or sociocultural systems, we can have, with some approximation). Factually, the situation is somewhat different and the principle of the immanent generation of the consequences becomes still more important. The point is that outside the experimental laboratory conditions, the discharge of the act A by the system changes not only the system but also the milieu, infinitesimally or greatly. The changes in the milieu produced by the act of the system now begin to react upon the system in a different way than before. Therefore, the system now has to act differently, not only because it is changed itself, but also because by its act it has changed the milieu, and these changes force the system to act differently than did the pressure of the milieu B, before it was changed by the act of the system. A given state declares war against another state. The act of warfare changes not only the first state but introduces a series of important consequences in the world external to it. Among these changes, the other state is forced to enter the warfare. In the process of war, the second state becomes victorious, invades and subjugates the first state. Thus the act of the first state immanently generated a series of changes in itself; a series of changes in the external world; internal and external changes in their turn have reacted forcibly upon the state and have led to its profound transformation, up to the loss of its sovereignty and independence. In this sense, any system not only bears in itself the seeds of its change, but generates the change incessantly, with every act, every reaction, every activity it discharges.

(B) PRINCIPLE OF IMMANENT SELF-DETERMINATION OF THE SYSTEM'S DESTINY (Existence Career)

The second fundamental implication of the principle of immanent change is the principle of immanent self-determination of the potentially given course of the existence of a sociocultural system. It may be formulated as follows: *As soon as a sociocultural system emerges, its essential and 'normal' course of existence, the forms, the phases, the activities of its life career or destiny are determined mainly by the system itself, by its potential nature and the totality of its properties. The totality of the external circumstances is relevant, but mainly in the way of retarding or accelerating the unfolding of the immanent destiny; weakening or reinforcing some of the traits of the system; or facilitating a realization of the immanent potentialities of the system; finally, in catastrophic changes, destroying the system; but these external circumstances cannot force the system to manifest what it potentially does not have; to become what it immanently cannot become; to do what it immanently is incapable of doing. Likewise, the external conditions can crush the system or terminate an unfolding of its immanent destiny at one of the earliest phases of its development (its immanent life career), depriving it of a realization of its complete life career; but they cannot fundamentally change the character and the quality of each phase of the development; nor can they, in many cases, reverse or fundamentally change the sequence of the phases of the immanent destiny of the system.*[1]

This proposition is a mere result of the principle of immanent change and immanent generation of the consequences. With all the traits at

1. A. Comte, in spite of his externalistic tendencies, well understood this. 'This human being cannot be modified indefinitely by exterior circumstances; such modifications can affect only the degrees of phenomena, without at all changing their nature; and again, when the disturbing influences exceed their general limits, the organism is no longer modified, but destroyed. All this is . . . more eminently true of the social than of the individual organism, on account of its higher complexity and position.' A. Comte, *The Positive Philosophy*, translated by H. Martineau (New York, 1853), Vol. II, p. 117.

a given moment (T^1), the system acts in the form of A; A introduces changes in the milieu and in the system itself. Therefore, for the next moment, T^1, the system's total situation is determined by the external consequences of the act A. This situation at T^1 is thus determined by the system's properties and activities at the moment T^1. The same is true for the moment T^2, T^3 ... T^n, up to the end of the existence of the system. This means that any sociocultural system, as soon as it emerges as a system, bears in itself its future destiny. To use Aristotle's example an acorn as soon as it emerges bears in itself its destiny, namely the unfolding destiny of an oak and of nothing else. So with the initial system of any plant or animal organism. The same is still truer of a sociocultural system: a moronic family cannot unfold itself into the Great Christian Church or develop the properties of the Royal Scientific Society; from an emerged contractual business concern one cannot expect the properties, functions, and life career of the early Christian monastery; from a Sensate 'Society of Conoisseurs of Wines and Women' the characteristics and destiny of an ascetic society; from the State, the functions and destiny of a sentimental philanthropic society; from a real university, the functions, behavior and life career of a criminal gang; and so on. As soon as a sociocultural system emerges, with all its properties and *modus vivendi* and *modus agendi*, it contains in itself its 'normal' future. At any moment of its existence and activity it creates it, controls it, determines it, and molds it. In this sense, to use the proverb, any sociocultural system is the molder of its own future.[2]

This does not deny the role of the external circumstances. But as mentioned, it specifies their functions. The external agencies may crush the system and in this way prevent it from a realization of its immanent destiny. Earthquake, fire, plague, inundation, war, and other agencies external to a given system – the family, the artistic society, the religious or political sect – can kill all or a part of its members; can destroy its property and other instrumentalities of its activities; can disperse the members; can destroy the scientific libraries and laboratories, art museums and churches, means of transportation and communication, food supply; and in hundreds of forms may put an end to the existence of the system. Still more frequently, the external circumstances many

2. Compare Aristotle's 'Natural things are exactly those which do move continuously, by virtue of a principle inherent in themselves, towards a determined goal.' 'The final development reached from any one principle (*e.g.*, human seed) is neither exactly the same for every individual (for no two men are exactly alike) nor yet is it any random result (*e.g.*, dog or horse). There is, however, in each species always a tendency towards an identical result if nothing interferes.' Aristotle, *The Physics*, Bk. II, 199b, pp. 176–77.

accelerate or retard, facilitate or hinder, reinforce or weaken a realization of the immanent potentialities of the system and therefore of its destiny. All this is granted as self-evident. And yet, all this does not determine fundamentally the 'normal' career and phases of the development of the system. All this does not and cannot force the system A (oak, man, criminal gang), destined to have a life career B to have a life career fundamentally different, for which A does not have any potentiality: for instance, for a female to become a male; for a criminal gang to change into a society of the real saints; for the State to become a night club; and so on. This 'normal' career or destiny is an unfolding of the immanent potentialities of the system given at the moment of its emergence.

(C) IMMANENT SELF-DETERMINISM AS SYNTHESIS OF DETERMINISM AND INDETERMINISM

The preceding analysis raises the question: *What is the relationship of the immanent principle to the problem of determinism-indeterminism?* Is the immanent principle of change a variety of determinism or is it that of indeterminism? *The answer is: neither or both.* So far as the immanent principle implies that the normal course and the essential traits of the system are greatly determined by the potentialities of the system at the moment of its emergence, it is deterministic. It is also deterministic so far as the influence of external factors is concerned, when it reaches beyond the margin of the system's autonomy. Considering, however, that the determining potentialities of the system are *the system itself* and are its immanent properties, *the determinism of the system turns into self-determinism. Self-determinism is the equivalent of freedom.* When we ourselves determine something, we feel ourselves free; and especially when this self-determination flows spontaneously from us as something quite natural to us and emanating from our very nature. The self-determination of a system is exactly this: it is rooted in the system; it expresses its very nature and its most essential potentialities; it flows spontaneously from the system and cannot do otherwise. For all these reasons the principle of immanent self-determination is equivalent to indeterminism. It is indeterministic also in the sense that the very notion of the potentialities of the system, as we shall see in the next paragraph, contains an element of indeterminacy on its fringes and in no way means a rigid necessity, as has been shown above. In all these aspects, the principle of immanent change of a system is indeterministic and implies a considerable margin of autonomy from all the agencies that are external to the system; and also some amount of indeterminacy

425

within the system itself, so far as realization of its potentialities is concerned.

Such is the definite and precise answer to the question raised. The answer appears to be more adequate and sound than the half-truths of pure determinism and indeterminism.[3] The stated principle organically and logically unites in itself the valid parts of either of these principles and is free from the fallacies of either. It clearly indicates in what sense and to what degree the sociocultural system is indeterministic or free, and in what respects it is deterministic. In application to man and man's sociocultural world it synthesizes the doctrine of 'free will' with the doctrine of determinism and 'predestination.' The next paragraph will specify still more fully the conclusion reached.

(D) PRINCIPLE OF DIFFERENTIAL DEGREES OF SELF-DETERMINATION AND DEPENDENCE FOR VARIOUS SOCIOCULTURAL SYSTEMS

If any sociocultural system bears in itself the reason of its change and determination of its destiny, three questions arise: 1. In the unfolding of the potentialities of the system in its life career, is there only one quite rigid and definite course for the system, or are there several possibilities or routes to be traveled? 2. Is the margin of self-determination of the system and its dependence upon the external conditions the same for all sociocultural systems or is it different for different systems? 3. If so, upon what conditions does the relative portion of self-determination and dependence upon external agencies in the systems depend?

These are the three questions to be answered. Turn to the first problem. Put in a more definite way, the first problem asks whether the destiny or the future life career of any sociocultural system is quite rigidly predetermined in one definite course, from the moment of the emergency of the system. If the question is answered positively, this

3. It seems also more consistent and less self-contradictory than some theories of the modern physicists, like Sir Arthur Eddington, who extends the law of chance or indeterminacy over the inorganic world but exempts from it the realm of life, consciousness and spirit, as governed in a considerable part by the 'objective law of direction'; or like Max Planck, who extends the 'dynamic and statistical' determinism over the inorganic phenomena but exempts from it the region of 'Ego' and 'free will'. Such a mechanical division can hardly be satisfactory and consistent, not to mention the conspicuous contradiction of the theories of Eddington and Planck, confronted with each other. See Sir Arthur Eddington, *The Philosophy of Physical Science* (New York, 1939), pp. 61, 89–90, 180–181, 220–21; Max Planck, *Where Science Is Going* (New York, 1932), pp. 145–169.

would mean that any system is devoid of any possibility of deviating from its predetermined course, and becomes what it shall become. Such an answer cannot be accepted in this rigid form. First, because it entirely ignores the role of the external conditions of the system. We have seen that though the external circumstances cannot fundamentally modify the 'normal' destiny of any system, nevertheless, they can crush it, can accelerate and retard, favor and disfavor the development of the 'native potentialities' of the system, and in this way can exert of considerable influence upon its life career. In some respects they play a role similar to the row of tracks at the railroad station: the train (the system) remains the same, but where it will go and what will be its destination depends upon what track it follows. Sometimes when it is shifted on to a wrong track, the result is a collision and catastrophe. *In other words, the very existence of the external conditions of a system makes its life career not absolutely predetermined at the moment of the emergence of the system.* The immanent potentialities of the system (at the moment of its emergence) can actualize in somewhat different life careers if the external conditions are different (for the same system) or when they change differently during the life career of the system. Second, the very conception of the immanent potentialities of a system (at the moment of its emergence) hardly entitles us to interpret their totality as something absolutely rigid, devoid of any elasticity. 'Potentiality' is only an approximately marked course of career or direction of development. It implies some leeway of variation in most of its detailed 'curves' and 'turns' and 'by-ways.' It is not one highway which a driver has to follow (though even on such a highway the actual trajectories of the cars passing upon it are also somewhat different and never absolutely the same), but reminds us rather of several different routes to the point of destination, which the drivers can take and do take indeed: 3, 3A, 3B, 3C, each leading in the same direction, but each being a different route from the others. *Potentiality has always a margin for variations, especially on its fringes.* These variations are never rigidly determined or excluded. They are always the given datum. Otherwise, 'potentiality' would not be 'potentiality' but absolutely determined actuality or necessity, which conception contradicts that of potentiality.[4] In empirical sociocultural reality, the leeway of variations of potentiality is rather considerable for most of the sociocultural systems. Even when we are reasonably certain that a given child is gifted, we never can tell

4. Compare Aristotle's 'There are different stages of potentiality. The learner is a potential thinker in any given science, in a different sense from that in which he is a potential thinker in it, when he has learned its principles but is not thinking about it.' *Physics*, 255b; also 199c.

exactly what his accomplishments will be. The same is still truer of a given family, state, business corporation, religious current, literary movement, or a fighting army, or what not. Considering the potentialities of each of these systems, we can expect roughly, that their course, under given conditions, would be approximately such and such, but only a fool or a charlatan can forecast all the details of this course.

Even in regard to the biological systems this leeway of a given potentiality is considerable. Having an acorn, we can reasonably expect the growth of an oak from it. But, how long actually the oak will live, what will be its shape, strength, height, size, the exact patterns of its branches, number of its leaves, and hundreds of other detailed characteristics, we cannot foresee.

Thus, the role of the external milieu and the nature of the immanent potentialities of any sociocultural system force us to admit a margin of indetermined possibilities in the development of the life career of the system. I say a 'margin,' not the complete indeterminacy. Such a margin means the rejection of a fatalistic and absolutely determined course of development of the system. Put in symbolic form, this thesis means that a given system A has an immanent potentiality B, which has to be unfolded in the course of its existence. But, granting even similar external circumstances, this B in one case will actualize into Ba, in another into Bb, in the third into Bc, and so on, up to Bn. In different external milieus, the difference between the actualizations of this B will be still greater.

Turn now to the second question: *Is the margin of self-determination of the future career of the system the same for all sociocultural systems?* Phrased in different form this question means: Are all the social and cultural systems equally dependent upon or independent of the external conditions in shaping their own destiny?

This destiny is shaped, as we have seen, by the immanent forces of the system itself and by the milieu in which it exists. Are the shares of both 'molders' constant for any system?

It seems almost axiomatic that the share of the immanent factor of self-determination and that of the external circumstances is different for different systems. Some social and cultural systems seem to be conditioned by external circumstances much more than others. In our daily observation we notice the individuals who are the playthings of circumstances and the individuals who are to a much greater degree the builders of their own destiny, often contrary to the most inimical conditions. There are 'soft and weak' persons and the persons with 'an iron will power and determination.' Likewise, we all know strong and weak families, unions, associations, states, governments. The strong weather many storms and stand firmly against many attacks, misfortunes, perturbations, while the weak fundamentally change or go to pieces after a slight inimical pressure of circumstances. The same is true about many systems of culture mentally (in religion, science, philosophy, art, law, literature, etc.). Some systems rise quickly, carried on by the wave of favorable circumstances, and as quickly decline when the luck of the circumstances changes; or rapidly change their character and individuality, adapting themselves to the external milieu and soon lose their identity, turning into a kind of formless and skeletonless protoplasma. Other systems persist and hold their identity, regardless of external circumstances. They remain equal to themselves under both adverse and favorable conditions; they display much less elasticity and versatility than the former; they ride the same ship in all weathers. Thus they show themselves much more immune to and independent from, the external conditions than the former. Facts of this kind are daily observations. They mean that the amount of self-determination of their own destiny or the amount of the dependence upon the external conditions is not constant for various sociocultural systems.

Logically, such a conclusion is also comprehensible. In order that all sociocultural systems shall be equally dependent on or independent of the external conditions in molding their own destiny, we should require: first, that all the systems be identical in all their potential nature, and therefore in their capacity to resist the influence of the external circumstances, or that all systems have the same immunity in this respect. To accept such an assumption would be a logical as well as a factual fallacy. A logical fallacy, because we here ascribe an identity to the systems which otherwise we recognize as different from one another. Since they are different in other respects they can hardly be equally immune to or dependent upon, the external conditions. Observationally, we know that various mechanical (*e.g.*, automobile), organic (different organisms), psychosocial (human individuals), and sociocultural systems have a different amount of 'immunity' in regard to many external conditions. A good automobile can continue to function on a poor road without difficulty, while an old and poor automobile would break down or have trouble. Some organisms are more immune to several kinds of germs, or weather or food conditions than many others. Many minds are influenced by the current fads and fashions much less than many others. Likewise, as mentioned, some married couples get divorced after some slight quarrel or 'incompatibility,' while some others remain married up to their death. Some societies and unions persist for decades and even centuries, amidst most different environmental circumstances; while others quickly die, after meeting the first adverse outside conditions. Thus logically and observationally, the degree of self-determination (or dependence upon the external conditions) in molding their own destiny is different for different systems.

Is it possible to indicate a few more or less general conditions upon which depends the amount of self-determination of its destiny by the system?

First of all, it depends upon the *kind of social or cultural system*. Different social and cultural systems, like different mechanical or organic systems are likely to have different degrees of dependence upon external conditions in unfolding their immanent potentialities. However, this does not get us far: the proposition does not answer exactly which traits and properties make the systems differently immune to the forces of the environment. Until these properties are pointed out, the answer is useless.

Second, the amount of self-determination of various systems depends also upon the *kind of milieu*. We have seen that the milieu may be favorable or unfavorable to the unfolding of the potentialities of the system. Sometimes it may even crush it and end its existence. This again does not lead us far: to be a real answer, the proposition must indicate what properties of the milieu are favorable or unfavorable.

Third, we must distinguish farther between *the total and the specific immunity* of the system from its environment, in the molding of its own destiny. An organism, for instance, may possess a specific immunity in regard to typhus or diphtheria forces of the environment; and yet, as a whole, be more dependent upon the milieu than another organism which does not have this specific immunity, but, as a whole, stands better all the shocks of the environment, lives longer, and unfolds its potentialities better than the first. Farther on, different organisms may have different specific immunities: one in regard to diphtheria, another in regard to tuberculosis, a third in regard to venereal disease. A similar situation is thinkable in regard to the social and cultural systems. Some of them may have a high specific immunity and low total immunity; some others may have a high total immunity and a low specific immunity. Some of them may be immune in regard to one set of specific forces of the environment, while others are immune in regard to different agencies of the milieu. For instance, a business firm may be very sensitive towards the economic conditions of its environment (have a low immunity) and quite insensitive towards the artistic or philosophical or family agencies of its milieu. An art association or a philosophical society may, on the contrary, be very immune towards the economic forces of the environment, and greatly dependent upon the nature of its artistic or philosophical atmosphere.

These preliminary remarks show all the complexity of the problem discussed and warn against its simplification. Before laying down the propositions answering the question, we must specify as exactly as possible under what conditions they can be valid and what kind of self-determination – general or special – they mean.

Let us assume, first, that we have social and cultural systems *of the same kind:* say, the family, or the State, or the business firm; or a philosophical school or an art system.

(E) OTHER CONDITIONS BEING EQUAL (INCLUDING THE MILIEU), IN THE SOCIAL AND CULTURAL SYSTEMS OF THE SAME KIND, THE GREATER AND BETTER IS THEIR INTEGRATION, THE GREATER IS THEIR SELF-DETERMINATION (AND AUTONOMY FROM THE ENVIRONMENT) IN MOLDING THEIR OWN DESTINY

By the greater and better integration of a social and cultural system or group is meant first, the existence and the degree of the causal and meaningful interdependence between its components; second, and this is very important, the solidarity (familistic, or at least, contractual) character of the relationship between the members or human agents; third, consistency between other components of the system.

Such is probably the most important condition of the amount of self-determination of the system, in unfolding its potentiality during its life career.

Unfolded, the proposition implies:

(1) *Other conditions being equal, of the social and cultural complexes, the least amount of self-determination is found in unorganized social groups and in cultural congeries.* An unorganized group of individuals (unintegrated social congeries) or an unintegrated cultural congeries is a mere collection of the elements of the social and cultural system. As such, it does not have any causal and meaningful cohesion and unity; any unified direction of its activities; any unified efforts towards a fuller unfolding of its potentialities; any unified end; and respectively, any unified system of forces directed towards the preservation of its identity and a realization of its destiny. Therefore, it cannot successfully oppose the adverse pressure of environmental forces, cannot press unifiedly against the agencies of the milieu and overcome their resistance. It is like a collection of individuals not organized into a disciplined army and therefore incapable of resisting the attack of the same number of individuals unified into a well-integrated military body. Such social and cultural congeries have only the atomized and divergent self-

determination of each of its elements, but no unified and therefore more powerful system of self-determination. Respectively, it is much more a plaything in the hands of the environmental forces than an integrated system of the same elements.

(2) Other conditions being equal, *the highest amount of self-determination belongs to those social and cultural systems which are most perfectly integrated, causally and meaningfully*, where the causal inter-dependence of the components and elements of the system is the greatest; and their relationship is the most solidary (among human agents) and most consistent among the components, where, neither actually nor potentially, is there any contradiction, any *Spannung*, any inner tension, antagonism or conflict. Out of similar families or states – the family or state which is perfectly integrated, where the relationships are solidary, where all members spontaneously and deliberately strive towards the same ends; have the same mentality and objectives; have a unified system of aims, efforts, and activities – such a family or state is a builder of its own future much more than the family or state with lower causal and meaningful integration, where the causal interdependence of the members is loose, relationships less solidary, and where heterogeneous aims, conflicts, and antagonisms exist.

Finally, *between these types stand the immediate systems, which are neither congeries nor perfectly integrated systems*. Such are the social systems where only the causal interdependence is found but where realtionships are not quite solidary; or the cultural systems where relationships of the elements of the system are somewhat eclectic, not quite consistent, and actually or latently conflicting between and in each of its components. In such systems there always is found what Max Weber, M. Scheler and E. Barthel style, *Spannung*, a kind of tension or latent antagonism; a hidden split or crack, which flares into an open split of the system as soon as the respective adverse interference of the external conditions takes place. For this reason, it is less capable of standing the modifying and breaking influence of the environmental forces, and depends upon them more than the systems with perfect integration. This again concerns a person, a social and cultural system. Fanatics, Don Quixotes, persons whith deep convictions and consistent systems of mentality, are examples of strongly integrated personalities. We all know that they are much more immune towards all the currents of fashions and fads in art and science, philosophy and religion, ideology and so forth, than the persons whose mentality is a kind of elastic attic, where side by side lie traditional religion and progressive diluted atheism; enthusiasm for American democracy and the Soviet paradise; parrot-like eulogy of Bach, and enjoyment of crooning and jazz; admiration of each succeeding best-seller, be it Papini's *Life of Christ*, Strachey's psychoanalytic biography, *Trader Horn*, *Anthony Adverse*, Thurman Arnold's *Folklore of Capitalism*, or what not. They follow any fad and fashion and are continually being passively molded – in their mentality and behavior – by the passing currents of their environment. They have little selective function: within their capacity they ingest all that environment gives to them, and therefore are playthings of the external forces.

The same, with a proper variation, can be said of the social and cultural systems. Any eclectic pseudo system of philosophy, art, religion, or law is similar to the above 'eclectic' and 'open-minded' persons. They seem to accept almost anything. As a result, they are always being changed by the passing currents of thoughts of their environment. As such, they seldom have any real individuality and remind us of something formless and shapeless, passively plastic, molded principally by their milieu and little by their own potentialities. This is the reason why the eclectic pseudo systems of culture mentality – in all the compartments of culture – do not last long, as an eclectic system of a *definite* sort (as endlessly varying complexes the eclecticism, like other congeries, is a perennial phenomenon). They leave faint traces in the annals of history. They come and go, while any consistent cultural systems, such as idealism and materialism, eternalism and temporalism, realism and nominalism, in philosophy; the visual and ideational styles in art; the classic, the Gothic, the baroque and other styles in architecture; the unified systems of religious beliefs or ethical teachings, persist for centuries and dominate for centuries. Even when they are on the decline, they still exist and are distinguishable; and – what is more – sooner or later they again ascend and become dominant (see Volumes One and Two). It is not incidental that, whether it be in the history of philosophy, art, ethical systems, scientific theories, religions, or law – in all such histories very little can be found about innumerable eclectic theories which existed, and still exist. The bulk of the histories deal with only the more or less perfectly integrated systems of philosophy of the great 'integrating minds,' or with the integrated systems of art, ethics, science, or religion. The greater the integration of the system, the more space is given to it, and the longer it persists, and often the greater the influence it exerts upon the destiny not only of its own but other cultural systems of mankind.

The same is true of the social systems. Unintegrated armies have always been beaten by integrated ones. Unintegrated states have always been short-lived compared with the integrated ones. A poorly integrated family, or business organization, or any 'eclectic social organization' has always been more dependent upon external forces and external 'good or bad luck,' and, as a rule, more quickly and frequently has come to an end (divorce, separation, disorganization and loss of independence, bankruptcy or dissolution) than similar but better integrated social systems.

One word of caution: *integration and lack of it should not be mixed with fashionable terms like 'plasticity,' 'capacity of adjustment to environment,' 'progressiveness,' and the like.* These terms are not equivalent to good or poor integration. A system may be well integrated, and yet may possess a high plasticity and versatility in its functioning activities and 'adjustment of the environment' to itself (in contra-distinction to the contemporary passive: 'adjustment to the environ-ment'). And vice versa, a system may be poorly integrated and yet be very rigid and unchangeable; for instance, in its vehicles, agents, and activities, in the perennial presence of antagonisms among its members, in its use of antiquated ways and means for a discharge of its functions, in the ossification of its activities and so on.

Well-integrated systems may be both elastic and rigid in their structure and tactics, according to the conditions; the same is true of the poorly integrated systems. In passing, it is to be noted that nowadays what is so widely extolled as the virtue of plasticity and 'capacity of adjustment' is often, in fact, a cult of a lack, or of a poor integration in a system, be it an individual or social body. If we are to believe the partisans of this theory, we all, it seems, should ingest all the best-sellers; follow all the fashions and fads; praise simultaneously democracy and fascism and communism, religion and atheism, capitalism and communism; if others become obsessed with cross-word puzzles, or bridge, or 'Informa-tion, Please,' we should 'adjust' ourselves by sharing the obsession; open widely all the organizations to everybody who wants to join them; follow simultaneously quite opposite and conflicting policies in our organizations; join quite unrelated movements; in brief, be spineless, skeletonless, unintegrated eclectics, passively 'adjusting ourselves' to everything from the last-minute conception of God, to the last-minute current fad of the artistic, scientific, philosophical, political, culinary, and what-not movement or organization.[5] Such a triumph of uninte-grated eclecticism and unintegrated passivity is in accordance with our

5. See P. Sorokin, 'Tragic Dualism of Sensate Culture,' *Science, Philo-sophy and Religion. Symposium* (New York, 1941). K. Horney accurately sees in such self-contradictory eclecticisms the tensions of our culture; in such tensions the source of many contemporary neuroses, and in such persons the neurotics of our time. Among tensions of our culture she emphasizes such contradictions as: the ideal of competition and success, on the one hand; on the other, the ideal of brotherly love and humility; the

super-ripe Sensate culture and society. But, as has been shown above, it is not the way of self-determination and control of one's own or the nation's or mankind's future destiny, as the partisans of this backbone-less eclecticism and passive environmentalism often claim. It is the most hopeless road to that end.

Of the other conditions relevant to the amount of self-direction of a system in molding its own destiny, the following ones can be mentioned:

(3) *Other conditions being equal (including the identical environment and the perfection of integration), the greater the power of the system, the greater its autonomy from the social, biological and cosmic environment, and the greater its self-control and self-direction.* Put in that form, the proposition is almost axiomatic. The more powerful system naturally has the greater chance to resist, overcome, and therefore to carry on its aims and potentialities, in its environment, than a less powerful system. The weakness of the proposition consists in the indeterminacy of the term 'power.' Left at that, it is valid, but fairly indefinite. What is the power of a sociocultural system? How can it be measured? And measured it must be, in order that we can say which system is more powerful.

I do not know any satisfactory device for a measurement as well as for a clear definition of the power of a social or cultural system. All that one can do is to indicate a few rough criteria which are somewhat measurable, and which can give at least a very rough, but nevertheless hardly misleading, 'index' of the power of the system.

Other conditions being equal, (*a*) *the greater the membership of a social system;* (*b*) *the better their biological and mental and social qualities;* (*c*) *the greater the sum total of real knowledge, experience, and wisdom at its disposal;* (*d*) *the more efficient its organization in the sense of the distribution of rights-duties-functions among its members* (including the distribution to everybody according to his talent and ability); (*e*) *the greater the sum total of the means and instruments of influencing human conduct as well as of modifying biological and cosmic nature; and*

---

stimulation of needs, and their frustrations in hundreds of ways; the freedom of the individual (in Sensate meaning) and his progressive limitation. Such eclecticisms and contradictory tensions breed poorly integrated neurotics. See K. Horney, *The Neurotic Personality of Our Time* (New York, 1937). And their number is far greater than the official statistics of the *Patients in Hospitals for Mental Diseases* give. Factually, all the enormous masses of the eclectics of the type described are potential neurotics. Their name is millions. *Cf.* A. J. Toynbee's theory of 'Syncretism' and 'Promiscuity' in the periods of disintegration of civilizations. *A Study of History*, Vol. V, pp. 376–569.

finally, (f) the better its solidary integration (discussed above); the greater is the power of the group – the more independent it is from the external conditions in the realization of its potentialities.

A few comments will make each of these conditions clear.

(a) That the power and influence of any social system depends upon its membership is self-evident: an army of one hundred soldiers will be beaten by one of ten thousand soldiers of similar quality. A labor union with a membership of one hundred can exert much less pressure upon the employers and other groups than a union with one million members And so in regard to any social group. The mere number of the members of a system is always a relevant component of its influence and power

(b) Besides the quantity, the quality of the members plays an important role in the influence, power, and realization of the system's ends. It is also evident that of the groups of equal size, the group consisting of the mentally talented, morally integrated, biologically healthy persons can do much more than a group whose members are either morons, or biologically weak, or morally disintegrated persons.

(c) Likewise, the important role of knowledge, experience, and wisdom that are in the possession of the system or group also needs no lengthy comment. This condition is specifically mentioned, because a group may be composed of good human material but, due to various conditions, may be deprived of an actual possession of knowledge, experience, and wisdom at a given moment. In such a case, for a given moment, the influence of the group would be less than that of another similar group in actual possession of the knowledge and experience. Military history furnishes many cases of this kind: the invaders (in the past or in the present) often have been little, if at all, superior to the nation invaded. But they had in their actual possession the knowledge of the military technique and the perfect military weapons which were lacking among the invaded people. As a result, even though not being superior either morally, mentally, or biologically, the invaders have often been able to subjugate the people of the invaded country and become victorious over them. It is not enough to be potentially talented; it is no less important actually to have the necessary knowledge and experience.

(d) The next important condition is the technical organization of the system; its social differentiation and stratification; the manner of distribution of rights, duties, functions among its members; and the kind of persons to whom these rights, duties, and functions are given. It must be evident, to begin with the simplest case, that, of two groups, the one where military command is given to an inborn Napoleon or Caesar; where moral and religious leadership is likewise entrusted to inborn moral and religious leaders; and where the governmental and other, including the humblest, functions are given to those who are most fitted for them – such a group will evidently be more efficient and powerful than a similar one where a potential Beethoven is made a captain of finances; an idiotic strategist, the commander-in-chief; an inborn slave, a ruler; a stupid person, a captain of science.

No less important, however, is the existence or nonexistence of the social stratification and differentiation, with their division of labor; and what kind of social organization is found in all these respects. Generally, division of functions of the members of the system increases the system's efficiency and power. Likewise, these greatly depend upon what kind of division of functions, or social organization, is carried through in the system: for instance, whether it is 'democratic,' or 'fascist,' or 'monarchical'; a system with masters and slaves; highly hierarchical or equalitarian; 'capitalistic' or 'communistic,' and so on. There is hardly any definite form of social organization which is most efficient for all the systems, at all times, and in all conditions and circumstances. On the contrary, the difference in the nature of the systems and their objectives makes certain that for widely different systems widely different forms of social organization are most efficient and best: the form of social organization of an army is little suited to a monastery of ascetics or a university or even a business corporation. And vice versa, the best form of organization of a preparatory school will be disastrous for an army. But for the same systems of the same kind, there are more and less fit, more and less perfect forms of organization. What they are for different groups is out of place to discuss here. The important fact is that the power and efficiency of the group depends greatly upon how fitted is its social organization to its nature and to its environment. Hence, its mention among other conditions.

(e) By means of influencing human behavior and of controlling the social, biological, and cosmic milieu in conformity with the ends of the system, is meant any instrumentality that serves the purpose: the total sum of the technical instruments and tools; machines, arms, weapons, factories, mills; wealth and money; means of communication and contact; army; police; prisons; electric chairs; and finally, the total sum of the talents mentioned above: preachers; teachers; orators; inventors; researchers; in brief, anything and anybody that helps to influence the human behavior of the members and outsiders to overcome the obstacles of the social, biological, and cosmic external world.

(f) Finally, the important role of perfect solidary integration of the system has been already discussed.[6]

6. On the power of social systems and its criteria see further details in P. Sorokin, *Sistema Soziologii* (Petrograd, 1920), Vol. II, pp. 45 ff., 83 ff.

With a slight modification, the same criteria are applicable to the comparative power of cultural systems. *The greater the number of the human agents of the system (of art, religion, philosophy, science, etc.); the better their biological, mental, moral, and social qualities; the greater the wisdom, knowledge, and value it incorporates* (value or system of meanings: religious, scientific, artistic, ethical, etc.); *the better it fits the social organization of its followers; the greater is its logico-causal integration* (within the system of meanings and between all its components); *the greater the sum total of means or vehicles for its unfolding, broadcasting, and maintenance at its disposal; the greater the power of the cultural system – the more independent it is from its environmental forces.*

Here, however, a greater emphasis is to be put upon the value (the system of meanings) the system incorporates and the consistency of the integration of its elements and components (see above, Chapter Two) than in the social system.

The rest of the conditions are in a sense derivative from these properties of the system. If the value it incarnates is great; and if this value is integrated perfectly into a system, the system is likely to have a large number of followers; be fitted to their social organization (because it incorporates a great value); and get an abundance of vehicles – means for its objectification, broadcasting, maintenance, and functioning.

Each of these conditions is unquestionably a basic constituent of the power of a social or cultural system. Taken separately, each condition cannot be an index of the power of the system. Taken together, they give a very approximate, but hardly misleading, indicator of that power.

This proposition then sums up, if not all, then probably the most essential uniform conditions of the comparative autonomy of the system (in building its destiny) from the external conditions, and explains the

---

The problem of the comparative powerfulness of social systems has been studied very little. Of the previous attempts to roughly elucidate it and even to give the definite index of powerfulness, the theory of A. Coste is probably most notable, but entirely unsatisfactory. (See P. Sorokin, *Contemporary Sociological Theories*, pp. 364 ff.)

The recent attempt of Bertrand Russell according to whom, 'The power of a community depends not only upon its numbers and its economic resources and its technical capacity, but also upon its beliefs,' plus upon a kind of organization, practically repeats (independently), in a vaguer and less systematic and complete way, the above criteria of mine, set forth in my Russian work. In other respects, the analysis of power given by Russell is rather patchy, superficial, and far from being 'A New Social Analysis' as the book claims to be. Bertrand Russell, *Power, A New Social Analysis* (New York, 1938), pp. 145, 158, *et passim*.

relative share of the system's self-control and self-regulation in molding its own destiny.

Summary

1. The reason or cause of a change of any sociocultural system is in the system itself, and need not be looked for anywhere else.

2. Additional reason for change of a system is its milieu, which is again composed mostly of the immanently changing systems.

3. Any sociocultural system changing immanently, incessantly generates a series of immanent consequences, which change not only the milieu of the system but also the system itself.

4. Bearing the seeds of its change in itself, any sociocultural system bears also in itself the power molding its own destiny or life career. Beginning with the moment of emergence, each sociocultural system is the main factor of its own destiny. This destiny, or the system's subsequent life career, represents mainly an unfolding of the immanent potentialities of the system in the course of its existence.

5. The environmental forces are not negligible, but their role consists essentially in retardation or acceleration; facilitation or hindrance; reinforcement or weakening, of the realization of the immanent potentialities of the system. Sometimes they can crush the system and put an end to its existence; or stop the process of unfolding the immanent potentialities at one of the early phases. They cannot, however, change fundamentally the immanent potentialities of the system and its normal destiny in the sense of making the life career of an unfolding acorn that of a cow, or vice versa.

6. So far as the system, since the moment of its emergence, bears in itself its future career, it is a determinate system and in this sense deterministic. So far as the future of the system is determined mainly not by external agents, but by the system itself, such a determinism is indeterministic or free, as flowing spontaneously, in accordance with its nature, from the system itself.

7. The process of unfolding the immanent potentialities of the emerged system is somewhat predetermined by the system, but this predetermination leaves a considerable margin for variations. In this sense it is not absolutely and narrowly preconditioned. Only the main direction and the main phases of the unfolding are predetermined; the rest, including most of the details, are 'free' and become an unforeseen and unpredictable matter of chance, environment, and free choice of the system.

8. Since the destiny or life career of any system is the result of the system's self-control and of the influence of the environmental forces, the relative share of each of these two factors in molding the system's

career is not constant for all sociocultural systems. The share of the self-control of the system is the greater, the more perfectly the system is integrated and the more powerful it is.

9. As a rough indicator of the elusive concept of the power of a sociocultural system, the following less elusive combination of the criteria is offered: the greater the membership of the system; the better the members biologically, mentally, morally and socially; the greater the actual wisdom, knowledge and experience the system has at its disposal; the better it is organized; the greater the total sum of means of influencing human behavior and forces of nature at its disposal; the more solidarily (or consistently) the system is integrated; the more powerful it is; the more independent from the forces of the environment, – the greater is the share of its own control in molding its destiny.

Vilfredo Pareto 1848–1923

Major works

Les Systèmes Socialistes (2 volumes, 1902–3)
Trattato di sociologia generale (2 volumes, 1916; translated as *The Mind and Society*)

The following extracts are reprinted from Vilfredo Pareto, *The Mind and Society*, edited by Arthur Livingston, translated by Andrew Bongiorno and Arthur Livingston (New York: Harcourt, Brace & Co., 1935), with the permission of the Pareto Fund.

2026. *Social* élites *and their circulation.*[1] Suppose we begin by giving a theoretical definition of the thing we are dealing with, making it as exact

1. Kolabinska, *La circulation des élites en France*, p. 5: 'The outstanding idea in the term "*élite*" is superiority. That is the only one I keep. I disregard secondary connotations of appreciation or as to the utility of such superiority. I am not interested here in what is desirable. I am making a simple study of what is. In a broad sense I mean by the *élite* in a society people who possess in marked degree qualities of intelligence, character, skill, capacity, of whatever kind ... On the other hand I entirely avoid any sort of judgment on the merits and utility of such classes.' [The phrase 'circulation of *élites*' is well established in Continental literature. Pareto himself renders it in Italian as 'circulation of the élite (selected, chosen, ruling, 'better') classes.' It is a cumbersome phrase and not very exact, and I see no reason for preferring it to the more natural and, in most connexions, the more exact, English phrase, class-circulation. – A. L.]

as possible, and then go on to see what practical considerations we can replace it with to get a first approximation. Let us for the moment completely disregard considerations as to the good or bad, useful or harmful, praiseworthy or reprehensible character of the various traits in individuals, and confine ourselves to degrees – to whether, in other words, the trait in a given case be slight, average, intense, or more exactly, to the index that may be assigned to each individual with reference to the degree, or intensity, in him of the trait in question.

2027. Let us assume that in every branch of human activity each individual is given an index which stands as a sign of his capacity, very much the way grades are given in the various subjects in examinations in school. The highest type of lawyer, for instance, will be given 10. The man who does not get a client will be given 1 – reserving zero for the man who is an out-and-out idiot. To the man who has made his millions – honestly or dishonestly as the case may be – we will give 10. To the man who has earned his thousands we will give 6; to such as just manage to keep out of the poor-house, 1, keeping zero for those who get in. To the woman 'in politics,' such as the Aspasia of Pericles, the Maintenon of Louis XIV, the Pompadour of Louis XV, who has managed to infatuate a man of power and play a part in the man's career, we shall give some higher number, such as 8 or 9; to the strumpet who merely satisfies the senses of such a man and exerts no influence on public affairs, we shall give zero. To a clever rascal who knows how to fool people and still keep clear of the penitentiary, we shall give 8, 9, or 10, according to the number of geese he has plucked and the amount of money he has been able to get out of them. To the sneak-thief who snatches a piece of silver from a restaurant table and runs away into the arms of a policeman, we shall give 1. To a poet like Carducci we shall give 8 or 9 according to our tastes; to a scribbler who puts people to rout with his sonnets we shall give zero. For chess-players we can get very precise indices, noting what matches, and how many, they have won. And so on for all the branches of human activity.

2028. We are speaking, remember, of an actual, not a potential, state. If at an English examination a pupil says: 'I could know English very well if I chose to; I do not know any because I have never seen fit to learn,' the examiner replies: 'I am not interested in your alibi. The grade for what you know is zero.' If, similarly, someone says: 'So-and-so does not steal, not because he couldn't but because he is a gentleman,' we reply: 'Very well, we admire him for his self-control, but his grade as a thief is zero.'

2029. There are people who worship Napoleon Bonaparte as a god. There are people who hate him as the lowest of criminals. Which are right? We do not choose to solve that question in connexion with a quite different matter. Whether Napoleon was a good man or a bad man, he was certainly not an idiot, nor a man of little account, as millions of others are. He had exceptional qualities, and that is enough for us to give him a high ranking, though without prejudice of any sort to questions that might be raised as to the ethics of his qualities or their social utility.

2030. In short, we are here as usual resorting to scientific analysis, which distinguishes one problem from another and studies each one separately. As usual, again, we are replacing imperceptible variations in absolutely exact numbers with the sharp variations corresponding to groupings by class, just as in examinations those who are passed are sharply and arbitrarily distinguished from those who are 'failed,' and just as in the matter of physical age we distinguish children from young people, the young from the aged.

2031. So let us make a class of the people who have the highest indices in their branch of activity, and to that class give the name of *élite*.

2032. For the particular investigation with which we are engaged, a study of the social equilibrium, it will help if we further divide that class into two classes: a *governing élite*, comprising individuals who directly or indirectly play some considerable part in government, and a *non-governing élite*, comprising the rest.[2]

2033. A chess champion is certainly a member of the *élite*, but it is no less certain that his merits as a chess-player do not open the doors to political influence for him; and hence unless he has other qualities to win him that distinction, he is not a member of the governing *élite*. Mistresses of absolute monarchs have oftentimes been members of the *élite*, either because of their beauty or because of their intellectual endowments; but only a few of them, who have had, in addition, the particular talents required by politics, have played any part in government.

2034. So we get two strata in a population: (1) A lower stratum, the *non-élite*, with whose possible influence on government we are not just here concerned; then (2) a higher stratum, *the élite*, which is divided into two: (*a*) a governing *élite*; (*b*) a non-governing *élite*.

2. Kolabinska, *Op. cit.*, p. 6: 'We have just enumerated different categories of individuals comprising the *élite*. They may also be classified in many other ways. For the purpose I have in view in this study it is better to divide the *élite* into two parts: one, which I will call *M*, will contain those individuals in the *élite* who share in the government of the state, who make up what may be more or less vaguely called "the governing class." The other part, *N*, will be made up of the remainder of the *élite* when the part *M* has been set off from it.'

2035. In the concrete, there are no examinations whereby each person is assigned to his proper place in these various classes. That deficiency is made up for by other means, by various sorts of labels that serve the purpose after a fashion. Such labels are the rule even where there are examinations. The label 'lawyer' is affixed to a man who is supposed to know something about the law and often does, though sometimes again he is an ignoramus. So, the governing *élite* contains individuals who wear labels appropriate to political offices of a certain altitude – ministers, Senators, Deputies, chief justices, generals, colonels, and so on – making the opposite exceptions for those who have found their way into that exalted company without possessing qualities corresponding to the labels they wear.

2036. Such exceptions are much more numerous than the exceptions among lawyers, physicians, engineers, millionaires (who have made their own money), artists of distinction, and so on; for the reason, among others, that in these latter departments of human activity the labels are won directly by each individual, whereas in the *élite* some of the labels – the label of wealth, for instance – are hereditary. In former times there were hereditary labels in the governing *élite* also – in our day hardly more than the label of king remains in that status; but if direct inheritance has disappeared, inheritance is still powerful indirectly and an individual who has inherited a sizable patrimony can easily be named Senator in certain countries, or can get himself elected to the parliament by buying votes or, on occasion, by wheedling voters with assurances that he is a democrat of democrats, a Socialist, an Anarchist. Wealth, family, or social connexions also help in many other cases to win the label of the *élite* in general, or of the governing *élite* in particular, for persons who otherwise hold no claim upon it.

2037. In societies where the social unit is the family the label worn by the head of the family also benefits all other members. In Rome, the man who became Emperor generally raised his freedom to the higher class, and oftentimes, in fact, to the governing *élite*. For that matter, now more, now fewer, of the freemen taking part in the Roman government possessed qualities good or bad that justified their wearing the labels which they had won through imperial bounty. In our societies, the social unit is the individual; but the place that the individual occupies in society also benefits his wife, his children, his connexions, his friends.

2038. If all these deviations from type were of little importance, they might be disregarded, as they are virtually disregarded in cases where a diploma is required for the practice of a profession. Everyone knows that there are persons who do not deserve their diplomas, but experience shows that on the whole such exceptions may be overlooked.

2039. One might, further, from certain points of view at least, disregard deviations if they remained more or less constant quantitatively – if there were only a negligible variation in proportions between the total of a class and the people who wear its label without possessing the qualities corresponding.

2040. As a matter of fact, the real cases that we have to consider in our societies differ from those two. The deviations are not so few that they can be disregarded. Then again, their number is variable, and the variations give rise to situations having an important bearing on the social equilibrium. We are therefore required to make a special study of them.

2041. Furthermore, the manner in which the various groups in a population intermix has to be considered. In moving from one group to another an individual generally brings with him certain inclinations, sentiments, attitudes, that he has acquired in the group from which he comes, and that circumstance cannot be ignored.

2042. To this mixing, in the particular case in which only two groups, the *élite* and the non-*élite*, are envisaged, the term 'circulation of élites' has been applied[3] – in French, *circulation des élites* [or in more general terms 'class-circulation'].

2043. In conclusion we must pay special attention (1), in the case of one single group, to the proportions between the total of the group and the number of individuals who are nominally members of it but do not possess the qualities requisite for effective membership; and then (2), in the case of various groups, to the ways in which transitions from one group to the other occur, and to the intensity of that movement – that is to say, to the velocity of the circulation.

2044. Velocity in circulation has to be considered not only absolutely but also in relation to the supply of and the demand for certain social elements. A country that is always at peace does not require many soldiers in its governing class, and the production of generals may be overexuberant as compared with the demand. But when a country is in a state of continuous warfare many soldiers are necessary, and though production remains at the same level it may not meet the demand. That, we might note in passing, has been one of the causes for the collapse of many aristocracies.[4]

3. And most inappropriately, for, in this sense, the phrase never meant more than circulation within the *élite*. Furthermore, the *élite* is not the only class to be considered, and the principles that apply to circulation within the *élite* apply to circulation within such lower classes as one may choose for one purpose or another to consider. – A. L.

4. Kolabinska, *Op. cit.*, p. 10: 'Inadequate recruiting in the *élite* does not result from a mere numerical proportion between new members and old.

2045. Another example. In a country where there is little industry and little commerce, the supply of individuals possessing in high degree the qualities requisite for those types of activity exceeds the demand. Then industry and commerce develop and the supply, though remaining the same, no longer meets the demand.

2046. We must not confuse the state of law with the state of fact. The latter alone, or almost alone, has a bearing on the social equilibrium. There are many examples of castes that are legally closed, but into which, in point of fact, new-comers make their way, and often in large numbers. On the other hand, what difference does it make if a caste is legally open, but conditions *de facto* prevent new accessions to it? If a person who acquires wealth thereby becomes a member of the governing class, but no one gets rich, it is as if the class were closed; and if only a few get rich, it is as if the law erected serious barriers against access to the caste. Something of that sort was observable towards the end of the Roman Empire. People who acquired wealth entered the order of the curials. But only a few individuals made any money. Theoretically we might examine any number of groups. Practically we have to confine ourselves to the more important. We shall proceed by successive approximations, starting with the simple and going on to the complex.

2047. *Higher class and lower class in general.* The least we can do is divide society into two strata: a higher stratum, which usually contains the rulers, and a lower stratum, which usually controls the ruled. That fact is so obvious that it has always forced itself even upon the most casual observation, and so for the circulation of individuals between the two strata. Even Plato had an inkling of class-circulation and tried to regulate it artificially. The 'new man,' the upstart, the *parvenu*, has always been a subject of interest, and literature has analysed him unendingly. Here, then, we are merely giving a more exact form to things that have long been perceived more or less vaguely. We noted a varying distribution of residues in the various social groupings, and chiefly in the higher and the lower class. Such heterogeneousness is a fact perceived by the most superficial glance.

2048. Changes in Class I and Class II residues occurring within the

---

Account has to be taken of the number of persons who possess the qualities required for membership in the governing *élite* but are refused admittance; or else, in an opposite direction, the number of new members the *élite* might require but does not get. In the first case, the production of persons possessing unusual qualities as regards education may far surpass the number of such persons that the *élite* can accommodate, and then we get what has been called an "intellectual proletariat".'

two social strata have an important influence in determining the social equilibrium. They have been commonly observed by laymen under a special form, as changes in 'religious' sentiments, so called, in the higher stratum of society. It has often been noted that there were times when religious sentiments seemed to lose ground, others when they seemed to gain strength, and that such undulations corresponded to social movements of very considerable scope. The uniformity might be more exactly described by saying that in the higher stratum of society Class II residues gradually lose in strength, until now and again they are reinforced by tides upwelling from the lower stratum.[5]

2049. Religious sentiments were very feeble in the higher classes in Rome towards the end of the Republic; but they gained notably in

5. Many writers who are not equipped with this general conception fall into contradictions. Sometimes the clarity of the facts forces itself upon them; then again preconceptions will blur their view of things. Taine is an example. In the *Ancien régime* he well notes (Chap. III) that the mind of the masses at large is steeped in prejudices (is, in our terms, under the sway of Class II residues). On that basis he should go on and conclude that the French Revolution was a particular case of the religious revolution, where popular faith overwhelms the scepticism of the higher classes. But, consciously or otherwise, he succumbs to the influence of the preconception that the higher classes are educators of the masses, and views unbelief and impiety in the nobility, the Third Estate, and the higher clergy as among the main causes of the Revolution. He notes the difference between France and England in that regard and seems on the verge of ascribing to that circumstance the fact that the revolution which occurred in France did not occur in England. Says he, Bk. IV, Chap. II, sec. 1 (Vol. II, p. 118): 'In England [the higher class] speedily perceived the danger. Philosophy was precocious in England, native to England. That does not matter. It never got acclimated there. Montesquieu wrote in his travel note-book in 1729 (*Notes sur l'Angleterre*, p. 352): "No religion in England. . . . If anyone brings up the subject of religion, he is laughed at." Fifty years later the public mind has about-faced: "all those who have a tight roof over their heads and a good coat on their backs" [The expression is Macaulay's.] have seen what these new doctrines mean. In any event they feel that speculations in the library must not become preachings on the streets. [They and Taine therefore believe in the efficacy of such preachings.] Impiety seems to them bad manners. They regard religion as the cement that holds public order together. That is because they are themselves public men, interested in doing things, participating in the government and well taught by daily personal experience. . . . [Yet a few lines before that Taine had refuted himself:] When you talk religion or politics with people, you find their minds almost always made up. Their preconceptions, their interests, their situation in life, have convinced them already, and they will listen to you only if you tell them

strength thereafter, through the rise to the higher classes of men from the lower, of foreigners that is, freedmen, and others, whom the Roman Empire raised in station. They gained still further in intensity in the days of the decadent Roman Empire, when the government passed into the hands of a military plebs and a bureaucracy originating in the lower classes. That was a time when a predominance of Class II residues made itself manifest in a decadence in literature and in the arts and sciences, and in invasions by Oriental religions and especially Christianity.

2050. The Protestant Reformation in the sixteenth century, the Puritan Revolution in Cromwell's day in England, the French Revolution of 1789, are examples of great religious tides originating in the lower classes and rising to engulf the sceptical higher classes. An instance in our day would be the United States of America, where this upward thrust of members of lower classes strong in Class II residues is very intense; and in that country one witnesses the rise of no end of

---

aloud things they have been thinking in silence.' If that is so, the 'preachings in the street' to which Taine alludes ought not to be very effective, and if they are, it cannot be that people 'will listen to you only if you tell them aloud things they have been thinking in silence.' As a matter of fact, it is these latter hypotheses that the more closely approximate experience. The mental state of the French people towards the end of the eighteenth century had been but little affected by the impiety of the higher classes, any more than the mental state of the Romans had been affected by the impiety of the contemporaries of Lucretius, Cicero, and Caesar, or the mental state of the European masses by the impiety of the nobility and higher clergy at the time of the Reformation. Belin, *Le commerce des livres prohibés à Paris de 1750 à 1789*, pp. 104–105: 'One may assert that the works of the philosophers did not directly reach the masses or the lower *bourgeoisie*. The working-men, the tradesmen, did not know Voltaire and Rousseau until the time of the Revolution, when their tribunes began to gloss them in inflammatory harangues or to translate their maxims into legislation. When they stepped into the limelight they had certainly not read the great books of the century, though they could not have missed entirely the more celebrated of the literary quarrels. The true disciples of the *philosophes*, the faithful patrons of the pedlars of forbidden literature, were the nobles, the abbés, the members of the privileged classes, idlers about the parlours of society who were on the look-out for some distraction from their relentless tedium and threw themselves headlong into philosophical discussions and soon let themselves be vanquished by the new spirit [That is all borne out by experience; the following less so.], without foreseeing the remoter consequences of the premises that they were adopting so gaily. ... [Belin makes a further point:] The privileged for that matter were the only ones who could afford the exorbitant prices that any lover of forbidden books had to pay.'

strange and wholly unscientific religions – such as Christian Science –
that are utterly at war with any sort of scientific thinking, and a mass
of hypocritical laws for the enforcement of morality that are replicas of
laws of the European Middle Ages.

2051. The upper stratum of society, the *élite*, nominally contains
certain groups of people, not always very sharply defined, that are
called aristocracies. There are cases in which the majority of individuals
belonging to such aristocracies actually possess the qualities requisite
for remaining there; and then again there are cases where considerable
numbers of the individuals making up the class do not possess those
requisites. Such people may occupy more or less important places in
the governing *élite* or they may be barred from it.

2052. In the beginning, military, religious, and commercial aristocracies and plutocracies – with a few exceptions not worth considering –
must have constituted parts of the governing *élite* and sometimes have
made up the whole of it. The victorious warrior, the prosperous
merchant, the opulent plutocrat, were men of such parts, each in his
own field, as to be superior to the average individual. Under those
circumstances the label corresponded to an actual capacity. But as time
goes by, considerable, sometimes very considerable, differences arise
between the capacity and the label; while on the other hand, certain
aristocracies originally figuring prominently in the rising *élite* end by
constituting an insignificant element in it. That has happened especially
to military aristocracies.

2053. Aristocracies do not last. Whatever the causes, it is an
incontestable fact that after a certain length of time they pass away.
History is a graveyard of aristocracies. The Athenian 'People' was an
aristocracy as compared with the remainder of a population of resident
aliens and slaves. It vanished without leaving any descent. The various
aristocracies of Rome vanished in their time. So did the aristocracies of
the Barbarians. Where, in France, are the descendents of the Frankish
conquerors? The genealogies of the English nobility have been very
exactly kept; and they show that very few families still remain to claim
descent from the comrades of William the Conqueror. The rest have
vanished. In Germany the aristocracy of the present day is very largely
made up of descendants of vassals of the lords of old. The populations
of European countries have increased enormously during the past few
centuries. It is as certain as certain can be that the aristocracies have not
increased in proportion.

2054. They decay not in numbers only. They decay also in quality,
in the sense that they lose their vigour, that there is a decline in the
proportions of the residues which enabled them to win their power and

hold it. The governing class is restored not only in numbers, but – and that is the more important thing – in quality, by families rising from the lower classes and bringing with them the vigour and the proportions of residues necessary for keeping themselves in power. It is also restored by the loss of its more degenerate members.

2055. If one of those movements comes to an end, or worse still, if they both come to an end, the governing class crashes to ruin and often sweeps the whole of a nation along with it. Potent cause of disturbance in the equilibrium is the accumulation of superior elements in the lower classes and, conversely, of inferior elements in the higher classes. If human aristocracies were like thoroughbreds among animals, which reproduce themselves over long periods of time with approximately the same traits, the history of the human race would be something altogether different from the history we know.

2056. In virtue of class-circulation, the governing *élite* is always in a state of slow and continuous transformation. It flows on like a river, never being today what it was yesterday. From time to time sudden and violent disturbances occur. There is a flood – the river overflows its banks. Afterwards, the new governing *élite* again resumes its slow transformation. The flood has subsided, the river is again flowing normally in its wonted bed.

2057. Revolutions come about through accumulations in the higher strata of society – either because of a slowing-down in class-circulation, or from other causes – of decadent elements no longer possessing the residues suitable for keeping them in power, and shrinking from the use of force; while meantime in the lower strata of society elements of superior quality are coming to the fore, possessing residues suitable for exercising the functions of government and willing enough to use force.

2058. In general, in revolutions the members of the lower strata are captained by leaders from the higher strata, because the latter possess the intellectual qualities required for outlining a tactic while lacking the combative residues supplied by the individuals from the lower strata.

2059. Violent movements take place by fits and starts, and effects therefore do not follow immediately on their causes. After a governing class, or a nation, has maintained itself for long periods of time on force and acquired great wealth, it may subsist for some time still without using force, buying off its adversaries and paying not only in gold, but also in terms of the dignity and respect that it had formerly enjoyed and which constitute, as it were, a capital. In the first stages of decline, power is maintained by bargainings and concessions, and people are so deceived into thinking that that policy can be carried on indefinitely. So the decadent Roman Empire brought peace of the

Barbarians with money and honours. So Louis XVI, in France, squandering in a very short time an ancestral inheritance of love, respect and almost religious reverence for the monarchy, managed, by making repeated concessions, to be the King of the Revolution. So the English aristocracy managed to prolong its term of power in the second half of the nineteenth century down to the dawn of its decadence, which was heralded by the 'Parliament Bill' in the first years of the twentieth . . .

Suppose we put in one category, which we may call S, individuals whose incomes are essentially variable and depend upon the person's wide-awakeness in discovering sources of gain. In that group, generally speaking and disregarding exceptions, will be found those promoters of enterprise – those *entrepreneurs* – whom we were considering some pages back; and with them will be stockholders in industrial and commercial corporations (but not bondholders, who will more fittingly be placed in our group next following). Then will come owners of real estate in cities where building speculation is rife; and also landowners – on a similar condition that there be speculation in the lands about them; and then stock-exchange speculators and bankers who make money on governmental, industrial, and commercial loans. We might further add all persons depending upon such people – lawyers, engineers, politicians, working-people, clerks – and deriving advantage from their operations. In a word, we are putting together all persons who directly or indirectly speculate and in one way or another manage to increase their incomes by ingeniously taking advantage of circumstances.

2234. And let us put into another category, which we may call R, persons who have fixed or virtually fixed incomes not depending to any great extent on ingenious combinations that may be conceived by an active mind. In this category, roughly, will be found persons who have savings and have deposited them in savings-banks or invested them in life-annuities; then people living on incomes from government bonds, certificates of the funded debt, corporation bonds, or other securities with fixed interest-rates; then owners of real estate and lands in places where there is no speculation; then farmers, working-people, clerks, depending upon such persons and in no way depending upon speculators. In a word, we so group together here all persons who neither directly nor indirectly depend on speculation and who have incomes that are fixed, or virtually fixed, or at least are but slightly variable.[6]

6. Monographs along the lines of Le Play's would be of great use in determining the character of the persons belonging in our S group, and those belonging to our R group. Here is one such, contributed by Prezzolini: *La Francia e i francesi del secolo XX osservati da un italiano.* I know it as

2235. Just to be rid of the inconvenience of using mere letters of the alphabet, suppose we use the term 'speculators' for members of category *S* and the French term *rentiers* for members of category *R*.[7] Within the two groups of persons we shall find analogous conflicts, economic and social, between them. In the speculator group Class I residues predominate, in the *rentier* group, Class II residues. That that should be the case is readily understandable. A person of pronounced capacity for economic combinations is not satisfied with a fixed income, often a very small one. He wants to earn more, and if he finds a favourable opportunity, he moves into the *S* category. The two groups perform functions of differing utility in society. The *S* group is primarily responsible for change, for economic and social progress. The *R* group, instead, is a powerful element in stability, and in many cases counter-

---

quoted by E. Cesari in the *Vita italiana*, Oct. 15, 1917, pp. 367–70. The person in question is a well-known member of the French parliament – we suppress the proper name; for us here, he is not a person, but just a type. The figures given by Prezzolini are those publicly declared by the member himself, Monsieur *X*. *X*'s fixed income yields a total of 17,500 francs, of which 15,000 are salary as a member of the parliament and 2,500 interest on his wife's dowry. Only the latter sum belongs in category *R* – the salary belongs rather in category *S*, because to get such a thing one must have the ability and the good fortune to be elected. *X*'s expense-account shows a total of 64,200 francs, divided as follows: household expenses, 33,800; office expenses, 22,550; expenses for his election district (avowable expenses), 7,850. There ought, therefore, to be a deficit of 45,700 francs; but the deficit is not only covered but changes into a surplus in view of the following revenues: contributions to newspapers and other publications, 12,500 francs; honorarium as general agent of the *A.B.C.* Company, 21,000 francs; commissions on sales, 7,500. In this connexion, Prezzolini notes that *X*, reporting on the war budget, enters 100,000 francs for supplies delivered to himself, as general agent of the *A.B.C.* Company: that gives *X* his 'sales commissions'. Finally, because of the influence that he enjoys, our member, *X*, receives a stipend of 18,000 francs from a newspaper. In all, these revenues, which clearly belong in the category *S*, yield a total of 50,000 francs. Prezzolini adds that the member in question is not the only one, nor the least, of his species. He is just a better-known and an honester type.

7. It might be well to repeat that our use of such terms is not based on their ordinary senses, nor upon their etymologies. We are to use them strictly in the sense defined in §§ 2233–34, and the reader must refer to those definitions whenever he encounters them in the remainder of this volume. [I keep the term 'speculator'. English ordinarily analyzes the matter embraced under Pareto's term, especially in slang. Pareto's 'speculator' is our 'hustler,' 'man of pep,' 'wide-awake individual,' 'live-wire,' and so on. – A. L.]

acts the dangers attending the adventurous capers of the S's. A society in which R's almost exclusively predominate remains stationary and, as it were, crystallized. A society in which S's predominate lacks stability, lives in a state of shaky equilibrium that may be upset by a slight accident from within or from without.

Members of the R group must not be mistaken for 'conservatives,' nor members of the S group for 'progressives,' innovators, revolutionaries. They may have points in common with such, but there is no identity. There are evolutions, revolutions, innovations, that the R's support, especially movements tending to restore to the ruling classes certain residues of group-persistence that had been banished by the S's. A revolution may be made against the S's – a revolution of that type founded the Roman Empire, and such, to some extent, was the revolution known as the Protestant Reformation. Then too, for the very reason that sentiments of group-persistence are dominant in them, the R's may be so blinded by sentiment as to act against their own interests. They readily allow themselves to be duped by anyone who takes them on the side of sentiment, and time and time again they have been the artisans of their own ruin. If the old feudal lords, who were endowed with R traits in a very conspicuous degree, had not allowed themselves to be swept off their feet by a sum of sentiments in which religious enthusiasm was only one element, they would have seen at once that the Crusades were to be their ruin. In the eighteenth century, had the French nobility living on income, and that part of the French *bourgeoisie* which was in the same situation, not succumbed to the lure of humanitarian sentiments, they would not have prepared the ground for the Revolution that was to be their undoing. Not a few among the victims of the guillotine had for long years been continually, patiently, artfully grinding the blade that was to cut off their heads. In our day those among the R's who are known as 'intellectuals' are following in the footprints of the French nobles of the eighteenth century and are working with all their might to encompass the ruin of their own class.

Nor are the categories R and S to be confused with groupings that might be made according to economic occupation. There again we find points of contact, but not full coincidence. A retail merchant often belongs to the R group, and a wholesale merchant too, but the wholesaler will more likely belong to the S group. Sometimes one same enterprise may change in character. An individual of the S type founds an industry as a result of fortunate speculations. When it yields or seems to be yielding a good return, he changes it into a corporation, retires from business, and passes over into the R group. A large number of stockholders in the new concern are also R's – the ones who bought stock when they thought they were buying a sure thing. If they are not mistaken, the business changes in character, moving over from the *S* type to the *R* type. But in many cases the best speculation the founder ever made was in changing his business to a corporation. It is soon in jeopardy, with the *R*'s standing in line to pay for the broken crockery. There is no better business in this world than the business of fleecing the lambs – of exploiting the inexperience, the ingenuousness, the passions, of the *R*'s. In our societies the fortunes of many many wealthy individuals have no other foundations.[8]

8. Many people conclude that such facts are enough to condemn our social organization, and hold it responsible for most of the pains from which we suffer. Others think that they can defend our present order, only by denying the facts or minimizing their significance. Both are right from the ethical standpoint, wrong from the standpoint of social utility experimentally considered. Obviously, if it be posited as an axiom that men *ought*, whatever happens, to observe certain rules, those who do not observe them necessarily stand condemned. If one goes on to say that the organization so condemned is in the main injurious to society, one must logically fall back on some premise that confuses morality and utility. On the other hand, if premises of those types are granted and one would, notwithstanding, still defend or approve the organization of our societies, there is nothing left but to deny the facts or say they are not significant. The experimental approach is altogether different. Anyone accepting it grants no axioms independent of experience, and therefore finds it necessary to discuss the premises of the reasonings mentioned. On so doing one soon perceives that it is a question of two phenomena that do indeed have points in common but are in no sense identical, and that in every particular case experience has to be called in to decide whether one is dealing with a point of contact or a point of divergence. An instant's reflection is enough to see that if one accepts certain conclusions one adopts by that fact the premises to which they are indissolubly bound. But the power of sentiment and the influence of habitual manners of reasoning are such that people disregard the force of logic entirely and establish conclusions without reference to the premises or, at the very best, accept the premises as axioms not subject to discussion. Another effect of such power and such influence will be that in spite of the warnings we have given and over and over again repeated, there will always be someone to carry the import of the remarks that he is here reading on the *R*'s and *S*'s beyond the limits we have so strictly specified, interpreting all that we have been saying against one of those groups as implying that the influence of the group is, on the whole, harmful to society and the group itself 'condemnable'; and all that we have been saying in its favour as a proof that the influence of the group is, in general, beneficial to society and the group itself worthy of praise. We have neither the means nor the least desire to prevent the fabrication of such interpretations. We are satisfied with recognizing them as one variety of our derivations.

2236. The differing relative proportions in which S types and R types are combined in the governing class correspond to differing types of civilization; and such proportions are among the principal traits that have to be considered in social heterogeneity. Going back, for instance, to the protectionist cycle, we may say that in modern democratic countries industrial protection increases the proportion of S's in the governing class. That increase in turn serves to intensify protection, and the process would go on indefinitely if counter-forces did not come into play to check it. (Vol. III, §§ 2026–59; Vol. IV, §§ 2233–6)

2170. Societies in general subsist because alive and vigorous in the majority of their constitutent members are sentiments corresponding to residues of sociality. But there are also individuals in human societies in whom some at least of those sentiments are weak or indeed actually missing. That fact has two interesting consequences which stand in apparent contradiction, one of them threatening the dissolution of a society, the other making for its progress in civilization. What at bottom is there is continuous movement, but it is a movement that may progress in almost any direction.

2171. It is evident that if the requirement of uniformity were so strongly active in all individuals in a given society as to prevent even one of them from breaking away in any particular from the uniformities prevalent in it, such a society would have no internal causes for dissolution; but neither would it have any causes for change, whether in the direction of an increase, or of a decrease, in the utility of the individuals or of the society. On the other hand if the requirement of uniformity were to fail, society would not hold together, and each individual would go on his own way, as lions and tigers, birds of prey, and other animals do. Societies that endure and change are therefore situated in some intermediate condition between those two extremes.

2172. A homogeneous society might be imagined in which the requirement of uniformity would be the same in all individuals, and would correspond to the intermediate state just mentioned. But observation shows that that is not the case with human societies. Human societies are essentially heterogeneous, and the intermediate state is attained because the requirement of uniformity is very strong in some individuals, moderately strong in others, very feeble in still others, and almost entirely absent in a few. The average is found not in each individual, but in the group comprising them all. One may add as a datum of fact that the number of individuals in whom the requirement of uniformity is stronger than the average requisite of the intermediate state in which the society is situated is much greater than the number of individuals in whom the requirement is weaker than that average, and very very much greater than the number in whom it is entirely missing.

2173. For the reader who has followed us thus far it is needless to add that, in view of the effects of this greater or lesser potency of the sentiments of uniformity, one may foresee out of hand that two theologies will put in an appearance, one of which will glorify the immobility of one or another uniformity, real or imaginary, the other of which will glorify movement, progress, in one direction or another. That is what has actually happened in history. There have been popular Olympuses where the gods fixed and determined once and for all how human society was to be; and then, too, Olympuses of utopian reformers, who derived from their exalted minds conceptions of forms from which human society was never more to deviate. On the other hand from the days of ancient Athens down to our own, the lord gods of Movement in a Certain Direction have listened to the prayers of their faithful and now sit triumphant in our latter-day Olympus, where Progress Optimus Maximus reigns in sovereign majesty. So that intermediate situation of society has usually been attained as the resultant of many forces, prominent among them the two categories mentioned, which envisage different imaginary goals and correspond to different classes of residues.

2174. To ask whether or not force ought to be used in a society, whether the use of force is or is not beneficial, is to ask a question that has no meaning; for force is used by those who wish to preserve certain uniformities and by those who wish to overstep them; and the violence of the ones stands in contrast and in conflict with the violence of the others. In truth, if a partisan of a governing class disavows the use of force, he means that he disavows the use of force by insurgents trying to escape from the norms of the given uniformity. On the other hand, if he says he approves of the use of force, what he really means is that he approves of the use of force by the public authority to constrain insurgents to conformity. Conversely, if a partisan of the subject class says he detests the use of force in society, what he really detests is the use of force by constituted authorities in forcing dissidents to conform; and if, instead, he lauds the use of force, he is thinking of the use of force by those who would break away from certain social uniformities.

2175. Nor is there any particular meaning in the question as to whether the use of violence to enforce existing uniformities is beneficial to society, or whether it is beneficial to use force in order to overstep them; for the various uniformities have to be distinguished to see which of them are beneficial and which deleterious to society. Nor, indeed, is that enough; for it is further necessary to determine whether the utility of the uniformity is great enough to offset the harm that will be done by using violence to enforce it, or whether detriment from the uniformity is great enough to overbalance the damage that will be caused by the use of force in subverting it; in which detriment and damage we must not forget to reckon the very serious drawback involved in the anarchy that results from any frequent use of violence to abolish existing uniformities, just as among the benefits and utilities of maintaining frankly injurious uniformities must be counted the strength and stability they lend to the social order. So, to solve the problem as to the use of force, it is not enough to solve the other problem as to the utility, in general, of certain types of social organization; it is essential also and chiefly to compute all the advantages and all the drawbacks, direct and indirect. Such a course leads to the solution of a scientific problem; but it may not be and oftentimes is not the course that leads to an increase in social utility. It is better, therefore, if it be followed only by people who are called upon to solve a scientific problem or, to some limited extent, by certain individuals belonging to the ruling class; whereas social utility is oftentimes best served if the members of the subject class, whose function is not to lead but to act, accept one of the two theologies according to the case – either the theology that enjoins preservation of existing uniformities, or the theology that counsels change . . .

2178. What now are the correlations that subsist between this method of applying force and other social facts? We note, as usual, a sequence of actions and reactions, in which the use of force appears now as cause, now as effect. As regards the governing class, one gets, in the main, five groups of facts to consider: 1. A mere handful of citizens, so long as they are willing to use violence, can force their will upon public officials who are not inclined to meet violence with equal violence. If the reluctance of the officials to resort to force is primarily motivated by humanitarian sentiments, that result ensues very readily; but if they refrain from violence because they deem it wiser to use some other means, the effect is often the following: 2. To prevent or resist violence, the governing class resorts to 'diplomacy,' fraud, corruption – governmental authority passes, in a word, from the lions to the foxes. The governing class bows its head under the threat of violence, but it surrenders only in appeances, trying to turn the flank of the obstacle it cannot demolish in frontal attack. In the long run that sort of procedure comes to exercise a far-reaching influence on the selection of the governing class, which is now recruited only from the foxes, while the lions are blackballed. The individual who best knows the arts of sapping the strength of the foes of 'graft' and to winning back by fraud and deceit what seemed to have been surrendered under pressure of force, is now leader of leaders. The man who has bursts of rebellion, and does not know how to crook his spine at the proper times and places, is the worst of leaders, and his presence is tolerated among them only if other distinguished endowments offset that defect. 3. So it comes about that the residues of the combination-instinct (Class I) are intensified in the governing class, and the residues of group-persistence debilitated; for the combination-residues supply, precisely, the artistry and resourcefulness required for evolving ingenious expedients as substitutes for open resistance, while the residues of group-persistence stimulate open resistance, since a strong sentiment of group-persistence cures the spine of all tendencies to curvature. 4. Policies of the governing class are not planned too far ahead in time. Predominance of the combination instincts and enfeeblement of the sentiments of group-persistence result in making the governing class more satisfied with the present and less thoughtful of the future. The individual comes to prevail, and by far, over family, community, nation. Material interests and interests of the present or a near future come to prevail over the ideal interests of community or nation and interests of the distant future. The impulse is to enjoy the present without too much thought for the morrow. 5. Some of these phenomena become observable in international relations as well. Wars become essentially economic. Efforts are made to avoid conflicts with the powerful and the sword is rattled only before the weak. Wars are regarded more than anything else as speculations. A country is often unwittingly edged towards war by nursings of economic conflicts which, it is expected, will never get out of control and turn into armed conflicts. Not seldom, however, a war will be forced upon a country by peoples who are not so far advanced in the evolution that leads to the predominance of Class I residues.

2179. As regards the subject class, we get the following relations, which correspond in part to the preceding: 1. When the subject class contains a number of individuals disposed to use force and with capable leaders to guide them, the governing class is, in many cases, overthrown and another takes its place. That is easily the case where governing classes are inspired by humanitarian sentiments primarily, and very very easily if they do not find ways to assimilate the exceptional individuals who come to the front in the subject classes. A humanitarian aristocracy that is closed or stiffly exclusive represents the maximum of insecurity. 2. It is far more difficult to overthrow a governing class that is adept in the shrewd use of chicanery, fraud, corruption; and in the highest degree difficult to overthrow such a class when it successfully assimilates most of the individuals in the subject class who show those same talents, are adept in those same arts, and might therefore become the leaders of such plebeians as are disposed to use violence. Thus left without leadership, without talent, disorganized, the subject class is almost always powerless to set up any lasting régime. 3. So the combination-residues (Class I) become to some extent enfeebled in the subject class. But that phenomenon is in no way comparable to the corresponding reinforcement of those same residues in the governing class; for the governing class, being composed, as it is, of a much smaller number of individuals, changes considerably in character from the addition to it or withdrawal from it of relatively small numbers of individuals; whereas shifts of identical numbers produce but slight effects in the enormously greater total of the subject class. For that matter the subject class is still left with many individuals possessed of combination-instincts that are applied not to politics or activities connected with politics but to arts and trades independent of politics. That circumstance lends stability to societies, for the governing class is required to absorb only a small number of new individuals in order to keep the subject class deprived of leadership. However, in the long run the differences in temperament between the governing class and the subject class become gradually accentuated, the combination-instincts tending to predominate in the ruling class, and instincts of group-persistence in the subject class. When that difference becomes sufficiently great, revolution occurs. 4. Revolution often transfers power to a new governing class, which exhibits a reinforcement in its instincts of group-persistence and so adds to its designs of present enjoyment aspirations towards ideal enjoyments presumably attainable at some future time – scepticism in part gives way to faith. 5. These considerations must to some extent be applied to international relations. If the combination-instincts are reinforced in a given country beyond a certain limit, as compared with the instincts of group-persistence, that country may be easily vanquished in war by another country in which that change in relative proportions has not occurred. The potency of an ideal as a pilot to victory is observable in both civil and international strife. People who lose the habit of applying force, who acquire the habit of considering policy from a commercial stand-point and of judging it only in terms of profit and loss, can readily be induced to purchase peace; and it may well be that such a transaction taken by itself is a good one, for war might have cost more money than the price of peace. Yet experience shows that in the long run, and taken in connexion with the things that inevitably go with it, such practice leads a country to ruin. The combination-instincts rarely come to prevail in the whole of a population. More commonly that situation arises in the upper strata of society, there being few if any traces of it in the lower and more populous classes. So when a war breaks out one gazes in amazement on the energies that are suddenly manifested by the masses at large, something that could in no way have been foreseen by studying the upper classes only. Sometimes, as happened in the case of Carthage, the burst of energy may not be sufficient to save a country, because a war may have been inadequately prepared for and be incompetently led by the ruling classes, and soundly prepared for and wisely led by the ruling classes of the enemy country. Then again, as happened in the wars of the French Revolution, the energy in the masses may be great enough to save a country because, though the war may have been badly prepared for by its ruling classes, preparations and leadership have been even worse in the ruling classes of the enemy countries, a circumstance that gives the constituent members of the lower strata of society time to drive their ruling class from power and replace it with another of greater energy and possessing the instincts of group-persistence in greater abundance. Still again, as happened in Germany after the disaster at Jena, the energy of the masses may spread to the higher classes and spur them to an activity that proves most effective as combining able leadership with enthusiastic faith.

2180. These, then, are the main, the outstanding phenomena, but other phenomena of secondary or incidental importance also figure. Notable among such is the fact that if a ruling class is unable or unwilling or incompetent to use force to eradicate violations of uniformities in private life, anarchic action on the part of the subject class tends to make up for the deficiency. It is well known to history that the private vendetta languishes or recurs in proportion as public authority continues or ceases to replace it. It has been seen to recur in the form of lynchings in the United States, and even in Europe. Whenever the influence of public authority declines, little states grow up within the state, little societies within society. So, whenever judicial process fails, private or group justice replaces it, and *vice versa*. In international relations, the tinselling of humanitarian and ethical declamation is just a dressing for an underlying force. The Chinese considered themselves the superiors in civilization of the Japanese, and perhaps they were, but they lacked a military aptitude that the Japanese, in virtue of a surviving remnant of feudal 'barbarism,' possessed in abundance. So the poor Chinese were attacked by hordes of Europeans – whose exploits in China, as Sorel well says, remind one of the feats of the Spanish *conquistadores* in the Americas. They suffered murder, rapine, and pillage at European hands, and then paid an indemnity into the bargain; whereas the Japanese came off victorious over the Russians and now exact respect from everybody. A few centuries back, the subtle diplomacy of the Christian lords of Constantinople did not save them from ruin under the impact of the fanaticism and might of the Turks; and now, in this year 1913, on the very same spot, the victors show that they have deteriorated in their fanaticism and in their power and, in their turn reposing illusory hopes in the diplomatic arts, are defeated and overthrown by the vigour of their sometime subjects. Grievous the hallucination under which those statesmen labour who imagine that they can replace the use of force with unarmed law. Among the many examples that one might point to are Sulla's constitution in ancient Rome and the conservative constitution of the Third Republic in France. Sulla's constitution fell because the armed force that might have compelled respect for it was not maintained. The constitution of Augustus endured because his successors were in a position to rely on the might of the legions. When the Commune had been defeated and overthrown, Thiers decided that his government ought to find its support rather in the law than in armed force. As a result his laws were scattered like leaves before the hurricane of democratic plutocracy. We need say nothing of Louis XVI of France, who thought he could halt the Revolution with his royal veto, for his was the illusion of a spineless weakling who was soon to lose what little head he had.

2181. All such facts as a rule present themselves in the guise of derivations. In one direction we get theories that condemn the use of violence by the subject class in whatever case, in the other direction theories that censure its use by public authority.

2182. Ruling-class theories, when the requirement of logic is not too keenly felt, appeal simply to sentiments of veneration for holders of power, or for abstractions such as 'the state' and to sentiments of disapprobation for individuals who try to disturb or subvert existing orders (§ 2192). Then when it is deemed advisable to satisfy the need of logic, the effort is to create a confusion between the violation of an established uniformity for the individual's exclusive profit and a violation designed to further some collective interest or some new uniformity. The aim in such a derivation is to carry over to the social or political act the reprobation that is generally visited upon common crime. Frequent in our day are reasonings in some way connected with the theology of Progress. Not a few of our modern governments have revolutionary origins. How condemn the revolutions that might be tried against them without repudiating the forefathers? That is attended to by invoking a new divine right: Insurrection was legitimate enough against governments of the past, where authority was based on force; it is not legitimate against modern governments, where the authority is based on 'reason.' Or else: Insurrection was legitimate against kings and oligarchies; it is never legitimate against 'the People.' Or again: Rebellion is justifiable where there is no universal suffrage, but not where that panacea is the law of the land. Or again: Revolt is useless and therefore reprehensible in all countries where 'the People' are able to express their 'will.' Then finally – just to give some little satisfaction to their Graces, the Metaphysicists: Insurrection cannot be tolerated where a 'state of law' exists. I hope I shall be excused if I do not define that very sweet entity here. For all of most painstaking researches on my part, it remains an entity altogether unknown to me, and I should much rather be asked to give the zoological pedigree of the Chimaera.

2183. Again as usual, no one of these derivations has any exact meaning. All governments use force, and all assert that they are founded on reason. In the fact, whether universal suffrage prevails or not, it is always an oligarchy that governs, finding ways to give to the 'will of the people' that expression which the new desire, from the 'royal law' that bestowed the *imperium* on the Roman Emperors down to the votes of a legislative majority elected in one way or another, from the plebiscite that gave the empire to Napoleon III down to the universal suffrage that is shrewdly bought, steered, and manipulated by our 'speculators.' Who is this new god called Universal Suffrage? He is no more exactly definable, no less shrouded in mystery, no less beyond the pale of reality, than the hosts of other divinities; nor are there fewer and less patent contradictions in his theology than in theirs. Worshippers of Universal Suffrage are not led by their god. It is they who lead him – and by the nose, determining the forms in which he must manifest himself. Oftentimes, proclaiming the sanctity of 'majority rule,' they resist 'majority rule' by obstructionist tactics, even though they form but small minorities, and burning incense to the goddess Reason, they in no wise disdain, in certain cases, alliances with Chicanery, Fraud, and Corruption.

2184. Substantially such derivations express the sentiments felt by people who have climbed into the saddle and are willing to stay there – along with the far more general sentiment that social stability is a good thing. If, the moment a group, large or small, ceased to be satisfied with certain norms established in the community of which it is a part, it flew to arms to abolish them, organized society would fall to pieces. Social stability is so beneficial a thing that to maintain it it is well worth while to enlist the aid of fantastic ideals and this or that theology – among the others, the theology of universal suffrage – and be resigned to putting up with certain actual disadvantages. Before it becomes advisable to disturb the public peace, such disadvantages must have grown very very serious; and since human beings are effectively guided not by the sceptical reasonings of science but by 'living faiths' expressed in ideals, theories such as the divine right of kings, the legitimacy of oligarchies, of 'the people,' of 'majorities,' of legislative assemblies, and other such things, may be useful within certain limits, and have in fact proved to be, however absurd they may be from the scientific standpoint.

2185. Theories designed to justify the use of force by the governed are almost always combined with theories condemning the use of force by the public authority. A few dreamers reject the use of force in general, on whatever side; but their theories either have no influence at all or else serve merely to weaken resistance on the part of people in power, so clearing the field for violence on the part of the governed. In view of that we may confine ourselves to considering such theories, in general, in the combined form.

2186. No great number of theories are required to rouse to resistance and to the use of force people who are, or think they are, oppressed. The derivations therefore are chiefly designed to incline people who would otherwise be neutral in the struggle to condemn resistance on the part of the governing powers, and so to make their resistance less vigorous; or at a venture, to persuade the rulers themselves in that sense, a thing, for that matter, that is not likely to have any great success in our day save with those whose spinal columns have utterly rotted from the bane of humanitarianism. A few centuries ago some results might have been achieved in our Western countries by working with religious derivations upon sincere Christians; and, in other countries, by working upon firm believers with derivations of the religion prevailing in the given case. Since humanitarianism is a religion, like the Christian, the Moslem, or any other, we may say, in general, that one may sometimes secure the aid of neutrals and weaken resistance on the part of people in power by using derivations of the religion, whatever it may be, in which they sincerely believe. But since derivations readily lend themselves to proving the pro and contra, that device is often of scant effect even when it is not a mere mask for interests.

2187. In our times conflicts are chiefly economic. If a government therefore sets out to protect employers or strike-breakers from violence by strikers, it is accused of 'interfering' in an economic matter that does not properly concern it. If the police do not allow their heads to be broken without using their weapons, they are said to have 'shown poor judgment,' to have acted 'impulsively,' 'nervously.' Like strike-breakers, they must be denied the rights to use arms whenever they are attacked by strikers, for otherwise some striker might be killed, and the crime of assault, assuming but not conceding that there has been such a crime, does not deserve the penalty of death. Court decisions are impugned as 'class decisions'; at any rate, they are always too severe. Amnesties, finally, must wipe out all remembrance of such unpleasantness. One might suppose that since the interests of employers and strikebreakers are directly contrary to the interests of the strikers, they would use the opposite derivations. But that is not the case, or if they do, they do it in a very mild, apologetic way. The reason is, as regards the 'strikebreaker,' the 'scab,' that he has, as a class, very little spirit. He is not inspired by any lofty ideal, he is almost ashamed of what he is doing, and does it with as little talk as possible. As regards employers of labour, the reason is that many of them are 'speculators' who hope to make up for their losses in a strike through government aid and at the expense of consumer or taxpayer. Their quarrels with strikers are quarrels between accomplices over the division of the loot. The strikers belong to the masses, where there is a wealth of Class II residues. They have not only interests but ideals. Their 'speculator' employers belong to a class that has grown rich in its aptitude for combinations. They are well supplied, over-supplied, with residues from Class I and so have interests chiefly, and few or no ideals. They spend their time in activities that are far more lucrative than the manufacture of theories. Among them are not a few plutocratic demagogues who are artists at the trick of turning to their advantage strikes that are in all appearances directed against them. There are general considerations, furthermore, that apply to both domestic and international conflicts. They come down, in brief, to an appeal to sentiments of pity for the sufferings that are caused by the use of force, disregarding entirely the reasons for which the force is used and the utility or the harm that results from using or not using it. They are often filled out with expressions of reverence, or at least of compassion, for the proletariat, which can never do wrong or at the very least is excusable for whatever it does. In a day gone by, similar derivations, corresponding to the very same sentiments, were used in favour now of royal, now of theocratic, now of aristocratic, rule.

2188. It is interesting, as in keeping with the essentially sentimental character of derivations, that theories that would be the soundest from the logico-experimental standpoint are as a rule neglected. In the Middle Ages an excellent argument might have been put forward in favour of the ecclesiastical power at a time when it was at war with imperial, royal, or baronial powers – the fact that it was virtually the only counterbalance to those other powers, and almost the only refuge of intelligence, science, and cultivation against ignorant brutal force. But that argument was seldom, if ever, used. People preferred to rely on derivations based on the doctrine of revelation and quotations from Scripture. Now employers who themselves enjoy economic protection manifest great indignation at strikers for trying to rid themselves of the competition of non-union workers. The rejoinder is never made that they are trying to keep others from doing what they are doing themselves, and that they fail to show how and why free competition is good for the workingman and bad for the employer of labour. An individual tries to slip across the Italian frontier with a few bags of saccharin. Customs officers come running and violently prevent such competition with Italian manufacturers of beet-sugar, going, on occasion, so far as to use their guns and sometimes to kill the smuggler whom nobody mourns. All the same it is owing to just such violence and such murders that now a few Italian 'sugar men' have managed to amass considerable fortunes and win public esteem, national honours, and even seats among the law-makers. One still has to be shown why violence cannot be used in the same way to increase wages.

2189. It may be objected that the violence that safe-guards the interests of the employer is legal and the violence used by the strikers on 'scabs' illegal. That transfers the question from the utility of the violence to the utility of the manner in which violence is applied – a matter of considerable importance, no one will deny. Legal violence is the consequence of the norms established in a society, and in general resort to it is more beneficial or at least less harmful than resort to private violence, which is designed as a rule to overthrow prevailing norms. The strikers might answer, and in fact sometimes do, that they are using illegal violence because they are cut off from using the legal variety. If the law were to constrain people by use of legal violence to give them what they demand, they would not need to resort to illegal violence. The same argument would serve in many other cases. People who use illegal violence would ask for nothing better than to be able to transmute it into legal violence.

2190. But the matter is not yet exhausted, and we now come to the salient point in question. Let us set the particular case aside and look at the problem in its general form. The dispute is really as to the relative merits of shrewdness and force, and to decide it in the sense that never, not even in the exceptional case, is it useful to meet wits with violence, it would be necessary first to show that the use of cunning is always, without exception, more advisable than the use of force. Suppose a certain country has a governing class, A, that assimilates the best elements, as regards intelligence, in the whole population. In that case the subject class, B, is largely stripped of such elements and can have little or no hope of ever overcoming the class A so long as it is a battle of wits. If intelligence were to combine with force, the dominion of the *A*'s would be perpetual, for as Dante says, *Inferno*, XXXI, vv. 55–57 (Fletcher translation):

> For if the machination of the mind
> To evil-will be added and to might,
> Of no defence is competent mankind.

But such a happy combination occurs only for a few individuals. In the majority of cases people who rely on their wits are or become less fitted to use violence, and *vice versa*. So concentration in the class *A* of the individuals most adept at chicanery leads to a concentration in class *B* of the individuals most adept at violence; and if that process is long continued, the equilibrium tends to become unstable, because the *A*'s are long in cunning but short in courage to use force and in the force itself; whereas the *B*'s have the force and the courage to use it, but are short in the skill required for exploiting those advantages. But if they chance to find leaders who have the skill – and history show that such leadership is usually supplied by dissatisfied *A*'s – they have all they need for driving the *A*'s from power. Of just that development history affords countless examples from remotest times all the way down to the present.

2191. In general terms, a revolution of that type is beneficial to a community – more so when a governing class is tending more and more towards humanitarianism, less so when it is made up of individuals who are tending more and more to use combinations instead of force, especially if the combinations result, even indirectly, in the material prosperity of the community.

Let us imagine a country where the governing class, *A*, is inclining more and more in the direction of humanitarianism, is fostering, in other words, only the more harmful group-persistences, rejecting the others as outworn prejudices, and, while awaiting the advent of the 'reign of reason,' is becoming less and less capable of using force and is so shirking the main duty of a ruling class. Such a country is on its way to utter ruin. But lo, the subject class, *B*, revolts against the class *A*. In fighting *A* it uses the humanitarian derivations so dear to the *A*'s, but underlying them are quite different sentiments, and they soon find expression in deeds. The *B*'s apply force on a far-reaching scale, and not only overthrow the *A*'s but kill large numbers of them – and, in so doing, to tell the truth, they are performing a useful public service something like ridding the country of a baneful animal pest. They bring with them to the seats of power a great abundance of group persistences; and little it matters, if it matters at all, that these group-

465

persistences be different in outward forms from the old. The important thing is that now they are functioning in the governing class and that owing to them the social fabric is acquiring stability and strength. The country is saved from ruin and is reborn to a new life.

If one judges superficially, one may be tempted to dwell more especially on the slaughter and pillaging that attend a revolution, without thinking to ask whether such things may not be manifestations – as regrettable as one may wish – of sentiments, of social forces, that are very salutary. If one should say that, far from being reprehensible, the slaughter and robbery are signs that those who were called upon to commit them deserved power for the good of society, he would be stating a paradox, for there is no relationship of cause and effect, nor any close and indispensable correlation, between such outrages and social utility; but the paradox would still contain its modicum of truth, in that the slaughter and rapine are external symptoms indicating the advent of strong and courageous people to places formerly held by weaklings and cowards. In all that we have been describing in the abstract many revolutions that have actually occurred in the concrete, from the revolution which gave imperial rule to Augustus down to the French Revolution of '89. If the class governing in France had had the faith that counsels use of force and the will to use force, it would never have been overthrown and, procuring its own advantage, would have procured the advantage of France. Since it failed in that function it was salutary that its rule should give way to rule by others; and since, again, it was the resort to force that was wanting, it was in keeping with very general uniformities that there should be a swing to another extreme where force was used even more than was required. Had Louis XVI not been a man of little sense and less courage, letting himself be floored without fighting, and preferring to lose his head on the guillotine to dying weapon in hand like a man of sinew, he might have been the one to do the destroying. If the victims of the September massacres, their kinsmen and friends, had not for the most part been spineless humanitarians without a particle of courage or energy, they would have annihilated their enemies instead of waiting to be annihilated themselves. It was a good thing that power should pass into the hands of people who showed that they had the faith and the resolve requisite for the use of force.

The advantage of the use of force to a society is less apparent when the governing class is made up of persons in whom the combination instincts are prevalent, and within certain limits there may be no advantage. But when a governing class divests itself too completely of the sentiments of group-persistence, it easily reaches a point where it is unfit to defend, let alone its own power, what is far worse, the independence of its country. In such a case, if the independence is to be deemed an advantage, it must also be deemed an advantage to be rid of a class that has become incompetent to perform the functions of defence. As a rule it is from the subject class that individuals come with the faith and the resolve to use force and save a country.

2192. The governing class, *A*, tries to defend its power and avert the danger of an uprising of the *B*'s in various ways. It may try to take advantage of the strength of the *B*'s, and that is the most effective policy. Or it may try to prevent its disaffected members from becoming leaders of the *B*'s, or rather, of that element among the *B*'s which is disposed to use force; but that is a very difficult thing to achieve. And the *A*'s use derivations to keep the *B*'s quiet (§ 2182), telling them that 'all power comes from God,' that it is a 'crime' to resort to violence, that there is no reason for using force to obtain what, if it is 'just,' may be obtained by 'reason.' The main purpose of such derivations is to keep the *B*'s from giving battle on their own terrain, the terrain of force, and to lead them to other ground – the field of cunning – where their defeat is certain, pitted as they will be against the *A*'s, who are immensely their superiors in wits. But as a rule the effectiveness of such derivations depends largely upon the pre-existing sentiments that they express, and only to a slight extent upon sentiments that they create.

2193. Those derivations have to be met with other derivations of equal effectiveness, and it will be better if some of them play upon sentiments that are acceptable to people who imagine that they are neutral, though in reality they may not be, who would prefer not to take sides with either the *A*'s or the *B*'s but to think solely of what is 'just' and 'honest.' Such sentiments are chiefly available in the group manifested by residues of sociality (Class IV) and more especially the sentiments of pity. For that reason, most of the derivations favouring the use of violence by the subject class defend it not so much directly as indirectly – condemning resistance on the part of the governing class in the name of sociality, pity, and repugnance to sufferings in others. These latter sentiments are almost the only ones that are exploited by many pacifists who can think of no other way to defend their thesis than by describing the 'horrors of war.' Derivations relating to the social struggle often have recourse, further, to sentiments of asceticism, which sometimes influence individuals among the *A*'s and so prove to be of no mean advantage to the *B*'s.

2194. At the bottom all such derivations express in chief, the sentiments of individuals who are eager for change in the social order, and they are therefore beneficial or harmful according as the change is beneficial or harmful. If one is going to assert that change is always for the worse, that stability is the supreme good, one ought to be ready to show either that it would have been to the advantage of human societies always to have remained in a state of barbarism, or that the transition from barbarism to civilization has been achieved, or *might have* been achieved, without wars and revolutions. This latter assertion is so grossly at variance with the facts as we learn them from history that it is absurd even to discuss it. So only the first is left, and it might be defended by giving a special meaning to the term 'utility' and adopting the theories that have sung the joys of a 'state of nature.' If one is unwilling to go as far as that, one cannot hold to the first proposition either; and so one is forced by the facts and by the logic to admit that wars and revolutions have sometimes been beneficial (which does not mean that they have always been so). And once that is admitted for the past, no bias whatever remains for showing that things will be otherwise in the future.

2195. So there we are again, and as usual, driven from the qualitative field, where derivations predominate, into the quantitative field of logico-experimental science. One cannot assert in general that stability is always beneficial or that change is always beneficial. Every case has to be examined on its particular merits and the utility and the detriment appraised to see whether the first overbalances the second, or *vice versa*.

2196. We have already found that in many cases stability is beneficial. We should find cases no fewer in number where violations of existing norms have also proved beneficial, provided we consider norms of an intellectual order along with norms of a material order. But keeping them separate, it will be apparent that – especially as regards violations by small numbers of individuals – many are the cases where violations of intellectual norms by individuals or by a few individuals prove advantageous, few the cases where violations of norms of a material order prove beneficial. For that reason, the implications of the formula stated in § 2176, whereby violations of norms of a material order should be the more vigorously suppressed, the more exclusively they are the work of individuals, the less so, the more they are the work of groups, do not in many cases take us too far astray from the maximum of social utility, as they would do if the formula were applied to violations of norms of an intellectual order. That, substantially, is the chief argument that can be advanced in favour of what is called 'freedom of thought.'

2197. Derivations do not run that way. Dissenters defend their opinions because they are 'better' than the opinions held by the majority; and it is a good thing that they have that faith, for it alone can supply them with the energy they need to resist the persecutions that they almost always incur. So long as they are few in numbers, they ask just for a little place in the Sun for their sect. In reality they are panting for the moment when they can turn from persecuted to persecutor, a thing that infallibly happens as soon as they have become numerous enough to enforce their will. At that moment the advantage of their past dissent is at an end, and the detriment resulting from their new orthodoxy begins to assert itself.

2198. In considering the use of force there is a stronger temptation than in other social connexions to think only of relationships of cause and effect: nor in many cases do we go very far wide of the mark in that. After all, in the sequence of actions and reactions that confronts one, the action of this or that force as producing this or that effect occupies a very considerable place. However, it is better not to stop at that, but go on to see whether phenomena that are more general should not be taken into account.

2199. We have previously compared the revolution in Rome at the time of Augustus with the revolution in France at the time of Louis XVI; and we saw that to understand those two events we had to look beyond the derivations to the sentiments and interests that the derivations represented. Advancing one step further, one notes that both in the fall of the Roman Republic and in the fall of the French monarchy, the respective governing classes were either unwilling or unable to use force, and were overthrown by other classes that were both willing and able to do that (§ 2191). Both in ancient Rome and in France the victorious element rose from the people and was made up in Rome of the legions of Sulla, Caesar, and Octavius, in France of the revolutionary mobs that routed a very feeble royal power, and then of an army that vanquished the very inefficient troops of the European potentates. The leaders of the victors spoke Latin, of course, in Rome, and French in France, and no less naturally used derivations that were suitable to the Romans and the French respectively. The Roman people was fed on derivations conforming with a feeling that substance might be changed so long as forms were kept, the French masses, on derivations inspired by the religion of 'Progress,' a faith surpassing dear to the French of that day. Not otherwise, in the days of the Puritan Revolution, did Cromwell and other foes of the Stuarts use biblical derivations.

2200. The French derivations are more familiar than the Roman not only because more documents have come down to us, but also, as seems very probable, because they were supplied in greater abundance. Had Octavius long continued in his rôle as defender of the Senate, he might have made very lavish use of them; but when, before Bologna, he came to an understanding with Antony and Lepidus, his fortunes came to rest altogether on the might of his legions; so he laid his derivations away in his arsenals as weapons no longer needed, not taking them out again till after his victory, when it was a question of smoothing the fur of old-timers in Rome, which might have been ruffled by the change in régime. Something of the same sort took place in France as regards Napoleon I; but before his time the Jacobins, who opened the road for him, found it impossible to play only the lion and had to resort to the tricks of the fox. With his own prestige as commander, Octavius had made sure of the support of an armed force, and at first with his own money, later on with the money that he was in a position to extort by force from others. The French revolutionary leaders were unable to do anything like that, in the beginning. They had to recruit their revolutionary army with derivations, which, expressing as they did the sentiments of many of the government's enemies, brought them in a flock to their standards, and, expressing also the sentiments of almost all members of the ruling classes, further served as an opiate to their already listless vigilance, and broke down their already feeble resistance. Later on, as soon as the revolution got possession of power, its leaders imitated the Roman triumvirs and many other masterful men of the same type, distributing among their followers the money and property of their adversaries.

2201. If the effects of derivations are much less considerable than the effects of residues, they are not, as we have many times seen, altogether without influence, serving primarily to give greater strength and effectiveness to the residues that they express. It would not therefore be exact to say that the historians who have made the derivations of the French Revolution their exclusive or at least their main concern have dealt with an entirely irrelevant aspect of that episode. They may be said to have erred in regarding as primary an aspect that was merely secondary. It has been a more serious error on their part not to consider the rôle played by force and the reasons why force was used by some parties, and not by others. The few who have considered the rôle of force at all have gone astray in assuming that this or that man in power refrained from using force in deference to derivations, whereas both derivations and the aversion to use of force had a common origin in the sentiments of those men. And yet – if one examines closely – the whole thing seems clear, with the proof and the counter-proof. Louis XVI fell because he was unwilling, unable, incompetent, to use force; the revolutionists triumphed because they were willing and able and competent. Not by any cogency in their theories but by sheer might of their followings did now this and now that revolutionary faction climb to power. Even the

Directory, which had saved itself by resorting to force in conflicts with weaker factions, succumbed to force in its struggle with Bonaparte, made the man of the hour by his victorious troops. And Napoleon lasts until he is worn down under the superior force of the Allies. And then – ever again: a succession of régimes in France, each falling because unwilling, unable, incompetent, to use force, and others rising on the use of force. That was observable on the fall of Charles X, on the fall of Louis Philippe, on the advent of Napoleon III; and one may go on and say that if the government of Versailles in 1871 managed to keep its feet in the face of the Commune, it was because it had a strong army at its disposal and knew enough to use it.

(Vol. IV, §§ 2170–75, 2178–201)

842. Since social phenomena appear in complex form in the concrete, we saw at once that it would be helpful to divide them into at least two elements, distinguishing logical from non-logical conduct; and that gave us a first conception of the nature of non-logical conduct and of its importance in human society. But at that point a question arose: If non-logical conduct plays such an important role in human life, why has it been so generally neglected? We found in reply that almost all writers on social or political subjects have indeed observed such conduct, or at least caught glimpses of it. Many elements, therefore, of the theory we are framing in these volumes are to be found scattered about here and there in the works of various writers, though often under hardly recognizable forms.

843. But we saw that all such writers had ideas of their own to which they very expressly attached capital importance – ideas on religion, morality, law, and the like, which have been battle-grounds for centuries. So, if they did recognize non-logical conduct implicitly, explicitly they glorified logical conduct, and most of them regarded it as the only conduct worth considering in social phenomena. We were therefore called upon to see what truth there was in theories of that type, and to decide whether we were to abandon the course on which we had set out or take heart and push on.

We then proceeded to examine those various manners of considering social phenomena, and we saw that from the logico-experimental standpoint they were devoid of all exactness and of any strict accord with the facts; though from another standpoint, we could not deny the great importance that they had had in history and in determining the social equilibrium. That discovery lent force to a suspicion which had already occurred to us, and which will acquire greater and greater prominence in the course of these volumes: that the experimental 'truth' of certain theories is one thing and their social 'utility' quite another, and that the two things are not only not one and the same but may, and often do, stand in flat contradiction.

844. We found that it was as important to separate those two things as it had been to distinguish logical from non-logical conduct, and our inductive survey showed that the failure to make such a distinction had been the main cause of error, from the scientific standpoint, in most social theories.

845. So we looked at them a little more closely and saw how and why they went astray, and how and why, though fallacious, they enjoyed and still enjoy such great prestige. In the course of that investigation we came upon things which we had not thought of at the outset. But we went on analyzing, distinguishing, and soon we observed another distinction that struck us as being quite as important as the others we had made – on the one hand an instinctive, non-logical element that was constant, on the other, a deductive element that was designed to explain, justify, demonstrate, the constant element. Arriving at that point, we found that induction had given us the elements of a theory.

846. Here, now, we are called upon to frame it, that is to say, we must now drop the inductive for the deductive method, and see what consequences result from the principles that we have found, or think we have found. After that we shall have to compare our inferences with the facts. If they fit, we shall keep our theory. If they fail to fit, we shall discard it.

847. In this chapter (and since the subject is a vast one, in the next two) we are to study the constant element a, going on, after that, to the deductive element b. But we are dealing with a very difficult matter, and a few more remarks in general on the elements a and b, and their resultant c, will not come amiss.

848. We saw in [an earlier section] that in the theories of the logico-experimental sciences one may discern a basic element A, and a deductive element B, which in some respects are analogous to, in some respects different from, the elements a and b in theories that are not strictly logico-experimental.

The social sciences as hitherto cultivated show elements that bear a closer resemblance to a than to A, through their failure to avoid intrusions of sentiments, prejudices, creeds, or other predilections, tendencies, postulates, principles, that carry the thinker outside the logico-experimental domain.

849. The deductive element in the social sciences as hitherto cultivated sometimes comes very close to B, and there are cases where the logic is so adequate that coincidence with B would be exact were it not for a lack of definiteness in the premises *a*, which deprives the reasoning of strict validity. But oftentimes in the social sciences the deductive element stands very close to *b*, as containing many non-logical and non-experimental principles and showing great susceptibility to inclinations, bias, and the like.

850. So let us make the elements *a* and *b* our main concern. The element *a* corresponds, we may guess, to certain instincts of man, or more exactly, men, because *a* has no objective existence and differs in different individuals; and it is probably because of its correspondence to instincts that it is virtually constant in social phenomena. The element *b* represents the work of the mind in accounting for *a*. That is why *b* is much more variable, as reflecting the play of the imagination.[1]

851. But if the element *a* corresponds to certain instincts, it is far from reflecting them all; and that is evident from the very manner in which we found it. We analyzed specimens of thinking on the look-out for a constant element. We may therefore have found only the instincts that underlay those reasonings. There was no chance of our meeting along that road instincts which were not so logicalized. Unaccounted for still would be simple appetites, tastes, inclinations, and in social relationships the very important class called 'interests.'

852. We may also have found only a part of one of the things *a*, the other part being a mere appetite. If the sex instinct tended only to unite the sexes it would not figure in our investigations. But that instinct is often enough logicalized and dissembled under guise of asceticism; there are people who preach virtue as a way of lingering, in their thoughts, on sex matters. Examining their thinking, we accordingly find an element *a* corresponding to the sex instinct, and an element *b* that is the reasoning under which it hides. Diligent search might reveal similar elements corresponding to the appetites for food and drink. But in those cases the role played by simple instinct is far more considerable, at any rate, than in the case of sex.

853. The fact of being provident or improvident depends upon certain instincts, certain tastes, and from that point of view it would not figure in *a*. But in the United States the improvident instinct has fathered a theory that people ought to spend all they can earn; and so analysis of that theory yields a quantum *a*, which will be improvidence.

854. A politician is inspired to champion the theory of 'solidarity' by an ambition to obtain money, power, distinctions. Analysis of that theory would reveal but scant trace of his motives, which are, after all,

1. As we have already seen, the part *b* has in its turn to be subdivided, since it varies all the way from one extreme, where it is pure logic, to another extreme where it is pure instinct and fancy.

the motives of virtually all politicians, whether they preach white or black. First prominence would be held by principles *a* that are effective in influencing others. If the politician were to say, 'Believe in "solidarity" because if you do it means money for me,' he would get many laughs and few votes. He therefore has to take his stand on principles that are acceptable to his prospective constituents.

If we stopped at that, it might seem that in the case before us the *a*'s were located not in the principles that suggested championing the theory to the politician, but in the principles that inspired acceptance of it by his hearers. But going a little deeper, such a distinction is seen not to hold. Oftentimes the person who would persuade others begins by persuading himself; and even if he is moved in the beginning by thoughts of personal advantage, he comes eventually to believe that his real interest is the welfare of others. Unbelieving apostles are rare and ineffective, but ubiquitous and ubiquitously effective is the apostle who believes, and he is the more effective, the more sincere his belief. The element *a* in a theory *c* is present both in the persons who accept and in the persons who propound it, but not to be overlooked in either case are the advantages accruing from the theory *c*, to the ones and the other.

855. In analyzing a theory *c*, we must keep the objective standpoint sharply distinguished from the subjective. The two researches are very often confused, and so two errors, in chief, arise. In the first place, as we have so often cautioned, the logico-experimental value of a theory is not kept distinct from its persuasive force or its social utility. Then again – and this is a peculiarly modern error – the objective study of a theory is replaced by a subjective research as to how and why it was evolved or adopted by its author. This second research certainly has its importance, but it ought to supplement the other, not replace it. Whether a theorem of Euclid is true or false, and how and why he came to discover it, are two separate questions, and the one does not preclude the other. If the *Principia* of Newton had been written by an unknown writer, would that in any way affect the value of the book? So two of the aspects under which a writer's theory may be considered become confused: (1) his manner of thinking, his psychic state, and how he came by it; (2) what he meant in a given passage. The first aspect, which is personal, subjective to him, is mixed in with the second, which is impersonal, objective. A factor in the confusion oftentimes is regard for the writer's authority. In deference to that sentiment it is assumed *a priori* that everything he thinks and believes must necessarily be 'true,' and that to determine his thought is tantamount to testing the 'truth' (or when the logico-experimental sciences are concerned, the accord with experience) of what he thought.

856. Long prevalent was an inclination to consider theories exclusively from the standpoint of their intrinsic merit (sometimes their logico-experimental soundness), which, much more often, was determined with reference to the sentiments of the critic or to certain metaphysical or theological principles. Nowadays the tendency is to consider them exclusively from the extrinsic standpoint, as to the manner of their genesis, that is, and the reasons for their acceptance. Both methods, if used exclusively, are equally incomplete and to that extent erroneous.

857. The second error (§ 855) is the opposite of the first. The first considered only the intrinsic merit of the theory; the second only its extrinsic merit. It appears in the abuse of the historical method, which is frequent enough nowadays, especially in the social and economic sciences. In the beginning, in their eagerness to free their science of contingencies of time and place, the fathers of political economy made the mistake of viewing their findings as absolutes. It was a salutary reaction, therefore, when just such contingencies came to be taken into account, and from that point of view the historical method was a notable contribution to the progress of science. And a forward step no less important was taken when the effort to derive the forms of social institutions from dogmatic absolutes was abandoned in favour of historical studies that made it possible to learn how institutions had developed, and their bearing on other social phenomena. We are altogether within the domain of logico-experimental science when we ask not what the family ought to be, but what it has actually been. But the historical study is to be thought of as supplementing, not as replacing, our inquiry into the relations between the constitution of the family and other social phenomena. It is useful to know how, historically, theories of income have been evolved: but it is also useful to know the relations of such theories to the facts – their logico-experimental value.

858. However, this latter type of research is much more difficult than the mere writing of history; and there are plenty of people who are utterly incapable of understanding, let alone of creating, a logico-experimental theory in political economy, yet who blithely presume to write histories of that science.

859. In the literary field historical studies often degenerate into mere collections of anecdotes that are easy to write and agreeable to read. To find out what a writer ate and drank, how he slept, the clothes he wore, is intellectually and scientifically easier than to deal with the relations between his theories and experimental realities. And if a critic can find something to say about a writer's love affairs, he is certain to make a very entertaining book indeed.

860. To study the element b is to study the subjective element in a theory. But the subjective element may be further subdivided into two: the general causes and the special causes that account for the genesis and success of a theory. General causes would be causes operative over fairly extensive periods of time and affecting considerable numbers of individuals. Special causes operate in an essentially contingent manner. If a theory comes into vogue because it serves the interests of a social class it has, in that fact, a general cause. If a writer invents a theory because he is paid to do so or because he wants to spite a rival, the cause is special.

861. Things that exert powerful effects upon the social order give rise to theories, and we shall find them, therefore, in the course of our quest for a's. In addition to such a's there are, as we have just seen, appetites and interests. Taking them all together we have the sum of the things that operate to any appreciable extent towards determining the social order (§ 851), bearing in mind of course that the social order reacts upon them, so that we are all along dealing not with a relationship of cause and effect, but with an interrelation or a relationship of interdependence. If we assume, as in fact seems probable, that animals have no theories, they cannot have an element a of any kind and perhaps not even interests – all that is left in their case is instincts. Uncivilized peoples, however close to animals they may seem to stand, do have theories of one sort or another, and an element a has to be considered in dealing with them. And beyond a doubt they have instincts and interests. Civilized peoples have theories for very very many of their instincts and interests. An element a figures through virtually the whole range of their social life.

862. In this volume we are to go looking for the element a. In many cases already we have distinguished a elements and b elements that we found combined and confused in some single phenomenon, c. That was in itself a start towards finding a norm for making such analyses. Suppose we get a still clearer view of the method from an example or two and then proceed with our systematic study.

863. *Example I.* Christians have the custom of baptism. If one knew the Christian procedure only one would not know whether and how it could be analyzed. Moreover, we have an explanation of it: We are told that the rite of baptism is celebrated in order to remove original sin. That still is not enough, if we had no other facts of the same class to go by, we should find it difficult to isolate the elements in the complex phenomenon of baptism. But we do have other facts of that type. The pagans too had lustral water, and they used it for purposes of purification. If we stopped at that, we might associate the use of water with the fact of purification. But other cases of baptism show that the use of water is not a constant element. Blood may be used for purification, and other substances as well. Nor is that all; there are numbers of rites that effect the same result. In cases where taboos have been violated, certain rites remove the pollution that a person has incurred in one set of circumstances or another. So the circle of similar facts widens, and in the great variety of devices and in the many explanations that are given for their use the thing which remains constant is the feeling, the sentiment, that the integrity of an individual which has been altered by certain causes, real or imaginary, can be restored by certain rites. The given case, therefore, is made up of that constant element, a, and a variable element, b, the latter comprising the means that are used for restoring the individual's integrity and the reasonings by which the efficacy of the means is presumably explained. The human being has a vague feeling that water somehow cleanses moral as well as material pollutions. However, he does not, as a rule, justify his conduct in that manner. The explanation would be far too simple. So he goes looking for something more complicated, more pretentious, and readily finds what he is looking for.

864. The nucleus a, now that we have found it, is seen to be made up of a number of elements: first of all an instinct for combinations; people want 'to do something about it' – they want to combine certain things with certain acts. It is a curious fact, also, that the ties so imagined persist in time. It would be easy enough to try some new combination every day. Instead there is one combination, fantastic though it be, that tends to prevail and sometimes does prevail over all competitors. Discernible, finally, is an instinct which inclines people to believe that certain combinations are suited to attaining certain objectives.[2]

865. *Example II*. We have seen many cases where people believed that they could raise or avert tempests. If we knew only one such case, we could make little or nothing of it. However, we know many cases and can identify a constant nucleus in them. Ignoring, for the moment, the element in the nucleus that relates, as in the case of baptism, to the persistence of certain combinations and the faith in their efficacy, we find a constant element, a, corresponding to the feeling, the sentiment,

2. As for 'causes' or 'origins,' we might guess that actually effective combinations, such as striking a flint to get a fire, may have led people to believe in the efficiency of imaginary combinations. But we need not, for the present, concern ourselves with that explanation or any other. We can rest content with establishing the fact, and stop at that. In some other connexion we might try to go further and explain the fact by other facts, then the latter by others still, and so on.

that a divinity exists and that, by a variable means, *b*, he (or 'it') may be made to interfere and influence the weather. And then, right away, there is another sort of belief, the belief that it is possible to produce the desired effect by certain rites or practices, which mean nothing in themselves – the practice, for instance, of tearing a white cock asunder and carrying the two halves around a field to protect it from drought. So the circle widens, and another constant *a* appears: an instinct for combinations, whereby things and acts designed for producing given effects are brought together haphazard.

866. *Example III.* Catholics believe that Friday is a day of evil omen as – so it is averred – the day of the Passion. If we knew just that, and nothing else of the kind, it would be difficult to determine which of the two facts, the evil omen or the Passion, was the main, and which the secondary, fact. But we do have other facts of the kind, many of them. The Romans had their 'black' or 'vicious' days (*dies atri* or *vitiosi*), which were days of evil omen – for instance, the eighteenth of July, the anniversary of their defeat by the Gauls at Allia, A.U.C. 365. That is one kind of *a* – the feeling that the day which is associated with some catastrophe is a day of evil omen. But there are other facts. Both the Romans and the Greeks had days of evil omen and days of good omen without there being any special causes in the nature of public successes or disasters. Hence there has to be a more comprehensive class of *a*'s, which includes the *a* just mentioned and expresses an impulse to combine days (and other things too) with good or evil omens.

867. These examples give us an inkling as to how a composite situation, *c*, may be broken up into *a* elements and *b* elements.[3]

868. Before going any farther it might perhaps be advisable to give word-names to the things we have been calling *a*, *b*, and *c*. To designate them by mere letters of the alphabet in a measure embarrasses our discussion and makes it harder to follow. For that reason, and for no other, suppose we call the things *a*, *residues*, the things *b*, *derivations*, and the things *c*, *derivatives*. But we must always and at all times remember that nothing, absolutely nothing, is to be inferred from the proper meanings of those words or their etymologies, that they mean respectively the things *a*, *b*, and *c* and nothing else.

3. [Pareto makes no very extensive use of the term 'derivative,' probably because its functions are filled just as well by the term 'theory,' or better, 'non-logico-experimental theory.' Etymologically, a 'residue' would be 'what is left' (the constant element) when the variable elements have been eliminated from an action or a reasoning by a comparative analysis. It is always reducible to the synonymous phrase: 'principle underlying a non-logical action or reasoning.' – A. L.]

869. As we have already seen, the residues *a* constitute a multifarious mass of facts, which have to be classified according to the mutual analogies they present. In that way we get 'classes,' 'genera,' and 'species.' And so for the derivations *B*.

870. Residues correspond to certain instincts in human beings, and for that reason they are usually wanting in definiteness, in exact delimitation. That trait, indeed, nearly always serves to distinguish them from scientific facts or principles *A*, which otherwise bear some resemblance to them. Many times *A*'s have come out of *a*'s as a result of making the *a*'s more exact. The term 'warm' is indefinite. Using it, it has been possible to say that well-water is 'warm' in winter and 'cold' in summer. But as used by physicists the term 'warm' corresponds to certain degrees of heat as registered by a thermometer; it is definite. That made it evident that the water in wells is not in that sense warmer in winter than in summer, for a thermometer lowered into a well registers about the same temperature in winter as in summer, or if anything a lower one.

871. Curious the number of different meanings the term 'warm' has in Macrobius, *Saturnalia*, VII, 6–8, all of them showing as their residue the sentiments that the term 'warm' awakens in the minds now of this, now of that, individual. The doctors say that wine is warm; but a character in the *Saturnalia* disagrees, finding wine by nature cold. A woman's body, says another, contains a large amount of cold. No, answers a companion, the female body is naturally warmer than the male – it is so warm, in fact, that when it was the custom to dispose of dead bodies by cremation, a female corpse was commonly burned with each ten males so that the latter might more quickly be consumed. Women have so much heat in their bodies that they are able to wear light clothing in winter. Heat, moreover, is the principle of conception. All that is disputed by another, except as regards conception, the cause of which seems really to be heat. Why is it that in a very hot country wine has the property of cold instead of heat? The reason is that when the air is hot it drives the cold into the ground. The air is always hot in Egypt, so the cold permeates the soil and reaches the vine-roots, imparting its own properties to the wine. And we are told why a fan cools.

872. That is the type of the metaphysical reasoning, whether ancient or modern. The premises contain terms altogether devoid of exactness, and from the premises, as from mathematical axioms presumably trustworthy, conclusions are drawn by strict logic. They serve, after all, to probe not things but the notions that given individuals have of things.[4]

4. Some people are willing as an extreme concession to bar that type of

873. The Macrobius example again shows how inexact terms may readily be used to prove both the pro and the contra. Women can wear lighter clothing than men because of the heat in their bodies. No, someone objects, it is because of the cold in their bodies.

874. In general terms, it is the indefiniteness of the residues a, chiefly, that unsuits them to serve as premises in strict reasonings, whereas A propositions can be and are constantly being so used in the sciences.

875. The residues a must not be confused with the sentiments or instincts to which they correspond. The residues are the manifestations of sentiments and instincts just as the rising of the mercury in a thermometer is a manifestation of the rise in temperature. Only elliptically and for the sake of brevity do we say that residues, along with appetites, interests, etc. are the main factors in determining the social equilibrium, just as we say that water boils at 100° Centigrade. The completed statements would be: 'The sentiments or instincts that correspond to residues, along with those corresponding to appetites, interests, etc. are the main factors in determining the social equilibrium.' 'Water boils when its calorific state attains the temperature of 100° as registered by a Centigrade thermometer.'

876. It is only by way of analysis and for the sole purposes of study that we distinguish various residues $a1$, $a2$, $a3$ ... What is at work in the individual is sentiments corresponding to the groups (a_1, a_2, a_3); (a_1, a_3, a_4); (a_3, a_5); and so on. These are composites as compared with the residues $a1$, $a2$ ... which are simpler. We might go on and break up $a1$, $a2$ ... as well into simpler elements; but we must know how to stop in time, because if made too general propositions end by meaning nothing. So the multifarious circumstances conditioning life on our globe may, in general, be reduced to solar light, the presence of an atmosphere, and so on; but the biologist needs conditions that are much less general than that as a basis for a greater number of biological laws.

877. It sometimes happens that a derivative, c, reached from a residue, a, by way of derivation, b, becomes in its turn the residue of other phenomena and itself subject to deviations. The bad omen, for instance, that is associated with the presence of thirteen persons at a table may be derivative from a sentiment of horror at Judas's betrayal followed by his suicide; but that derivative has become a residue by this time, and people feel ill at ease at a table of thirteen without the least thought of Judas.

---

reasoning from the physical sciences, but insist on retaining it for the social sciences. If we keep within experimental limits, however, there is nothing to justify any such distinction.

878. All the pointers just given must be kept in mind at all times in the investigations following. Anyone forgetting them will get everything askew.

879. This research as so far outlined has certain points of analogy with the ordinary researches of philology that deal with the roots and derivatives in which the words of a language originate. The analogy is not altogether artificial. It arises in the fact that products of the mental activity of the human being are involved in both cases, that their processes are the same. Take, for instance, Greek. The words in that language may be grouped in families, each family having its own root. There are the nouns meaning 'anchor' ($ἄγχυρα$), 'fish-hook' ($ἄγκιστρον$), 'curved object' ($ἀγκαλη$), 'bent arm' ($ἀγκαλίς$), 'bend of the arm' ($ἀγκύλη$), 'elbow' ($ἀγκών$); the adjectives 'curved' ($ἀγκύλος$) and 'hook-shaped' ($ἀγκιστωτρός,-ή-όν$); the verbs 'to fish with a hook' ($ἀγκιστρεύω$) and 'to bend' ($ἀγκυλῶ$). They all have the same root (residue) $ἀγκ$, which originates in, and expresses, the rather vague notion of something curved, hooked, crooked. By processes of derivation, which have their rules, words are derived from these roots, just as the derivatives, c, are derived from the residues, a. We find combinations of roots just as we find combinations of residues. The adjective 'biting a hook' ($ἀγκιστροφάγος$) has $ἀγκ$ and $φαγ$ for its roots, the first referring to something vaguely hook-shaped, the second eating. There are some very common derivations in Greek. The suffix $ματ$, for instance, combining with various roots, gives large numbers of words designating the effects of the actions indicated by the roots. So in social phenomena, certain derivations are very common. The Will of the Divinity, for instance, serves to justify no end of prescriptions. Combined with the residue of filial love, it yields the precept: 'Honour thy father and thy mother, for God so ordains.'

880. Actually observable in society are certain derivatives, c, that derive from residues, a, by way of derivations, b. Other derivatives ($γ$) may be as regularly deducible from the residues as the c's but are not observable in the concrete.

881. That situation has its philological counterpart in regular and irregular verbs. In point of fact such terms must not be taken literally. A so-called irregular verb is as regular as any other. The difference lies in the differing methods of derivation. A process of derivation used for certain roots gives a class of verbs that actually occur in the language. Used for other roots, it gives verbs that do not occur in the language. Conversely, the process of derivation used for these second roots yields verbs that occur in the language, but non-existent verbs when used for the other roots.

882. Derivatives treated as residues have their counterparts in language. The word ἀγκιστροφάγος ('biting a hook') was not derived directly from the roots ἀγκ and φαγ, but from ἀγκιστρον and φαγεῖν. Inflections, conjugations, comparatives, superlatives, locatives, to mention only a few, are examples of derivations based on other derivations.

883. That is not all. The philologists of our time know that the language is an organism which has developed according to its own laws and is not an artificial invention. Only a relatively few technical terms, such as 'oxygen,' 'meter,' 'thermometer,' and the like, are products of logical activity on the part of scholars. Such terms would correspond to 'logical actions' in society. The majority of the words in ordinary usage correspond in their formation to 'non-logical' actions.[5]

884. We have noted these analogies merely to facilitate a clear comprehension of the theories that we are expounding. They of course are not and could not be offered as proofs. Proof must come from direct examination of the facts and in no other way. The method that relies on analogies is a very bad method.

885. Investigations into the 'origins' of social phenomena, which have so far concerned sociology in the main, have oftentimes been, though their authors were not aware of the fact, searches for residues.

5. It is high time that sociology were making some progress and trying to get to the level that philology has already reached. Many other analogies between the two sciences might be noted – to mention just one, the analogy between the abuse of the historical method in sociology and of hyper-criticism of texts in philology. Reinach, *Manuel de philologie*, Vol. I, § 3, p. 48: 'Boeckh has very properly called attention to a vicious circle to which philological criticism is not immune. In order to explain a text it has to be read under a certain form, and to read it under that form *without change* one has to be able to understand it and explain it. Hence a tendency in many scholars to correct or suppress all passages they do not understand. [That is a way also with writers interested in the "origins" of (social or historical) phenomena.] Says Nauck, in Schneidewin's edition of Sophocles: "The conjecture that can claim plausibility is the conjecture that best realizes from every point of view what the most exacting mind would like to find in a Greek tragic author." Boeckh seems almost to have been writing for Nauck's benefit when he said: "The Athenians, at the suggestion of Lycurgus, had forbidden any alteration in the texts of the tragic authors. One could almost wish the ancient classics were protected by a similar law today." ' Nowadays, in the quest for 'origins' everybody takes account of the facts that agree with his notions, and nothing else. Show me if you can the humanitarian who will accept an account of facts that runs counter to his beliefs, or the Marxian who does not test all facts by his doctrine of capitalism!

It was taken for granted, more or less vaguely, that the simple must have preceded the complex – that the residue must have been anterior to the derivative. When Herbert Spencer locates the chronological origin of religion in the deification of human beings, he thinks he has found the residue of all religions phenomena, the simple phenomenon from which the complex religious observable in our day derive.

886. Two criticisms are to be made of that view. 1. No proof is offered of the hypothesis that knowledge of the residue is chronologically anterior to knowledge of the derivative. That has been the case in some instances, but certainly not in others. So in chemistry certain chemical compounds have been discovered later in time than the elements of which they are compounded, but many other compounds have been known earlier in time. In sociology the 'latent' principles of law are an excellent example of derivatives that were known before their residues. An illiterate peasant woman in the mountains around Pistoia knows the conjugations of many Italian verbs by practice perfectly well and much better than any number of educated people; but she has not the remotest idea of the rules that govern the derivation of those conjugations from their roots. 2. Even if knowledge of the residue is anterior in time to knowledge of the derivative, it is better to follow a course directly opposite to the one that has so far been followed. A chronological quest for the residue a is difficult, often impossible, because there are no documents for times so remote from ours; and it is illegitimate to take the imagination and the 'common sense' of the modern man as substitutes for them. Imagination and common sense may, to be sure, yield fascinating theories, but they have little or nothing to do with the facts. To try to discover in primitive periods the residue, a, from which the phenomena, c, observable today, are derived is to try to explain the known by the unknown. To the precise contrary, the less well known must be inferred from the better known: one must try to discover the residues, a, in the phenomena, c, that are observable today and then see whether there are traces of a in documents of the past. If in so doing we find that a existed before c was known we might conclude that a is anterior in time to c, and that, in the particular case, the *origin* is one and the same with the *residue*. Where such proof is lacking no such identity can legitimately be assumed.

887. So far in these volumes we have tried, and we shall continue at all times trying, to explain facts of the past by other facts that we are able to observe in the present; and in any event, we shall always be at the greatest pains to work from the better known to the less known. We are not dealing with 'origins' here, not because origins are not important historically, but because the question of origins has little or no

bearing on the inquiry into the conditions determining the social equilibrium with which we are at present engaged. Of great moment, instead, are the instincts and sentiments that correspond to residues.

(Vol. II, §§ 842–87)

Ralph Linton 1893–1953

Major works

The Tanala, a Hill Tribe of Madagascar (1933)
The Study of Man: An Introduction (1936)
The Cultural Background of Personality (1940)
The Tree of Culture (1955)

The following extracts are reprinted from Ralph Linton, *The Study of Man: An Introduction* (New York: Appleton-Century-Crofts, 1936), with the permission of the publishers. Copyright © D. Appleton-Century Co., Inc., 1936.

In the preceding chapter we discussed the nature of society and pointed out that the functioning of societies depends upon the presence of patterns for reciprocal behavior between individuals or groups of individuals. The polar positions in such patterns of reciprocal behavior are technically known as *statuses*. The term *status*, like the term *culture*, has come to be used with a double significance. *A status*, in the abstract, is a position in a particular pattern. It is thus quite correct to speak of each individual as having many statuses, since each individual participates in the expression of a number of patterns. However, unless the term is qualified in some way, *the status* of any individual means the sum total of all the statuses which he occupies. It represents his position with relation to the total society. Thus the status of Mr Jones as a member of his community derives from a combination of all the statuses which he holds as a citizen, as an attorney, as a Mason, as a Methodist, as Mrs Jones's husband, and so on.

A status, as distinct from the individual who may occupy it, is simply a collection of rights and duties. Since these rights and duties can find expression only through the medium of individuals, it is extremely hard for us to maintain a distinction in our thinking between statuses and the people who hold them and exercise the rights and duties which constitute them. The relation between any individual and any status he holds is somewhat like that between the driver of an automobile and the driver's place in the machine. The driver's seat with its steering wheel, accelerator, and other controls is a constant with ever-present potentialities for action and control, while the driver may be any member of the family and may exercise these potentialities very well or very badly.

A *role* represents the dynamic aspect of a status. The individual is socially assigned to a status and occupies it with relation to other statuses. When he puts the right and duties which constitute the status into effect, he is performing a role. Role and status are quite inseparable, and the distinction between them is of only academic interest. There are no roles without statuses or statuses without roles. Just as in the case of *status*, the term *role* is used with a double significance. Every individual has a series of roles deriving from the various patterns in which he participates and at the same time *a role*, general, which represents the sum total of these roles and determines what he does for his society and what he can expect from it.

Although all statuses and roles derive from social patterns and are integral parts of patterns, they have an independent function with relation to the individuals who occupy particular statuses and exercise their roles. To such individuals the combined status and role represent the minimum of attitudes and behavior which he must assume if he is to participate in the overt expression of the pattern. Status and role serve to reduce the ideal patterns for social life to individual terms. They become models for organizing the attitudes and behavior of the individual so that these will be congruous with those of the other individuals participating in the expression of the pattern. Thus if we are studying football teams in the abstract, the position of quarter-back is meaningless except in relation to the other positions. From the point of view of the quarter-back himself it is a distinct and important entity. It determines where he shall take his place in the line-up and what he shall do in various plays. His assignment to this position at once limits and defines his activities and establishes a minimum of things which he must learn. Similarly, in a social pattern such as that for the employer-employee relationship the statuses of employer and employee define what each has to know and do to put the pattern into operation. The employer does not need to know the techniques involved in the employee's labor, and the employee does not need to know the techniques for marketing or accounting.

It is obvious that, as long as there is no interference from external sources, the more perfectly the members of any society are adjusted to their statuses and roles the more smoothly the society will function.

In its attempts to bring about such adjustments every society finds itself caught on the horns of a dilemma. The individual's formation of habits and attitudes begins at birth, and, other things being equal, the earlier his training for a status can begin the more successful it is likely to be. At the same time, no two individuals are alike, and a status which will be congenial to one may be quite uncongenial to another. Also, there are in all social systems certain roles which require more than training for their successful performance. Perfect technique does not make a great violinist, nor a thorough book knowledge of tactics an efficient general. The utilization of the special gifts of individuals may be highly important to society, as in the case of the general, yet these gifts usually show themselves rather late, and to wait upon their manifestation for the assignment of statuses would be to forfeit the advantages to be derived from commencing training early.

Fortunately, human beings are so mutable that almost any normal individual can be trained to the adequate performance of almost any role. Most of the business of living can be conducted on a basis of habit, with little need for intelligence and none for special gifts. Societies have met the dilemma by developing two types of statuses, the *ascribed* and the *achieved*. *Ascribed* statuses are those which are assigned to individuals without reference to their innate differences or abilities. They can be predicted and trained for from the moment of birth. The *achieved* statuses are, as a minimum, those requiring special qualities, although they are not necessarily limited to these. They are not assigned to individuals from birth but are left open to be filled through competition and individual effort. The majority of the statuses in all social systems are of the ascribed type and those which take care of the ordinary day-to-day business of living are practically always of this type.

In all societies certain things are selected as reference points for the ascription of status. The things chosen for this purpose are always of such a nature that they are ascertainable at birth, making it possible to begin the training of the individual for his potential statuses and roles at once. The simplest and most universally used of these reference points is sex. Age is used with nearly equal frequency, since all individuals pass through the same cycle of growth, maturity, and decline, and the statuses whose occupation will be determined by age can be forecast and trained for with accuracy. Family relationships, the simplest and most obvious being that of the child to its mother, are also used in all societies as reference points for the establishment of a whole series of statuses. Lastly, there is the matter of birth into a particular socially established group, such as a class or caste. The use of this type of reference is common but not universal. In all societies the actual ascription of statuses to the individual is controlled by a series of these reference points which together serve to delimit the field of his future participation in the life of the group.

The division and ascription of statuses with relation to sex seems to be basic in all social systems. All societies prescribe different attitudes and activities to men and to women. Most of them try to rationalize these prescriptions in terms of the physiological differences between the sexes or their different roles in reproduction. However, a comparative study of the statuses ascribed to women and men in different cultures seems to show that while such factors may have served as a starting point for the development of a division the actual ascriptions are almost entirely determined by culture. Even the psychological characteristics ascribed to men and women in different societies vary so much that they can have little physiological basis. Our own idea of women as ministering angels contrasts sharply with the ingenuity of women as torturers among the Iroquois and the sadistic delight they took in the process. Even the last two generations have seen a sharp change in the psychological patterns for women in our own society. The delicate, fainting lady of the middle eighteen-hundreds is as extinct as the dodo.

When it comes to the ascription of occupations, which is after all an integral part of status, we find the differences in various societies even more marked. Arapesh women regularly carry heavier loads than men 'because their heads are so much harder and stronger.' In some societies women do most of the manual labor; in others, as in the Marquesas, even cooking, housekeeping, and baby-tending are proper male occupations, and women spend most of their time primping. Even the general rule that women's handicap through pregnancy and nursing indicates the more active occupations as male and the less active ones as female has many exceptions. Thus among the Tasmanians seal-hunting was women's work. They swam out to the seal rocks, stalked the animals, and clubbed them. Tasmanian women also hunted opossums, which required the climbing of large trees.

Although the actual ascription of occupations along sex lines is highly variable, the pattern of sex division is constant. There are very few societies in which every important activity has not been definitely assigned to men or to women. Even when the two sexes coöperate in a particular occupation, the field of each is usually clearly limited. Thus in Madagascar rice culture the men make the seed beds and terraces and prepare the fields for transplanting. The women do the work of transplanting, which is hard and back-breaking. The women weed the crop, but the men harvest it. The women then carry it to the threshing

487

floors, where the men thresh it while the women winnow it. Lastly, the women pound the grain in mortars and cook it.

When a society takes over a new industry, there is often a period of uncertainty during which the work may be done by either sex, but it soon falls into the province of one or the other. In Madagascar, pottery is made by men in some tribes and by women in others. The only tribe in which it is made by both men and women is one into which the art has been introduced within the last sixty years. I was told that during the fifteen years preceding my visit there had been a marked decrease in the number of male potters, many men who had once practised the art having given it up. The factor of lowered wages, usually advanced as the reason for men leaving one of our own occupations when women enter it in force, certainly was not operative here. The field was not overcrowded, and the prices for men's and women's products were the same. Most of the men who had given up the trade were vague as to their reasons, but a few said frankly that they did not like to compete with women. Apparently the entry of women into the occupation had robbed it of a certain amount of prestige. It was no longer quite the thing for a man to be a potter, even though he was a very good one.

The use of age as a reference point for establishing status is as universal as the use of sex. All societies recognize three age groupings as a minimum: child, adult, and old. Certain societies have emphasized age as a basis for assigning status and have greatly amplified the divisions. Thus in certain African tribes the whole male population is divided into units composed of those born in the same years or within two- or three-year intervals. However, such extreme attention to age is unusual, and we need not discuss it here.

The physical differences between child and adult are easily recognizable, and the passage from childhood to maturity is marked by physiological events which make it possible to date it exactly for girls and within a few weeks or months for boys. However, the physical passage from childhood to maturity does not necessarily coincide with the social transfer of the individual from one category to the other. Thus in our own society both men and women remain legally children until long after they are physically adult. In most societies this difference between the physical and social transfer is more clearly marked than in our own. The child becomes a man not when he is physically mature but when he is formally recognized as a man by his society. This recognition is almost always given ceremonial expression in what are technically known as puberty rites. The most important element in these rites is not the determination of physical maturity but that of social maturity. Whether a boy is able to breed is less vital to his society than whether he is able to do a man's work and has a man's knowledge. Actually, most puberty ceremonies include tests of the boy's learning and fortitude, and if the aspirants are unable to pass these they are left in the child status until they can. For those who pass the tests, the ceremonies usually culminate in the transfer to them of certain secrets which the men guard from women and children.

The passage of individuals from adult to aged is harder to perceive. There is no clear physiological line for men, while even women may retain their full physical vigor and their ability to carry on all the activities of the adult status for several years after the menopause. The social transfer of men from the adult to the aged group is given ceremonial recognition in a few cultures, as when a father formally surrenders his official position and titles to his son, but such recognition is rare. As for women, there appears to be no society in which the menopause is given ceremonial recognition, although there are a few societies in which it does alter the individual's status. Thus Comanche women, after the menopause, were released from their disabilities with regard to the supernatural. They could handle sacred objects, obtain power through dreams and practise as shamans, all things forbidden to women of bearing age.

The general tendency for societies to emphasize the individual's first change in age status and largely ignore the second is no doubt due in part to the difficulty of determining the onset of old age. However, there are also psychological factors involved. The boy or girl is usually anxious to grow up, and this eagerness is heightened by the exclusion of children from certain activities and knowledge. Also, society welcomes new additions to the most active division of the group, that which contributes most to its perpetuation and well-being. Conversely, the individual who enjoys the thought of growing old is atypical in all societies. Even when age brings respect and a new measure of influence, it means the relinquishment of much that is pleasant. We can see among ourselves that the aging usually refuse to recognize the change until long after it has happened.

In the case of age, as in that of sex, the biological factors involved appear to be secondary to the cultural ones in determining the content of status. There are certain activities which cannot be ascribed to children because children either lack the necessary strength or have not had time to acquire the necessary technical skills. However, the attitudes between parent and child and the importance given to the child in the family structure vary enormously from one culture to another. The status of the child among our Puritan ancestors, where he was seen and not heard and ate at the second table, represents one extreme. At the other might be placed the status of the eldest son of a Polynesian chief. All the *mana* (supernatural power) of the royal line converged upon such a child. He was socially superior to his own father and mother, and any attempt to discipline him would have been little short of sacrilege. I once visited the hereditary chief of a Marquesan tribe and found the whole family camping uncomfortably in their own front yard, although they had a good house built on European lines. The eldest son, aged nine, had had a dispute with his father a few days before and had tabooed the house by naming it after his head. The family had thus been compelled to move out and could not use it again until he relented and lifted the taboo. As he could use the house himself and eat anywhere in the village, he was getting along quite well and seemed to enjoy the situation thoroughly.

The statuses ascribed to the old in various societies vary even more than those ascribed to children. In some cases they are relieved of all heavy labor and can settle back comfortably to live off their children. In others they perform most of the hard and monotonous tasks which do not require great physical strength, such as the gathering of firewood. In many societies the old women, in particular, take over most of the care of the younger children, leaving the younger women free to enjoy themselves. In some places the old are treated with consideration and respect; in others they are considered a useless incumbrance and removed as soon as they are incapable of heavy labor. In most societies their advice is sought even when little attention is paid to their wishes. This custom has a sound practical basis, for the individual who contrives to live to old age in an uncivilized group has usually been a person of ability and his memory constitutes a sort of reference library to which one can turn for help under all sorts of circumstances.

In certain societies the change from the adult to the old status is made more difficult for the individual by the fact that the patterns for these statuses ascribe different types of personality to each. This was the case among the Comanche, as it seems to have been among most of the Plains tribes. The adult male was a warrior, vigorous, self-reliant, and pushing. Most of his social relationships were phrased in terms of competition. He took what he could get and held what he had without regard to any abstract rights of those weaker than himself. Any willingness to arbitrate differences or to ignore slights was a sign of weakness resulting in loss of prestige. The old man, on the other hand, was expected to be wise and gentle, willing to overlook slights and, if need be, to endure abuse. It was his task to work for the welfare of the tribe, giving sound advice, settling feuds between the warriors, and even preventing his tribe from making new enemies. Young men strove for war and honor, old men strove for peace and tranquillity. There is abundant evidence that among the Comanche the transition was often a difficult one for the individual. Warriors did not prepare for old age, thinking it a better fate to be killed in action. When waning physical powers forced them to assume the new role, many of them did so grudgingly, and those who had strong magic could go on trying to enforce the rights which belonged to the younger status. Such bad old men were a peril to young ones beginning their careers, for they were jealous of them simply because they were young and strong and admired by the women. The medicine power of these young men was still weak, and the old men could and did kill them by malevolent magic. It is significant that although benevolent medicine men might be of any age in Comanche folklore, malevolent ones were always old.

Before passing on, it might be well to mention still another social status which is closely related to the foregoing. This is the status of the dead. We do not think of the dead as still members of the community, and many societies follow us in this, but there are others in which death is simply another transfer, comparable to that from child to adult. When a man dies, he does not leave his society; he merely surrenders one set of rights and duties and assumes another. Thus a Tanala clan has two sections which are equally real to its members, the living and the dead. In spite of rather half-hearted attempts by the living to explain to the dead that they are dead and to discourage their return, they remain an integral part of the clan. They must be informed of all important events, invited to all clan ceremonies, and remembered at every meal. In return they allow themselves to be consulted, take an active and helpful interest in the affairs of the community, and act as highly efficient guardians of the group's mores. They carry over into their new status the conservatism characteristic of the aged, and their invisible presence and constant watchfulness does more than anything else to ensure the good behavior of the living and to discourage innovations. In a neighboring tribe there are even individual statuses among the dead which are open to achievement. Old Betsileo men and women will often promise that, after their deaths, they will give the living specific forms of help in return for specified offerings. After the death of one of these individuals, a monument will be erected and people will come to pray and make offerings there. If the new ghost performs his functions successfully, his worship may grow into a cult and may even have a priest. If he fails in their performance, he is soon forgotten.

Biological relationships are used to determine some statuses in all societies. The mere fact of birth immediately brings the individual within the scope of a whole series of social patterns which relate him to his parents, either real or ascribed, his brothers and sisters, and his parents' relatives. The biological basis for the ascription of these family statuses is likely to blind us to the fact that the physiological factors which may influence their content are almost exactly the same as those affecting the content of sex and age statuses. While there is a special relationship between the young child and its mother, based on the child's dependence on nursing, even this is soon broken off. After the second year any adult woman can do anything for the child that its mother can do, while any adult male can assume the complete role of the father at any time after the child is conceived. Similarly, the physiological factors which might affect the statuses of uncle and nephew, uncle and neice, or brother and sister are identical with those affecting the relations of persons in different age or sex groupings. This lack of physiological determinants may be responsible in part for the extraordinarily wide range of variation in the contents of the statuses ascribed on the basis of biological relationships in various societies . . .

The bulk of the ascribed statuses in all social systems are parceled out to individuals on the basis of sex, age, and family relationships. However, there are many societies in which purely social factors are also used as a basis of ascription. There seems to be a general tendency for societies to divide their component individuals into a series of groups or categories and to ascribe to such categories differing degrees of social importance. Such divisions may originate in many different ways. They may grow out of individual differences in technical skill or other abilities, as in the case of craft groups or the aristocracies of certain Indian tribes, membership in which was determined by the individual's war record. They may also originate through the conscious formation of some social unit, such as the first college fraternity or the first business men's club, which is usually followed by the formation of a series of similar units organized upon nearly the same lines. Lastly, such divisions may originate through the subjugation of one society by another society, with the subsequent fusion of both into a single functional unit, as in the case of Old World aristocracies deriving from conquest. Even when the social divisions originate in individual differences of ability, there seems to be a strong tendency for such divisions to become hereditary. The members of a socially favored division try to transmit the advantages they have gained to their offspring and at the same time to prevent the entry into the division of individuals from lower divisions. In many cases these tendencies result in the organization of the society into a series of hereditary classes or castes. Such hereditary units are always used as reference points for the ascription of status.

The factor of social class or caste rarely if ever replaces the factors of sex, age, and biological relationship in the determination of status. Rather, it supplements these, defining the roles of individuals still more clearly. Where the class system is strong, each class becomes almost a society in itself. It will have a series of sex, age, and relationship statuses which are peculiar to its members. These will differ from the statuses of other classes even when both are determined by the same biological factors. Not only is the commoner debarred from the occupation of aristocratic statuses, but the aristocrat is similarly debarred from the occupation of common statuses. It may be mentioned in passing that this arrangement is not always entirely to the advantage of the members of the upper class. During the nineteenth century the aristocratic prohibition against engaging in trade condemned many aristocrats to genteel poverty.

Feudal Europe offers an excellent example of the ascription of statuses on the basis of social class. A man born into the noble class could look forward to being a bachelor, in the technical sense of a boy beginning his training for knighthood, a squire, and lastly a knight and lord of a manor. The performance of the roles connected with the final status required a long and arduous training both in the use of arms and in administration. The woman born into the same class could also look forward to being lady of a manor, a task which entailed special knowledge and administrative ability fully on a par with that of her husband. A man born into the peasant class could look forward only to becoming a tiller of the soil. He would pass through no statuses corresponding to those of bachelor or squire, and although he might be trained to the use of weapons, these would be different weapons from those used by the knight. The woman born in this class could only look forward to becoming a simple housewife. and her necessary training for this status was limited to a knowledge of housekeeping and baby-tending. The third class in medieval society, the burghers, also had its own series of statuses, the boy looking forward to becoming first an apprentice and then a master training apprentices in turn. All these divergent, class-determined statuses were mutually interdependent, and all contributed to the successful functioning of medieval society. The noble provided protection and direction, the peasant provided food, and the burgher took care of trade and manufactures.

Ascribed statuses, whether assigned according to biological or to social factors, compose the bulk of all social systems. However, all these symptoms also include a varying number of statuses which are open to individual achievement. It seems as though many statuses of this type were primarily designed to serve as baits for socially acceptable behavior or as escapes for the individual. All societies rely mainly on their ascribed statuses to take care of the ordinary business of living. Most of the statuses which are thrown open to achievement do not touch this business very deeply. The honored ones are extremely satisfying to the individuals who achieve them, but many of them are no more vital to the ordinary functioning of the society than are honorary degrees or inclusions in 'Who's Who' among ourselves.

Most societies make only a grudging admission of the fact that a limited number of statuses do require special gifts for their successful performance. Since such gifts rarely manifest themselves in early childhood, these statuses are, of necessity, thrown open to competition. At the same time, the pattern of ascribing all vital statuses is so strong that all societies limit this competition with reference to sex, age, and social affiliations. Even in our own society, where the field open to individual achievement is theoretically unlimited, it is strictly limited in fact. No woman can become President of the United States. Neither could a Negro nor an Indian, although there is no formal rule on this point, while a Jew or even a Catholic entering the presidential race would be very seriously handicapped from the outset. Even with regard to achievable statuses which are of much less social importance and which perhaps, require more specific gifts, the same sort of limited competition is evident. It would be nearly if not quite impossible for either a woman or a Negro to become conductor of our best symphony orchestra, even if better able to perform the duties involved than anyone else in America. At the same time, no man could become president of the D.A.R., and it is doubtful whether any man, unless he adopted a feminine *nom de plume*, could even conduct a syndicated column on advice to the lovelorn, a field in which our society assumes, *a priori*, that women have greater skill.

These limitations upon the competition for achieved statuses no doubt entail a certain loss to society. Persons with special talents appear to be mutants and as such are likely to appear in either sex and in any social class. At the same time, the actual loss to societies through this failure to use their members' gifts to the full is probably a good deal less than persons reared in the American tradition would like to believe. Individual talent is too sporadic and too unpredictable to be allowed any important part in the organization of society. Social systems have to be built upon the potentialities of the average individual, the person who has no special gifts or disabilities. Such individuals can be trained to occupy almost any status and to perform the associated role adequately if not brilliantly. The social ascription of a particular status, with the intensive training that such ascription makes possible, is a guarantee that the role will be performed even if the performance is mediocre. If a society waited to have its statuses filled by individuals with special gifts, certain statuses might not be filled at all. The ascription of status sacrifices the possibility of having certain roles performed superlatively well to the certainty of having them performed passably well.

When a social system has achieved a good adjustment to the other sectors of the group's culture and, through these, to the group's environment, it can get along very well without utilizing special gifts. However, as soon as changes within the culture or in the external environment produce maladjustments, it has to recognize and utilize these gifts. The development of new social patterns calls for the individual qualities of thought and initiative, and the freer the rein given to these the more quickly new adjustments can be arrived at. For this reason, societies living under new or changing conditions are usually characterized by a wealth of achievable statuses and by very broad delimitations of the competition for them. Our own now extinct frontier offered an excellent example of this. Here the class lines of the European societies from which the frontier population had been drawn were completely discarded and individuals were given an unprecedented opportunity to find their place in the new society by their own abilities.

As social systems achieve adjustment to their settings, the social value of individual thought and initiative decreases. Thorough training of the component individuals becomes more necessary to the survival and successful functioning of society than the free expression of their individual abilities. Even leadership, which calls for marked ability under conditions of change, becomes largely a matter of routine activities. To ensure successful training, more and more statuses are transferred from the achieved to the ascribed group, and the competition for those which remain is more and more rigidly delimited. To put the same thing in different terms, individual opportunities decrease. There is not an absolute correlation between the degree of adjustment of a social system to its setting and the limitation of individual opportunity. Thus if the group attaches a high value to individual initiative and individual rights, certain statuses may be left open to competition when their ascription would result in greater social efficiency. However, well-adjusted societies are, in general, characterized by a high preponderance of ascribed over achieved statuses, and increasing perfection of adjustment usually goes hand in hand with increasing rigidity of the social system.   (pp. 113–23, 126–30)

We have seen in the previous chapter how the particular culture within which any inventor works directs and circumscribes his efforts and determines whether his inventions will be socially accepted. Because of this the number of successful inventions originating within the confines of any one linked society and culture is always small. If every human group had been left to climb upward by its own unaided efforts, progress would have been so slow that it is doubtful whether any society by now would have advanced beyond the level of the Old Stone Age. The comparatively rapid growth of human culture as a whole has been due to the ability of all societies to borrow elements from other cultures and to incorporate them in their own. This transfer of culture elements from one society to another is known as *diffusion*. It is a process by which mankind has been able to pool its inventive ability. By diffusion an invention which has been made and socially accepted at one point can be transmitted to an ever-widening group of cultures until, in the course of centuries, it may spread to practically the whole of mankind.

Diffusion has made a double contribution to the advance of mankind. It has stimulated the growth of culture as a whole and at the same time has enriched the content of individual cultures, bringing the societies which bore them forward and upward. It has helped to accelerate the evolution of culture as a whole by removing the necessity of every society to perfect every step in an inventive series for itself. Thus a basic invention which has been made at one point will ultimately be brought to the attention of a great number of inventors and its potentialities for use and improvement thoroughly explored. As more minds are put to work upon each problem the process of culture advance is accelerated. The rapidity of progress during the past century is certainly due in large part to the development of means for easy and rapid communication plus techniques for ensuring to the inventor the economic rewards of his labors. Patents have made secrecy unnecessary. They impose a temporary tax upon the use of inventions but make the idea available to all. Any invention which is made at the present time is promptly diffused over a wide area and becomes part of the store of knowledge available to hundreds of inventors. Prior to the development of the present conditions it took centuries for any new element of culture to diffuse over the same territory to which it is now extended in a few months or years.

The slow cultural advance of societies which are left to their own abilities is well illustrated by the conditions in isolated human groups. Perhaps the oustanding example is the Tasmanians. These people were cut off from the rest of mankind at least 20,000 years ago. When they reached their island they seem to have had a culture which, in its material development at least, corresponds roughly to that of Europe during the Middle Paleolithic. They were still in this stage when Europeans first visited them during the eighteenth century. During the long period of isolation they had no doubt made some minor advances and improvements, but their lack of outside contacts was reflected in a tremendous culture lag. To cite a much less extreme example, the culture of some of our own isolated mountain communities still corresponds in many respects to that of the pioneers of a century ago. The first settlers of these isolated regions brought this culture with them, and their unaided efforts have contributed little to it. In general, the more opportunities for borrowing any society has the more rapid its cultural advance will be.

The service of diffusion in enriching the content of individual cultures has been of the utmost importantce. There is probably no culture extant today which owes more than 10 per cent of its total elements to inventions made by members of its own society. Because we live in a period of rapid invention we are apt to think of our own culture as largely self-created, but the rôle which diffusion has played in its growth may be brought home to us if we consider the beginning of the average man's day. The locations listed in the following paragraphs refer only to the origin points of various culture elements, not to regions from which we now obtain materials or objects through trade.

Our solid American citizen awakes in a bed built on a pattern which originated in the Near East but which was modified in Northern Europe before it was transmitted to America. He throws back covers made from cotton, domesticated in India, or linen, domesticated in the Near East, or wool from sheep, also domesticated in the Near East, or silk, the use of which was discovered in China. All of these materials have been spun and woven by processes invented in the Near East. He slips into his moccasins, invented by the Indians of the Eastern woodlands, and goes to the bathroom, whose fixtures are a mixture of European and American inventions, both of recent date. He takes off his pajamas, a garment invented in India, and washes with soap invented by the ancient Gauls. He then shaves, a masochistic rite which seems to have been derived from either Sumer or ancient Egypt.

Returning to the bedroom, he removes his clothes from a chair of southern European type and proceeds to dress. He puts on garments whose form originally derived from the skin clothing of the nomads of the Asiatic steppes, puts on his shoes made from skins tanned by a process invented in ancient Egypt and cut to a pattern derived from the classical civilizations of the Mediterranean, and ties around his neck a strip of bright-colored cloth which is a vestigial survival of the shoulder shawls worn by the seventeenth-century Croatians. Before

497

going out for breakfast he glances through the window, made of glass invented in Egypt, and if it is raining puts on overshoes made of rubber discovered by the Central American Indians and takes an umbrella, invented in southeastern Asia. Upon his head he puts a hat made of felt, a material invented in the Asiatic steppes.

On his way to breakfast he stops to buy a paper, paying for it with coins, an ancient Lydian invention. At the restaurant a whole new series of borrowed elements confronts him. His plate is made of a form of pottery invented in China. His knife is of steel, an alloy first made in southern India, his fork a medieval Italian invention, and his spoon a derivative of a Roman origin. He begins breakfast with an orange, from the eastern Mediterranean, a cantaloupe from Persia, or perhaps a piece of African watermelon. With this he has coffee, an Abyssinian plant, with cream and sugar. Both the domestication of cows and the idea of milking them originated in the Near East, while sugar was first made in India. After his fruit and first coffee he goes on to waffles, cakes made by a Scandinavian technique from wheat domesticated in Asia Minor. Over these he pours maple syrup, invented by the Indians of the Eastern woodlands. As a side dish he may have the egg of a species of bird domesticated in Indo-China, or thin strips of the flesh of an animal domesticated in Eastern Asia which have been salted and smoked by a process developed in northern Europe.

When our friend has finished eating he settles back to smoke, an American Indian habit, consuming a plant domesticated in Brazil in either a pipe, derived from the Indians of Virginia, or a cigarette, derived from Mexico. If he is hardy enough he may even attempt a cigar, transmitted to us from the Antilles by way of Spain. While smoking he reads the news of the day, imprinted in characters invented by the ancient Semites upon a material invented in China by a process invented in Germany. As he absorbs the accounts of foreign troubles he will, if he is a good conservative citizen, thank a Hebrew deity in an Indo-European language that he is 100 per cent American.

The foregoing is merely a bit of antiquarian virtuosity made possible by the existence of unusually complete historic records for the Eurasiatic area. There are many other regions for which no such records exist, yet the cultures in these areas bear similar witness to the importance of diffusion in establishing their content. Fairly adequate techniques have been developed for tracing the spread of individual traits and even for establishing their origin points and there can be no doubt that diffusion has occurred wherever two societies and cultures have been brought into contact.

In view of the tremendous importance of this mechanism for

the enrichment of culture, it is rather surprising that so little is still known about the actual dynamics of the diffusion process. Most of the students who have been interested in this field have considered the study of diffusion little more than a preliminary to historic reconstruction. They have spent much time and effort in tracing the distribution of culture elements, but have been content with the formulation of two or three basic principles of diffusion which were immediately applicable to their historic studies. Such studies are by no means the mere satisfactions of idle curiosity which some of their opponents would have them to be. The content of a culture at any point in its history can only be explained in terms of its past and any light which can be thrown upon that past contributes to our understanding of the present. Even the study of the functions of the various elements within a culture becomes largely meaningless unless we can determine the factors to which these elements owe their form and consequently their potentialities for function. This matter will be discussed at length in a later chapter. For the present we need only point out that the more exact our knowledge of the dynamics of the diffusion process the greater will be the possiblity of making valid historic reconstructions from trait distributions.

A real understanding of the dynamics of diffusion can be arrived at only by observing the process in actual operation. A thorough study of the current spread of any new culture element, the factors responsible for this spread, the reactions which the new element has evoked in different societies, and the adaptations which the acceptance of the new trait into various cultures has entailed would do more to put diffusion studies on a sound basis than twenty studies of trait distributions at a given point in time. Unfortunately there is hardly a single study of this sort extant. In the discussion which follows we must, therefore, raise far more questions than we can answer. Nevertheless, there are a few generally recognized principles of diffusion, and we may begin our investigation with these.

The first of these is that, *other things being equal, elements of culture will be taken up first by societies which are close to their points of origin and later by societies which are more remote or which have less direct contacts.* This principle derives from the fact that the diffusion of any element obviously requires both contact and time. It is impossible for any trait to spread to a culture unless there is contact with some other culture which already has it. Thus if we have three tribes, A, B, and C, with the territory of B intervening between that of A and C and preventing any direct contact between them, no new culture trait which A may develop can reach C until after it has been accepted by B. From this it also follows that the trait will be received later by C than by B.

There is abundant historic evidence of the general validity of this principle. Thus the alphabet, which seems to have been invented in the general region of the Sinai peninsula, was taken up first by the Semitic groups which immediately adjoined this area and transmitted by them to the Phoenicians. These carried it by sea to the Greeks and Romans, from whom it was diffused into northern Europe. It did not appear in Scandinavia until about 2,000 years after its invention and reached this region by way of a series of intermediary cultures each of which had had certain effects on the alphabet's development.

From this principle of the diffusion of traits to more and more remote localities a second principle emerges, that of *marginal survivals*. Let us suppose that a new appliance has been developed by a particular society and is spreading to the neighboring societies in an ever-widening circle. At the same time it may very well be undergoing changes and improvements at its point of origin. These improvements will, in turn, be diffused to the neighboring societies, but since this diffusion will begin at a later point in time, the improved appliance will have a tendency to lag behind the original one in its spread. Long after the new appliance has completely supplanted the ancestral one at its point of origin, the ancestral one will continue in use about the margins of the diffusion area. This principle may be illustrated by the present distribution of telephone types in the United States. The earliest telephones had cranks for calling central. At the present time the crank telephone is still used in the more remote rural districts but has completely disappeared in the cities. The desk type of telephone, with automatic call, is used over an intermediate zone, while the hand telephone, first used in New York in 1927, is still largely confined to city use. Lastly, dial telephones are making rapid headway in the larger cities, but are only beginning to spread to the smaller ones and have not reached any rural districts. The example may not be considered a perfect one, since the diffusion of the telephone has obviously been influenced by such atypical factors as the monopoly of telephone service and desire of the company to use old equipment already in existence, but it does serve to illustrate the principle.

The simile most commonly applied to the diffusion process is that of the ripples sent out by dropping a stone into still water. The last ripples will still be moving outward when the center has once more become quiet. While such a constant and uniform spread of traits from a single center in order of their development may be used as a hypothetical case to illustrate the principle, actual historic records show that it never occurs in fact. Even traits which originate in the same center spread irregularly and travel at different spreads. A few examples will make this clear.

Everything indicates that the cultivation of maize in America was a culture trait which originated in Mexico. From there it spread widely over the Mississippi Valley and eastern United States and also took firm root in the Southwest. While in the East it reached New England, the Dakotas and the peninsula of Michigan, in the West it barely penetrated southern California. This in spite of the fact that this region was in fairly close touch with the Southwest, where maize culture was highly developed and where there were adequate techniques for growing the crop under semi-arid conditions. Again, the California Indians, outside a small area in the south, failed to take over pottery although they were close to an area of high pottery development and although the rather sedentary life of most California tribes would have given it great utility. Our present fairly accurate knowledge of Southwestern time sequences proves that tribes on the margin of the California area must have been exposed to both maize and pottery for at least 1,500 years, yet they failed to accept either.

Such reluctance to accept new elements of culture slows down their rate of speed even when it does not completely inhibit their diffusion in certain directions. A group which is reluctant to take over a new trait interposes a bar between the origin point of that trait and more remote groups which might be quite willing to accept it if given the opportunity. Even if the reluctance of the intermediary culture is finally broken down, much time will have been lost. Because of this varying coefficient of receptivity, traits always spread from their origin points irregularly and certain traits may be diffused with amazing speed while others diffuse slowly, if at all. One of the most striking examples of extremely rapid diffusion is that afforded by the spread of certain New World food crops, especially maize, during the first 300 years following Columbus's discovery. By the end of this period these crops had penetrated practically all areas of Europe, Asia, and Africa in which they could be raised and in many places had profoundly altered the patterns of native life. Thus the Betsimisaraka of Madagascar, who could scarcely have received maize before 1600, have a myth that it was given to them by the Creator at the same time that he gave rice to the Plateau tribes of the island. They meet any suggestion that it might be a fairly recent introduction by the simple statement that it cannot be, since the people could not live without it.

The spread of tobacco after the discovery of the New World is a still more striking example of rapid diffusion and has the advantage of being well documented. For once, popular traditions seem to be correct in their ascription of the introduction of smoking into England to Sir Walter Raleigh. At least the first mention of it there is in connection with the return of his Virginia colonists, and we know that Ralph Lane, the first governor, presented Raleigh with an Indian pipe in 1586 and instructed him in its use. This launched the custom of smoking in court circles, and from there it spread to the common people with amazing speed. It should be noticed that tobacco had also been introduced into Spain by Francisco Fernandez in 1558, but it came in the guise of a medicine and there was considerable delay in its acceptance for purely social purposes.

These two points of introduction became, in turn, centers for the diffusion of tobacco over the Old World. England was the main donor to northern Eurupe. Smoking was introduced into Holland in 1590 by English medical students, and the English and Dutch together spread the new habit by sea into the Baltic countries and Scandinavia and overland through Germany into Russia. By 1634, forty-eight years after its first appearance in northern Europe, it had become a nuisance in Russia and laws were enacted against it. Nevertheless its spread eastward continued unchecked, and within 200 years it had crossed the steppes and mountains of Siberia and was reintroduced into America at Alaska. This rapid diffusion is the more remarkable since in much of this northern region the plant had to be obtained by trade over great distances.

From Spain and Portugal tobacco was diffused throughout the Mediterranean countries and into the near East. The dates here are less certain, but Sultan Murad of Turkey passed laws against its use in 1605. The Dutch and Portuguese together carried it to Africa and southeastern Asia. In far-off Japan it was accepted so quickly that by 1605 it was found necessary to limit the amount of ground which could be devoted to its cultivation. In South Africa tobacco became the regular medium of exchange between the Dutch and the natives, a cow being valued at its over-all length in tobacco leaves. In spite of frequent official opposition and drastic laws, the new element of culture spread almost as fast as men could travel.

It has been observed that while elements of culture may be diffused alone they are more likely to travel in groups of elements which are functionally related. This point is also illustrated by the spread of tobacco, since with the plant there were diffused various methods of using it. The linking of these methods with the various lines of diffusion can be traced back even to the New World. The Indians used tobacco in different ways in different regions. Those of the eastern coast of North America smoked it in elbow pipes, which became the prototypes of the modern English briars. Although this form of pipe underwent various modifications along the northern route of diffusion, all the people who derived their tobacco habit by way of England have remained predominant pipe-smokers. The Indians of Brazil, with whom the Portuguese had most contact, preferred cigars, as did some of the Antillean groups. The Mexicans, on the other hand, preferred the cigarette and gave it to the Spaniards. From them it passed to the other Mediterranean cultures, a fact reflected in our own preference for Turkish and Egyptian cigarettes. Since the Portuguese and Dutch acted simultaneously in the diffusion of tobacco to southeastern Asia, that region received both the pipe and the cigar, and the two still exist side by side there in many localities. Some tribes even preserve complete neutrality by rolling their tobacco into cigars and then smoking these in pipes. In Africa, where the Dutch won in the struggle against the Portuguese, the pipe became the regular appliance.

In the course of its diffusion tobacco even developed two new methods of use, the water-pipe and snuff. The water-pipe originated in the Near East and never diffused far beyond that region. Snuff seems to have originated in Spain and grew out of the medicinal application of tobacco. It had no prototype in America. Some of the Antillean and South American tribes did use snuff, but it was not made from tobacco. On the other hand snuffs of one sort or another had been used in Europe for centuries. Apparently this was a result of a mistaken attempt to reach the brain through the nasal passages. The first tobacco sent from Portugal to France was in the form of snuff, and the habit to taking tobacco in this way became established at the French court and spread from there to the whole of European polite society. In fact, it seems for a time to have threatened the existence of smoking in higher social circles. Toward the close of the eighteenth century the high tide of snuff began to recede, and it now survives only in marginal areas and even there is at a social disadvantage.

The last chapter in the diffusion of methods of smoking is curious enough to deserve special mention. The cigarette, in spite of its general acceptance in the Mediterranean area, did not spread to northern Europe or the United States until very recent times. It was not introduced into England until after the close of the Crimean War, when the custom of cigarette smoking was brought back by officers who had learned it from their Turkish allies. It reached the United States still later, within the memory of many persons now alive, and there encountered vigorous opposition. Although there seems to be no proof that the cigarette is any more harmful than the virile corn-cob or the chewing tobacco which was the American pioneer's special contribution to the tobacco complex, laws against its use are still to be found on many statute books. It was considered not only harmful but also effeminate, and traces of the latter attitude survive even to-day. He-men who enjoy their cigarette can console themselves with the knowledge that many a 'hard-boiled' Aztec priest must have indulged in one before beginning his 'daily dozen' of human sacrifices.

It should be plain from the foregoing that no simple mechanistic interpretation of diffusion will prove adequate to the needs of even the rather limited field of historic reconstruction. Diffusion required not only a donor but also a receiver, and the rôle of this receiver is certainly the more important. As we have seen in the case of the California Indians with regard to maize and pottery, exposure to a culture trait is not necessarily followed by acceptance. Diffusion really includes three fairly distinct processes: presentation of the new culture element or elements to the society, acceptance by the society, and the integration of the accepted element or elements into the preëxisting culture. Each of these is influenced by a large number of variable factors most of which still require study.

The presentation of new elements to a society always presupposes contact. The society with which this contact is established may, of course, be either the originator of the new culture element or simply an intermediary in its spread. This factor can have little influence on the process. However, the nature of the contact is of tremendous importance. Such contacts vary from those in which two societies and cultures are brought into a close relationship as wholes to sporadic trade contacts of those in which a single individual from one society settles in another society. Complete contacts are decidedly rare. It is difficult to find examples of them except in the case of conquering groups who settle among and exploit the conquered or in that of immigrant groups such as we still have in many parts of America. Such contacts have a somewhat different quality from those involved in the ordinary diffusion process, and the process of culture change under these conditions is usually termed *acculturation*. Apparently the use of this term, which was first applied to the study of changes in immigrant groups, is based on the rather naïve belief that one of the societies thus brought into contact completely abandons its former culture and completely accepts that of the others. Actually such close and complete contacts always result in an exchange of culture elements. In the long run both the originally diverse societies and their cultures will fuse to form a new society and culture. In this final product elements from both will be represented, although they may be represented in widely varying proportions. Thus the Italians in America usually lose their identity as a distinct society by the third or fourth generation and accept the culture in which they then find themselves. At the same time this culture is not the same which their ancestors encountered on arrival. It has been enriched by the American acceptance of such originally Italian elements as a popular interest in grand opera, spaghetti dinners, and superior techniques for racketeering.

Taking the world as a whole, the type of contact which makes acculturation possible is more likely to arise through conquest and the settlement of the conquering groups among the vanquished than through anything else. In such cases the normal numerical superiority of the conquered is likely to be balanced to a considerable extent by the superior prestige of the conquerors, so that the two cultures stand on fairly equal terms in their contribution to the new culture which always arises under such conditions. Such hybrid cultures usually present the aspects of a chemical rather than a mechanical mixture. In addition to traits drawn from both the parent cultures they possess qualities foreign to both. However, we must return to the more normal forms of culture contact and the dissemination of culture elements which these make possible.

It goes without saying that contacts between cultures can only be established through the medium of individuals. We have pointed out in a previous chapter that no individual participates completely in the culture of his own society. This means that under ordinary conditions the full culture of the donor society is never offered to the receiving society. The only elements made available to them are those with which the contact individuals are familiar. Thus if a trade relation exists between two tribes, the trade being carried on by men, the product of the women's industries in one tribe may become familiar to the other tribe, but the techniques will not be transmitted with it. The men who do the trading, even if they do not guard these techniques as valuable commercial secrets, will have only a vague idea of how the things are made. If the receiving tribe becomes accustomed to the use of this product and then finds the supply suddenly cut off, it may develop quite different techniques for the manufacture of equivalent articles. It is interesting to conjecture whether the extreme diversity of techniques of pottery manufacture in the Melanesian region may not have arisen in this way. There are many tribes here who regularly use pottery without manufacturing it, and it is easy to imagine the members of such a group working out a method of making the familiar and necessary pots if their normal source was removed.

The differential which is introduced into diffusion by this varying participation of individuals in their own culture is just as strongly operative when the contact-individuals from the donor group settle among the receiving group. The trader, missionary, or government official can transmit no more of his culture than he himself knows. If the contact-individual is a male, he usually can transmit very little from the female half of his own culture, and the female elements which he can transmit are likely to be heterogeneous and to bear little functional relation to each other. I knew a French official who was the envy of all his colleagues because he had been able to teach his native mistress how to starch and iron his white shirts. His knowledge of this technique had been acquired by accident, and he knew no more about other aspects of housekeeping than the average male. Conversely, if the contact-individual is a female she can transmit female techniques but is most unlikely to pass on such purely masculine items as a new form of metal-working or a new war magic. It is easy to imagine situations in which, due to this contact differential, many elements from certain sections of a culture will have been presented and even accepted while few or none have been presented from other sections. Thus the natives on an island which has been a regular port of call for whaling vessels may have absorbed a good many of the cultural elements connected with the industry and even a fair number of the habits and attitudes of whalemen. They may learn to build whaleboats and dress in European garments gotten from the whalers, while they still have no idea that drawing-rooms exist, still less of the behavior appropriate to them. To cite a less extreme case, a native group might have had close contact with half a dozen missionaries and their wives without receiving any inkling of the evolutionary theories which now influence so much of European thought or of modern European trends in dress and interior decoration.

When two societies are in long-continued contact, as in the case of two tribes who live side by side and are generally on friendly terms, sooner or later the entire culture of each will be made available to the other. The long series of contacts with individuals, each of whom is a partial participant, will have a cumulative effect. When, on the other hand, the contacts of one society are exclusively with selected groups of individuals from the other society, the receiving group may never be exposed to the totality of the donor group's culture. This situation holds true to a very large extent for regions to which whites come as traders or administrators, but never as artisans or laborers.

A second factor which exercises a strong influence upon diffusion is what, for lack of a better term, may be called the inherent communicability of the culture elements themselves. This has nothing to do with the attitudes of the receiving group or with its preëxisting culture configurations. Although this aspect of the diffusion problem has never been studied, it seems probable that we are dealing here with something which is fairly constant. In a previous chapter we have pointed out that culture is itself a socio-psychological phenomenon and that the various forms of behavior which we are able to observe and record are simply its overt expressions. Certain elements of culture can be much more readily expressed than others, whether this expression takes the form of ordinary acts or verbalizations. Since it is only through the observation of these overt expressions that culture elements can be transmitted from one individual to another or from one society to another, it follows that those cultural elements which can be most readily and completely expressed will be those which are the most readily available for acceptance. Among the varied elements which go to make up the totality of a culture, the techniques for food-getting and manufacturing take precedence in this respect. These can be made clear to a bystander without the medium of speech. If he wishes to acquire such techniques, all he has to do is to imitate the worker's movements carefully and exactly. Although he may lack the proper muscular control at first, this can be acquired through practice. The same holds for manufactured objects. Even when the techniques have not been observed, the members of the receiving culture can fix the details of the object firmly in their memory and proceed to reproduce it at leisure The tendency which the Japanese still show to study and reproduce imported objects would be a case in point.

As soon as we pass from such simple culture elements as techniques and their material products, we encounter increasing difficulties in communication. Although it is quite possible to describe such an element of culture as the ideal pattern for marriage and even to express it in non-verbal behavior, this expression is much less complete than that which is possible with regard to such a culture element as basket-making. The most thorough verbalization has difficulty in conveying the series of associations and conditioned emotional responses which are attached to this pattern and which give it meaning and vitality within our own culture configuration. In all our overt expressions of such a pattern these things are taken for granted, but the individual to whom we are attempting to convey a sense of the pattern can know nothing of them. Even when language difference has ceased to be a serious barrier to the conveyance of such patterns, it is extremely difficult to put them across. This is even more true of those concepts which, while a part of culture, find no direct expression in behavior aside from verbalizations. There is a story of an educated Japanese who was trying to understand the nature of the Trinity and after a long discussion with a European friend burst out with: 'Oh, I see now. It is a committee.' Such a remark gives a shock to any good Christian. The Trinity certainly is not a committee, but it may bring the point home to the reader if he pictures himself as trying to explain to this Japanese student just how and why he was in error.

Lastly, we have in all cultures those vital attitudes and values which lie largely below the level of individual consciousness and which the average member of a society rarely tries to verbalize even to himself. The practical impossibility of making such elements available for borrowing by the members of some other society is obvious. This part of any culture simply is not susceptible to diffusion. It can never be presented in sufficiently concrete and objective terms. Such things as religions or philosophical concepts can be communicated after a fashion, although probably never in their entirety. Patterns of social behavior can also be transmitted in the same uncertain way, but the associations which give them genuine potentialities for function cannot be transmitted. A borrowing group may imitate their outward forms, but it will usually be found that it has introduced new elements to replace those which could not be genuinely communicated to it. The institution of marriage as it exists among our own Southern Negroes would be a good example of such incomplete transmission of a pattern and its consequent modifications. As a matter of fact, the material techniques and their products are probably the only elements of culture which can be completely communicated, and it is significant that it is usually these elements which are accepted most readily and retained in most nearly their received form. It is obvious that such inherent differences in communicability must be of tremendous importance in diffusion, especially through their influence upon completeness of transmission and rate of transmission.

Our discussion hitherto has dealt with donor cultures and the qualities of culture elements. Let us turn now to what is the real core of the problem of diffusion, the reaction of the accepting group to the elements presented to it. In its acceptance or rejection of these elements a society exercises free will. There may be a few exceptions to this in cases in which a socially dominant group seeks to impose its culture forcibly upon a subject society, but these are less important than they might appear. In the first place, such a dominant group rarely, if ever, attempts to impose its culture as a whole. It is content with the imposition of a few selected elements, such as outward adherence to its religion or the custom of wearing trousers. Obviously no amount of force can introduce into another culture any element which is not constantly and directly reflected in overt behavior. The conquered can be forced to attend church regularly, and it may even become a habit with them, something which produces no emotional response, but they cannot be forced to accept the new faith emotionally or be prevented from praying to their own gods alone and in private. At the same time the very use of force makes the proscribed elements of the native culture symbols of revolt, and this inspires a stronger attachment to them. Under a veil of superficial compliance a persecuted group can maintain its own ideals and values intact for generations, modifying and reinterpreting the superficial elements of culture which are forced upon it in such a way that they will do these no violence.

With very few exceptions, therefore, every new element which a society incorporates into its culture, it accepts of its own free will. This acceptance, in turn, is controlled by a large number of variable factors. The only constant in the situation is that such elements are always taken at their face value. A society can apprehend only those parts of a total complex which can be communicated to it plainly and directly. Thus a woman from one tribe who copies the design which she has seen on a basket made by some other tribe does so simply because its esthetic qualities appeal to her. She knows nothing of the symbolism which may surround this design or of what the original makers consider appropriate or inappropriate uses for it. Similarly when a new appliance, say a rifle, is presented to any group, they accept or reject it not on the basis of its associations and functions in the donor culture but on the potentialities for use which they perceive for it in their own. This perception never extends beyond the limits of immediate utility. There is no perception of the modifications in preëxisting patterns which the adoption of the new element will entail. In fact it is doubtful whether any mind is ever able to foresee any but the most immediate of these. Even in our own culture no one could have foretold the profound changes which have come in the wake of the acceptance of the automobile, changes which have affected our social patterns even more deeply than they have affected our economic ones.

The factors which control the receptivity of a society toward any new element of culture are, after all, very much the same whether this element originates inside or outside of their culture, i.e., whether it comes to them through invention or through diffusion. The main difference between these two processes lies in the fact that, if society rejects an invention, that addition to the sum total of culture is permanently lost, while if it rejects an element presented by diffusion this element is not lost but remains in the hands of the donor culture and may crop up at a later time when the society's reaction to it may be quite different.

New traits are accepted primarily on the basis of two qualities, utility and compatibility: in other words, on the basis of what they appear to be good for and how easily they can be fitted into the existing culture configuration. Both these qualities are, of course, relative to the receiving culture and are influenced by such a long series of factors that an outsider can hardly ascertain all of them. We have mentioned elsewhere that culture change is mainly a matter of the replacement of old elements by new ones and that every culture normally includes adequate techniques for meeting all the conscious needs of the society's members. When a new trait presents itself its acceptance depends not so much on whether it is better than the existing one as on whether it is enough better to make its acceptance worth the trouble. This in turn must depend upon the judgment of the group, their degree of conservatism, and how much change in existing habits the new appliance will entail. Even in the simplest form of diffusion, that of mechanical appliances, superiority cannot be judged simply in terms of increased output. There are pleasant and unpleasant forms of work, and even such a simple change as that from the use of adzes to axes for tree-felling entails a change in muscular habits which is unpleasant for the time being. In many parts of Oceania the natives have been receptive to European plane irons, which they could haft and use like their original stone adzes, but have refused to accept the vastly more efficient axe simply because they did not like to work with it.

Very much the same situation holds with regard to the problem of compatibility. The acceptance of any new culture element entails certain changes in the total culture configuration. Although the full extent of these changes can never be forecast, certain of them are usually obvious. If the new trait is of such a sort that its acceptance will conflict directly with important traits already present in the culture, it is almost certain to be rejected. One cannot conceive of techniques of mass production being accepted by a culture which had a pattern of uniqueness. There actually are societies which believe that no two objects should ever be the same and never make any two things exactly alike.

One very good example of such a conflict is afforded by the reactions of the Apache to peyote, a narcotic cactus used by many Indian tribes to induce visions and through these to put the individual in close touch with the supernatural. The Apache attach as much importance to visions as any other tribe, but each individual hoards the power which comes to him through his supernatural experiences, and such power can be stolen by other medicine men. The regular pattern of peyote use is that of eating it in a group ceremonial. After a tentative and partial acceptance of the new idea the Apache rejected it. The opportunities for stealing power which contact in the assembly would provide, especially if an individual were under the influence of the drug and thus off guard, were too dangerous. It was felt that a man was likely to lose more power than he could gain. As a result, the use of peyote in this tribe has become infrequent and even then is limited to men of no importance who have little power to lose.

Most conflicts between new elements and preëxisting elements are less direct and obvious. In the matter of compatibility as in that of utility there is a broad zone of uncertainty. There are new elements which may be recognized as slightly superior to existing ones and other elements which may be seen to be somewhat incompatible, but not enough so as to make their acceptance impossible. Very often the advantages and disadvantages are so evenly balanced that the acceptance of the new trait may seem desirable to certain members of the society and undesirable to others. The ultimate acceptance or rejection of elements which fall within this zone is controlled by still another series of variable factors about which we know very little. One of the most important of these is certainly the particular interests which dominate the life of the receiving group. A new trait which is in line with these interests will be given more serious consideration and has a better chance of adoption than one which is not. A slight gain along the line of these interests is felt to be more important than a larger one in some other line in which the group takes little interest. Thus the Hindus have always been highly receptive to new cults and new philosophic ideas as long as these did not come into too direct conflict with their existing patterns, but have shown an almost complete indifference to improved techniques of manufacture. The material world was felt to be of so little importance that minor advances in its control were not considered worth the trouble of changing established habits.

There are other factors beside those of the receiving group's interests and evaluations which may help to weight the scales for or against a new element of culture. One of the most important of these is the prestige of the donor group. There are many different grades and kinds of prestige. Occasionally one encounters a society which seems to have a genuine inferiority complex with regard to some other and to consider everything which this admired society has superior to the corresponding elements in its own culture. Such a group will borrow almost anything from its model that it has an opportunity to borrow. An example of this would be the indiscriminate acceptance of elements of European culture by the Japanese during the latter half of the nineteenth century. Such an attitude usually ends either in thorough disillusionment or in the disappearance of the borrowing society as a distinct cultural entity.

Such a condition is unusual. Donor prestige is usually a much more limited type, referring only to certain aspects of culture. The average society believes in its general superiority to the rest of mankind, but at the same time admits that some other society or societies are superior in particular respects. Thus although Americans feel a certain condescension toward French culture as a whole, it has become almost an article of faith that the French are superior to us in the designing of women's wear. When an American woman is called upon to choose between a Paris model and a Chicago model, this feeling is strong enough to give the Paris model a distinct advantage. Conversely, a style which was advertised as originating in Germany would get less consideration than even the Chicago one, since we believe that dress-designing is not along the line of Germany's best efforts. In other words, Paris styles are aided in their American diffusion by French prestige, while Berlin styles are hampered in their American diffusion by a lack of prestige. Even in primitive society there are always neighboring tribes who are admired in certain respects and other tribes who are despised. Any trait which comes from the admired source will at least be given serious consideration, while one which comes from the despised source must be markedly advantageous to win acceptance.

A further factor which influences the acceptance of new culture elements is the prestige of the individuals under whose auspices the new thing is presented to the society. In diffusion as in invention, acceptance of a new trait begins with a single individual or at most a small group of individuals. It makes a great deal of difference who these innovators happen to be. If they are persons whom the society admires and is accustomed to imitate, the way for the general acceptance of the new trait is smoothed from the start. If the innovators happen to be personally unpopular or of low social status, the new element immediately acquires undesirable associations which may outweigh any intrinsic advantages. Thus in our own society no one would try to launch a new and daring style through the cheap dress shops. It would not take even in the social group which patronizes these shops, since the wearing of the new style would then be a mark of a social status about which its holders were not enthusiastic. The same style launched from the highest point in the social ladder which its designers could reach would be eagerly accepted by the cheap-shop patrons.

Lastly, there is the factor of what can only be termed 'faddism.' It is an observed fact that certain new elements of culture will be eagerly accepted by groups when there are no discernible reasons of either utility or prestige. Major elements are unlikely to be introduced into any culture in this way, but a whole series of minor ones may be. We ourselves have witnessed the arrival and departure of such items as the ankle watch, sunburn initials, etc. Moreover, such fads are by no means limited to effete civilizations. Primitive tribes also have their changes of fashion and their borrowing of intrinsically useless items of culture which happen to catch their fancy. Thus among the Bara of Madagascar the past twenty years have witnessed the introduction of fantastic haircuts among the men, while prior to this time there was a rather simple uniform mode of tribal hairdressing. The style is said to have owed its origin to an enterprising Imerina barber who settled in the Bara territory and sought an outlet for his professional gifts. The young men who accepted it were severely ridiculed at first, but once done it could not be undone and they thus had a strong incentive to make converts to the new idea. Beginning with no utility and a rather negative prestige, it has now become firmly established as a part of Bara culture.

All this will indicate the great number of variable factors which enter into both the presentation and the acceptance of new culture elements. Until we know more about the operation of these factors we can have only a very imperfect understanding of the diffusion process. The last step in this process, that of the changes and readjustments which inevitably follow the adoption of any new trait, will be treated in the next chapter. (pp. 324–46)

Talcott Parsons born 1902

Major works

The Structure of Social Action (1937)
Essays in Sociological Theory (1949)
The Social System (1951)
The Large Scale Society as a Social System (1964)
Sociological Theory and Modern Society (1969)
Co-author of:
Family, Socialization and Interaction Process (1955)
Co-editor of:
Toward a General Theory of Action (1951)

The following article, 'The Social Structure of the Family', is reprinted from *The Family: Its Function and Destiny*, revised edition, edited by Ruth Nanda Anshen (New York: Harper & Brothers, 1949), pp. 241–5, with the permission of Harper & Row, Publishers, Inc. Copyright © Harper & Row, Publishers, Inc., 1949; Ruth Nanda Anshen, 1959.

The scientific study of the social relationships of everyday life presents peculiar difficulties. We are continually living in and through them and hence do not find it easy to view them from the outside. The problem may be compared to grammar and the other aspects of language which interest the technical linguist. Every ordinary person speaks his native language reasonably correctly and without effort, without necessarily being even aware that those technical aspects exist. In the social field these considerations are pre-eminently applicable to the family, for no aspect of social life is more deeply imbedded in laters of sentiment and of motivation of which we are normally scarcely even aware. Hence the difficulty is often more a matter of the perspective in which the facts are seen than of their unfamiliarity or difficulty of ascertainment as such.

In attaining this perspective social science has been greatly aided by the comparative study of the structure and functioning of different societies. Seen in these terms the contemporary American family and kinship system is not simply the natural way to live but constitutes a highly exceptional mode of the patterning of relationships in this area.

It can perhaps be regarded as established that, with proper precautions, analysis of kinship terminology can serve as a highly useful approach to the study of the functioning social structure. In the case of the English language two precautions in particular, over and above those commonly observed, need to be explicitly mentioned; for such analysis alone cannot serve to bring out what is distinctly American because the terminology has been essentially stable since before the settlement of America, and today there is no significant terminological difference as between England and the United States. Moreover, the differences in this respect between English and the other modern European languages are minor. Hence all that an analysis of terminology can do is to indicate a very broad type within which the more distinctively American system falls.

As shown in the accompanying diagram [page 516][1] the American family is perhaps best characterized as an open, multilineal, conjugal system.

1. The diagramming conventions adopted in this chapter are somewhat different from those commonly used by anthropologists. They are imposed by the peculiar structural features of our system, especially

(a) Its openness, i.e., absence of preferential mating. Hence the two spouses of any given conjugal family are not structurally related by family of orientation and it is not possible to portray *the* system in terms of a limited number of lines of descent. Each marriage links 'ego's' kinship system to a complete system.

(b) The consequent indefinite dispersion of the lines of descent.

The conjugal family unit of parents and children is one of basic significance in any kinship system. What is distinctive about our system is the absence of any important terminologically recognized units which cut across conjugal families, including some members and excluding others. The only instances of such units are *pairs* of conjugal families each with *one* common member. Terminologically, in common speech, it is significant that we have only the words 'family,' which generally[2] refers to the conjugal unit, and 'relatives,' which refers not to *any* solitary unit at all but only to anyone who is a kinsman.

Ours then is a conjugal[3] system in that it is made up exclusively of interlocking conjugal families. The principle of the structural relation of these families is founded on the fact that, as a consequence of the incest taboo, 'ego' in the structurally normal[4] case is always a member not of one but of two conjugal families, those which Warner usefully distinguishes as the 'family of orientation,' into which he is born as a child, and the 'family of procreation,' which is founded by his marriage. Moreover, he is the *only* common member of the two families.

From ego's point of view, then, the core of the kinship system is constituted by families 1 and 2 in the diagram – in the one case his father, mother, brothers, and sisters; in the other his spouse (wife or husband according to ego's sex), sons, and daughters. Monogamy is reflected in the fact that parent and other parent's spouse are termin-

---

The best that can be done in two dimensions is to take ego as a point of reference and show his significant kin. It is strictly impossible to diagram the system as a whole – that would require a space of n-dimensions. Similarly, vertical and horizontal or lateral axes have only a very limited meaning. Lines of descent and generations are significant. But there is a geometrically progressive increase in the number of lines of descent with each generation away from ego, and the distinctions cannot be made in terms of a linear continuum. I am indebted to Miss Ai-li Sung of Radcliffe College for assistance in drafting the diagram.

2. The most important exception is its usage in upper-class circles to denote what Warner calls a 'lineage,' i.e., a group possessing continuity over several generations, usually following the 'name line,' e.g., the 'Adams family.' See W. L. Warner and P. S. Lunt, *Social Life of a Modern Community* (New Haven: Yale University Press, 1941). The significance of this exception will be commented upon below. [See especially pp. 517–20, *infra*. – ED.]

3. See Ralph Linton, *The Study of Man* (New York: D. Appleton-Century Company, 1936), chap. viii, for the very useful distinction between conjugal and consanguine kinship types.

4. Excluding, of course, those who do not marry. But failure to marry has no positive structural consequences in relation to kinship – only negative.

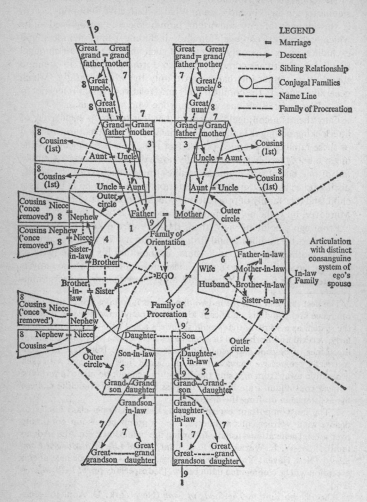

[Diagram of the American Family (see page 514).]

Types of Families:
1. Ego's family of orientation (1 only)
2. Ego's family of procreation (1 only)
3. First-degree ascendant families (2)
4. First-degree collateral families (number indefinite, 2 types)
5. First-degree descendant families (number indefinite, 2 types)
6. In-law family (1 only)
7. Second-degree ascendant and descendant families (4 ascendant, descendant indefinite, 4 types)
8. Second-degree collateral families (all children ego's cousins)

Structural Groupings of Families:
I. 1 + 2 – Inner circle
II. 3, 4, 5 + 6 – Outer circle
III. 1, 2, 3, 5, 7 – Families in line of descent
IV. 4, 8 – Collateral families
V. 2, 6 – Articulation of consanguine systems

No difference according to sex of ego, except in the term for spouse and the fact that, if ego is female, name line does not extend below ego in line of descent.

ologically identical, modified only by the prefix 'step' to take account of second or later marriages, and in the fact that the terms father and mother, husband and wife, can each apply to only *one* person at a time. It is also notable that no distinction on the basis of birth order is made – all brothers are terminologically alike. But most notable of all is the fact that *none* of these seven kinship personalities is terminologically identified with *any* relative outside the particular conjugal family in which he is placed. A brother is specifically distinguished from any male cousin, the father from any uncle, the mother from any aunt, and so on. These two conjugal families may conveniently be treated as constituting the inner circle of the kinship structure. Relative priorities within them will be discussed below.

Now *each* member of ego's inner kinship circle is the connecting link with one other terminologically recognized conjugal family. Moreover, he links the family of orientation or procreation, as the case may be, with only one father conjugal family, and each individual with a separate one. The kinship personalities of this outer circle, however, are not always terminologically separate, a fact which will be shown to be of paramount importance.

The first pair of outer-circle families, which may be called the first ascendant, are the families of orientation of ego's parents; besides the articulating personality, each consists of the four kinship personalities of grandfather, grandmother, uncle, and aunt. The most significant fact is the lack of terminological distinction between the paternal and the maternal families of orientation – grandparents, uncles, and aunts are alike regardless of which side they are on. The only important exception to this lies not in the kinship terminology as such but in the patrilineal inheritance of the family name, giving rise to a unilateral 'name line.' Since the same principle of lack of distinction by sex of intervening relatives applies to still higher ascendant generations – the four great- and eight great-great-grandfathers – it is perhaps more accurate to speak of a multilineal than of a bilateral system. Any one of an indefinite number of lines of descent may be treated as significant. Above all, the extension from the principle of bilaterality, as applied to the first ascendant (and descendant) families, to that of multilineality in succeeding generations is completely incompatible with any tendency to bifurcate the kin group on the basis of lines of descent.

The same fundamental principles govern the terminology of the first collateral families – the families of procreation of ego's siblings – and the first descendant families, the families of procreation of his children. It is noteworthy that siblings' spouses are terminologically assimilated to sibling status with the suffix 'in-law' – generally not used in address or the more intimate occasions of reference – and that nephews and nieces are the same whether they are brothers' or sisters' children and regardless of the sex of ego. Similarly, spouses of children are assimilated to the status of children by the same terminological device, and sons' and daughters' children are all indiscriminately grandchildren. Finally, both siblings-in-law and children-in-law are terminologically segregated from any kinship status relative to ego except that in the particular conjugal family which is under consideration.

The last outer-circle family, the in-law family, has a very particular significance. It is the only one of those linked to ego's inner circle to which he is bound not by descent and consanguinity but only by affinity, and this fact is of paramount importance, signalizing as it does the openness of our system. In other words, preferential mating on a kinship basis is completely without structural significance, and every marriage in founding a new conjugal family brings together (in the type case) two completely unrelated kinship groups which are articulated on a kinship basis only in this one particular marriage. Seen from a somewhat more generalized point of view, if we take the total inner and outer circle group of ego's kin as a system, it is articulated to another entirely distinct system of the same structure by every peripheral relative (one who is not a connecting link between the inner and outer circles), except in the direct lines of descent. The consequence is a maximum of dispersion of the lines of descent and the prevention of the structuring of kinship groups on any other principle than the 'onion' principle, which implies proportionately increasing distances with each circle of linked conjugal families.[5]

Another way of throwing the significance of this basic open-multilineal structure into relief is to recall the fact that ego's family of orientation and his in-law family are, from the point of view of his children, both first ascendant families whose members are equally grandparents, aunts, and uncles.

In principle it is possible to distinguish, beyond the outer circle, further layers of the so-called onion indefinitely. It is significant, however, that our kinship terminology ceases at this point to apply at all specific terms, fundamentally recognizing only two elements. The first is the line of descent designated by the ascendant and descendant family terms with the addition of the reduplicating prefix 'great' – as in a great-grandfather and greatgrandson. The second is the indiscriminate category 'cousins' into which all collaterals are thrown, with only the descriptive[6] devices of 'first,' 'third,' 'once removed,' and so forth to distinguish them by.

This onion structure of interlocking conjugal families differs above all from most other kinship systems in the fact that the conjugal family is so isolated by the unusual symmetry of its relationships to all the other conjugal units with each of which it is linked by one common member. It is not particularly closely integrated with any one or two of these in a larger solidary grouping which would bias this symmetry of relationship

5. In any finite population, lines of descent are bound to cross somewhere, and in our society the marriage of close relatives is not infrequent. But there is no consistent pattern in this intermarriage, hence it is without structural consequences.

Most of the essentials of an open conjugal system can be maintained, while a high level of generation continuity in at least one line is also maintained, by a systematic discrimination between lines of descent – especially through primogeniture. The extent to which this has and has not occurred is the most important range of variation within the basic pattern and will have to be discussed in some detail below.

6. It should perhaps be stated explicitly that, though sometimes called a descriptive system by some of the older anthropologists, our terminology is by no means literally descriptive of exact biological relationships. Above all it fails to distinguish relatives whose relation to ego is traced through different lines of descent. But it also fails to distinguish by birth order, or to distinguish siblings' spouses from spouses' siblings – both are brothers- or sisters-in-law. Finally, as just noted, it stops making distinctions very soon and treats all collaterals as cousins.

to others. Above all there is no strong emphasis on a line of descent which would ensure conformity of status of the kinship unit from generation to generation.[7]

How far can this distinctive terminology be said to reflect the actual institutional structure of kinship? In a broad way it certainly does this. We clearly have none of the extended kin groupings so prevalent among non-literate peoples, such as patrilineal or matrilineal clans; we have no exogamy except that based on degree of relationship; we have no preferential mating – all these are a matter of the simplest common knowledge. But to get a clearer conception of the more specific structure it is essential to turn to a different order of evidence.

In the first place, the importance of the isolated conjugal family is brought out by the fact that it is the normal household unit. This means it is the unit of residence and the unit whose members as a matter of course pool a common basis of economic support – especially, as with us, money income. Moreover, in the typical case neither the household arrangements nor the source of income bears any specific relation to the family of orientation of either spouse, or, if there is any, it is about as likely to be to the one as to the other. But the typical conjugal family lives in a home segregated from those of both pairs of parents (if living) and is economically independent of both. In a large proportion of cases this geographical separation is considerable. Furthermore, the primary basis of economic support and of many other elements of social status lies typically in the husband's occupational status – his job, which typically he holds independently of any particularistic relation to kinsmen.

The isolation of the conjugal unit in this country is in strong contrast to that common in the historic structure of European society, where a much larger and more important element have inherited home, source of economic support, and specific occupational status (especially a farm or family enterprise) from their fathers. This of course has had to involve discrimination between siblings, since the whole complex of property and status has to be inherited intact.[8]

7. A well-known example of the latter type is the traditional Chinese gentry family with its three- or four-generation household, consisting of an older couple, their married sons, wives, and children, and perhaps even grandchildren in the male line. A different type is that common among European peasants; here the holding and corresponding status in the community is passed down intact to one son, and the others must leave the agricultural community.

8. Though perhaps the commonest pattern, primogeniture has by no means been universal. Cf. Arensberg and Kimball, *Family and Community*

Hence considerable significance attaches to our patterns of inheritance of property. Here the important thing is the absence of any specific favoring of any particular line of descent. Formally, subject to protection of the interest of widows, complete testamentary freedom exists. The American law of intestacy, however, in specific contrast to the older English Common Law tradition, gives equal shares to all children, regardless of sex or the order of birth. But, even more important, the actual practice of wills overwhelmingly conforms to this pattern. Where deviations exist they are not bound up with the kinship structure as such but are determined by particular relationships or situations of need. There is also noticeable in our society a relative weakness of pressure on a person to leave all or even most property to kin.[9]

It is probably safe to assume that an essentially open system, with a primary stress on the conjugal family and a corresponding absence of groupings of collaterals cutting across conjugal families, has existed in Western society since the period when the kinship terminology of the European languages took shape. The above evidence, however, is sufficient to show that within this broad type the American system, by contrast with its European forebears, has developed far in the direction of a symmetrically multilineal type. The relative absence of any structural bias in favor of solidarity with the ascendant and descendant families in any one line of descent has enormously increased the structural isolation of the individual conjugal family. This isolation, a manifestation of the almost symmetrical onion-type structure, is the most distinctive feature of the American kinship system and underlies most of its peculiar functional and dynamic problems

Before entering into a few of these it should be made clear that the incidence of the fully developed type in the American social structure is uneven and that important tendencies to deviation from it are found in certain structural areas. In the first place, in spite of the extent to which American agriculture has become commercialized, the economic and social conditions of rural life place more of a premium on continuity of occupation and status from generation to generation than do urban conditions; hence, especially perhaps among the more solidly established rural population, something approaching Le Play's *famille souche* is not unusual.

---

in Ireland (Cambridge: Harvard University Press, 1940), and G. C. Homans, *English Villagers of the 13th Century* (Cambridge: Harvard University Press, 1941).

9. Indeed a wealthy man who completely neglected philanthropies in his will would be criticized.

Second, there are important upper-class elements in this country for which an élite status is closely bound up with the status of ancestry, hence the continuity of kinship solidarity in a – mainly patrilineal – line of descent, in lineages.[10] Therefore in these 'family élite' elements the symmetry of the multilineal kinship structure is sharply skewed in the direction of a patrilineal system with a tendency to primogeniture – one in many respects resembling that historically prevalent among European aristocracies, though considerably looser. There is a tendency for this in turn to be bound up with family property, especially an ancestral home, and with continuity of status in a particular local community.

Finally, there is evidence that in lower-class situations, in different ways both rural and urban, there is another type of deviance from the main kinship pattern. This type is connected with a strong tendency to an instability of marriage and to a mother-centered type of family structure – found both in Negro and white population elements.[11] I would not disturb the multilineal symmetry of the system but would favor a very different type of conjugal family, even if it tended to be as nearly isolated as the main type from other kinship groups. This situation, however, has not been at all adequately studied from a functional point of view.

Thus what is here treated as the focal American type of kinship structure is most conspicuously developed in the urban middle-class areas of the society. This fact is strong evidence of the interdependence of kinship structure with other structural aspects of the same society, notably the occupational system.

In approaching the functional analysis of the central American kinship type, the focal point of departure must lie in the crucial fact that ego is a member not of one but of two conjugal families. This fact naturally

10. Cf. Warner and Lunt, op. cit., and Allison Davis and B. B. and M. R. Gardner, *Deep South* (Chicago: Chicago University Press, 1941).

11. Cf. Davis and Gardner, op. cit., chap. vi; E. Franklin Frazier, *The Negro Family in the United States* (Chicago: Chicago University Press, 1939), and Robert S. Lynd, *Middletown in Transition* (New York: Harcourt, Brace & Company, 1937). Dr Florence Kluckholm has called my attention to a fourth deviant type which she calls the 'suburban matriarchy.' In certain urban areas, especially with an upper-middle-class population, the husband and father is out of the home a large proportion of the time. He tends to leave by far the greater part of the responsibility for children to his wife and also to participate in the affairs of the local community either not at all or only at the insistence of his wife. This would apply to informal social relationships where both entertaining and acceptance of invitations are primarily arranged by the wife or on her initiative.

is of central significance in all kinship systems, but in our own it acquires a special importance because of the structural prominence of the conjugal family and its peculiar isolation. In most kinship systems many persons retain throughout the life cycle a fundamentally stable – though changing – status in one or more extended kinship units.[12] In our system this is not the case for anyone.

The most immediate consequence lies in the structural significance of the marriage relationship, especially in relation to the lines of descent and to the sibling tie. That is, in ours as compared with other kinship systems, ego by his marriage is drastically segregated from his family of orientation – both from his parents and their forebears and from his siblings. His first kinship loyalty is unequivocally to this spouse and then to their children if and when any are born. Moreover, his family of procreation, by virtue of a common household, income, and community status, becomes a solidary unit in the sense in which the segregation of the interests of individuals is relatively meaningless, whereas the segregation of these interests of ego from those of the family of orientation tends relatively to minimize solidarity with the latter.

For ego as an adult the strong emphasis on the marriage relationship at the expense of his relationship to parents and siblings is directly correlative with the symmetrical multilineality of the system. From the standpoint of the marriage pair, in other words, neither family of orientation, particularly neither parental couple, has a structurally sanctioned priority of status. Thus in a sense there is a balance-of-power situation in which the independence of the family of procreation is favored by the necessity of maintaining impartiality as between the two families of orientation.[13]

12. This, in a unilateral clan system, is conspicuously true, for example, of the members of the sex group on which the continuity of the clan rests. On the other hand, the situation of the other, the out-marrying sex, is quite different.

13. See Simmel's well-known essay on the significance of number in social relationships (*Soziologie*, chap. ii). This is an illuminating case of the 'triadic' group. It is not, however, institutionally that of *tertius gaudens*, since that implies one 'playing off the other two against each other,' though informally it may sometimes approach that. Institutionally, however, what is most important is the requirement of impartiality between the two families of orientation. Essentially the same considerations apply as between an older couple and two or more of their married children's families of procreation – impartiality irrespective of sex or the order of birth is expected.

From this it seems legitimate to conclude that in a peculiar sense which is not equally applicable to other systems the marriage bond, in our society, is the main structural keystone of the kinship system. This results from the structural isolation of the conjugal family and the fact that the married couple is not supported by comparably strong kinship ties to other adults. Closely related to this situation is that of the choice of a marriage partner. It is not only an open system in that there is no preferential mating on a kinship basis, but, since the new marriage is not typically incorporated into an already existing kinship unit, the primary structural reasons for an important influence on marriage choice being exerted by the kin of the prospective partners are missing or at least minimized.

It is true that something approaching a system of arranged marriages does persist in some situations, especially where couples brought up in the same local community marry and expect to settle down there – or where there are other particularistic elements present, as in cases of 'marrying the boss's daughter.' Our open system, however, tends very strongly to a pattern of purely personal choice of marriage partner without important parental influence. With increasing social mobility – residential, occupational, and other – it has clearly become the dominant pattern. Though not positively required by the kinship structure, freedom of choice is not impeded by it, and the structure in various ways is probably connected with the motivation of this freedom, an important aspect of the 'romantic love' complex.

A closely related functional problem touches the character of the marriage relationship itself. Social systems in which a considerable number of individuals are in a complex and delicate state of mutual interdependence tend greatly to limit the scope of 'personal' emotional feelings, or at least its direct expression in action. Any considerable range of affective spontaneity would tend to impinge on the statuses and interests of too many others, with disequilibrating consequences for the system as a whole. This need to limit affective spontaneity is fundamentally the reason why arranged marriages tend to be found in kinship systems where the newly married couple is incorporated into a larger kin group, but it also strongly colors the character of the marriage relationship itself and tends to place the primary institutional sanctions upon matters of objective status and obligation to other kin, rather than on subjective sentiment.[14] Thus the structural isolation of

14. This tendency for multiple-membered social systems to repress spontaneous manifestations of sentiment should not be taken too absolutely. In such phenomena as cliques, there is room for the following of personal

the conjugal family tends to free the affective inclination of the couple from a whole series of hampering restrictions.

Nevertheless these restrictive forces, which in other kinship systems inhibit affective expression, have positive functional significance in maintaining the solidarity of the effective kinship unit. Very definite expectations in the definition of the different roles, combined with a complex system of interrelated sanctions, both positive and negative, go far to guarantee stability and the maintenance of standards of performance. In the American kinship system this kind of institutionalized support of the role of marriage partner through its interlocking with other kinship roles is, if not entirely lacking, at least much weaker. A functionally equivalent substitute in motivation to conformity with the exceptions of the role is clearly needed. Hence it may be suggested that the institutional sanction placed on the proper subjective sentiments of spouses, in short the expectation that they have an obligation to be 'in love,' has that significance. This in turn is related to the personal choice of a marriage partner, since affective devotion – particularly in our culture – is linked to a presumption of the absence of any element of coercion.

inclinations within the framework of institutionalized statuses. It is probable, however, that it is more restrictive in groups where, as in kinship, the institutionalized relationships are particularistic and functionally diffuse than in universalistic and functionally specific systems such as modern occupational organizations. In the latter case, personal affective relationships can, within considerable limits, be institutionally ignored as belonging to the sphere of private affairs.

Robert K. Merton born 1910

Major works

Mass Persuasion (1946)
Social Theory and Social Structure (1949; revised 1957)
Co-editor of a number of volumes including:
*Continuities in Social Research: Studies in the Scope and Method of
'The American Soldier'* (1950)
Reader in Bureaucracy (1952)
Sociology Today (1959)

The following paper, 'The Bearing of Empirical Research upon the Development of Social Theory', was read before the annual meeting of the American Sociological Society, Cleveland, Ohio, 1–3 March 1946; it may be identified as Publication No. A–89 of the Bureau of Applied Social Research, Columbia University. It is reprinted here from the *American Sociological Review*, XIII (1948), 505–15, with the permission of the author and the American Sociological Association.

History has a certain gift for outmoding stereotypes. This can be seen, for example, in the historical development of sociology. The stereotype of the social theorist high in the empyrean of pure ideas uncontaminated by mundane facts is fast becoming no less outmoded than the stereotype of the social researcher equipped with questionnaire and pencil and hot on the chase of the isolated and meaningless statistic. For in building the mansion of sociology during the last decades, theorist and empiricist have learned to work together. What is more, they have learned to talk to one another in the process. At times, this means only that a sociologist has learned to talk to himself since increasingly the same man has taken up both theory and research. Specialization and integration have developed hand in hand. All this has led not only to the realization that theory and empirical research *should* interact but to the result that they *do* interact.

As a consequence, there is decreasing need for accounts of the relations between theory and research to be wholly programmatic in character. A growing body of theoretically oriented research makes it progressively possible to discuss with profit the actual relations between the two. And, as we all know, there has been no scarcity of such discussions. Journals abound with them. They generally center on the role of theory in research, setting forth, often with admirable lucidity, the functions of theory in the initiation, design and prosecution of empirical inquiry. But since this is not a one-way relationship, since the two *inter*act, it may be useful to examine the other direction of the relationship: the role of empirical research in the development of social theory. That is the purpose of this paper.

THE THEORETIC FUNCTIONS OF RESEARCH

With a few conspicuous exceptions, recent sociological discussions have assigned but one major function to empirical research: 'testing' or 'verification' of hypotheses. The model for the proper way of performing this function is as familiar as it is clear. The investigator begins with a hunch or hypothesis, from this he draws various inferences and these, in turn, are subjected to empirical test which confirms or refutes the hypothesis.[1] But this is a logical model, and so fails, of course, to describe much of what actually occurs in fruitful investigation. It presents a set of logical norms, not a description of the research experience. And, as logicians are well aware, in purifying the experience, the logical model may also distort it. Like other such models, it abstracts from the temporal sequence of events. It exaggerates the creative role of explicit theory just as it minimizes the creative role of observation. For research is not merely logic tempered with observation. It has its psychological as well as its logical dimensions, although one would scarcely suspect this from the logically rigorous sequence in which research is usually reported.[2] It is both the psychological and logical pressures of research upon social theory which we seek to trace.

It is my central thesis that empirical research goes far beyond the passive role of verifying and testing theory: it does more than confirm or refute hypotheses. Research plays an active role: it performs at least four major functions which help shape the development of theory. It *initiates*, it *reformulates*, it *deflects* and *clarifies* theory.

1. See, for example, the procedural review of Stouffer's 'Theory of intervening opportunities' by G. A. Lundberg, 'What are Sociological Problems?', *American Sociological Review*, VI (1941), 357–9.
2. See R. K. Merton, 'Science, Population and Society,' *Scientific Monthly*, XLIV (1937), 170–71; the apposite discussion by Jean Piaget, *Judgment and Reasoning in the Child* (London, 1929), chaps. v, ix, and the comment [on the methodological procedures of scientific research] by William H. George, *The Scientist in Action* (London, 1936), p. 153. 'A piece of research does not progress in the way it is "written up" for publication.'

Modern American Sociology

1. THE SERENDIPITY PATTERN

(The unanticipated, anomalous and strategic datum exerts a pressure for initiating theory.)

Under certain conditions, a research finding gives rise to social theory. In a previous paper, this was all too briefly expressed as follows: 'Fruitful empirical research not only tests theoretically derived hypotheses; it also originates new hypotheses. This might be termed the 'serendipity' component of research, *i.e.*, the discovery, by chance or sagacity, of valid results which were not sought for.'[3]

The serendipity pattern refers to the fairly common experience of observing an *unanticipated, anomalous* and *strategic* datum which becomes the occasion for developing a new theory or for extending an existing theory. Each of these elements of the pattern can be readily described. The datum is, first of all, unanticipated. A research directed toward the test of one hypothesis yields a fortuitous by-product, an unexpected observation which bears upon theories not in question when the research was begun.

Secondly, the observation is anomalous, surprising,[4] either because it seems inconsistent with prevailing theory or with other established facts. In either case, the seeming inconsistency provokes curiosity; it stimulates the investigator to 'make sense of the datum,' to fit it into a broader frame of knowledge. He explores further. He makes fresh observations. He draws inferences from the observations, inferences depending largely, of course, upon his general theoretic orientation. The more he is steeped in the data, the greater the likelihood that he will hit upon a fruitful direction of inquiry. In the fortunate circumstance that his new hunch proves justified, the anomalous datum leads ultimately to a new or extended theory. The curiosity stimulated by the anomalous datum is temporarily appeased.

3. R. K. Merton, 'Sociological Theory,' *American Journal of Sociology*, L (1945), 469n. Interestingly enough, the same outlandish term 'serendipity' which has had little currency since it was coined by Horace Walpole in 1754 has also been used to refer to this component of research by the physiologist Walter B. Cannon. See his *The Way of an Investigator* (New York: W. W. Norton, 1945), chap. vi, in which he sets forth numerous instances of serendipity in several fields of science.

4. Charles Sanders Peirce had long before noticed the strategic role of the 'surprising fact' in his account of what he called 'abduction,' that is, the initiation and entertaining of a hypothesis as a step in inference. See his *Collected Papers* (Harvard University Press, 1931–5), VI, 522–8.

And thirdly, in noting that the unexpected fact must be 'strategic,' *i.e.*, that it must permit of implications which bear upon generalized theory, we are, of course, referring rather to what the observer brings to the datum than to the datum itself. For it obviously requires a theoretically sensitized observer to detect the universal in the particular. After all, men had for centuries noticed such 'trivial' occurrences as slips of the tongue, slips of the pen, typographical errors, and lapses of memory, but it required the theoretic sensitivity of a Freud to see these as strategic data through which he could extend his theory of repression and symptomatic acts.

The serendipity pattern, then, involves the unanticipated, anomalous and strategic datum which exerts pressure upon the investigator for a new direction of inquiry which extends theory. Instances of serendipity have occurred in many disciplines, but I should like to draw upon a current sociological research for illustration. In the course of our research into the social organization of Craftown,[5] a suburban housing community of some 700 families, largely of working class status, we observed that a large proportion of residents were affiliated with more civic, political and other voluntary organizations than had been the case in their previous places of residence. Quite incidentally, we noted further that this increase in group participation had occurred also among the parents of infants and young children. This finding was rather inconsistent with commonsense knowledge. For it is well known that, particularly on the lower economic levels, youngsters usually tie parents down and preclude their taking active part in organized group life outside the home. But Craftown parents themselves readily explained their behavior. 'Oh, there's no real problem about getting out in the evenings,' said one mother who belonged to several organizations. 'It's easy to find teen-agers around here to take care of the kids. There are so many more teen-agers around here than where I used to live.'

The explanation appears adequate enough and would have quieted the investigator's curiosity, had it not been for one disturbing datum: like most new housing communities, Craftown actually has a very small proportion of adolescents – only 3.7%, for example, in the 15–19 year age group. What is more, the majority of the adults, 63%, are under 34 years of age, so that their children include an exceptionally large proportion of infants and youngsters. Thus, far from there being many adolescents to look after the younger children in Craftown, quite the contrary is true: the ratio of adolescents to children under ten years of

5. Drawn from continuing studies in the Sociology and Social Psychology of Housing, under a grant from the Lavanburg Foundation.

age is 1:10, whereas, in the communities of origin, the ratio hovers about 1:1.5.[6]

We were at once confronted, then, by an anomalous fact which was certainly no part of our original program of observation. This should be emphasized. . . . Here was an observation both unanticipated and anomalous. Was it also strategic? We did not prejudge its 'intrinsic' importance . . .

The clue was inadvertently provided by further interviews with residents. In the words of an active participant in Craftown affairs, herself the mother of two children under six years of age:

> 'My husband and I get out together much more. You see, there are more people around to mind the children. *You feel more confident about having some thirteen-or-fourteen-year-old in here when you know most of the people. If you're in a big city, you don't feel so easy about having someone who's almost a stranger come in.*'

This clearly suggests that the sociological roots of the 'illusion' are to be found in the structure of community relations in which Craftown residents are enmeshed. The belief is an unwitting reflection, not of the statistical reality, but of the community cohesion. It is not that there are objectively more adolescents in Craftown, but more who are *intimately known* and who, therefore, *exist socially* for parents seeking aid in child supervision. Most Craftown residents having lately come from an urban setting now find themselves in a community in which proximity has developed into reciprocal intimacies. The illusion expresses the perspective of people for whom adolescents as potential child-care aides 'exist' only if they are well-known and therefore merit confidence. In short, perception was a function of confidence and confidence, in turn, was a function of social cohesion.[7]

6. Essentially the same discrepancies in age distribution between Craftown and communities of origin are found if we compare proportions of children under ten with those between 10 and 19. If we make children under five the basis for comparison, the disproportions are even more marked.

7. Schedule data from the study provide corroborative evidence. In view of the exceptionally high proportion of young children, it is striking that 54 per cent of their parents affirm that it is 'easier in Craftown to get people to look after our children when we want to go out' than it was in other places where they have lived; only 21 per cent say it is harder and the remaining 25 per cent feel there is no difference. Those who come from the larger urban communities are more likely to report greater ease in obtaining assistance in Craftown. Moreover, as we would expect from the hypothesis, those residents who are more closely geared in with Craftown, who identify

From the sociological viewpoint, then, this unanticipated finding fits into and extends the theory that 'social perception' is the product of a social framework. It develops further the 'psychology of social norms,'[8] for it is not merely an instance of individuals assimilating particular norms, judgments, and standards from other members of the community. The social perception is, rather, a by-product, a derivative, of the structure of human relations.

This is perhaps sufficient to illustrate the operation of the serendipity pattern: an unexpected and anomalous finding elicited the investigator's curiosity, and conducted him along an unpremeditated by-path which led to fresh hypothesis.

2. THE RECASTING OF THEORY

(New data exert pressure for the elaboration of a conceptual scheme.)

But it is not only through the anomalous fact that empirical research invites the extension of theory. It does so also through the repeated observation of hitherto neglected facts. When an existing conceptual scheme commonly applied to a given subject-matter does not adequately take these facts into account, research presses insistently for its reformulation. It leads to the introduction of variables which have not been systematically included in the scheme of analysis. Here, be it noted, it is not that the data are anomalous or unexpected or incompatible with existing theory; it is merely that they have not been considered pertinent. Whereas the serendipity pattern centers in an apparent inconsistency which presses for resolution, the reformulation pattern centers in the hitherto neglected but relevant fact which presses for an extension of the conceptual scheme.

Examples of this in the history of social science are far from limited. Thus it was a series of fresh empirical facts which led Malinowski to incorporate new elements into a theory of magic. It was his Trobrianders, of course, who gave him the clue to the distinctive feature of his theory. When these islanders fished in the inner lagoon by the reliable method of poisoning, an abundant catch was assured and danger was absent. Neither uncertainty nor uncontrollable hazards were involved. And

---

themselves most fully with it, are more likely to believe it easier to find such aid; 61 per cent of these do so as against 50 per cent of those who identify with other communities, whereas only 12 per cent find it more difficult in comparison with 26 per cent of the latter group.

8. Muzafer Sherif's book by this title should be cited as basic in the field, although it tends to have a somewhat limited conception of 'social factors,' *The Psychology of Social Norms* (New York, 1936).

here, Malinowski noted, magic was not practiced. But in the open-sea fishing, with the uncertain yield and its often grave dangers, the rituals of magic flourished. Stemming from these pregnant observations was his theory that magical belief arises to bridge the uncertainties in man's practical pursuits, to fortify confidence, to reduce anxieties, to open up avenues of escape from the seeming impasse. Magic was construed as a supplementary technique for reaching practical objectives. It was these empirical facts which suggested the incorporation of new dimensions into earlier theories of magic – particularly the relations of magic to the fortuitous, the dangerous and the uncontrollable. It was not that these facts were *inconsistent* with previous theories; it was simply that these conceptual schemes had not taken them adequately into account. Nor was Malinowski testing a preconceived hypothesis – he was developing an enlarged and improved theory on the basis of suggestive empirical data.

For another example of this pressure of empirical data for the recasting of a specific theory we turn closer home. The investigation dealt with a single dramatic instance of mass persuasion: broadcasting at repeated intervals over a span of eighteen hours. Kate Smith, a radio star, sold large quantities of war-bonds in the course of the day. It is not my intention to report fully on the dynamics of this case of mass persuasion;[9] for present purposes, we are concerned only with the implications of two facts which emerged from the study.

First of all, in the course of intensive interviews many of our informants – New Yorkers who had pledged a bond to Smith – expressed a thorough disenchantment with the world of advertising, commercials and propaganda. They felt themselves the object of manipulation – and resented it. They objected to being the target for advertising which cajoles, insists and terrorizes. They objected to being engulfed in waves of propaganda proposing opinions and actions not in their own best interests. They expressed dismay over what is in effect a pattern of *pseudo-Gemeinschaft* – subtle methods of salesmanship in which there is the feigning of personal concern with the client in order to manipulate him the better. As one small businessman phrased it, 'In my own business, I can see how a lot of people in their business deals will make some kind of gesture of friendliness, sincerity and so forth, most of which is phony.' Drawn from a highly competitive, segmented metropolitan society, our informants were describing a climate of reciprocal distrust, of *anomie*, in which common values have been submerged in the welter of private interests. Society was experienced as an arena for

9. R. K. Merton, M. Fiske and A. Curtis, *Mass Persuasion* (New York: Harper, 1946).

rival frauds. There was small belief in the disinterestedness of conduct.

In contrast to all this was the second fact: we found that the persuasiveness of the Smith bond-drive among these same informants largely rested upon their firm belief in the integrity and sincerity of Smith. And much the same was found to be true in a polling interview with a larger cross-section sample of almost a thousand New Yorkers. Fully 80% asserted that in her all-day marathon drives, Smith was *exclusively* concerned with promoting the sale of war bonds, whereas only 17% felt that she was *also* interested in publicity for herself, and a negligible 3% believed she was *primarily* concerned with the resulting publicity . . .

In short, it was not so much what Smith *said* as what she *did* which served to validate her sincerity. It was the presumed stress and strain of an eighteen-hour series of broadcasts, it was the deed not the word which furnished the indubitable proof. Listeners might question whether she were not unduly dramatizing herself, but they could not escape the incontrovertible evidence that she was devoting the entire day to the task. Appraising the direct testimony of Smith's behavior, another informant explains that 'she was on all day and the others weren't. So it seemed that she was sacrificing more and was more sincere.' Viewed as a process of persuasion, the marathon converted initial feelings of scepticism and distrust among listeners into at first a reluctant, and later, a full-fledged acceptance of Smith's integrity. The successive broadcasts served as a fulfillment in action of a promise in words. The words were reinforced by things she has actually done. The currency of talk was accepted because it is backed by the gold of conduct. The gold reserve, moreover, need not even approximate the amount of currency it can support.

This empirical study suggests that propaganda-of-the-deed may be effective among the very people who are distrustful of propaganda-of-the-word. Where there is social disorganization, *anomie*, conflicting values, we find propaganditis reaching epidemic proportions. Any statement of value is likely to be discounted as 'mere propaganda.' Exhortations are suspect. But the propaganda of the deed elicits more confidence. Members of the audience are largely permitted to draw their conclusions from the action – they are less likely to feel manipulated. When the propagandist's deed and his words symbolically coincide, it stimulates belief in his sincerity. Further research must determine whether this propaganda pattern is significantly more effective in societies suffering from *anomie* than in those which are more fully integrated. But not unlike the Malinowski case-in-point, this may illustrate the role of research in suggesting new variables to be incorporated into a specific theory.

3. THE RE-FOCUSSING OF THEORETIC INTEREST

(New methods of empirical research exert pressure for new foci of theoretic interest.)

To this point we have considered the impact of research upon the development of particular theories. But empirical research also affects more general trends in the development of theory. This occurs chiefly through the invention of research procedures which tend to shift the foci of theoretic interest to the growing points of research.

The reasons for this are on the whole evident. After all, sound theory thrives only on a rich diet of pertinent facts and newly invented procedures help provide the ingredients of this diet. The new, and often previously unavailable, data stimulate fresh hypotheses. Moreover, theorists find that their hypotheses can be put to immediate test in those spheres where appropriate research techniques have been designed. It is no longer necessary for them to wait upon data as they happen to turn up – researches directed to the verification of hypotheses can be instituted at once. The flow of relevant data thus increases the tempo of advance in certain spheres of theory whereas in others, theory stagnates for want of adequate observations. Attention shifts accordingly.

In noting that new centers of theoretic interest have followed upon the invention of research procedures, we do not imply that these alone played a decisive role.[10] The growing interest in the theory of propaganda as an instrument of social control, for example, is in large part a response to the changing historical situation, with its conflict of major ideological systems; new technologies of mass communication which have opened up new avenues of propaganda; and the rich research treasuries provided by business and government interested in this new weapon of war, both declared and undeclared. But this shift is also a by-product of accumulated facts made available through such newly developed, and confessedly crude, procedures as content-analysis, the panel technique and the focussed interview.

Examples of this impact in the recent history of social theory are numerous but we have time to mention only a few. Thus, the increasing concern with the theory of character and personality formation in relation to social structure became marked after the introduction of new projective methods; the Rorschach test, the thematic apperception

10. It is perhaps needless to add that these procedures, instruments and apparatus are in turn dependent upon prior theory. But this does not alter their stimulating effect upon the further development of theory. Cf. Merton, 'Sociological Theory,' 463n.

test, play techniques and story completions being among the most familiar. So, too, the sociometric techniques of Moreno and others, and fresh advances in the technique of the 'passive interview' have revived interest in the theory of interpersonal relations. Stemming from such techniques as well is the trend toward what might be called the 'rediscovery of the primary group,' particularly in the shape of theoretic concern with informal social structures as mediating between the individual and large formal organizations. This interest has found expression in an entire literature on the role and structure of the informal group, for example, in factory social systems, bureaucracy and political organizations. Similarly, we may anticipate that the recent introduction of the panel technique – the repeated interviewing of the same group of informants – will in due course more sharply focus attention of social psychologists upon the theory of attitude formation decisions among alternative choices, factors in political participation and determinants of behavior in cases of conflicting role demands, to mention a few types of problems to which this technique is especially adapted.

Perhaps the most direct impact of research procedures upon theory has resulted from the *creation* of sociological statistics organized in terms of theoretically pertinent categories. Talcott Parsons has observed that numerical data are scientifically important only when they can be fitted into analytical categories and that 'a great deal of current research is producing facts in a form which cannot be utilized by any correct generalized analytical scheme.'[11] These well-deserved strictures of a scant decade ago are proving progressively less applicable. In the past, the sociologist has largely had to deal with *pre-collected series* of statistics usually assembled for non-sociological purposes and, therefore, not set forth in categories directly pertinent to any given theoretical system. As a result, at least so far as quantitative facts are concerned, the theorist was compelled to work with makeshift data bearing only a tangential relevance to his problems. This not only left a wide margin for error – consider the crude indexes of social cohesion upon which Durkheim had to rely – but it also meant that theory had to wait upon the incidental and, at times, almost accidental availability of relevant data. It could not march rapidly ahead. This picture has now begun to change.

11. Talcott Parsons, 'The Role of Theory in Social Research,' *American Sociological Review*, III (1938), 19; cf. his *Structure of Social Action* (New York, 1937), pp. 328–9n. [Note his statement that] '. . . in the social field most available statistical information is on a level which cannot be made to fit directly into the categories of analytical theory.'

No longer does the theorist depend exclusively upon the consensus of administrative boards or social welfare agencies for his quantitative data. Tarde's programmatic sketch[12] a half-century ago of the need for statistics in social psychology, particularly those dealing with attitudes, opinions and sentiments, has become a half-fulfilled promise. So, too, investigators of community organization are creating statistics on class structure, association behavior, and clique formations, and this has left its mark on theoretic interests. Ethnic studies are beginning to provide quantitative data which are reorienting the theorist. It is safe to suppose that the enormous accumulation of sociological materials during the war – notably by the Research Branch of the Information and Education Division of the War Department – materials which are in part the result of new research techniques, will intensify interest in the theory of group morale, propaganda and leadership. But it is perhaps needless to multiply examples.

What we have said does not mean that the piling up of statistics of itself advances theory; it does mean that theoretic interest tends to shift to those areas in which there is an abundance of *pertinent* statistical data. Moreover, we are merely calling attention to this shift of focus, not evaluating it. It may very well be that it sometimes deflects attention to problems which, in a theoretic or humanistic sense, are 'unimportant'; it may divert attention from problems with larger implications onto those for which there is the promise of immediate solutions. Failing a detailed study, it is difficult to come to any overall assessment of this point. But the pattern itself seems clear enough in sociology as in other disciplines: as new and previously unobtainable data become available through the use of new techniques, theorists turn their analytical eye upon the implications of these data and bring about new directions of inquiry.

4. THE CLARIFICATION OF CONCEPTS

(Empirical research exerts pressure for clear concepts.)

A good part of the work called 'theorizing' is taken up with the clarification of concepts – and rightly so. It is in this matter of clearly defined concepts that social science research is not infrequently defective. Research activated by a major interest in methodology may be centered on the *design* of establishing causal relations without due regard for analysing the variables involved in the inquiry. This methodological empiricism, as the design of inquiry without correlative concern with

12. Gabriel Tarde, *Essais et mélanges sociologiques* (Paris, 1895), pp. 230–70.

the clarification of substantive variables may be called, characterizes a large part of current research. Thus, in a series of effectively designed experiments, Chapin finds that 'the rehousing of slum families in a public housing project results in improvement of the living conditions and the social life of these families.'[13] Or through controlled experiments, psychologists search out the effects of foster home placement upon children's performances in intelligence tests.[14] Or, again through experimental inquiry, researchers seek to determine whether a propaganda film has achieved its purpose of improving attitudes toward the British. These several cases, and they are representative of a large amount of research which has advanced social science method, have in common the fact that the empirical variables are not analyzed in terms of their conceptual elements.[15] As Rebecca West, with her characteristic lucidity, put this general problem of methodological empiricism, one might 'know that A and B and C were linked by certain causal connexions, but he would never apprehend with any exactitude the nature of A or B or C.' In consequences, these researches further the procedures of inquiry, but their findings do not enter into the repository of cumulative social science theory.

But in general, the clarification of concepts, commonly considered a province peculiar to the theorist, is a frequent result of empirical research. Research sensitive to its own needs cannot avoid this pressure for conceptual clarification. *For a basic requirement of research is that the concepts, the variables, be defined with sufficient clarity to enable the research to proceed*, a requirement easily and unwittingly not met in the kind of discursive exposition which is often miscalled 'sociological theory.'

The clarification of concepts ordinarily enters into empirical research in the shape of establishing *indices* of the variables under consideration. In non-research speculations, it is possible to talk loosely about 'morale' or 'social cohesion' without any clear conceptions of what is entailed by these terms, but they *must* be clarified if the researcher is to go about his

13. F. S. Chapin, 'The effects of slum clearance and rehousing on family and community relationships in Minneapolis,' *American Journal of Sociology*, XLIII (1938), 744–63.

14. R. R. Sears, 'Child Psychology,' in Wayne Dennis, ed., *Current Trends in Psychology* (University of Pittsburgh Press, 1947), pp. 55–56. Sears' comments on this type of research state the general problem admirably.

15. However crude they may be, procedures such as the focused interview are expressly designed as aids for detecting possibly relevant variables in an initially undifferentiated situation. See R. K. Merton and P. L. Kendall, 'The Focused Interview,' *American Journal of Sociology*, LI (1946), 541–57.

business of systematically observing instances of low and high morale, of social cohesion or cleavage. If he is not to be blocked at the outset, he must devise indices which are observable, fairly precise and meticulously clear. The entire movement of thought which was christened 'operationalism' is only one conspicuous case of the researcher demanding that concepts be defined clearly enough for him to go to work.

This has been typically recognized by those sociologists who combine a theoretic orientation with systematic empirical research. Durkheim, for example, despite the fact that his terminology and indices now appear crude and debatable, clearly perceived the need for devising indices of his concepts. Repeatedly, he asserted that 'it is necessary . . . to substitute for the internal fact which escapes us an external fact that symbolizes it and to study the former through the latter.'[16] The index, or sign of the conceptualized item, stands ideally in a one-to-one correlation with what it signifies (and the difficulty of establishing this relation is of course one of the critical problems of research). Since the index and its object are so related, one may ask for the grounds on which one is taken as the index and the other as the indexed variable. As Durkheim implied and as Suzanne Langer has indicated anew, the index is that one of the correlated pair which is perceptible and the other, harder or impossible to perceive, is theoretically relevant.[17] Thus, attitude scales make available indices of otherwise not discriminable attitudes, just as ecological statistics represent indices of diverse social structures in a given area.

What often appears as a tendency in research for quantification (through the development of scales) can thus be seen as a special case of attempting to clarify concepts sufficiently to permit the conduct of empirical investigation. The development of valid and observable indices becomes central to the use of concepts in the prosecution of research. A final illustration will indicate how research presses for the clarification of ancient sociological concepts which, in the plane of discursive exposition, have remained ill-defined and unclarified.

A conception basic to sociology holds that individuals have multiple social roles and tend to organize their behavior in terms of the structurally defined expectations assigned to each role. Further, it is said, the

16. Émile Durkheim, *Division of Labor in Society* (New York: Macmillan, 1933), p. 66; also his *Les règles de la méthode sociologique* (Paris, 1895), pp. 55–58; *Le Suicide* (Paris, 1930), pp. 356 and *passim*. Cf. R. K. Merton, 'Durkheim's Division of Labor in Society,' *American Journal of Sociology*, XL, 1934, esp. 326–7 which touches on the problem of indices.

17. Suzanne K. Langer, *Philosophy in a New Key* (New York: Penguin Books, 1948), pp. 46–47.

less integrated the society, the more often will individuals be subject to the strain of incompatible social roles. Type-cases are numerous and familiar: the Catholic Communist subjected to conflicting pressures from party and church, the marginal man suffering the pulls of conflicting societies, the professional woman torn between the demands of family and career. Every sociological textbook abounds with illustrations of incompatible demands made of the multiselved person.

Perhaps because it has been largely confined to discursive interpretations and has seldom been made the focus of systematic research, this central problem of conflicting roles has yet to be materially clarified and advanced beyond the point reached decades ago. Thomas and Znaniecki long since indicated that conflicts between social roles *can* be reduced by conventionalization and by role-segmentation (by assigning each set of role-demands to different situations).[18] And others have noted that frequent conflict between roles is dysfunctional for the society as well as for the individual. But all this leaves many salient problems untouched: on which grounds does one predict the behavior of persons subject to conflicting roles? And when a decision must be made, which role (or which group solidarity) takes precedence? Under which conditions does one or another prove controlling? On the plane of discursive thought, it has been suggested that the role with which the individual identifies most fully will prove dominant, thus banishing the problem through a tautological pseudo-solution. Or, the problem of seeking to predict behavior consequent to incompatibility of roles, a research problem requiring operational clarification of the concepts of solidarity, conflict, role-demands and situation, has been evaded by observing that conflicts of roles typically ensue in frustration.

More recently, empirical research has pressed for clarification of the key concepts involved in this problem. Indices of conflicting group pressures have been devised and the resultant behavior observed in specified situations. Thus, as a beginning in this direction, it has been shown that in a concrete decision-situation, such as voting, individuals subject to these cross-pressures respond by delaying their vote-decision. And, under conditions yet to be determined, they seek to reduce the conflict by escaping from the field of conflict: they 'lose interest' in the political campaign. Finally, there is the intimation in these data that in cases of cross-pressures upon the voter, it is socio-economic position which is typically controlling.[19]

18. W. I. Thomas and F. Znaniecki, *The Polish Peasant* (New York: Knopf, 1927), pp. 1866–70, 1888, 1899 ff.

19. P. F. Lazarsfeld, Bernard Berelson and Hazel Gaudet, *The People's Choice* (New York: Duell, Sloan & Pearce, 1944), chap. vi.

However this may be, the essential point is that, in this instance as in others, the very requirements of empirical research have been instrumental in clarifying received concepts. The process of empirical inquiry raises conceptual issues which may long go undetected in theoretic inquiry.

There remain, then, a few concluding remarks. My discussion has been devoted exclusively to four impacts of research upon the development of social theory: the initiation, reformulation, refocusing and clarification of theory. Doubtless there are others. Doubtless, too, the emphasis of this paper lends itself to misunderstanding. It may be inferred that some invidious distinction has been drawn at the expense of theory and the theorist. That has not been my intention. I have suggested only that an explicitly formulated theory does not invariably precede empirical inquiry, that as a matter of plain fact the theorist is not inevitably the lamp lighting the way to new observations. The sequence is often reversed. Nor is it enough to say that research and theory must be married if sociology is to bear legitimate fruit. They must not only exchange solemn vows – they must know how to carry on from there. Their reciprocal roles must be clearly defined. This paper is a brief essay toward that definition.

Charles Wright Mills 1916–62

Major works

From Max Weber: Essays in Sociology (edited and translated with H. H. Gerth, 1946)
White Collar: The American Middle Classes (1951)
The Power Elite (1956)
The Sociological Imagination (1959)

Perhaps the most fruitful distinction with which the sociological imagination works is between 'the personal troubles of milieu' and 'the public issues of social structure.' This distinction is an essential tool of the sociological imagination and a feature of all classic work in social science.

Troubles occur within the character of the individual and within the range of his immediate relations with others; they have to do with his self and with those limited areas of social life of which he is directly and personally aware. Accordingly, the statement and the resolution of troubles properly lie within the individual as a biographical entity and within the scope of his immediate milieu – the social setting that is directly open to his personal experience and to some extent his willful activity. A trouble is a private matter: values cherished by an individual are felt by him to be threatened.

Issues have to do with matters that transcend these local environments of the individual and the range of his inner life. They have to do with the organization of many such milieux into the institutions of an historical society as a whole, with the ways in which various milieux overlap and interpenetrate to form the larger structure of social and historical life. An issue is a public matter: some value cherished by publics is felt to be threatened. Often there is a debate about what that value really is and about what it is that really threatens it. This debate is often without focus if only because it is the very nature of an issue, unlike even widespread trouble, that it cannot very well be defined in terms of the immediate and everyday environments of ordinary men. An issue, in fact, often involves a crisis in institutional arrangements, and often too it involves what Marxists call 'contradictions' or 'antagonisms.'

In these terms, consider unemployment. When, in a city of 100,000, only one man is unemployed, that is his personal trouble, and for its relief we properly look to the character of the man, his skills, and his immediate opportunities. But when in a nation of 50 million employees, 15 million men are unemployed, that is an issue, and we may not hope to find its solution within the range of opportunities open to any one individual. The very structure of opportunities has collapsed. Both the correct statement of the problem and the range of possible solutions require us to consider the economic and political institutions of the society, and not merely the personal situation and character of a scatter of individuals.

Consider war. The personal problem of war, when it occurs, may be how to survive it or how to die in it with honor; how to make money out of it; how to climb into the higher safety of the military apparatus; or how to contribute to the war's termination. In short, according to one's values, to find a set of milieux and within it to survive the war or make one's death in it meaningful. But the structural issues of war have to do with its causes; with what types of men it throws up into command; with its effects upon economic and political, family and religious institutions, with the unorganized irresponsibility of a world of nation-states.

Consider marriage. Inside a marriage a man and a woman may experience personal troubles, but when the divorce rate during the first four years of marriage is 250 out of every 1,000 attempts, this is an indication of a structural issue having to do with the institutions of marriage and the family and other institutions that bear upon them.

Or consider the metropolis – the horrible, beautiful, ugly, magnificent sprawl of the great city. For many upper-class people, the personal solution to 'the problem of the city' is to have an apartment with private garage under it in the heart of the city, and forty miles out, a house by Henry Hill, garden by Garrett Eckbo, on a hundred acres of private land. In these two controlled environments – with a small staff at each end and a private helicopter connection – most people could solve many of the problems of personal milieux caused by the facts of the city. But all this, however splendid, does not solve the public issues that the structural fact of the city poses. What should be done with this wonderful monstrosity? Break it all up into scattered units, combining residence and work? Refurbish it as it stands? Or, after evacuation, dynamite it and build new cities according to new plans in new places? What should those plans be? And who is to decide and to accomplish whatever choice is made? These are structural issues; to confront them and to solve them requires us to consider political and economic issues that affect innumerable milieux.

In so far as an economy is so arranged that slumps occur, the problem of unemployment becomes incapable of personal solution. In so far as war is inherent in the nation-state system and in the uneven industrialization of the world, the ordinary individual in his restricted milieu will be powerless – with or without psychiatric aid – to solve the troubles this system or lack of system imposes upon him. In so far as the family as an institution turns women into darling little slaves and men into their chief providers and unweaned dependents, the problem of a satisfactory marriage remains incapable of purely private solution. In so far as the overdeveloped megalopolis and the overdeveloped automobile are built-in features of the overdeveloped society, the issues of urban living will not be solved by personal ingenuity and private wealth.

What we experience in various and specific milieux, I have noted, is often caused by structural changes. Accordingly, to understand the changes of many personal milieux we are required to look beyond them. And the number and variety of such structural changes increase as the institutions within which we live become more embracing and more intricately connected with one another. To be aware of the idea of social structure and to use it with sensibility is to be capable of tracing such linkages among a great variety of milieux. To be able to do that is to possess the sociological imagination.

What are the major issues for publics and the key troubles of private individuals in our time? To formulate issues and troubles, we must ask what values are cherished yet threatened, and what values are cherished and supported, by the characterizing trends of our period. In the case both of threat and of support we must ask what salient contradictions of structure may be involved.

When people cherish some set of values and do not feel any threat to them, they experience *well-being*. When they cherish values but *do* feel them to be threatened, they experience a crisis – either as a personal trouble or as a public issue. And if all their values seem involved, they feel the total threat of panic.

But suppose people are neither aware of any cherished values nor experience any threat? That is the experience of *indifference*, which, if it seems to involve all their values, becomes apathy. Suppose, finally, they are unaware of any cherished values, but still are very much aware of a threat? That is the experience of *uneasiness*, of anxiety, which, if it is total enough, becomes a deadly unspecified malaise.

Ours is a time of uneasiness and indifference – not yet formulated in such ways as to permit the work of reason and the play of sensibility. Instead of troubles – defined in terms of values and threats – there is often the misery of vague uneasiness; instead of explicit issues there is often merely the beat feeling that all is somehow not right. Neither the values threatened nor whatever threatens them has been stated; in short, they have not been carried to the point of decision. Much less have they been formulated as problems of social science.

In the 'thirties there was little doubt – except among certain deluded business circles – that there was an economic issue which was also a pack of personal troubles. In these arguments about 'the crisis of capitalism,' the formulations of Marx and the many unacknowledged re-formulations of his work probably set the leading terms of the issue, and some men came to understand their personal troubles in these terms. The values threatened were plain to see and cherished by all; the structural contradictions that threatened them also seemed plain. Both were widely and deeply experienced. It was a political age.

But the values threatened in the era after World War Two are often neither widely acknowledged as values nor widely felt to be threatened. Much private uneasiness goes unformulated; much public malaise and many decisions of enormous structural relevance never become public issues. For those who accept such inherited values as reason and freedom, it is the uneasiness itself that is the trouble; it is the indifference itself that is the issue. And it is this condition, of uneasiness and indifference, that is the signal feature of our period.

All this is so striking that it is often interpreted by observers as a shift in the very kinds of problems that need now to be formulated. We are frequently told that the problems of our decade, or even the crises of our period, have shifted from the external realm of economics and now have to do with the quality of individual life – in fact with the question of whether there is soon going to be anything that can properly be called individual life. Not child labor but comic books, not poverty but mass leisure, are at the center of concern. Many great public issues as well as many private troubles are described in terms of 'the psychiatric' – often, it seems, in a pathetic attempt to avoid the large issues and problems of modern society. Often this statement seems to rest upon a provincial narrowing of interest to the Western societies, or even to the United States – thus ignoring two-thirds of mankind; often, too, it arbitrarily divorces the individual life from the larger institutions within which that life is enacted, and which on occasion bear upon it more grievously than do the intimate environments of childhood.

Problems of leisure, for example, cannot even be stated without considering problems of work. Family troubles over comic books cannot be formulated as problems without considering the plight of the contemporary family in its new relations with the newer institutions of the social structure. Neither leisure nor its debilitating uses can be understood as problems without recognition of the extent to which malaise and indifference now form the social and personal climate of contemporary American society. In this climate, no problems of 'the private life' can be stated and solved without recognition of the crisis of ambition that is part of the very career of men at work in the incorporated economy.

It is true, as psychoanalysts continually point out, that people do often have 'the increasing sense of being moved by obscure forces within themselves which they are unable to define.' But it is *not* true, as Ernest Jones asserted, that 'man's chief enemy and danger is his own unruly nature and the dark forces pent up within him.' On the contrary: 'Man's chief danger' today lies in the unruly forces of contemporary society itself, with its alienating methods of production, its enveloping techniques of political domination, its international anarchy – in a word, its pervasive transformations of the very 'nature' of man and the conditions and aims of his life.

It is now the social scientist's foremost political and intellectual task – for here the two coincide – to make clear the elements of contemporary uneasiness and indifference. It is the central demand made upon him by other cultural workmen – by physical scientists and artists, by the intellectual community in general. It is because of this task and these demands, I believe, that the social sciences are becoming the common denominator of our cultural period, and the sociological imagination our most needed quality of mind.

In every intellectual age some one style of reflection tends to become a common denominator of cultural life. Nowadays, it is true, many intellectual fads are widely taken up before they are dropped for new ones in the course of a year or two. Such enthusiasms may add spice to cultural play, but leave little or no intellectual trace. That is not true of such ways of thinking as 'Newtonian physics' or 'Darwinian biology.' Each of these intellectual universes became an influence that reached far beyond any special sphere of idea and imagery. In terms of them, or in terms derived from them, unknown scholars as well as fashionable commentators came to re-focus their observations and re-formulate their concerns.

During the modern era, physical and biological science has been the major common denominator of serious reflection and popular metaphysics in Western societies. 'The technique of the laboratory' has been the accepted mode of procedure and the source of intellectual security. That is one meaning of the idea of an intellectual common denominator: men can state their strongest convictions in its terms; other terms and other styles of reflection seem mere vehicles of escape and obscurity.

That a common denominator prevails does not of course mean that no other styles of thought or modes of sensibility exist. But it does mean that more general intellectual interests tend to slide into this area, to be formulated there most sharply, and when so formulated, to be thought somehow to have reached, if not a solution, at least a profitable way of being carried along.

The sociological imagination is becoming, I believe, the major common denominator of our cultural life and its signal feature. This quality of mind is found in the social and psychological sciences, but it goes far beyond these studies as we now know them. Its acquisition by individuals and by the cultural community at large is slow and often fumbling; many social scientists are themselves quite unaware of it. They do not seem to know that the use of this imagination is central to the best work that they might do, that by failing to develop and to use it they are failing to meet the cultural expectations that are coming to be demanded of them and that the classic traditions of their several disciplines make available to them.

Yet in factual and moral concerns, in literary work and in political analysis, the qualities of this imagination are regularly demanded. In a great variety of expressions, they have become central features of intellectual endeavor and cultural sensibility. Leading critics exemplify these qualities as do serious journalists – in fact the work of both is often judged in these terms. Popular categories of criticism – high, middle, and low-brow, for example – are now at least as much socio-logical as aesthetic. Novelists – whose serious work embodies the most widespread definitions of human reality – frequently possess this imagin-ation, and do much to meet the demand for it. By means of it, orienta-tion to the present as history is sought. As images of 'human nature' become more problematic, an increasing need is felt to pay closer yet more imaginative attention to the social routines and catastrophes which reveal (and which shape) man's nature in this time of civil unrest and ideological conflict. Although fashion is often revealed by attempts to use it, the sociological imagination is not merely a fashion. It is a quality of mind that seems most dramatically to promise an under-standing of the intimate realities of ourselves in connection with larger social realities. It is not merely one quality of mind among the contem-porary range of cultural sensibilities – it is *the* quality whose wider and more adroit use offers the promise that all such sensibilities – and in fact, human reason itself – will come to play a greater role in human affairs.

The cultural meaning of physical science – the major older common denominator – is becoming doubtful. As an intellectual style, physical science is coming to be thought by many as somehow inadequate. The adequacy of scientific styles of thought and feeling, imagination and sensibility, has of course from their beginnings been subject to religious doubt and theological controversy, but our scientific grandfathers and fathers beat down such religious doubts. The current doubts are secular, humanistic – and often quite confused. Recent developments in physical science – with its technological climax in the H-bomb and the means of carrying it about the earth – have not been experienced as a solution to any problems widely known and deeply pondered by larger intellectual communities and cultural publics. These developments have been correctly seen as a result of highly specialized inquiry, and improperly felt to be wonderfully mysterious. They have raised more problems – both intellectual and moral – than they have solved, and the problems they have raised lie almost entirely in the area of social not physical affairs. The obvious conquest of nature, the overcoming of scarcity, is felt by men of the overdeveloped societies to be virtually complete. And now in these societies, science – the chief instrument of this conquest – is felt to be footloose, aimless, and in need of re-appraisal.

The modern esteem for science has long been merely assumed, but now the technological ethos and the kind of engineering imagination associated with science are more likely to be frightening and ambiguous than hopeful and progressive. Of course this is not all there is to 'science,' but it is feared that this could become all that there is to it. The felt need to reappraise physical science reflects the need for a new common denominator. It is the human meaning and the social role of science, its military and commercial issue, its political significance that are undergoing confused re-appraisal. Scientific developments of weaponry may lead to the 'necessity' for world political rearrangements – but such 'necessity' is not felt to be solvable by physical science itself.

Much that has passed for 'science' is now felt to be dubious philosophy; much that is held to be 'real science' is often felt to provide only confused fragments of the realities among which men live. Men of science, it is widely felt, no longer try to picture reality as a whole or to present a true outline of human destiny. Moreover, 'science' seems to many less a creative ethos and a manner of orientation than a set of Science Machines, operated by technicians and controlled by economic and military men who neither embody nor understand science as ethos and orientation. In the meantime, philosophers who speak in the name of science often transform it into 'scientism,' making out its experience to be identical with human experience, and claiming that only by its method can the problems of life be solved. With all this, many cultural workmen have come to feel that 'science' is a false and pretentious Messiah, or at the very least a highly ambiguous element in modern civilization.

But there are, in C. P. Snow's phrase, 'two cultures': the scientific and the humanistic. Whether as history or drama, as biography, poetry or fiction, the essence of the humanistic culture has been literature. Yet it is now frequently suggested that serious literature has in many ways become a minor art. If this is so, it is not merely because of the development of mass publics and mass media of communication, and all that these mean for serious literary production. It is also owing to the very quality of the history of our times and the kinds of need men of sensibility feel to grasp that quality.

What fiction, what journalism, what artistic endeavor can compete with the historical reality and political facts of our time? What dramatic vision of hell can compete with the events of twentieth-century war? What moral denunciations can measure up to the moral insensibility of men in the agonies of primary accumulation? It is social and historical reality that men want to know, and often they do not find contemporary literature an adequate means for knowing it. They yearn for facts, they search for their meanings, they want 'a big picture' in which they can believe and within which they can come to understand themselves. They want orienting values too, and suitable ways of feeling and styles of emotion and vocabularies of motive. And they do not readily find these in the literature of today. It does not matter whether or not these qualities *are* to be found there; what matters is that men do not often find them there.

In the past, literary men as critics and historians made notes on England and on journeys to America. They tried to characterize societies as wholes, and to discern their moral meanings. Were Tocqueville or Taine alive today, would they not be sociologists? Asking this question about Taine, a reviewer in *The Times* (London) suggests:

> Taine always saw man primarily as a social animal and society as a collection of groups: he could observe minutely, was a tireless field worker and possessed a quality . . . particularly valuable for perceiving relationships between social phenomena – the quality of springliness. He was too interested in the present to be a good historian, too much of a theorist to try his hand as a novelist, and he thought of literature too much as documents in the culture of an age or country to achieve first-class status as a critic . . . His work on English literature is less about English literature than a commentary on the morality of English society and a vehicle for his positivism. He is a social theorist before all else.[1]

That he remained a 'literary man' rather than a 'social scientist' testifies perhaps to the domination of much nineteenth-century social science by the zealous search for 'laws' presumably comparable to those imagined to be found by natural scientists. In the absence of an adequate social science, critics and novelists, dramatists and poets have been the major, and often the only, formulators of private troubles

1. *Times Literary Supplement*, 15 November 1957.

and even of public issues. Art does express such feelings and often focuses them – at its best with dramatic sharpness – but still not with the intellectual clarity required for their understanding or relief today. Art does not and cannot formulate these feelings as problems containing the troubles and issues men must now confront if they are to overcome their uneasiness and indifference and the intractable miseries to which these lead. The artist, indeed, does not often try to do this. Moreover, the serious artist is himself in much trouble, and could well do with some intellectual and cultural aid from a social science made sprightly by the sociological imagination.

Twentieth-century Sociology: Sociology in France, England and Germany

The dominating influence of Durkheim on French sociology had the effect of bringing together a heterogeneous group of scholars who applied his methodology and approach to their different fields of study. In effect a Durkheimian school of sociology, unlike anything that occurred elsewhere, was formed. It had a peculiar orientation, and it was inspired by a high-minded elevation of thought and imbued with a single-minded devotion to further sociological thought. Whatever one thinks of the ultimate results of their work, there is no doubt that this kind of scholarly fraternity, with all its members sharing the same presuppositions, produced a coherent, unmistakably characteristic body of work distinguished for its originality and uniqueness. Durkheim himself died in 1919, a disillusioned man, having lost his son in the war. The war took a severe toll of many of the young and promising members of the school, and the *Année sociologique* had, of course, to suspend its publication; but somehow enough of the movement survived to enable the sociologists to get together again and resume their collaborative work. One man more than anybody else was responsible for this, and to him is owed almost everything that was done in France in the fields of sociology and social anthropology in the inter-war years. He was Marcel Mauss, Durkheim's nephew and his right-hand man for many years. He set the tone and the pace. He revived the *Année sociologique* which came out at infrequent intervals in the inter-war period.

Mauss made Durkheim's *The Elementary Forms of Religious Life* the starting point of many of his own contributions. Perhaps

Durkheim was never more original than in those few pages at the end of his work in which he related the categories of thought of a group to its social life. In this way, he can be said to have pioneered a new branch of sociology, which has come to be known as the sociology of knowledge. This branch of sociology, which has grown in importance and significance since his day, deals not only with the processes of thought that are socially conditioned but also with the results of literary, artistic and scientific thought, which can only be adequately understood in terms of the social organization of society. This was perhaps the most distinctive contribution of the French school of sociology. Mauss himself, taking his cue from Durkheim's sociology of knowledge, tried to prove that the classifications of logic reflect the structure of the group. Gifted as he was in so many fields of scholarship, he preferred to encourage the works of others rather than write himself. Nevertheless he published brilliant essays on Eskimo society, *The Gift*, and, in collaboration with Henri Hubert, the essay on *Sacrifice: Its Nature and Function*.

Perhaps even more than Mauss, Marcel Granet (1884–1940), whose works on Chinese history and civilization are classics, elaborated on the ideas of Durkheim, applying them to the social system of the Chinese as reflected in their language and thought.

The theories of primitive thought, mentality and religion of another writer, Lucien Lévy-Bruhl (1857–1939), almost rivalled those of Durkheim in their influence. Lucien Lévy-Bruhl was a prolific writer who, starting with works on philosophical themes, especially morals, ended by writing one work after another on primitive thought and religion. He was perhaps the last of the so-called armchair social anthropologists in France. He believed, as Durkheim did, in the existence of collective ideas or representations which were irrational, even 'mystical' and therefore non-scientific, and which entirely determined the thought structure of primitive people. So he coined a new term to describe this type of thought, which he called pre-logical. On this basis he explained all the so-called irrational or non-rational practices and beliefs of primitive people. Primitive religion came under this condemnation, and, by the same token, all religion, although Lévy-Bruhl would not admit it, was a species of irrational and superstitious belief.

At the same time as these ideas of Lévy-Bruhl were being acclaimed uncritically for their insight and originality, British anthropologists, as will be shown presently, were slowly but surely by their patient field work undermining the quite false dichotomy between primitive and civilized thought.

In political thought, the most outstanding writer in France was undoubtedly Célestin Bouglé (1870–1940), and many of the prominent political thinkers of today were his pupils. Bouglé revived the ideas of Saint-Simon and Proudhon, commented on them, and showed their relevance to contemporary thought. Like de Tocqueville, he was interested in the rise of egalitarianism in modern society. He attributed the rise of modern individualism to the spread of the egalitarian ethos. Such individualism is diametrically opposed to the caste system, which is based on a rigid social hierarchy. In modern European history, particularly in the last century or so, there has been a gradual disintegration of the hierarchical system of life.

The theme of social classes was taken up by another writer, Maurice Halbwachs (1877–1945). Halbwachs made a serious attempt to understand the nature of social classes and he carried out empirical research on the working class. His view, expressed in a number of works, was that class cannot be determined either by occupation or by income but by certain behaviour patterns. His views on urbanization led him to modify the conclusions on suicide arrived at by Durkheim. According to Halbwachs, suicide resulting from anomie may well occur as a result of inadequate adaptation due to rapid urbanization. This kind of suicide is invariably individually motivated. Like the other members of the Durkheimian school, Halbwachs made important contributions to the sociology of knowledge; in particular he presented a new angle to the phenomenon of memory. His view was that memory is the result of our social life. Each and every one of our recollections is related in manifold ways to the life of society, particularly by language. Our recollection, therefore, operating within an area defined by our social life, has a limit in time and place.

French sociology was certainly very much alive in the inter-war period in spite of the many handicaps and tribulations it encountered. But somehow it was insulated and tied down by too many rigid preconceptions. Once an idea was launched, all facts, however awkward, had to fit into the preconceived scheme. There was a predilection for polarization of ideas – sacred and profane, right and left, gift and reciprocity, and lastly, as with Claude Lévi-Strauss, nature and culture. In this respect, it was rationalistic in the best tradition of French thought, and open therefore to easy refutation.

In England, sociology as such had never been an academic discipline, though some economists, like Marshall, toyed with the idea that sooner or later sociology might well encompass much of what is known as social science, including economics. Having made a very promising beginning with works by Buckle, Mill, Bagehot and especially Spencer, and with interest in Comte and Le Play still very strong, British sociology fizzled out by the end of the nineteenth century. There were two main reasons for this. The first was that it was associated in the British mind with social reform, and therefore it was to some extent seen as having a political purpose. But the second reason was by far the more important one. All those writers who produced work on one or other aspect of sociology were outside the academic fraternity, and therefore their views and writings, however distinguished or popular, were not regarded as academically respectable. In addition, the philosophical tradition in British universities in the second half of the nineteenth century came under the influence of German idealistic philosophy and turned away from the typical British empirical school of thought, in particular the associationist school of psychology, which still had adherents like Spencer and Mill. The latter could not resist the powerful assaults made on them by the academic philosophers of the day, and when Spencer died in 1900 he and his works were completely forgotten. More than anywhere else it proved a hard struggle to find a place for sociology in the academic world. Two of the finest scholars, whom any country would have been proud of, occupied the only chairs of sociology in England, at the London School of Economics, L. T. Hobhouse (1864–1929) and E. A. Westermarck (1862–1939). They produced between them works of scholarship unequalled in range and depth. Both of them were interested in the place of morality in social life. Westermarck was, in addition, a keen anthropologist who spent a number of years in Morocco, as a result of which he wrote works on *Ritual and Belief in Morocco* (1926) and collected a large number of proverbs. His two masterpieces were *The History of Human Marriage* (1891) and *The Origin and Development of the Moral Ideas* (1906, 1908). Westermarck's view was that there is no such thing as universal moral principles governing human conduct, that morality, basically, is a question of sentiment, and that moral ideas can be shown to have a history during which they undergo change and development. Thus morality is an important subject matter for both sociology and psychology.

Hobhouse was the more philosophical thinker. In his monumental work *Morals in Evolution* (1906), he attempted to trace the stages of mental as well as social development, between which he discovered a correlation. This kind of development he described as occurring in the direction of greater rationality and a wider concept of goodness. For Hobhouse, human evolution meant evolution towards 'the rational good'. He repudiated the crude evolutionism of Spencer and the nineteenth-century writers. There are stages of progress as well as regress in human history. There are variations from one society to another but, by and large, one can discern a movement towards a more humane and moral society. A pioneering work in sociology was produced by Hobhouse in collaboration with G. C. Wheeler and M. Ginsberg called *The Material Culture and Social Institutions of the Simpler Peoples* (1915), in which it was proved that social systems may vary enormously in their institutions while possessing identical economic structures.

Nevertheless, the influence of Hobhouse and Westermarck as sociologists was minimal. Neither of them showed any acquaintance with the seminal works that were being produced in France and Germany, not to speak of those that were coming out in America. Properly speaking, they were not moving in the main stream of sociological thought. It was other British writers, mainly political writers of socialist leanings, like Graham Wallace, Laski and Tawney, who contributed more than Hobhouse or Westermarck to the development of sociological thought. Their works must be seen as part of the whole process of British thought and writings which were directly aimed at bringing about a change in social policy. It is in this light that works of people like Rowntree, the Webbs and Beveridge must be seen, works on the social and industrial aspects of society which were largely responsible, not only for awakening the social consciousness of the people, but for legislation which changed the social system of Britain.

In another very important respect, British writers made a lasting and profound contribution to sociological knowledge. The Victorian social anthropologists, the most popular writer of whom was Frazer, used material at second hand to speculate about early primitive society. One and all, in their different ways they were determined to prove that the institutions of early society were part of the childhood of the human race and, as such, need not be taken seriously, being a product of ignorance, fear and superstition. If religion which had a permeating influence on early society has no claim to rational belief, then all religion is equally irrational. This was one way in which these writers could rationalize their disbelief and agnosticism. Nothing of any value could be derived from the lucubrations of these armchair writers. The man who more than anybody else delivered the *coup de grâce* to this kind of thought was Bronislaw Malinowski (1884–1942).[1] His field work among Trobriand islanders and other small-scale societies in the Pacific set the standard for the kind of anthropological research which has been followed by all his successors. Once for all, he proved that the social institutions of primitive or savage people are just as complex as those of more advanced civilizations, that these institutions comprise a culture which has the sanction of tradition behind it and, what is more important, that the differences in thought processes between primitive and more civilized people are differences not in kind but only in degree. At the same time, Malinowski revived the concept of functionalism as a method of investigation to denote that institutions, because they have survived in society, must therefore serve a function and can only be understood in terms of the needs they fulfil. Malinowski even grandiloquently claimed that he had discovered the theory of functionalism. The extreme view he himself took can be reduced

1. See also Chapter 6, pp. 402–3.

to a tautology, and logically implies that institutions are what they are because they are what they are. They should be regarded as serving an essential purpose and should not be tampered with. It is quite obvious that, even if we take the concept of need as a point of departure, it does not follow that the same need cannot be fulfilled by a change in the institution or by another institution.

Of equal influence were the contributions of A. R. Radcliffe-Brown (1881–1953). In his first major work, *The Andaman Islanders* (1922), and in a succession of other works, notably *Structure and Function in Primitive Society: Essays and Addresses* (1923–49), Radcliffe-Brown undertook to explain social phenomena, that is, the social facts that are the data for the anthropologist, as persistent systems of adaptation and integration. For him, any social system must be viewed in terms of structure and function. Social structure involves the study of interests or values which determine social relations, while function leads to the study of institutions. A social system must possess a persistent structure in order to experience any changes at all. To retain and maintain an equilibrium, it must have a certain recognizable arrangement of roles and activities. Only in this way can evolution be regarded as a gradual process to higher integration and differentiation. Radcliffe-Brown went even further than Spencer in drawing the analogy between a social system or society and a biological organism. While such an analogy is a useful methodological device in showing the interdependence of parts with each other, to say, as Radcliffe-Brown did, that each part is functionally necessary to the other parts and the whole is logically wrong.

Mainly through Malinowski's method of field work and his voluminous writings, England became the centre of the most brilliant school of social anthropology in this century. In the twenties and thirties a whole generation of outstanding young anthropologists, working directly under him or inspired by his work and writings, began to produce work that was destined to add significantly to our knowledge of the culture, thought patterns and institutions of primitive small-scale societies.

The picture in Germany was altogether deplorable. The deaths of Weber and Simmel brought to an end an era of German thought, writing and research of great depth and originality. During the brief period of the Weimar republic, some attempts were made to branch out into new fields of sociological research, mainly in the fields of communication, mass media and the cinema. The conditions, however, were not ripe for sustained and continuous research, apart from the fact that the period of the republic was too brief to allow for the necessary readjustments and reorientations to take place. The most influential sociologist of that period was Leopold von Wiese (1876–1962), whose major work, *General Sociology*, was published in 1924; the second revised edition appeared in 1932. With the advent of the Nazi regime in 1933, sociology as such ceased to exist in Germany, and all sociological societies and journals were suspended.

Marcel Mauss 1872–1950

Major works

The Gift: Forms and Functions of Exchange in Archaic Societies (1925)
Sociology and Anthropology (1950)
Co-author of:
Primitive Classification (with Émile Durkheim, 1963)
Sacrifice: Its Nature and Function (with Henri Hubert, 1964)

The following extracts are reprinted from Marcel Mauss, *The Gift*, translated by Ian Cunnison (London: Cohen & West, 1966, 1969), pp. 1–2, 3, 10–12, 69, 77, with the permission of the publishers.

We intend in this book to isolate one important set of phenomena: namely, prestations which are in theory voluntary, disinterested and spontaneous, but are in fact obligatory and interested. The form usually taken is that of the gift generously offered; but the accompanying behaviour is formal pretence and social deception, while the transaction itself is based on obligation and economic self-interest. We shall note the various principles behind this necessary form of exchange (which is nothing less than the division of labour itself), but we shall confine our detailed study to the enquiry: *In primitive or archaic types of society what is the principle whereby the gift received has to be repaid? What force is there in the thing given which compels the recipient to make a return?* We hope, by presenting enough data, to be able to answer this question precisely, and also to indicate the direction in which answers to cognate questions might be sought. We shall also pose new problems. Of these, some concern the morality of the contract: for instance, the manner in which today the law of things remains bound up with the law of persons; and some refer to the forms and ideas which have always been present in exchange and which even now are to be seen in the idea of individual interest . . .

In the systems of the past we do not find simple exchange of goods, wealth and produce through markets established among individuals. For it is groups, and not individuals, which carry on exchange, make contracts, and are bound by obligations; the persons represented in the contracts are moral persons – clans, tribes, and families; the groups, or the chiefs as intermediaries for the groups, confront and oppose each other. Further what they exchange is not exclusively goods and wealth, real and personal property, and things of economic value. They exchange rather courtesies, entertainments, ritual, military assistance, women, children, dances, and feasts; and fairs in which the market is but one element and the circulation of wealth but one part of a wide and enduring contract. Finally, although the prestations and counter-prestations take place under a voluntary guise they are in essence strictly obligatory, and their sanction is private or open warfare. We propose to call this the system of *total prestations* . . .

The Obligation to Give and the Obligation to Receive

To appreciate fully the institutions of total prestation and the potlatch we must seek to explain two complementary factors. Total prestation not only carries with it the obligation to repay gifts received, but it implies two others equally important: the obligation to give presents and the obligation to receive them. A complete theory of the three obligations would include a satisfactory fundamental explanation of this form of contract among Polynesian clans. For the moment we simply indicate the manner in which the subject might be treated.

It is easy to find a large number of facts on the obligation to receive. A clan, household, association or guest is constrained to demand hospitality, to receive presents, to barter or to make blood and marriage alliances. The Dayaks have even developed a whole set of customs based on the obligation to partake of any meal at which one is present or which one has seen in preparation.

The obligation to give is no less important. If we understood this, we should also know how men came to exchange things with each other. We merely point out a few facts. To refuse to give, or to fail to invite, is – like refusing to accept – the equivalent of a declaration of war; it is a refusal of friendship and intercourse. Again, one gives because one is forced to do so, because the recipient has a sort of proprietary right over everything which belongs to the donor. This right is expressed and conceived as a sort of spiritual bond. Thus in Australia the man who owes all the game he kills to his father- and mother-in-law may eat nothing in their presence for fear that their very breath should poison his food. We have seen above that the *taonga* sister's son has customs of this kind in Samoa, which are comparable with those of the sister's son (*vasu*) in Fiji.

In all these instances there is a series of rights and duties about consuming and repaying existing side by side with rights and duties about giving and receiving. The pattern of symmetrical and reciprocal rights is not difficult to understand if we realize that it is first and foremost a pattern of spiritual bonds between things which are to some extent parts of persons, and persons and groups that behave in some measure as if they were things.

All these institutions reveal the same kind of social and psychological pattern. Food, women, children, possessions, charms, land, labour, services, religious offices, rank – everything is stuff to be given away and repaid. In perpetual interchange of what we may call spiritual matter, comprising men and things, these elements pass and repass between clans and individuals, ranks, sexes and generations . . .

Political and Economic Conclusions

Our facts do more than illumine our morality and point out our ideal; for they help us to analyse economic facts of a more general nature, and our analysis might suggest the way to better administrative procedures for our societies.

We have repeatedly pointed out how this economy of gift-exchange fails to conform to the principles of so-called natural economy or utilitarianism. The phenomena in the economic life of the people we have studied (and they are good representatives of the great neolithic stage of civilization) and the survivals of these traditions in societies closer to ours and even in our own custom, are disregarded in the schemes adopted by the few economists who have tried to compare the various forms of economic life. We add our own observations to those of Malinowski who devoted a whole work to ousting the prevalent doctrines on primitive economics.

Here is a chain of undoubted fact. The notion of value exists in these societies. Very great surpluses, even by European standards, are amassed; they are expended often at pure loss with tremendous extravagance and without a trace of mercenariness; among things exchanged are tokens of wealth, a kind of money. All this very rich economy is nevertheless imbued with religious elements; money still has its magical power and is linked to clan and individual. Diverse economic activities – for example, the market – are impregnated with ritual and myth; they retain a ceremonial character, obligatory and efficacious; they have their own ritual and etiquette. Here is the answer to the question already posed by Durkheim about the religious origin of the notion of economic value. The facts also supply answers to a string of problems about the forms and origins of what is so badly termed exchange – the barter or *permutatio* of useful articles. In the view of cautious Latin authors in the Aristotelian tradition and their *a priori* economic history, this is the origin of the division of labour. On the contrary, it is something other than utility which makes goods circulate in these multifarious and fairly enlightened societies. Clans, age groups and sexes, in view of the many relationships ensuing from contacts between them, are in a state of perpetual economic effervescence which has little about it that is materialistic; it is much less prosaic than our sale and purchase, hire of services and speculations.

We may go farther than this and break down, reconsider and redefine the principal notions of which we have already made use. Our terms 'present' and 'gift' do not have precise meanings, but we could find no others. Concepts which we like to put in opposition – freedom and obligation; generosity, liberality, luxury on the one hand and saving, interest, austerity on the other – are not exact and it would be well to put them to the test. We cannot deal very fully with this; but let us take an example from the Trobriands. It is a complex notion that inspires the economic actions we have described, a notion neither of purely free and gratuitous prestations, nor of purely interested and utilitarian production and exchange; it is a kind of hybrid.

Malinowski made a serious effort to classify all the transactions he witnessed in the Trobriands according to the interest or disinterestedness present in them. He ranges them from pure gift to barter with bargaining, but this classification is untenable. Thus according to Malinowski the typical 'pure gift' is that between spouses. Now in our view one of the most important acts noted by the author, and one which throws a strong light on sexual relationships, is the *mapula*, the sequence of payments by a husband to his wife as a kind of salary for sexual services. Likewise the payments to chiefs are tribute; the distributions of food (*sagali*) are payments for labour or ritual accomplished, such as work done on the eve of a funeral. Thus basically as these gifts are not spontaneous so also they are not really disinterested. They are for the most part counter-prestations made not solely in order to pay for goods or services, but also to maintain a profitable alliance which it would be unwise to reject, as for instance partnership between fishing tribes and tribes of hunters and potters. Now this fact is wide-spread – we have met it with the Maori, Tsimshian and others. Thus it is clear wherein this mystical and practical force resides, which at once binds clans together and keeps them separate, which divides their labour and constrains them to exchange. Even in these societies the individuals and the groups, or rather the sub-groups, have always felt the sovereign right to refuse a contract, and it is this which lends an appearance of generosity to the circulation of goods. On the other hand, normally they had neither the right of, nor interest in, such a refusal; and it is that which makes these distant societies seem akin to ours.

The use of money suggests other considerations. The Trobriand *vaygu'a*, armshells and necklaces, like the North-West American coppers and Iroquois *wampum*, are at once wealth, tokens of wealth, means of exchange and payment, and things to be given away or destroyed. In addition they are pledges, linked to the persons who use them and who in turn are bound by them. Since, however, at other times they serve as tokens of money, there is interest in giving them away, for if they are transformed into services or merchandise that yield money then one is better off in the end. We may truly say that the Trobriand or Tsimshian chief behaves somewhat like the capitalist who knows how to spend his money at the right time only to build his capital up again. Interest and disinterestedness taken together explain this form of the circulation of wealth and of the circulation of tokens of wealth that follows upon it.

Even the destruction of wealth does not correspond to the complete disinterestedness which one might expect. These great acts of generosity are not free from self-interest. The extravagant consumption of wealth, particularly in the potlatch, always exaggerated and often purely destructive, in which goods long stored are all at once given away or destroyed, lends to these institutions the appearance of wasteful expenditure and child-like prodigality. Not only are valuable goods thrown away and foodstuffs consumed to excess but there is destruction for its own sake – coppers are thrown into the sea or broken. But the motives of such excessive gifts and reckless consumption, such mad losses and destruction of wealth, especially in these potlatch societies, are in no way disinterested. Between vassals and chiefs, between vassals and their henchmen, the hierarchy is established by means of these gifts.

To give is to show one's superiority, to show that one is something more and higher, that one is *magister*. To accept without returning or repaying more is to face subordination, to become a client and subservient, to become *minister*.

The magic ritual in the *kula* known as *mwasila* contains spells and symbols which show that the man who wants to enter into a contract seeks above all profit in the form of social – one might almost say animal – superiority. Thus he charms the betelnut to be used with his partners, casts a spell over the chief and his fellows, then over his own pigs, his necklaces, his head and mouth, the opening gifts and whatever else he carries; then he chants, not without exaggeration: 'I shall kick the mountain, the mountain moves ... the mountain falls down ... My spell shall go to the top of Dobu Mountain ... My canoe will sink ... My fame is like thunder, my treading is like the roar of flying witches ... Tudududu.' The aim is to be the first, the finest, luckiest, strongest and richest and that is how to set about it. Later the chief confirms his *mana* when he redistributes to his vassals and relatives what he has just received; he maintains his rank among the chiefs by exchanging armshells for necklaces, hospitality for visits, and so on. In this case wealth is, in every aspect, as much a thing of prestige as a thing of utility. But are we certain that our own position is different and that wealth with us is not first and foremost a means of controlling others?

Let us test now the notion to which we have opposed the ideas of the gift and disinterestedness: that of interest and the individual pursuit of utility. This agrees no better with previous theories. If similar motives animate Trobriand and American chiefs and Andaman clans and once animated generous Hindu or Germanic noblemen in their giving and spending, they are not to be found in the cold reasoning of the business man, banker or capitalist. In those earlier civilizations one had interests but they differed from those of our time. There, if one hoards, it is only to spend later on, to put people under obligations and to win followers. Exchanges are made as well, but only of luxury objects like clothing and ornaments, or feasts and other things that are consumed at once. Return is made with interest, but that is done in order to humiliate the original donor or exchange partner and not merely to recompense him for the loss that the lapse of time causes him. He has an interest but it is only analogous to the one which we say is our guiding principle.

Ranged between the relatively amorphous and disinterested economy within the sub-groups of Australian and North American (Eastern and Prairie) clans, and the individualistic economy of pure interest which our societies have had to some extent ever since their discovery by Greeks and Semites, there is a great series of institutions and economic events not governed by the rationalism which past theory so readily took for granted.

The word 'interest' is recent in origin and can be traced back to the Latin *interest* written on account books opposite rents to be recovered. In the most epicurean of these philosophies pleasure and the good were pursued and not material utility. The victory of rationalism and mercantilism was required before the notions of profit and the individual were given currency and raided to the level of principles. One can date roughly – after Mandeville and his *Fable des Abeilles* – the triumph of the notion of individual interest. It is only by awkward paraphrasing that one can render the phrase 'individual interest' in Latin, Greek or Arabic. Even the men who wrote in classical Sanskrit and used the word *artha*, which is fairly close to our idea of interest, turned it, as they did with other categories of action, into an idea different from ours. The sacred books of ancient India divide human actions into the categories of law (*dharma*), interest (*artha*) and desire (*kama*). But *artha* refers particularly to the political interest of king, Brahmins and ministers, or royalty and the various castes. The considerable literature of the *Niticastra* is not economic in tone.

It is only our Western societies that quite recently turned man into an economic animal. But we are not yet all animals of the same species. In both lower and upper classes pure irrational expenditure is in current practice: it is still characteristic of some French noble houses. *Homo oeconomicus* is not behind us, but before, like the moral man, the man of duty, the scientific man and the reasonable man. For a long time man was something quite different; and it is not so long now since he became a machine – a calculating machine.

In other respects we are still far from frigid utilitarian calculation. Make a thorough statistical analysis, as Halbwachs did for the working classes, of the consumption and expenditure of our middle classes and how many needs are found satisfied? How many desires are fulfilled that have utility as their end? Does not the rich man's expenditure on luxury, art, servants and extravagances recall the expenditure of the nobleman of former times or the savage chiefs whose customs we have been describing?

It is another question to ask if it is good that this should be so. It is a good thing possibly that there exist means of expenditure and exchange other than economic ones. However, we contend that the best economic procedure is not to be found in the calculation of individual needs. I believe that we must become, in proportion as we would develop our wealth, something more than better financiers, accountants and administrators. The mere pursuit of individual ends is harmful to the ends and peace of the whole, to the rhythm of its work and pleasures, and hence in the end to the individual.

We have just seen how important sections and groups of our capital industries are seeking to attach groups of their employees to them. Again all the syndicalist groups, employers' as much as wage-earners', claim that they are defending and representing the general interest with a fervour equal to that of the particular interests of their members, or of the interests of the groups themselves. Their speeches are burnished with many fine metaphors. Nevertheless, one has to admit that not only ethics and philosophy, but also economic opinion and practice, are starting to rise to this 'social' level. The feeling is that there is no better way of making men work than by reassuring them of being paid loyally all their lives for labour which they give loyally not only for their own sakes but for that of others. The producer-exchanger feels now as he has always felt – but this time he feels it more acutely – that he is giving something of himself, his time and his life. Thus he wants recompense, however modest, for this gift. And to refuse him this recompense is to incite him to laziness and lower production.

We draw now a conclusion both sociological and practical. The famous Sura LXIV, 'Mutual Deception,' given at Mecca to Mohammed, says:

15. Your possessions and your children are only a trial and Allah it is with whom is a great reward.

16. Therefore be careful [of your duty to] Allah as much as you can, and hear and obey and spread (*sadaqa*), it is better for your souls; and whoever is saved from the greediness of his soul, these it is that are the successful.

17. If you set apart from Allah a goodly portion, He will double it for you and forgive you; and Allah is the multiplier of rewards, forebearing.

18. The knower of the unseen and the seen, the mighty, the wise.

Replace the name of Allah by that of the society or professional group, or unite all three, replace the concept of alms by that of co-operation, of a prestation altruistically made; you will have a fair idea of the practice which is now coming into being. It can be seen at work already in certain economic groups and in the hearts of the masses who often enough know their own interest and the common interest better than their leaders do.

Sociological and Ethical Conclusions

We may be permitted another note about the method we have used.

We do not set this work up as a model; it simply proffers one or two suggestions. It is incomplete: the analysis could be pushed farther. We are really posing questions for historians and anthropologists and offering possible lines of research for them rather than resolving a problem and laying down definite answers. It is enough for us to be sure for the moment that we have given sufficient data for such an end.

This being the case, we would point out that there is a heuristic element in our manner of treatment. The facts we have studied are all 'total' social phenomena. The word 'general' may be preferred although we like it less. Some of the facts presented concern the whole of society and its institutions (as with potlatch, opposing clans, tribes on visit, etc.); others, in which exchanges and contracts are the concern of individuals, embrace a large number of institutions.

These phenomena are at once legal, economic, religious, aesthetic, morphological and so on. They are legal in that they concern individual and collective rights, organized and diffuse morality; they may be entirely obligatory, or subject simply to praise or disapproval. They are at once political and domestic, being of interest both to classes and to clans and families. They are religious; they concern true religion, animism, magic and diffuse religious mentality. They are economic, for the notions of value, utility, interest, luxury, wealth, acquisition, accumulation, consumption and liberal sumptuous expenditure are all present, although not perhaps in their modern senses. Moreover, these institutions have an important aesthetic side which we have left unstudied; but the dances performed, the songs and shows, the dramatic representations given between camps or partners, the objects made, used, decorated, polished, amassed and transmitted with affection, received with joy, given away in triumph, the feasts in which everyone participates – all these, the food, objects and services, are the source of aesthetic emotions as well as emotions aroused by interest.

Bronislaw Malinowski 1884–1942

Major works

The Family Among the Australian Aborigines (1913)
Sex and Repression in Savage Society (1926)
Coral Gardens and Their Magic (2 volumes, 1935)
The Foundations of Faith and Morals (1936)

The following extract is reprinted from Bronislaw Malinowski, *Magic, Science, and Religion* (first published in *Science, Religion and Reality*, edited by Joseph Needham, London: Society for Promoting Christian Knowledge, 1926; Glencoe, Ill.: The Free Press, 1948, pp. 29–35), with the permission of the Society for Promoting Christian Knowledge.

Of all sources of religion, the supreme and final crisis of life – death – is of the greatest importance. Death is the gateway to the other world in more than the literal sense. According to most theories of early religion, a great deal, if not all, of religious inspiration has been derived from it – and in this orthodox views are on the whole correct. Man has to live his life in the shadow of death, and he who clings to life and enjoys its fullness must dread the menace of its end. And he who is faced by death turns to the promise of life. Death and its denial – Immortality – have always formed, as they form today, the most poignant theme of man's forebodings. The extreme complexity of man's emotional reactions to life finds necessarily its counterpart in his attitude to death. Only what in life has been spread over a long space and manifested in a succession of experiences and events is here at its end condensed into one crisis which provokes a violent and complex outburst of religious manifestations.

Even among the most primitive peoples, the attitude at death is infinitely more complex and, I may add, more akin to our own, than is usually assumed. It is often stated by anthropologists that the dominant feeling of the survivors is that of horror at the corpse and of fear of the ghost. This twin attitude is even made by no less an authority than Wilhelm Wundt the very nucleus of all religious belief and practice. Yet this assertion is only a half-truth, which means no truth at all. The emotions are extremely complex and even contradictory; the dominant elements, love of the dead and loathing of the corpse, passionate attachment to the personality still lingering about the body and a shattering fear of the gruesome thing that has been left over, these two elements seem to mingle and play into each other. This is reflected in the spontaneous behavior and in the spiritual proceedings at death. In the tending of the corpse, in the modes of its disposal, in the post-funerary and commemorative ceremonies, the nearest relatives, the mother mourning for her son, the widow for her husband, the child for the parent, always show some horror and fear mingled with pious love, but never do the negative elements appear alone or even dominant.

The mortuary proceedings show a striking similarity throughout the world. As death approaches, the nearest relatives in any case, sometimes the whole community, forgather by the dying man, and dying, the most private act which a man can perform, is transformed into a public, tribal event. As a rule, a certain differentiation takes place at once, some of the relatives watching near the corpse, others making preparations for the pending end and its consequences, others again performing perhaps some religious acts at a sacred spot. Thus in certain parts of Melanesia the real kinsmen must keep at a distance and only relatives by marriage perform the mortuary services, while in some tribes of Australia the reverse order is observed.

As soon as death has occurred, the body is washed, anointed and adorned, sometimes the bodily apertures are filled, the arms and legs tied together. Then it is exposed to the view of all, and the most important phase, the immediate mourning begins. Those who have witnessed death and its sequel among savages and who can compare these events with their counterpart among other uncivilized peoples must be struck by the fundamental similarity of the proceedings. There is always a more or less conventionalized and dramatized outburst of grief and wailing in sorrow, which often passes among savages into bodily lacerations and the tearing of hair. This is always done in a public display and is associated with visible signs of mourning, such as black or white daubs on the body, shaven or dishevelled hair, strange or torn garments.

The immediate mourning goes on round the corpse. This, far from being shunned or dreaded, is usually the center of pious attention. Often there are ritual forms of fondling or attestations of reverence. The body is sometimes kept on the knees of seated persons, stroked and embraced. At the same time these acts are usually considered both dangerous and repugnant, duties to be fulfilled at some cost to the performer. After a time the corpse has to be disposed of. Inhumation with an open or closed grave; exposure in caves or on platforms, in hollow trees or on the ground in some wild desert place; burning or setting adrift in canoes – these are the usual forms of disposal.

This brings us to perhaps the most important point, the two-fold contradictory tendency, on the one hand to preserve the body, to keep its form intact, or to retain parts of it; on the other hand the desire to be done with it, to put it out of the way, to annihilate it completely. Mummification and burning are the two extreme expressions of this two-fold tendency. It is impossible to regard mummification or burning or any intermediate form as determined by mere accident of belief, as a historical feature of some culture or other which has gained its universality by the mechanism of spread and contact only. For in these customs is clearly expressed the fundamental attitude of mind of the surviving relative, friend or lover, the longing for all that remains of the dead person and the disgust and fear of the dreadful transformation wrought by death.

One extreme and interesting variety in which this double-edged attitude is expressed in a gruesome manner is sarco-cannibalism, a custom of partaking in piety of the flesh of the dead person. It is done with extreme repugnance and dread and usually followed by a violent vomiting fit. At the same time it is felt to be a supreme act of reverence, love, and devotion. In fact it is considered such a sacred duty that among the Melanesians of New Guinea, where I have studied and witnessed it, it is still performed in secret, although severely penalized by the white Government. The smearing of the body with the fat of the dead, prevalent in Australia and Papuasia is, perhaps, but a variety of this custom.

In all such rites, there is a desire to maintain the tie and the parallel tendency to break the bond. Thus the funerary rites are considered as unclean and soiling, the contact with the corpse as defiling and danger-ous, and the performers have to wash, cleanse their body, remove all traces of contact, and perform ritual lustrations. Yet the mortuary ritual compels man to overcome the repugnance, to conquer his fears, to make piety and attachment triumphant, and with it the belief in a future life, in the survival of the spirit.

And here we touch on one of the most important functions of religious cult. In the foregoing analysis I have laid stress on the direct emotional forces created by contact with death and with the corpse, for they primarily and most powerfully determine the behavior of the survivors. But connected with these emotions and born out of them, there is the idea of the spirit, the belief in the new life into which the departed has entered. And here we return to the problem of animism with which we began our survey of primitive religious facts. What is the substance of a spirit, and what is the psychological origin of this belief?

The savage is intensely afraid of death, probably as the result of some deep-seated instincts common to man and animals. He does not want to realize it as an end, he cannot face the idea of complete cessation, of annihilation. The idea of spirit and of spiritual existence is near at hand, furnished by such experiences as are discovered and described by Tylor. Grasping at it, man reaches the comforting belief in spiritual continuity and in the life after death. Yet this belief does not remain unchallenged in the complex, double-edged play of hope and fear which sets in always in the face of death. To the comforting voice of hope, to the intense desire of immortality, to the difficulty, in one's own case, almost the impossibility, of facing annihilation there are opposed powerful and terrible forebodings. The testimony of the senses, the gruesome decomposition of the corpse, the visible disappearance of the personality – certain apparently instinctive suggestions of fear and horror seem to threaten man at all stages of culture with some idea of annihilation, with some hidden fears and forebodings. And here in this play of emotional forces, into this supreme dilemma of life and final death, religion steps in, selecting the positive creed, the comforting view, the culturally valuable belief in immortality, in the spirit independent of the body, and in the continuance of life after death. In the various ceremonies at death, in commemoration and communion with the departed, and worship of ancestral ghosts, religion gives body and form to the saving beliefs.

Thus the belief in immortality is the result of a deep emotional revelation, standardized by religion, rather than a primitive philosophic doctrine. Man's conviction of continued life is one of the supreme gifts of religion, which judges and selects the better of the two alternatives suggested by self-preservation – the hope of continued life and the fear of annihilation. The belief in spirits is the result of the belief in immortality. The substance of which the spirits are made is the full-blooded passion and desire for life, rather than the shadowy stuff which haunts his dreams and illusions. Religion saves man from a surrender to death and destruction, and in doing this it merely makes use of the observations of dreams, shadows, and visions. The real nucleus of animism lies in the deepest emotional fact of human nature, the desire for life.

Thus the rites of mourning, the ritual behavior immediately after death, can be taken as pattern of the religious act, while the belief in immortality, in the continuity of life and in the nether world, can be taken as the prototype of an act of faith. Here, as in the religious ceremonies previously described, we find self-contained acts, the aim of which is achieved in their very performance. The ritual despair, the obsequies, the acts of mourning, express the emotion of the bereaved and the loss of the whole group. They endorse and they duplicate the natural feelings of the survivors; they create a social event out of natural fact. Yet, though in the acts of mourning, in the mimic despair of wailing, in the treatment of the corpse and in its disposal, nothing ulterior is achieved, these acts fulfil an important function and possess a considerable value for primitive culture.

What is the function? The initiation ceremonies we have found fulfil theirs in sacralizing tradition; the food cults, sacrament and sacrifice bring man into communion with providence, with the beneficent forces of plenty; totemism standardizes man's practical, useful attitude of selective interest towards his surroundings. If the view here taken of the biological function of religion is true, some such similar role must also be played by the whole mortuary ritual.

The death of a man or woman in a primitive group, consisting of a limited number of individuals, is an event of no mean importance. The nearest relatives and friends are disturbed to the depth of their emotional life. A small community bereft of a member, especially if he be important, is severely mutilated. The whole event breaks the normal course of life and shakes the moral foundations of society. The strong tendency on which we have insisted in the above description; to give way to fear and horror, to abandon the corpse, to run away from the village, to destroy all the belongings of the dead one – all these impulses exist and if given way to would be extremely dangerous, disintegrating the group, destroying the material foundations of primitive culture. Death in a primitive society is, therefore, much more than the removal of a member. By setting in motion one part of the deep forces of the instinct of self-preservation, it threatens the very cohesion and solidarity of the group, and upon this depends the organization of that society, its tradition, and finally the whole culture. For if primitive man yielded always to the disintegrating impulses of his reaction to death, the continuity of tradition and the existence of material civilization would be impossible.

We have seen already how religion, by sacralizing and thus standardizing the other set of impulses, bestows on man the gift of mental integrity. Exactly the same function it fulfils also with regard to the whole group. The ceremonial of death which ties the survivors to the body and rivets them to the place of death, the beliefs in the existence of the spirit, in its beneficent influences or malevolent intentions, in the duties of a series of commemorative or sacrificial ceremonies – in all this religion counteracts the centrifugal forces of fear, dismay, demoralization, and provides the most powerful means of reintegration of the group's shaken solidarity and the re-establishment of its morale.

In short, religion here assures the victory of tradition and culture over the mere negative response of thwarted instinct.

With the rites of death we have finished the survey of the main types of religious acts. We have followed the crises of life as the main guiding thread of our account, but as they presented themselves we also treated the side issues, such as totemism, the cults of food and of propagation, sacrifice and sacrament, the commemorative cults of ancestors and the cults of the spirits. To one type already mentioned we still have to return – I mean, the seasonal feasts and ceremonies of communal or tribal character – and to the discussion of this subject we proceed now.

The following extracts are reprinted from Bronislaw Malinowski, *The Foundations of Faith and Morals*, Seventh Series of Riddell Memorial Lectures delivered before the University of Durham at Armstrong College, Newcastle upon Tyne, in 1935 (London: Oxford University Press, Humphrey Milford, 1936), Chapter i, pp. 1–8, and Chapter vii, pp. 58–82, with the permission of the University of Newcastle upon Tyne.

The Three Aspects of Religion

Religion is a difficult and refractory subject of study. It seems futile to question that which contains the answers to all problems. It is not easy to dissect with the cold knife of logic what can only be accepted with a complete surrender of heart. It seems impossible to comprehend with reason that which encompasses mankind with love and supreme wisdom.

Nor is it easier for an atheist to study religion than for a deeply convinced believer. The rationalist denies the reality of religious experience. To him, the very fact of religion is a mystery over which he may smile, or by which he may be puzzled, but which, by his very admission, he is not qualified to fathom; it is difficult to study seriously facts which appear merely a snare, a delusion, or a trickery. Yet how can even a rationalist lightly dismiss those realities which have formed the very essence of truth and happiness to millions and hundreds of millions over thousands of years?

In another way the believer, too, is debarred from impartial study. For him one religion, his own, presents no problems. It is the Truth, the whole Truth, and nothing but the Truth. Especially if he be a fundamentalist, that is, unable to understand the foundations of human faith, he will simply disregard most religious phenomena as 'superstitions' and will uphold his own views as Absolute Truth. And yet every one, the bigoted fundamentalist always excepted, might well pause and reflect on the way of his Providence which has vouchsafed the Truth to a small part of humanity, and has kept the rest of mankind in a state of perpetual darkness and error and thus condemned them to eternal perdition. Yet there may perhaps be room for a humble approach to all facts of human belief, in which the student investigates them with a sympathy which makes him almost a believer, but with an impartiality which does not allow him to dismiss all religions as erroneous whilst one remains true.

It is in this spirit that the Anthropologist must approach the problems of primitive religion if they are to be of use in the understanding of the religious crises of our modern world. We must always keep in sight the relation of faith to human life, to the desires, difficulties, and hopes of human beings. Beliefs, which we so often dismiss as 'superstition,' as a symptom of savage crudeness or 'prelogical mentality,' must be understood; that is, their culturally valuable core must be brought to light. But belief is not the alpha and omega of religion: it is important to realize that man translates his confidence in spiritual powers into action; that in prayer and ceremonial, in rite and sacrament, he always attempts to keep in touch with that supernatural reality, the existence of which he affirms in his dogma. Again, we shall see that every religion, however humble, carries also instructions for a good life; it invariably provides its followers with an ethical system.

Every religion, primitive or developed, presents then three main aspects, dogmatic, ritual, and ethical. But the mere division or differentiation into three aspects is not sufficient. It is equally important to grasp the essential interrelation of these three aspects, to recognize that they are really only three facets of the same essential fact. In his dogmatic system, man affirms that Providence or Spirits or Supernatural Powers exist. In his religious ritual he worships those entities and enters into relation with them, for revelation implies that such a relation is possible and necessary. Spirits, ancestral ghosts, or gods refuse to be ignored by man, and he in turn is in need of their assistance. The dependence on higher powers implies further the mutual dependence of man on his neighbour. You cannot worship in common without a common bond of mutual trust and assistance, that is, of charity and love. If God had created man in His own image. one image of God may not debase, defile, or destroy the other.

In discussing dogmatics, especially in primitive relations, we shall be met by what might be described as the mystery of myth. In all religions, Christianity and Judaism not excepted, we find that every tenet of belief, every dogmatic affirmation, has a tendency to be spun out into a long narrative. In other words, the abstract system of dogmatic principles is invariably bound up with a sacred history.

Minor characteristics, extravagances, and peculiarities of mythology have mostly attracted the interest of the student in the past and aroused his passion to explain them. The stories are at times crude, in some cases even obscene. This, within the general scope of our analysis, we shall not find difficult to understand: religious beliefs enter deeply into the essential facts of life, of which fertility and procreation are an essential part. Another peculiarity of myth is the frequent reference to natural phenomena, to features of the landscape, to quaint habits of animals and plants. This has often been accounted for in learned theories by the assumption that mythology is primitive science, and that its main function is to explain natural phenomena and the mysteries of the Universe. Such theories we shall to a large extent have to dismiss or at least to correct. Primitive man has his science as well as his religion; a myth does not serve to explain phenomena but rather to regulate human actions.

The main problem of myth is, in my opinion, its relation to dogma; the fact that myth is an elaboration of an act of faith into an account of a definite concrete miracle. Why is this necessary? In the course of our analysis I hope to show that this is due to the very nature of life and faith. Faith is always based on primeval revelation, and revelation is a concrete event. In revelation, God, or ancestral spirits, or culture heroes create and mould the Universe, manifest their will and power to man. All this is a temporal process, a concrete sequence of activities, a set of dramatic performances. Man in turn reacts to this manifestation of supernatural power, he rebels and sins, gains knowledge, loses grace and regains it once more. Small wonder, then, that most of the dogmatic systems of mankind occur as a body of sacred tradition, as a set of stories stating the beginning of things and thus vouching for their reality. Again, since in myth we have an account of how Providence created man and revealed its reality to him, we usually find that myth contains also the prescription of how man has to worship Providence in order to remain in contact with it.

Thus the discussion of myth leads us directly to the riddle of ritual. Here, again, we shall not tarry over the sensational peculiarities of detail. We shall proceed at once to the central and fundamental problem: 'Why ritual?' We may start here with the extreme Puritan's scorn and rejection of all ritualism, for this represents the voice of reason against the sensuous, almost physiological attitude of naïve faith. Incense, pictures, processions, fireworks are as incomprehensible, hence repugnant, to the highly refined and relective type of religious conscious- ness as they are to the anti-religious rationalist. Ritualism is to reason, pure, or sublimated in religious feeling, always a form of idolatry, a return to magic. To the dispassionate student of all religions, who is not prepared to discount Roman Catholicism because he feels a deep admiration for the religion of Friends, not to dismiss Totemism because he appreciates its distance from the religion of Israel, ritual still remains a problem. Why has man to express such simple affirmations as the belief in the immortality of the soul, in the reality of a spiritual world, by antics, dramatized performances, by dancing, music, incense, by an elaboration, richness, and an extensiveness of collective action which often consumes an enormous amount of tribal or national energy and substance?

Here, again, our argument will not be a mere tilting at windmills. The usual scientific treatment of ritual, primitive and civilized, does not seem to me to be quite satisfactory. The conception, for instance, of primitive magic as 'a false scientific technique' does not do justice to its cultural value. Yet one of the greatest contemporary anthropologists, Sir James Frazer, has to a certain extent given countenance to this conception. Freud's theory that magic is man's primitive belief in the 'omnipotence of thought' would also dismiss primitive ritual as a colossal piece of pragmatic self-deception. The views here advanced will be that every ritual performance, from a piece of primitive Australian magic to a Corpus Christi procession, from an initiation ceremony to the Holy Mass, is a traditionally enacted miracle. In such a miracle the course of human life or of natural events is remodelled by the action of supernatural forces, which are released in a sacred, traditionally standardized act of the congregation or of the religious leader. The fact that every religious rite must contain an element of the miraculous will not appear to us an outgrowth of human childishness, of primeval stupidity (*Urdummheit*), nor yet a blind alley of primitive pseudo- science. To us it represents the very essence of religious faith. Man needs miracles not because he is benighted through primitive stupidity, through the trickery of a priesthood, or through being drugged with 'the opiate for the masses,' but because he realizes at every stage of his development that the powers of his body and of his mind are limited. It is rather the recognition of his practical and intellectual limitations, and not the illusion of the 'omnipotence of thought,' which leads man into ritual- ism; which makes him re-enact miracles, the feasibility of which he has accepted from his mythology.

The enigma of ethics, the question why every religion carries its own morals, is simpler. Why, in order to be decent and righteous, must man believe in the Devil as well as in God, in demons as well as in spirits, in the malice of his ancestral ghosts as well as in their benevolence? Here once more, we have a host of theoretical conceptions, or misconceptions, dictated by hostility to religion or by the partisanship of sectarians. In order to safeguard ourselves against invented hell-fire so as to cow believers into doing what it wishes, we shall have to make an attempt at a real understanding of the phenomena. For, with all our sympathy for the religious attitude, we shall also have to reject the theological view that morality must be associated with dogma, because both have been vouchsafed to mankind by the One True Revelation. The correct answer to our problem lies in the social character of religion. That every organized belief implies a congregation, must have been felt by many thinkers instructed by scholarship and common sense. Yet, here again, science was slow to incorporate the dictates of simple and sound reason. Tylor and Bastian, Max Müller and Mannhardt treat religious systems as if initiative in putting the sociological aspect of religion on the scientific map came from the Scottish divine and scholar, Robertson Smith. It was elaborated with precision, but also with exaggeration, by the French philosopher and sociologist, Durkheim.

The essentially sound methodological principle is that worship always happens in common because it touches common concerns of the community. And here, as our analysis will show, enters the ethical element intrinsically inherent in all religious activities. They always require efforts, discipline, and submission on the part of the individual for the good of the community. Taboos, vigils, religious exercises are essentially moral, not merely because they express submission of man to spiritual powers, but also because they are a sacrifice of man's personal comfort for the common weal. But there is another ethical aspect which, as we shall see, makes all religions moral in their very essence. Every cult is associated with a definite congregation: ancestor-worship is primarily based on the family; at times even on a wider group, the clan; at times it becomes tribal, when the ancestor spirit is that of a chief. The members of such a group of worshippers have natural duties towards each other. The sense of common responsibility, of reciprocal charity and goodwill, flows from the same fundamental idea and sentiment which moves clansmen, brothers, or tribesmen to common worship. I am my tribesman's brother, or my clansman's totemic kinsman, because we are all descended from the same being whom we worship in our ceremonies, to whom we sacrifice, and to whom we pray. We have only to change the word *descended* into *created* in order to pass to those religions which maintain as a fundamental principle the brotherhood of man, because he owes his existence to a Creator whom he addresses as 'Our Father which art in Heaven.' The conception of the Church as a big family is rooted in the very nature of religion.

These conclusions may seem simple, once they are stated directly. Fundamental scientific truths in physics and biology, as in the science of man, are never sophisticated. Yet, even now anthropologist and missionary alike deny ethics to the heathen.

Conclusions on the Anatomy and Pathology of Religion

The scientific analysis of religion is systems as regards substance, form, and function. Every organized faith must carry its specific apparatus, by which it expresses its substance. There must be a dogmatic system backed by mythology or sacred tradition; a developed ritual in which man acts on his belief and communes with the powers of the unseen world; there must also be an ethical code of rules which binds the faithful and determines their behaviour towards each other and towards the things they worship. This structure or form of religion can be traced in Totemism and Animism, in ancestor-worship as well as in the most developed monotheistic systems.

We find, moreover, that there exists an intrinsically appropriate subject-matter in every religious system, a subject-matter which finds its natural expression in the religious technique of ritual and ethnics, and its validation in sacred history. This subject-matter can be summed up as the twin beliefs in Providence and in Immortality. By belief in Providence we understand the mystical conviction that there exist in the universe forces or persons who guide man, who are in sympathy with man's destinies, and who can be propitiated by man. This concept completely covers the Christian's faith in God, One and Indivisible though present in Three Persons, who has created the world and guides it to-day. It embraces also the many forms of polytheistic paganism: the belief in ancestor ghosts and guardian spirits. Even the so-called totemic religions, based on the conviction that man's social and cultural order is duplicated in a spiritual dimension, through which he can control the natural forces of fertility and of the environment, are but a rude version of the belief in Providence. For they allow man to get in touch with the spiritual essence of animal or plant species, to honour them and fulfil duties towards them, in return for their yielding to his needs. The belief in Immortality in our higher religions is akin to that of private creeds, some of which only affirm a limited continuance after death, while others assume an immortality consisting in repeated acts of reincarnation.

The substance of all religion is thus deeply rooted in human life; it grows out of the necessities of life. In other words, religion fulfils a definite cultural function in every human society. This is not a platitude. It contains a scientific refutation of the repeated attacks on religion by the less enlightened rationalists. If religion is indispensable to the integration of the community, just because it satisfies spiritual needs by giving man certain truths and teaching him how to use these truths, then it is impossible to regard religion as a trickery, as an 'opiate for the masses,' as an invention of priests, capitalists, or any other servants of vested interests.

The scientific treatment of religion implies above all a clear analysis of how it grows out of the necessities of human life. One line of approach consists in the study of sacraments, that is, those religious acts which consecrate the crises of human life, at birth, at puberty, at marriage, and above all at death. In these religion gives a sense and a direction to the course of life and to the value of personality. It bonds the individual to the other members of his family, his clan or tribe, and it keeps him in constant relation with the spiritual world.

Another empirical approach shows how magical and religious phenomena are directly dictated to man by the stresses and strains of life, and the necessity of facing heavy odds; how faith and ritual must follow the darker, more dangerous, and more tragic aspects of man's practical labours. Here the material foundations of man's life ought to be scrutinized. Agriculture, with its principal condition of rainfall and sunshine, leads to the magic of fertility, to an elaborate ritual of sowing, flowering, harvest, and first-fruits, and to the institution of divine kings and chiefs. Primitive food-gathering produces ceremonies of the Intichiuma type. Hazardous pursuits, such as hunting and fishing, sailing and distant trading, yield their own type of ritual, belief, and ethical rules. The vicissitudes of war and love are also rich in magical concomitants. Religion, no doubt, combines all these elements in a great variety of designs or mosaics. It is the object of science to discover the common elements in them, though it may be the task of the artist or of the mystic to depict or to cherish the individual phenomenon. But I venture to affirm that in not a single one of its manifestations can religion be found without its firm roots in human emotion, which again always grows out of desires and vicissitudes connected with life.

Two affirmations, therefore, preside over every ritual act, every rule of conduct, and every belief. There is the affirmation of the existence of powers sympathetic to man, ready to help him on condition that he conforms to the traditional lore which teaches how to serve them, conjure them, and propitiate them. This is the belief in Providence, and this belief assists man in so far as it enhances his capacity to act and his readiness to organize for action, under conditions where he must face and fight not only the ordinary forces of nature, but also chance, ill luck, and the mysterious, ever incalculable designs of destiny.

The second belief is that beyond the brief span of natural life there is compensation in another existence. Through this belief man can act and calculate far beyond his own forces and limitations, looking forward to his work being continued by his successors in the conviction that, from the next world, he will still be able to watch and assist them. The sufferings and efforts, the injustices and inequalities, of this life are thus made up for. Here again we find that the spiritual force of this belief not only integrates man's own personality, but is indispensable for the cohesion of the social fabric. Especially in the form which this belief assumes in ancestor-worship and the communion with the dead do we perceive its moral and social influence.

In their deepest foundations, as well as in their final consequences, the two beliefs in Providence and Immortality are not independent of one another. In the higher religions man lives in order to be united to God. In the simpler forms, the ancestors worshipped are often mystically identified with environmental forces, as in Totemism. At times they are both ancestors and carriers of fertility, as the Kachina of the Pueblos. Or again the ancestor is worshipped as the divinity, or at least as a culture hero.

The unity of religion in substance, form, and function is to be found everywhere. Religious development consists probably in the growing predominance of the ethical principle and in the increasing fusion of the two main factors of all belief, the sense of Providence and the faith in Immortality.

The conclusions to be drawn with regard to contemporary events I shall leave to the reader's own reflection. Is religion, in the sense in which we have just defined it – the affirmation of an ethical Providence, of Immortality, of transcendental value and sense of human life – is such religion dead? Is it going to make way for other creeds, perhaps less exacting, perhaps more immediately repaying and grossly satisfactory, but creeds which, nevertheless, fail to satisfy man's craving for the Absolute; fail to answer the riddle of human existence, and to convey the ethical message which can only be received from a Being or Beings regarded as beyond human passions, strife, and frailties? Is religion going to surrender its own equipment of faith, ritual, and ethics to cross-breeds between superstition and science, between economics and credulity, between politics and national megalomania? The dogmatic affirmations of these new mysticisms are banal, shallow, and they pander directly to the lowest instincts of the multitude. This is true of the belief in the absolute supremacy of one race and its right to bully all others; the belief in the sanctity of egoism in one's own nationality; the conviction of the value of war and collective brutality; the belief that only manual labour gives the full right to live and that the whole culture and public life of a community must be warped in the interests of the industrial workers.

Those of us who believe in culture and believe in the value of religion, though perhaps not in its specific tenets, must hope that the present-day misuse of the religious apparatus for partisan and doctrinaire purposes is not a healthy development of religion, but one of the many phenomena in the pathology of culture which seem to threaten the immediate development of our post-war western society. If this be so, these new pseudo-religions are doomed to die. Let us hope that our whole society will not be dragged with them to destruction. Let us work for the maintenance of the eternal truths which have guided mankind out of barbarism to culture, and the loss of which seems to threaten us with barbarism again. The rationalist and agnostic must admit that even if he himself cannot accept these truths, he must at least recognize them as indispensable pragmatic figments without which civilization cannot exist.

The following extract is reprinted from Bronislaw Malinowski, *Magic, Science, and Religion* (first published in *Science, Religion and Reality*, edited by Joseph Needham, London: Society for Promoting Christian Knowledge, 1926; Glencoe, Ill.: The Free Press, 1948, pp. 8–18), with the permission of the Society for Promoting Christian Knowledge.

The problem of primitive knowledge has been singularly neglected by anthropology. Studies on savage psychology were exclusively confined to early religion, magic and mythology. Only recently the work of several English, German, and French writers, notably the daring and brilliant speculations of Professor Lévy-Bruhl, gave an impetus to the student's interest in what the savage does in his more sober moods. The results were startling indeed: Professor Lévy-Bruhl tells us, to put it in a nutshell, that primitive man has no sober moods at all, that he is hopelessly and completely immersed in a mystical frame of mind. Incapable of dispassionate and consistent observation, devoid of the power of abstraction, hampered by 'a decided aversion towards reasoning,' he is unable to draw any benefit from experience, to construct or comprehend even the most elementary laws of nature. 'For minds thus orientated there is no fact purely physical.' Nor can there exist for them any clear idea of substance and attribute, cause and effect, identity and contradiction. Their outlook is that of confused superstition, 'prelogical,' made of mystic 'participations' and 'exclusions.' I have here summarized a body of opinion, of which the brilliant French sociologist is the most decided and competent spokesman, but which numbers besides, many anthropologists and philosophers of renown.

But there are also dissenting voices. When a scholar and anthropologist of the measure of Professor J. L. Myres entitles an article in *Notes and Queries* 'Natural Science,' and when we read there that the savage's 'knowledge based on observation is distinct and accurate,' we must surely pause before accepting primitive man's irrationality as a dogma. Another highly competent writer, Dr. A. A. Goldenweiser, speaking about primitive 'discoveries, inventions and improvements' – which could hardly be attributed to any pre-empirical or pre-logical mind – affirms that 'it would be unwise to ascribe to the primitive mechanic merely a passive part in the origination of inventions. Many a happy thought must have crossed his mind, nor was he wholly unfamiliar with the thrill that comes from an idea effective in action.' Here we see the savage endowed with an attitude of mind wholly akin to that of a modern man of science!

To bridge over the wide gap between the two extreme opinions current on the subject of primitive man's reason, it will be best to resolve the problem into two questions.

First, has the savage any rational outlook, any rational mastery of his surroundings, or is he, as M. Lévy-Bruhl and his school maintain, entirely 'mystical'? The answer will be that every primitive community is in possession of a considerable store of knowledge, based on experience and fashioned by reason.

The second question then opens: Can this primitive knowledge be regarded as a rudimentary form of science or is it, on the contrary, radically different, a crude empiry, a body of practical and technical abilities, rules of thumb and rules of art having no theoretical value? This second question, epistemological rather than belonging to the study of man, will be barely touched upon at the end of this section and a tentative answer only will be given.

In dealing with the first question, we shall have to examine the 'profane' side of life, the arts, crafts and economic pursuits, and we shall attempt to disentangle in it a type of behavior, clearly marked off from magic and religion, based on empirical knowledge and on the confidence in logic. We shall try to find whether the lines of such behavior are defined by traditional rules, known, perhaps even discussed sometimes, and tested. We shall have to inquire whether the sociological setting of the rational and empirical behavior differs from that of ritual and cult. Above all we shall ask, do the natives distinguish the two domains and keep them apart, or is the field of knowledge constantly swamped by superstition, ritualism, magic or religion?

Since in the matter under discussion there is an appalling lack of relevant and reliable observations, I shall have largely to draw upon my own material, mostly unpublished, collected during a few years' field-work among the Melanesian and Papuo-Melanesian tribes of Eastern New Guinea and the surrounding archipelagoes. As the Melanesians are reputed, however, to be specially magic-ridden, they will furnish an acid test of the existence of empirical and rational knowledge among savages living in the age of polished stone.

These natives, and I am speaking mainly of the Melanesians who inhabit the coral atolls to the N.E. of the main island, the Trobriand Archipelago and the adjoining groups, are expert fishermen, industrious manufacturers and traders, but they rely mainly on gardening for their subsistence. With the most rudimentary implements, a pointed digging stick and a small axe, they are able to raise crops sufficient to maintain a dense population and even yielding a surplus, which in olden days was allowed to rot unconsumed, and which at present is exported to feed plantation hands. The success in their agriculture depends – besides the excellent natural conditions with which they are favored – upon their extensive knowledge of the classes of the soil, of the various cultivated plants, of the mutual adaptation of these two factors, and, last not least, upon their knowledge of the importance of accurate and hard work. They have to select the soil and the seedlings, they have appropriately to fix the times for clearing and burning the scrub, for planting and weeding, for training the vines of the yam-plants. In all this they are guided by a clear knowledge of weather and seasons, plants and pests, soil and tubers, and by a conviction that this knowledge is true and reliable, that it can be counted upon and must be scrupulously obeyed.

Yet mixed with all their activities there is to be found magic, a series of rites performed every year over the gardens in rigorous sequence and order. Since the leadership in garden work is in the hands of the magician, and since ritual and practical work are intimately associated, a superficial observer might be led to assume that the mystic and the rational behavior are mixed up, that their effects are not distinguished by the natives and not distinguishable in scientific analysis. Is this so really?

Magic is undoubtedly regarded by the natives as absolutely indispensable to the welfare of the gardens. What would happen without it no one can exactly tell, for no native garden has ever been made without its ritual, in spite of some thirty years of European rule and missionary influence and well over a century's contact with white traders. But certainly various kinds of disaster, blight, unseasonable droughts and rains, bush-pigs and locusts, would destroy the unhallowed garden made without magic.

Does this mean, however, that the natives attribute all the good results to magic? Certainly not. If you were to suggest to a native that he should make his garden mainly by magic and scamp his work, he would simply smile on your simplicity. He knows as well as you do that there are natural conditions and causes, and by his observations he knows also that he is able to control these natural forces by mental and physical effort. His knowledge is limited, no doubt, but as far as it goes it is sound and proof against mysticism. If the fences are broken down, if the seed is destroyed or has been dried or washed away, he will have recourse not to magic, but to work, guided by knowledge and reason. His experience has taught him also, on the other hand, that in spite of all his forethought and beyond all his efforts there are agencies and forces which one year bestow unwonted and unearned benefits of fertility, making everything run smooth and well, rain and sun appear at the right moment, noxious insects remain in abeyance, the harvest yield a super-abundant crop; and another year again the same agencies bring ill-luck and bad chance, pursue him from beginning till end and thwart all his most strenuous efforts and his best-founded knowledge. To control these influences and these only he employs magic.

Thus there is a clear-cut division: there is first the well-known set of conditions, the natural course of growth, as well as the ordinary pests and dangers to be warded off by fencing and weeding. On the other hand there is the domain of the unaccountable and adverse influences, as well as the great unearned increment of fortunate coincidence. The first conditions are coped with by knowledge and work, the second by magic.

This line of division can also be traced in the social setting of work and ritual respectively. Though the garden magician is, as a rule, also the leader in practical activities, these two functions are kept strictly apart. Every magical ceremony has its distinctive name, its appropriate time and its place in the scheme of work, and it stands out of the ordinary course of activities completely. Some of them are ceremonial and have to be attended by the whole community, all are public in that it is known when they are going to happen and anyone can attend them.

They are performed on selected plots within the gardens and on a special corner of this plot. Work is always tabooed on such occasions, sometimes only while the ceremony lasts, sometimes for a day or two. In his lay character the leader and magician directs the work, fixes the dates for starting, harangues and exhorts slack or careless gardeners. But the two roles never overlap or interfere: they are always clear, and any native will inform you without hesitation whether the man acts as magician or as leader in garden work.

What has been said about gardens can be paralleled from any one of the many other activities in which work and magic run side by side without ever mixing. Thus in canoe-building empirical knowledge of material, of technology, and of certain principles of stability and hydrodynamics, function in company and close association with magic, each yet uncontaminated by the other.

For example, they understand perfectly well that the wider the span of the outrigger the greater the stability yet the smaller the resistance against strain. They can clearly explain why they have to give this span a certain traditional width, measured in fractions of the length of the dug-out. They can also explain, in rudimentary but clearly mechanical terms, how they have to behave in a sudden gale, why the outrigger must be always on the weather side, why the one type of canoe can and the other cannot beat. They have, in fact, a whole system of principles of sailing, embodied in a complex and rich terminology, traditionally handed on and obeyed as rationally and consistently as is modern science by modern sailors. How could they sail otherwise under eminently dangerous conditions in their frail primitive craft?

But even with all their systematic knowledge, methodically applied, they are still at the mercy of powerful and incalculable tides, sudden gales during the monsoon season and unknown reefs. And here comes in their magic, performed over the canoe during its construction, carried out at the beginning and in the course of expeditions and resorted to in moments of real danger. If the modern seaman, entrenched in science and reason, provided with all sorts of safety appliances, sailing on steel-built steamers, if even he has a singular tendency to superstition – which does not rob him of his knowledge or reason, nor make him altogether pre-logical – can we wonder that his savage colleague, under much more precarious conditions, holds fast to the safety and comfort of magic?

An interesting and crucial test is provided by fishing in the Trobriand Islands and its magic. While in the villages on the inner lagoon fishing is done in an easy and absolutely reliable manner by the method of poisoning, yielding abundant results without danger and uncertainty, there are on the shores of the open sea dangerous modes of fishing and also certain types in which the yield varies according to whether shoals of fish appear beforehand or not. It is most significant that in the Lagoon fishing, where man can rely completely upon his knowledge and skill, magic does not exist, while in the open-sea fishing, full of danger and uncertainty, there is extensive magical ritual to secure safety and good results.

Again, in warfare the natives know that strength, courage, and agility play a decisive part. Yet here also they practice magic to master the elements of chance and luck.

Nowhere is the duality of natural and supernatural causes divided by a line so thin and intricate, yet, if carefully followed up, so well marked, decisive, and instructive, as in the two most fateful forces of human destiny: health and death. Health to the Melanesians is a natural state of affairs and, unless tampered with, they human body will remain in perfect order. But the natives know perfectly well that there are natural means which can affect health and even destroy the body. Poisons, wounds, burns, falls, are known to cause disablement or death in a natural way. And this is not a matter of private opinion of this or that individual, but it is laid down in traditional lore and even in belief, for there are considered to be different ways to the nether world for those who died by sorcery and those who met 'natural' death. Again, it is recognized that cold, heat, overstrain, too much sun, over-eating, can all cause minor ailments, which are treated by natural remedies such as massage, steaming, warming at a fire and certain potions. Old age is known to lead to bodily decay and the explanation is given by the natives that very old people grow weak, their oesophagus closes up, and therefore they must die.

But besides these natural causes there is the enormous domain of sorcery and by far the most cases of illness and death are ascribed to this. The line of distinction between sorcery and the other causes is clear in theory and in most cases of practice, but it must be realized that it is subject to what could be called the personal perspective. That is, the more closely a case has to do with the person who considers it, the less will it be 'natural,' the more 'magical.' Thus a very old man, whose pending death will be considered natural by the other members of the community, will be afraid only of sorcery and never think of his natural fate. A fairly sick person will diagnose sorcery in his own case, while all the others might speak of too much betel nut or over-eating or some other indulgence.

But who of us really believes that his own bodily infirmities and the approaching death is a purely natural occurrence, just an insignificant event in the infinite chain of causes? To the most rational of civilized men health, disease, the threat of death, float in a hazy emotional mist, which seems to become denser and more impenetrable as the fateful forms approach. It is indeed astonishing that 'savages' can achieve such a sober, dispassionate outlook in these matters as they actually do.

Thus in his relation to nature and destiny, whether he tries to exploit the first or to dodge the second, primitive man recognizes both the natural and the supernatural forces and agencies, and he tries to use them both for his benefit. Whenever he has been taught by experience that effort guided by knowledge is of some avail, he never spares the one or ignores the other. He knows that a plant cannot grow by magic alone, or a canoe sail or float without being properly constructed and managed, or a fight be won without skill and daring. He never relies on magic alone, while, on the contrary, he sometimes dispenses with it completely, as in fire-making and in a number of crafts and pursuits. But he clings to it, whenever he has to recognize the impotence of his knowledge and of his rational technique.

I have given my reasons why in this argument I had to rely principally on the material collected in the classical land of magic, Melanesia. But the facts discussed are so fundamental, the conclusions drawn of such a general nature, that it will be easy to check them on any modern detailed ethnographic record. Comparing agricultural work and magic, the building of canoes, the art of healing by magic and by natural remedies, the ideas about the causes of death in other regions, the universal validity of what has been established here could easily be proved. Only, since no observations have methodically been made with reference to the problem of primitive knowledge, the data from other writers could be gleaned only piecemeal and their testimony though clear would be indirect.

I have chosen to face the question of primitive man's rational knowledge directly: watching him at his principal occupations, seeing him pass from work to magic and back again, entering into his mind, listening to his opinions. The whole problem might have been approached through the avenue of language, but this would have led us too far into questions of logic, semasiology, and theory of primitive languages. Words which serve to express general ideas such as *existence*, *substance*, and *attribute*, *cause* and *effect*, the *fundamental* and the *secondary*; words and expressions used in complicated pursuits like sailing, construction, measuring and checking; numerals and quantitative descriptions, correct and detailed classifications of natural phenomena, plants and animals – all this would lead us exactly to the same conclusion: that primitive man can observe and think, and that he possesses, embodied in his language, systems of methodical though rudimentary knowledge.

Similar conclusions could be drawn from an examination of those mental schemes and physical contrivances which could be described as diagrams or formulas. Methods of indicating the main points of the compass, arrangements of stars into constellations, co-ordination of these with the seasons, naming of moons in the year, of quarters in the moon – all these accomplishments are known to the simplest savages. Also they are all able to draw diagrammatic maps in the sand or dust, indicate arrangements by placing small stones, shells, or sticks on the ground, plan expeditions or raids on such rudimentary charts. By co-ordinating space and time they are able to arrange big tribal gatherings and to combine vast tribal movements over extensive areas. The use of leaves, notched sticks, and similar aids to memory is well known and seems to be almost universal. All such 'diagrams' are means of reducing a complex and unwieldy bit of reality to a simple and handy form. They give man a relatively easy mental control over it. As such are they not – in a very rudimentary form no doubt – fundamentally akin to developed scientific formulas and 'models,' which are also simple and handy paraphrases of a complex or abstract reality, giving the civilized physicist mental control over it?

This brings us to the second question: Can we regard primitive knowledge, which, as we found, is both empirical and rational, as a rudimentary stage of science, or is it not at all related to it? If by science be understood a body of rules and conceptions, based on experience and derived from it by logical inference, embodied in material achievements and in a fixed form of tradition and carried on by some sort of social organization – then there is no doubt that even the lowest savage communities have the beginnings of science, however rudimentary.

Most epistemologists would not, however, be satisfied with such a 'minimum definition' of science, for it might apply to the rules of an art or craft as well. They would maintain that the rules of science must be laid down explicitly, open to control by experiment and critique by reason. They must not only be rules of practical behavior, but theoretical laws of knowledge. Even accepting this stricture, however, there is hardly any doubt that many of the principles of savage knowledge are scientific in this sense. The native shipwright knows not only practically of buoyancy, leverage, equilibrium, he has to obey these laws not only on water, but while making the canoe he must have the principles in his mind. He instructs his helpers in them. He gives them the traditional rules, and in a crude and simple manner, using his hands, pieces of wood, and a limited technical vocabulary, he explains some general laws of hydrodynamics and equilibrium. Science is not detached from the craft, that is certainly true, it is only a means to an end, it is crude, rudimentary, and inchoate, but with all that it is the matrix from which the higher developments must have sprung.

If we applied another criterion yet, that of the really scientific attitude, the disinterested search for knowledge and for the understanding of causes and reasons, the answer would certainly not be in a direct negative. There is, of course, no widespread thirst for knowledge in a savage community, new things such as European topics bore them frankly and their whole interest is largely encompassed by the traditional world of their culture. But within this there is both the antiquarian mind passionately interested in myths, stories, details of customs, pedigrees, and ancient happenings, and there is also to be found the naturalist, patient and painstaking in his observations, capable of generalization and of connecting long chains of events in the life of animals, and in the marine world or in the jungle. It is enough to realize how much European naturalists have often learned from their savage colleagues to appreciate this interest found in the native for nature. There is finally among the primitives, as every field-worker well knows, the sociologist, the ideal informant, capable with marvelous accuracy and insight to give the *raison d'être*, the function, and the organization of many a simpler institution in his tribe.

Science, of course, does not exist in any uncivilized community as a driving power, criticizing, renewing, constructing. Science is never consciously made. But on this criterion, neither is there law, nor religion, nor government among savages.

The question, however, whether we should call it *science* or only *empirical and rational knowledge* is not of primary importance in this context. We have tried to gain a clear idea as to whether the savage has only one domain of reality or two, and we found that he has his profane world of practical activities and rational outlook besides the sacred region of cult and belief.

A. R. Radcliffe-Brown 1881–1955

Major works

The Andaman Islanders (1922)

Structure and Function in Primitive Society: Essays and Addresses 1923–49 (1952)

Method in Social Anthropology: Selected Essays (edited by M. N. Srinwas, 1958)

The following extract is reprinted from A. R. Radcliffe-Brown, *The Andaman Islanders* (London: Cambridge University Press, 1922), pp. 238–57, with the permission of the Cambridge University Press.

In the peace-making ceremony of the North Andaman, the meaning is easily discovered; the symbolism of the dance being indeed at once obvious to a witness, though perhaps not quite so obvious from the description given. The dancers are divided into two parties. The actions of the one party throughout are expressions of their aggressive feelings towards the other. This is clear enough in the shouting, the threatening gestures, and the way in which each member of the 'attacking' party gives a good shaking to each member of the other party. On the other side what is expressed may be described as complete passivity; the performers stand quite still throughout the whole dance, taking care to show neither fear nor resentment at the treatment to which they have to submit. Thus those of the one side give collective expression to their collective anger, which is thereby appeased. The others, by passively submitting to this, humbling themselves before the just wrath of their enemies, expiate their wrongs. Anger appeased dies down; wrongs expiated are forgiven and forgotten; the enmity is at an end.

The screen of fibre against which the passive participants in the ceremony stand has a peculiar symbolic meaning that will be explained later in the chapter. The only other elements of the ceremony are the weeping together, which will be dealt with very soon, and the exchange of weapons, which is simply a special form of the rite of exchanging presents as an expression of good-will. The special form is particularly appropriate as it would seem to ensure at least some months of friendship, for you cannot go out to fight a man with his weapons while he has yours.

The purpose of the ceremony is clearly to produce a change in the feelings of the two parties towards one another, feelings of enmity being replaced through it by feelings of friendship and solidarity. It depends for its effect on the fact that anger and similar aggressive feelings may be appeased by being freely expressed. Its social function is to restore the condition of solidarity between two local groups that has been destroyed by some act of offence.

The marriage ceremony and the peace-making dance both afford examples of the custom which the Andamanese have of weeping together under certain circumstances. The principal occasions of this ceremonial weeping are as follows: (1) when two friends or relatives meet after having been for some time parted, they embrace each other and weep together; (2) at the peace-making ceremony the two parties of former enemies weep together, embracing each other; (3) at the end of the period of mourning the friends of the mourners (who have not themselves been mourning) weep with the latter; (4) after a death the relatives and friends embrace the corpse and weep over it; (5) when the bones of a dead man or woman are recovered from the grave they are wept over; (6) on the occasion of a marriage the relatives of each weep over the bride and bridegroom; (7) at various stages of the initiation ceremonies the female relatives of a youth or a girl weep over him or her.

First of all it is necessary to note that not in any of the above-mentioned instances is the weeping simply a spontaneous expression of feeling. It is always a rite the proper performance of which is demanded by custom. (As mentioned in an earlier chapter, the Andamanese are able to sit down and shed tears at will.) Nor can we explain the weeping as being an expression of sorrow. It is true that some of the occasions are such as to produce sorrowful feelings (4 and 5, for example), but there are others on which there would seem to be no reason for sorrow but rather for joy. The Andamanese do weep from sorrow and spontaneously. A child cries when he is scolded or hurt; a widow weeps thinking of her recently dead husband. Men rarely weep spontaneously for any reason, though they shed tears abundantly when taking part in the rite. The weeping on the occasions enumerated is therefore not a spontaneous expression of individual emotion but is an example of what I have called ceremonial customs. In certain circumstances men and women are required by custom to embrace one another and weep, and if they neglected to do so it would be an offense condemned by all right-thinking persons.

According to the postulate of method laid down at the beginning of the chapter we have to seek such an explanation of this custom as will account for all the different occasions on which the rite is performed, since we must assume that one and the same rite has the same meaning in whatever circumstances it may take place. It must be noted, however, that there are two varieties of the rite. In the first three instances enumerated above the rite is reciprocal, i.e. two persons or two distinct groups of persons weep together and embrace each other, both parties to the rite being active. In the other four instances it is one-sided; a person or group of persons weeps over another person (or the relics of a person) who has only a passive part in the ceremony. Any explanation, to be satisfactory, must take account of the difference between these two varieties.

I would explain the rite as being an expression of that feeling of attachment between persons which is of such importance in the almost domestic life of the Andaman society. In other words the purpose of the rite is to affirm the existence of a social bond between two or more persons.

There are two elements in the ceremony, the embrace and the weeping. We have already seen that the embrace is an expression, in the Andamans as elsewhere, of the feeling of attachment, i.e. the feeling of which love, friendship, affection are varieties. Turning to the second element of the ceremony, we are accustomed to think of weeping as more particularly an expression of sorrow. We are familiar, however, with tears of joy, and I have myself observed tears that were the result neither of joy nor of sorrow but of a sudden overwhelming feeling of affection. I believe that we may describe weeping as being a means by which the mind obtains relief from a condition of emotional tension, and that it is because such conditions of tension are most common in feelings of grief and pain that weeping comes to be associated with painful feelings. It is impossible here to discuss this subject, and I am therefore compelled to assume without proof this proposition on which my explanation of the rite is based. My own conclusion, based on careful observation, is that in this rite the weeping is an expression of what has been called the tender emotion. Without doubt, on some of the occasions of the rite, as when weeping over a dead friend, the participants are suffering a painful emotion, but this is evidently not so on all occasions. It is true, however, as I shall show, that on every occasion of the rite there is a condition of emotional tension due to the sudden calling into activity of the sentiment of personal attachment.

When two friends or relatives meet after having been separated, the social relation between them that has been interrupted is about to be renewed. This social relation implies or depends upon the existence of a specific bond of solidarity between them. The weeping rite (together with the subsequent exchange of presents) is the affirmation of this bond. The rite, which, it must be remembered, is obligatory, compels the two participants to act as though they felt certain emotions, and thereby does, to some extent, produce those emotions in them. When the two friends meet their first feeling seems to be one of shyness mingled with pleasure at seeing each other again. This is according to the statements of the natives as well as my own observation. Now this shyness (the Andamanese use the same word as they do for 'shame') is itself a condition of emotional tension, which has to be relieved in some way. The embrace awakens to full activity that feeling of affection or friendship that has been dormant and which it is the business of the rite to renew. The weeping gives relief to the emotional tension just noted, and also reinforces the effect of the embrace. This it does owing to the fact that a strong feeling of personal attachment is always produced when two persons join together in sharing and simultaneously expressing one and the same emotion. The little ceremony thus serves to dispel the initial feeling of shyness and to reinstate the condition of intimacy and affection that existed before the separation.

In the peace-making ceremony the purpose of the whole rite is to abolish a condition of enmity and replace it by one of friendship. The once friendly relations between the two groups have been interrupted by a longer or shorter period of antagonism. We have seen that the effect of the dance is to dispel the wrath of the one group by giving it free expression. The weeping that follows is the renewal of the friendship. The rite is here exactly parallel to that on the meeting of two friends, except that not two individuals but two groups are concerned, and that owing to the number of persons involved the emotional condition is one of much greater intensity. Here therefore also we see that the rite is an affirmation of solidarity or social union, in this instance between the groups, and that the rule is in its nature such as to make the participants feel that they are bound to each other by ties of friendship.

We now come to a more difficult example of the rite, that at the end of mourning. It will be shown later in the chapter that during the period of mourning the mourners are cut off from the ordinary life of the community. By reason of the ties that still bind them to the dead person they are placed, as it were, outside the society and the bonds that unite them to their group are temporarily loosened. At the end of the mourning period they re-enter the society and take up once more their place in the social life. Their return to the community is the occasion on which they and their friends weep together. In this instance also, therefore, the rite may be explained as having for its purpose the renewal of the social relations that have been interrupted. This explanation will seem more convincing when we have considered in detail the customs of mourning. If it be accepted, then it may be seen that in the first three instances of the rite of weeping (those in which the action is reciprocal) we have conditions in which social relations that have been interrupted are about to be renewed, and the rite serves as a ceremony of aggregation.

Let us now consider the second variety of the rite, and first of all its meaning as part of the ceremony of marriage. By marriage the social bonds that have to that time united the bride and bridegroom to their respective relatives, particularly their female relatives such as mother, mother's sister, father's sister and adopted mother, are modified. The unmarried youth or girl is in a position of dependence upon his or her older relatives, and by the marriage this dependence is partly abolished. Whereas the principal duties of the bride were formerly those towards her mother and older female relatives, henceforth her chief duties in life will be towards her husband. The position of the bridgeroom is similar, and it must be noted that his social relations with his male relatives are less affected by his marriage than those with his female relatives. Yet, though the ties that have bound the bride and bridegroom to their relatives are about to be modified or partially destroyed by the new ties of marriage with its new duties and rights they will still continue to exist in a weakened and changed condition. The rite of weeping is the expression of this. It serves to make real (by feeling), in those taking part in it, the presence of the social ties that are being modified.

When the mother of the bride or bridegroom weeps at a marriage she feels that her son or daughter is being taken from her care. She has the sorrow of a partial separation and she consoles herself by expressing in the rite her continued feeling of tenderness and affection towards him in the new condition that he is entering upon. For her the chief result of the rite is to make her feel that her child is still an object of her affection, still bound to her by close ties, in spite of the fact that he or she is being taken from her care.

Exactly the same explanation holds with regard to the weeping at the initiation ceremonies. By these ceremonies the youth (or girl) is gradually withdrawn from a condition of dependence on his mother and older female relatives and is made an independent member of the community. The initiation is a long process that is only completed by marriage. At every stage of the lengthy ceremonies therefore, the social ties that unite the initiate to these relatives are modified or weakened, and the rite of weeping is the means by which the significance of the change is impressed upon those taking part in it. For the mother the weeping expresses her resignation at her necessary loss, and acts as a consolation by making her feel that her son is still hers, though now being withdrawn from her care. For the boy the rite has a different meaning. He realizes that he is no longer merely a child, dependent upon his mother, but is now entering upon manhood. His former feelings towards his mother must be modified. That he is being separated from her is, for him, the most important aspect of the matter, and therefore while she weeps he must give no sign of tenderness in return but must sit passive and silent. So also in the marriage ceremony, the rite serves to impress upon the young man and woman that they are, by reason of the new ties that they are forming with one another, severing their ties with their families.

When a person dies the social bonds that unite him to the survivors are profoundly modified. They are not in an instant utterly destroyed, as we shall see better when we deal with the funeral and mourning customs, for the friends and relatives still feel towards the dead person that affection in which they held him when alive, and this has now become a source of deep grief. It is this affection still binding them to him that they express in the rite of weeping over the corpse. Here rite and natural expression of emotion coincide, but it must be noted that the weeping is obligatory, a matter of duty. In this instance, then, the rite is similar to that at marriage and initiation. The man is by death cut off from the society to which he belonged, and association with his friends, but the latter still feel towards him that attachment that bound them together while he lived, and it is this attachment that they express when they embrace the lifeless corpse and weep over it.

There remains only one more instance of the rite to be considered. When the period of mourning for a dead person is over and the bones are recovered the modification in the relations between the dead and the living, which begins at death, and is, as we shall see, carried out by the mourning customs and ceremonies, is finally accomplished. The dead person is now entirely cut off from the world of the living, save that his bones are to be treasured as relics and amulets. The weeping over the bones must be taken, I think, as a rite of aggregation whereby the bones as representative of the dead person (all that is left of him) are received back into the society henceforth to fill a special place in the social life. It really constitutes a renewal of social relations with the dead person, after a period during which all active social relations have been interrupted owing to the danger in all contact between the living and the dead. By the rite the affection that was once felt towards the dead person is revived and is now directed to the skeletal relics of the man or woman that once was their object. If this explanation seem unsatisfactory, I would ask the reader to suspend his judgment until the funeral customs of the Andamans have been discussed, and then to return to this point.

The proffered explanation of the rite of weeping should now be plain. I regard it as being the affirmation of a bond of social solidarity between those taking part in it, and as producing in them a realization of that bond by arousing the sentiment of attachment. In some instances the rite therefore serves to renew social relations when they have been interrupted, and in such instances the rite is reciprocal. In others it serves to show the continued existence of the social bond when it is being weakened or modified, as by marriage, initiation or death. In all instances we may say that the purpose of the rite is to bring about a new state of the affective dispositions that regulate the conduct of persons to one another, either by reviving sentiments that have lain dormant, or producing a recognition of a change in the condition of personal relations.

The study of these simple ceremonies has shown us several things of importance. (1) In every instance the ceremony is the expression of an affective state of mind shared by two or more persons. Thus the weeping rite expresses feelings of solidarity, the exchange of presents expresses good-will. (2) But the ceremonies are not spontaneous expressions of feeling; they are all customary actions to which the sentiment of obligation attaches, which it is the duty of persons to perform on certain definite occasions. It is the duty of everyone in a community to give presents at a wedding; it is the duty of relatives to weep together when they meet. (3) In every instance the ceremony is to be explained by reference to fundamental laws regulating the affective life of human beings. It is not our business here to analyse these phenomena but only to satisfy ourselves that they are real. That weeping is an outlet for emotional excitement, that the free expression of aggressive feelings causes them to die out instead of smouldering on, that an embrace is an expression of feelings of attachment between persons: these are the psychological generalizations upon which are based the explanations given above of various ceremonies of the Andamanese. (4) Finally, we have seen that each of the ceremonies serves to renew or to modify in the minds of those taking part in it some one or more of the social sentiments. The peace-making ceremony is a method by which feelings of enmity are exchanged for feelings of friendship. The marriage rite serves to arouse in the minds of the marrying pair a sense of their obligations as married folk, and to bring about in the minds of the witnesses a change of feeling towards the young perople such as should properly accompany their change of social status. The weeping and exchange of presents when friends come together is a means of renewing their feelings of attachment to one another. The weeping at marriage, at initiation, and on the occasion of a death is a reaction of defence or compassion when feelings of solidarity are attacked by a partial breaking of the social ties that bind persons to one another.

In the ceremonial life of the Andamans some part is played by dancing, and it will be convenient to consider next the meaning and function of the dance. It is necessary, however, to deal very briefly with this subject and omit much that would have to be included in an exhaustive study. Thus the ordinary Andaman dance may be looked upon as a form of play; it also shows us the beginnings of the arts of dancing, music and poetry; and therefore in any study pretending to completeness it would be necessary to discuss the difficult problem of the relation between art, play and ceremonial in social life, a subject of too wide a scope to be handled in such an essay as this. For our present purpose we are concerned with the dance only as a form of social ceremonial.

If an Andaman Islander is asked why he dances he gives an answer that amounts to saying that he does so because he enjoys it. Dancing is therefore in general a means of enjoyment It is frequently a rejoicing. The Andaman Islanders dance after a successful day of hunting; they do not dance if their day has been one of disappointment.

Pleasurable mental excitement finds its natural expression in bodily activity, as we see most plainly in young children and in some animals. And in its turn mere muscular activity is itself a source of pleasure. The individual shouts and jumps for joy; the society turns into a dance, the shout into a song.

The essential character of all dancing is that it is rhythmical, and it is fairly evident that the primary function of this rhythmical nature of the dance is to enable a number of persons to join in the same actions and perform them as one body. In the Andamans at any rate it is clear that the spectacular dance is a late development out of the common dance. And it is probable that the history of the dance is everywhere the same, that it began as a common dance in which all present take some active part, and from this first form (still surviving in our ball-room dances) arose the spectacular dance in which one or more dancers perform before spectators who take no part themselves.

In the Andamans the song is an accompaniment of the dance. The dancing and singing and the marking of the rhythm by clapping and by stamping on the sounding-board are all parts of the one common action in which all join and which for convenience is here spoken of as the dance. It is probable that here again the Andamanese practice shows us the earliest stage in the development of the song, that song and music at first had no independent existence but together with dancing formed one activity. It is reasonable to suppose that the song first came into general use in human society because it provides a means by which a number of persons can utter the same series of sounds together and as with one voice, this being made possible by the fixed rhythm and the fixed pitch of the whole song and of each part of it (i.e. by melody). Once the art of song was in existence its further development was doubtless largely dependent upon the esthetic pleasure it is able to give. But in the Andamans the esthetic pleasure that the natives get from their simple and monotonous songs seems to me of quite secondary importance as compared with the value of the song as a joint social activity.

The movements of the ordinary Great Andaman dance do not seem to me to be in themselves expressive, or at any rate they are not obviously mimetic like the movements of the dances of many primitive folk. Their function seems to be to bring into activity as many of the muscles of the body as possible. The bending of the body at the hips and of the legs at the knees, with the slightly backward poise of the head and the common position of the arms held in line with the shoulders with the elbows crooked and the thumb and first finger of each hand clasping those of the other, produce a condition of tension of a great number of the muscles of the trunk and limbs. The attitude is one in which all the main joints of the body are between complete flexion and complete extension so that there is approximately an equal tension in the opposing groups of flexor and extensor muscles. Thus the whole body of the dancer is full of active forces balanced one against another, resulting in a condition of flexibility and alertness without strain.

While the dance thus brings into play the whole muscular system of the dancer it also requires the activity of the two chief senses, that of sight to guide the dancer in his movements amongst the others and that of hearing to enable him to keep time with the music. Thus the dancer is in a condition in which all the bodily and mental activities are harmoniously directed to one end.

Finally, in order to understand the function of the Andamanese dance it must be noted that every adult member of the community takes some part in it. All the able-bodied men join in the dance itself; all the women join in the chorus. If anyone through ill-health or old age is unable to take any active part, he or she is at least necessarily a spectator for the dance takes place in the centre of the village in the open space towards which the huts usually face.

The Andamanese dance (with its accompanying song) may therefore be described as an activity in which, by virtue of the effects of rhythm and melody, all the members of a community are able harmoniously to cooperate and act in unity; which requires on the part of the dancer a continual condition of tension free from strain; and which produces in those taking part in it a high degree of pleasure. We must now proceed to examine very briefly the chief effects on the mental condition of those taking part.

First let us consider some of the effects of rhythm. Any marked rhythm exercises over those submitted to its influence a constraint, impelling them to yield to it and to permit it to direct and regulate the movements of the body and even those of the mind. If one does not yield to this constraining influence it produces a state of restlessness that may become markedly unpleasant. One who yields himself utterly to it, as does the dancer when he joins in the dance, still continues to feel the constraint, but so far from being unpleasant it now produces a pleasure of a quite distinct quality. The first point for us to note therefore is that through the effect of rhythm the dance affords an experience of a constraint or force of a peculiar kind acting upon the individual and inducing in him when he yields himself to it a pleasure of self-surrender. The peculiarity of the force in question is that it seems to act upon the individual both from without (since it is the sight of his friends dancing and the sound of the singing and marking time that occasions it), and also from within (since the impulse to yield himself to the constraining rhythm comes from his own organism).

A second effect on the rhythm of the dance is due to the well-known fact that series of actions performed rhythmically produces very much less fatigue than actions not rhythmical requiring the same expenditure of muscular energy. So the dancer feels that in and through the dance he obtains such an increase in his personal energy that he is able to accomplish strenuous exertions with a minimum of fatigue. This effect is reinforced by the excitement produced by the rapid movements of the dancers, the loud sounds of the song and clapping and sounding-board, and intensified, as all collective states of emotion are intensified, by reason of being collective; with the result that the Andaman Islanders are able to continue their strenuous dancing through many hours of the night.

There is yet a third most important effect of rhythm. Recent psychology shows that what are called the esthetic emotions are largely dependent upon motor images. We call a form beautiful when, through the movements of the eye in following it, we feel it as movement, and as movement of a particular kind which we can only describe at present by using such a word as 'harmonious.' Similarly our esthetic appreciation of music seems to be largely dependent on our feeling the music as movement, the sounds appealing not to the ear only but to stored-up unconscious motor memories. With regard to dancing, our pleasure in watching the graceful, rhythmical and harmonious movements of the dancer is an esthetic pleasure of similar nature to that obtained from the contemplation of beautiful shapes or listening to music. But when the individual is himself dancing it does not seem quite fitting to call his pleasure esthetic. Yet the dance, even the simple dance of the Andamans, does make, in the dancer himself, partly by the effect of rhythm, partly by the effect of the harmonious and balanced tension of the muscles, a direct appeal to that motor sense to which the contemplation of beautiful forms and movements makes only an indirect appeal. In other words the dancer actually feels within himself that harmonious action of balanced and directed forces which, in the contemplation of a beautiful form we feel as though it were in the object at which we look. Hence such dancing as that of the Andaman Islanders may be looked upon as an early step in the training of the esthetic sense, and to recognize all that the dance means we must make allowance for this fact that the mental state of the dancer is closely related to the mental state that we call esthetic enjoyment.

Let us now consider the effects of the dance as a social or collective activity. First, the dance affords an opportunity for the individual to exhibit before others his skill and agility and so to gratify his personal vanity. It is very easy to observe the action of this harmless vanity in the dancers, and particularly in the man who takes the place at the sounding-board and acts as soloist or leader of the chorus. The dancer seeks to feel, and does feel, that he is the object of the approbation and admiration of his friends. His self-regarding sentiments are pleasantly stimulated, so that he becomes conscious, in a state of self-satisfaction and elation, of his own personal value. This stimulation of the self-regarding sentiment is an important factor in the total effect produced by the dance.

Secondly, the dance, at the same time that it stimulates pleasantly the self-regarding sentiment, also affects the sentiments of the dancer towards his fellows. The pleasure that the dancer feels irradiates itself over everything around him and he is filled with geniality and good-will towards his companions. The sharing with others of an intense pleasure, or rather the sharing in a collective expression of pleasure, must ever incline us to such expansive feelings. It is certainly a readily observable fact that in the Andamans the dance does produce a condition of warm good-fellowship in those taking part in it. There is no need to enquire more closely into the mental mechanisms by which this is brought about.

The Andaman dance, then, is a complete activity of the whole community, in which every able-bodied adult takes some part, and is also an activity in which, so far as the dancer himself is concerned, the whole personality is involved, by the innervation of all the muscles of the body, by the concentration of attention required, and by its action on the personal sentiments. In the dance the individual submits to the action upon him of the community; he is constrained, by the immediate effect of rhythm as well as by custom, to join in, and he is required to conform in his own actions and movements to the needs of the common activity. The surrender of the individual to this constraint or obligation is not felt as painful, but on the contrary as highly pleasurable. As the dancer loses himself in the dance, as he becomes absorbed in the unified community, he reaches a state of elation in which he feels himself filled with energy or force immensely beyond his ordinary state, and so finds himself able to perform prodigies of exertion. This state of intoxication, as it might almost be called, is accompanied by a pleasant stimulation of the self-regarding sentiment, so that the dancer comes to feel a great increase in his personal force and value. And at the same time, finding himself in complete and ecstatic harmony with all the fellow-members of his community, experiences a great increase in his feelings of amity and attachment towards them.

In this way the dance produces a condition in which the unity, harmony and concord of the community are at a maximum, and in which they are intensely felt by every member. It is to produce this condition, I would maintain, that is the primary social function of the dance. The well-being, or indeed the existence, of the society depends on the unity and harmony that obtain in it, and the dance, by making that unity intensely felt, is a means of maintaining it. For the dance affords an opportunity for the direct action of the community upon the individual, and we have seen that it exercises in the individual those sentiments by which the social harmony is maintained.

It was formerly the custom, I was told, always to have a dance before setting out to a fight. The reason for this should now be clear. When a group engages in a fight with another it is to revenge some injury that has been done to the whole group. The group is to act as a group and not merely as a collection of individuals, and it is therefore necessary that the group should be conscious of its unity and solidarity. Now we have seen that the chief function of the dance is to arouse in the mind of every individual a sense of the unity of the social group of which he is a member, and its function before setting out to a fight is therefore apparent. A secondary effect of the dance before a fight is to intensify the collective anger against the hostile group, and thereby and in other ways to produce a state of excitement and elation which has an important influence on the fighting quality of the Andaman warrior.

An important feature of the social life of the Andamans in former times was the dance-meetings that were regularly held and at which two or more local groups met together for a few days. Each local group lived for the greater part of the year comparatively isolated from others. What little solidarity there was between neighbouring groups therefore tended to become weakened. Social relations between two groups were for the most part only kept up by visits of individuals from one group to another, but such visitis did not constitute a relation between group and group. The function of the dance-meetings was therefore to bring the two groups into contact and renew the social relations between them and in that way to maintain the solidarity between them. Those meetings, apart from the provision of the necessary food, were entirely devoted to the exchange of presents and to dancing, the two or more parties of men and women joining together every night in a dance. We have already seen that the exchange of presents is a means of expressing solidarity of mutual good-will. It is now clear that the dance serves to unite the two or more groups into one body, and to make that unity felt by every individual, so creating for a few days a condition of close solidarity. The effects of the meeting would gradually wear out as months went by, and therefore it was necessary to repeat the meeting at suitable intervals.

Thus it appears that not only the ordinary dance, but also the war-dance, and the dance-meetings owe their place in the life of the Andaman Islanders to the fact that dancing is a means of uniting individuals into a harmonious whole and at the same time making them actually and intensely experience their relation to that unity of which they are the members. The special dances at initiation ceremonies and on other occasions will be delt with later in the chapter, on the basis of the general explanation given above.

On the occasion of a dance, particularly if it be a dance of some importance, such as a war-dance, or a dance of two groups together, the dancers decorate themselves by putting on various ornaments and by painting their bodies with red paint and white clay. The explanation of the dance cannot therefore be regarded as complete till we have considered the meaning of this personal adornment connected with it.

If the Andaman Islander be asked why he adorns himself for the dance, his reply is invariably that he wishes to look well, to improve his personal appearance. In other words his conscious motive is personal vanity.

One of the features of the dance, and a not unimportant one, is that it offers an opportunity for the gratification of personal vanity. The dancer, painted, and hung over with ornaments, becomes pleasantly conscious of himself, of his own skill and agility, and of his striking or at least satisfactory appearance, and so he becomes also conscious of his relation to others, of their admiration, actual or possible, and of the approval and good-will that go with admiration. In brief, the ornamented dancer is pleasantly conscious of his own personal value. We may therefore say that the most important function of any such adorning of the body is to express or mark the personal value of the decorated individual.

This explanation only applies to certain bodily ornaments and to certain ways of painting the body. It applies to the painting of white clay, with or without red paint, that is adopted at dances and on other ceremonial occasions. It applies to such personal ornaments as those made of netting and *Dentalium* shell which constitute what may be called the ceremonial costume of the Andamanese. It is of these that the natives say that they use them in order to look well.

The occasions on which such personal decoration is used are strictly defined by custom. In other words the society dictates to the individual when and how he shall be permitted to express his own personal value. It is obvious that personal vanity is of great importance in directing the conduct of the individual in his dealings with his fellows, and much more amongst a primitive people such as the Andamanese than amongst ourselves, and it is therefore necessary that the society should have some means of controlling the sentiment and directing it towards social ends. We have seen that the dance is the expression of the unity and harmony of the society, and by permitting at the dance the free expression of personal vanity the society ensures that the individual shall learn to feel, even if only subconsciously, that his personal value depends upon the harmony between himself and his fellows.

The bride and bridegroom are painted with white clay, and wear ornaments of *Dentalium* shell on the day following their marriage. We have seen that marriage involves a change of social status, and we may say that it gives an increased social value to the married pair, the social position of a married man or woman being of greater importance and dignity than that of a bachelor or spinster. They are, after marriage, the objects of higher regard on the part of their fellows than they were before. It is therefore appropriate that the personal value of the bride and bridegroom should be expressed so that both they themselves and their fellows should have their attention drawn to it, and this is clearly the function of the painting and ornaments.

After the completion of any of the more important of the initiation ceremonies, such as the eating of turtle, the initiate is painted with white clay and red paint and wears ornaments of *Dentalium* shell. This is exactly parallel to the painting of the bride and bridegroom. The initiate, by reason of the ceremony he has been through, has acquired new dignity and importance, and by having fulfilled the requirements of custom has deserved the approval of his fellows. The decoration of his body after the ceremony is thus the expression of his increased social value.

A corpse, before burial, is decorated in the same manner as the body of a dancer. This, we may take it, is the means by which the surviving relatives and friends express their regard for the dead, i.e. their sense of his value. We need not suppose that they believe the dead man to be conscious of what they are doing. It is to satisfy themselves that they decorate the corpse, not to satisfy the spirit. When a man is painted he feels that he has the regard and good-will of his fellows, and those who see him, at any rate in the instance of a bridegroom or initiate, realize that he has deserved their regard. So, to express their regard for the dead man they paint the inanimate body. Hence it is that the greater the esteem in which the dead man or woman is held, the greater is the care bestowed on the last painting.

We may conclude therefore that the painting of the body with white clay and the wearing of ornaments of *Dentalium* shell is a rite or ceremony by which the value of the individual to the society is expressed on appropriate occasions. We shall find confirmation of this later in the chapter.

Before passing on to consider the meaning of other methods of decorating the body there is one matter that is worthy of mention. It is often assumed or stated that both personal ornament and dancing, amongst uncivilized peoples, are connected with sexual emotion. It is, of course, extremely difficult to disprove a statement of this sort. So far as the Andamanese are concerned I was unable to find any trace whatever of a definitely sexual element in either their dances or their personal adornment. It may be recalled that both men and women wear exactly the same ornaments on ceremonial occasions, and this is to some extent evidence that such have no sexual value. It is possible that some observers might see in the dance of the women (which is only performed on rare occasions) a suggestion of something of a sexual nature. I was unable to find that the natives themselves consider that there is anything suggestive of sex in either the dance of the men or that of the women. If it were true that the most important feature of the dance was that it appealed in some way to sexual feelings it is difficult to see how we are to explain the different occasions on which dancing takes place, as before a fight, at the end of mourning, etc., whereas these are adequately accounted for by the hypothesis that the dance is a method of expressing the unity and harmony of the society. Similarly the explanation of personal ornament as being connected with sexual feeling would fail to account for the occasions on which it is regarded as obligatory. There is therefore, I believe, no special connection between the dancing and personal ornament of the Andamanese and sexual feeling. It would still be possible to hold that there is a general connection of great importance between the affective dispositions underlying these and other customs and the complex affective disposition that we call the sex instinct. The nature of that connection, important as it is, lies outside the scope of this work.

I remarked above that the explanation which I have given of the meaning of personal ornament does not apply to all the objects that the Andaman Islanders wear on their body, but only to certain of them. If an Andaman Islander be asked why he paints himself with white clay, or why he wears a belt or necklace of *Dentalium* shell he replies that he does so in order to look well; but if he be asked why he wears a string of human bones round his head or neck or waist, he gives quite a different answer, to the effect that he does so in order to protect himself from dangers of a special kind. According to circumstances he will say either that he is wearing the bones to cure himself of illness, or else that he wears them as a protection against spirits. Thus while some things are worn on the body in order to improve the personal appearance, and consequently, as explained above, to give the individual a sense of his own value, others are worn because they are believed to have a protective power, and thereby arouse in the person a sense of security. Exactly the same sort of protective power is attributed to things that cannot be worn on the body, such as fire, and it will therefore be convenient to consider together all the things that afford this kind of protection, whether they can be worn on the body or not.

The interpretation here offered is that the customs connected with this belief in the protective power of objects of various kinds are means by which is expressed and thereby maintained at the necessary degree of energy a very important social sentiment, which, for lack of a better term, I shall call the sentiment of dependence. In such a primitive society as that of the Andamans one of the most powerful means of maintaining the cohesion of the society and of enforcing that conformity to custom and tradition without which social life is impossible, is the recognition by the individual that for his security and well-being he depends entirely upon the society.

The following extract is reprinted from A. R. Radcliffe-Brown, *Structure and Function in Primitive Society* (London: Cohen & West; Glencoe, Ill.: The Free Press, 1952), pp. 136–52, with the

I have purposely chosen from our society two examples of ritual avoidances which are of very different kinds. The rule against eating meat on Friday or in Lent is a rule of religion, as is the rule, where it is recognized, against playing golf or tennis on Sunday. The rule against spilling salt, I suppose it will be agreed, is non-religious. Our language permits us to make this distinction very clearly, for infractions of the rules of religion are sins, while the non-religious avoidances are concerned with good and bad luck. Since this distinction is so obvious to us it might be thought that we should find it in other societies. My own experience is that in some of the societies with which I am acquainted this distinction between sinful acts and acts that bring bad luck cannot be made. Several anthropologists, however, have attempted to classify rites into two classes, religious rites and magical rites.

For Emile Durkheim the essential distinction is that religious rites are obligatory within a religious society or church, while magical rites are optional. A person who fails in religious observances is guilty of wrong-doing, whereas one who does not observe the precautions of magic or those relating to luck is simply acting foolishly. This distinction is of considerable theoretical importance. It is difficult to apply in the study of the rites of simple societies.

Sir James Frazer defines religion as 'a propitiation or conciliation of superhuman powers which are believed to control nature and man,' and regards magic as the erroneous application of the notion of causality. If we apply this to ritual prohibitions, we may regard as belonging to religion those rules the infraction of which produces a change of ritual status in the individual by offending the superhuman powers, whereas the infraction of a rule of magic would be regarded as resulting immediately in a change of ritual status, or in the misfortune that follows, by a process of hidden causation. Spilling salt, by Sir James Frazer's definition, is a question of magic, while eating meat on Friday is a question of religion.

An attempt to apply this distinction systematically meets with certain difficulties. Thus with regard to the Maori Sir James Frazer states that 'the ultimate sanction of the taboo, in other words, that which engaged the people to observe its commandments, was a firm persuasion that any breach of those commandments would surely and speedily be punished by an *atua* or ghost, who would afflict the sinner with a painful malady till he died.' This would seem to make the Polynesian taboo a matter of religion, not of magic. But my own observation of the Polynesians suggests to me that in general the native conceives of the change in his ritual status as taking place as the immediate result of such an act as touching a corpse, and that it is only when he proceeds to rationalize the whole system of taboos that he thinks of the god and spirits – the *atua* – as being concerned. Incidentally it should not be assumed that the Polynesian word *atua* or *otua* always refers to a personal spiritual being.

Of the various ways of distinguishing magic and religion I will mention only one more. For Professor Malinowski a rite is magical when 'it has a definite practical purpose which is known to all who practise it and can be easily elicited from any native informant,' while a rite is religious if it is simply expressive and has no purpose, being not a means to an end but an end in itself. A difficulty in applying this criterion is due to uncertainty as to what is meant by 'definite practical purpose.' To avoid the bad luck which results from spilling salt is, I suppose, a practical purpose though not very definite. The desire to please God in all our actions and thus escape some period of Purgatory is perhaps definite enough, but Professor Malinowski may regard it as not practical. What shall we say of the desire of the Polynesian to avoid sickness and possible death which he gives as his reason for not touching chiefs, corpses and newly-born babies?

Seeing that there is this absence of agreement as to the definitions of magic and religion and the nature of the distinction between them, and seeing that in many instances whether we call a particular rite magical or religious depends on which of the various proposed definitions we accept, the only sound procedure, at any rate in the present state of anthropological knowledge, is to avoid as far as possible the use of the terms in question until there is some general agreement about them. Certainly the distinctions made by Durkheim and Frazer and Malinowski may be theoretically significant, even though they are difficult to apply universally. Certainly, also, there is need for a systematic classification of rites, but a satisfactory classification will be fairly complex and a simple dichotomy between magic and religion does not carry us very far towards it.

Another distinction which we make in our own society within the field of ritual avoidances is between the holy and the unclean. Certain things must be treated with respect because they are holy, others because they are unclean. But, as Robertson Smith and Sir James Frazer have shown, there are many societies in which this distinction is entirely unrecognized. The Polynesian, for example, does not think of a chief or a temple as holy and a corpse as unclean. He thinks of them all as things dangerous. An example from Hawaii will illustrate this fundamental identity of holiness and uncleanness. There, in former times, if a commoner committed incest with his sister he became *kapu* (the Hawaiian form of tabu). His presence was dangerous in the extreme for the whole community, and since he could not be purified he was put to death. But if a chief of high rank, who, by reason of his rank was, of course, sacred (*kapu*), married his sister he became still more so. An extreme sanctity or untouchability attached to a chief born of a brother and sister who were themselves the children of a brother and sister. The sanctity of such a chief and the uncleanness of the person put to death for incest have the same source and are the same thing. They are both denoted by saying that the person is *kapu*. In studying the simpler societies it is essential that we should carefully avoid thinking of their behaviour and ideas in terms of our own ideas of holiness and uncleanness. Since most people find this difficult it is desirable to have terms which we can use that do not convey this connotation. Durkheim and others have used the word 'sacred' as an inclusive term for the holy and the unclean together. This is easier to do in French than in English, and has some justification in the fact that the Latin *sacer* did apply to holy things such as the gods and also to accursed things such as persons guilty of certain crimes. But there is certainly a tendency in English to identify sacred with holy. I think that it will greatly aid clear thinking if we adopt some wide inclusive term which does not have any undesirable connotation. I venture to propose the term 'ritual value.'

Anything – a person, a material thing, a place, a word or name, an occasion or event, a day of the week or a period of the year – which is the object of a ritual avoidance or taboo can be said to have ritual value. Thus in Polynesia chiefs, corpses and newly-born babies have ritual value. For some people in England salt has ritual value. For Christians all Sundays and Good Friday have ritual value, and for Jews all Saturdays and the Day of Atonement. The ritual value is exhibited in the behaviour adopted towards the object or occasion in question. Ritual values are exhibited not only in negative ritual but also in positive ritual, being possessed by the objects towards which positives rites are directed and also by objects, words or places used in the rites. A large class of positive rites, those of consecration or sacralization, have for their purpose to endow objects with ritual value. It may be noted that in general anything that has value in positive ritual is also the object of some sort of ritual avoidance or at the very least of ritual respect.

The word 'value,' as I am using it, always refers to a relation between a subject and an object. The relation can be stated in two ways by saying either that the object has a value for the subject, or that the subject has an interest in the object. We can use the terms in this way to refer to any act of behaviour towards an object. The relation is exhibited in and defined by the behaviour. The words 'interest' and 'value' provide a convenient shorthand by which we can describe the reality, which consists of acts of behaviour and the actual relations between subjects and objects which those acts of behaviour reveal. If Jack loves Jill, then Jill has the value of a loved object for Jack, and Jack has a recognizable interest in Jill. When I am hungry I have an interest in food, and a good meal has an immediate value for me that it does not have at other times. My toothache has a value to me that it does not have at other times. My toothache has a value for me as something that I am interested in getting rid of as quickly as possible.

A social system can be conceived and studied as a system of values. A society consists of a number of individuals bound together in a net-work of social relations. A social relation exists between two or more persons when there is some harmonization of their individual interests, by some convergence of interest and by limitation or adjustment of divergent interests. An interest is always the interest of an individual. Two individuals may have similar interests. Similar interests do not in themselves constitute a social relation; two dogs may have a similar interest in the same bone and the result may be a dog-fight. But a society cannot exist except on the basis of a certain measure of similarity in the interests of its members. Putting this in terms of value, the first necessary condition of the existence of a society is that the individual members shall agree in some measure in the values that they recognize.

Any particular society is characterized by a certain set of values – moral, aesthetic, economic, etc. In a simple society there is a fair amount of agreement amongst the members in their evaluations, though of course the agreement is never absolute. In a complex modern society we find much more disagreement if we consider the society as a whole, but we may find a closer measure of agreement amongst the members of a group or class within the society.

While some measure of agreement about values, some similarity of interests, is a prerequisite of a social system, social relations involve more than this. They require the existence of common interests and of social values. When two or more persons have a common interest in the same object and are aware of their community of interest a social relationship is established. They form, whether for a moment or for a long period, an association, and the object may be said to have a social value. For a man and his wife the birth of a child, the child itself and its well-being and happiness or its death, are objects of a common interest which

607

binds them together and they thus have, for the association formed by the two persons, social value. By this definition an object can only have a social value for an association of persons. In the simplest possible instance we have a triadic relation; Subject 1 and Subject 2 are both interested in the same way in the Object and each of the Subjects has an interest in the other, or at any rate in certain items of the behaviour of the other, namely those directed towards the object. To avoid cumbersome circumlocutions it is convenient to speak of the object as having a social value for any one subject involved in such a relation, but it must be remembered that this is a loose way of speaking.

It is perhaps necessary for the avoidance of misunderstanding to add that a social system also requires that persons should be objects of interest to other persons. In relations of friendship or love each of two persons has a value for the other. In certain kinds of groups each member is an object of interest for all the others, and each member therefore has a social value for the group as a whole. Further, since there are negative values as well as positive, persons may be united or associated by their antagonism to other persons. For the members of an anti-Comintern pact the Comintern has a specific social value.

Amongst the members of a society we find a certain measure of agreement as to the ritual value they attribute to objects of different kinds. We also find that most of these ritual values are social values as defined above. Thus for a local totemic clan in Australia the totem-centres, the natural species associated with them, i.e. the totems, and the myths and rites that relate thereto, have a specific social value for the clan: the common interest in them binds the individuals together into a firm and lasting association.

Ritual values exist in every known society, and show an immense diversity as we pass from one society to another. The problem of a natural science of society (and it is as such that I regard social anthropology) is to discover the deeper, not immediately perceptible, uniformities beneath the superficial differences. This is, of course, a highly complex problem which will require the studies begun by Sir James Frazer and others to be continued by many investigators over many years. The ultimate aim should be, I think, to find some relatively adequate answer to the question – *What is the relation of ritual and ritual values to the essential constitution of human society?* I have chosen a particular approach to this study which I believe to be promising – to investigate in a few societies studied as thoroughly as possible the relations of ritual values to other values including moral and aesthetic values. In the present lecture, however, it is only one small part of this study in which I seek to interest you – the question of a relation between ritual values and social values.

One way of approaching the study of ritual is by the consideration of the purposes or reasons for the rites. If one examines the literature of anthropology one finds this approach very frequently adopted. It is by far the least profitable, though the one that appeals most to common sense. Sometimes the purpose of a rite is obvious, or a reason may be volunteered by those who practise it. Sometimes the anthropologist has to ask the reason, and in such circumstances it may happen that different reasons are given by different informants. What is fundamentally the same rite in two different societies may have different purposes or reasons in the one and in the other. The reasons given by the members of a community for any custom they observe are important data for the anthropologist. But it is to fall into grievous error to suppose that they give a valid explanation of the custom. What is entirely inexcusable is for the anthropologist, when he cannot get from the people themselves a reason for their behaviour which seems to him satisfactory, to attribute to them some purpose or reason on the basis of his own preconceptions about human motives. I could adduce many instances of this from the literature of ethnography, but I prefer to illustrate what I mean by an anecdote.

A Queenslander met a Chinese who was taking a bowl of cooked rice to place on his brother's grave. The Australian in jocular tones asked if he supposed that his brother would come and eat the rice. The reply was 'No! We offer rice to people as an expression of friendship and affection. But since you speak as you do I suppose that you in this country place flowers on the graves of your dead in the belief that they will enjoy looking at them and smelling their sweet perfume.'

So far as ritual avoidances are concerned the reasons for them may vary from a very vague idea that some sort of misfortune or ill-luck, not defined as to its kind, is likely to befall anyone who fails to observe the taboo, to a belief that non-observance will produce some quite specific and undesirable result. Thus an Australian aborigine told me that if he spoke to any woman who stood in the relation of mother-in-law to him his hair would turn grey.[1]

1. In case it may be thought that this is an inadequate supernatural punishment for a serious breach of rules of proper behaviour a few words of explanation are necessary. Grey hair comes with old age and is thought to be usually associated with loss of sexual potency. It is thus premature old age with its disadvantages but without the advantages that usually accompany seniority that threatens the man who fails to observe the rules of avoidance. On the other hand when a man's hair is grey and his wife's

The very common tendency to look for the explanation of ritual actions in their purpose is the result of a false assimilation of them to what may be called technical acts. In any technical activity an adequate statement of the purpose of any particular act or series of acts constitutes by itself a sufficient explanation. But ritual acts differ from technical acts in having in all instances some expressive or symbolic element in them.

A second approach to the study of ritual is therefore by a consideration not of their purpose or reason but of their meaning. I am here using the words symbol and meaning as coincident. Whatever has a meaning is a symbol and the meaning is whatever is expressed by the symbol.

But how are we to discover meanings? They do not lie on the surface. There is a sense in which people always know the meaning of their own symbols, but they do so intuitively and can rarely express their understanding in words. Shall we therefore be reduced to guessing at meanings as some anthropologists have guessed at reasons and purposes? I think not. For as long as we admit guess-work of any kind social anthropology cannot be a science. There are, I believe, methods of determining, with some fair degree of probability, the meanings of rites and other symbols.

There is still a third approach to the study of rites. We can consider the effects of the rite – not the effects that it is supposed to produce by the people who practise it but the effects that it does actually produce. A rite has immediate or direct effects on the persons who are in any way directly concerned in it, which we may call, for lack of a better term, the psychological effects. But there are also secondary effects upon the social structure, i.e. the network of social relations binding individuals together in an ordered life. These we may call the social effects. By considering the psychological effects of a rite we may succeed in defining its psychological function; by considering the social effects we may discover its social function. Clearly it is impossible to discover the social function of a rite without taking into account its usual or average psychological effects. But it is possible to discuss the psychological effects while more or less completely ignoring the more remote sociological effects, and this is often done in what is called 'functional anthropology.'

Let us suppose that we wish to investigate in Australian tribes the totemic rites of a kind widely distributed over a large part of the continent. The ostensible purpose of these rites, as stated by the natives

---

mother has passed the age of child-bearing the taboo is relaxed so that the relatives may talk together if they wish.

themselves, is to renew or maintain some part of nature, such as a species of animal or plant, or rain, or hot or cold weather. With reference to this purpose we have to say that from our point of view the natives are mistaken, that the rites do not actually do what they are believed to do. The rain-making ceremony does not, we think, actually bring rain. In so far as the rites are performed for a purpose they are futile, based on erroneous belief. I do not believe that there is any scientific value in attempts to conjecture processes of reasoning which might be supposed to have led to these errors.

The rites are easily perceived to be symbolic, and we may therefore investigate their meaning. To do this we have to examine a considerable number of them and we then discover that there is a certain body of ritual idiom extending from the west coast of the continent to the east coast with some local variations. Since each rite has a myth associated with it we have similarly to investigate the meanings of the myths. As a result we find that the meaning of any single rite becomes clear in the light of a cosmology, a body of ideas and beliefs about nature and human society, which, so far as its most general features are concerned, is current in all Australian tribes.

The immediate psychological effects of the rites can be to some extent observed by watching and talking to the performers. The ostensible purpose of the rite is certainly present in their minds, but so also is that complex set of cosmological beliefs by reference to which the rite has a meaning. Certainly a person performing the rite, even if, as sometimes happens, he performs it alone, derives therefrom a definite feeling of satisfaction, but it would be entirely false to imagine that this is simply because he believes that he has helped to provide a more abundant supply of food for himself and his fellow-tribesmen. His satisfaction is in having performed a ritual duty, we might say a religious duty. Putting in my own words what I judge, from my own observations, to express what the native feels, I would say that in the performance of the rite he has made that small contribution, which it is both his privilege and his duty to do, to the maintenance of that order of the universe of which man and nature are interdependent parts. The satisfaction which he thus receives gives the rite a special value for him. In some instances with which I am acquainted of the last survivor of a totemic group who still continues to perform the totemic rites by himself, it is this satisfaction that constitutes apparently the sole motive for his action.

To discover the social function of the totemic rites we have to consider the whole body of cosmological ideas of which each rite is a partial expression. I believe that it is possible to show that the social structure of an Australian tribe is connected in a very special way with these cosmological ideas and that the maintenance of its continuity depends on keeping them alive, by their regular expression in myth and rite.

Thus any satisfactory study of the totemic rites of Australia must be based not simply on the consideration of their ostensible purpose and their psychological function, or on an analysis of the motives of the individuals who perform the rites, but on the discovery of their meaning and of their social function.

It may be that some rites have no social function. This may be the case with such taboos as that against spilling salt in our own society. Nevertheless, the method of investigating rites and ritual values that I have found most profitable during work extending over more than thirty years is to study rites as symbolic expressions and to seek to discover their social functions. This method is not new except in so far as it is applied to the comparative study of many societies of diverse types. It was applied by Chinese thinkers to their own ritual more than twenty centuries ago.

In China, in the fifth and sixth centuries B.C., Confucius and his followers insisted on the great importance of the proper performance of ritual, such as funeral and mourning rites and sacrifices. After Confucius there came the reformer Mo Ti who taught a combination of altruism – love for all men – and utilitarianism. He held that funeral and mourning rites were useless and interfered with useful activities and should therefore be abolished or reduced to a minimum. In the third and second centuries B.C., the Confucians, Hsün Tze and the compilers of the *Li Chi* (Book of Rites), replied to Mo Ti to the effect that though these rites might have no utilitarian purpose they none the less had a very important social function. Briefly the theory is that the rites are the orderly (the *Li Chi* says the beautiful) expression of feelings appropriate to a social situation. They thus serve to regulate and refine human emotions. We may say that partaking in the performance of rites serves to cultivate in the individual sentiments on whose existence the social order itself depends.

Let us consider the meaning and social function of an extremely simple example of ritual. In the Andaman Islands when a woman is expecting a baby a name is given to it while it is still in the womb. From that time until some weeks after the baby is born nobody is allowed to use the personal name of either the father or the mother; they can be referred to by teknonymy, i.e. in terms of their relation to the child. During this period both the parents are required to abstain from eating certain foods which they may freely eat at other times.

I did not obtain from the Andamanese any statement of the purpose or reason for this avoidance of names. Assuming that the act is symbolic, what method, other than that of guessing, is there of arriving at the meaning? I suggest that we may start with a general working hypothesis that when, in a single society, the same symbol is used in different contexts or on different kinds of occasions there is some common element of meaning, and that by comparing together the various uses of the symbol we may be able to discover what the common element is. This is precisely the method that we adopt in studying an unrecorded spoken language in order to discover the meanings of words and morphemes.

In the Andamans the name of a dead person is avoided from the occurrence of the death to the conclusion of mourning; the name of a person mourning for a dead relative is not used; there is avoidance of the name of a youth or girl who is passing through the ceremonies that take place at adolescence; a bride or bridegroom is not spoken of or to by his or her own name for a short time after the marriage. For the Andamanese the personal name is a symbol of the social personality, i.e. of the position that an individual occupies in the social structure and the social life. The avoidance of a personal name is a symbolic recognition of the fact that at the time the person is not occupying a normal position in the social life. It may be added that a person whose name is thus temporarily out of use is regarded as having for the time an abnormal ritual status.

Turning now to the rule as to avoiding certain foods, if the Andaman Islanders are asked what would happen if the father or mother broke his taboo the usual answer is that he or she would be ill, though one or two of my informants thought it might perhaps also affect the child. This is simply one instance of a standard formula which applies to a number of ritual prohibitions. Thus persons in mourning for a relative may not eat pork and turtle, the most important flesh foods, and the reason given is that if they did they would be ill.

To discover the meaning of this avoidance of foods by the parents we can apply the same method as in reference to the avoidance of their names. There are similar rules for mourners, for women during menstruation, and for youths and girls during the period of adolescence. But for a full demonstration we have to consider the place of foods in Andamanese ritual as a whole, and for an examination of this I must refer to what I have already written on the subject.

I should like to draw your attention to another point in the method by which it is possible to test our hypotheses as to the meanings of rites. We take the different occasions on which two rites are associated together, for example the association of the avoidance of a person's name with the avoidance by that person of certain foods, which we find in the instance of mourners on the one hand and the expectant mother and father on the other. We must assume that for the Andamanese there is some important similarity between these two kinds of occasions – birth and death – by virtue of which they have similar ritual values. We cannot rest content with any interpretation of the taboos at childbirth unless there is a parallel interpretation of those relating to mourners. In the terms I am using here we can say that in the Andamans the relatives of a recently dead person, and the father and mother of a child that is about to be, or has recently been, born, are in an abnormal ritual status. This is recognized or indicated by the avoidance of their names. They are regarded as likely to suffer some misfortune, some bad luck, if you will, unless they observe certain prescribed ritual precautions of which the avoidance of certain foods is one. In the Andaman Islands the danger in such instances is thought of as the danger of illness. This is the case also with the Polynesian belief about the ritual status of anyone who has touched a corpse or a newly-born baby. It is to be noted that for the Polynesians as well as for the Andamanese the occasion of a birth has a similar ritual value to that of a death.

The interpretation of the taboos at childbirth at which we arrive by studying it in relation to the whole system of ritual values of the Andamanese is too complex to be stated here in full. Clearly, however, they express, in accordance with Andamanese ritual idiom, a common concern in the event. The parents show their concern by avoiding certain foods; their friends show theirs by avoiding the parents' personal names. By virtue of these taboos the occasion acquires a certain social value, as that term has been defined above.

There is one theory that might seem to be applicable to our example. It is based on a hypothesis as to the psychological function of a class of rites. The theory is that in certain circumstances the individual human being is anxious about the outcome of some event or activity because it depends to some extent on conditions that he cannot control by any technical means. He therefore observes some rite which, since he believes it will ensure good luck, serves to reassure him. Thus an aeronaut takes with him in a plane a mascot which he believes will protect him from accident and thus carries out his flight with confidence.

The theory has a respectable antiquity. It was perhaps implied in the *Primus in orbe deos fecit timor* of Petronius and Statius. It has taken various forms from Hume's explanations of religion to Malinowski's explanation of Trobriand magic. It can be made so plausible by a suitable selection of illustrations that it is necessary to examine it with particular care and treat it with reasonable scepticism. For there is always the danger that we may be taken in by the plausibility of a theory that ultimately proves to be unsound.

I think that for certain rites it would be easy to maintain with equal plausibility an exactly contrary theory, namely, that if it were not for the existence of the rite and the beliefs associated with it the individual would feel no anxiety, and that the psychological effect of the rite is to create in him a sense of insecurity or danger. It seems very unlikely that an Andaman Islander would think that it is dangerous to eat dugong or pork or turtle meat if it were not for the existence of a specific body of ritual the ostensible purpose of which is to protect him from those dangers. Many hundreds of similar instances could be mentioned from all over the world.

Thus, while one anthropological theory is that magic and religion give men confidence, comfort and a sense of security, it could equally well be argued that they give men fears and anxieties from which they would otherwise be free – the fear of black magic or of spirits, fear of God, of the Devil, of Hell.

Actually in our fears or anxieties as well as in our hopes we are conditioned (as the phrase goes) by the community in which we live. And it is largely by the sharing of hopes and fears, by what I have called common concern in events or eventualities, that human beings are linked together in temporary or permanent associations.

To return to the Andamanese taboos at childbirth, there are difficulties in supposing that they are means by which parents reassure themselves against the accidents that may interfere with a successful delivery. If the prospective father fails to observe the food taboo it is he who will be sick, according to the general Andamanese opinion. Moreover, he must continue to observe the taboos after the child is safely delivered. Further, how are we to provide a parallel explanation of the similar taboos observed by a person mourning for a dead relative?

The taboos associated with pregnancy and parturition are often explained in terms of the hypothesis I have mentioned. A father, naturally anxious at the outcome of an event over which he does not have a technical control and which is subject to hazard, reassures himself by observing some taboo or carrying out some magical action. He may avoid certain foods. He may avoid making nets or tying knots, or he may go round the house untying all knots and opening any locked or closed boxes or containers.

I wish to arouse in your minds, if it is not already there, a suspicion that both the general theory and this special application of it do not give the whole truth and indeed may not be true at all. Scepticism of plausible but unproved hypotheses is essential in every science. There is at least good ground for suspicion in the fact that the theory has so far been considered in reference to facts that seem to fit it, and no systematic attempt has been made, so far as I am aware, to look for facts that do not fit. That there are many such I am satisfied from my own studies.

The alternative hypothesis which I am presenting for consideration is as follows. In a given community it is appropriate that an expectant father should feel concern or at least should make an appearance of doing so. Some suitable symbolic expression of his concern is found in terms of the general ritual or symbolic idiom of the society, and it is felt generally that a man in that situation ought to carry out the symbolic or ritual actions or abstentions. For every rule that *ought* to be observed there must be some sort of sanction or reason. For acts that patently affect other persons the moral and legal sanctions provide a generally sufficient controlling force upon the individual. For ritual obligations conformity and rationalization are provided by the ritual sanctions. The simplest form of ritual sanction is an accepted belief that if rules of ritual are not observed some undefined misfortune is likely to occur. In many societies the expected danger is somewhat more definitely conceived as a danger of sickness or, in extreme cases, death. In the more specialized forms of ritual sanction the good results to be hoped for or the bad results to be feared are more specifically defined in reference to the occasion or meaning of the ritual.

The theory is not concerned with the historical origin of ritual, nor is it another attempt to explain ritual in terms of human psychology; it is a hypothesis as to the relation of ritual and ritual values to the essential constitution of human society, i.e. to those invariant general characters which belong to all human societies, past, present and future. It rests on the recognition of the fact that while in animal societies social coaptation depends on instinct, in human societies it depends upon the efficacy of symbols of many different kinds. The theory I am advancing must therefore, for a just estimation of its value, be considered in its place in a general theory of symbols and their social efficacy.

By this theory the Andamanese taboos relating to childbirth are the obligatory recognition in a standardized symbolic form of the significance and importance of the event to the parents and to the community at large. They thus serve to fix the social value of occasions of this kind. Similarly I have argued in another place that the Andamanese taboos relating to the animals and plants used for food are means of affixing a definite social value to food, based on its social importance. The *social* importance of food is not that it satisfies hunger, but that in such a community as an Andamanese camp or village an enormously large proportion of the activities are concerned with the getting and consuming of food, and that in these activities, with their daily instances of collaboration and mutual aid, there continuously occur those interrelations of interests which bind the individual men, women and children into a society.

I believe that this theory can be generalized and with suitable modifications will be found to apply to a vast number of the taboos of different societies. My theory would go further for I would hold, as a reasonable working hypothesis, that we have here the primary basis of all ritual and therefore of religion and magic, however those may be distinguished. The primary basis of ritual, so the formulation would run, is the attribution of ritual value to objects and occasions which are either themselves objects of important common interests linking together the persons of a community or are symbolically representative of such objects. To illustrate what is meant by the last part of this statement two illustrations may be offered. In the Andamans ritual value is attributed to the cicada, not because it has any social importance itself but because it symbolically represents the seasons of the year which do have importance. In some tribes of Eastern Australia the god Baiame is the personification, i.e. the symbolical representative, of the moral law of the tribe, and the rainbow-serpent (the Australian equivalent of the Chinese dragon) is a symbol representing growth and fertility in nature. Baiame and the rainbow-serpent in their turn are represented by the figures of earth which are made on the sacred ceremonial ground of the initiation ceremonies and at which rites are performed. The reverence that the Australian shows to the image of Baiame or towards his name is the symbolic method of fixing the social value of the moral law, particularly the laws relating to marriage.

In conclusion let me return once more to the work of the anthropologist whom we are here to honour. Sir James Frazer, in his *Psyche's Task* and in his other works, set himself to show how, in his own words, taboos have contributed to build up the complex fabric of society. He thus initiated that functional study of ritual to which I have in this lecture and elsewhere attempted to make some contribution. But there has been a shift of emphasis. Sir James accounted for the taboos of savage tribes as the application in practice of beliefs arrived at by erroneous processes of reasoning, and he seems to have thought of the effects of these beliefs in creating or maintaining a stable orderly society as being accidental. My own view is that the negative and positive rites of savages exist and persist because they are part of the mechanism by which an orderly society maintains itself in existence, serving as they do to establish certain fundamental social values. The beliefs by which the rites themselves are justified and given some sort of consistency are the rationalizations of symbolic actions and of the sentiments associated with them. I would suggest that what Sir James Frazer seems to regard as the accidental results of magical and religious beliefs really constitute their essential function and the ultimate reason for their existence.

8   Conclusion

By 1950 the dominance of American sociology was over. Not that the massive output of sociological works diminished, or that the expansion of research projects was halted; nor had the popularity of the course programmes in the schools or the number of graduates declined. Quite the contrary; it may even be claimed that the proportionate increase in sociological teaching, writing and research in America was greater than in any other country. It is only to say that other countries for the first time caught up, not only by the quality of the work they produced, but, more importantly, by their independence and individuality. Many factors contributed to this changing situation, not the least of which were the rapid means of communication and easy access to funds which enabled sociologists from Western Europe, and indeed from all over the world, to observe and study the American scene on the spot and to apply on their return the knowledge and techniques they had acquired. At the same time, the expansion of higher education everywhere, made possible by economic reconstruction and growth, forced the newer and older universities alike to make provision for and offer courses in the newer social sciences, in particular psychology, sociology and social anthropology. In one respect greater affluence succeeded in containing the conflicts of society and assuaging their excesses, but in another respect it had the effect of exacerbating them by bringing them up to the surface, and at the same time creating new problems and sources of conflict. For once society was aware of the complexity of the multitudinous problems confronting it. Social thought assumed a new dimension, and the upsurge everywhere in sociological studies must be seen in the light of the response to this situation. Whether the interest engendered in this way was directed to the right end and whether those who had shown it were equipped by the intellectual training they were given to make a positive approach to ideas and solutions are debatable matters. The American scene is one in which these aspects of the case can be seen in their most extreme and revealing form.

The trend that was visible in the early forties towards large-scale research and the increasing application of novel techniques was intensified after the war. Foundations and government departments with unlimited resources outbid each other in the award of funds for research into this or that topic, irrespective of its intrinsic importance or of its relevance to social policy. Sociology became a highly lucrative profession, and as with all professions its success was measured by its ability to deliver the goods in an acceptable form. The sociologist, for the first time perhaps, ceased to be a scholar, and became a hack with some technical expertise which he paraded as the epitome of the latest wisdom. No university department was immune to the blandishments of high finance, and only a few sociologists succeeded in fulfilling the double role of swimming with the tide and retaining a high concept of their vocation. Nevertheless amidst widespread confusion, ambiguity and misdirected effort, there were elements in American sociology that were inspired by scholarly zeal and endeavour. The latent idea that sociology was a wide-ranging cultural discipline was given positive expression by the respect shown to an older generation of sociologists, Becker, Lynd, Benedict, Chapin, as well as by the avid and uncritical reception accorded to high-powered theoretical contributions like those of MacIver and Davis. None of this surpassed the vogue that Talcott Parsons's work created in the fifties. The sheer bulk of his output could not but evoke ungrudging admiration. But its widespread influence could only be accounted for by the unconscious assumption that sociology must be grounded on some basic theory. That Parsons's theory was an over-blown affair, and inconsistent at that, did not matter. It represented a healthy symptom of a sociological imperative. Much the same thing could be said of Sorokin's rehabilitation in the mid-sixties after years of neglect and oblivion, even if his theoretical assumptions were very shaky. Twenty years have elapsed since the publication of Merton's work, but they have not dimmed its beneficent influence in provoking new thought and initiating new research, however vulnerable are some of its basic presuppositions. The fulminations and prophecies of doom in the fifties of Wright Mills, incontestably the greatest mind in American sociology, have produced a salutary effect. If he has not left a school of thought behind, he has had at least a respectable and distinguished following, who have not only kept his memory fresh but have been inspired by his example and method to make sociology a constructive and intellectually honest undertaking. Whether in the periphery or in the centre of sociological thought, works of sound scholarship, in some cases of great originality, have appeared. Apart from the contributions of Wright Mills, one could cite in particular Riesman's *The Lonely Crowd*, a work in which characterology is placed in a social context, Becker's revised edition of *From Lore to Science*, a standard work of great historical insight and learning, Gunnar Myrdal's *An American Dilemma*, which deals primarily with the Negro, Franz Neumann's *Behemoth*, Paul Tillich's *The Courage to Be* and *The Protestant Era*, Lasswell's and Kaplan's *Power and Society*, while the works of Schumpeter and Galbraith are significant for their insight into the social and political consequences of the economic structure. It has to be admitted, however, that in spite of the sterling quality of these works, their influence has not penetrated deep enough into the American sociological scene to effect a radical change in its orientation and methods. It is still parochial, and lacks a sound philosophical and conceptual base, while its unhistorical perspective gives it an air of ephemeral insubstantiality. Its recent attraction to futurology is a symptom of this. Wedded to government or institutional grants as much of its research is, it displays its mediocrity in the choice of subjects for investigation and in the parade of computerized data. Hardly a single article in the *American Journal of Sociology* is without its rows of figures and square roots to prove either something that is not worth proving or something that any intelligent child can tell, or quite literally to prove nothing at all. Couched as it most often is in language of ineffable turgidity and pedantry, it is an unequalled example of the capacity of the human mind to fool itself and to fool others, the more degrading as it is done with complete impunity and with official backing and encouragement.

Another feature of the American scene has been the proliferation of departments of anthropology. In spite of the much-vaunted interdisciplinary character of the faculty courses, the rivalry between the three disciplines, sociology, social anthropology and social psychology, for priority consideration has become acute at a time when the lines of demarcation between them have become blurred and their overlapping interests more conspicuous. At present, the whole of what is called the developing world has been appropriated, the Pacific area, South-East Asia, Africa and Latin America, where a continuous procession of young people, recipients of handsome grants, are being sent to investigate heaven knows what. The pitiful results may be gauged from the infantile contents of some of the articles, such as the sexual habits of some obscure tribe in an island in the Pacific or the terminology of medicinal herbs in another, published in *Ethnography* and other journals, which have not even the merit of exotic novelty or the fascination of heightened curiosity.

Lastly, the American scene is being bedevilled, with consequences that nobody can foretell, by a new phenomenon, which briefly, if inadequately, may be described as ideological. The conflict overtaking American society is no longer one between right and left, urban and rural, Jew and Gentile, old and young, or even rich and poor; nor is it, as it is commonly thought, between white and black. These are symptoms of a much deeper malaise which is misunderstood on the one hand and reviled on the other, because where it is articulate it takes on all sorts of grotesque forms. It is an expression of a deep-seated discontent and is motivated by an implicit or explicit repudiation of the basis of organized society. The university people, in particular the sociologists and social scientists, were the only ones in a position to confront this new movement, go to the bottom of it and make sense of it, and, if possible, to contain it and direct it to constructive purposes. If it was furthermore necessary, as it always is, to reorganize courses to make them more relevant to contemporary movements of thought, they were again eminently competent to do this in conformity with well-tried methods and procedures.

Instead they either took a stand in a reactionary but futile attempt at suppression, or, what was even more reprehensible, supinely yielded to the raucous clamour of irrational agitation for change. The establishment of new studies and the rewriting of books to appease this clamour are a disservice to truth and a piece of craven folly.

As has already been noted, during the inter-war period in the other centres of learning, sociology proceeded at a more leisurely pace, if it was not altogether in doldrums, and for this reason its achievements in the post-war period were all the more impressive. In England the expansion in sociological studies occurred initially, as was to be expected, in London, at the London School of Economics. The great rush for admission to degree courses in sociology at L.S.E. was symptomatic of what was to follow very shortly in the rest of the country. The tradition begun by L. T. Hobhouse and Westermarck was carried on by Morris Ginsberg and T. H. Marshall. The broad outline of the curriculum, with a very strong historical and philosophical bias, had already been drawn up in the 1930s, and served as a model for degree courses in some of the new overseas universities which stood in a special relationship with London University.

However, the proliferation of departments of sociology in British universities – there is hardly a university without one – and the great vogue of sociology as a vocational or academic discipline have accentuated the divisions of thought which were a feature of the British scene before the war. One can discern as many as half a dozen schools of thought. The traditional London idea that sociology, if anything, must be philosophical, historical and critical, has not been universally accepted. Even in London, though that is still the aim, it is being diluted to some extent and undermined in view of the desire to broaden the course and in face of the persistent clamour for quick results and solutions.

Again following an old British tradition is the idea that there are important social issues requiring study with the object of producing a change in social policy. The creation of the Welfare State is evidence of the effectiveness and necessity of such empirical studies. Social problems are still with us: poverty, housing, education. Large-scale investigations into these problems are still needed, and sociology must address itself to them. So sociology becomes, in this view, an empirical study of social problems, and ideally its aim must be to make people embarking on its study dedicated social reformers.

Closely allied to this school of thought is another, which is relatively of recent origin but is growing at a pace which may well place it at the head of sociological disciplines. This is Social Administration. It is a discipline which is exclusively vocationally oriented, not in terms of large-scale empirical research with the object of influencing policy, but in terms of effective implementation of social welfare policy. The need for trained social workers is not in question. But the distinguishing features of the British system is the established practice of making social administration an academic discipline on a par with the others, offering it as a degree course of its own. The combination of vocational training and sociological theory produces a kind of mish-mash which is often confusing and rarely helpful. It is the case, however, that the only jobs availabe for most of those who have read sociology or social administration are those connected with the social welfare services of one kind or another. Whether this answers their original purpose of wishing to study the subject because it is 'about people' is quite another question.

What has been said about social administration as an autonomous discipline applies, with perhaps greater justification, to two other branches of sociology, demography and criminology, the former attracting statisticians, economists and biologists, the latter lawyers and psychologists. There is, however, another discipline, social anthropology, whose autonomy is perhaps of greater significance than anything that has occurred in the British scene, as it has a bearing on sociology proper with regard to what it should teach, how it should be taught and what methods and conceptual tools it should use. The fact that it has had a less popular appeal than sociology is largely due to the reluctance, on very sound principles, on the part of its practitioners to incorporate it in the undergraduate syllabus. As a branch of sociology, however, if not its veritable trunk, social anthropology has not only retained but has significantly added to the renown it has so deservedly acquired. Many of those who were trained in the late twenties and thirties under the new dispensation are still with us, Evans-Pritchard, Fortes, Daryll Forde, Raymond Firth, Lucy Mair, Leonard Schapiro, and they are being followed by another generation of equal eminence. There is now so much agreement about the approach and method of dealing with anthropological problems that it can be said they all belong to the same school of thought. As a result, significant progress can be registered in all the fields of investigation. One need only compare the works in social anthropology that have been published in the last thirty years with those of the older generation to be convinced of this. Our conceptions of religion, witchcraft, magic, political and economic organization have been transformed and placed on a firmer scientific basis. All this has been done without the quest for non-existent causal laws of society, without any theoretical presuppositions about society, but entirely through careful research in the field and through an analysis which explains a matter under investigation dynamically in terms of its functional and structural place in the system as a whole. The 'theoretical capital' of social anthropology consists of certain analytical notions like 'rite', 'solidarity', 'kinship', 'structure', which in themselves have a neutral meaning but when applied to social phenomena can lead to valuable insights. The concepts of 'exchange' and 'gift', for example, have proved in the hands of social anthropologists to be of great significance when their application has been extended to wider spheres of social life. If this technique in the use of general categories of thought does not enable the social anthropologist to formulate general laws or theories of society, this can hardly be counted as a failing as this is not at all its purpose, which is primarily to make social life intelligible; and this the social anthropologist does extremely well.

Because of its constructive and scholarly progress and its massive contributions to our knowledge of all aspects of social life, it is a moot point whether social anthropology has not completed its mission and has nothing new to say to us. It would seem that all small-scale societies, in their 'primitiveness', isolation and self-sufficiency, have been studied in depth, and their social systems, with the aggregate of all the institutions, familial, religious, political and economic, which comprise them, have been mapped out, as it were, classified and brought under a logical and coherent scheme. What seems to be happening now is that a new work is no more than a refinement, reformulation and at most only a trivial critique of what has already been written. This is an exercise whose benefit is incommensurate with the effort that has gone to its undertaking. This is tied up with another factor which leads one to feel that social anthropology has had its day. The kinds of society which were the subject of study by social anthropology are passing away, if they have not already virtually disappeared. The divisions between village and town are breaking down and becoming very tenuous. The most remote and inaccessible hamlet has been incorporated into a larger system, political, economical and social. It is thus no longer 'particularistic' but increasingly 'universalistic'. The separation of social anthropology and sociology is no longer needed, even in a very conservatively academic sense, and the sooner they merge as one integrated discipline and are dealt with comparatively, the better, because town and country are themselves merging and there is no such thing as a static social system; even a whole society, while its problems may be peculiar to itself, must be seen in the context of its relationship to other societies.

If there is one area of interests which constitutes the main preoccupation of British sociology, it is the class structure of Britain in its various manifestations. This is understandable in view of the rigid class divisions that historically have characterized British society. With the industrial, economic and social changes brought about by the war and the establishment of the welfare state, a re-examination of the class structure was called for. T. H. Marshall was perhaps the first post-war writer to deal with this problem, in his book *Citizenship and Social Class* (1950). This was followed by *The English Middle Class* (1953) by R. Lewis and A. Maude and, in rapid succession, T. B. Bottomore's book *Classes in Modern Society* (1955), G. D. H. Cole's *Studies in Class Structure* (1955) and T. P. Pear's *English Social Differences* (1955). A few works dealt with industry and business. Perhaps the most ambitious and comprehensive sociological study to be published in Britain in recent years was *The Affluent Worker* by a team of workers led by John Goldthorpe. The idea of this project was to test empirically the widely accepted thesis of working-class embourgeoisement. The conclusion published in the third part of the monograph, *The Affluent Worker*, on the class structure is a model of powerful but clearly reasoned argument. Nevertheless, the perspective is narrow and concerned with certain specific issues which bear very little relation to the wider issues which affect not only the industrial workers but the whole of society. Very important investigations have been carried out on the structure of the language of schoolchildren by Basil Bernstein, while a scholarly and theoretical interest in sociological problems is being maintained by such writers as Donald MacRae, Ernest Gellner, Alisdair MacIntyre, W. G. Runciman and Dorothy Emmett.

In view of the divisions of thought in the British scene, to which reference has already been made, it is only to be expected that there should be confusion, disarray, a lack of common perspective and purpose, an absence of a cohesive centre whose effectiveness and strength will be continually renewed through the allegiance that it inspires. Every university department has its own course programme depending on what it believes is needed, on the extent to which it believes it can attract students and perhaps ultimately on the fancies and predilections of the Head. The bewildering variety of the courses offered is reflected in the bewilderment with which the undergraduate goes through the course and his complete befuddlement as to what sociology is about. The effect of this may be gauged by the sort of outbursts and pronouncements to which they are not infrequently prone. Perhaps reflecting negatively or positively the bias of their teachers, and without a prior preparation for some rigorous thinking, they seize hold of a few ideas to which they have been introduced or which they have picked up, like alienation, authoritarianism, bureaucracy, class, capitalism, and with these as their sole intellectual pabulum they believe they are entitled to lay down the law and launch a campaign for the regeneration of society. Faced with the realities of life and under the necessity of standing on their own feet, some of them might, for their own good, forget completely the titbits of undigested knowledge which they have acquired, while retaining a healthy appreciation of the spirit of sociological thought. Others may well find the harsh realities of life, to which no alternative to submission is possible, a confirmation of a sour disillusionment to which they have succumbed and which they will hug as a boon companion for the rest of their lives. It is hoped that the resilience of which human nature is capable, and in particular with the reputed common sense, humour and intellectual indolence of the British people, the number of such people will always be few and far between and that they will remain their own sufferers.

In this connection it is pertinent to ask whether sociology would not be a more meaningful discipline if people came to it with a more mature approach, whether a training in another discipline, literature, philosophy, law, history, economics, psychology, even biology – since sociology is about any or all these things and more besides – is not an indispensable requirement for sociological understanding, and, lastly, whether sociology on its own, severed as it is from any of these other disciplines, is not a barren pursuit, a mere froth and bubble of very little substantive significance.

In contrast the French, among the leading sociologists of the world, were the last to have made sociology a separate discipline leading to a *licence* in the universities. Their reluctance to follow the American and other people's example was as much due to their conservatism in academic matters as to their conviction, having a long historical tradition to support it, that sociology requires a philosophical basis of thought and that it is more likely to be effective when it is allied to other branches of thought than if it existed independently. There is an unbroken and distinct line of development in French sociology that can be traced back to Descartes, Bodin, Rousseau and Montesquieu and continues in the highly structured, speculative and complex system of Claude Lévi-Strauss. The leading writers and exponents of sociological thought after the war, like Aron, Gurvitch, Duverger and Cuvillier, received their formative education before the war and they set the pace for the expansion in sociology that occurred after the war. The influence of Durkheim and his school as represented by

Marcel Mauss and Maurice Halbwachs is still considerable in the works of present-day sociologists, social psychologists and ethnologists in France. For a few years after the war, the leading figure in French sociology was Georges Gurvitch. He became internationally known on account of the book *Twentieth-century Sociology*, which was issued in collaboration with W. E. Moore in 1946. He was also responsible for editing the *Bibliothèque de sociologie contemporaine* and *Cahiers internationaux de sociologie*. But soon, in the fifties, it was realized that Gurvitch's whole approach to sociology, with its tendency to highly abstract formalization and a jugglery with neologisms like 'dialectical hyper-empiricism', was leading to a dead end. The borrowed ideas from psychoanalysis and psychological thought were evident in his advocacy of 'depth sociology', a perfectly meaningless concept. The whole compendium of Gurvitch's work happily, but not unexpectedly, died with him.

As elsewhere, an interest in practical research and investigation grew in France. A powerful institution, the Centre d'Études Sociologiques, was founded as a subordinate unit of the governmental Centre Nationale de la Recherche Scientifique, which is responsible for the allocation of research grants. To a large extent influenced by American techniques and methodology, a great deal of experimental work was chanelled into problems which are regarded as the province of social psychology, like group dynamics, public opinion research and so forth. At the same time, the industrial rehabilitation of France after the Second World War and the growth of an industrial economy inevitably created problems which a newer school of young industrial sociologists attempted to investigate. The most outstanding of the writers in industrial sociology are Alan Touraine and Michel Crozier. Mention must also be made of the remarkable work being done by the Institut National d'Études Démographiques, whose official organ, *Population*, is deservedly famous for its contributions to basic sociological problems.

It remains, however, the case that those who were mainly responsible for giving a specific tone and character to French sociology after the war were those who were brought up under the old system and who belong, in spite of their divergent interests, to the same tradition of sociological thought. Raymond Aron and Maurice Duverger are the direct heirs of Mosca, Michels and Weber and have brought to political sociology and the philosophy of history a fresh and incisive orientation, without which French sociology would have been all that much poorer. In the same philosophical and historical tradition must be placed Armand Cuvillier and Georges Friedmann, both pupils of C. Bouglé. Both are interested in looking at society in the round in order to discover how it is moving, and the historical processes that are responsible for moulding society amidst all the changes and upheavals which are overtaking it. Cuvillier is an outstanding scholar, whose masterpiece, *Manual of Sociology*, is more than a summary of what has been said and thought by sociologists; it is a brilliant synthesis of ideas that have shaped sociological thought since its inception in ancient Greece to the present day. Friedmann looks at the future of society in terms of the changes brought about by modern industry. The theme of many of his works, like *The Human Problems of Mechanization* (1947), *Whither Human Labour* (1951) and the *Atomization of Labour* (1956), consists of the view that a more equitable and a happier order of society may well develop from these violent changes.

With the same end in view, Henri Lefebvre, a prolific writer, while insisting as he does in his *Critique of Everyday Life* (1947) that sociology must deal with problems of everyday life, believes that a synthesis between sociology and social history is called for. This means in effect that the present can only be understood in terms of the past. In this way a dynamic consideration of the present will reveal a clue to the future.

As has already been indicated, the Durkheimian school after the First World War concentrated its efforts almost exclusively in the direction of ethnography and social anthropology. At the same time a basis was laid for what can broadly be called colonial sociology. In the works of Georges Balandier and Paul Mercier, this branch of investigation has been developed to include the ethnology of under-developed countries in all its aspects. This is the main function and purpose of the celebrated Musée de l'Homme. The works of Claude Lévi-Strauss, though not much to the taste or even understanding of English readers, bear testimony not only the extraordinary vogue that 'primitivism' has in France but also to the unbroken tradition which French sociologists, especially those of the Durkheimian school, have maintained in ethnography and social anthropology. His debt to that school is perfectly obvious. His use of the concept of 'exchange', which Marcel Mauss first made famous in his essay on *The Gift*, to formulate a theory of the formation of human society is one celebrated example. He has also made an attempt to incorporate psychoanalytic ideas and Marxism into his own peculiar theory of the interaction of the two polar opposites 'nature' and 'culture'.

By and large, French sociology, including social anthropology, has not yet been able to divest itself of the incubus of the realistic, *a priori*, cartesian mode of thought. Consequently, it is often dogmatic and influenced by political presuppositions of one kind or another. So we have a sociology in France, much of which is politicized, which means it is question-begging, because it starts with those very assumptions which, in fact, have to be proved.

Unlike any other country, Germany after the Second World War was faced with the formidable task of reconstituting the whole sociological movement, including the publication of journals, the founding of societies and the establishment of chairs. Strange enough, a few of the older sociologists of the Weimar republic like Leopold von Wiese and Alfred Weber survived the Nazi régime and reappeared to play a leading part in the revival of German sociology. The going, however, was very slow. A number of memorial editions for von Wiese, A. Vierkandt, R. Thurnwald and Max Horkheimer appeared between 1948 and 1955, by which time the establishment of fruitful contact with developments elsewhere was getting under way. At the same time a number of German sociologists, like Adorno and Bettelheim, who had sought refuge in the United States, returned to Germany. The German Sociological Society was reconstituted in 1946. The Institute of Social Research was re-formed in Frankfurt, and, very soon after, the leading German sociological periodical reappeared under the new extended title of *Journal of Sociology and Social Psychology*. An interest in rural sociology was revived,

Conclusion

and René Konig and his co-workers were engaged in research on the sociology of the family. On the whole, however, sociology in Germany in the 1950s was a period of consolidation, and the main inspiration came from the older sociologists. This was seen particularly in the case of Ralf Dahrendorf, who can be said to have been the most outstanding representative of the younger generation of sociologists in Germany. He reintroduced into German sociology the methodology and the theoretical framework of Weber's sociology through its revised, truncated and in many respects distorted version in American sociology as it was used by Talcott Parsons. Nevertheless, Dahrendorf's early works on class conflict and industrial sociology displayed a brilliance and originality of a rare kind, and their influence was widespread. By the sixties, however, Dahrendorf was being supplanted by a younger generation of sociologists, who distrusted this kind of theoretical approach to sociological problems and who felt that a greater measure of empiricism was needed to deal with concrete and practical problems.

Much of this work, even more so than in France, was concerned with factory organization, the place and status of workers in that organization. Industrial sociology in general thus played a dominant role in sociological research in Germany. The research workers received encouragement from the trade unions as well as from factory owners and they were given every opportunity to examine the situation at first hand by actually participating in the industrial process at all levels. This was done on both an individual and team basis. The approach and methodology were quite other than the ones that were practised in America and elsewhere. The research workers in Germany did not feel that it was sufficient to obtain a coefficiency of correlation between two variables, A and B, in a situation – say, between the attitude of workers to their trade unions and their satisfaction or otherwise in their work. It is necessary to regard A and B as dependent variables which must be related to a much wider social context, C. Obviously this is a formidable undertaking and probably the results would prove inconclusive, but neverthless, the repudiation of the trivial research that hitherto had gone by the name of industrial sociology in America is a sign that sociology in Germany has reached maturity and is following a line that is sociologically sounder.

The sociological 'explosion' after the war was the most significant development in the academic world of modern times. Every respectable university everywhere in the world, not to be left behind, established a department of sociology, and research units, frequently at national levels, were set up to launch and co-ordinate and publish the results of large-scale research projects. The kind of research that was carried out in each country by individual scholars or teams of workers was largely determined obviously by specific local or national problems. Nowhere was this more so than in Eastern Europe. In the nineteenth and especially in the first half of the twentieth century, specifically sociological problems were bound up with the nationalistic struggles and the search for a viable economic structure of society. By the 1950s, with all of Eastern Europe under the influence of Russia and established communist régimes, two almost contradictory phenomena resulted. Whilst sociology took on a new lease of life, it was strictly within a predetermined pattern, and there was a complete divorce not only from previous national thought but from the rest of the world. Whilst Russia was slow in modifying its view that all sociology is bourgeois sociology, the satellite countries of Eastern Europe continued to maintain that sociology can still perform a useful function in a communist state. However, this sociology was really a misnomer. For Russia and the satellite countries of Eastern Europe, the laws of society have already been discovered. Marxism, which embodies these laws, has now been established as the only true ideology of the people. This dogma implies that, as is in fact explicitly stated by the communist countries, absolute truth has now been attained, and there is nothing in their society which is not in accordance with the scientific laws of society. Therefore any sociological problems as such do not exist; society, being marxist, must be immune to any criticism and therefore sociology must only be concerned with isolated problems of how groups in society interact and what is the effect of this or that social phenomenon on this or that group of people. The improved situation in the last ten years or so, with more contacts taking place between east and west, has not made the division in thought any less acute. The two sides, though making an outwardly polite but basically hypocritical show of mutual collaboration and understanding, are simply speaking at cross purposes, in fact, speaking different languages, with the absolute rigid stance of the one and the more flexible relativistic stance of the other. Again by a kind of paradox, one senses a convergence between the two extremes, say, the Russian and the American. Both regard the systems prevailing in their societies as the best and not to be questioned. Therefore the main role of sociology is not to be a critique of society – this is forbidden in Russia and is not done in America – but rather to tinker with this problem or another and provide it with a mass of data and figures, inventing if possible highly refined mathematical models for them, with no other view in mind than stating the problem and producing a result which is involved, incomprehensible or trivial as the case may be.

Apart from this division of thought in sociology between east and west, there is another equally fundamental problem which has not yet been faced, much less resolved. It is the problem of the function, purpose, even subject matter of sociology. It can be stated in this form. Assuming there is complete agreement about the subject matter, can we regard sociology as an intellectual discipline having for its purpose an enlarged and more perfect understanding of society, human society as such, and not only a particular society in which we happen to live? Is it therefore a new attitude of mind that we wish to cultivate in studying sociology and a fresh approach to the operations of society? In which case, can we say of sociology what Hume said of philosophy: 'And though a philosopher may live remote from business, the genius of philosophy, if carefully cultivated by several, must gradually diffuse itself throughout the whole society, and bestow a similar correctness on every art and calling'? The answer is unfortunately 'no'. There is as yet no such thing as a climate of sociological thought; there is not even a fashion in sociology as there is in philosophy, art and history. This is because there is a fundamental confusion, running right through the sociological world, between sociology as a study of human society in its dynamic processes and sociology as a study of applied science dealing with problems that appear to be of interest to a worker or a team of workers. No matter how comprehensive or detailed the investigation of such a problem is, it is invariably a case of learning about something which has already happened and hardly ever one which is designed to make a difference to the problem. Beyond those who are engaged in this kind of research, is it of any use, benefit or interest to anybody else? Most of the resources and a great deal of the time and effort of sociologists are devoted to this kind of research. If we take the vast body of research in sociology during the last twenty years all over the world, can we think of any change, social, political, what-have-you, that has been effected as a result of this research? One has to go back to the great social surveys which were carried out in Britain in the last hundred years or so for examples of research that had a direct effect on national policy. This was because these surveys were conducted for a purpose, they were undertaken by individuals or groups of people who were imbued with a social sense, a sense of justice, in the conviction that if the facts were assembled and brought to light, public conscience would be aroused and national policy changed. Such surveys are needed everywhere and at all times.

This kind of so-called 'applied' sociology must be completely separated from sociology proper. Without underestimating the importance of the former, the latter is an intellectual discipline which has to take in, if it is to be meaningful and culturally relevant, history, psychology and philosophy. Essentially a sociologist tries to make sense of what is happening against a background of what has happened, so that some clue could be obtained of what is likely to happen. For this, an insight into human reactions in terms of people's psychological conditioning is required. The example of the methods used by social anthropologists may be cited as the way to go about this task. From an inchoate mass of social practices, habits, beliefs and so forth they try, as with a jig-saw puzzle, to fit all the pieces together functionally and structurally to present a coherent and logical whole. It is for others to say whether the interpretation they provide is the right one, but the aim is the correct one, and in pursuing it they can bring to light underlying thoughts, ideas, aspects of which the very people they are studying may be, and usually are, entirely unaware. This is essentially the aim also of the sociologist and it is hopelessly wrong to think that this aim should include the discovery of laws. All he is entitled to do is to hazard generalizations, with the proviso that they are valid only to the situation under consideration and to no other. Nor is his aim the formulation of a theory, except in the trivial sense where 'theory' means an explanation. What is important and essential is the ability, capacity and knowledge to place a phenomenon in a historically and dynamically determined context so that its relationship to the other parts of the system and to the system as a whole may be significantly traced. It is no mean achievement if a sociologist is able to say, through the different techniques he uses, why a thing should happen to be what it is. For this task, a philosophical or speculative approach is relevant, desirable, and indeed essential. A sociologist cannot separate his own deep feelings, which are the motive force of his philosophical attitude and convictions, from the subject that he is studying. He has, therefore, to bring his own values to bear on it, and, whether by implication or explicitly, he must, if it is to have any value at all, pass a judgement of it. The stark alternatives between the 'live' and 'lifeless' ways of doing sociology have never been expressed more sharply and clearly than in the words of Wright Mills:

There is no way in which any social scientist can avoid assuming choices of value and implying them in his work as a whole. Problems, like issues and troubles, concern threats to expected values, and cannot be clearly formulated without acknowledgement of those values. Increasingly, research is used, and social scientists are used, for bureaucratic and ideological purposes. This being so, as individuals and as professionals, students of man and society face such questions as whether they are aware of the uses and values of their work, whether these may be subject to their own control, whether they want to seek to control them . . . All social scientists, by the fact of their existence, are involved in the struggle between enlightenment and obscurantism.

C. Wright Mills, *The Sociological Imagination*

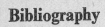

Bibliography

Bibliography

Howard Becker and Harry E. Barnes, *Social Thought from Lore to Science* (3 volumes, New York: Dover Publications Inc., revised edition 1966): the most outstanding, scholarly and comprehensive work ever undertaken on the development of social thought from the earliest times to the present day (1960) wherever it occurred. Unlikely to be superseded or supplemented for a very long time.

Pitirim A. Sorokin, *Contemporary Sociological Theories* (New York: Harper & Row, 1928) and *Sociological Theories of Today* (New York: Harper & Row, 1966): the earlier work became a classic as soon as it was published. It was the first work of its kind in which nearly all modern theories were critically examined and analysed. The second work follows the same pattern in dealing with the more recent theories, but with one important difference, that it does so in the light of Sorokin's own theories.

Nicholas S. Timasheff, *Sociological Theory: its nature and growth* (New York: Random House, revised edition 1966): not strictly historical, but a very lucid and critical outline of the most influential modern social theories in terms of their approaches and orientations.

Don Martindale, *The Nature and Types of Sociological Theory* (London: Routledge & Kegan Paul, 1961): the work deals with modern theories, classified in terms of schools of thought. The exposition is both sound and scholarly, and a judicious assessment is made of the theories.

H. E. Barnes (ed.), *An Introduction to the History of Sociology* (Chicago: University of Chicago Press, 1948): a huge work consisting of essays of varying length and competence, by different authors, on the founders of modern sociology.

Raymond Aron, *Main Currents in Sociological Thought* (2 volumes, London: Weidenfeld & Nicolson, 1965–8, Penguin Books, 1968–70): a great work, written with distinction and style, on some of the great historical figures who have moulded sociological thought.

Werner Stark, *A Short History of Sociology* (London: Routledge & Kegan Paul, 1960): a useful work of reference, but too concise, in view of the amount of material covered, to be very enlightening.

H. Maus, *A Short History of Sociology* (London: Routledge & Kegan Paul, 1965): a highly condensed but very detailed, if uncritical, account of the history of modern sociology up to 1950. A good book of reference.

Armand Cuvillier, *Manuel de sociologie* (3 volumes, Paris: Presses Universitaires de France, 4th edition 1960): a masterpiece of immense learning and scholarship. It deals with every known contribution to sociological thought in terms of subject matter like morals, religion, art, law, etc. Not least of its merits is its comprehensive bibliography.

Two introductory works on sociology contain an outline of the development of sociological thought:

J. Rumney and I. Maier, *The Science of Society* (London: Duckworth, 1958);

J. H. Abraham, *Sociology* (Teach Yourself Series, London: English Universities Press, 1966).

Index

Index

Index

Index

Index

Index